KINGDOM
in the
WEST
The Mormons and the American Frontier

Will Bagley, series editor

VOLUME 12

In 1875 Nancy Saphrona Huff Cates gave the most compelling survivor's account of the massacre. She is pictured here with her husband, Dallas Cates, whom the *Dardanelle Independent* called an "Estimable Gentleman in Yell County," about the time her statement was published. In December 2006 the Mountain Meadows Monument Foundation provided a marker for her grave at the Antioch Cemetery near Perryville, Arkansas. *Courtesy of the Will Bagley Collection.*

INNOCENT BLOOD

Essential Narratives of the Mountain Meadows Massacre

Edited by
DAVID L. BIGLER AND WILL BAGLEY

THE ARTHUR H. CLARK COMPANY
An imprint of the University of Oklahoma Press
Norman, Oklahoma
2008

———————————

Library of Congress Catalog Card Number 2008018696
ISBN 978-0-87062-362-2 (hardcover edition)
ISBN 978-0-87062-364-6 (collector's edition)
ISBN 978-0-87062-274-8 (entire series)

———————————

Library of Congress Cataloging-in-Publication Data
Innocent blood : essential narratives of the Mountain Meadows Massacre /
edited by David L. Bigler and Will Bagley.
    p. cm. — (Kingdom in the West : the Mormons and the American
frontier ; v. 12)
    Includes bibliographical references and index.
    1. Mountain Meadows Massacre, Utah, 1857—Sources. 2. Mormon pio-
neers—Utah—History—Sources. 3. Mormon pioneers—Utah—Biography.
I. Bigler, David L., 1927– II. Bagley, Will, 1950– III. Title. IV. Series.

F826.I56 2008
979.2'02—DC22

            2008018696

———————————

The paper in this book meets the guidelines for permanence and durability
of the Committee on Production Guidelines for Book Longevity
of the Council on Library Resources. ∞

For the families of those who died at Mountain Meadows

Whatever is has already been, and what will be has been before; and God will call the past to account.

Hyrum Smith was forty-four years old in February, 1844, and Joseph Smith was thirty-eight in December, 1843; and henceforward their names will be classed among the martyrs of religion . . . They were innocent of any crime, as they had often been proved before, and were only confined in jail by the conspiracy of traitors and wicked men; and their *innocent blood* on the floor of Carthage jail is a broad seal affixed to "Mormonism" that cannot be rejected by any court on earth, and their *innocent blood* on the escutcheon of the State of Illinois, with the broken faith of the State as pledged by the governor, is a witness to the truth of the everlasting gospel that all the world cannot impeach; and their *innocent blood* on the banner of liberty, and on the *magna charta* of the United States, is an ambassador for the religion of Jesus Christ, that will touch the hearts of honest men among all nations; and their *innocent blood*, with the *innocent blood* of all the martyrs under the altar that John saw, will cry unto the Lord of Hosts till he avenges that blood on the earth. Amen.

Doctrine and Covenants *of the Church of Jesus Christ of Latter-day Saints*, 135:6–7

CONTENTS

ILLUSTRATIONS

Maps

PREFACE

A s dawn broke on a late summer morning in 1857 at a lush alpine oasis in southwestern Utah Territory, a volley of gunfire from nearby ravines and hilltops suddenly ripped through the camp of a dozen large families and their hired hands on the way to California. The fusillade and subsequent attack killed or wounded about a quarter of the able-bodied men. The surviving Arkansans dragged their scattered wagons into a corral and leveled their long rifles at their hidden, painted attackers, stopping a brief frontal assault in its tracks. The men quickly built a wagon fort and dug a pit at its center to protect the women and children. Cut off from water and under siege, the emigrants fended off their assailants for five hellish days.

Finally, on Friday, 11 September 1857, hope appeared in the form of a white flag. The emigrants let the emissary, a Mormon from the nearby settlement of Cedar City, into their fort, and then the local Indian agent, John D. Lee, entered the camp. Lee told them the Indians had gone, and if the Arkansans would lay down their arms, his men would escort them to safety. The desperate emigrants trusted Lee's honor and agreed to his bizarre terms. They separated into three groups—the wounded and youngest children, who led the way in two wagons; the women and older children, who walked behind; and then the men, each escorted by an armed member of the "Nauvoo Legion," the local militia. Some say the surviving men cheered their rescuers as they fell in with their escort.

Lee led this strange cavalcade, which included almost a hundred women and children, about a mile from the campground to the rim of the Great Basin, where a single shot rang out, followed by an order: "Do your duty!" The escorts turned and shot down the unarmed men as painted "Indians" jumped out of oak brush to cut down the women and children. Lee directed the murder of the wounded. Within five minutes, a brutal act of religious terror was over, not to be surpassed in America until another bright September day exactly 144 years later.

Almost every man who executed this fearful atrocity, including the handful of Indians who participated, had been baptized as members of The Church of Jesus Christ of Latter-day Saints, today known as the Mormon or LDS church. Virtually all of them were decent, God-fearing husbands and fathers, and some of them had sacrificed everything they owned for their religion, not once or twice but three or four times. They had been raised in a culture in which it was a man's duty to lay down his life rather than see violence done to women and children. While some believe that the massacre was an act of simple larceny, the notion that some seventy men executed such an atrocity to acquire a few cows and gowns ignores the magnitude of the crime and uses a gross oversimplification to deny its complexity. To know what led these heads of families to deceive, betray, and murder other God-fearing men and their wives and children is to ask one of life's most perplexing question: why do deeply religious, upright men commit terrible acts? To ask this question is to stare evil in the face.

As Utah-born historians, we both learned the story of Mountain Meadows from official texts that tried to explain the "tragedy" in reassuring terms. One told how the taunts and depredations of a group of evildoers known as the "Missouri Wildcats" goaded Utah's peaceful settlers "to a point of extreme bitterness." These miscreants poisoned the meat of a dead ox, which "thoroughly aroused" the Paiutes who ate it and whose "law demanded blood vengeance against any of the offending tribe." So several hundred Indians attacked the emigrants on the eighth or ninth of September, and then "a number of white men arrived." In the final betrayal, white men shot down the males, but "hundreds of Indians who had lain in ambush rushed on the hapless party" and killed the women and children. "Unfortunately, no thorough investigation to bring the perpetrators to justice was held until twenty years later." Brigham Young swore in an 1875 deposition that he had urged his replacement as governor to take a federal judge to southern Utah, where Young pledged to provide "sufficient aid to investigate the matter and bring the offenders to justice." But the judge was more interested in convicting Brigham Young of murder than in endeavoring "to punish the actual perpetrators of the crime."[1]

---

[1]Berrett, *The Restored Church*, 335–37.

This history covered all the bases, explaining motive, means, and opportunity. Irony and tragedy mingled in the tale of a messenger sent from Cedar City asking what to do with the pesky wagon train and his heroic ride to deliver Brigham Young's response: "The emigrants must not be meddled with, if it takes all Iron county to prevent it. They must go free and unmolested." Unfortunately, the message arrived too late. The evidence that Mormon officials gave him persuaded H. H. Bancroft to argue that Mountain Meadows "was the crime of an individual"—John D. Lee—"the crime of a fanatic of the worst stamp."[2]

Yet somehow, this was not entirely comforting or even believable. We later found a much more honest story told in Juanita Brooks's courageous monograph, *The Mountain Meadows Massacre*. Her account established that much of the official story was obviously untrue. And as our mutual fascination with the American West led us to become historians, we discovered ourselves again and again confronted with that long ago and now largely forgotten September day. Due to the difficult problems with the sources that tell this story, neither of us was particularly interested in becoming entangled in it. Yet circumstances, notably the events sparked when massacre descendants successfully built a monument to the victims in 1990, drew us back to Mountain Meadows and its problems as relentlessly as Charybdis ensnared Odysseus. We came to appreciate the event as an inescapable vortex in Mormon history. Together, we are among the most widely published authorities on this dismal subject, a not entirely wished-for claim to fame.

Why return to this awful tale? Juanita Brooks's diligent work put all the essential evidence she could find into her books and her co-edited publication of John D. Lee's journals. Over the last decade, the Internet revolution has made many key Mountain Meadows sources, ranging from James Carleton's 1859 report to Brigham Young's 1875 affidavit, easily available to an international audience. Yet over the years we have turned up a wealth of evidence that casts entirely new light on the event.

We have attempted to assemble this material into a compelling record that presents the key aspects of the story and the divergent perspectives on it. At the same time, these records should help dispel the mystery and confusion surrounding the crime. Much of this evidence has been suppressed for more than a century, and it deserves to see the light of day—it is all the more

---

[2]Bancroft, *History of Utah*, 544, 567.

important because it survived the extensive purging of sources mentioned in the historical record that are now altered, missing, or destroyed. To help readers gain an insight into how the story of the massacre was first revealed and how it evolved over time, we have presented the material basically in a chronological sequence. Since the contemporary record contains the best historical evidence, we encourage readers to note how quickly the facts of the crime emerged from the "fog of war," and how much of what later historians came to believe was true was, in fact, based on fables fabricated many years later.

This volume looks at the combination of dogmas and events that led to the massacre. At the same time, we caution readers that the version of Mormonism described in these pages has little if anything to do with the modern institution. These documents show how rank-and-file Latter-day Saints such as James Skinner considered the crime "a dastardly outrage" even in the nineteenth century.[3] Some Utah Mormons, notably George A. Hicks, heroically opposed official efforts to protect the killers.

This volume publishes a selection of the essential documents, many for the first time, that we believe reveal the truth about the Mountain Meadows massacre. Having spent years wrestling with this horrific tale, we have definite opinions about how and why it happened, and obviously many will look at the evidence presented here and draw different conclusions. We long ago realized, as a wise friend once said with only slight exaggeration, that no faithful Mormon will ever accept that Brigham Young had anything to do with the massacre, while no non-Mormon will ever believe otherwise. We have done our best to explain the complex context that led to the creation of these documents and the crime they describe. In the process, we have tried to keep our editorial comments as few and dispassionate as possible—a task that may be impossible when dealing with such a hotly contested subject. We present our conclusions, based on sources slowly revealed over the years, in the Afterword. This new evidence refutes many of the old deceits and justifications and, although circumstantial, paints a convincing picture that the Fancher train's destruction was inescapable from the start of its *jornado del muerto* across Utah.

---

[3]Skinner, Reminiscences, 1915, 1.

Editorial Procedures

T his collection of Mountain Meadows narratives and documents attempts to represent faithfully the original records in a readable format. With noted exceptions, these transcriptions preserve the grammar, spelling, and diction of the originals. We capitalized the first letters of sentences and of personal names and added periods to the ends of sentences; where the case used in the manuscript is ambiguous, we follow standard capitalization. Where a writer employed commas in the place of periods, they are converted to periods, but otherwise we maintained the punctuation (or its absence) of the original.

We use [*sic*] more often than is our usual practice. Brackets enclose added letters, missing words, and conjectural readings. [Blank] indicates a blank space, while other bracketed comments, such as [*tear*], note physical defects in the manuscript. We placed interlined insertions in their logical location in the text. Abbreviations A.M. and P.M. are set in small caps. Underlined text is italicized, while crossed-out text is rendered as ~~strikethroughs~~. We used ellipses consisting of three periods throughout.

We have cited materials from the Archives of the Church of Jesus Christ of Latter-day Saints as "LDS Archives." The Journal History of the LDS church, a daily "scrapbook" of Mormon history consisting of journals, minutes, letters, and articles extracted (and expurgated) from church records by Andrew Jenson, is cited as Journal History. "Romney Typescript" refers to transcriptions that church secretary Edyth Romney made for Leonard Arrington's Mormon History Trust, which were sometimes provided to us with or in place of the original documents.

The material is organized into chapters, sections, and documents. Each document contains an abbreviated heading identifying the source and its location. Headings and footnotes citing newspaper articles contain the complete information needed to locate them. Full citations for other items, including manuscript numbers, are found in the bibliography. Footnotes cite published sources by author, title, and page number. Where available, newspaper citations are to page/column: 2/3. The bibliography contains a complete listing of all the books, articles, newspapers, journals, and manuscripts referenced in the footnotes. We have italicized book titles and put article, thesis, and dissertation titles in quotation marks. Manuscript citations appear in plain text without quotation marks. Quoted material from the sources reproduced in this volume is often not footnoted.

This volume contains an interview with Paiute tribal elder Clifford Jake, the series' first venture into oral history. The former first chairman of the Indian Peaks Band of the Paiute Tribe of Utah, Jake was of Southern Paiute and Western Shoshone ancestry. He died at age 85 on 23 May 2005 at his home in Enoch, Utah, leaving behind many descendants, including three great-great-grandchildren. His interview is presented with only minor editorial intervention.

The purpose of this work is to provide access to important documentary evidence about one of the most notorious and contentious crimes in the history of the West. In the interest of letting the material speak for itself, we have chosen to forgo detailed citations to the vast (and, in our view, often absurd) modern literature that seeks either to attack or defend the LDS church and its role in the massacre. Readers will find detailed references to the best of this material in other KINGDOM IN THE WEST volumes and in our own writings. We have consciously decided not to debate or respond to the personal attacks of our critics, which include assertions that question our integrity as historians: we believe the quality and balance of our work speaks for itself. To avoid being self-referential and tedious, we have chosen to rarely cite our previous books and articles, which examine many of the controversial subjects addressed here in detail. Where the reader finds an explanatory comment or note lacking, these works will provide additional background. We believe the documentary approach is especially appropriate for this highly contentious subject, since a close examination of the evidence is the only way to understand this particularly relevant episode in our nation's history.

Acknowledgments

W e must begin our thanks with a general appreciation of western history archives throughout the United States, including the staffs of the University of California's Bancroft Library, Yale University's Beinecke Library, the Henry E. Huntington Library, the California Historical Society, the California State Archives, the California State Library, the International Society, Daughters of Utah Pioneers, the Utah State Historical Society, the University of Utah's Marriott Library, Weber State University's Stewart Library, Southern Utah University's Gerald R. Sherratt Library, and Brigham Young University's Harold B. Lee Library. The support of the Beinecke Library with a research grant is deeply appreciated.

Archivist Ronald E. Romig, Assistant Archivist Barbara Bernauer, and Librarian Sue McDonald of the Library and Archives of the Community of Christ in Independence, Missouri, provided us with invaluable assistance. Deputy Director Russell Baker and Librarian Sheila Bevill of the Arkansas History Commission helped survey their Mountain Meadows materials and locate several significant newspaper accounts. Shirley Pyron has shared the files of the Carroll County Historical Society. Gary Tom of the Paiute Indian Tribe of Utah arranged a meeting with tribal elder Clifford Jake. Logan Hebner, John Alley, Lora Tom, and many tribal elders have contributed to our understanding of the Paiute people. Floyd A. O'Neil has shared his decades of scholarship and wide-ranging knowledge of the National Archives.

The staff of the Family and Church History Department of The Church of Jesus Christ of Latter-day Saints (formerly the Church Historian's Office or the Historical Department) have been extremely helpful.

Lora Blair, Roger P. Blair, M.D., Phil Bolinger, Lynn-Marie Dixon Fancher, Paul Fancher, Gary Fancher, Burr and Ada Fancher, Roger Logan, Patricia Norris, and Lesley Wischmann provided valuable information about the victims' families.

A hardy band of independent historians has greatly aided our undertaking. Polly Aird has contributed her invaluable store of insights. Blaine M. Simons gave us access to his seventy years of research on the subject, while William P. MacKinnon has contributed his almost fifty years of analysis of Utah Territory's conflicts with the United States. We wish to thank a number of transcribers, including Jane Carpenter, Lyndia Carter, Robert Carter, Jerry Dunton, John Eldredge, Michele Margetts, and our late friend, Harold Schindler. We especially acknowledge our debt to Ardis E. Parshall, who has provided access to some of her transcriptions of vital source documents.

We must recognize the contributions of Robert A. Clark and Charles E. Rankin, two great editors and friends, and we would be remiss not to thank Chuck for suggesting this volume's subtitle.

Finally, we treasure the enduring support of Evah Bigler and Laura Bayer.

INTRODUCTION

For as long as the American republic endures, 11 September 2001 will live in the memory of its people. In terms of lives taken, terrorists that day executed the deadliest attack on civilians in the nation's history. Yet the day also marks the anniversary of another terrible act of violence. On the same date in 1857, white settlers, with help from a few Indians, deceived, betrayed, and murdered over a hundred men, women, and children at a remote spot in southern Utah known as Mountain Meadows. No one knows for sure the exact number they killed because there were no survivors old enough to tell, but a reasonable estimate would be some thirty unarmed men, about forty women, most of them young mothers, and as many as fifty or more terrified children. They struck them down one at a time, face to face, with knives, hatchets, pistols, and muskets at point-blank range. Mercy was shown only to those too young to give credible testimony and who qualified as "innocent blood" under a doctrine revealed in Joseph Smith's last revelation.[1]

For those who died from a shot to the head or a knife to the throat, it was over in minutes. But for the seventy or more white men who did the killing, the wounds from that day were soul-deep and lasting. For them, it was never over; the horror never stopped. According to family tradition, it drove George Spencer to suicide. Delirious and dying, eighty-four-year-old Nephi Johnson preached in Indian tongues, sang hymns, and prayed. Suddenly his eyes opened wide, staring straight up, and he cried, "Blood! BLOOD! BLOOD!" He was reliving the horror, and he was afraid to die.

In 1999 president Gordon B. Hinckley of the LDS church spoke at the dedication of a new monument at Mountain Meadows. Except for the absence of a cross, it was patterned after the one that U.S. Army brevet major James

---

[1] *Doctrine and Covenants*, 132:19, 20, 26, 27.

H. Carleton and the men of Company K, First Dragoons, had raised there 140 years earlier. President Hinckley placed the entire blame on local settlers, ruled out Brigham Young's involvement, and said it could never be known why many members of his church had killed without mercy so many helpless victims.

"We can't understand it at this time," he said. He could not imagine how it could happen, because the crime was such a shocking deviation from the accepted history of Utah's pioneers, as well as from his church's deserved reputation today as a model of civic order and a defender of traditional American moral and civic values. "None of us can place ourselves in the moccasins of those who lived there at the time," he said later. It made no sense. It did not fit. Moreover, it was so long ago. "Let the book of the past be closed," Hinckley declared.[2]

Yet the nation's deadliest attack on innocent civilians prior to the Oklahoma City bombing is not an event lost in the mists of time, but as recent as yesterday. A daughter of Mountain Meadows survivor William Twitty Baker is still alive as we write this in January 2007. The descendants of the ones who did the killing and those who died at their hands are but three or four generations removed from that bloody field. The massacre was also not an aberration brought about by a strange movement of the stars or a foreign substance in the water. It can be understood only by examining the forgotten religious beliefs and events that led inexorably to it and throw needed light on the darkest day in Utah's history.

For good reason Mormons today often cannot understand how faithful husbands and devoted fathers could kill young mothers and their children. The story that they have been taught is fundamentally out of touch with the actual events as revealed in the documents presented here, for reasons George Orwell described: "The past is whatever the records and the memories agree upon." For those who are in full control of all records, the past is whatever they choose to make it.[3] Early LDS church historians long portrayed the Fancher party, made up mostly of women and children, as coming to Utah to torment a citizenry of nearly forty thousand, boasting a military force of some six thousand men. Having suffered so much persecution in the past, this story goes, southern Utah settlers could not take it anymore and went berserk. Behind

---

[2]Christopher Smith, "The Dilemma of Blame," *Salt Lake Tribune*, 14 March 2000, 1/1–3; 4/1–5.
[3]Howe, *Orwell's Nineteen Eighty-Four*, 95.

this story lies long-forgotten doctrines that shaped events and led the men who committed a terrible atrocity to believe they were doing God's work.

Foremost of these was the visionary imperative to establish the Kingdom of God as a sovereign political entity in North America's Great Basin as a condition of Jesus Christ's Second Coming. To believers, the Mormon theocracy was the stone envisioned by the prophet Daniel, "cut out of the mountain without hands," that would supersede all other systems of government, including that of the United States, within their own lifetime.[4] Highly confrontational was the purpose "to reduce all nations and creeds to one political and religious standard."[5]

Hardly had they opened their march to universal dominion, however, when Mexico in 1848 ceded to the United States the place that Brigham Young had chosen in 1847 to build the earthly Kingdom of God. Congress further violated the hope of divine rule three years later by reducing Deseret, the Almighty's projected domain, to the lowly status of a territory with the unwanted name of Utah, presided over by presidential appointees. These developments reopened earlier conflicts between a theocracy, ruled by God through inspired men, and a republic, governed by elected representatives of its people. Civil warfare in Missouri and Illinois had already shown the incompatibility of these two forms of government.

Over the next six years, nearly a dozen federal officials or employees took flight from the frustration of finding that it was impossible to do their jobs or out of fear of violence. When several Arkansas emigrant parties arrived in August 1857, the last non-Mormon federal officer in Utah was about to flee for his life.[6] Only one man, Brigham Young, then controlled a slice of the American West large enough to encompass New England, New York, Pennsylvania, and Ohio and which contained the major lines of east–west travel and communications between the Missouri River and California.

The implications of such power were ominous in light of Mormon doctrines concerning American Indians. Believing they and Indians shared the same Hebrew ancestry, Mormon missionaries encouraged the natives to identify themselves with the millennial movement rather than the U.S. The doctrine that the tribes would become an instrument of vengeance against the

---

[4]Dan. 3:45.
[5][Pratt], *Proclamation of the Twelve Apostles*, 6–7.
[6]He was U.S. Indian agent Garland Hurt.

enemies of Zion had been a source of conflict between the Mormons and their neighbors from the first days of the faith. As Young moved to assert a sovereign position in 1855, his call of hundreds of missionaries to forge alliances with the tribes set off alarms across the frontier. Chief Kanosh's Pahvants in central Utah and the Southern Paiutes, also called Piedes, on the Santa Clara River accepted the overture. The tribal lands of both lay across the southern trail linking Great Salt Lake City to southern California.

The red thread of vengeance that ran through Mormon history during this period was not limited to relations with the Indians. The memory of the murder of the founding prophet of the church and his brother thirteen years earlier was still bitter. Hundreds had taken an oath in the Nauvoo, Illinois, temple "to avenge the blood of the anointed ones," Joseph and Hyrum Smith, as well as other martyrs of the faith, upon a guilty nation.[7] The oath became applicable and compelling with Apostle Parley P. Pratt's 1857 murder in northwestern Arkansas while the emigrant train from that part of the state was on its way west. Pratt was struck down at the peak of a radical LDS revival known as the Reformation that was intended to cleanse latter-day Israel and prepare the people for the Second Coming. The uncontrolled religious frenzy saw the promulgation of the doctrine that some sins, such as adultery and apostasy, were not covered by Christ's atonement, but could only be redeemed by the sinner's own blood. Known as blood atonement, it stressed unquestioning obedience to church authorities.

Historians often ignore such long-since shelved and forgotten motives. Yet without their influence on events, President James Buchanan would never have found it necessary in 1857 to designate a new governor to replace Brigham Young, whose four-year term had expired three years earlier.[8] And without them, the emigrants from Arkansas would have rolled across the territory to their California destination as peacefully as thousands of others had done before them.

As it was, an American president used his constitutional power to appoint a new governor and order the U.S. Army to escort him west and restore federal law. James Buchanan's imposition of Washington's thumb on God's Kingdom touched off an explosive reaction. "As for any nation's coming to destroy

---

[7]Heber C. Kimball Journal, 21 December 1845.

[8]Young kept his seat under a provision of the territory's 1850 organic act that specified the governor would "hold his office for four years, and until his successor shall be appointed and qualified."

this people," Young thundered, "God Almighty being my helper, they cannot come here."[9] The appointed governor of an American territory, who kept his seat for lack of a replacement, asserted his own understanding of constitutional authority. He threw off the federal yoke and seized all of present Utah, most of Nevada, and portions of Colorado and Wyoming. The Mormon leader prepared to defend a sovereign position.[10]

So it was that four years before the South seceded from the Union, an American territory moved militantly to establish and uphold an independent state. On 15 September 1857, four days after the massacre at Mountain Meadows, just as long as it would take for the word to reach him at Salt Lake, Brigham Young declared martial law, shut down travel without a permit across much of the West, and mobilized the Mormon theocracy's military arm, the Nauvoo Legion, also known as the Utah militia, to repel the threatened "invasion." (He never addressed the question of whether an American army could invade an American territory.) Privately he also sent agents to warn the Indians that the Mormons' enemies were also their enemies and "they must be our friends and stick to us." If Young's actions seem incomprehensible today, they were in perfect harmony with the prophetic mission that the stone of Daniel, "cut out of the mountains" of western America, would establish the Kingdom of God, "which shall fill the whole earth, and shall stand for ever." There was no alternative to sovereignty.[11]

As the U.S. Army's Utah Expedition marched west from Fort Leavenworth, a Mormon express bore news of its coming to Great Salt Lake. Riding in the wagon was the last of Parley P. Pratt's many widows, the emotionally unhinged Eleanor McLean Pratt. She cried for his "innocent blood" to be avenged, a cry that was echoed throughout the Mormon settlements. She called down vengeance on her legal husband, Hector McLean, who had taken revenge on the apostle for stealing his wife and children. And she called for vengeance on the state of Arkansas and the country at large for allowing McLean to do it.

Into this aroused hive of resentment and religious fervor came several parties of farm families from northwest Arkansas. Unlike unruly companies of

---

[9]Brigham Young, 13 September 1857, *Journal of Discourses*, 4:226.

[10]For some of many reports of Young's declaration of independence, see Oliver Lee Robinson Diary, 13 September 1857; Joseph Harker Journal, 21 October 1857; Milton D. Hammond Journal, 13 September 1857; Salmon River Mission Journal, 22 October 1857; and Brooks, ed., *On the Mormon Frontier: The Diary of Hosea Stout*, 2:636.

[11][Pratt], *Proclamation of the Twelve Apostles*, 1.

gold seekers, hell-bent on "seeing the elephant," they were moving west to make new homes in California and were taking all they owned with them. Much of their wealth was in the form of large droves of cattle, but some carried significant amounts of cash as well. Their leaders were tested trail captains taking their wives and children over a route they had traveled before. These trains had left Arkansas weeks before Pratt's murder, but rumors in those days spread fast and seldom accurately. One rumor claimed some of the Arkansans had taken part in Pratt's murder. Another had it that others had helped kill the Mormon prophets, Joseph and Hyrum Smith. For a century and a half, those who controlled the memory of the past, as George Orwell described, have maligned the emigrants' character and falsified who they were and what happened to them.

It was a bad time in Utah for apostates and the enemies of Zion. The culture of fear and hostility is hard to imagine today. Forty years later, John M. Higbee, whose order began the slaughter at Mountain Meadows, said, "there was with many a GREAT REFORMATION, with others a craze of fanaticism, stronger than we would be willing to admit."[12] Level-headed men did what they were told out of fear for their own lives and the welfare of family members, as Homer Brown at Nephi explained: "The Bishop wanted those that would rather have their right arms severed from their body than to back out of defending this people to raise their hands," he said. "(I think all hands were raised.)"[13] No doubt those who were more afraid *not* to kill that day at Mountain Meadows outnumbered the fanatics.

The LDS church built a new monument at Mountain Meadows in 1999: except for the lack of a cross, it was a replica of the cairn the First Dragoons raised at the site in 1859. At outdoor services that September in the little valley near the rim of the Great Basin, several hundred descendants and relatives from across America gathered to memorialize their slain kinfolk and inter the bones of twenty-eight men, women, and children found during the construction of the cenotaph. Escorted by an honor guard of local Boy Scouts, family members reverently carried the bones in small handmade wooden arks to the new monument, where they were buried in soil from Arkansas.

---

[12]John Higbee, 1896 Statement, MMM File, LDS Archives.

[13]Journal of Homer Brown, 9 August 1857, LDS Archives.

As a deep stillness fell over the little mountain valley, Stanton Cram, pastor of the Friendship Baptist Church in Springdale, Arkansas, asked the question that mattered most for the living. No one knows the hour or the way he will be called home, the Reverend Cram said. If it would be today at this place, as it was for those slain here so long ago, he asked, "Are you ready?" A profound silence and an inexpressible sense of sadness then fell over those assembled as the Baptist preacher sang a familiar gospel song that seemed composed for just that moment.

> I am a poor, wayfaring stranger,
> A travelin' through this world below,
> But there's no sickness, toil, nor danger,
> In that bright land to which I go.
> I know dark clouds are going to gather 'round me.
> I know my way'll be rough and steep,
> But beautiful fields lie just before me,
> Where God's redeemed their vigils keep.
> I'm going there to see my mother,
> She said she'd meet me when I come,
> I'm only going over Jordan,
> I'm only going over home.
> I'm going there to see my Savior,
> I'll dwell with Him and I'll never roam.
> Oh I'm just goin' over Jordan.
> I'm only goin' over home.

This is the story of the wayfaring strangers remembered in this old hymn.

Chapter 1

"I Am a Poor Wayfaring Stranger"
The Arkansas Families

The first reports of the murder of some 120 men, women, and children who had set out for California from rural communities in the Ozark Mountains in April 1857 reached northwestern Arkansas before Christmas, and detailed accounts of the crime appeared in eastern newspapers early in 1858. At first the stories of the horrible fate that befell the dozen families or more who made up this wagon train of prosperous farmers and cattlemen must have seemed unbelievable to the husbands, fathers, mothers, children, and cousins they left behind.

Over the next three years, the relatives of the victims in Arkansas and elsewhere sought to learn what had happened—and why. They successfully pressured the federal government to recover the children who had survived the atrocity, and they lobbied, unsuccessfully, that justice be done to their murdered kinfolk. They sought to document the dead, filing detailed affidavits that, although long buried in government files, describe the fortunes of the victims and provide insights into the character of the people slain in September 1857 at a lonely oasis on the wagon road to California.

Examining the first reports of this event and the reaction of the families who suffered its consequences drives home the human consequences of the most violent act to occur in the thirty-year history of America's overland wagon roads.

Seeming to Exult in Their Crimes

The news "that a whole train of emigrants from Salt Lake city, for San Bernardino, composed of twenty-five families ... had been cruelly massacred" in Utah

Territory appeared in the *Los Angeles Star* on 3 October 1857, less than a month after the murders. "Although the rumor was generally believed in San Bernardino," wrote the *Star*, "we confess our unwillingness to credit such a wholesale massacre."[1]

The first reports to reach the American people blamed the Indians, but added justification for their committing the atrocity. Religious authorities in southern Utah and the Mormon colony at San Bernardino, near Los Angeles, tried to manipulate information about the killings. Col. William Dame, commander of the Nauvoo Legion's Iron County Brigade, allowed two independent witnesses to travel to California with a Mormon freight train, apparently believing their reports would be helpful. Given what George Powers and P. M. Warn did report, Dame made a major miscalculation about his ability to hide what had transpired and who actually committed the murders at Mountain Meadows.

"THE LATE HORRIBLE MASSACRE,"
LOS ANGELES STAR, 17 OCTOBER 1857, 2/2-3.

... As each will draw his own conclusions from the narrative, without further comment we give the statements of Messrs. Powers and Warn, regarding the late Massacre of the Plains.

Mr. George Powers, of Little Rock, left Arkansas, and with his train arrived at Salt Lake in August. He says:—

We found the Mormons making very determined preparations to fight the United States troops, whenever they may arrive. On our way in, we met three companies of 100 men each, armed and on the road towards the pass above Fort Bridger. I was told at Fort Bridger, that at Fort Supply, twelve miles this side of Fort Bridger, there were 400 armed Indians awaiting orders; they also said that there were 60,000 pounds of flour stored at Fort Bridger for the use of their army. We found companies drilling every evening in the city. The Mormons declared to us that no U.S. troops should ever cross the mountains; and they talked and acted as if they were willing to take a brush with Uncle Sam.

We remained in Salt Lake five days, and then pushed on, hoping we might overtake a larger train, which had started ten days ahead of us, and which proved to be the train that was massacred. We came on to Buttermilk Fort near the lone cedar, 175 miles, and found the inhabitants greatly enraged at the train which had just passed, declaring that they had abused the Mormon women, calling them w——s, &c, and letting on about the men. The people had refused to sell that train any provisions, and told us they were sorry they had not killed them there; but, they knew it would be done before they got

---

[1] *Los Angeles Star*, 3 October 1857, 2/3. For this and the other early newspaper reports, see Chapter 5.

in. They stated further, that they were holding the Indians in check until the arrival of their chief, when he would follow the train and cut it in pieces.

We attempted to purchase some butter here; the women set it out to us, and as we were taking it away, the men came running and charging, and swore we should not have it, nor anything else, as we had misused them. They appeared to be bitterly hostile, and would hardly speak to us. We were unable to get anything we stood in need of. We camped at this place but one night.

At Corn Creek, we found plenty of Indians, who were all peaceable and friendly. We learned nothing of the train, except that it had passed that place several days before, and we were glad to find we had gained so much on them. The next place where we heard of the Train was on our arrival at Beaver, 230 miles from Salt Lake. Here we learned, that when the train ahead were camped at Corn Creek, which was thirty-five miles back, and at which place we found the Indians so friendly, an ox died, and the Indians asked for it. Before it was given to them, a Mormon reported that he saw an emigrant go to the carcass and cut it with his knife, and as he did so, would pour some liquid into the cut from a phial. The meat was eaten by the Indians, and three of them died, and several more were sick and would die. The people of Beaver seemed also to be incensed against the train, for the same reason as before reported. I asked an Indian, at Beaver, if there was any truth in the poisoned meat story; he replied in English, that he did not know, that several of the Indians had died and several were sick; he said their water melons made them all sick, and he believed that the Mormons had poisoned them.

We laid by at Beaver several days, as the Bishop [Philo Farnsworth] told us it was dangerous for so small a company as ours to go on. Our train consisted of only three wagons, and we were hurrying on to join the larger one.

While waiting here, the train of Wm. Mathews and Sidney Tanner of San Bernardino came up, and I made arrangements to come on with them.[2] We came on to Parowan, and here we learned that the train ahead had been attacked by the Indians, at the Mountain Meadows, fifty miles from Parowan, and had returned upon their road five miles to a spring, and fortified themselves. We then drove out of Parowan five or six miles, and camped at what is called the Summit [on 8 September 1857].

Next morning an express arrived from Mr. Dame, President of Parowan, requesting us not to proceed any further that day if we pleased; also that Mathews and Tanner should return to Parowan, and bring me along with them. We returned, and a council was held, at which it was advised by Mr. Dame, that I should go back to my own train, as they did not wish to have strangers in their train. He also stated, that at two o'clock that morning [9 September

---

[2]Mathews and Tanner were members of the San Bernardino Stake High Council, and Mathews was a counselor in the stake presidency. Earlier that year, he had brought arms and ammunition to Utah. On reaching San Bernardino, he reported, "the ammunition we will make every exertion to get as soon as we can but we have to work exceedingly carefull to avoid suspicion." See Mathews to Young, 7 October 1857.

As commander of the Nauvoo Legion's Iron County Brigade, Col. William H. Dame issued the order to kill the emigrants at Mountain Meadows. He later threatened to "put the saddle on the right horse" if blamed for the murders. Despite his involvement in the atrocity, Dame remained president of the Parowan Stake of Zion until 1880.
Courtesy Special Collections, Southern Utah University.

1857], he had received an express from the train ahead, stating they were surrounded by Indians, who had killed two or three of their number, and asking for assistance. While we were talking, an express came in from Beaver, stating that the Indians had attacked my train in the streets of the place, and were fighting when he left. One reason given, was that ten miles the other side of Beaver, an emigrant train had shot an Indian, which greatly enraged them; that the people of Beaver went out in the night and brought the emigrants in, and were followed by the Indians, who made the attack after their arrival.

On the receipt of this news, another private council was held; after which I was called in and told, that in consequence of the fight behind, it would be for their advantage to bring me through, provided I would obey council and the rules of the train. To this I assented, being anxious to get on, and asked what was required of me. Mr. Dame replied, that in passing through the Indian country, it might be necessary for me to be laid flat in the wagon and covered with blankets, for two or three days, as the Indians were deadly hostile to all Americans; that if I was seen, it would endanger the safety of the whole train. My friend Mr. Warn, was told that he could also go on upon the same conditions.

At Parowan, it seems, when it was "for their interest" to bring us through, the Elders had no control over the Indians; while at Buttermilk Fort, they were able to restrain them, as they declared, under great provocation.

On Friday, the 18th [11th] day of September, we left Parowan, and arrived at Cedar City, some eighteen miles, about one o'clock. During the afternoon, an express arrived from the Indians, stating that one of their warriors had run up and looked into the corral, and he supposed that "only five or six of the emigrants were killed yet." These were the words of the expressman. The same night, four men were sent out from Parowan, to go and learn what was the fate of the train, and, as they pretended, to save, if possible, some of its members.

I omitted to mention, in the proper place, that Mr. Dame informed me that the attack on the train commenced on Monday, the 14th of September.[3] I asked him if he could not raise a company, and go out and relieve the besieged train. He replied, that he could go out and take them away in safety, but he dared not; he dared not disobey counsel.[4]

On Saturday [12 September], at twelve o'clock, we left Cedar City. About the middle of the afternoon, we met the four men who were sent out the night previous, returning in a wagon. Mathews and Tanner held a council with them apart, and when they left, Mathews told me the entire train had been cut off; and as it was still dangerous to travel the road, they had concluded it was better for us to pass the spot in the night. We continued on, without much conversation, and about dusk met Mr. Dame, (I did not know that he had left Cedar City) and three other white men, coming from the scene of the slaughter, in company with a band of some twenty Indian warriors.[5] One of the men in company with Mr. Dame, was Mr. Haight, President of Cedar City. Mr. Dame said they had been out to see to the burying of the dead; but the dead were not buried. From what I heard, I believe the bodies were left lying naked upon the ground, having been stripped of their clothing by the Indians. These Indians had a two-horse wagon; [it was] filled with something I could not see, as blankets were carefully spread over the top. The wagon was driven by a white man, and beside him there were two or three Indians in it! Many of them had shawls, and bundles of women's clothes were tied to their saddles. They were also all supplied with guns or pistols, besides bows and arrows. The hindmost Indians were driving several head of the emigrants' cattle. Mr. Dame and Mr. Haight, and their men, seemed to be on the best of terms with the Indians, and they were all in high spirits, as if they were mutually pleased with the accomplishment of some desired object. They thronged around us, and greeted us with noisy cordiality. We did not learn much from them. They passed on, and we drove all night in silence, and at daylight camped, and were told we were three miles beyond the scene of the slaughter. We lay by here two or three hours to rest, and then drove all day, twenty miles, at night camping on the Santa Clara River, near the Chief Jackson's village.

---

[3] This statement provides surprising evidence that the massacre happened a week later than most experts believe, but given when he arrived in California, Powers's date appears to be incorrect.

[4] The only "counsel" William Dame was compelled to obey as a Latter-day Saint would have to come from a higher LDS priesthood authority. As stake presidents, Dame and Isaac Haight were the highest ranking priesthood officials in southern Utah. The only higher priesthood officer they had talked to for months was Apostle George A. Smith.

[5] The editor of another southern California paper spoke with Powers and Warn when they arrived in Los Angeles and concluded there were no Indians engaged in the affair, but that the Indians they had seen were Mormons in disguise. See "The Federal Government and Utah," *Southern Vineyard*, 29 May 1858, 2, Chapter 6.

Next morning, after driving a few miles, we stopped to water. Jackson and his band soon came to us; and in a few minutes pointed out Mr. Warn as an American. The Mormon boys denied it, but the Indians were dissatisfied, and appeared restive. The Chief came up and accused me of being an American; appeared mad; stepped round; shook his head, and pulled his bowstring. He then sent several men on our road ahead. Mr. Mathews advised us to leave there as quick as possible, as it was getting dangerous.

At Jackson's, we engaged Mr. [Ira] Hatch to go on to the Muddy as an interpreter. It was a fortunate circumstance for us that this Mr. Hatch arrived at our camp at the very moment that we were wishing for him most. Mr. Mathews told me he was an Indian missionary, and of great influence among them. He could do more with them than anybody else; and if he could not get me over the road, nobody could. Mr. Tanner had declared that he would not go on without Mr. Hatch, and pretended to be afraid of the dangers of the road.[6]

Next morning, Mr. Hatch left us and went on to the Muddy. About a day's drive, the other side of the Muddy, we met him returning in company with two young men, brothers Young, horse-thieves, who were escaping from justice in San Bernardino; having been assisted in getting away by those who had them in custody. Mr. Hatch stated, that when he reached the Muddy he found the Young boys, in company with an emigrant who had escaped the massacre. That on his arrival, there was not an Indian in sight, and that he had to give the whoop to call them from concealment. He said in continuation, without appearing to notice the discrepancy, that on his arrival he found the Indians hotly pursuing the three men; and that they jumped upon the emigrant and killed him before his eyes, before he could interfere to prevent it. He said he threw himself between the boys and the Indians, and had great difficulty in saving them. The Indians were in a great excitement, as he said, but that as Mathews and Tanner were Mormons, they could pass without danger.

We arrived at the Muddy the day after we met Mr. Hatch, and the Young boys. We found here 30 or 40 Indians, and the mail riders from Los Angeles, who had come in that morning. The Indians were very friendly, and shook hands with everybody. No expression of hostility to Americans was heard, but that was accounted for on the ground that this was a Mormon train.

At the Vegas we found another band of Indians. The chief asked our interpreter whether our captain had brought him no word from Brigham Young, whether he was nearly ready to fight the Americans yet; adding that he was ready, had got his arrows poisoned, &c &c.

---

[6]Warn told correspondent "Yo Mismo" (William Wallace) of the *Alta California* that mail carrier William Hyde joined the Mathews-Tanner train two days out of San Bernardino. Hyde told Warn that Jackson had "a little book or journal of one of the emigrants in which was written the name, 'William B. Jones, Caldwell County, Missouri.'" See "Later from the South: The Murders at Mountain Canon Confirmed," *Alta California*, 27 October 1857, 1/4.

MAJ. ISAAC C. HAIGHT, CIRCA 1857
Along with Col. William Dame, Haight issued
the orders to "decoy and exterminate" the
Fancher party. Like John D. Lee, Haight was
sealed to another wife by Brigham Young in
January 1858, which critics naturally perceived
as a reward for carrying out difficult orders.
Haight was excommunicated from the LDS
church in 1870, but Young quietly reinstated
him in 1874. *Courtesy of the Will Bagley Collection.*

At the Cotton Woods, 15 miles from the Vegas, the chief, called Brigham
Young, said he was afraid of the emigrant train behind, and wished to know
if they would shoot.

On the 1st October, we arrived at San Bernardino, and I was advised by
Mr. Mathews, who I learned, was a President or Elder in that place, not to
associate with the damned apostates, that they were cut throats of the worst
character. If I wished, they would give me constant work at their mill in the
mountains, and I must be careful not to talk too much of what I had seen.

Whilst in San Bernardino I heard many persons express gratification at the
massacre. At the church services on Sunday, Capt. [Jefferson] Hunt occupied
the pulpit, and among other things, he said that the hand of the Lord was in
it; whether it was done by white or red skins, it was right! The prophesies concerning Missouri were being fulfilled, and they would all be accomplished.

Mr. Matthews said the work had just begun, and it should be carried on
until Uncle Sam and all his boys that were left, should come to Zion and beg
for bread.

I did not stay in San Bernardino, because it did not appear to be a free
country, for I am an American, and like freedom of thought and speech.

Thus far the narrative of Mr. Powers.

On being asked, if he did not at any time express any feeling, in the company, at the wholesale massacre of his countrymen. He replied, it was not safe
to express an opinion. The men he was with were unscrupulous, and would

not have hesitated to kill him for any unguarded words. When the Indians passed by him, wearing the garments of American women, and seeming to exult in their crimes, his blood boiled, but he dared not speak; and after they were gone, he asked Matthews, with earnestness, why it had been done. Matthews replied, that he must not grieve or take on, for the women were all prostitutes, that their bodies had been examined by President Dame, and this ought to console him. Matthews rejoiced greatly at the massacre, and considered it the beginning of long delayed vengeance.

Mr. Tanner regretted it, and seemed to be deeply grieved.

It is supposed that one hundred and eighteen (118) persons were killed of whom fifty six (56) were men, and that fifteen (15) children were taken back to Cedar City—of whom, not one was over six years old. It was reported, that but one Indian was killed.

Mr. P. M. Warn, of Bergen, Genesee county, New York; who was a fellow-traveler with Mr. Powers, on that fatal journey, corroborates the statements of Powers, so far as he was acquainted with the facts, and gives the following additional particulars, which did not come under the observation of Mr. Powers:

Mr. Warn states that there was a coolness between himself and Mr. Matthews, arising from the frankness with which he expressed his opinions, and in consequence of this, he was not treated with as much confidence as Mr. Powers.

Mr. Warn arrived at Salt Lake, via Independence, on the 7th of April last, and remained until the 26th [of August 1857], on which day he started for California, as a passenger in Matthews and Tanner's train. He states, that on his journey through the settlements, which was a week or ten days subsequent to the passage of the murdered train, he every where heard the same threats of vengeance against them, for their boisterousness and abuse of Mormons and Mormonism, as was reported, and these threats seemed to be made with the intention of preparing the mind to expect a calamity, and also when a calamity occurred, it should appear to fall upon transgressors, as a matter of retribution.

Mr. Warn says according to his memorandum, "On the 5th of September we encamped at Corn Creek. Here I had conversation with the Indian agent, concerning the poisoning of the ox. He said that six Indians had died; that others were sick and would die. Upon one of them, the poison had worked out all over his breast, and he was dead next morning, as reported.[7] After-

---

[7] If this man was a government agent, he was probably George W. Armstrong, a Mormon hired by Brigham Young. "Pilgrim," a member of the Dukes company, said the poison story was "regarded by every person in this train as a fabrication, on the part of the Mormons to clear themselves of suspicion, and to justify the Indians in murdering that company of emigrants." The correspondent said his company camped at Corn Creek with William Mathews, the San Bernardino Mormon official "who started the tale," ten days after the Fancher party, "but during our stay, we never heard anything of the poisoning. We used the same water, and between five and six hundred head of our cattle and horses used the same water, yet we discovered no poison, nor heard anything of it, till we got to Parowan, 85 miles from Corn Creek, where Mathews started the story." See "Letter from San Bernardino," *San Francisco Evening Bulletin*, 12 November 1857, 2/3.

wards, I conversed with an Indian, said to be the war chief Ammon, who spoke good English. I inquired how many of his tribe had died from eating the poisoned animal. He replied not any—but some were sick. He did not attribute the sickness to poison, nor did he give any reason for it. His manner, and that of all his people towards us, was not only friendly, but cordial; and he did not mention the train which had been doomed. Besides the Mormon train, there were camped at this place two or three emigrants trains, amounting to fifteen or eighteen wagons, with whom the Indians were as friendly as with ourselves. From Corn Creek, nothing of importance occurred more than is related by Mr. Powers, until we arrived at Cedar City. Here the four men, spoken of by Mr. Powers, (and among whom I recognized Mr. Dame,) arrived at our camp; they wished to get fresh animals, that they might go on that night to the besieged party. This was on Friday night, the night on which the slaughter was completed. They rested an hour or two, and took refreshments. In the conversation which ensured, one of our party said, "be careful, and don't get shot, Mr. Haight." Mr. H. replied, "we shall have no shooting;" emphasizing the we, and throwing up his head, as if he meant to imply that the shooting would be all over before he arrived. They left us in good spirits."

One reason that may be assigned for the massacre of this train, is, that it was known to be in possession of considerable valuable property, and this fact excited the cupidity of the Mormons. It was said, they had over 400 head of stock, besides mules, &c. They were well supplied with arms and ammunition, an element of gain which enters largely into all Mormon calculations. The train was composed of families who all seemed to be in good circumstances, and as they were moving to California, their outfit indicated that they might be in possession of considerable funds. The men were very free in speaking of the Mormons; their conduct was said to have been reckless, and they would commit little acts of annoyance for the purpose of provoking the saints. Feeling perfectly safe in their arms and numbers, they seemed to set at defiance all the powers that could be brought against them. And they were not permitted to feel the dangers that surrounded them, until they were cut off from all hope of relief.

Mr. Warn states, in speaking of the emigrant who escaped and was killed at the Muddy, that at Painter Creek, some six or seven miles on the other side of the place of massacre, a Mormon told him that one of the little girls who was taken back, and who is about six years old, said that she saw her mother killed by an arrow, and that her father had escaped to California.[8] This was before Hatch joined the train. The matter of the escaped was talked over by the Mormon captains, and Mathews made the remark, "If the man comes into our train, he shall not be received!"

---

[8]Circumstantial evidence indicates this child was Mary Miller; her father and perhaps one of the messengers was Joseph Miller, age 30.

As P. M. Warn observed, everywhere he spoke with local settlers he heard "the same threats of vengeance" against the Arkansas emigrants "for their boisterousness and abuse of Mormons and Mormonism." But he clearly doubted the tales he heard of emigrant depredations. "These threats seemed to be made with the intention of preparing the mind to expect a calamity," he observed, "and also when a calamity occurred, it should appear to fall upon transgressors, as a matter of retribution."

WHY ALL THIS CONCEALMENT?

As increasingly detailed reports of the massacre reached the Mississippi Valley early in 1858, relatives of the three hundred or so Arkansans who had set out for California the previous spring clung to hope that their loved ones had somehow escaped such a terrible fate. This optimism vanished for the Fancher, Cameron, Dunlap, Baker, Mitchell, Jones, and Tackitt families when reports drawn from the *Alta California* containing "particulars about the murdered emigrants" arrived from San Francisco and appeared in local newspapers.

P., "THE IMMIGRANT MASSACRE," *DAILY ALTA CALIFORNIA*, 17 OCTOBER 1857.

Angels [Camp], October 14, 1857

Editors Alta: This morning, while conversing with some immigrants, who have lately arrived via the Plains from Arkansas, and are living within a few miles of this place, I related to them the circumstances of the massacre.[9] They immediately informed me that they knew who the parties were. They stated that there were three, and perhaps four, companies from Arkansas, while the balance of the company was made up of Missourians, who fell in with them; of these latter, they knew nothing, but the Arkansas companies, consisted of Faziers [Fanchers], Camerons and the two Dunlaps, and perhaps Bakers. They were from the counties of Marion, Harrol [*sic*] and Johnson. They say when they saw them, they were encamped six miles from Salt Lake City [in Emigration Canyon], that they had been there for some time, and that they intended to stay there until the weather got cool enough for them to come by the South Pass [the Southern Route], expecting to make a stay of eight weeks all together. Baker had not arrived there when they left, but as they can learn nothing from him or his company, they concluded that he had fallen in and decided to come into California with these companies. The two Dunlaps had each nine children, some of them well grown. If these are the persons who were

---

[9] Very likely, this group included Basil Parker, who mentioned passing through Angel's Camp in 1857 in his memoirs.

slaughtered, who can be so blind as not to see that the hands of Mormons are stained with this blood. How could so large a company remain among them for two months and they not learn one name? and why would the Indians kill every being, except those that were too young to communicate anything to their friends, or hardly tell a name, or tell who were the murderers of their parents, and brothers and sisters; or even discriminate between white men and Indians? Why all this concealment? and in the very face of it the Indians tell what they have done and sell all their spoils to the whites. It will do to lay this blood upon them, but I feel certain that investigation will throw it off. P.

P., "Letter from Angel's Camp,"
Daily Alta California, 1 November 1857, 1/3.

Further particulars about the murdered emigrants—
their names and circumstances—the Mormons guilty
of the crime—how they should be punished.

Angel's, October 29, 1857

By the late news from Los Angeles, I see that the information given by me in my last letter, in reference to the names of the murdered emigrants, is about to prove true. In view of this fact, I went out this morning to see the immigrants that gave me the information, to learn further particulars from them. I called on but one of the families, and they informed me that in Arkansas they lived but three miles from Baker's farm, and that he was generally known by the name of "Jack" or "Captain Jack," Baker. He was reported to be wealthy, and left home with four hundred head of cattle, accompanied by his two sons. One son, named George, had spent some years in California, and had lived about Stockton, Sonora and Columbia. The other son was single. The old man intended, as soon as he could settle here, to return by water and bring out the remainder of his family. In his company were two brothers, by the name of Mitchel, (one of whom had his family,) a man named Milam Jones, and a widow named Tacket, who was coming to live with her son in California. I think this son is living near Tuttletown. My informants saw all these persons at Fort Bridger, about the last of July. Fancier (I wrote Fazier by mistake in my other letter) had spent some years in California, but my informant did not know in what part. They think the whole company had at least a thousand head of cattle with them. They also had many splendid rifles and guns, and plenty of them. My informants tell me, that the day they passed the junction of the Cut-off and the main road through Salt Lake City, (thirty miles this side of the city,) they saw a party of Indians enjoying a feast given them by the Mormons. The Mormons said they had just finished a treaty with the Indians, the purpose of which was that the Indians were not to trouble the whites who travelled through by the Salt Lake route, as they wanted them to pass that way in order to trade with them.

The last news also confirms my opinion as to who were the perpetrators of this deed. There were some facts connected with the first information given by the Mormons of this slaughter, that convinced me that the murderers were not Indians. It may be true that Indians took part in the work, but the blame rests with those who led them on. The first of these facts is, that the young children were saved. This was no Indian act, but was natural for the Mormons, who wanted to train them to their faith. The second is, the suppression of all the names. Now, if no one of that large company did not tell his name to any Mormon, they certainly left some evidence among the property as to who they were and where they were from. The third is, the statement that the Indians had told the whites what they had done.

We are all at a loss to know what is to be done with these people, and we dread to contemplate the horrors of the future. If soldiers must be sent to conquer them, rivers of blood must flow through their valleys before it will be done. If they are to be left alone to do as they will, the great highway of travel between the Atlantic States and the Pacific will be closed, and Utah will be the place of refuge for all the villains who escape from justice in the States, and a worse set will be gathered there than the world has ever seen.

The only remedy seems to be to dissolve the Territorial government, declare their laws null and void, send large bodies of soldiers to be stationed at every town and settlement in the Territory, let martial law prevail, then hang or shoot every man that rebels, punish every one according to the crime he commits, and give encouragement to the Gentiles to settle there. By this policy the country will fill up with Gentiles. P.

One Company in Family Groups: The 1860 Arkansas Depositions

On a 1988 business trip to Washington, D.C., related to his work as an aerospace engineer, Ronald Loving, a descendant of John Fancher, whose brother Alexander died at Mountain Meadows, made what many consider the single most significant archival discovery related to the Mountain Meadows massacre. At the National Archives, in a green metal box containing the U.S. Senate's copy of the State Department's Territorial Papers of Utah, Loving found eight folders holding seventeen depositions that consisted of fifty-eight handwritten pages of testimony taken in Arkansas between 22 and 26 October 1860 from relatives of victims of the massacre.[10]

The folded cover sheet for William C. Mitchell's statement defined its purpose: "Papers in relation to the claims of the heirs of persons killed at the

[10]Loving, "Captain John Baker," 2.

Mountain Meadow in Utah Territory, for property lost." The depositions provided detailed information about the composition of seven families, their personal wealth, and their plans to make a new life in the West. Although the National Archives had microfilmed the depositions in 1953, historians remained unaware of their existence.

Beyond the stated purpose of Mitchell's claim, the intent of the depositions is not clear, but they may have been taken as a preliminary step to filing Indian depredation claims with the federal government, which had accepted responsibility for such losses in 1796.[11] If similar depositions were taken from other families who had relatives in the Fancher party, they may have been among the many Arkansas records destroyed during the Civil War.

PAPERS PERTAINING TO THE TERRITORY OF UTAH,
RECORDS OF THE U.S. SENATE, RG 46, NATIONAL ARCHIVES.

State of Arkansas
County of Carroll

Be it remembered that on this 22nd day of October, 1860 personally came and appeared before me the undersigned, John Bunch, an acting and duly commissioned Justice of the Peace, Mary Baker, the widow of John T. Baker Deceased, to me, personally, well known to be the widow of said John T. Baker, deceased, and who after being duly sworn according to law, to Testify the truth, the whole truth, and nothing but the truth, in regard to the matters in ~~controversy~~ and about the amount, kind, and quality of property, which John T. Baker had in his possession, and owned in his own right when he left the county of Carroll and state of Arkansas in the month of April AD 1857. Deposed as follows;

MARY BAKER

My name is Mary Baker;[12] I was lawfully married to John T Baker in the county of Madison and State of Alabama on or about [blank] of [blank] A D 1823; we emigrated to Arkansas in the year 1849, where we resided together as man and wife, and until John T. Baker left his home in Carroll County with a lot of cattle [and] horses . . . I have been informed and truly believe that after John T. Baker had proceeded as far as a place in the west known as "Mountain Meadows," he, together with a large number of persons in company with him, were murdered, and their property all stolen and appropriated by the mur-

---

[11]See Skogen, *Indian Depredations Claims*, 23–51.

[12]Beginning here, the depositions have been edited for readability, eliminating redundancies and formal legal language such as "as aforesaid," "in the above facts," and "hereto annexed" without notation. They do not include the long testimonials of authenticity made by the authorities who took the statements. Ellipses identify longer cuts in the text, none of which contain significant information. This transcription has been closely corrected against copies of the original manuscript, but for an alternate version, consult Judge Roger V. Logan, Jr.'s, 1992 edited copy in "New Light on the Mountain Meadows Caravan," 224–37.

derers; and . . . I have not at any time incurred any pay, or return of any of the property that John T Baker left with. The object my husband had in going to California was to sell a large lot of cattle, and when he left here in April 1857 for California he started with the following personal property:

138 head of fine stock-cattle
8 yoke of work oxen
1 yoke of work oxen, extra
2 mules
1 mare
1 large ox wagon
Provisions, cloathing, and camp Equipage for himself and five hands.

The cattle were all good stock, and all three years old and upwards—were picked cattle and such as in this market at the date of his departure from this place were worth at the lowest cash price twenty dollars per head and which would amount to the sum of $2760
The nine yoke of work oxen were worth in this market at the date of Departure, fifty dollars per yoke   450
The ox wagon was worth   100
The mules were worth each $125 [or]   250
The mare was worth   100
He had in cash the morning he left the sum of $98 in cash   98
The cloathing, provisions, Tents camp Equipage &c, was worth here   350
1 fine rifle Gun worth   25
1 Colts repeater   15
Amounting in all as far as I now remember to the sum of Four $4148.00
Thousand one hundred Forty Eight dollars in this market—I have placed this Estimate of the cattle and oxen at low figures, as I know that such oxen as those my husband left here with could not have been purchased at a lower price than from fifty five to seventy dollars per yoke—The stock cattle had been bought with the view to make quick sales on arriving at California, and were a well selected lot of cattle—My husband was a good trader and would not, and did not purchase any inferior cattle for the out fit—I believe that the foregoing statement of amounts, numbers and descriptions of personal property, is a true and correct inventory of the amounts property that John T Baker left this county with in the month of April 1857—and I am fully persuaded and verilly believe that property was worth at "Mountain Meadows," where my husband, as I am informed and believe, was murdered, the sum of about Ten Thousand dollars— I can only make this statement from information received from others, and here say of course, that I only form my opinion from "here say"—But be this estimate over, or under the amount that the property was worth at Mountain Meadows, I have stated truly, and faithfully upon my own knowledge, and upon such

information as I deem reliable, and I make this statement upon a full knowledge of the facts as being within my own knowledge, so help me God—

Her
Mary "X" Baker
Mark

JOHN H. BAKER, 22 OCTOBER 1860.

My name is John H Baker—I am a son of the witness Mary Baker . . . and John T Baker deceased— . . . I have of my own knowledge and recollection [and] full belief that her statements and calculations are correct—I was living only [one] half mile from my father when he started to Calafornia in April 1857, and Know that he had the number of cattle and other personal property set forth by Mary Baker; I was well acquainted with the price of stock at that time; was also well acquainted with the kind quality and worth of the property as mentioned in the tabular statement made in the deposition of Mary Baker, and I Know that the personal property was the property of my father, and that he started to california with all and more personal property than mentioned he had more Guns, saddles, bridles &c than is mentioned—I Know that such oxen as John T Baker took with him could not have been purchased in this market and got fixed and ready for the trip under a cost of from sixty to seventy dollars; I Know also that the mare and mules are put down at a low estimate, and as to the amount of Provisions, camp Equipage & my opinion is that it is below the real value, but of this I can not say with so much certainty—I have been in calafornia was there in the latter part of the year 1852, stayed there untill the month of September 1854, and from my knowledge of the country, and the price of property I think the property that John T Baker left here with in April 1857, would have been worth at Mountain Meadows, the full sum of Ten Thousand dollars—This statement however is only made from such general Knowledge as I have from the western trade, and also from the information of other Traders—I can not now state what amount of money my Father started with—But I know he had money with him . . . The stock cattle were a well selected lott of cattle, and were low in this market at Twenty dollars per head—I have a good knowledge of the quality of cattle, for I helped my father collect the cattle and also went a few days travel with him when he started to Calafornia, and have of my own personal knowledge gave the statements as regards the value of this property here—So help me God.

JOHN CRABTREE, 22 OCTOBER 1860.

I was well acquainted with John T Baker in his life time, and was living about a half or three quarters of a mile from him when he left, in April 1857 for calafornia—Mr Baker was a very industrious man, and a shrewd, good trader—I saw the cattle and property that John T Baker owned and started with to Calafornia—I can not give the exact number of cattle he started with but he had somewhere between one hundred and thirty and forty head of cattle—he had Two mules—and one mare 1 large ox waggon, Provisions, camp Equipage, and a general outfit for a trip from here to Calafornia—As to the amount of money he started with I do not Know—I believe the cattle he had and started with were worth in cash in this market the sum of Twenty dollars per head—I think the oxen he started with would have been worth fifty five or sixty dollars per yoke—I think the mules were worth at the time he left here ~~worth~~ one hundred and fifty dollars each—The mare was well worth in this market one hundred dollars—The ox waggon was worth one hundred and Twenty five dollars—And from my knowledge of the outfit, and the amount of Provisions necessary for the support of John T and his five hired hands I would say that the estimate made by Mary Baker at three hundred and fifty dollars is a very low estimate, and I think it would ~~have~~ more nearly have reached the sum of Five hundred dollars: I was at the house of John T Baker, frequently while he was collecting the cattle, and I was present in April 1857 when Baker started for Calafornia, and I had a good opportunity to notice the quality and condition of the stock and outfit and I have made the above estimate of the prices and value of the stock of cattle, oxen, mules, waggon, mare, &c on my own Judgement, and from my knowledge of the value of property at that time— and I think and believe that the estimate made by Mary Baker is below the real value of the amount of property that Baker owned, had in his possession, and took away with him when he started to Calafornia in the spring of the year 1857; I was present when he started and aided and assisted him on his way a few miles when he started—The John T. Baker of whome I speak was the same Baker of whom rumor says, was murdered in the west at a Place known as "Mountain Meadows"—I also know that the witness Mary Baker now lives at the same place where she did, where the said John T. Baker started in April 1857, for Calafornia, and I have been acquainted with the family and have lived a close neighbor for over 4 years next, before Baker left, and have lived a close neighbor to his widow ever since, so help me God.[13]

WILLIAM C. MITCHELL, 22 OCTOBER 1860.

I was personally well acquainted with Charles and Joel Mitchell—They were my sons, and I assisted them in making their outfit for the trip in the spring of 1857. They left in company with John T Baker and many others, and were murdered, as I am informed and believe, at "mountain meadows" in september—They were on their way to California, and when they left here they had in their possession and under their control the following personal property—

They had in cash when they left this county, in April 1857, about the sum of Two hundred and seventy five dollars.

---

[13]Here Hugh A. Torrance, who worked for John T. Baker, made a statement that essentially repeated the information in John Crabtree's affidavit.

They had thirteen yoke of good work oxen. They had Sixty Two head of other cattle and when they reached Washington county, they wrote to me that they had bought Ten head more and intended getting two more so as to make one hundred head in all. I have no doubt from all the information I have on this subject . . . that when they left the state they had with them one hundred head of good saleable cattle—The[y] one horse, saddle, and bridle—They had one large ox wagon, log chains, &c—They had their wearing apparel, beds, and bedding and cooking utensils—They had guns, pistols and Bowe [Bowie] knives. The property they had with them when they left for California in April 1857 was worth in this market, at the date of their departure, at a fair and reasonable cash valuation as follows:

13 yoke of work oxen @ $60.00 per yoke	$780.00
74 head of other cattle, cows, steers @ $12	$888.00
cash on hand when they left here	$275.00
1 large wagon, chains, &c	$120.00
1 horse saddle & bridle	$100.00
Guns, fire arms, knives, &c	$50.00
Clothing, beds, and bedding, Provisions, cooking utencils, camp equipage &c	$300.00
	$2513.00

. . . I have made the above estimate at what the said property was worth here, and . . . I believe that the amount is a fair estimate of the value of said property at the time said parties left. As to the value of said property at "Mountain Meadows" where the parties were murdered and robed, I have no knowledge [but] am informed and believe that said property was of double the value there to what it was here—and from all the information I have been enabled to obtain I believe that property at Mountain Meadows could have been worth the sum of about five or six thousand dollars—This last statement is only given as the information of others—so help me God.

Wm C Mitchell

SAMUEL MITCHELL, 22 OCTOBER 1860.

I am a brother to Charles R. and Joel D. Mitchell . . . I was well acquainted with the outfit of the parties, and acquainted with all the property . . . and from my knowledge . . . I believe that the value given and estimated, is a fair cash valuation of the property and its value in this market at the date of the departure of said parties for California—They left this county in company of John T. Baker and many others, all bound for California, and I have no doubt but what they were all murdered at a place known as "Mountain Meadows" so help me God—

Samuel Mitchell

JOSEPH B. BAINS, 23 OCTOBER 1860.

I have lived in Carroll County, Arkansas for a number of years, and was living here in the month of April 1857, and was living in ¼ of a mile of John T Baker when the parties all left for calafornia in April 1857. I now reside . . . within ¼ of a mile of Mary Baker, the widow of John T. Baker. George W Baker was the son of the same John T. Baker and Mary Baker, and I know that George W. left here about the same time of his father in April 1857—when George W Baker left he . . . had in his possession a considerable amount of cash and personal property, and had sold out his lands and was moving to calafornia—He had a wife and four children when he left here. He was Guardian of Melissa Ann Beller and she was also in company with him and he had in his possession as Guardian of Melissa Ann Beller, the sum of seven hundred dollars in cash—I had paid him as Guardian that amount for the Melissa Ann . . . I think Melissa Ann had a bed, bedding, wearing apparel, but of what value I cannot say. The amount of personal property within the possession of George W. Baker . . . was as follows:

2 ox waggons chains &c each worth at $125	$250
Had in cash on hand about	$500
He had beds & Beding, wearing apparel for himself and family, provisions for himself and family, worth	$500
3 young mares worth $100 each	$300
1 rifle gun	$25
1 double barrel shot gun	$25
136 head of cattle (or about that number) (worth in this market @ 20.00 each)	$2720
	$4320

. . . Baker had a good out fit, and his family was well provided for in the way of wearing apparel and provisions, &c, and I have placed the estimate at a sum that I am satisfied is a low estimate of what property was worth in this outfit. The cattle were a very good lot, and taking into consideration the demand for cattle at that time, I think the estimate is strictly within the cash limits of the market price here. The estimate of the cash paid him as Guardian for Melissa Ann Beller, may have been paid out in the stock purchased. But of this I am not positive; if the whole amount was expended in buying cattle, then the amount included the value of George W Bakers property and Melissa Ann Beller's estate. If perhaps all of said estate of Melissa Ann Beller was not expended here for stock, then the estimate is below the real amount of the value of said property. I have no doubt but what George W Baker, his wife, Melissa Ann, and all others in his family, except three children were murdered at the massacre of Mountain Meadows. Three of his children have been returned to this county, and now living within ¼ mile of me at their grandmothers, Mary Baker. The oldest of the children were recognized by their friends and relations here, as soon as they returned and this fact convinces me that said Baker and family, except the children, were all murdered at, Mountain Meadows, and further this deponent saith not, so help me God.

William C. Beller, 23 October 1860.

I was well acquainted with George W Baker, and . . . I was present when he started to move to Calafornia in April 1857, and saw his cattle and out fit for the trip—I think that George W Baker had, when he started from here, one hundred and fifty or sixty head of cattle, in which was included about eight yoke of work oxen . . . Now if the amount of cattle George W. Baker started with, was one hundred and sixty head and then out of that number the 8 yoke of oxen are taken, this would leave one hundred and fifty four head of stock cattle which at $15.00 per head would amount to the sum of $2160.00

8 yoke of oxen @ $55.00 per yoke	$440.00
3 horses, or mares 3 years old, and worth in cash in this market, $125.00 each	$375.00
2 ox wagons worth in cash & the cost him here	$260.00
About $400.00 in cash	$400.00
Beds, bedding, clothing for himself, & family, provisions	$500.00
1 shot gun, worth	$30.00
1 rifle, worth (cost him $45.00)	$30.00
	$4195.00

. . . I believe that the above is a low cash estimate of the property carried off with him when he left here in April 1857; He was moving to Calafornia, and had his wife, 4 children, Melissa Ann Beller, D. W. Beller, and 2 hired hands with him and was well supplied with provisions and cloathing &c for the trip—I have no doubt but what George W and all his family who started with him were all killed at "Mountain Meadows" except three of his children, who have been brought back to this county all of whome I could pick out of the crowd of children when they were brought back here—I know they are the children of George W Baker, and from all I can learn . . . I am fully satisfied that all were killed except children, who were in the train at Mountain Meadows and further this deponent saith not, so help me God.

John H. Baker, 23 October 1860.

George W Baker . . . left for Calafornia in April 1857, and had with him his wife, 4 children; Melissa Ann Beller, D. W. Beller, and Two hired hands—He had about 136 head of stock cattle—he had Eight yoke of work oxen which he worked to his waggons, and I think several extra yoke—he had 3 head of horses—Two ox waggons—Guns, provisions, cloathing, camp Equipage &c [worth] $3815.00

As to the cash on hand when he started, I do not now remember—and can not say what amount he had—I know he had money but the amount I do not Know—I have made the above estimate at that I think the property was worth here; that is at what it could have been cashed for.

I know the 3 children brought back here to be the children of George W Baker, and from what information I have been able to gather from them, and from information received from others, I am fully satisfied that George W Baker and all who went with him except the three children who have been brought back here were all killed at a place known as "Mountain Meadows."

IRVIN T. BELLER, 23 OCTOBER 1860.

I was well acquainted with George W. Baker, and I went with him when he started to move to calafornia [for] two days—I was acquainted with his property and outfit, and know the amount of property he had with him when he stated to move—He had the use of one hundred and sixty head of cattle, including work oxen and stock cattle and they worth in cash in this market at the time he left here, at least twenty dollars per head. $3,200.00

2 ox wagons, worth in cash	$275.00
3 mares were worth, $125.00	$375.00
1 shot gun, worth in cash:	$35.00
1 rifle, worth in cash:	$50.00
His out fit including beds and bedding, wearing apparel, provisions	$700.00
He had cash on hand about:	$500.00
	$5,135.00

I was there at the house of George W Baker most of the time he was making preparations to move, and was well acquainted with his arrangements, and make the above estimate from my own personal knowledge of the amount, quality and value of his property . . .

JAMES DESHAZO, 23 OCTOBER 1860.

I was well acquainted with Allen P DeShazo who left this county in the month of April 1857, bound for Calafornia—He left in company of John T Baker and I have no doubt but what he was murdered in the mountain meadows massacre—He left here with . . . seventeen head of stock cattle—The most of the lot were likely heifers and were worth in cash over two hundred dollars the morning he left here—I do not think he had but one steer in the lot, and they were a likely well selected lot of cattle—This together with his wearing apparel worth over fifty dollars, and a violin worth Ten dollars was all the property that I now remember that Allen P. had when he left—I believe that his cattle, cloathing and all he started with the morning he left here for calafornia was worth in cash in this market the sum of Three hundred dollars—Allen P DeShazo was my son . . .

Hugh A. Torrance, 23 October 1860.

I was acquainted with Allen P Deshazo who left here in company with John T Baker in the month of April 1857 bound for Calafornia—He had sixteen head of as likely young cattle as I ever saw in my life—They were all heifers and young cows, and were a well selected lot of cattle—Taking into consideration the Kind of cattle he had, and the cost trouble and expense attendant on getting said cattle together I would say that the morning he left here, they were worth at a low cash price the sum of Fifteen dollars per head, and I have no idea that Allen P Deshazo would have taken Twenty five dollars per head for the lot of cattle when he started with them . . . I suppose it would be a low estimate to put the amount of what his property was worth the morning he left here, at Three hundred dollars—and perhaps a larger sum.

Lorenzo D. Rush, 23 October 1860.

I . . . was well acquainted with the parties, or a great many of them who left in company with John T. Baker in the month of April, in the year 1857—I had a son who left in the same crowd, and who no doubt was with the crowd when they were all murdered at Mountain Meadows—From my knowledge of the county, the price of cattle, &c in the spring of 1857, I think the estimate made by witness James Deshazo and H A Torrance as to the worth of the property which Allen P Deshazo started with to California, is correct, and that estimate is a reasonable one . . .

I am the father of Milam Rush, and Know that he left here in the month of April 1857, bound for Calafornia; he left in company with John T Baker and many others, all of whom were murdered, as I am informed and believe, at Mountain Meadows, in Utah Territory in September of same year, and their property all carried away, or disappeared by the murderers—When my son Milam L. Rush left here he was the owner of . . . from ten to twelve head of cattle [and] he had one rifle Gun—Three Blankets—knives, and his wearing apparel, and also about Twenty five dollars in cash—I think his cattle were worth at a fair cash price at the morning he left here with them at least fifteen dollars per head—I think his wearing apparel, Rifle Gun, and other articles were worth in cash the sum of sixty three dollars—The estimate I make of the whole matter is this, I think that he had twelve head of cattle at $15 per head: $180.00

Cash on hand:	$25.00
His wearing apparel, gun, &c	$63.00
	$268.00

. . . I have no doubt but what said property was worth a much larger amount than the above estimate at the place where the parties were murdered.

Francis M. Rowan, 24 October 1860.

. . . In April 1857, I was residing in the county of washington, in this state, and John M. Jones and his Brother Newton Jones, on their way to California,

camped some 10 or 15 days within five or six miles of where I lived at that time—
I had been acquainted with the Jones' boys for a number of years previous to
that time, and when they camped there, I was frequently with the boys; I was
at their camp, and saw their property, and being well acquainted with the boys,
Milam Jones, and Newton Jones particularly, pointed out the property that
they owned—showed me their cattle and oxen—Of course I did not pay that
attention to the property that I would have done had I believed that I would
have ever been called upon to Testify about it—But my recollection is that the
two Jones boys owned four yoke of work oxen—one large ox waggin—John
M. Jones was married and had his wife and two children with him, and was
moving to Calafornia—He had with him the widow Tackett and three or four
of her children: Newton Jones, John M. Jones, his wife and two children, widow
[Cynthia] Tackett and three or four children, and Sebrun Tackett constituted
one company in family groups—The Jones boys owned the waggin, oxen and
out fit, and the others seemed to be living with them and depending on the
Jones boys for their support—The waggin was large and very hevier [heavily]
loaded; I suppose John M Jones had a gun and other fire arms but of what
value or number I do not Know—Newton Jones had a fine rifle Gun; they
appeared to be all well supplied with beds and beding and wearing apparel for
an excursion of that kind, and also with provisions—I know that there was in
the corral sixty six, or sixty eight head of stock cattle, but how many they had,
that is how many the Jones' had I do not now remember, but according to the
best of my recollection, Milam Jones had only about 8 head of the stock cattle as near as I can now Estimate. The value of the property owned by the two

Jones' boys I would say that the large ox waggin was worth in cash:	$125.00
4 yoke of work oxen at 65.00 per yoke	$260.00
8 head of stock cattle at 20.00 per head	$160.00
I would say that from my Knowledge of the number of persons along, that the beds, bedding, wearing apparel, provisions, furniture, camp Equippage, &c was worth:	$500.00
They had cash on hand but how much I know not—	
Newton Jones had over Twenty that I know of	$20.00.
The rifle gun was worth;	<u>$15.00</u>
	$1075.00

. . . There were several other persons along, and who had separate waggins—There were 3 men by the name of Peteat, or Pilleats—The oldest one
of the Peteats was a married man, had his wife and children along; They had
a separate camp and waggin; there was an other man Pleasant Tackett who
had a separate waggin; and before they started George W Baker drove up and
camped near the others—The Peteats and Pleasant Tackett had oxen and other
property but I can not say how many—They had horses, and camp equipage,
provisions &c, and appeared to be well fixed for the out fit—But it is impossible for me to separate the several claimants, or the amounts that each one

owned, only . . . I am well satisfied that the amount of property . . . was worth several thousand dollars—I have no doubt but what all the parties were murdered at "Mountain Meadows" in September 1857, except a fiew children who have been sent back to the states—and I further state that I believe that the property above described was lost or destroyed at Mountain Meadows in 1857—and further this deponent saith not—So help me God.

F. M. Rowan

FIELDING WILBURN, 24 OCTOBER 1860.

. . . I was living near the Indian line in washington county Arkansas in the month of April 1857—I was personally well acquainted with John M Jones, and Newton Jones, Pleasant Tackett, and the widow Tackett . . . when the parties were on their way to Calafornia, and while they were in camp on the Indian line. I was at their camp & stayed with them two or three days—I was well acquainted, and on intimate terms with the Jones boys, and saw their property . . . John M. Jones & his Brother had to my own knowledge; one large good ox waggin, 4 yoke of first rate work oxen—Their wagon was very heavily laden, with cloathing, beds and beding, Provisions, &c—The few stock cattle they had some six or eight in all were good cattle, and were all no doubt wirth the prices named [by] Francis M. Rowan. I know that there was about sixty head of stock cattle over and above the amount owned by the Jones Boys—But to whome it belonged I can not say—The widow Tackett, Pleasant Tackett, Peteats, and several others were in the crowd and all left the State of Arkansas for Calafornia together—They left sometime in the month of April 1857. The Peteats, Basham, and Tacketts had three waggins, several yoke of good oxen to each waggin and had one horse—had apparently plenty of provisions, cloathing and a general out fit to make the trip comfortable.

F. Wilburn

FELIX W. JONES, 24 OCTOBER 1860.

. . . I was well and intimately acquainted with John M. and Newton Jones who left Arkansas in April 1857, for Calafornia. They were my brothers. John M was Married and started with his wife and two children—He was moving to California—Newton was a young man, and was going with his Brother to Calafornia—I only knew [of] the waggon, and one yoke of oxen [but] I believe they had all the property mentioned in the statement of witness Rowan—The waggin was worth at the time the parties left here in cash one hundred and Twenty five dollars—The yoke of oxen I knew were worth sixty five dollars—The stears I mention, and one half the waggin belonged to Newton Jones—The other half of the wagon belonged to John M Jones—and the other oxen, and cattle &c spoken of by Rowan, and Wilburn belonged to John M., I suppose—I do not know how much money the boys had when they left—But Newton had thirty dollars or upwards—Newton also had a rifle Gun and John M Jones had a shot gun—worth perhaps fifteen or Twenty dollars each—I do not know what the provisions, cloathing and general outfit was worth, but from all the information I have been able to get in relation to the provisions, Tents cloathing and out fit, I would say that it was worth in cash between five and six hundred dollars.

Felix W. Jones

William C. Mitchell, 26 October 1860.

On this 26th day of October A.D. 1860, personally appeared before me, Moses P. Ray an acting justice of the peace . . . , William C Mitchell to me well known and made oath in due form of Law. That he was made acquainted with Lorenzo D. Dunlap, who left Marion County Arkansas in April 1857. On route for Calafornia in ~~Capt~~ John T. Baker Company and that Dunlap had a wife and Eight children who was all killed at or near a place called the Mountain Meadows—Utah Territory—except two small daughters who is at this time in my care . . .

I was appointed Special Agent to secure and take charge of the Children Survivors of the Mountain Meadows Massecre and secured the Children above mention at Fort Leavenworth in Kansas Territory in August A D 1859 and delivered them at Carrollton Arkansas in September 1859—and have no doubt of the Death of L D. Dunlap and was Killed at or near the Mountain Meadows in Utah Territory

Four yoke of oxen at $60 each	$240.00
12 head of cattle worth $15 each	$180.00
3 guns, pistols, knives, the worth	$50.00
1 wagon log chains, the worth 100	$100.00
Provisions, cooking articles and camp fixings, &c	<u>$350.00</u>
	$920.00

William C. Mitchell[14]

James D. Dunlap, 26 October 1860.

Jesse Dunlap and family of Marion County . . . was in company of Capt. John T. Baker and all of his family with the exception of three small daughters, I have no doubt was killed at or near the Mountain Meadows, in Utah Territory. And said Jesse Dunlap left with the following property, nine yoke of oxen worth sixty dollars per yoke, thirty head of cattle worth twelve dollars per head, two head of horses worth one hundred dollars cash, three wagon log chains the worth one hundred dollars each, three guns, pistols and knives worth fifty dollars. Cash at the time of his departure, three hundred and twenty dollars. Provisions, camp fixins, cooking articles, worth four hundred dol-

---

[14]In the next deposition, Samuel Mitchell, James D. Dunlap, and Adam P. Dunlap supported Mitchell's statement.

lars. The Dunlap family consisted at the time he left, a wife and nine children. The three youngest was delivered at Carrollton, Arkansas, in charge of William C. Mitchell, Special Agent in September, A.D. 1859, and said survivors of Jesse Dunlap is at this time in my possession. Jesse Dunlap, deceased, was my brother. The worth of property is estimated at its worth in the State of Arkansas at the time of his departure

Nine yoke of oxen $60.00 per yoke	$540.00
Thirty head of cattle at $12.00 per head	$360.00
2 head of horses at $100.00 each	$200.00
3 wagon log chains and fixtures, $100 ea	$300.00
3 guns, pistols, knives, at $50.00	$50.00
Money when he left, $320.00	$320.00
Provision, bedding, blankets & cooking utensils	$400.00
	$2110.00[15]

WILLIAM C. MITCHELL, 26 OCTOBER 1860.

The statement made by James D. Dunlap . . . is correct, as I went with him twenty five miles the time he left Arkansas and I have no doubt of his death at or near the Mountain Meadows in Utah Territory. I acted as special agent of the General government and delivered the three children spoken of as survivors of the Mountain Meadows Massacre in September 1857, at Carrollton Arkansas in September 1859, and James D. Dunlap has the children at his house which is their home at this time.[16]

On 9 January 1861 these petitions were sent to the U.S. Senate's Committee on Indian Affairs, which dissolved the next month after its chairman, Arkansas senator William Sebastian, resigned and Arkansas left the Union. In the chaotic days at the beginning of the Civil War, these powerful statements were filed and forgotten for more than a century and a quarter.

Of the ninety-seven members of the Fancher-Baker party who can be reasonably identified, forty were men, fifteen were women, and thirty-nine were children under the age of 18.[17] Mormon frontiersman Jacob Hamblin, who saw the party at Corn Creek, near Fillmore, Utah, described them in 1859 as "ordinary frontier 'homespun' people." No contemporary evidence described drunken or violent behavior. The earliest documents tell the story of a band of ordinary American families that inadvertently stumbled into a hornet's nest of rancor, religious fervor, war hysteria, hostility, and fear.

---

[15]This sum is incorrect; the figures add up to $2,170.00.

[16]In addition to these statements, Adam P. Dunlap and Samuel Mitchell gave a short affidavit on 26 October 1860.

[17]This does not count those whose names are merely associated with the train.

Cedar Stake High Councilman Ira Allen served as a second
lieutenant in Company E of the Nauvoo Legion's Iron
County Brigade. Philip Klingensmith testified that Allen told
him "that the decree had passed, devoting [the Arkansas] company to destruction" and that Allen "put the Church Brand"
on the Fancher party's cattle. After Judge Cradlebaugh
issued a warrant for his arrest in 1859, Allen fled to northern Utah. He helped found the town of Hyrum at Cache
Valley in April 1860 and lived there peacefully until his death
in 1900. *Courtesy Jeff Petersen.*

Chapter 2

"TRAVELIN' THROUGH THIS WORLD BELOW"
The Mormon Reformation

After more than three months on the trail, the Arkansas emigrants reached Great Salt Lake City in August 1857, still at least two months short of their destination. They came at the wrong time to the wrong place. After years of conflict in Missouri and Illinois, relations between a people ruled by God and citizens of a republic governed by its people had at last come to a head on a national level. As the Arkansans journeyed west, President James Buchanan ordered the U.S. Army to impose federal authority in the first territory or state to assert its independence from the Union, and escort Indian Affairs bureaucrat Alfred Cumming of Georgia to replace Brigham Young as governor. The Mormon theocracy and its parent republic headed into a military showdown.

The news that U.S. soldiers were marching west from Fort Leavenworth, which came just before the Arkansas wagon train arrived, shocked Mormon settlements along the Wasatch Mountains. If it came sooner than expected, however, it did not take LDS leaders by surprise. The year before they had ignited one of the most intense and disturbing religious revivals in the nation's history—the Reformation, now at its peak—to sanctify the body of Israel and justify divine support in the conflict, which they had foreseen. The Arkansans came to a place unlike any other in the American republic, then or since.

ELISHA GROVES:
THE ANGEL OF VENGEANCE SHALL BE WITH THEE

The Kingdom's move to sovereignty began with the call for hundreds of Indian missionaries in 1855 to go out to dozens of tribes west of the Missouri River to restore native peoples to the faith of their Hebrew ancestors and forge alliances with them. Under doctrines of the faith, American Indians were a "remnant of Jacob" known as "Lamanites" and cousins of Mormons by right of the "blood of Israel"—that is, the Indians as descendants of Manasseh and Mormons as the literal offspring of the biblical Joseph's youngest son, Ephraim. The surge in Indian outreach followed the success of Mormon missionaries among the Southern Paiutes, whose lands the Arkansans were about to cross.

Other Mormon doctrines at that time regarding American Indians bore sobering implications for travelers on the nation's overland wagon roads. For when Zion was redeemed, recorded *Book of Mormon* prophet 3rd Nephi, echoing the Old Testament prophet Micah, the American remnant of Israel, or Jacob, would rage among unrepentant Gentiles "as a lion among the beasts of the forest, and as a young lion among the flocks of sheep, who, if he goeth through both treadeth down and teareth in pieces."[1] In patriarchal blessings, spiritual leaders foretold the future of followers who remained true to the faith, and in them they often bestowed promises bristling with militant imagery. Consider, for example, the blessing that John Smith bestowed upon John Borrowman at Council Bluffs, shortly after he enlisted in the Mormon Battalion in 1846.

> Patriarchal Blessing of John Borrowman, son of William and Marion Borrowman, born in the town of Glasgow, Scotland, May 13th., 1816. Brother John, I lay my hands upon your head, in the name of Jesus, I place upon thee all the blessings of the true and everlasting covenant. I also seal upon thee the power to overcome all thine enemies. Thou shalt be able to escape the edge of the sword although thousands may fall on thy right hand and on thy left, thou shalt not be hurt. Thou shalt have an inheritance in the land of Zion with the children of Ephraim, thy brethren. Thousands shall rejoice because of thy wisdom, thou shalt be able to confound all the wise and the learned of this generation and bring many thousands to a knowledge of the truth and when the remnants of Jacob go through among the Gentiles like a lion among the beasts of the forest, as the prophets have spoken, thou shalt be in their midst and shall be a captain of hundreds and shall be satisfied with the prosperity of Zion. Thou shalt have a family that shall be very great. Thy name shall not be blotted out of the Lamb's book of life but shall have every desire of thy heart in time and to all eternity, even so, amen.[2]

Even more alarming were the promises that Patriarch Elisha Groves bestowed at Cedar City on 20 February 1854 on William Dame, later the commander of the Nauvoo Legion's Iron County Brigade.

---

[1]See *The Book of Mormon*, 3 Nephi 20:15-16; also Micah 5:8.
[2]Patriarchal Blessing, 20 July 1846, in Extracts, Journal of John Borrowman.

... Thou shalt be called to act at the head of a portion of thy brethren and of the Lamanites in the redemption of Zion and the avenging of the blood of the prophets upon them that dwell on the earth. The angel of vengeance shall be with thee shall nerve and strengthen thee. Like unto Moroni no power shall be able to stand before thee till thou hast accomplished thy work. Thou art one of the Horns of Joseph that shall assist in the accomplishment of the gathering of Israel. Thou shalt be able to fill any mission or station in which thou shalt be called to act. No miracle shall be too hard for thee to perform which shall be for the advancement of thy Redeemers Kingdom on earth. Thou shalt behold the winding up scene the reign of peace the coming of thy Redeemer ... Thou shalt receve [sic] many blessings and privileges in the Temple in Zion thou shalt be numbered with the hundred forty and four thousand and receive thy Crown Kingdom Dominon power and Eternal Increase ...[3]

Early in 1857, Brigham Young sent letters to southern Utah stake presidents, including Dame at Parowan and Haight at Cedar City. The epistles directed them to be ready "to pursue, retake & punish" two Californians recently released from the territorial penitentiary. "We do not expect there would be any prosecutions for false imprisonment or tale bearers left for witnesses," Young wrote. "Make no noise about it and keep this letter safe. We write for your eye alone and to men that can be trusted." Unlike earlier letters to bishops Aaron Johnson, John L. Butler, and George W. Bradley, "they did not state that a penalty was to be imposed only after the theft of stock." The men had passed before Colonel Dame received Young's letter, but Dame informed the governor that he "was surprised to see them here" and had kept a close eye on them. "Word any time is comforting," Dame replied. "We try to live so when your finger crooks, we move."[4] At 4:00 A.M. the next morning, unknown assailants launched a furious attack on John Tobin (a Mormon) and three companions camped near Santa Clara Canyon. Ironically, none of them were the California drifters.[5]

JEDEDIAH M. GRANT: LET YOUR BLOOD BE SHED

As Indian missionaries spread out to tribes across central and western America, Brigham Young and his fiery second counselor, Jedediah M. Grant, in

---

[3]Patriarchal Blessing, 1854, in William Horne Dame Papers, 1838–84.

[4]Young to Bishops and Presidents South, 6 February 1857, in Parshall, "'Pursue, Retake & Punish,'" 64. Tobin was the son-in-law of Apostle Charles C. Rich. The 18 February 1857 attack took place near the spot where the Nauvoo Legion later planned to attack the Fancher party.

[5]Parshall, "'Pursue, Retake & Punish,'" 64, 72, 74–75, 86. The Nauvoo Legion later planned to attack the Fancher party near this spot in Santa Clara Canyon.

September 1856 launched the great revival, known as the Reformation, so as to merit God's backing in the impending conflict with the U.S. They touched off a spiritual firestorm that yielded a flood of confession, repentance, rebaptism, and fear in settlements throughout the territory.

In some places, the flames of reform flared out of control, and disillusioned settlers tried to get away by joining passing wagon parties. At Springville, William Parrish and his son Beason were killed, and their Judas guide, who led them into an ambush, was shot dead by mistake.[6] Like the Parrishes, other frightened settlers sought to escape and keep their property by joining passing emigrant parties. The exact number or fate of such so-called apostates or outsiders who joined the doomed Baker-Fancher train will never be known. Jedediah Grant, called "the Sledgehammer of Brigham," launched this impassioned revival so "that the sinners in Zion may be afraid." It worked.

"REMARKS BY JEDEDIAH M. GRANT, BOWERY, SUNDAY MORNING, SEPT. 21, 1856," *DESERET NEWS*, GREAT SALT LAKE CITY, 1 OCTOBER 1856, 6:30, 235.

I feel that the remarks which we have heard this morning are true, and they apply directly to you who are now present, and to the inhabitants of this city and of the Territory generally, and we do not excuse any of you . . . Some have received the Priesthood and a knowledge of the things of God, and still they dishonor the cause of truth, commit adultery and every other abomination beneath the heavens, and then meet you here or in the street and deny it.

These are the abominable characters that we have in our midst, and they will seek unto wizards that peep, and to star-gazers and soothsayers, because they have no faith in the holy Priesthood, and then when they meet us they want to be called Saints.

The same characters will get drunk and wallow in the mire and filth, and yet they call themselves Saints and seem to glory in their conduct, and they pride themselves in their greatness and in their abominations.

They are the old hardened sinners, and are almost—if not altogether—past improvement, and are full of hell, and my prayer is that God's indignation may rest upon them, and that He will curse them from the crown of their heads to the soles of their feet.

I say that there are men and women that I would advise to go to the President [Brigham Young] immediately, and ask him to appoint a committee to attend to their case; and then let a place be selected, and let that committee shed their blood.

[6]For more on the Parrish-Potter murders, see Aird, " 'You Nasty Apostates, Clear Out,' " 129–207.

We have those amongst us that are full of all manner of abominations, those who need to have their blood shed, for water will not do, their sins are of too deep a dye.

You may think that I am not teaching you Bible doctrine, but what says the apostle Paul? I would ask how many covenant breakers there are in this city and in this kingdom. I believe that there are a great many; and if they are covenant breakers we need a place designated, where we can shed their blood . . .

We have men who are incessantly finding fault, who get up little party spirits, and criticise the conduct of men of God. They will find fault with this, that, and the other, and nothing is right for them, because they are full of all kinds of filth and wickedness.

And we have women here who like any thing but the celestial law of God; and if they could break asunder the cable of the Church of Christ, there is scarcely a mother in Israel but would do it this day.[7] And they talk it to their husbands, to their daughters, and to their neighbors, and say they have not seen a week's happiness since they became acquainted with that law, or since their husbands took a second wife. They want to break up the Church of God, and to break it from their husbands and from their family connections.

Then again there are men that are used as tools by their wives, and they are just a little better in appearance and in their habits than a little black boy. They live in filth and nastiness, they eat it and drink it, and they are filthy all over.

We have Elders and High Priests that are precisely in this predicament; and yet they are wishing for more of the Holy Ghost, they wish to have it in larger doses. They want more revelation, but I tell you that you now have more than you live up to, more than you practise and make use of.

If I hurt your feelings let them be hurt. And if any of you ask, "do I mean you?" I answer, yes. If any woman asks, "do I mean her?" I answer, yes. And I want you to understand that I am throwing the arrows of God Almighty among Israel; I do not excuse any.

I am speaking to you in the name of Israel's God, and you need to be baptized and washed clean from your sins, from your backslidings, from your apostacies, from your filthiness, from your lying, from your swearing, from your lusts, and from every thing that is evil before the God of Israel.

We have been trying long enough with this people, and I go in for letting the sword of the Almighty be unsheathed, not only in word, but in deed . . .

Brethren and sisters, we want you to repent and forsake your sins. And you who have committed sins that cannot be forgiven through baptism, let your blood be shed, and let the smoke ascend, that the incense thereof may come up before God as an atonement for your sins, and that the sinners in Zion may be afraid.

---

[7] A reference to the revealed nature of plural marriage or polygamy.

Brigham Young:
To Have Their Blood Spilt upon the Ground

The most frightening feature of the great Mormon Reformation was the doctrine of blood atonement made public by Brigham Young and Jedediah Grant in 1856, less than a year before the Arkansas train arrived. Young followed Grant to the stand on Sunday, 21 September 1856, and described the creed. He "made the H[e]arts of many tremble," wrote Apostle Wilford Woodruff, a likely understatement.[8]

"Discourse By President Brigham Young,"
21 September 1856, *Deseret News*, 1 October 1856, 6:30, 235–36.

. . . We need a reformation in the midst of this people; we need a thorough reform, for I know that very many are in a dozy condition with regard to their religion; I know this as well as I should if you were now to doze and go to sleep before my eyes.

You are losing the spirit of the gospel, is there any cause for it? No, only that which there is in the world. You have the weakness of human nature to contend with, and you suffer that weakness to decoy you away from the truth, to the side of the adversary; but now it is time to awake, before the time of burning.

Whether the time of burning will be this week, or the next, or next year, I do not know that I care; and I do not know that I would ask, if I was sure the Lord would tell me. But I tell you that which I do know, and that is sufficient.

I do know that the trying day will soon come to you and to me; and ere long, we will have to lay down these tabernacles and go into the spirit world. And I do know that as we lie down so judgment will find us, and that is scriptural; "as the tree falls so it shall lie," or, in other words, as death leaves us so judgment will find us.

I will explain how judgment will be laid to the line. If we all live to the age of man the end thereof will soon be here, and that will burn enough, without anything else; and the present is a day of trial, enough for you and me.

We have got to be rightly prepared to go into the spirit world, in order to become kings. That is, so far as the power of satan is concerned you and I have got to be free from his power, but we cannot be while we are in the flesh.

Here we shall be perplexed and hunted by him; but when we go into the spirit world there we are masters over the power of satan, and he cannot afflict us any more, and this is enough for me to know.

Whether the world is going to be burned up within a year, or within a

---

[8]Kenny, ed., *Wilford Woodruff's Journal*, 4:448.

thousand years, does not matter a great [deal] to you and me. We have the words of eternal life, we have the privilege of obtaining glory, immortality, and eternal lives, now will you obtain these blessings?

Will you spend your lives to obtain a seat in the kingdom of God, or will you lie down and sleep, and go down to hell?

I want all the people to say what they will do, and I know that God wishes all his servants, all his faithful sons and daughters, the men and the women that inhabit this city, to repent of their wickedness, or we will cut them off.

I could give you a logical reason for all the transgressions in this world, for all that are committed in this probationary state, and especially for those committed by men.

There are sins that men commit for which they cannot receive forgiveness in this world, or in that which is to come, and if they had their eyes open to see their true condition, they would be perfectly willing to have their blood spilt upon the ground, that the smoke thereof might ascend to heaven as an offering for their sins; and the smoking incense would atone for their sins, whereas, if such is not the case, they will stick to them and remain upon them in the spirit world.

I know, when you hear my brethren telling about cutting people off from the earth, that you consider it is strong doctrine; but it is to save them, not to destroy them.

Of all the children of Israel that started to pass through the wilderness, none inherited the land which had been promised, except Caleb and Joshua, and what was the reason? It was because of their rebellion and wickedness; and because the Lord had promised Abraham that he would save his seed.

They had to travel to and fro to every point of the compass, and were wasted away, because God was determined to save their spirits. But they could not enter into his rest in the flesh, because of their transgressions, consequently he destroyed them in the wilderness.

I do know that there are sins committed, of such a nature that if the people did understand the doctrine of salvation, they would tremble because of their situation. And furthermore, I know that there are transgressors, who, if they knew themselves and the only condition upon which they can obtain forgiveness would beg of their brethren to shed their blood, that the smoke thereof might ascend to God as an offering to appease the wrath that is kindled against them, and that the law might have its course. I will say further; I have had men come to me and offer their lives to atone for their sins.

It is true that the blood of the Son of God was shed for sins through the fall and those committed by man, yet men can commit sins that it can never remit. As it was in ancient days, so it is in our day; and though the principles are taught publicly from this stand, still the people do not understand them; yet the law is precisely the same. There are sins that can be atoned for by an

offering upon an altar as in ancient days; and there are sins that the blood of
a lamb, or a calf, or of turtle doves, cannot remit, but they must be atoned
for by the blood of the man. That is the reason why men talk to you as they
do from this stand; they understand the doctrine and throw out a few words
about it. You have been taught that doctrine, but you do not understand it.

Jedediah M. Grant:
Let Their Names Be Written Down

The Reformation's most intrusive aspect was the cross-examination, known
as the catechism, for interrogating church members and exposing their sins.
Jedediah Grant told local authorities to enter every house and "find out who
are not disposed to do right." He instructed, "Let their names be written
down and let the offence and place of residence be written against the same."[9]
Hannah Tapfield King said the list of questions was over a foot long. "The
people shrunk, shivered, wept, groaned like whipped children," she said. "They
were told to get up in meeting and confess their sins. They did so 'till it was
sickening, and brought disease."[10] The questions varied somewhat from place
to place, but following is a representative sample.

Diary of John Moon Clements, 4 November 1856.

Have you ever committed adultery?

Have you ever spoken evil of Authorities or anointed of the Lord?

Have you ever betrayed your brethren?

Have you ever stolen or taken anything that was not your own?

Have you ever took the name of God in vain?

Have you ever been drunk?

Have you ever taken any poles from the big field or fences or taken your
brothers hay?

Have you ever picked up anything that did not belong to you and kept it
without seeking to find out the owner?

Have you made promises and not performed them?

Do you pay all your Tithing?

Do you labor faithfully and diligently for your employer?

Do you preside over your Family as a servant of God or are they subject
to you?

---

[9] Jedediah M. Grant, 2 November 1856, *Journal of Discourses*, 4:83–87. For another version of the catechism, see Ekins, ed., *Defending Zion*, 216–18.

[10] Journals of Hannah Tapfield King, 8 October 1856.

Do you teach your children the gospel?
Do you attend your Ward meetings?
Do you pray in your families night and morning?
Do you pray in secret?
Do you wash your bodies once a week?

JACOB BIGLER:
THAT THE GENTILE BANDS MAY BE BROKEN

When the Mass Quorum of Seventies met in Nephi, Utah, on 30 December 1856, they invited the priesthood's lesser-ranking Elders Quorum "to attend this meeting owing to a letter coming from President [Jacob G.] Bigler" to the presidents of both quorums. Like many Mormon leaders, Bigler held multiple offices, including bishop of Juab County, legislative assembly representative, and officer of the Nauvoo Legion.

Bishop Bigler's letter reported the fiery spirit of Reformation that had gripped Utah's territorial legislature, which would dispatch a message to Washington defying the authority of the national government before it adjourned. His letter captured the spirit of religious zeal and political rebellion that characterized the flaming revival in Utah. The call to Mormon colonies at Carson Valley and San Bernardino as early as 1856 to return and defend Zion revealed that Brigham Young was fully aware of the provocative course he was pursuing.

Mormon historians usually terminate the Reformation with the death of Jedediah Grant on 1 December 1856, but as Bigler's letter and the documents that follow it reveal, the legislature kindled the hottest flames of the revival in Utah's frontier settlements during 1857.

JACOB G. BIGLER TO JOHN PYPER AND DAVID WEBB, 22 DECEMBER 1856.

GT S.L. CITY DEC. 22ᴰ 1856

Brothers John Pyper David Webb and your councelors.

Respected Brethren, After hearing what I have since I have been here I fell to say to you arise on the strength of Israels God. Get the power of God upon you for you ~~for you~~ have not [got] it. You should have it, for a Trying day is is [sic] nigh, I was at a meeting last night where the fire of God burned. The Twelve where [sic] there & the first Presidents of the seventies (Joseph excepted) when called upon to go to the first Presidency of the church and

CEDAR CITY'S FIRST ORGANIZED CHOIR, CIRCA 1865
(*left to right, standing*) Annie Wood, Eliza Hunter, Margaret Heyborne, Mary Corlett,
Tillie Macfarlane, Lizzie Corry, Ellen Lunt. (*seated*) Alice Bulloch, Sarah Chatterly,
William Unthank, Daniel Macfarlane, John M. Macfarlane, John Chatterly, Joseph
Smith, John Lee Jones. John D. Lee's *Confessions* listed the Macfarlane brothers and
Joseph Smith as participants in the Mountain Meadows massacre. *Courtesy of the Will
Bagley Collection.*

to surrender that responsibility & if he is a mind to fill their places with men
who have the fire of God burning in them and in the Vigor of youth who
can fight the Devil whether in tabernacles or not, and at this time I hear the
voice of Bro W. Woodruff roaring like the trumpet of the Angel of God in
the room under me he is Awake, & the power of God is upon on him he hard-
ley rests any night. And the word is [if] Presidents & Bishops do not do their
duty and get the Holy Ghost they will be drop[p]ed and that soon for it is
to[o] late in the day for people to sleep. So arise let the light shine, let no
man stand in the gap. I want you to show what the holey ghost has done in
former days & then you will see what It will do In our day, go to the scrip-
tures & see what the men of God has done under the Influance of the holey
Ghost, when it cleansed Israil. Put the gavaline [javelin] to the hearts of wicked
Rulers kicked out the bowels of a Judas.

Dec 24 11 oclock. Yesterday the two houses with a few more met in the council Room and continued there untill 4 PM. & such a meeting I never enjoyed before. The fire of God is burning here and I command you and your Quorums to scour up your armer both temporally & spiritual[l]y. What I say I me[a]n you to understand literal[l]y. Tell Bro George, Kendall & Bro [Samuel] Pitchforth to roar God Bless you bretheren. Go a head & your power shall encrease. I wish I was there two hours before the people of Nephi but I will say for your sake & for my sake also [?] to Wake Up Wake Up Wake Up. Let those who think they stand be the more faithfull lest they fall. The Quorums are commanded to cut off the dead branches that the tree may Grow and not let the lower Branches suck the sap of the bodey. I attended the meeting of the Bishops & Missionarys last night. Bros Hyde Woodruff Snow & Richards[11] ware there and shurley God speaks through them. The Saints in Carson & Sanbernidino are called to Come Home Come Home Come Home. I felt last night as though I did not want to go to bed or sleep. I was preaching to the people of Nephi City things that I dont feel to Write. Prepare your selves to stand by me when Israil is to be cleansed for this has got to be done that the Gentile bands may be Broken.[12]

THE CEDAR STAKE MINUTES:
COME FORTH TO SLAY THE WICKED

The unique nature of the violence against women and children at Mountain Meadows raises a disturbing question. What could have motivated intensely religious men to breach one of the most deeply engrained social obligations of the nineteenth century—a man's duty to defend the lives and honor of women and children with his life? Since no American soldier ever murdered a woman or child during the Civil War without facing summary judgment, rampant violence is not adequate to explain what happened in Utah in 1857. The answer requires knowing what was going on in this particular time and place, and it begins with understanding the social and psychological forces set loose during the Mormon Reformation. The fiery revival harped on the sins of God's people, but its main theme was obedience to authority. Members were told to mind their own business, but every private aspect of their own lives became their leaders' business.

Illustrating the forces at work in Utah during the Reformation are the minutes of the Thursday and Sunday church meetings at Cedar City between

---

[11] Apostles Orson Hyde, Wilford Woodruff, Lorenzo Snow, and Franklin D. Richards.

[12] In the interests of full disclosure, Jacob G. Bigler was editor David L. Bigler's great-great-grandfather.

December 1856 and July 1857, which vividly illustrate the all-encompassing nature of the faith that dominated this remote village on the Mormon frontier.

CEDAR STAKE JOURNAL, DECEMBER 1856–AUGUST 1859.

Dec 19th 1856 . . . Bishop P K Smith Spoke of the necesity of this people being organized in all our buisness opperations; and of us being diligent if we cherrish the principle of Reformation . . . Prest. John M Higbee Spoke of the benifits of the society and of us not encouraging those blood sucking gentiles that bring us their goods . . .

Dec 21st 1856. Sunday . . . Elder Rufus Allen Made remarks of the necesity of the Saints being faithful in all circumstances and of doing the will of the Lord in all things. Elder Laban Morrell Spoke of his backwardness in the cause of truth, and of faithfulness. Elder Ira Allen Spoke upon the principle of family government . . . Prest John M Higbee Made remarks of the necesity of us as saints living in subjection unto those who are placed over us in the Lord. And of the Lord not giving us any commandments that we cannot Keep &c . . .

Dec 28th 1856. Sunday . . . Prest John M Higbee Made remarks upon the saints living their religion; and of doing our duties as people of God, and of having the spirit of God to discern good from evil, also showed forth that those who have a good spirit will counsel at all times . . .

Jan 11th 1857 Sunday . . . Elder Jno D Lee (from Harmony) Made remarks upon the reformation and of the saints living according to the order of God . . .

Jan 18th 1857. Sunday . . . Prest Jno M Higbee. Exhorted to faithfulness, and felt to bless the people, 'said' it is necessary of us to bring our minds to live to the Lord and fulfil our duties as saints and live humble, and to be kind and affectionate to each other, by so doing we may save a soul. For many times we need kindness. Many men act as if their wives were slaves for them, some men are all right to have but one wife, it is the duty of all good men to get more wives, but some will not believe it and will not give their daughters to good men who has got a wife. Let us reform and try to live according to the law of the Lord, for at present there are but few of us ready to live according to that law, therefore let us try to have the knots trimed off us. Let us consider that we must take a course to save ourselves. What is our duties as servants of God? We have got to show that we have to fight the devil; in this God will not do all the work we have got to do our part, he will do what we cannot do. Let us love our brethren and not take advantage of them, when we promise let us do as we say if it takes our shirt; let us rise our prayers continually in the behalf of each other; let us mind our own buisness, and not others, and especially those whom God has place[d] in authority . . . Bishop P. K Smith Spoke of the necesity of the bitter branches been [being] cut off from the church . . .

Jan 15th [22] 1857. Thursday . . . A letter was read from Prest I C Haight exhorting the saints to faithfulness; also another was read that the bishop had received from Prest Brigham Young calling for some men to go to the Las Vagus to assist the brethren at the lead mines and to take flower and cattle to sustain the whole company . . .[13]

Jan 18th [25] 1857. Sunday . . . Pres Elias Morris Remarked that he for one was happy to receive the instructions from our president. Spoke upon the reformation and that now is the day for us to repent and now is the time to wake up. The bishop is going to send round the questions and we want you to read them and examine yourselves by them honestly before God, the time has come when if we do not repent we cannot stand; if we hear of any man or woman that reviles against the authorities crossed in their path you are not to know it: you who have got the Priesthood of God help to put down the enemies of God. We want to clothe ourslves [sic] with the gospel of Christ and be faithful therein. Elder Ruffus Allen Spoke upon the reformation and of living humbly before God, and be prepared to meet every thing necesary for the advancement of the Kingdom of God . . . Bishop P. K Smith Exhorted us to dig about ourselves, and be on hand for the building up of the Kingdom of God. Elder Wm W Willis Spoke of the Indians hearing and obeying the gospel at the Big Muddy. Also spoke of the mercy of God towards the Saints, and of the spirit of the reformation which is in our midst . . .

Jan. 29th 1857 . . . Prest Isaac C Haight (having returned from the sitting of the Legislature) Arose to address the saints. Brethren and Sisters I feel to speak to you and rejoice that I am again in your midst; while away from you I rejoiced in having the privilege of meeting with the first Presidency and the reason of the legislature adjourned unto Great Salt Lake was inconsequence of the health of the first presidency been preserved, and it has been a school of the prophets unto us. The remarks of Bro: Harrison are true, the sins of this people has caused the blessings of God to be withheld from them. It is true Prest B Young was a— [sic] about to take up his knapsack and go preaching unto the people for he said I cannot stand it any longer, Prest J M Grant took this burden upon himself and through the same he wore out his body and fallen, and now the twelve Apostles have took upon themselves the burden, and they have sent us out with a portion of that burden and priesthood. Brigham laid down his priesthood at the feet of the Twelve then the Twelve turned round and laid down their priesthood and authority at the feet of Brigham, and it is for Brigham to send out such men as are worthy . . . We

---

[13]Young to Klingensmith, 7 January 1857. On the same day in a letter to Elder Samuel Thompson at Las Vegas, Young indicated why he wanted aid sent to the settlement: "We like the idea of your holding meetings with the Indians at their wick-e-ups at [sic] trust that it will have a salutary influence over them. We also wish that you would aid by your influence and by furnishing such assistance as can be spared to Bro Jones in the lead business, also endeavoring to conciliate the Indians and protect the stock. Work harmoniously together with every interest which has for its object the promotion of the great cause in which we are all enlisted." Both Indians and lead would be essential resources in the pending struggle for "the great cause."

preached reformation; the next day we were told there was to be no more legislature unless we as a body repented of our sins and was rebaptized, and then
go on with the legislature in righteousnes—for the good of this people because
the first presidency loves this people. Some of you have made restitution and
some of you have not done it, and will not yet do it, but you should let that
be your first buisness of life. The chief sins of this people are disrespect to the
holy priesthood and the pruning time has come, and those who hold the priesthood must wake up and magnify their calling and then we shall be saved, every
one of us who have got the holy priesthood upon us know these are great sins
and you who know most must repent of most & all forsake your sins, and if
you do not this when the servants of God will come forth to slay the wicked.
Who of you can do this. I am for the Lord come life or death . . .

Feb: 22th 1857. Sunday . . . Elder Saml McMurdie Spoke upon the principle of obedience. Elder Wm Wesley Willis also spoke upon obedience. Prest
John M Higbee Spoke upon the principle of honoring the priesthood and
of the mercy of Our God towards us and of every word of God being ful-
filed; we have got to trim up ourselves that we may stand and be on hand for
the rolling forth of the truth[;] we have got to keep the commandments of
the authorities and rise up and Magnify the Priesthood that is put upon us
that we may live long upon the earth and not sink back into the lethargy we
once were in. Bp P K Smith. Bore testimony to what Bro Higbee had said,
and of Apostates going to hell . . .

March 29th 1857. Sunday . . . Prest Jno M Higbee Spoke of preparing ourselves for every thing, and [d]o every thing required at our hands . . .

May 3th 1857. Sunday . . . Prayer by Bp P. K. Smith . . . Followed by Prest
Elias Morris . . . The people of this place of late are indulging in liquir, the
women even take the whiskey jug into their tea parties and must treat a friend.
I say let the men women and Children who indulgue in it leave it off unless
you will go down and be condemned, such is in opposition to the spirit of
the Lord, and if my Brethren & Sisters want to have respect for each other
do not hand them the whiskey jug, it is useless for me to have a name in the
Kingdom of God unless I merit it.

2 o'clock PM . . . Bp P K Smith . . . Fulfill you[r] covenants with each other,
and make your confessions unto those who come to catachize you and do not
lie unto them. I have been one choosen to catachize the people and I Know
some lied, I do not want any to go and be baptized who have not confessed
their sins. You need not be afraid of your sins been talked about for if those
who catachize you talk about them they forfiet their lives.[14]

---

[14]Among the men named in the Cedar Stake Journal, the following were reportedly at Mountain Meadows at the time of the massacre: Philip Klingensmith, John Higbee, William Bateman, John D. Lee, Charles
Hopkins, Samuel McMurdy, Daniel Macfarlane, John Urie, William Tate, Richard Harrison, Nephi Johnson, Joel White, Ira Allen, Jonathan Pugmire, and Eleazer Edwards.

Cedar City records are not the only church minutes that capture the raging fires of the Reformation. Even before news broke of an approaching U.S. Army, the frenzy that gripped Utah during 1857 was mirrored by Provo Stake president James C. Snow, who warned: "Hell's Kitchen is now boiling over—some men from this Territory have written back some of the most disgraceful letters that could be written & they are on the way back—they have written about the Consecration or purification Law as they term it—and all you Danites had better be on the look out," he said.[15] "I told you last winter that undue Sympathy would distroy a good many—therefore be on your guard & if your nerves are weak take givers & molasses & nerve root—that your nerves may be strong."

Garland Hurt: The Bitterest Agonies of Soul

U.S. Indian agent Garland Hurt's reports to the Office of Indian Affairs from 1855 to 1859 are among the most important of the reliable sources that describe conditions in Utah at this period. Excerpts from his letter at Fort Bridger to Alfred Cumming, Utah's new governor, describe the fearful nature of the Reformation from an outsider's perspective.

Garland Hurt to Alfred Cumming, 17 December 1857, National Archives.

Sir,

As I have been thrown in concert with the opposers of Mormonism and Mormon authority, I avail myself of the liberty of addressing you a brief summary of the reasons by which I have been activated in this course. And in doing so, I would promise, that I came to Utah three years ago, fully resolved to divest myself of any predilections or prejudices, either for, or against any of the people of the Territory, knowing that I would have an opportunity of having an acquaintance with them and personal observations, and I determined to make that the basis of my [estimations] in regard to them. Consequently, I endeavored from the outset to render myself in every respect as courteous and affable as I could towards them.

Under this course, it is not [remarkable] that I acquired my friends among the laboring masses, with whom I necessarily associated much, and for whom

---

[15]The oath-bound Danites were organized in 1838 to execute judgment on apostates and take vengeance on enemies of the Mormon movement in Missouri. Utah Stake Minutes, 28 June 1857, General Meetings 1855–60, 873.

I confess I contracted sympathizing regard. It was not long however, till I recognized among them the existence of a heartfelt hatred for the people of the
United States, and with surprise and regret, was I compelled to witness that
this hatred was fed and sustained by harangues from those in authority of the
Church, whom I have never known to loose [sic] an opportunity for fanning
the flames of this rebellious spirit.

Under a series of the most flimsy pretexts, and by distorting the history
of their connection with the government and people of the United States,
they present to the world, a list of grievances, which constitute the theme of
every orator, the initiatory lessons of every convert, and the intuitive teaching of almost every mother to her child.

This state of things rendered my position among these people not [by]
any means uninteresting or impossible. With a lively interest for their pecu-
niary and political prospect, I could not avoid inter[posing], as occasion would
offer, an effort to correct the [wrong] and misguided impressions under which
I conceived them to be laboring: but on [occasions] endeavoring to act with
becoming defference for their feelings.

In this cause I labored with [zeal], but with doubtful prospects of success,
till the autumn of 1856; when matters assumed such an [aspect] that it required
not prophet or visionary power to discern [in] the minds of the of the people, a disposition to assert their Constitutional rights—a spirit of independence was evidently abroad among them, and gradually in[serting] itself into
their thoughts and actions; but the eye of the Priesthood was upon them. I
watched with no ordinary solici[tude] the course of events, till at length, with
one vast stroke of the sub[t]le machinery of Priestcraft all our hopes were
blasted [and] the voice of liberty hushed throughout the length and breadth
of his dominions. This feat of miraculous interposition was conducted under
the name of a religious reformation . . .

Ordering the reformation [was] a proclamation issued from the Lord's
anointed, announcing the solemn fact, that the people had violated their
covenants with God, and commanding them indiscriminately to bow at the
confessional, and repair to the streams of the mountains and be rebaptized
forth with. Under the execution of this measure, thousands now in Utah, will
not be surprised when I say that I have seen men and women, weeping in the
bitterest agonies of soul; and when I attempted to console them would say,
they abhorred the idea of being forced into a confessional but dared not refuse.
They would say they knew not where they had sinned, but dare not disobey
this counsel. They will not be surprised when I say, that I have heard their
teachers, announce on numerous occasions, in round terms, that if they refused
to obey this mandate, they would get their damned throats cut.

Brigham Young: The Way to Love Mankind

Joseph Smith, Mormonism's first prophet, revealed the doctrine of blood atonement not to punish those who had accepted the faith's covenants, but to save them. Sins requiring such extreme expiation included breaking sacred vows, apostasy, and shedding innocent blood. The latter included children under age 8 and Mormons with special temple endowments—those of "spotless garments" ready to meet the returning messiah.[16]

While the doctrine remains shrouded in mystery—and confusion—it became an ongoing theme of sermons during the Reformation. Mormon historians have argued that blood atonement only expressed support for capital punishment and that Brigham Young's comments on the subject were purely rhetorical. This may not have been apparent to those listening to his discourses.

"Discourse by Brigham Young," 8 February 1857,
Deseret News, 18 February 1857, 6:50, 396–97.

. . . And I will say that the time will come, and is now nigh at hand, when those who profess our faith, if they are guilty of what some of this people are guilty of, will find the axe laid at the root of the tree and they will be hewn down. What has been must be again, for the Lord is coming to restore all things. The time has been in Israel under the law of God, the celestial law, or that which pertains to the celestial law, for it is one of the laws of that kingdom where our Father dwells, that if a man was found guilty of adultery he must have his blood shed, and that is near at hand. But now I say, in the name of the Lord, that if this people will sin no more, but faithfully live their religion, their sins will be forgiven them without taking life . . .

Now take a person in this congregation who has knowledge with regard to being saved in the kingdom of our God and our Father, and being exalted, one who knows and understands the principles of eternal life, and sees the beauty and excellency of the eternities before him compared with the vain and foolish things of the world, and suppose that he is overtaken in a gross fault; that he has committed a sin that he knows will deprive him of that exaltation which he desires and that he cannot attain to it without the shedding of his blood, and also knows that by having his blood shed he will atone for that sin and be saved and exalted with the Gods, is there a man or woman in this house but what would say, "shed my blood that I may be saved and exalted with the Gods?"

---

[16]Faithful Mormons who had been through the temple ceremonies wore special underclothes with sacred markings called garments to remind them of their vows.

All mankind love themselves, and let these principles be known by an individual, and he would be glad to have his blood shed. That would be loving themselves, even unto an eternal exaltation. Will you love your brothers or sisters likewise, when they have committed a sin that cannot be atoned for without the shedding of their blood? Will you love that man or woman well enough to shed their blood? That is what Jesus Christ meant. He never told a man or woman to love their enemies in their wickedness, never. He never intended any such thing; his language is left as it is for those to read who have the Spirit to discern between truth and error; it was so left for those who can discern the things of God. Jesus Christ never meant that we should love a wicked man in his wickedness.

Now take the wicked, and I can refer to where the Lord had to slay every soul of the Israelites that went out of Egypt, except Caleb and Joshua. He slew them by the hands of their enemies, by the plague, and by the sword, why? Because He loved them, and promised Abraham that He would save them. And He loved Abraham because he was a friend to his God and would stick to Him in the hour of darkness, hence He promised Abraham that He would save his seed. And He could save them upon no other principle, for they had forfeited their right to the land of Canaan by transgressing the law of God, and they could not have atoned for the sin if they had lived. But if they were slain the Lord could bring them up in the resurrection and give them the land of Canaan, and He could not do it on any other principle.

I could refer you to plenty of instances where men have been righteously slain, in order to atone for their sins. I have seen scores and hundreds of people for whom there would have been a chance in the last resurrection there will be if their lives had been taken and their blood spilled on the ground as a smoking incense to the Almighty, but who are now angels to the devil, until our elder brother Jesus Christ raises them up—conquers death, hell, and the grave. I have known a great many men who have left this church for whom there is no chance whatever for exaltation, but if their blood had been spilled, it would have been better for them. The wickedness and ignorance of the nations forbid this principle's being in full force, but the time will come when the law of God will be in full force.

This is loving our neighbour as ourselves; if he needs help, help him; and if he wants salvation and it is necessary to spill his blood on the earth in order that he may be saved, spill it. Any of you who understand the principles of eternity, if you have sinned a sin requiring the shedding of blood, except the sin unto death, would not be satisfied nor rest until your blood should be spilled, that you might gain that salvation you desire. That is the way to love mankind.

Chapter 3

"Dark Clouds Are Going to Gather 'Round Me"
The Murder of Parley Parker Pratt

> *Got the news of the Death of Parley P Pratt Who was Murdered by Hector McLane. The U.S. have stopped our eastern Mail and the People of the U.S. are persecuting the saints there. O Ye fools your time is short when the Lord will avenge the Blood of the Prophets.*
>
> Charles L. Walker, 21 July 1857

Not only did the doomed emigrants come *to* the wrong place in August 1857, but they also came *from* the wrong place. The former home of most of them was only one county removed from the place in Arkansas where the jealous husband of Eleanor McLean had struck down Mormon apostle Parley P. Pratt that spring for claiming Eleanor as his twelfth polygamous wife. Brigham Young himself had sealed her to Pratt for time and eternity in Salt Lake's Endowment House while she was still married to Hector McLean, who pursued and killed the beloved apostle.[1]

Adding to the emotions already inflamed by the Reformation, Pratt's distraught widow arrived in Great Salt Lake on 23 July, eleven days before the emigrants, in a mail wagon driven by Mormon gunman Porter Rockwell. Church officials in Missouri had arranged to rush Eleanor to Utah, where she delivered her cry for vengeance and an impassioned account of Pratt's murder to church officials.

---

[1]Under Mormon marriage doctrines at this time, it was not uncommon for undivorced women, who had been joined to their husbands for life outside the church, to be sealed in religious rites to male priesthood holders for time and eternity.

ELEANOR McLEAN: FATAL CURIOSITY

The conversion and odyssey of Eleanor McComb McLean and her two husbands had all the elements of nineteenth-century Victorian melodrama. For most Americans, the story was one of adultery, delusion, betrayal, and righteous vengeance, to which was added the salacious feature of polygamy. To the Mormon people, however, it was a crime of the highest magnitude—the unpunished martyrdom of yet another of their beloved prophets. As the following account shows, those not of the faith saw it differently.

"SAD STORY OF MORMONISM.—THE MOTHER AND CHILDREN,"
NEW ORLEANS BULLETIN, 19 DECEMBER 1856. REPRINTED IN
THE MORMON, 14 MARCH 1857, 2/7.

A few years since, a gentleman, his wife, and two infant children, like thousands of others, left this city for the golden shores of the Pacific, the husband and wife, dreaming doubtless that in the land of the shining ore they should soon realize a fortune for themselves and their children. The lady, we may premise, possessed more than an ordinary share of intellect, which had been cultivated to a highly respectable degree, by the care of fond and adoring parents, who little thought of the use to which that intellect would in after years be devoted, or how their devotion would be repaid. Alas! they can feel "how sharper than a serpent's tooth it is to have a thankless child," or one that brings them only sorrow instead of joy.

The family is settled in San Francisco. Some time afterward, the gentleman and his wife, in connection with a brother of the latter, chanced to step in on a Sunday to hear a Mormon missionary from Utah, who was holding forth in San Francisco. They were prevented by the bad weather, and walking from attending their usual place of worship, and as the house from where the Mormon was speaking happened to be in their way, they concluded, after leaving home, and from mere curiosity, to go in and hear him. Fatal curiosity! Inauspicious day! . . . After coming out, the husband and brother expressed themselves very freely upon the merits of what they had heard, and pronounced some of it little, if any, short of blasphemy. To the utter astonishment of both, however, the wife and sister expressed herself highly pleased with it!

As a probable solution of such a mystery, . . . it subsequently turned out that she had heard a Mormon missionary while a young lady residing in one of the port towns in Mississippi. Polygamy was at that time carefully concealed from the outside Gentiles by the Apostles of Joe Smith, and stoutly denied. Probably the young lady was fascinated by the romance which the Mormon may have skilfully woven into his discourse, and the seeds of blasting ruin thus lodged in her mind to spring up healthy and bear apples of Sodom to turn out ashes in the tasting many days afterwards. Be this as it may, the

lady soon became strongly attached to the Mormon faith and went frequently, if not constantly to hear its Apostles. In a short time he had acquired sufficient influence over her to cause her to resolve to quit her husband—if he
would not accompany her—and repair to the grand re[n]dezvous of the Latter Day Saints, as they style themselves, at Salt Lake City.

The determination once taken, nothing could dissuade her from her purpose. But the children, what was to become of them? The mother was devot-
edly, passionately attached to them and she determined to take them with her.
The father and brother of course became alarmed. To prevent her from going
they knew well would be impossible, but they resolved to save the children
from the yawning gulf which was about opening to receive them; and in pursuance of this resolution, they determined to send them to their grand parents in this city. They were therefore taken when the mother was absent, placed
on board a steamer, and safely reaching New Orleans, were soon under the
loving care and hospitable roof of their grand parents.

Who, however, can baffle or circumvent a determined woman, fanatic tho'
she be, when her feelings, her pride and her affections all combine to spur her
on to the accomplishment of her object? The very next steamer that sailed
brought that mother to this city, chaffing like an enraged tigress, whose young
had been taken from her. Her parents who had been made aware of the circumstances, now determined that she should not take her children from them,
and that if she was bent upon dooming herself to destruction, she should not
drag her innocent babes down into the foul abyss with her . . . How completely her whole soul had become wrapped in the gross and disgusting deception
which had seized upon her like a giant, the reader can judge when we inform
him that rather than relinquish joining the vile horde which contaminate the
air of Great Salt Lake by their abominations, she actually tore herself from
the children of her heart, and went without them.

She did not, however, abandon her purpose. Finding herself baffled for
the time being, she determined to change her tactics, the more certain to secure
at a future day, what she could not then effect. She went to Salt Lake City via
St. Louis, and her parents had the melancholy satisfaction to know that if she
was lost, that her children were at least safe. These, brother and sister, under
the bountiful and fostering care which they received, budded, like the opening rose beneath the sweet and genial influences of the Southern spring.

They heard nothing more of her till one day last week, when they were
struck almost dumb with amazement by her entrance into the family mansion.
. . . She had been to Utah and had been a teacher there, had *boarded* at Gov.
Brigham Young's, only *boarded*, had seen much suffering there from famine, and
had seen also the error of her ways! Said she had been mad, had now left the
Mormons and had come to live with her parents and children, and to do what
she could to make them happy. She asked them to restore her once more to
their confidence. Of course, the delight of her parents was boundless. She did

not profess, however to have renounced Mormonism, but wished not to return to Utah, and still insisted that the Mormons were good people, and Brigham and his associates in office true Prophets. If these drawbacks upon the value of her repentance created a regret or a lingering suspicion in the minds of her parents, they did not express it, grateful and happy that she had done so much as she had, and made even a quasi confession as to the impropriety of her past conduct; and hoping, doubtless, that time would accomplish what was lacking in her complete recovery from her horrible delusion.

On last Saturday morning, she requested permission to take her children into town (her parents live in the suburbs) to go shopping, and promising to return by five, or at most six o'clock in the evening. The permission was readily granted, and they have seen neither her nor the children since. She has accomplished her purpose; and she is, of course, on her way back to Utah with her children, to be thrust into the opening throat of the grim visaged and horrible monster, who sits midway upon the Rocky Mountains, lapping his repulsive jaws, and eager to devour new victims as they become entangled in his foul, his leprous coils.

Her dissimulation was profound—was perfect. So much for Mormonism!

The same issue of *The Mormon* that reprinted "Sad Story of Mormonism," issued Parley P. Pratt's rebuttal, "Sad Story of Presbyterianism," telling Eleanor's story of the "threats, railings and abuses" of her "brutish husband" and the plots of "her bigoted and hard-hearted Presbyterian parents and brothers and sisters." But when Pratt returned to Missouri in March, he found McLean and his friends "hunting him as bloodhounds would a hare."

PARLEY P. PRATT:
McLean and His Friends Will Kill Me

Hector McLean finally caught up with his estranged wife and Parley P. Pratt in Indian Territory. With the help of federal authorities and soldiers, McLean had them arrested, and the couple was taken for a hearing before a magistrate in Van Buren in western Arkansas, near the border. Eleanor McLean's account scrupulously noted the men involved in the arrest.

ELEANOR J. McCOMB [McLEAN], ACCOUNT OF
THE DEATH OF PARLEY P. PRATT, LDS ARCHIVES, 1–4.

On the 6 of May I was journeying with my children through the Creek Nation, west of the state of Arkansas when McLean (the murderer) met us.

We were in a lone wagon owned and driven by a man who was not a Mormon. He had a wife and three children; and was en route from Texas to Nebraska. It was about the middle of the day, when the D . . . [Devil] on horseback accompanied by one other man rode in front of our wagon. The scene that was then and there enacted could be seen, and felt but never described. Had a raging beast come and draged my lambs to his den, the shrieks of anguish and despair could not have been exceeded. Yet he has no mercy! he dragged them out of the wagon—threw one on each horse in front of their saddles; and with fearful speed they disappeared in the distance. And the last I heard of my darling children was their cries of unmingled despair as they were borne from my sight by the unrelenting tyrant!

In about three hours after the above scene I was arrested by a man styled the "State's Marshall" upon a charge of Larceny of clothing belonging to Albert & Annie McLean to the amount of ten dollars (10$).

In the same charge there was three other names read "Parley P Pratt— James Gammell & Elias J. Gammell."[2] There was with this Marshall a the same man who was with McLean, whom they called Perkins.

They took me to a kind of hotel in the indian town ("North fork") kept by an Indian named John Smith, where I saw on the gallery twelve armed men who appeared to be in a state of great excitement . . .

Next morning they put me on a horse and the crowd set off all on horse back at an early hour. When we had rode I suppose fifteen miles I being in the special custody of *"Thomas [Hall?]!!"* He asked me if I would like to see Mr. Pratt? I replied "Not in tribulation such as I am in." "He is a good man, and I know his family and would be sorry to see him as a prisoner! "Is *he* in this part of the country"? I inquired. "Well he's not 40 miles from here!" was the answer.

This was the first intimation I had that Mr. P. was in that country. I asked the marshall if he was going to arrest him. He answered, I am bound to if I see him.

We rode untill noon and stopped at an Indian house for dinner. While at the table I saw that the excitement greatly increased, and the number of men increased. They brandished their weapons, rode to and fro, and spoke to each other in a subdued voice, as if planning some fearful and deadly combat. But few attempted to eat. The marshall however stayed close to me, and when ready to mount our horses I saw McLean who had the children in a carriage at a distance from the house commit the lines [reins] to another person; put on an extra weapon a sword handed him by a man on horseback examined his pistols ect [*sic*]—Just then the Marshall said to me, "They have arrested Pratt, and McLean is *determined to kill him, but he shall not do* it while he is a pris-

[2]Brigham Young sent Elder James Gemmell (in Mormon records, Gammell or Gamwell) on a mission to Texas, where Eleanor Pratt had taken refuge near Houston "at the home of Wm. Gambell [*sic*], who is a man of no religion." Mrs. Pratt left Houston with Gemmell on 4 March 1857 for Ellis County, Kansas, "where the Mormon emigration was fitting out for a trip across the plains." See Eleanor McLean to Mr. Editor, 18 May 1857, *The Mormon*, 13 June 1857, 3. For Gemmell's colorful career, see anthropologist Stuart D. Scott's "A Frontier Spirit: The Life of James Gemmell," 55–115.

oner! I told Cap [Lewis Henry] Little of the military to protect him and McLean shall not molest him while in my custody."

We were soon upon our horses and in about ½ mile from the house came in sight of the military troops, who had arrested Mr. Pratt. As ~~I~~ we drew near I saw the man of God upon the ground. He lay near a stream of water in a beautifuly green spot, with his hand under his head. He looked like a man who had stopped to rest in a shady place, while his horse ~~was grazing~~ might graze. His calm penetrating look as he lay viewing the crowd around him, formed a striking contrast with the *pale, trembling fiendish looking* beings, who were a perfect personification of *fear, hate & guilt.* There was Cap Little ~~(Remember it all ye Mormon boys)~~ with a company of U.S. Soldiers. And there was many armed men beside—Indians and white men old and young. One old man I would not fail to name, he is about Mr. Pratt's size & age but for [illegible] His name is Shaw. He is a merchant in Fort Gibson and of all the crowd seemed to enjoy the most guilt himself [?] in what was being done, and I believe *he* is the man who handed ~~McLean~~ the sword to McLean ~~(Mark this wherever there is Mormon blood a saint of God~~.

One more man of that rabble I would describe. The man Perkins (but I do not think his right name) he is of medium size and heavy black whiskers, heavy eyebrows, and I think gray eyes. The expression of his mouth is spiteful, and his eyes rather bold but his general bearing cowardly. This man charged round and with a hateful grin of triumph said "That's *one of the apostles!!* "One *of the twelve!* "Now we've got somebody hav'nt [sic] we?!" Come down and see him!! he looks like a lion don't he?"

George B. Higginson had spent much of April 1857 trying to intercept Eleanor McLean on the road between Indian Territory and Texas and was arrested along with Pratt.[3] Feeling that fate was closing in on him, the apostle gave his companion a "sacred request."

We then rode back to Fort Gibson, where we were lodged in prison, in separate rooms for the night. The next day I was taken into the same room that Brother Parley was occupying. He asked me of my welfare, and said, "I am happy we have been permitted to converse with each other; I feel the hand of the Lord is in it." He said: "McLean and his friends will kill me. They have arrested me to put me in his power." He said: "You will probably escape alive, and I have a sacred request to make of you: that is to go and see my family

---

[3]Higginson immigrated to the United States from Liverpool in 1853 at age 22 with his wife, Mary. Called as a missionary to the Indians in 1855, he arrived in today's Oklahoma in November, where he served in the Choctaw Nation until October 1856 "without being able to baptize any one." That month the Cherokees ordered "all Mormon Elders to leave the nation forthwith," and Higginson served in the Creek Nation until Parley P. Pratt asked him "to travel towards Texas and look out for the Texas emigration for Utah" in early April 1857. See Foreman, "Missionaries of the Latter Day Saints Church in Indian Territory," 197, 202–203, 211–12; and Journal History, 13 May 1857, 12.

and tell them I am perfectly reconciled to my fate. I am in the hands of the Lord and He can do what he likes with me. I had rather die than live. I have no desire to live except to do good and my way appears hedged up on every hand." He also desired me, if I could, to wait in Van Buren and see what became of him, and if he was murdered to make a full report to President Brigham Young of the true circumstances of his death and trial.[4]

The next morning, Pratt and Higginson were "both chained together and marched off for Van Buren" with the marshal and an escort of two soldiers. "We were treated with great kindness by them during the journey, which lasted three days," Higginson reported. "On arriving in Van Buren, the excitement was intense. Threats, the most awful to utter, were made on the person of Brother Pratt."[5]

On the morning of 12 May, Pratt was charged with stealing the McLean children's clothes. Hector McLean testified at the hearing. "I was allowed to state the history of my grievances, and to read the evidences of my wrongs to the court," he recalled, "to about five hundred spectators." He implicated "the scoundrel in court, Parley Parker Pratt, as the principal cause of all my sorrows" and succeeded "in producing the most intense excitement." McLean inflamed the crowd against Pratt until the aggrieved husband felt they were about "to lay hold of him and tear him to pieces."[6] Determined to stop a lynching, the officials postponed the case until the next day. "Next morning Mr. Pratt was released, put on his horse, which was a very good one," court official James Orme told a Mormon missionary years later. McLean quickly learned of the discharge and followed Pratt with two friends. Twelve miles northwest of Van Buren, they overtook Pratt, and McLean "at once opened fire on him with a six shooter. Two balls fired by McLain entered the back of Mr. Pratt's saddle, one of these balls cutting a hip strap; several balls passed through his clothing, but none entered his body," Orme recalled. Pratt abandoned the road and plunged his horse into a thicket, followed closely by McLean. McLean emerged from the copse, got a derringer from one of his companions, went back into the thicket, and fired several shots. McLean and his friends returned to Van Buren, while the Mormon apostle bled to death in front of a farmhouse.[7]

---

[4]Journal History, 13 May 1857, 13.

[5]Ibid., 14.

[6]"The Killing of Pratt—Letter from Mr. McLean," *Alta California*, 9 July 1857.

[7]James Orme, Quoted in Journal of James G. Duffin, 3 September 1903, Journal History, 13 May 1857, 7–8.

Eleanor McLean:
The Blood of This Man upon Her Soil

Eleanor McLean was a gifted, deeply emotional woman, but the loss of her two children and the murder of her beloved second husband drove her to the edge of reason. Immediately after Pratt's murder, his widow wrote this impassioned report to Apostle Erastus Snow at St. Louis.

> May 15th I went yesterday to see the dead body of my beloved Parley. I saw his wounds—saw his blood dripping from his heart making a puddle on the floor and spattering a vessel put to catch it. Saw his coat full of holes where the balls passed through, and two rents made by the knife which gave him the death wound on his left breast, one straight across and the other precisely the shape of the marks on his garments; and one did not penetrate through the lining. I went and examined the spot where he died, and where he bore his dying testimony while his precious blood was dripping on the ground. I picked up some leaves that were matted with blood & although it had rained heavily when I pulled them apart the blood looked fresh and warm. And I said in my head Oh! God of Israel let the blood of beloved Parley come up before thee. Let it plead the cause of the innocent, and condemn the guilty!! Brother Higinson and myself shrouded him in fine linen. He with assistance first putting on his garments and then we commenced at his feet and [rolled?] his body to his arms, then passed it under his left arm and across his breast then under his right arm and from thence to his feet tying it with a ribband [sic] on his right shoulder and around his feet. It was a very fine piece of linen beautifully white, and when we got through he looked very well. While we were doing it there were a number of persons present, and I said aloud, "Parley thou are not dead but sleeping. And thy innocent blood and thy wounds are before the God of Israel, to plead for the innocent, and call forth vengeance on the guilty.["] I could not wait to see him put in the ground, fore [sic] was with me the Marshall who went for my protection and it grew late. But brother Higinson said he would see it done and then make his escape in the night.[8]

The widow's subsequent report of Pratt's murder to the Church Historian's Office ranks among the most remarkable documents connected to the massacre at Mountain Meadows—and like many such documents, its origin is clouded. Wilford Woodruff "got an account of the death and burial of Elder P. P. Pratt" from Pratt's widow on 1 August 1857, which she read aloud in the Church Historian's Office three weeks later.[9] However, the document

---

[8]Eleanor J. McComb to Erastus Snow, 14, 15 May 1857, LDS Archives.

[9]Kenny, ed., *Wilford Woodruff's Journal*, 1 August 1857, 5:71; and Historical Department, Journals, 24 August 1857.

that survives at LDS Archives is probably a second version prepared at the request of church historian George A. Smith, who conducted an overhaul of church records in the wake of the 1859 federal investigation of the massacre and other crimes in Utah. In April 1860 Woodruff showed the document to Brigham Young and asked his advice "about its being published in England. He said He did not wish it published but wished it retained in the office."[10]

ELEANOR J. McCOMB, ACCOUNT OF THE DEATH
OF PARLEY P. PRATT, LDS ARCHIVES, 23–38.

Late in the evening, the real Marshall (Mr. Hays) called with bro. Higinson to inform me that ~~Mr.~~ bro. Pratt was acquitted by the court and was only kept in the jail for his own personal safety, and would be let out at the first moment ~~thought safe~~ that might promise security from his enemies, either that night or the next morning. Said the court had appointed the trial for 11 o'clock next day on purpose to deceive McLean and afford the prisoner a chance to escape.

Wednesday morning 13th May about 9 o'clock I was informed that ~~Mr.~~ bro. P had been released, and that McLean with two other men was only ten minutes behind him—And a few minutes later I heard that many men on horseback were in close pursuit, and that some had stated what they meant to do, which was to my mind far worse than death, and I prayed earnestly to my father in heaven that he would not suffer them to mangle the body of his faithful servant, and leave him to linger in pain in a land of strangers, and perhaps remote from the dwelling of any human beings. And I felt a confidence that such would not be the case.

I suppose it was about half past twelve when a lady in the Hotel told me, news had come that they had shot ~~Mr.~~ him all to pieces & A little after another report that he was wounded but not dead. And in a few minutes more McLean with his party were drinking in the bar room of the Hotel in which I was, and very soon the Landlord (Mr. Smith) came and told me he could not ascertain what they had done. Said he asked MacLean "What have you done?" to which he replied "Well I've done a good work" and the demons whispered and winked at each other, but would not say aloud what they had done. One said "Come now let us lynch her, t'will not do to let her escape." But Mr. Smith checked him. Said *"how dare you speak in that manner in my house. If any man attempts to molest that lady while she is in my house, he must do it over my dead body, for I will protect her while she is under my roof & the man that would so disgrace his kind as to suggest such a thing, had better not be seen again on my premises."*

A few minutes more and McLean was crossing the Arkansas River which flowed immediately in front of the Hotel. And I stood on the upstairs front

---

[10]Kenny, ed., *Wilford Woodruff's Journal*, 30 April 1860, 5:453.

gallery and saw him alone in the boat holding his horse. And at the same time I saw the man Perkins in front of the bar room door, on a horse, and holding a horse apparently for some other man, and his countenance was more dark and fiendish looking than I could untill that moment have concieved of.

Mr. Smith came again to my room and said he felt assured they had killed Mr. Pratt. Said that McLean spoke to a man on the side of the street as he went to the boat as follows "Sir if you will go out 8 or 10 miles on a Certain road, you might do a deed of humanity" and then passed on.

I suppose it was an hour after all this when a man came from the scene of the murder and reported that Mr. Pratt was dead. That he was killed near to a house, and that the man of the house saw all that was done.

About dusk that evening the Marshall (Mr. Hays) came to my room and talked a considerable time. Said he regretted exceedingly the deed that had been done. That the tone of feeling in the place had greatly changed between the rising and setting of the sun that day; and there was a disposition to punish the murderers, not so much McLean as the citizens of Van Buren who were equally guilty.

I appealed to him to know if I could go to the dead body. I told him I was the only person in that land who knew the murdered man and his family, and said I "they are noble and faithful & pure & he was a faith[ful] servant of God. he was a mighty orator & Poet—beloved by tens of thousands, and prized by his bretheren as one of superlative worth—And shall he not receive the burial of a simple Saint of God?"

I asked him if he would protect brother Higinson and myself to go and clothe the body for the grave. "Yes Madam you shall do any thing you wish to do, as far as my influence or protection goes."

He spoke with apparent emotion of the quiet uncomplaining manner of the deceased. Said he *"I never saw a man like him!"* And again when speaking of ~~the~~ his manner when leaving the jail he said, *"I never saw the like of it!"* Then said he "our citizens know not of any evil he has done, and McLean failed to substantiate any thing against him. And it is my feeling that those two men who took part in the murder *shall suffer* the ~~pene~~ penalty of the law *for they were in no way agrieved.* Many of the people feel that McLean was deeply wronged, and perchance they would clear him, but popular sentiment is against our citizens, who have aided in bringing this man's blood upon ~~the~~ our soil."

Ah! yes Sir, and it is innocent blood—You might have killed a million of men in this state and perhaps not not [*sic*] have shed one drop of innocent blood. Tis the innocence of this man, that will give power to the cry of his blood, when it comes before the God of Israel. And tis better for the state of Arkansas ~~and the United States~~ to have suffered seven years famine, than to have the blood of this man upon her soil!

As agreed upon he came next morning with his carriage to take me to the place of the murder. Mr. Smith came and told me there was about a hundred men gathered to see me come out. I requested him to have the carriage driven in the Alley that led back by the stable, which he did, & I was in in a moment, and the Marshall drove out the back way, and escaped the crowd of idle gazers.

He drove past his residence, and proposed that if it would be agreeable to me, a lady, the wife of a Methodist minister would go along and drive the carriage, while he would ride with brother H on horseback. This was done and two friends of the man and we rode along quietly over rough hills, through wood land, and over a number of beautiful streams of water—and about the middle of the day came to the house where the dead body ~~of the beloved~~ brother Parley lay.

There was a great number of horses hitched to the fence and bushes, for it was a quiet forest place and but a small lot of ground cleared, and the house was a small log building, divided into two rooms there being an arena between, and a porch on the back of the building. The direction of the road was north and the house on the right hand side.

We entered by the arena and through a door to the right, and there on our right, lay the body of the man of God, upon a board. He had on the same blue check shirt, but other pants, and the blood was still dripping from his side. ~~There was a number of respectable looking~~ If he had been on a bed I should have thought him only asleep for the expression of his countenance was lifelike. There was no rigidity or congealed look to the skin or flesh, and he was limber, ~~and~~ yet warm about his heart. There was a great deal of blood on the floor and a vessel about two thirds full in the midst of it.

I have often thanked my God that I had never been called upon to witness a scene of human blood greater than a small wound on the hand or foot. But now I was called to look upon a ~~livid~~ crimson flood that had ~~lately~~ but yesterday filled the veins of one who was beloved by all ~~who~~ the lovers of virtue & truth, who ever knew him.

The grand jury were sitting around a table on the back porch, and there was a number of respectable looking women, apparently the mothers and their daughters, in the room and they all looked serious. They all appeared to feel that a terrible thing had been done in their neighbourhood.

A man who saw him die took me to the place and showed me the tracks of the horses, and the place where he fell, and then the spot where he breathed his last breath.

The man (Mr. Winn) living at the place, heard the approach of horses as he worked in his shop on the road side ran to the door and stood and saw the men comeing. His testimony read about as follows. I saw a lone man comeing in the road and soon after three others, who appeared to be pursuing the first man. One rode in advance of the other two; increased the speed of his horse and was soon close upon the first man, and when nearly touching him fired. ~~The first man turned out of the road,~~ and in a backward direction through the bushes, and the other after still firing untill I heard the sixth ball. Cannot swear that the one man fired all six. By this time they were again in the road, and one of the other men had got in advance, and headed the first man round, and ~~then~~ forced him into close colision with his ~~person~~ assassin, and then he aimed two blows at his heart with a knife. They were now a little across the road, and I saw the man fall to the ground, and his horse stood off about the length of himself, and stood perfectly still.

The three men then rode away out of sight. But in a ~~few moments~~ little time perhaps ten minutes one came back got down from his horse and placin~~g~~ed a pistol I think nearly touching the man's neck and fired, and then mounted his horse and rode away.

I did not go to the wounded man for I thought he was dead, I heard no noise nor did I see him move. I got my horse and went for my neighbours which I suppose occupied an hour. When we came near ~~to~~ the man turned over and said "Sir will you please give me a drink of water for I am very thirsty; and raise my head if you please[."] This we did and then I asked him, "What is your name? He answered "My name is Parley P Pratt"

"Who is your murderer?"

"He is one McLean[."]

"Of what did he accuse you?"

"He accused me of taking his wife and children I *did not do it they were oppressed, and I did for them what I would do for the oppressed any where!*"

~~Did you see~~ "Was there any persons with McLean[?"]

["]I saw ~~persons~~ other men but I do not know them[.]"

["]Are you confident it was McLean killed you[?"]

"Yes. He shot me here["] (pointing to his neck) "and cut me here" (pointing to his side).

"Have you any family?"

"Yes. I have a family in Salt Lake City Utah Territory and that is my home. My gold is in this pocket (pointing to his pants) and my gold watch in this and I want them with all my effects sent to my family in Salt Lake. Write to ~~a man the~~ Mr. [Crouch?] Flint Post Office Cherokee Nation and let him have all my things to send to my family."

This is the testimony of Mr. Winn and several other men who stood near while the man of God lay bleeding and dying upon the ground[.]

They consulted about sending for Doctors But he said, "I want no Doctors for I will be dead in a few minutes."

I inquired if he groaned or appeared to suffer much? The answer was No!

He lay still and complained of nothing but thirst and his last breath was like a man going to sleep. This was the Language of Mrs [W]inn in reply to my question. She said she was by him the last half hour.

~~After we had heard I here perhaps~~ The place where he fell was near to a stump, and looked as though he might have struggled a good deal, for the leaves were rubbed from the ground and matted with the gore in a kind of circle, there was also a bunch of paper about as large as a common egg bloody on one end, and looked as though he had endeavored to stop the bleeding by putting this into the wound! Oh! my soul was it so that the "Beloved Parley" lay one hour alone bleeding & thirsty, without one wife or child or even a friend to raise his head or give him a drink of cold water, an[d] to whom he could express his dying wish!

Eleanor McLean ended her impassioned report with a poem that imagined a haunting wail that was "the voice of wives and children wild with grief."

> The wail increased, untill it reached the throne of God,
> And Elohim himself did take his mighty rod,
> And said I'll cut *them* down and blot *them* from the earth,
> Who've slain my prophets on the soil that gave them birth!
>
> I'l[l] send upon them *"famine pestilence & war!"*
> And I'll call my legions from the northern realms afar,
> And they *shall hunt them down in every land & place*
> That's stained with the blood of one of Joseph's race.
>
> The blood of Parley shall not long before me plead,
> For wrath on him or them who did the hellish deed,
> And ere it cease to cry, that nation shall atone,
> For every widow's tear & every orphan's moan.
>
> And every drop of guiltless blood they ever shed,
> Shall quickly come upon their own devoted head.

Exactly how and when Parley Pratt's last widow reached Utah ahead of the Fancher party is a question that has long puzzled historians. It is now known that as Mormon luminaries made their way up Big Cottonwood Canyon on the evening of 23 July to celebrate the tenth anniversary of Brigham Young's arrival in Salt Lake, Orrin Porter Rockwell drove a light buckboard into the valley. The legendary Mormon frontiersman delivered confirmation of the news heard weeks before that President Buchanan had appointed a new governor and ordered some twenty-five hundred troops to march to Utah. Riding with

Rockwell were Abraham O. Smoot, Judson Stoddard—and Eleanor Pratt. From Fort Laramie, Rockwell had rushed the widow Pratt to Salt Lake in an amazing five days and three hours, perhaps passing the Arkansans on the trail.[11]

"When news of his death arrived in Salt Lake City, the Presidency were spending the holiday, July 24th, in Big Cottonwood Canyon," recalled one of Pratt's widows, Ann Agatha Walker Pratt. As soon as the First Presidency returned from Big Cottonwood, they visited Pratt's widows to "mingle their grief and sorrow with ours," she wrote. President Young told her how moved he had been by Apostle Pratt's death. "Nothing has happened so hard to reconcile my mind to since the death of Joseph," Young said. "Brother Parley has done more good on this short mission than many elders will do in their whole life."[12]

On the penultimate page of her report of the death of Parley Pratt, Eleanor McLean gave her final accounting of the ones she held most accountable for the murder:

> I believe I have not yet named the two men who accompanied him [McLean].— *Howell and John Cornell!* Mark it ye hosts of Israel. And there was one N. D. Collins, a young lawyer, who acknowledged to me that he went along to "see and assist" in mangling the body of the deceased.[13] This young man called to see me to explain what he had done. Said he understood I had his name written down and he did not wish me to leave under any false impression. But the more he explained the better I understood his guilt and told him his name would stand where I put it.

"If I were appointed Executioner, and murder was the crime, I would feel no compunctions of law in beheading this man," wrote Eleanor McLean. "I believe he is a murderer at heart."[14] The grim widow described the spot where Pratt had bled to death: "Oh! My soul, what a sight! and what a fountain of

---

[11]Kenny, ed., *Wilford Woodruff's Journal*, 5:69; Schindler, *Orrin Porter Rockwell*, 246–47; and Thomas, ed., *Elias Smith's Journal*, 23 July 1857. Smith's report that Eleanor McLean arrived with Rockwell might appear to be an unimportant detail, but the fact that historian Harold Schindler, who spent more than forty years relentlessly researching Rockwell's career, never learned how Pratt's widow arrived in Utah indicates how scrupulously this information was suppressed.

[12]Pratt, "His Last Mission," 17:234.

[13]Since Mormon vengeance was never visited on McLean, there is no reason to think that any of his accomplices suffered violent ends. Eleanor McLean's demand for beheading may refer either to the Utah capital punishment law, which gave the convicted a choice of death by hanging, firing squad, or beheading, or the blood-atonement doctrine introduced during the Reformation.

[14]McComb, Account of The Death of Parley P. Pratt, 61. The microfilm of this document at LDS Archives omits the last two pages, but the editors have seen the original.

blood was there opened!! perchance many thousands in the State of Arkansas might have lost their blood and yet not a drop of innocent blood, raised a cry from the ground."[15]

PARLEY P. PRATT:
THE BLOOD OF INNOCENCE CRIES FOR VENGEANCE

The *Western Standard*, the voice of the LDS church in California, published the "melancholy and heart-sickening intelligence" of Pratt's murder on 3 July. The paper correctly predicted that this "diabolical transaction" would "be the signal for a general jubilee throughout California, as it has already been in the East," and would "be a cause of rejoicing among all those who hate the servants of God." It mourned Pratt as "a martyr for the cause of truth" and foresaw that "God will, ere long, come out of his hiding place" and call "*this* generation" to account for "all the righteous blood which has been shed from the time of Jesus to the present."[16]

Mormon resentment against the United States and its failure to prosecute the men who had martyred its prophets ran deep. In 1845, on the first anniversary of Joseph Smith's murder, the Quorum of the Twelve met in a prayer circle and Willard Richards presented a formal prayer for vengeance on those who had shed the blood of the prophets. This "prayer of vengeance" (often called an oath) became part of the Nauvoo temple endowment.[17] Apostle George Q. Cannon recalled that during this rite, "he took an oath against the murderers of the Prophet Joseph as well as other prophets."[18] In September 1857 Heber C. Kimball said "the whole people of the United States are under condemnation. They consented to the death of Joseph, Hyrum, David [Patten], Parley, and lots of men, women, and children."[19] The Arkansas emigrants had left for California weeks before Pratt's death, but to Mormon believers, Pratt was not the victim of a marital dispute: he was another martyr whose death cried out for vengeance.

Hector McLean's account of the murder appeared in San Francisco's *Alta California*, claiming "it as the best act of my life. And the people of West

[15]"More Particulars of the Assassination of Parley P. Pratt," *Millennial Star*, 29 August 1857, 528.

[16]"The Assassination of President P. P. Pratt," *Western Standard*, 3 July 1857, 2/2–3.

[17]Quinn, *The Mormon Hierarchy: Origins of Power*, 179.

[18]Horne, ed., *An Apostle's Record: The Journals of Abraham H. Cannon*, 6 December 1889, 114.

[19]Heber C. Kimball, *Journal of Discourses*, 20 September 1857, 5:253.

Arkansas agree with me." The *Alta*—which had long been sympathetic to Mormonism—had remarkable insights into the Saints. On 9 July 1857 the paper asked:

> . . . whether the hot blood which must now be seething and boiling in the veins of Brigham Young and his satellites, at Salt Lake, is to be cooled by the murder of Gentiles who pass through their territory, whether the "destroying angels" of Mormondom, are to be brought into requisition to make reprisals upon travelers, or, whether, as has been done before, "Saints" disguised as Indians are to constitute themselves the supposed ministers of God's vengeance in this case, we are not informed, but have no doubt that such thoughts, such intentions as these, are prevalent among those saintly villains, adulterers and seducers, of Salt Lake.[20]

Meanwhile, Mormon authorities in Great Salt Lake City knew of Parley Pratt's murder as early as 23 June. "We learn that all Hell is boiling over against the saints in Utah," Wilford Woodruff reported after noting that Pratt's murder was painful news to his family. "The papers of the United States are filled with bitter revileings against us. The devil is exceding mad."[21] Oddly, the *Deseret News* barely mentioned Pratt's murder, and Mormon leaders in Utah had little to say about it in their discourses or official pronouncements. If this silence reflected a calculated policy, knowledge of it did not reach England. Asa Calkins, editor of the 1858 volume of the *Journal of Discourses*, the collected speeches of Mormon leaders, included the text of Parley P. Pratt's last sermon in Great Salt Lake City on "the blood of innocence."

"REMINISCENCES AND TESTIMONY OF PARLEY P. PRATT," *JOURNAL OF DISCOURSES*, 7 SEPTEMBER 1856, 5:197–98.

When that [*The Book of Mormon*] was printed in English, an ancient prophecy in it stated that it should come to the knowledge of the Gentiles in the latter day, at a time when the blood of the Saints would cry from the ground because of secret murders, and the works of darkness, and wicked combinations. And not only the blood of Saints, but the blood of husbands and fathers should cry from the ground for vengeance on the workers of iniquity, and the cries of widows and orphans would come up before God, against those that committed those crimes.

The blood of innocence cries for vengeance, because its enemies have not administered justice. They have not carried out the constitutional guarantees,

---

[20]"The Killing of Pratt," *Daily Alta California*, 9 July 1857, 2/1–2. For the complete McLean letter and other documents on Pratt's murder, see Ekins, ed., *Defending Zion*, 319–22.

[21]Kenny, ed., *Wilford Woodruff's Journal*, 23 June 1857, 5:61.

but have suffered innocent blood to flow. They have not administered justice nor law in the case, but have allowed wholesale murderers to run at large in Missouri and Illinois. And many of the people and of their rulers have consented to the shedding of that innocent blood, and the result is that the cries of widows and orphans ascend to God.

On the day he learned of Pratt's murder, Brigham Young asked George A. Smith "if it was not Hard to Acknowledge the hand of God in the death of Parley P Pratt" by a man as wicked as Hector McLean. "Yet we will have to do it."[22] Young saw Pratt's fate as unfortunate: "I regret exceeding to hear of the death of Bro Parley, but the Lords not my will be done," he wrote to George Q. Cannon. "The day will come when the kingdom of God will be triumphant, and none will dare to raise their hand against those who bear His name."[23] Early in 1858 G. A. Smith told his fellow apostles that he had advised Pratt not to go to Arkansas but to "take care of himself." Smith warned Pratt that if he tried to protect Eleanor and her children, he would lose his life. "But He did not take Care of himself" or follow Smith's counsel, Wilford Woodruff noted, with inevitable consequences.[24] George Higginson later complained, "it has been remarked 'Died Parley as a fool dieth.' "[25] But ordinary Mormons reacted to the news with mingled grief and outrage. Philip Margetts and other eastbound missionaries "felt like young lions and almost as savage in consequence of hearing of the assassination of our beloved P. P. Pratt."[26] Editors, priests, and people were "rejoicing over the murder of Br. Parley," William I. Appleby reported from New York. "Their joy will be turned into mourning before long."[27]

[22]Ibid., 25 June 1857, 5:62.

[23]Young to Cannon, 4 July 1857, Brigham Young Collection, LDS Archives.

[24]Kenny, ed., *Wilford Woodruff's Journal*, 3 January 1858, 5:153.

[25]Spencer W. Kimball to George L. Higginson, 20 October 1950, copy in Pratt family possession.

[26]Carter, ed., "Journal of Philip Margetts," *Heart Throbs*, 6:400.

[27]Appleby to Young, 11 June 1857, Brigham Young Collection, LDS Archives.

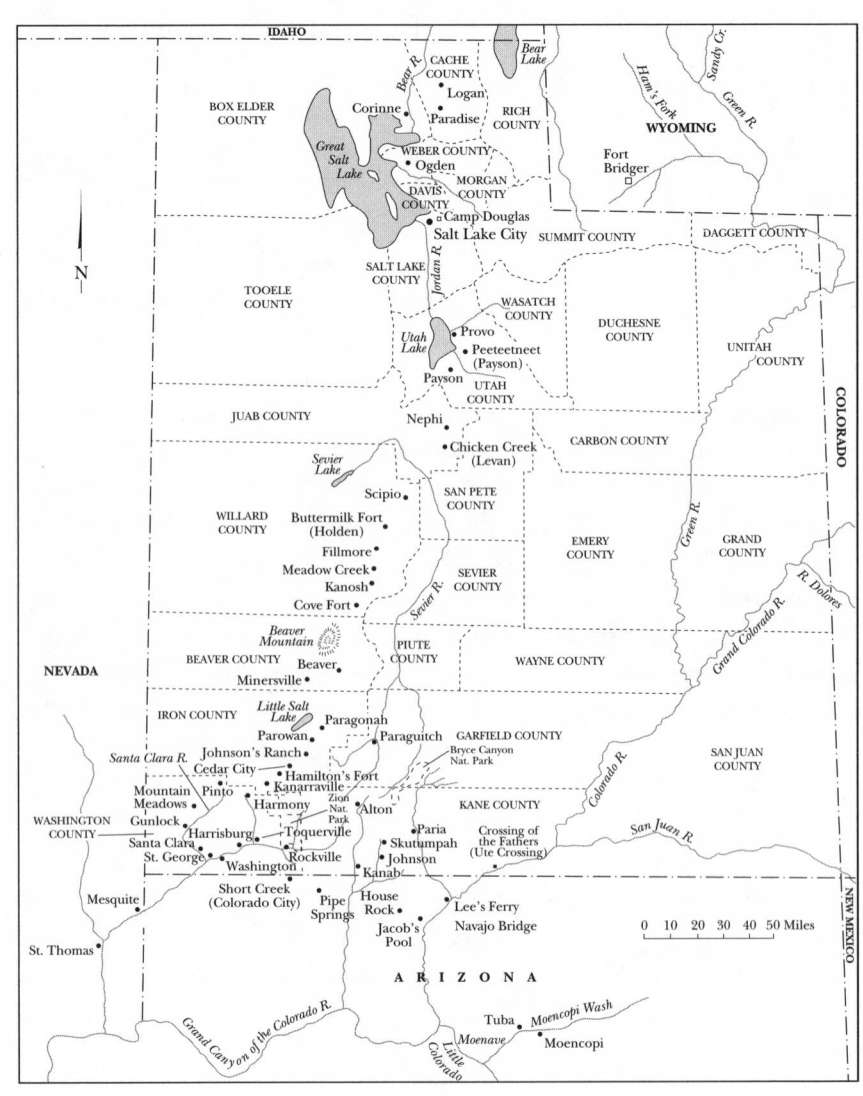

Utah Territory, based on a map from
Juanita Brooks, *John Doyle Lee: Zealot, Pioneer Builder, Scapegoat.*
Courtesy of the Arthur H. Clark Company.

Chapter 4

"My Way'll Be Rough and Steep"
The Emigrants Go South

The Arkansas emigrants on their way to California entered a world of religious fervor, rampant rumor, and bombastic defiance in Utah Territory. Malinda Cameron Scott Thurston, a member of one company, in 1877 fixed the date of her arrival in the Mormon capital—3 August 1857. As "P.," the *Alta California's* anonymous correspondent, reported in October 1857, the Camerons were one of "three, and perhaps four, companies from Arkansas" that soon formed what is now known as the Fancher party. As Thurston indicates, the emigrants split and took either the northern or southern route to California. From that day forward, the first southbound company was a marked train.

At daybreak on the day that the Camerons arrived, Apostle George A. Smith took off by buggy and raced south to visit the string of Mormon settlements that stretched over 250 miles from Great Salt Lake City to the rim of the Great Basin, near Cedar City.[1] Thurston and her four children escaped the fate of the southbound wagon train because her husband took them west via the northern route.[2] But on the advice of unidentified Mormons, her parents, William and Martha Cameron, and five brothers stuck with the ill-fated companies that followed Smith over the trail south.

[1]The Great Basin is a vast region of high-altitude deserts and north-south-running ranges that encompasses parts of six western states from which no water flows to any ocean. Its southern rim crossed Mountain Meadows.

[2]The northern route, also known as Hensley's Salt Lake Cutoff, headed due north from Great Salt Lake City and followed the line of present I-84 and Utah Highway 30 to the California Trail near present Almo, Idaho.

Malinda Cameron Scott Thurston parted
from her family and the Fancher train in
Great Salt Lake City in 1857 and survived
to file Indian depredation claims for the
property that the Cameron family lost
at Mountain Meadows. *Courtesy of
Cheryl Gremaux, Will Bagley Collection.*

MALINDA THURSTON: VIOLENTLY KILLED AND MURDERED

Years later, Malinda Cameron Scott Thurston reaffirmed her testimony and
added new information about the Fancher party. She said the emigrants numbered about 100 when they reached Great Salt Lake City on 3 August 1857,
where other people with wagons joined the company. The estimated 120 who
died in the massacre, plus 17 surviving children, came to about 140 and support her statement of the company's size.[3] Some have speculated that the
newcomers were hell-raising Missourians, whose bad behavior led southern
Utah settlers to commit the massacre. Subsequent news reports make clear
that the only identifiable Missourians on the southern trail traveled with the
parties that followed the Fancher company. It is now apparent that others
who joined the southbound train were dissident Mormons who wanted to
escape but were afraid to attempt it on their own after others who had tried
were killed at Provo and Springville.

[3]See Depositions, Malinda Thurston, Joel Scott, Frederick Arnold, and Andrew Wolf, 2 May 1911,
Thurston vs. the United States, Indian Depredation Claim 8479, RG 123, National Archives.

MALINDA THURSTON, DEPOSITION IN SUPPORT OF
H.R. 1459 AND H.R. 3945, 15 OCTOBER 1877.

Your petitioner, Mrs. Malinda Thurston, of San Joaquin county, in the State of California, respectfully represents that she is fifty-eight years of age, that she has been twice married, and that her first husband's name was Henry D. Scott and her maiden name was Malinda Cameron, and that her father's name was William Cameron and her mother's Martha Cameron. She further represents that in the year eighteen hundred and fifty-seven her said father, William Cameron, her mother, Martha Cameron, her brothers, Tilghman, Ison, Henry, James, and Larkin Cameron, her sisters, Martha Cameron, and Mathilda Miller, her brother-in-law, Joseph Miller and their children, named William Miller, Alfred Miller, Eliza Miller, and Joseph Miller, her cousin, named Nancy Cameron, her husband, Henry D. Scott, and herself, with their three children, and her husband's brother-in-law, were in a wagon train en route for California from the East and that on or about the third of August in said year eighteen hundred and fifty-seven they all arrived at Salt Lake City; that at the solicitation and under the advice of the Mormons and the representations that the stock could better be provided with feed, the train was divided, with the understanding that it was to be united outside of Salt Lake City and proceed by the northern route; and under said advice her husband, his brother-in-law, herself, and their three children and others started from Salt Lake and made one day's journey, on the third of August, in said mentioned year, and there encamped to await her father's part of said train; and that they remained at said camp until the seventh day of August in said year, when her husband was killed by one of the men of the train (but not by the Mormons). She further says that on the tenth of said month of August she was confined and was thus left with four small children; that after waiting for her father's part of the train a long and reasonable time the train proceeded on, and she eventually reached California. She further represents that her said father, while at Salt Lake City, at the time mentioned, was advised to and persuaded to take the southern route, as the Mormons represented the food for their stock was better and more plenty by said southern route; and that her said father, the said William Cameron, acting on said advice (although contrary to the agreement with her husband); did take said southern route, and that when some two or three days journey from Salt Lake City the said Mormons, under the authority of Brigham Young, with force of arms, violently killed and murdered the following persons, to wit, her father, William Cameron, her mother, Martha Cameron, her brothers, Tilghman Cameron, Ison Cameron, Henry Cameron, James Cameron, and Larkin Cameron, her sister, Martha Cameron, her sister, Mathilda Miller, Joseph Miller and their child, William Miller; and also killed other persons to her whose names are unknown; and captured Joseph and Mathilda Miller's children, named Alfred, Eliza, and Joseph, and her cousin, Nancy Cameron, who is yet with the Mormons, and who is aged about thirty-two years at this time.

Wagonmaster Basil Parker reached Great Salt Lake City in August 1857 to find the town teeming with hostile Indians. His friend Jack Baker's party was only two days ahead of him, he recalled, but Baker's wagons had already left when Parker arrived. He heard them charged with abusing the Mormons, and in his own tent "a Mormon threatened Baker's train, but as Capt. Jack was already far on his way, on the South Pass [*sic*] route, I could not warn him of the threat without seriously involving myself and train." Realizing he was in "a very close place," Parker behaved cautiously, believing the Mormons wanted "to create a disturbance as an excuse to slaughter the entire train." He took with him a lifelong opinion that there was "every reason to believe that the Baker party was doomed to destruction before it left Salt Lake City."[4]

Records even closer to these events create a similar impression.

Brigham Young:
Keep Your Guns and Pistols in Good Order

The LDS church's Journal History and historical department journals are important sources, but they are not daily accounts of events as they take place. These records are compilations of many sources, prepared well after the actions that they describe. This allowed the compiler an opportunity to alter information or reject any troublesome material altogether. While both records have been so altered for the days the Arkansans passed through Utah, a side-by-side comparison shows some revealing differences.

For example, the Journal History reported the arrival of the Baker-Fancher train on 3 August, but oddly neglected to mention the hurried departure of George A. Smith from Great Salt Lake that same day. Instead, as if to separate Smith's mission from the Arkansas party, it reported that Smith left Provo the following day, 4 August. Moreover, on 25 August, it reported that Smith camped "with a party of emigrants" at Corn Creek, near Fillmore, but failed to identify them as the Arkansas train. Neither journal mentioned that the apostle escorted as many as a dozen southern Utah chiefs to Great Salt Lake City to meet with Brigham Young and separated their arrival from Smith's.

These and other differences in the two records, both edited to start with, can be seen from the following comparison. The Historical Department Journal is presented in italic.

---

[4]Parker, *The Life and Adventures*, 62. In *Recollections of the Mountain Meadows Massacre*, 8–9, Parker wrote that Baker's train "was almost threatened in my presence."

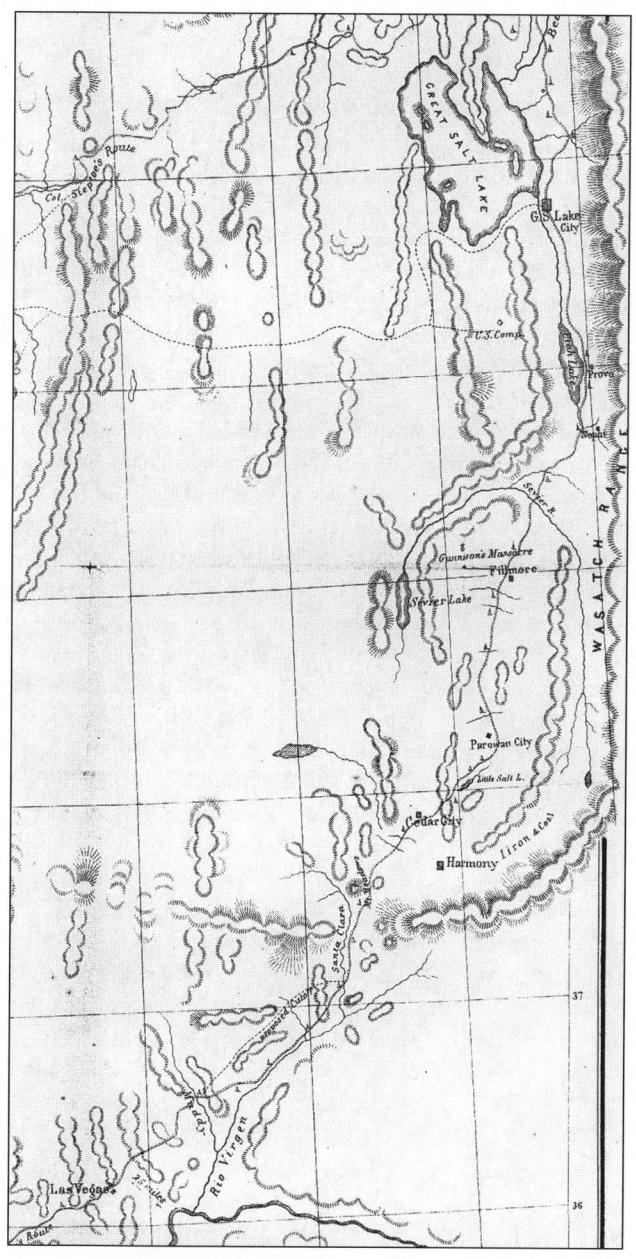

"Sketch of the march of a detachment of
U.S. Troops from Salt Lake, Utah to Ft. Tejon," 1855.
Lt. Sylvester Mowry's map shows the settlements strung along the
southern wagon road to Los Angeles at the time of the Mountain
Meadows massacre. *Courtesy of the National Archives.*

JOURNAL HISTORY, JULY–AUGUST 1857;
AND HISTORICAL DEPARTMENT JOURNALS,
23 JULY TO 6 SEPTEMBER 1857, LDS ARCHIVES.

July 20, 1857, Monday: About noon, a company of emigrants, mostly from Illinois, enroute for California, arrived in G.S.L. City . . .

July 25, 1857. Saturday: A company of California emigrants arrived in the city. Richard Pettit and Joseph Tompson [sic], overhearing C. J. Landon, an apostate, telling the emigrants what damned rascals the "Mormons" were, gave him a tremendous thrashing . . .[5]

July 27, 1857: Another company of emigrants arrived in G.S.L. City . . .

August 3, 1857. Monday: A company of emigrants arrived in G.S.L. City with a large herd of cattle . . .[6]

G.A.S. started at daybreak for Iron Co.—with Saml. Lewis . . . A company of emigrants arrived with a large herd of young cattle . . . G.A.S. spent several hours at Lehi and travelled to Provo in the evening. Delivered General orders from Gen Wells to Col Pace.

August 4, 1857. Tuesday: Another emigrant train with a large drove of cattle arrived in G.S.L. City. Geo. A. Smith left Provo at noon and delivered general orders to Gen. Aaron Johnson at Springville. Near Santaquin he broke his wagon and remained until the next day.

. . . Another emigrant train with a large drove of cattle arrived. G.A.S. left Provo at Noon. Delivered Gen Orders to Gen Aaron Johnson at Springville. Near Santaquin broke a felloe about 9 P.M. & stopped to get it repaired. Slept till 4 A.M. of the 5th.[7]

August 5, 1857: Another very large company of emigrants enroute to California arrived in G.S.L. City. At 4 A.M. Geo. A. Smith and company ~~started for~~ continued the journey to Nephi, where they delivered Gen. Wells orders to Major Bradley and camped for the evening 4 miles south of the Sevier river . . .

Thursday August 6. 1857 . . . G.A.S. Started at daylight & drove to Fillmore to dinner, delivered Gen. Orders to Maj McCullough.—Camped in evening at Corn Creek with Barney & Charley Carter of Parowan, coming north with lumber.[8]

Friday August 7. 1857 . . . G.A.S. Dined at Cove Creek with Jos. Adair & others on their return from the Cotton farm. Camped at 12 at night on Indian Creek.

August 8, 1857. Saturday: Another large company of emigrants enroute to California arrived in G.S.L. City. Geo. A. Smith breakfasted with Bishop

---

[5]For a report from the receiving end of this attack, see Landon to Burr, 18 September 1857, in *The Utah Expedition*, House Doc. 71, Serial 956, 122–23.

[6]This may well be the Fancher party.

[7]The below, or felly, is the exterior wooden rim, or segment of the rim, of a wheel supported by the spokes.

[8]William Leany, Sr., recalled "the day the picket was broke on my head" for giving onions from his yard to William Aden, a member of the Fancher party. "For that slight act of reciprocal kindness the bishop of Parowan sent two young men by the name of Carter to Laney's house," wrote Josiah Gibbs. "The latter was called out to the sidewalk where one of the young thugs beat him into insensibility with a club." See Leany to Steele, 17 February 1883, and Gibbs, *The Mountain Meadows Massacre*, 17–18.

Farnsworth at Beaver and later arrived in Parowan, where he delivered general orders to Col. William H. Dame.

> *... Another company of Cala emigrants arrived. G.A.S. Breakfasted with Bishop Farnsworth at Beaver. Arrived at Parowan at 5 P.M. Found the 1st Battalion on Parade & delivered General Orders to Col Dame, and at their request made a speech. Found his wife Zelpha & children well.*

August 10, 1857. Monday. The day was very hot in G.S.L. City. Another large company of emigrants arrived in G.S.L. City.

> *... More emigrants & cattle.*

August 11, 1857. Tuesday: It was a cloudy day in G.S.L. City. Another large company of emigrants passed through G.S.L. City. Geo. A. Smith went to Paragoona, where he preached in the forenoon. The prospects look bright for the raising of between four and five thousand bushels of wheat at that place.

> *... Emigrants & cattle continue passing.*

> *August 12, 1857 . . . More emigrants & cattle.*

> *August 15, 1857 . . . G.A.S. went to Cedar accompanied by his wife, Col. Dame & wife, Silas S. & Jesse N. Smith, Dr. Pendleton. The 2 & 3 Battalion mustered. Col. Dame drilled them & G.A.S. addressed them. Visited the Iron works & the improvements of the new city. I. C. Haight has built a house faced with burnt brick the only one in the Territory.*[9]

> *Sunday August 16th 1857 . . . G.A.S. preached twice & then went to Sidon & took supper with Bro Hambleton & then went to Harmony—staid for the night with Judge J. D. Lee.*[10] *Here met I. C. Haight who joined our party.*

> *Monday August 17 1857 . . . G.A.S preached to the people in Harmony meeting house.*[11] *Dame drilled the militia. Maj J. D. Lee & Capt Ingraham joined our part—Crossed Peters Leap and camped at Grape Vine Springs at 8 P.M.*[12] *The road rugged & rough the country a desert. Preached in afternoon. Dame drilled military—Bishop Covington brought in a load of melons from the field—Visited Tutsegabbit's corn field—he will have about 300 bushels. Ther.*

---

[9]Jesse N. Smith, a cousin of the Mormon prophet, wrote that an emigrant train passed Paragonah, about twenty-six miles north of Cedar City, on 3 September. His reconstructed journal claimed that he "went home and sold them some flour and salt; this company was afterwards massacred at Mountain Meadows." Smith, ed., *Six Decades in the Early West*, 27. Smith's date appears to be accurate and reveals that the Fancher party arrived in southern Utah later than many sources indicate.

[10]Both Smith and Lee, an Iron County probate judge, belonged to the ultra-secret Council of Fifty, organized in 1844 by Joseph Smith to establish the Kingdom of God as an earthly state that was to rule the world after the Second Coming.

[11]At New Harmony, "the brethren paraded in order to show the Officers of this place how to disipline their men right," Rachel Lee reported. "President G A Smith delivered a discourse on the Spirit that actuated the United States towards this people—full of hostility and virulence, [and] all felt to rejoice in the Lord God of our Fathers. After the singing prayer of Prest I. C. Haight the company left for the Rio Virgin." In a boastful and sarcastic sermon that Smith gave on his return to Salt Lake, the apostle admitted he "was perfectly running over with it." See Diary of Rachel Andora Woolsey Lee, Huntington Library, 47; and *Deseret News*, 23 September 1857, 227/1.

[12]Peter Shurtz opened a route south from Cedar City over the imposing Black Ridge. At one point it was necessary to dismantle wagons to get over, hence the name Peters Leap. Grape Vine Springs was also located on the early trail to Washington City.

*at 103° in the shade & people said it was unusually cool. Started at dusk drove 10 miles &
camped at Allen's farm. Several Indians accompanied us & took care of our horses—road awful*

August 18, 1857 . . . G.A.S started & travelled 10 miles—overtaken by Judge [Tarlton]
*Lewis with a Gen Order, directing people to save their grain—Arrived at Washington City
at 9 A.M. It consists of about 50 families camped in Wagons & tents on a sand bank & surrounded by a desert. Their fields are a piece of Sandy desert level enough to spread water over—
some 500 acres of which are in cultivation in corn, cotton & vines.*

*August 19, 1857 . . . Drove to Hamblin's Fort, the Santa Clara had dried up. It was dif-
ficult to get water to drink. They had raised a heavy crop of corn though it had suffered some
from drouth. Cotton indigo melons & peach trees & grape vines looked well, tho' all suffered
for want of water. Preached to the people. About 4 P.M. started for the Mountain Meadows.
Passed some 13 indian corn fields on the way up. Bro. Hamblin & associates are doing much
for the benefit of these Indians. Ther 103° in shade & 136 in sun. The people called it cool.
The fort is a good stone building about 120 ft. sq. & 9 or 10 high. The country round is desert.
About 9 P.M. surrounded by Indians who urged us to camp—tooke care of our horses, roast-
ed up corn &c. of which they had a plenty.*

*August 20, 1857. G.A.S. travelled to Mountain Meadows—took dinner. Ther at 72°. Arrived
at Penter* [Pinto] *in Evening. At Mountain Meadows there are about 30 souls herding cattle &
sheep belonging to the Santa Clara Mission. They fed us on toast & cheese. At Penter preached
at the house of Rufus Allen, the house crowded. Some came 25 miles to meeting.*

*August 21, 1857 . . . G.A.S. Drove to Cedar City & found the furnace in blast. A cloud
had just burst on the mountains covering the country with water and doing much damage. Bro.
Haight sent a specimen of iron to Prest. Young. Returned to Parowan arriving at 11 PM. Night
cold & wet. Travelled 46 miles that day.* [Since] *the time he left Parowan had travelled 186
miles, some of it the worst road any one ever took a wagon over.*

*Saturday August 22. 1857 . . . G.A.S. preached in the morning, & afternoon, & attend-
ed Council in the evening.*

Monday August 24. 1857. Fine day W[ilford]. *W*[oodruff]. *Hearing Helena Eleanor
Pratt read her A/c of Parley death . . . Col Dame took G.A.S.'s wife & daughter and carried them to Paragonah—took breakfast with Silas S. Smith. Bro. Orson B. Adams took them
in his carriage to Beaver (30 miles). S. S. Smith accompanied them on horseback. Preached 1
hour & 20 min in the evening at the School House which was crowded—Stayed with Sime-
on Howd. Married 3 couple*[s].

August 25, 1857. Geo. A. Smith arrived at Cove [Corn] Creek where he
camped with a party of emigrants.

*. . . G.A.S. left his wife to return to Parowan with Bro Adams, Bishop Philo Farnsworth
took his wagon & horses & carried him, accompanied by S. S. Smith & Elisha Hoopes 52
miles to Corn Creek. Camped with a party of emigrants who seemed to be much excited and
placed on a double guard as soon as we arrived. Bro. Jacob Hamblin, Tutsegabbit & Ammon
travelled & camped with them.*[13]

August 26, 1857 . . . G.A.S. took breakfast on Meadow Creek & reached Fillmore at 10

---

[13]The appearance of a Mormon apostle escorting a dozen Indian chiefs to Great Salt Lake City gave
the Arkansans much to be excited about.

A.M. gave out an appointment & preached 1½ hours to a crowded house at 5 P.M. Stayed with Saml. P. Hoyt.

August 27, 1857 ... Geo Pierce took G.A.S. in his waggon, was accompanied by the Bishop & S. S. Smith to Unionville 10 miles. There Bishop Bronson, & S. S. Smith left him & returned. Camped on the Sevier river with Ammon, Kanoshe & other Indians.

August 28, 1857 ... A train of emigrants for Cala arrived at 2 PM. with over 400 head of young stock. G.A.S. travelled to Nephi, arriving at noon. Preached in the evening 2 hours & 20 without knowing he had spoken so long.

August 29, 1857 ... Bishop Bigler got John Cazier to take his horses & carry G.A.S. to Provo. Arriving there at 5 PM.

August 31, 1857. Monday: At 2 p.m. a train of goods for Levi Stewart and Isaac Bowman arrived in G.S.L. City. Geo. A. Smith arrived in G.S.L. city at 4 p.m. having traveling 400 miles and preached in all the settlements in Iron, Washington and Beaver counties.

September 1, 1857. Tuesday: Pres. Young was in his office from 10 A.M. until late in the afternoon. At 4:45 an Indian by the name of John who had come all the way from Peetneet came into the office and asked Pres. Young to administer to him as he was very sick. Pres. Young, Geo. A. Smith and Wilford Woodruff administered to him.

Bro. Jacob Hamblin arrived in G.S.L. City from the Santa Clara Mission with 12 Indian Chiefs who had come to see Pres. Young. One of them was the head chief; his name was Tutsigabot. There was also the chief of the Piedes and of the Deserts and Santa Clara, and Rio Virgen, and of Harmony; also Kanosh, chief of the Pahvants, and Ammon, Walker's brother were in the company. Pres. Young had an interview for about one hour with the Indians ... *Tutsegabot, Kanoshe & Ammon had an interview with Prest B.Y. this evening ...*

Sunday Sept. 6, 1857. G.A.S. & R.L.C. [clerk Robert L. Campbell] writing letters to Wm. H. Dame ...[14]

Brigham Young: Those Who Persist in Selling Grain to the Gentiles

The orders that George A. Smith carried to military and settlement leaders along the wagon road from Great Salt Lake City to the Spanish Trail were warlike in tone and breathed armed defiance toward the approaching U.S. Army and bitter resentment toward the U.S. government. Especially noteworthy is Young's letter on 4 August to Isaac C. Haight, head of Zion's Cedar Stake and commander of the Nauvoo Legion battalion at Cedar City, "to pay strict attention" to the instructions he sent by Smith, no doubt verbal-

---

[14]These letters do not survive in LDS church records or William Dame's papers.

ly. Also significant is Young's replacing as head of the Santa Clara Indian Mission moderate Rufus C. Allen with the more trusted Jacob Hamblin.

WELLS TO DAME, 1 AUGUST 1857,
PALMER COLLECTION, SOUTHERN UTAH UNIVERSITY.

Sir,

Reports tolerably well authenticated, have reached this office that an army from the United States is now en route to invade this Territory.

The people of this Territory having lived in strict obedience to the Laws of the parent and home governments, and ever jealous of the supremacy of the Constitution and the rights guaranteed thereby, in such times when anarchy takes the place of orderly government and mobocratic tyranny usurp the power to rule; they are left to their inalienable right to defend themselves against aggression against their constitutional privileges. It is enough that for successive years they have witnessed the desolation of their homes; the barbarous wrath of mobs poured upon their unoffending brethren and sisters; their leaders arrested, incarcerated, and slain; and themselves driven to cull life from the hospitality of the desert and the Savage. They are not willing to endure longer these unceasing outrages; but, if an exterminating war is purposed against them, and blows alone can cleanse pollution from the nations bulwarks: to the God of our fathers let the appeal be made. You are instructed to hold your command in readiness to march at the shortest notice to any part of the Territory. See that the law is strictly enforced in regard to arms and ammunition and as far as practicable that each Ten shall be provided with a good wagon and four horses or mules, as well as the necessary clothing &c for a winter campaign. Particularly let your influence be used for the preservation of grain and report without delay any person from your district that disposes of a kernal of grain to any Gentile merchant or temporary sojourner or suffers to let it go to waste. Avoid all excitement but Be ready.

<table>
<tr><td>By order of the General Comm'd
James Ferguson, Adjt General</td><td>/s/ Daniel H. Wells
Lieut. Gen'l Comm'd</td></tr>
</table>

JACOB HAMBLIN: A MAN WITHOUT CONSCIENTIOUS SCRUPLE OR PHYSICAL FEAR

Early in 1858 at Fort Bridger, Albert G. Browne, Horace Greeley's correspondent with the Utah Expedition, received a remarkable set of internal Mormon documents. Copies of the original letters at LDS Archives match Browne's transcriptions of Brigham Young's private correspondence word for word, with only some variation in punctuation. Isaac Haight's letter to Rufus Allen survives nowhere else. Browne's introductory paragraph reveals that the

Americans who learned about the atrocity while it was still known as "the Santa Clara massacre" had little doubt about who instigated it or the character of the Mormon prophet's "confidential agents."

ALBERT G. BROWNE, "LETTER FROM THE UTAH ARMY . . .
INTERESTING MORMON DOCUMENTS,"
NEW-YORK DAILY TRIBUNE, 7 JULY 1858.

The following letters, which I have copied from the originals, add to the light which has already been thrown on the Santa Clara massacre. It seems that Brigham Young did not consider Elder Allen a man of sufficient ability for the work which he intended should be performed at his mission, and so Elder Jacob Hamblin, a man without conscientious scruple or physical fear, was sent in his place. Elder Haight is a confidential agent of Brigham, to whom is consigned the care of superintending the southern mission.

PRESIDENT'S OFFICE GREAT, SALT LAKE CITY

Aug 2, 1857

President J. [*sic*] C. Haight—*Dear Brother*:

I wish you to notify all Bishops and Presiding Elders in and south of Iron County to have the brethren in their various districts to save their grain, nor let a kernal go to waste or be sold to our enemies; and those who persist in selling grain to the Gentiles, or suffer their stock to trample it into the earth, *you will please note as such*. Let the Bishops get all the grain not required for use into their hands if possible . . .

Save your ammunition, keep your guns and pistols in good order, and prepare yourselves in all things, particularly in living your religion, for that which may hereafter come to pass. Praying that God may add to you his blessing
Your Brother in Christ,

BRIGHAM YOUNG.

BROTHER ALLEN: I wish you to read this to the brethren and govern yourselves accordingly, and hold themselves in readiness to march at a moment's warning. Gen. Wells has ordered that each ten shall provide a baggage wagon and four horses or mules, and clothing for a Winter campaign, as there are troops on the way to the valley to exterminate the Mormons.
Yours, truly,

J. C. HAIGHT.

PRESIDENT'S OFFICE GREAT, SALT LAKE CITY

Aug. 4, 1857

Rufus C. Allen—*Dear Brother:* As you have long been deprived of the society of your friends, and the health of your mother is not good, I have thought

A comparison of this retouched photo of Jacob Hamblin with the original reveals
how much both the appearance and reputation of John D. Lee's "Dirty Fingered
Jake" were rehabilitated to transform the roughhewn Mormon frontiersman into
the legendary "Apostle in Buckskin." *Courtesy of the Will Bagley Collection.*

best to release you from your missionary labors south and give you permission to return to this place if you choose to do so. *I have appointed Elder Jacob
Hamblin as your successor as President of the Indian Mission on Santa Clara.* You have
my blessing and best wishes for future prosperity.

For general news I refer you to Elder G. A. Smith. We have every prospect
of warm times. Uncle Sam, it appears, has seen fit to appoint a new Governor, Secretary, Judges, Postmaster and Marshall, and to send 2,500 troops with
fifteen months provisions. All this vast array were to leave Fort Leavenworth
July 15. In consideration of these tidings, it behooves all Elders of Israel to
be laboring for the welfare of Zion.

All is peace and plenty here. The Saints feel to renew their diligence before
the Lord, and *the day is near at hand when the Lord will cut short his work in righteousness.
That we may be in that day be enabled to triumph is the ardent wish of your*
Brother in Christ,

BRIGHAM YOUNG.

I am glad to learn that you are doing so well, in starting your machinery. My patience is not in the least exhausted, and I do most confidently expect, that in course of a year or two, we shall get a piece of home made iron, of good quality full as large as an ounce ball. My wish is, that you may succeed beyond your most sanguine expectations in the manufacture of Iron.[15]

I have written by this mail to release Bror. Rufus C. Allen, and have appointed Elder Jacob Hamblin, his successor. Although I believe Bro Rufus to be a good man, I think it more to the interest of the "Kingdom," that his labors should be directed in another sphere.

For the general news I refer you to Elder G. A. Smith who is well acquainted with the things transpiring in the lower world. I wish you to pay strict attention to the instructions which I forwarded to you by him.

We are going to send an express to the States in a week or ten days; and we shall continue sending every month, more or less, and forward letters for the saints, by their putting stamps upon the letters to prepay postage; and paying 50 cents to bear expenses.

Desiring that God may ever bless you I remain your Brother in Christ.

Brigham Young

Brigham Young: The Redemption of Zion Draweth Nigh

As George A. Smith carried orders to southern leaders, Brigham Young revealed his larger vision of Mormon theocracy's destiny to a trusted lieutenant. Andrew Cunningham, one of Young's finest military commanders, had been sent to establish a mail station at Genoa on the Loup River as part of the Brigham Young Express and Carrying Company. Now Young ordered him to convert the station into a relief settlement for Mormon emigrants being called to Utah as part of a planned separation from the United States. This significant letter sets forth the millennial expectancy behind the 1857 military confrontation, the design to establish a sovereign position, and the role of American Indians in sustaining an independent theocracy.

Dear Brother, Our Brethren Saml W Richards and George Snider who are the bearers of this note will explain to you the nature of their mission and our

---

[15]Haight was in charge of the iron works, which overland traveler Jotham Goodell heard was intended to manufacture cannon. In early 1857 the Deseret Iron Company paid Brigham Young $2,181 for a 13,000-pound steam engine that had been hauled into Salt Lake using oxen diverted from the handcart relief at Fort Bridger. The engine never actually worked. Shirts and Shirts, *A Trial Furnace*, 379–80.

wishes in relation to your station. We wish to have you keep it up as the brethren will be directed to come up to your place and to the settlement on Deer Creek as fast as possible. We also wish for you to keep about thirty animals for Express purposes. We expect to ~~call in all the~~ discontinue all the stations except yours and Bro Jones at Deer Creek. We wish for the rest to [be] sent into this City. We want you to pick them up from among the brethren at your place to keep these animals in good condition for service as we shall do our expressing on the North side of the Platt and shall want to change animals at your place. We wish to have every reliable information of consequence forwarded to us. We look upon the taking away of our Mail and the sending forth an army against us as strong indications that the Lord is hastening his work and that the "Redemption of Zion draweth nigh." Make yourself acquainted with the Indians and let them understand that they must be our friends. Have the brethren learn their language that we may have free communication with them. If they permit our enemies to kills us they will then kill them also, let them understand this but move in wisdom and be discreet in all you do, not to bring them nor yourselves into difficulty but open up communication with them as fast as you can. Conciliate them and make them your friends for the prospect is *that all Isreal* [*sic*] *will be needed to carry on the work of the last days*.[16] We trust that they our enemies will have plenty to do for the present and thereby hinder them from troubling us. The saints will soon find the gate shut down so that they cannot gather up through the states if these troubles continue, they had therefore better improve the present opportunity to come while the way is open before them and had not better let another army depart for this place before they do lest they should undertake to stop them on the road. They should start early in the season & what can should come up to your place and to Deer Creek this fall—but our Brethren S. W. Richards & Geo Snider will assist in the work. Lay up provision for all you can, cut and put up hay and be prepared as well as may be for any emergency that may occur. Provide yourself with guns and plenty of ammunition and if you can send us a little, although we expect to make those who cause us trouble to supply us in this respect. Of course we shall want a station at or near Florence[17] but we would recommend it not to be known [one word illegible] but have the boys understand what they are about keep their ears and eyes open and their mouths shut. May the Lord bless you with wisdom to know and understand all things pertaining to the duties incumbent upon you and help us to triumph of [over?] our enemies and finally attain salvation in his celestial Kingdom. I remain as ever your Brother in the gospel of salvation.

B.Y.

P.S. So soon as you can find a man who is and will be faithful prompt and trustworthy to take your place you are at liberty to come home.

---

[16]The term "all Israel" expresses the family relationship between Mormons and Indians.

[17]Florence was the main Mormon emigration base, now part of Omaha, Nebraska.

In keeping with the design that Young revealed to Cunningham, George A. Smith fanned the flames of the Reformation as he traveled south, damning the United States in "war sermons" filled with venom and hostility.[18] About the time the Arkansas train reached Utah Valley, James C. Snow, the head of Zion's Provo Stake, took up the themes that the apostle had introduced as he passed through five days earlier, as did other settlement leaders along the Mormon corridor.

> Prest J. C. Snow said it seemd from the remarks of Bro Whipple that he is getting warm on the subject of Uncle Sam. He was speaking about Charity I consider that many will have their damd throats cut—thereby we will cover up a multitude of sins, this is pure Charity—now do not run off & say to Brigham that Bro Snow says that in order to have Charity you must cut mens throats . . . Uncle Sam is determind to make us gain our independance as did the people of the U.S. from Great Briton—Now if any of you wants to go to the States go as quick as you please & the quicker the better—many have gone this season & they would give all of the luxurous of Egypt if they were back here for they do not find things as they expected . . .[19]

At Parowan, near the southern extremity of Mormon settlements, Apostle Smith spoke twice on 9 August, and both times the meeting place was so crowded that it would not hold all the people at the same time. Smith admitted that he "found himself preaching a military discourse."[20] According to legend, he told them that the bones of American soldiers would make good food for fruit trees.

SAMUEL PITCHFORTH: WE ARE AMERICAN CITIZENS

Moving more slowly than Smith, the Arkansans followed his buggy south on the line of today's I-15, the first train to take the southern route that season. The refusal of settlers to sell flour or vegetables was a continual reminder that they were crossing hostile ground. A more serious irritant was the damage wrought to Mormon pastures by the caravan's herd, numbering by various estimates from three hundred to one thousand cattle. To the settlers, the land was divinely reserved for their use; to the Arkansans such grounds were federal property and open to all citizens until surveyed and sold under federal land laws. English convert Samuel Pitchforth, whose diary is the only

---

[18]The phrase is from Martineau, My Life, 9 and 21 August 1857, Huntington Library.
[19]Utah Stake Minutes, 8 August 1857, LDS Archives.
[20]George A. Smith, Deseret News, September 23, 1857, 226–27.

contemporary account of the Baker-Fancher party's passage through Utah, illustrated the conflict in concepts of land ownership at Nephi settlement.

DIARY OF SAMUEL PITCHFORTH, BYU LIBRARY.

Satterday 15th August [1857] ... There is a company of Gentiles at Millers Springs[21] who have 300 head of Cattle. The Bishop [Jacob Bigler] sent out to them requesting them to move for they were distroying our winter feed. They answered that they were American Citizens and should not move.

Monday 17th [August 1857] The company of Gentiles passed through this morning—they wanted to purchase Flour—

Sunday 30th August ... I herd there is a company of gentiles at Millers Spring with 1000 head of cattle.

Wednesday 9th [September 1857] an expres[s] went through yesterday from Iron Co—to Pres Young bringing information the the [sic] emegrants who went through a short time since was acting very mean—Threatening the Bishops life—[22]

Wednesday 30th [September 1857] ... a Bro Elliot & wife [came] from Fillmore. Bro Bradshaw said It was True about the Indians Killing the emegrant—he also said that 2 Thousand Indians could be raised shortly if needed.

MORMON ULYSSES:
JOHN HAWLEY REMEMBERS THE FANCHER PARTY

Early Mormon convert John Pierce Hawley went with Apostle Lyman Wight after the death of Joseph Smith in 1844 to establish the Kingdom of God in Texas. On the failure of this ill-starred venture, he journeyed to Utah in 1856 and joined the church under Brigham Young. He was sent to southern Utah, where he later served as the bishop of Pine Valley.

Referring to the Reformation and doctrine of blood atonement, Hawley on one occasion reminded Wilford Woodruff "about the excitable times we had had and I told him I took no stock in a good many revengful speeches that had been indulged in by some of my brethren. He said he was satisfied that some of our brethren had gone farther with this reformation and vengeance than they ought." In August 1857 the independent-minded Mormon traveled south for three days with the Fancher train in Utah and afterward drew a favorable, and probably accurate, description of its members. His recollection provides evidence that "Lee and other officials" began assembling a force to attack

---

[21]Miller's Springs is at present Mona, Utah.

[22]This was express rider James Haslam, dispatched on 7 September to find out if Brigham Young truly intended for white settlers to participate in the massacre.

John Pierce Hawley recalled traveling through Utah with the Fancher party, whose captain told him, "we intend to observe the laws and rules of the territory." John D. Lee claimed that Hawley participated in the massacre, a charge that Hawley convincingly denied. *Courtesy of the Community of Christ Archives, Independence, Missouri.*

the Fancher party even before the emigrants reached Parowan. Hawley later joined the Reorganized Church of Jesus Christ of Latter Day Saints.

AUTOBIOGRAPHY OF JOHN PIERCE HAWLEY,
COMMUNITY OF CHRIST ARCHIVES.

We left Provo and drove for our home in the south. We travailed 150 miles and then overtook the Company that was masacred at Mountain Meadows and we travailed in company with them 3 days and we discovered that they was pretty much all men of famileys and had a quite large drove of cattle all going to locate in California. The captain of the Company told me that they had some trouble with the Mormons in two of their settlements. Salt Creek being one and Provo being the other. He said, "We have a Dutchman with us, a single man, and he has given us all the trouble we have had. He would not obey orders but was sassy with officers in these places and it all originated by our cattle being grazed on there herd ground, but we intend to observe the laws and rules of the territory." I am satisfied the Saints gave them more trouble than they ought.

Well we left this camp as we travailed faster than they did. By the time we got home which by the way was called Washington [Utah,] Jno D Lee and other officials was having their interpreters stirring up the Indians to commit hostilities on this Camp of emigrants, but however they landed safe in their destind stopping place, Mountain Meadows. Here they were to wait till the other Co[mpany] came up and then ware both travel together from here, but alas they met with death by the Indians and whites. Worse than all their

fate come unto them after they Surrendered and gave up their arms according to report. To say least of this tragedy, it must have of been heart rending
to those that witnessed and helped to do the deed.

Here, let me say I took a bold stand against this masacree, which there is
some here in Iowa and a great many in Utah that can bare witness. I remember well a conversation I had with J. D. Lee in Cedar City, Iron Co[unty, Utah,]
on the subject of this masacree and I told him in the presence of Isaac Hait's
son-in-law and family with Bishop Gardner and a few others, that he kneed
think for a moment that he could face the Judge at the last day with a clear
conscience before God if half that is reported that he did were true. He said
he had received more persecution from me about that mountain affair than all
the rest and he wished me to understand that he would look for a reward in
heaven for my persecuting him. I told him if I had accused him wrongfully he
might, but not without, the conversation ended with a mad Spirit in him.

I would not have been so bold had it not of been I was appointed by the
Bishop of Washington to do some preaching in this city, for we often had
missionaries to stir up the different settlers to a sense of duty. With one more
incident we will let this year pass, and that is concerning the Mountain Meadow affair. After the deed was done, there was a great deal of excitement about
it and those that were at the scene of death was the most excited, that is those
of our Settlement. They concluded that the dividing line had been drawn
between Mormons and gentyles and all that came in the Territory must be
cut off and the Bishop's first counselor, Harrison Pierce, was apparently the
most excited. He stated in a public meeting that he could see all the Gentyles
strippt naked and lashed on their backs and have the Sun scorch them to death
by inches and after 2 others had made similar speeches I was called upon to
report as I had just come down from head quarters this being customary when
one had been to head quarters and returned. So I continued the death text
and I had to proclaim against the position they had taken and I said I should
have to know it would be saving my own life before I would take the life of
my fellow man, and as far as the avenging the blood of the prophets that so
much has been said to day, who of you know this Co[mpany] had any hand
in killing the prophets? I understand my oath requires me to act upon one of
my senses and I must know before I would be justified to kill any man and I
knew when I took the oaths I had no way of knowing, neither do I think you
have, you only suppose and that will not do for me.

This was a bold act and the Bishop's counselor called a secret council to
take my case under advisement. I had the balance of power and came off unhurt
but some of the council said I ought to die, but the[y] sent a man by the name
of Young, better known by [the name of] Uncle Billy Young. He said to me
he and others plead[ed] for me as I would have been put out of the way, but
I am sent to tell you to be more on guard and not oppose authority. But my
answer was I don't know but what I was as well prepared to die now as ever,
and you may tell the council I will stand on the same ground I took yesterday.

Jacob Hamblin: A Strange Atmosphere

George A. Smith's diary of his seven-hundred-mile round trip to southern Utah is more noteworthy for what he does not say than for what he does. He does not reveal that he stayed the night with John D. Lee, who was later executed for his role in the massacre, and met with Isaac Haight. He does not reveal the verbal orders that he gave them and other LDS leaders.[23] On his return, he met the Arkansas emigrants at Corn Creek, south of Fillmore, "who seemed much excited." He did not say what upset them, but the sight of a Mormon apostle delivering ten or twelve southern Utah chiefs, from the very region the train would have to cross, to confer in Salt Lake with Brigham Young may have contributed to their alarm. Moreover, the Mormon reputation for complicity with their "Lamanite" cousins was by then well established on the frontier.

From Great Salt Lake City, the doomed party had traveled at a leisurely rate of seven to eight miles a day, allowing the cattle to feed after more than three months on the trail. But from Corn Creek, its members hurried to their final resting place at more than twelve miles a day, about as fast as they could go with a large herd. The implication is that the emigrants were not looking for trouble: they were trying to get away.

As noted, Brigham Young on 4 August abruptly ordered the trusted Jacob Hamblin to replace the independent-minded Rufus C. Allen as head of the Santa Clara Indian Mission. Known to history as "the buckskin apostle," Hamblin escorted the Southern Paiute chiefs in Smith's party to the territorial capital to meet with Young. At Corn Creek he described the reaction of the Arkansans at seeing the native leaders in Apostle Smith's company.

> From this time forth the Mision prosprd the influance of the ~~began to prosper~~ Misionarys Spread among the diferante bands. Nothing of note transpird until August 1857 when President R. C. Allen was caled home and I was apointed to preside over the Southern Indian Mision. I receivd my apoint from Pres Brigham Young. Before ~~I Pres~~ I received this apointment we had a fast meeting. President R. C Allen was thare. He [treated] me very roughly for Some little thing that did not Sut him. I [was] grieved and vext [and] felt as tho I was not in the falt. We Bro [Samuel] knites and my Self and Br. [Ira] Hatch Preyd that thare mite be Some one apointed to Preside over us that we had confidence in. I felt the influance of of [*sic*] the Spirit resting on me. I tol the Brotheren that the man that now presited over us would not Presite long. Doe

---

[23]Smith's August 1857 diary was largely incorporated in the Historical Department Journal quoted above. A variant is available in Jarvis, comp., *Ancestry, Biography, and Family of George A. Smith*, 215–17.

you ~~Poory~~ Provicy [prophesy] that asked the Brotheren. I answerd yes. They
Said we believe it will be fulifilled. A few Days after I was apointed to take
charge of the Mision. I Started for ~~G S A~~ G. S. L C. in company with Thales
Hascal and Titsegar vats the yanawant Chief. He had felt anxious for a long
time to visit Brigham young. We fel in company with George A. Smith. Conosh
the Pauvant Chief joined us [and] other Indian Chiefs joined in our company. When we arrived in the City thare was .10. of them. We went up to See
Brigham the great Morman chief. We encamp on corn Creek while on our
way nere a company of emigrants from Arcan Saw on thare way to Calafornia. Thare was a Strang atmosphere Serounded them. George A Spoke of it.
Said he beliedd [*sic*] Some evle would befall them before they got through.
[In Salt Lake] the Chiefs was treted with mutch resect [and] was taken to the
work Shops gardens orchards and other plases to Show them the advantages
of industry and incourag Same or induce them them [*sic*] to labor for a living. While I was in the citty I was Several times invited in in [*sic*] to the council of the first presidency and questioned concening the mision and cashing.[24]

DANIEL H. WELLS:
TELL THEM OUR ENEMIES ARE THEIR ENEMIES

There was good reason for the Baker-Fancher train to take alarm. The order
from Mormon general Daniel H. Wells to Iron County militia commander
William H. Dame and other military officers and settlement leaders along the
southern route illustrates that an orchestrated effort had already begun to win
the allegiance of the Indians in the coming showdown with the United States.

WELLS TO DAME, 13 AUGUST 1857,
PALMER COLLECTION, SOUTHERN UTAH UNIVERSITY LIBRARY.

Sir;
    You are hereby instructed to keep one or two tens out in the mountains
upon the approaches to the settlements as a corps of observation that we may
not be taken at any point by surprise.
    Get the Indians in your vicinity also to watch & take the most effective
measures to be in readiness & to have all the grain secured. Be careful that not
a kernel is wasted. Do not have it foolishly and needlessly fed to horses, but
let it be preserved, and instruct the people to be economical in using it, use
potatoes and vegetables that cannot be preserved and save the grain; have your
eye out for good safe places in the mountains where grain can be cached and

[24]Hamblin Daybook, Journals and Letters, 46–48, BYU Library. Juanita Brooks noted that pages 39–40
in Hamblin's "journal" at LDS Archives describing this encounter are missing. By "cashing," Hamblin refers
to Mormon plans to store food stocks in the mountains to support a scorched-earth policy of resistance
to the U.S. Army.

where women and children can be safe in case we have to take to the mountains. Drop other business and thrash out the grain, and secure it the first thing. This is the first business to attend to. The time may come when we shall have to lay every thing waste & go into the mountains, therefore let us be preparing for such an event; be storing up clothing of a substantial Kind. Fix up and keep in repair our wagons and take care of our property and not let anything go to waste.

Instruct the Indians that our enemies are also their enemies & how they are continually fighting against them somewhere and that it will be come upon them as well as the Sioux & Cheyennes in due time, that they must be our friends and stick to us, for if our enemies kill us off, they will surely be cut off by the same parties.

Find safe retreats in the Mountains for Stock as well as families, and cache some grain to learn how to do it so it will keep. A little "practice you know makes perfect," and it is well to be preparing.

Advise with this Office and keep us posted with every important item of reliable information which you can obtain. Be vigilant and active.

/s/ Daniel H. Wells
Lieut Gen. Commanding
Nauvoo Legion

Brigham Young: The Indians Will Use Them Up

As the Arkansas train slowly moved south, Brigham Young ripped the U.S. government and vowed his love of the American Constitution in virtually the same breath.[25] He included a veiled threat to loose the Indians on the overland lines of travel. If intimidating to the uninformed, his listeners surely knew better. Of the Southern Paiutes, U.S. Indian agent Garland Hurt wrote that "ten men well armed could defend themselves against the largest force that this band could muster."[26]

A Discourse by President Brigham Young, 16 August 1857, lds Archives.

. . . My mind was often exercised concerning the propriety of the affliction which continually came upon the Saints. It has become natural and easy to my understanding. [Yet] I have thought how long, how long, O lord, shall

---

[25]Young and his followers believed that God had inspired the Constitution's framers to create a land of religious freedom where His Kingdom could be restored, making the Constitution an intermediate step toward millennial rule, not an end in itself. Young therefore denounced federal officials who subverted its divine purpose and lauded the document in the same breath. His fealty was first, last, and always to the Kingdom of God.   [26]Simpson, *Report of Explorations across the Great Basin of the Territory of Utah*, 462.

we have to endure these afflictions and persecutions of the wicked, and tamely submitt to the Government—to their ruling? Of late in referring to the words of Joseph on which he promises the saints, tho there was enough said by him, but since we have heard that the Government under which we live have realy come out, not openly and boldly, but underhandedly, and sneekingly, raskaly—in the form of a mobb—again to pour their [intolerant persecution] upon this people and break them up, and ruin them—to destroy and kill them—as they have done in other times. They have already been the means of the death of thousands and thousands of men, women and children. They have whipped and otherwise abused many, and many they have killed outright. They killed Joseph and Hiram [*sic*] in prison, while they were under the pledge of the Government of the State of Illinoi[s], and they have killed a great many others, they have killed Parley lately. What do you see here, ask any man that has been to the United States in the east. Ask every man person that has been to the state of California, ask those that came from England, and from the uttermost parts of the earth where "Mormonism" has been preached, and I will tell you that every man that can boast that he has had a hand in shedding the blood of a Latter day Saint he is praised for the noble deed, he is blessed, he is looked upon as a man of honer, and varasity, he is caressed and received into the affections of the people, and the prevalent feeling is, 'if you can kill a latterday Saint, you have my friendship.'

All these things have been before me, and now I am going to tell you what I have concluded upon. I have come to this decision, if this people feel like joining me, that the last mobb has come to afflict this people that ever has come . . . [Let any] people whatever rise up against this people to destroy them, and in the name of Israel's God I say, lift the sword and slay them. (A unanimous shout, "Amen.")

Let it be treason, or not. We know that they turn every thing into treason. No 'Mormon' can say or do anything but what it is wicked in their eyes, when in reality we do and will (as we always have) take the institution of Constitution and the laws of the United States and the Declaration of Independence and we will walk in the path of our fathers. We have as good a right to declare the Constitution of the United States as any other people, and that guarantees to every man, and to every family and to every community, life and liberty.[27]

. . . The Governor of the United States is sending soldiers here with sealed orders, I know what they are, as well as though I had had the papers and read them. Their sealed orders amount to this, 'go to Utah, build your stations, distribute your troops, decoy away every man and woman you can, and bring them to our standard, hatch up any pretext, no matter what, and use up the

---

[27]Although Watt's transcription does not ascribe to Young a "declaration of Independence," others reported hearing him do exactly that. For one of many examples, see "Memorandum. August 16th, 1857. At 8 o'clock A.M. news was brought to me of the birth of my grandson, Brigham Young Hampton, being the morning on which Brother Young declared the independence of our people of the United States." See Journals of Hannah Tapfield King.

leaders, break up their organization, disperse the people, and call in our Gentile brethren and break up this kingdom called [the] Latter Day Saints.' That is the purport [*sic*] of their sealed orders. Now do it as pacifically as Franklin told the House of Lords in London, says he 'do you want us to stand still and let you run a hot iron into us, while you say, 'hold still, we are not going to hurt you,' and run it in another inch, saying, 'hold still, we are your friends?' That is the way they intend to treat us, but I tell you, the Lord Almighty and the Elders of Israel being our helpers, they shall not come to this territory. I will fight them and I will fight all hell.

Now suppose you are brought to that test, let me point it out to you that they cannot do anything this fall. We will say we know we are good for them this fall, anyhow, and they may send all they can get here, but in another year, suppose they send 50,000 or 100,000 troops against us, how many is there of the Elders of Israel and this community that will go with me, do as I do (here the speaker was interrupted with voices all over the congregation one after another saying, "We are ready.") and take the road I shall travel? I will tell you what it is, before I ask you to do it or not. If they come here, and if it is necessary I will tell you what I shall do. I shall lay this building in ashes, I shall lay my dwelling house in ashes, I shall lay my mills in ashes, I shall cut every shrub and tree in the Valley, every pole, every inch of board, and put it all into ashes. I will burn the grass and the stubble and lay it waste, and make a Moscow of every settlement, and then I guess we will make a Potter's field of every Canyon they go into. Dare you all go into the Mountains? (The congregation, at the tops of their voices, shouted, "Yes.") . . .

I have no objections to their sending Governors and judges here, but I do object to their injuring this people, and I do not mean they shall do it as they have hitherto. As stated in the last weeks paper the only fault that can be found with this people is that we did not hand [hang?] up certain poor miserable curses before they got out of this place. I will tell you further, every man and woman that do not calculate to take this shoot with me, if we are obliged to, and it is necessary upon natural principles, I want you to pick up and leave now while you can go in peace, for if a man refuses to come to the scratch if the time ever should come that I lay waste to everything, if a man rises up saying 'You cannot touch my building,' we will hew him down as a cumberer [*sic*] of the ground, and lay waste his heritage . . . Can you make the sacrifice? You know I despise that word, [for] it is the height of folly to me for people to talk about making sacrifices pertaining to the things of this world, when they have the privilege of gaining all eternity. Now who can stand it? Can you flee to the mountains, men, women and children, and lay wast[e] and desolate every thing before them? (Voices, "Yes.") If you can, show your hands. (All hands were up and not contented with this the whole congregation of thousands of Saints Claped [*sic*] their hands. The feeling that prevailed in the meeting cannot be described.)

Now some of you may say, 'Why, bro., Brigham, you are unwise to tell this.' Not so, and I will tell you why. In the first place, I will commence a little from this. You know that they alledge [*sic*] against me almost every thing they can imagine to my character, proclaiming that I have been the means of doing this mischeif [*sic*] and that and of killing emagrants [*sic*], and they have laid the death of Gunnison upon me, and the distroying [*sic*] of United States records, every partical [*sic*] of which is a lie. I have treated them kindly. I have done everything I could to make them happy. Don't you see I am clear, I am free? Don't you see I can call upon God to assist me in time of need? Now then, if I warn them, and forewarn them, what fault can they find? None at all.

If our enemies come here we shall surely lay them waste. Report it, ye gentiles, you hickory Mormons, write to them, publish it abroad, that we calculate to sweep the platter, and to lay this Territory wast[e], and then we will take it Indian fashion in the Mountains, and see what you can do with us. Now you need not any of you ask me where you will go, but you just wait until the time comes and it shall be told you. That I shall keep to my self. But I warn them and forewarn them to let this people alone. The Elders of Israel are Almighty, and it will soon be said, 'let us not go up to Zion, for the inhabitants of Zion are terrible' and it will soon be the case. They do not know the strength and power there is in a man by the faith of Jesus Christ. They have never had the trial, and when it comes they will find every man to be a host. I have now warned them and forewarned them . . .

I have strove [uniformly striven] to my uttermost, since I have been in this Territory, to make peace with the Indians, [and still] they have all the times been troubling emagrants, more or less. I have been sending out and expending [means among them] until the Government of the United States now owes me in my financial capacity some forty or fifty thousand dollars which I have expended for them more than they have paid me. I need not tell you [that] if they get any property in here, that I mean to put my hand on it to pay myself.

I have preached to the Indians, sent them presents, visited them and prayed for them, that they might become peacable [*sic*], and let the traveler alone. This Year they are [again] mischieveous [*sic*] on the North rout[e], and our brethren [who have lately come from California and Carson Valley] when they came through expected to have a fuss with them. The Indians tried to rob them, but they found them too many of them. Now let me say if the United States send their army here and war commences, the travel must stop; your trains must not cross this continent [back and forth]. To accomplish this I need only say [a word] to the[m] for the Indians will use them up; unless I continually strive to restrain [them]. I will say no more to the Indians, let them alone, but do as you please. And what is that? It is to use them up; and they will do it. With all my exertions this year, they have killed a good many of the emagrants, and it is a matter of regret.

I warn them and fore warn them [United States, that] if they commence on us, they need not expect me to hold the Indians while they shoot them. What did the first party of Emagrants going to the States do this year? I will show you the foolery of it. Every Indian they saw, they shot at. This raised the ire of the Indians to that degree [that] I cannot keep them peaceable . . . I have no ill feelings; I wish no man evil. I can say to our friends who have taken our money, millions of it, to make themselves rich, cease your operations, cease to peddle our blood for our money. Write to your friends, if the United States Armies come, but I do not believe they can get here, then say to your friends don't pretend to cross this Contenant [sic] [by the overland route], for I will tell you honestly, and plainly, and in all good feeling, [that] I will not hold the Indians while you [the emigrants] shoot them, as you have hitherto, but I will say to them, go and do as you please. I tell you that if it was not for the 'Mormons' in these mountains, this emagration that has past over this contenant this season would have been cut off [by the Indians], 19 out of 20. It would have be[e]n stopped. Had it not been for the settlements here, the overland emigration would have been stopped years ago, and [yet] they turn round and condemn me and this people for conniving with the Indians. This people have done the travelers good, they have kept the Indians from injuring them and we have done all in our [power] to save the lives of men, women and children, but [all] this will cease to be, if they commence on us.

In addition to George D. Watt's report of Brigham Young's August 16 discourse, Apostle Wilford Woodruff prepared a synopsis of the sermon.

WILFORD WOODRUFF, SYNOPSIS OF BRIGHAM YOUNG'S
16 AUGUST 1857 ADDRESS, ROMNEY TYPESCRIPT, LDS ARCHIVES, 168–69.

"I have had to hold the Indians here for years from destroying the emigrants. I have had to give them many thousands of dollars to keep them from killing the Gentile emigration to California. The United States Government now owe me $50,000 in my official capicity and they will not pay me a dime but are sending armies at a great expence to destroy me and this people. But I will now inform them and all people that if they attempt to make war upon me [?] I shall not attempt to restrain them any more but I shall let them do as they please."

"I now wish to say to all Gentiles. Send word to your friends that they must stop crossing this Continent to California for the Indians will kill them for the emigrants have slaughtered the Indians without any cause or provocation and if the United States make war upon me I shall not attempt to restrain them any longer. I will give all people in this Territory who wish to leave ~~the privilege to leave~~. I want all to leave who are not willing to follow me. If there is any of my family my wives who wish to leave I will send my teams and carry them wherever they wish to go. If it is to hell I will drive them to the gate but will not let my teams go into hell but they must turn round and come back but those who wish can enter in."

George A. Smith:
I Propose That We Have Some Danites

On the way back to Great Salt Lake City with the southern Utah Indian leaders, George A. Smith stopped at Provo to call for a restoration of the feared Danites, a secret paramilitary outfit from the Missouri period. He was followed by Bishop Elias H. Blackburn. "I propose that we have some Danites as their has been none for the last 19 years. You know that Dan was to be an adder in the path & I propose that we have some now to help to carry out the purposes of God," said Smith. "Let Dan be on the alert & meet them on the way." Meanwhile, the local bishop boasted that the Indian attacks that Mormon authorities had encouraged on the northern route to California were underway.

> Bishop E H Blackburn said he felt first rate Bro Brigham says that Enemy is in our hands if we will do right—A Co of 25 Indians on the Mallad found a Co of emigrants & they made a Stamped which caused their animals to flee from them amounting to some 600 head of Cattle & horses & left them without any, on foot. Our Prophet says he has held the Indians back for 10 years past but shall do it no longer as soon as this word went out they have commenced upon our enemies.[28]

Brigham Young: The Lamanites Will
Be Prepared to Fill Their Mission

As the Arkansas emigrants neared their last resting place, Mormon leaders met on Sunday 30 August and heard Brigham Young predict that the Indians would be prepared to fulfill their destiny foretold in *The Book of Mormon*. Two days later George A. Smith and Jacob Hamblin arrived with the Southern Paiute and Pahvant chiefs.

Wilford Woodruff Collection,
Romney Typescript, lds Archives, 171–72.

> On Sunday the 30th of August we had a good day. The Presidency and several others of the leaders spoke In the evening at the Prayer Circle . . . President Young said that many of the brethren had many fears about the Lamanites because the Gentiles were making them presents. You need have no fears upon the subject for if the nation gives them a few million it will not be all that is their due and then they will turn round and take the rest. We need have

---

[28]Utah Stake Minutes, 30 August 1857.

no fears but what the Lamanites will be prepared to fill their mission. I cannot feel that the time has come for us to do a great deal of hard fighting. We shall have help and strength and the promises of God will be verified unto us.

On the 1st of September brother Hamlin arrived from santa Clara mission with some 12 Indian Chiefs who had come to see President Young. One was the Chief. His name is Totse-I-gavets the Chief of the Pieds of the Deserts and Santa Clara and Rio Virgin. He had a Chief with him of the Indians of Harmony Kanosh the Chief of the Parvants and Amon Walker's brother. President Young had an interview with the Indians for about one hour . . .

DIMICK B. HUNTINGTON: I GAVE THEM ALL THE CATTLE

After Brigham Young publicly vowed he would no longer "hold the Indians" while emigrants shot at them, his personal ambassador to the tribes invited native chiefs to attack passing emigrants. As Young delivered his mid-August sermons railing against the U.S., New Yorker Dimick Huntington urged Shoshone, Ute, and Goshute chiefs to join Mormons in making war on approaching American soldiers. "If the troops killed us they would then kill them," he told them. Said he: "they & the mormans was one but the Lord had thrown the Gentiles a way."

Huntington then met on 30 August with chiefs of northern Utah bands and "gave them" all the cattle and horses on the "North rout[e]." It was an invitation to attack emigrant trains on the roads that joined the California Trail in the Silent City of Rocks, near Almo, Idaho. Two days later, he met with the Southern Paiute chiefs, who had come to Great Salt Lake City with George A. Smith, and held out to them the same incitement. He "gave them" the cattle "that had gone" to California on the southern trail. The Paiute leaders knew what cattle he meant because they had seen them at Corn Creek only days before meeting with Brigham Young. The cattle in question were not Young's to give. They belonged to the Fancher train.

DIMICK BAKER HUNTINGTON, JOURNAL,
AUGUST 1857–MAY 1859, LDS ARCHIVES.

[August] 16. Antero Qyeahoo & wife & 8 more Yam-pah Uts came to see Brigham & to have a talk. [He] exprest great fears about the troops [and] said he would go to the mountains & wait & see how we gut along through the fight. I told him that was good for [we] did not want any help with these. We could get along with[out] them but he might look out when the troops had killed us they would then kill all of them, but the Indians might runn off but God would

Dimick Baker Huntington's family history,
Wallace Stegner wrote, was a compendium
"of sacrifice, devotion and fanaticism."
Pictured here in his old age, Huntington was
not yet fifty years old when his diary recorded
the 1 September 1857 meeting between Brigham
Young and Indian leaders from southern Utah.
From Orson Whitney's History of Utah.

feel after them & they had gut to fight them when the Lord wanted them to
fight & they would not then be a fraid of them. I told them how the Gentiles
had treated the Indians in times past & [Antero] said he would think of it.

18 [August 1857]. 5 Goshah Uts came from Toeilla [Tooele. They] stayed
all Knight [and] had a talk with them. They exprest great sorrow on account
of the Lack of Amunition [and] said they was afraid of the troops & would
go home & wait and see how the troops came out. I told them that if the
troops killed us they would then kill them. I told them all that they & the
mormans was one but the Lord had thrown the Gentiles a way.

Sept 30 [August 1857]. An expres came in from Webber vally stating that thare
was a great many Indians a gathering at that place & their intentions ware not
known. The President told me to go & see to it. I started the same day & went
to Farmington [and] stayed all Knight with Thomas Smith.[29] Next morning
Brother [Marcus?] Shepherd took his Horses & Carriage & carrying me to the
place whare the Indians ware encamped Accompanyed by Bishop Stoker[30] &
his whare [?] We found one hundred & twenty lodges & about one thousand
men Women & Children. We met Bishop C West from ogden with 4 Waggon
Loads of Corn & mellons for the Indians. We gave them 4 beef Cattle & stayed
all Night & never saw so good a spirit before. I told them that the Lord had

---

[29]New Yorker Thomas S. Smith was on leave from his duties as president of the Salmon River Mission at Fort Limhi, near Salmon, Idaho. As Mormon colonists in Carson Valley and southern California returned to defend Zion, in October Smith lead some seventy families north to strengthen the outpost in Oregon Territory.

[30]Probably John Stoker, bishop of the North Creek Ward (today's Bountiful).

come out of his Hiding place & they had to commence their work. I gave them all the Beef Cattle & horses that was on the Road to California [by] the North Rout that they must put them into the mountains & not kill any thing as Long as they can help it but when they do kill take the old ones & not kill the cows or young ones. They sayed it was some thing new. They wanted to Council & think of it. Ben Simons a Delaware Indian was thare.[31] I told him all a Bout the Book of Morman. & he said his Father had told him about the same thing that they would have to rise up to fight but he did not think it was so near. He said tell Brother Brigham that we are his friends & if he says the soldiers must not come it is anough. The[y] wont come in, he said. Tell B that he can Depend upon us & I come down to see & if he talk as you do it is enough.

Tuesday 1st Sept 57. Konosh the Pahvant Chief, Ammon & wife (C[hief] Walkers Brother) & 11 Pahvants came in to see B[righam Young] & D [Dimick Huntington?] & find out about the soldiers.[32] Tutseygubbit a Piede Chief over 6 Piedes Band[33] Youngwuds[34] another Piede Chief & I gave them all the cattle that had gone to Cal [by] the south rout. It made them open their eyes. They sayed that you have told us not to steal. So I have but now they have come to fight us & you for when they kill us they will kill you. They sayd the[y] was afraid to fight the Americans & so would raise [grain] and we might fight.[35]

Sept 1/57. Anterro came to see the Pres & he told him to be at peace with all men except the Americans. & when an Indian stole from an other not to be mad with any one else but the one that stole & when a Ute stole from the Snakes give up that man that stole to the Snakes & let them do with him as they had a mind But be at peace with all other tribes.

Sept 8. Powder wich a Gosha Ute came to see us & was told the same.

[31]Ben Simons reported his conversation to Indian Agent Garland Hurt: "Huntington, (interpreter for Brigham Young,) and Bishop West, of Ogden, came to the Snake village, and told the Indians that Brigham wanted them to run off the emigrants' cattle, and if they would do so, they might have them for their own." Simons claimed that he advised the chiefs "to have nothing to do with the cattle," and implied that the Mormons hired Little Soldier to seize about four hundred animals from an emigrant named Squires. See Hurt to Forney, 4 December 1857, in Buchanan, *Massacre at Mountain Meadows*, Sen. Doc. 42, Serial 1033, 96–97.

[32]Brigham Young made Kanosh leader of the Pahvant Utes, who ranged the country around Sevier Lake and settled on Hurt's Indian Farm at Corn Creek. Garland Hurt identified "a chief named Ammon, on Beaver creek, in Beaver county," who led "a small band of Utahs and Piedes." Ibid., 93. As noted in the *Los Angeles Star*, Ammon was at Beaver during the attack on the Turner-Dukes train.

[33]Indian farmer John D. Lee identified "Tatsegobbotts" as "the Head Chief of the Piedes in this range." After the massacre, Brigham Young ordained the Southern Paiute leader an elder in the Mormon priesthood, but sources provide conflicting dates for the ordination. Wilford Woodruff, a reliable diarist, dated the ordination to 16 September 1857.

[34]Youngwuds (or Yungweids) was, Wilford Woodruff wrote, the chief "of the Indians of Harmony." In his confessions John D. Lee referred to "Tennquiches Band, Harmony." See Bishop, ed., *Mormonism Unveiled*, 256.

[35]Juanita Brooks concluded the Indians immediately returned south. Huntington billed Brigham Young $33.90 on 11 September 1859 for lodging Indians "on a visit to the superintendent of Indian affairs at Great Salt Lake City," including $20.40 on "Sept. 1 Kanosh and fourteen of the band, Ammon and wife, four days, at thirty cents." Huntington explained, "August 8 to September 1 was a time of great excitement among the Indians, and because I spoke their language, I was overrun with them." See "Accounts of Brigham Young," 1862, 85.

10 [September 1857]. Tutsegubbets & Yungweids 2 Piede Chievs came from
the Santa Clarra. Brigham ordained Tutsegubeds an elder & said that the 2
Nephites that was to tarry[36] should administer to him & to let him to go &
preach the Gospel & Baptise among the House of Israel.

The Battle Axe of the Lord

At meetings held at Cedar City in August and September 1857, Mormon leaders drove home their message of obedience and fear of approaching "enemies." The men who would order and commit a horrific mass murder during the time these minutes were taken—Isaac Haight, William Dame, John
M. Higbee, Philip Klingensmith, Thomas Willis, Ira Allen, and William Bateman—appear swept up in the exhortations to live their religion and "to be
faithful unto their calling." The minutes of the meetings held only two days
after the atrocity show neither remorse nor regret over what had taken place.
Instead they celebrated "the battle axe of the Lord," "cousin Lamuel being
fired up," and their "faithfulness in the gospel."

CEDAR STAKE JOURNAL, AUGUST–SEPTEMBER 1857,
PALMER COLLECTION, SOUTHERN UTAH UNIVERSITY LIBRARY.

August 7 [1857]. Sunday . . . Elders called upon to speak as they were lead
by the holy Spirit . . . 2 o'clock PM. Meeting opened with singing and Prayer.
Sacramont administerd and several of the Elders were called upon to speak
and exhort the Saints to be faithful unto their calling and to Live the lives of
Saints . . .

August 16th 1857 Sunday . . . Apostle G A Smith Addressed us on the necesity of living our religion and of preparing for every immergency. Singing . . .
2 o'clock PM . . . Elder Jesse N Smith (Parowan) made some remarks upon
faithfulness. Prest I C Haight. Exhorted us to be faithful in our callings as
saints . . . Apostle G A Smith. Spoke of the present state of the United States
and of Mormonism. Prest Wm H Dame (Parowan) Made some remarks about
the troubles of the Saints . . . Benidiction by Apostle G. A Smith.

Aug 23rd 1857. Sunday . . . Patriarch Elisha H Groves Made remarks upon
the principles of the gospel. Prest I C Haight also made remarks upon the
principles of the gospel. Singing . . .
2 o'clock PM . . . Elders Thos J Willis. Elias Morris, Ira Allen. Solomon

---

[36]The Nephites were a *Book of Mormon* people. According to LDS belief, when Christ visited America
after his crucifixion, he called twelve apostles and assigned three of them to live until "I shall come in my
glory with all the powers of heaven." See 3 Nephi 28:7. Typically, they are referred to as the Three Nephites,
but the Huntington manuscript clearly reads "2."

Chamberlain and Prest Jno M Higbee. Exhorted us to live our religion and put our trust in god and be prepared for every immergency . . .

Aug. 30th 1857. Sunday. 10 o'clock AM Meeting . . . Bishop P. K Smith Spoke upon the principle of restoration, and of our enemies coming and of our escaping if we are faithful. Prest I C Haight Made remarks about our enemies coming; and of our faithfulness . . .—2 o'clock PM . . . Brough[t] William Bateman before the people to know if they would again accept him as a member of the Church. William Bateman Said you all know what I want and what I have done in going off to California. I have come back and desire again to become a member of the Church and I will endeavor to do better. Voted that William Bateman be received again a member of the Church. Bp P. K. Smith. Made remarks upon the course those take who go to California . . .

Sep 10th [6th?] 1857. Sunday . . . 10 o'clock AM . . . Elder Edward Dalton (Parowan) Spoke of the necesity of living our religion and of standing up for the same and even to fight for it, and to keep all the commandments of God. Elder William Adams (Parowan) Bore his testimony to what had been said and exhorted to obedience. Elder Wm W. Willis. Exhorted us to live our religion . . . 2 o'clock PM . . . Elders James W. Bay. William Dalley. Priest. Francis Webster and Elder Jno Morris Spoke. Prest I C Haight Made remarks of having confidence in the Presidency and of being in subjection to the Holy Priesthood . . .

Sep 13. 1858 [1857]. Sunday At 10 o'clock AM . . . Patriarch Elisha H Groves spoke upon the principles of the gospel, and of the Lamanites been [sic] the battle axe of the Lord and of our faithfulness in the gospel. Bp Wm R Davies Bore testimony to what had been said and spoke of faithfulness in the gospel. Prest Elias Morris Made remarks upon living our religion . . .—2 o'clock PM . . . singing[.] Prayer by Prest I C Haight. Singing. Elder Benjamine R Hulse. Spoke upon the principles of faithfulness unto the gospel then the blessings will be given unto the sants [sic] of God. Prest I C Haight Spoke upon the spirit of the times, and of cousin Lamuel being fired up with the spirit of their fathers . . . [37]

BRIGHAM YOUNG: TO WREAK THEIR VENGEANCE

On the day after the massacre at Mountain Meadows, Brigham Young wrote to the U.S. commissioner of Indian Affairs complaining that the approaching army and abusive emigrants were driving Utah's Indians to war. By 12 September, he was aware he was no longer governor and his replacement was on the way. He also knew his appointment had expired three years before

[37]The expression "Cousin Lemuel" was a reference to the Indians. According to *The Book of Mormon*, Lemuel was a brother of Laman, after whom the Lamanites were named.

and he kept his office only under a provision of the territorial organic act that allowed him to stay "until his successor shall be appointed and qualified."[38] Yet three days later, just as long as it would take for a report of the massacre to reach him, he declared martial law, ordered the territorial militia to repel American soldiers, and shut down all travel across the Great Basin without a permit. By these actions, a lame-duck governor of an American territory seized control of over 220,000 square miles of the American west from the Rocky Mountains to the Sierra Nevada.

If diplomatic in tone, Young's letter of 12 September had the ring of an ultimatum. Making it clear that he ruled the vast region within the territory's borders, he told Commissioner of Indian Affairs James W. Denver that if the U.S. government wanted peace on the emigrant roads across Utah, it must meet three conditions: first, make emigrants stop shooting Indians; second, send more money; and, third, keep U.S. soldiers away. In another letter that same day to a trusted associate, he sounded even more bellicose and threatening.

YOUNG TO J. W. DENVER, 12 SEPTEMBER 1857,
"*THE UTAH EXPEDITION*," HOUSE EXEC. DOC. 71, 183–85.

. . . West and along the line of the California and Oregon travel, they [the Indians] continue to make their contributions, and, I am sorry to add, with considerable loss of life to the travellers. This is what I have always sought by all means in my power to avert, but I find it the most difficult of any portion to control. I have for many years succeeded better than this. I learn by report that many of the lives of the emigrants and considerable quantities of property have been taken. This is principally owing to a company of some three or four hundred returning Californians who travelled those roads last spring to the Eastern States, shooting at every Indian they could see—a practice utterly abhorrent to all good people, yet I regret to say, one which has been indulged in to a great extent by travellers to and from the eastern States and California; hence the Indians regard all white men alike their enemies, and kill and plunder whenever they can do so with impunity, and often the innocent suffer for the deeds of the guilty. This has always been one of the greatest difficulties that I have had to contend with in the administration of Indian affairs in this Territory. It is hard to make an Indian believe that the whites are their friends, and the Great Father wishes to do them good, when, perhaps, the very next party which crosses their path shoots them down like wolves.

This trouble with the Indians only exists along the line of travel west, and beyond the influence of our settlements. The Shoshones are not hostile to travellers, so far as they inhabit in this Territory, except, perhaps, a few called

[38]See "An Act to Establish a Territorial Government for Utah," *Acts, Resolutions and Memorials.*

"Snake Diggers," who inhabit, as before stated, along the line of travel west of the settlements. There have, however, been more or less depredations the present season north, and more within the vicinity of the settlements, owing to the causes above mentioned, and I find it of the utmost difficulty to restrain them. The sound of war quickens the blood and nerves of an Indian. The report that troops were wending their way to this Territory has also had its influence upon them. In one or two instances this was the reason assigned why they made the attacks which they did upon some herds of cattle. They seemed to think if it was to be war; they might as well commence and begin to lay in a supply of food, when they had a chance. If I am to have the direction of the Indian affairs of this Territory, and am expected to maintain friendly relations with the Indians, there are a few things that I would most respectfully suggest to be done:

First. That travellers omit their infamous practise of shooting them down when they happen to see one. Whenever the citizens of this Territory travel the roads they are in the habit of giving the Indians food, tobacco, and a few other presents, and the Indians expect some such trifling favor, and they are emboldened by this practise to come up to the road with a view of receiving such presents. When, therefore, travellers from the States make their appearance they throw themselves in sight with the same view, and when they are shot at, some of their number killed, as has frequently been the case, we cannot but expect them to wreak their vengeance upon the next train.

Secondly. That the government should make more liberal appropriations to be expended in presents. I have proven that it is far cheaper to feed and clothe the Indians than to fight them. I find, moreover, that after all, when the fighting is over, it is always followed by extensive presents, which, if properly distributed in the first instance, might have averted the fight. In this case, then, the expense of presents are the same, and it is true in nine-tenths of the cases that have happened.

Thirdly. The troops must be kept away, for it is a prevalent fact that, whereever there are the most of these we may expect to find the greatest amount of hostile Indians and the least security to persons and property.

If these three items could be complied with, I have no hesitation in saying that, so far as Utah is concerned, that travellers could go to and from, pass and repass and no Indian would disturb or molest them or their property.

In regard to my drafts it appears that the department is indisposed to pay them; for what reason I am at a loss to conjecture. I am aware that Congress separated the office of superintendent of Indian affairs from that of governor; that the salary of governor remained the same for his gubernatorial duties, and that the superintendent's was fifteen hundred. I do think that, inasmuch as I perform the duties of both offices, that I am entitled to the pay appropriated for it, and trust that you will so consider it.

I have drawn again for the expenditure of this present quarter, as above set forth. Of course you will do as you please about paying, as you have with the drafts for the two last quarters.

The department has often manifested its approval of the management of the Indian affairs in this superintendency, and never its disapproval. Why, then, should I be subjected to such annoyance in regard to obtaining the funds for defraying its expenses? Why should I be denied my salary; why should appropriations made for the benefit of the Indians of this Territory be retained in the treasury and individuals left unpaid? These are questions I leave for you to answer at your leisure, and, meanwhile, submit to such course in relation thereto as you shall see fit to direct.

Brigham Young had met with U.S. Army quartermaster Capt. Stewart Van Vliet, who arrived in Great Salt Lake on 8 September without his escort to arrange a camping place and supplies for the approaching U.S. Army expedition. Young told the officer that American soldiers would not be allowed to enter the Mormon stronghold unopposed. The coyotes had begun to feed on the bodies of the murdered Arkansans when Young wrote to one of his favorite stalwarts, Jeter Clinton, a missionary in Philadelphia, whose career blossomed as a Salt Lake City councilman, justice of the peace, probate judge alderman, coroner, and sergeant-at-arms in the territorial legislature. Clinton later had a falling out with Young, but in 1857 he clearly had his confidence. Young described his meeting with Van Vliet and his feeling that "we may depend upon the Captain to use his best efforts in staving off the expedition this year. But even should they keep away for the present, we cannot place any confidence in their assurances of amity and peaceful relations." His feeling was, Young wrote, "to be ready for them."

> For years I have been holding the Indians, [but] the check rein has broken, and cousin Lemuel is out at large, in fact he has been already collecting some of his annuities. Day after day I am visited by their chiefs to know if they may strike while the iron is hot. My answer depends on Mr. Buchanan's policy—if he do[es] not mete out justice to us; the war cry will resound from the Rio Colorado to the head waters of the Missouri—from the Black hills to the Sierra Nevada—travel will be stopped across the continent—the deserts of Utah become a battle ground for freedom. It is peace and our rights—or the knife and tomahawk—let Uncle Sam chose.[39]

---

[39]Young to Jeter Clinton, Philadelphia, 12 September 1857. With the possible exception of the Southern Paiutes, native leaders showed little inclination to join their Mormon "cousins" in opposing the U.S. Army.

The next day, Wilford Woodruff reported Brigham Young's final meeting with Captain Van Vliet.

> In the evening I went to Captain Hooper's and met with Captain Van Vleit . . . President Young said he wished Captain Van Vleit to report at Washington just as things are here . . . Again if they commence the war I shall not hold the Indians still by the wrist any longer for white man to shoot at them, but I shall let them go ahead and do as they please and I shall carry the war into their own land and they will want to let out the job before they get half through . . . Again you may tell them they must stop all emigration across this Continent for they cannot travel in safety. The Indians will kill all who attemp[t] it.[40]

FEMALE BENEVOLENT SOCIETY: AVENGE THE BLOOD OF THE PROPHETS

Mormon leaders at Cedar City, near the massacre site, hardly needed fiery rhetoric out of Great Salt Lake to fan the flames of reformation, to whip up resentment over past persecution, real and imagined, and instill blind obedience in their followers. Even women had a part to play in executing judgment on wrongdoers, said the wife of Cedar Stake President Isaac Haight, who gave the word "benevolent" new meaning. She told the members of the settlement's Benevolent Society to implant in their children's hearts a desire "to avenge the blood" of the slain prophets, Joseph and Hyrum Smith.

As this record shows, the day before the Mountain Meadows massacre, the women of Cedar City knew what their men were about.

> [The sisters are told] not to be fearful in these troublesome times . . . [Sister Haight] said that these were squally times, and we ought to attend to secret prayer in behalf of our husbands, sons, fathers, and brothers. Instructed the sisters to teach their sons & daughters the principles of righteousness and to implant a desire in their hearts to avenge the blood of the Prophets. Sister Hopkins said that she with sister White had visited the sisters in the middle lines, that they felt well and manifested a good spirit, and was desirous to do well, and to improve,—advised them to attend strictly to secret prayer in behalf of the brethren that are out acting in our defence.[41]

---

[40]Woodruff, 13 September 1857, Wilford Woodruff Collection, 178–90.
[41]Minutes of the Female Benevolent Society of Cedar City, 10 September 1857.

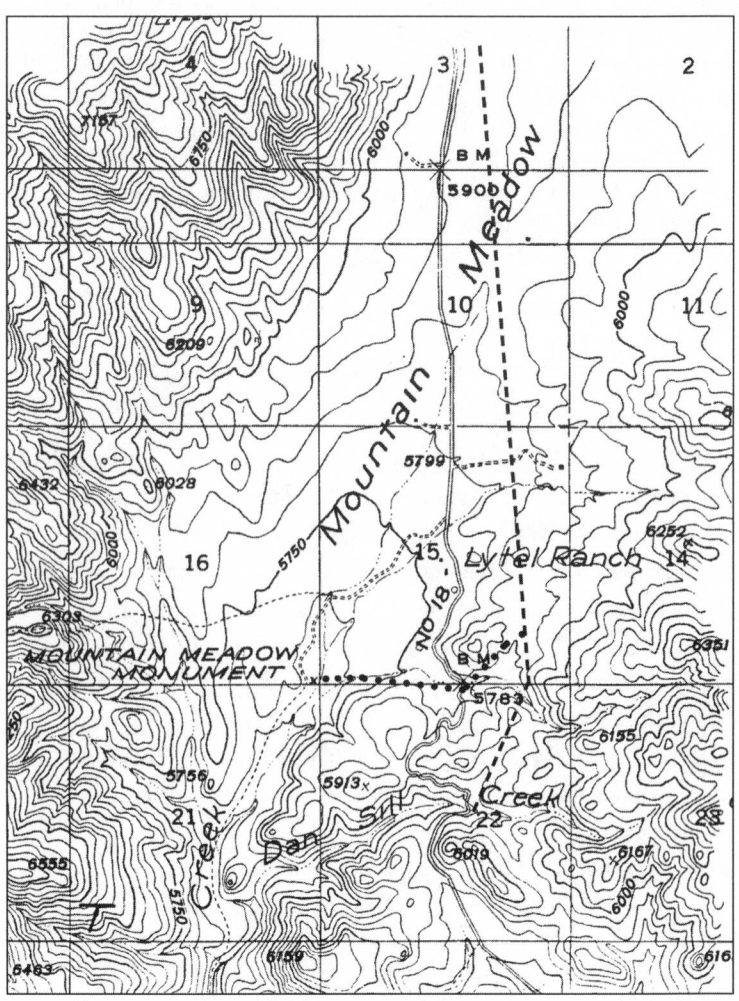

- - - - - Modern Highway 18
• • • • • Unpaved Road to 1932 Cairn

"Mountain Meadows, Utah."
The map shows the most likely route of the detour from the California
Trail to the Fancher party campsite. Today's Highway 18 appears as a dot-
ted line, while dots represent the unpaved road to the siege site and 1999
monument. *Based on the 1938 USGS Bull Valley District Map.*

Chapter 5

"I'm Only Going over Jordan"
First Reports of the Emigrant Massacre

Hurrying to get away from the hostility they encountered, the Fancher train reached Mountain Meadows late on Sunday, 6 September 1857, and camped at the spring in the narrow southern end of the verdant resting place on the Spanish Trail. At this peaceful mountain valley on the headwaters of the Virgin River, a tributary of the Colorado, the Arkansas travelers apparently thought they were out of harm's way: the tired company did not even circle their wagons. Thirty-five miles beyond the last major Mormon settlement at Cedar City, they must have felt they were safely on their way to California. But out of the darkness early the next morning a deadly fire opened on them that cut down as many as a dozen men as they stood by the campfire. The final act of deception and murder was played out five terrible days later on Friday, 11 September.

The perpetrators of the massacre took an oath of secrecy, but it proved impossible to hide their bloody deed. Mountain Meadows was far from major population centers, but squarely on the Spanish Trail, the Interstate 15 of that time, which ran from southern Utah through the Mormon colony at San Bernardino to Los Angeles. Over this artery news traveled fast. The best the killers could do was to concoct a story that would conceal Mormon participation in the crime from public view.

The earliest report of the massacre coming out of Utah was a story that justified the atrocity and laid the blame entirely on the victims and the Indians whom they had supposedly abused and provoked. Across the frontier, the killing of even a handful of white Americans would and did demand an immediate and lethal response from federal officials and local authorities. Utah's officials did not take enough interest in the largest slaughter of American civilians in the nation's history to even investigate and identify, let alone punish, the perpetrators.

The reports about the massacre passing through the office of the governor and Indian superintendent at Great Salt Lake City had very little to do with the facts. Less than three weeks after the murders, Mormon freighters and mail carriers delivered the same artful lies along the trail to California, where the authorities at San Bernardino fed them to the newspapers. This brazen attempt to manage the news unraveled when eyewitnesses to the strange circumstances surrounding the massacre began pouring into Los Angeles. When their chilling accounts appeared in the press, Americans got a shadowed glimpse of what had taken place at Mountain Meadows.

Rachel Woolsey Lee: The Test That Was Near at Hand

For a people so renowned for their dedicated record keeping, the paucity of contemporary records about the Mountain Meadows massacre is surprising and revealing. One of the most important of the still-extant documents is the handwritten diary of Rachel Woolsey Lee, the fifth or sixth wife of John D. Lee, for it establishes a likely date that Lee set out for Mountain Meadows. But like many Mormon records, it raises as many questions as it answers. The critical entry is misdated to "Decr," instead of September, and whether the day is the fifth or the sixth is open to question. A ragged tear mars the last lines at the bottom of the page, but it seems to be carefully made, since the previous and next pages were not affected. Two later pencil notations, not in Rachel Lee's handwriting, point out the diary's most significant information: the dates "J Lee went south" and "Lee return[ed] from MMM."

DIARY OF RACHEL WOOLSEY LEE, 1857, HUNTINGTON LIBRARY.

Decr 5th [corrected to 6?] the threshers have completed thrashing all the wheat at this place which amounted to 1000 Bushels. Sunday the thrashing machine ret [*tear*]

Bro: J. D. Lee went on an expedition South [*tear*]

Lee & B[isho]p Davis went to conference S.L.

Sept

Sunday at 2 o clock meeting was held singing prayer by H. Barney Bro: Prhrem [?] E. H. Groves. & A. G. Ingram spoke from the Stand on the test that was near at hand aluding to the troops &c. A good spirit prevaild Pres[ided over?] by E. H. Groves

13th this morning a great number of Indians returned from an expedition South west. Also with Bro J. D. Lee. Meeting was commenced in the afternoon

20th His Bishop and J. D. Lee went to conference at S.L. City in the afternoon meeting was held only a few of the Saints convend many being absent. Henry Barney presiding . . .

John D. Lee: They Killd an Ox & Poisened It

On 20 September John D. Lee headed north to report to Brigham Young; a few days later Dame, Haight, Klingensmith, and others involved in the massacre followed. On his way to the territorial capital, Lee addressed the general meeting of the Utah Stake of Zion at Provo on Sunday and related the official account.

UTAH STAKE MINUTES, 27 SEPTEMBER 1857, LDS ARCHIVES, 945–46.

[Stake president James] Br Snow Introduced Judge Lee from Washington Co. He said that he was a stranger to most of you &c & that you would like too hear from Re[garding] Lemuel [Indians] &c. There was some Emigrants passd through & boasted verry much & they killd an ox & poisened it for the Indians. Four or five of them Died one Mormon boy died[1] & the marshall arrested one of them & they said where is your Damd Bishop & such like conduct. They then went out, & Cousin Lemuel told them that they was friends too the cause of Isreal but they were enemies too the gentiles & they killd all but three that got away in the night. One was overtaken the next day & they was on the track of the other two. That this was the condition of the Lamonites out where he was living & many other things. He said of them seventeen Children was saved & brought intoo the settlements & that he was trying too live near untoo the lord that we all might have an interest in the Kingdom that we might be permitted too return too our father & mother in peace for which may the Lord Bless you all amen.

Br. Snow then aroze & said how do you like it for I was in hopes that Every Damd shit ass had left the territory that there was. I talk plain & shall talk plain all the time . . . I have no sympathy for such people but there is a sympathy that is for the good of the Saints & that is right & saints should know when too sympathize we should too it when it is right . . .

[1] These minutes show Lee inventing a story that would become part of the "evil emigrant" lore. On his way north, Lee learned that Proctor Robison had died at Fillmore on 21 September 1857, almost a month after the Fancher party passed through, far too long for them to have had any role in the boy's death. Robison's reported symptoms suggest he died of anthrax.

Garland Hurt: Mormons, and Not Indians, Had Killed the Americans

Even as Lee was speaking at Provo, a half-dozen Utes were rushing into the office of U.S. Indian agent Garland Hurt at the nearby Spanish Fork Indian farm crying, "Friend! Friend! the Mormons will kill you."[2] For nearly two weeks the last non-Mormon official in the territory had been investigating reports about the massacre. Now he looked out his window and saw a hundred mounted Nauvoo Legion troops coming to arrest him.[3] With the help of his Ute allies, the agent managed to escape and join the U.S. Army near South Pass. At Fort Bridger he wrote one of the first non-Mormon reports about the massacre, considerably at variance from the story being told by the church authorities.

On the tenth of September, Mormon merchant George W. Hancock from nearby Payson visited the Spanish Fork Indian farm and mentioned "he had learned that the California emigrants on the southern route had got themselves into a very serious difficulty with the Piedes [Southern Paiutes], who had given them to understand that they could not pass through their country, and on attempting to disregard this injunction, found themselves surrounded by the Indians, and compelled to seek shelter behind their wagons." Hancock's informant was "an express man, who passed his house that morning with a message from the Indians to President Young, inquiring of him what they must do with the Americans." Hurt's report confirmed that courier James Haslam "had been allowed one hundred consecutive hours in which to perform the trip of nearly three hundred miles and return, which Mr. Hancock felt confident he would do." The next day, a Ute who had been gathering pine nuts—an essential September task for Utah's Indians—informed Hurt that "the Mormons had killed all the emigrants. He said he learned this news from a band of the Piedes, but could not tell when the fight occurred, or how many had been killed."

Another Ute named Spoods arrived the farm early on 14 September "and also confirmed the report of the difficulty between the emigrants and the Piedes, but stated that when his brother Ammon (chief who lives in the Piede

---

[2]Hurt to Forney, 24 October 1857, *The Utah Expedition*, House Doc. 71, Serial 956, 206.

[3]"I am glad we did not get him," recalled Lt. George A. Hicks, one of the Legionnaires ordered to capture Hurt, "for more than likely he would have been killed if we had." See Hicks, Family Record and History, 32.

country,) went to Iron county to persuade the Piedes to leave the road, the bishop told him he had no business with the Piedes, and had better leave, where upon an altercation arose between the bishop and the chief." Spoods believed that the Mormons "had set the Piedes upon the emigrants." The farm's employees concluded "that all the emigrants on the southern road had been killed by the Piede Indians, and the report was confirmed by several other persons who visited the farm; but Indians insisted that Mormons, and not Indians, had killed the Americans."

Three days later Hurt dispatched "an Indian boy, named Pete, who speaks the English language quite fluently, with instructions to proceed to Iron county on a secret route, and to learn from the Piedes if possible, and also from the Utahs, what the nature of the difficulty was, and who were the instigators of it." Pete returned on the twenty-third, having gone only as far as Ammon's village near Beaver, where he met a large band of Paiutes just returned from Iron County.

> They acknowledged having participated in the massacre of the emigrants, but said that the Mormons persuaded them into it. They said that about ten or eleven sleeps ago, John D. Lee came to this village, and told them Americans were very bad people, and always made a rule to kill Indians whenever they had a chance. He said, also, that they had often killed the Mormons, who were friends to the Indians. He then prevailed on them to attack the emigrants, who were then passing through the country, (about one hundred in number,) and promised them that if they were not strong enough to whip them, the Mormons would help them. The Piedes made the attack, but were repulsed on three different occasions, when Lee and the bishop of Cedar City, with a number of Mormons, approached the camp of the emigrants, under pretext of trying to settle the difficulty, and with lying, seductive overtures, succeeded in inducing the emigrants to lay down their weapons of defense and admit them and their savage allies inside of their breastworks, when the work of destruction began, and in the language of the unsophisticated boy, "they cut all of their throats but a few that started to run off, and the Piedes shot them!"

Pete even reported "that there were some fifteen or sixteen small children that were not killed, and were in charge of the bishop." Over a thousand head of livestock went to Lee and the bishop, "as also a large amount of money." The Mormons, Hurt reported, claimed the emigrants had given the Paiutes "beef with strychnine upon it, and that when Brigham learned this fact, he sent word back to them 'to do with the Americans as they thought proper.' "

Hurt had been unable "to learn that the strynchaine [*sic*] had killed any of the Indians, or even made them sick."[4]

George W. Armstrong: Shameful Treatment

On 30 September, nineteen days after the massacre, Mormon Indian agent George W. Armstrong, who was stationed in Utah Valley, finally reported the crime and its alleged causes to Brigham Young. Armstrong began by discussing "the shameful treatment which many of the Indians receive at the hands of emigrants passing to and from California," and he then described the "poisoning a part of the band of Parvantes" during September by an emigrant company:

> While the company were camped a short distance from Fillmore City for the purpose of recruiting their teams a number of the Parvantes visited the emigrant camp which is their custom for the purpose of begging. They asked for something to eat which was denied them, but was answered if they did not immediately leave that they would receive a volley of bullets. This answer displeased the Indians, when some of the citizens of the settlement interfered and to prevent bloodshed informed the camp that they had better give the Indians a small present which would settle the difficulty. The captain of the Emigrant train after consultation with his company told the Indians that they would give them a beef the next day but claimed the privilege of killing it themselves. The Indians then left but previous to their return . . . the beef was killed and poisoned and given to the Indians. They cut up the beef and packed it to their lodges several miles distant from the emigrant camp. After partaking of the beef four of the Indians died and a large number taken dangerously sick.

The Pahvants, in Armstrong's account, "determined to be revenged upon the camp" when they discovered "the cause of this unhappy circumstance," despite the efforts of citizens at Fillmore "to appease their savage vengeance." The Indians followed the emigrants to Mountain Meadows, attacked the camp, "and after a desperate fight they killed fifty-seven men and nine women." Similar acts of cruelty had been practiced against the tribes on the northern route to California with similar results, "and until emigrants will learn to use wisdom and prudence in their treatment of the untutored savage they may expect to be severely handled by them," the agent concluded. With his report, which

---

[4]Hurt's "Report" first appeared in 1858 in *The Utah Expedition*, Serial 956, 199–205, and is easily accessible in Brooks, *Mountain Meadows Massacre*, 251–53.

stands in stark contrast to Garland Hurt's intelligence, a story of poison and
retribution took its initial shape and was inserted into church and federal records.[5]

WILFORD WOODRUFF: THEY POISONED BEEF

Years later Lee claimed that Stake President Isaac C. Haight told him to "go
to Salt Lake City and lay the whole matter before Brigham Young" because
Lee was "like a member of Brigham's family, and can talk to him privately
and confidentially."[6] Lee was more than "like" a member of Young's family.
He was "sealed" to Young at Nauvoo under the law of adoption, a now-dis-
continued temple ordinance. "All persons are required to be adopted to some
of the leading men of the Church," Lee himself explained, to form "the links
of the chain of priesthood back to the father, Adam, and so on to the second coming of the Messiah." Under this covenant, Lee swore his obedience
to Young as his father and god throughout this life and eternity. There is no
possibility that a zealot like Lee would attempt something so futile as trying to deceive Young. "I am watching you," Brigham Young had said on 8
October 1855. "Do you know that I have my threads strung all through the
Territory, that I may know what individuals do?"[7]

Lee later recalled that nearly three weeks after the massacre, he "gave to
Brigham Young a full, detailed statement of the whole affair, from first to
last." Young told him to keep the matter absolutely secret and asked him to
come back the next morning. When Lee returned, Young said he "went right
to God with it" and made the matter a subject of prayer. "I have evidence
from God that He has overruled it all for good, and the action was a righteous one and well intended."[8]

"Reports reached town that the companies of Cala. Emigrants going south
were all used up by the Indians—100 men. & 1000 head of cattle,—at Mountain Meadows," the Historian's Office Journal reported the day after Lee spoke
at Provo. "A bro from Iron Co. came into the office & confirmed the report
of yesterday," it recorded on Tuesday, 29 September 1857.[9] Apostle Wilford

---

[5]Armstrong to Superintendent Brigham Young, 30 September 1857, in Brooks, *The Mountain Meadows Massacre*, 143.
[6]Bishop, ed., *Mormonism Unveiled*, 165; and Collier, *Adoption—Law of the Kingdom—Forgotten Doctrine of Mormonism*, 2, 3.
[7]Brigham Young, 8 October 1855, *Journal of Discourses*, 3:122
[8]See Bishop, ed., *Mormonism Unveiled*, 251–54.
[9]Church Historian's Office Journal, 28, 29 September 1857.

Woodruff, assistant church historian, made no mention of the original report in his diary. Young's knowledge of the facts was thus denied, but if anyone would have known the futility of lying to the Mormon prophet about the actual events, it would have been John D. Lee. "Brigham Young was not a credulous simpleton: he was not duped or hoodwinked: he was not misinformed," Juanita Brooks and Robert Glass Cleland concluded. "He knew the true story of the Mountain Meadows Massacre, about which the most damning reports were soon published in the hostile Gentile world and widely circulated even among the Mormons themselves, as well as any man in Utah; and he knew the names of the individual Mormons, whether prominent or obscure, who participated in the wholesale atrocities."[10]

The story told in Wilford Woodruff's journal, purporting to show Lee lying to Brigham Young, apparently reflects a meeting the two men staged for the benefit of other church leaders. Woodruff's report put the official lie on record, but his account has several problems, not the least of which is Young's failure to do anything about Lee's purported deception after Jacob Hamblin told him "the whole facts" about the massacre in June 1858. But in recounting the false story, Apostle Woodruff unwittingly added Lee's assertion that there was no innocent blood in the emigrant camp, which unveiled the involvement of white Mormons. For if the Indians alone were guilty there would have been no need to worry over such unforgivable sins as shedding innocent blood.

WILFORD WOODRUFF COLLECTION,
ROMNEY TYPESCRIPT, LDS ARCHIVES, 83–84.

On the 29th of September Elder John D Lee arrived from Harmony with an express and an awful tale of blood. A company of California emigrants of about 150 men women and children many of them belonging to the mobbers of Missouri and Illinois had been massacred. They had many cattle and horses with them as they travelled along South they went damning Brigham Young Heber C Kimball and the heads of the Church saying that Joseph Smith ought to have been shot long before he was. They wanted to do all the evil they could so they poisoned beef and gave it to the Indians and some of them died. They pois[on]ed the Springs of water and several of the Saints died. The Indians became enraged at their conduct and they surrounded them on a Prairie and the emigrants formed a bulwark of their waggons; but the Indians fought them

[10]Cleland and Brooks, eds., *A Mormon Chronicle*, 1:xiii–xiv. Brooks and Cleland noted that Mormon leaders in Salt Lake "not only failed to bring the murderers to justice but for nearly twenty years effectively used their authority and influence to prevent the federal officers from arresting the offenders. It is obvious, moreover, that Brigham Young and his highest advisers were fully informed of the massacre soon after it occurred and knew to what degree each participant was accountable for its initiation and execution."

Historian Juanita Brooks standing by the John D. Lee monument about the time she published her epic biography, *John Doyle Lee: Zealot, Pioneer Builder, Scapegoat. Courtesy of Robert A. Clark.*

five days untill they killed all their men about 60 in number. They then rushed into the correll and cut the throats of their woman and children except some 8 or 10 children which they brought and sold to the whites. The Indians stripped the men and women naked and left them stinking in the boiling sun. When brother Lee found it out he took some men and went and buried their bodies. It was a horrid job The whole air was filled with an awful stench. Many of the men and women were rotten with the foul disease before they were hurt by the Indians.[11] The Indians obtained all their property cattle horses and guns &c.

Their was another large company of emigrants who had 1000 head of cattle who was also damning both Indians and Mormons they were afraid of sharing the same fate. Brother Lee had to send interpreters with them to the Indians to try to save their lives while at the same time they were trying to kill us.

Brother Brigham while speaking of the cutting of the throats of women and children as the Indians had done South said that it was heartrending that emigration must stop as he before said.

Brother Lee remarked that he did not think that there was a drop of innocent blood in the camp of the emigrants who were slain by the Indians. He had two of the surviving children and he could get but one to kneel in prayer time and the other would laugh at her for doing it and they would sware like pirates.

THE MURDER OF AN ENTIRE TRAIN OF EMIGRANTS

Days after Lee told Brigham Young about the massacre, newspapers broke the story at Los Angeles. William Mathews and Sidney Tanner, both Mormon religious officials, carried the first report west. Their detailed story was delivered to San Bernardino, where J. W. Christian, another member of the faith, added further information and sent it on to G. N. Whitman, a fourth Mormon, for delivery to the *Los Angeles Star*. So it happened that the story that appeared on the third and tenth of October on the West Coast was surprisingly similar to the report of the version John D. Lee delivered to Great Salt Lake City on 29 September.

Both versions held the Indians solely responsible, but excused them for what they had done. Both explained that the Arkansans had poisoned the natives at Corn Creek and thereby brought the awful retribution on them-

---

[11]In addition to other slander, Woodruff said many of the emigrants possessed a venereal disease, commonly called "the pox" or "the foul disease."

selves. The similarity in the two stories, the speed with which they traveled to widely separated points, and their variance from the facts that have subsequently been revealed over time were an early indication that the atrocity was being covered up. Moreover, subsequent reports from emigrants who followed the Fancher train, in light of past stories about Mormons inciting the natives to attack overland travelers, increasingly pointed to white involvement.

Several California newspapers had a long tradition of attacking Mormonism, but two of the state's most influential journals, the *Alta Californian* and the *Los Angeles Star*, had long been sympathetic to the Latter-day Saints. The Utah War closed the LDS church's West Coast newspaper, *The Western Standard*, and the conflict's worst atrocity eliminated whatever compassion Californians might have felt for the frontier theocracy.[12] The stories published immediately after the massacre incorporated much of the best and most reliable information on how and why it happened. These articles contain the initial Mormon stories and document the growing suspicion as more accurate reports arrived.

"RUMORED MASSACRE ON THE PLAINS," *LOS ANGELES STAR*, 3 OCTOBER 1857, 2/3.

We have just been informed by Judge [John] Brown of San Bernardino, who has arrived in town from that city, that a rumor was prevalent there, and had obtained general belief, that a whole train of emigrants from Salt Lake city, for San Bernardino, composed of twenty-five families, comprising ninety-five persons, men and women, had been cruelly massacred on the road, between the last settlements in Utah Territory and the boundary of this State.

All the property of the company had been carried off, and only the children left, who were picked up on the ground, and were being conveyed to San Bernardino.

This intelligence was brought on by another party who had started from the city after the reported missing company, and who had overtaken the mail carrier in the Cajon Pass, where he is said to have encamped on Wednesday night.

No further particulars are known, nor any names given or any account of the finding and disposition of the bodies. We give the rumor for what it is worth. The alleged facts are without authenticity as yet, the party not having arrived in San Bernardino at the time our informant left.

Although the rumor was generally believed in San Bernardino, we confess our unwillingness to credit such a wholesale massacre.

---

[12]See Ekins, ed., *Defending Zion*, for details of California's Mormon newspaper wars.

"Horrible Massacre of Emigrants!!"
Los Angeles Star, 10 October 1857, 2/2–3.

In our last publication, we gave the substance of a rumor which had just then reached us, of the massacre of a large party of emigrants on their way to this State, by Great Salt Lake city. We were unwilling at first to credit the statement and hoped that rumor had exaggerated the facts, but the report has been confirmed, and the loss of life is even greater than at first reported. This is the foulest massacre which has ever been perpetrated on this route, and one which calls loudly for the active interposition of the Government. Over one hundred persons have fallen by the hands of the merciless destroyer, and we hope that immediate steps will be taken by the authorities to inflict a terrible retribution on those concerned. There is no longer reason to doubt the facts—we have them from different parties, and all agree in placing the number of the slain at over one hundred souls, men, women and children.

The details as far as yet known, are these: A train of emigrants, from Missouri and Arkansas, for this State, were waylayed and cruelly butchered on the route, at a place called Santa Clara Cañon, near the rim of the Great Basin, about 300 miles from Salt Lake city. The scene of the massacre is differently designated as Santa Clara Cañon, the Mountain Springs, and the Mountain Meadows.[13] But all agree in locating it near the rim of the Great Basin, and about fifty miles from Cedar City, the most southern of the Mormon settlements. Of a party of about 130 persons, only fifteen infant children were saved. The account was given by the Indians themselves to the Mormons at Cedar City, to which place they brought the children, who were purchased from them by the people of that city. Whether the cause assigned is sufficient to account for the result, or whether a different cause is at the bottom of the transaction, we will leave the reader to form his own conclusion. We can scarcely believe that a party traveling along a highway would act in the manner described, that is to poison the carcass of an ox, and also the water, thus endangering the lives of those who were coming after them. Yet this is the story told by all who have spoken of the massacre. It is stated, the emigrants had an ox which died, and they placed poison in the body and also poisoned the water standing in pools, for the purpose of killing the Indians; that several of the tribe had died from this cause, and that the whole force mustered, pursued the train, and coming up with them at the above named place, which favored their purpose, attacked and murdered the whole party, except a few infant children. The Indians state that they made but one charge on the party, in which they cut off the greater portion of the men, and then guarded the outlets of the cañon, and shot the men and women down as they came out for water; that one man was making his escape with a few children, and they followed him, killed him, and took

---

[13]Several massacre participants later said that the Nauvoo Legion planned to attack the Arkansas emigrants at the head of Santa Clara Canyon rather than at Mountain Meadows.

the children fifteen in number, the eldest under five years of age. The report was brought to San Bernardino by Messrs. Sidney Tanner and W. Mathews.

The following letter from Mr. J. W. Christian, of San Bernardino, to Mr. G. N. Whitman, of this city, has been kindly placed at our disposal, and we give it at length, as it is the fullest report of the massacre, and the cause which led to it, that has reached us. The writer seems to intimate that the Mormons will be held responsible for the murder, and in this respect he is fully borne out by present indications, for a general belief pervades the public mind here that the Indians were instigated to this crime by the "Destroying Angels" of the church, and that the blow fell on these emigrants from Arkansas, in retribution of the death of Parley Pratt, which took place in that State. The truth of the matter will not be known until the Government make an investigation of the affair. This should be done, to place blame in the right quarter, as well as to inflict chastisement on the immediate actors in the fearful-tragedy, who are reported to be the Santa Clara tribe of Indians. The following is the letter:—

SAN BERNARDINO, October 4th, 1857.

I take this opportunity of informing you of the murder of an entire train of emigrants, on their way from Missouri and Arkansas to this State, via Great Salt Lake city; which took place, according to the best information I can possibly acquire, (which is, primarily, through Indians,) at the Mountain Meadows, which are at or near the Rim of the Great Basin, and some distance south of the most southern Mormon settlements, between the 10th and 12th ultimo. It is absolutely one of the most horrible massacres I have ever had the painful necessity of relating.

The company consisted of about 130 or 135 men, women and children, and including some forty or forty-five capable of bearing arms. They were in possession of quite an amount of stock consisting of horses, mules and oxen. The encampment was attacked about daylight in the morning, so say the Indians, by the combined forces of all the various tribes immediately in that section of the country. It appears that the majority of them were slain at the first onset made by the Indians. The remaining forces formed themselves into the best position there circumstances would allow; but before they could make the necessary arrangement for protecting themselves from the arrows, there were but few left who were able to bear arms. After having corralled their wagons, and dug a ditch for their protection, they continued to fire upon the Indians for one or two days, but the Indians had so secreted themselves that, according to their own statement, there was not one of them killed, and but few wounded. They (the emigrants) then sent out a flag of truce, borne by a little girl, and gave themselves up to the mercy of the savages, who immediately rushed in and slaughtered all of them, with the exception of fifteen infant children, that have since been purchased, with much difficulty, by the Mormon interpreters.

I presume it would be unnecessary, for all practical purposes, to relate the causes which gave rise to the above described catastrophe, from the simple fact that it will be attributed to the Mormon people, let the circumstances of the case be what they may. But it seems, from a statement which I received from Elders Wm. Mathew[14] and Wm. Hyde, who were in Great Salt Lake city at the time the train was there, recruiting their "fit out;" and were on the road to this place at the time when they were murdered, but several days' journey in the rear—somewhere about the Beaver Mountains, which is between Parawan [sic] and Fillmore cities—that the causes were something like these: The train camped at Corn Creek, near Fillmore City, where there is an Indian village, the inhabitants of which have raised a crop of wheat, and a few melons &c. And in trading with the Indians they gave them cash for wheat, and they not knowing the value of coin were severely cheated. They wanted a blanket for a sack of wheat, but they gave them fifty cents, and told them that amount would buy a blanket. They also had an ox with them which had died, and they put strychnine in him, for the purpose of poisoning the Indians; and also put poison of some description in the water, which is standing in holes. This occasioned several deaths among them, within a few days after the departure of the train. And upon this, it seems, the Indians gathered themselves together, and had, no doubt chose the place of attack, and arranged everything before the train arrived at the place where they were murdered.

It was ascertained by some of the interpreters, from a few of the Indians who were left at Corn Creek, that most of the Indians in the country had left; but they could not learn for what purpose, and before any steps could be taken to ascertain for certain what was the cause, the story was told—they were all killed. Yours truly, —J. WARD CHRISTIAN.

"THE DUTY OF THE GOVERNMENT,"
LOS ANGELES STAR, 17 OCTOBER 1857, 2/1.

It may be superfluous in us, on reviewing the facts detailed elsewhere, to say anything to urge the Federal Government at Washington to take prompt measures to investigate the last sanguinary tragedy on the Salt Lake route to California. The facts set forth, that one hundred and eighteen Americans, men, women, and children, have been cruelly butchered on the nation's highway, by a band of ruthless savages, are in themselves sufficiently startling and appalling, to arouse the energies of the most dormant. From time to time, outrages have been perpetrated by the Indians on passing emigrants, of which no notice have been taken by the authorities. It would seem as if those who set out to make their homes in this State, are deemed to have left behind them all claim on the Government for protection; and that they are doomed to death, if unable to defend themselves against the sudden attack of an ambushed enemy,

[14]William Mathews was Christian's father-in-law.

or unfortunate in contending against the unknown and unforeseen dangers of the route.

It is certainly the duty of the Government to afford both assistance and protection to its citizens, whilst traveling over territory under its own immediate supervision. In this respect, it has been heretofore remiss. It is not enough to keep troops stationed at certain points along the road. These troops should be kept on patrol duty along the route, at least during the season of emigration, and by this means not only would the Indians be kept in check, but assistance would be always at hand to help the weary traveler whilst suffering under the thousand and one exigencies of the long and tedious journey . . .

The Complicity of the Mormon Leaders

Brigham Young's insistence that he and he alone had kept the peace between Indians and emigrants on the overland road was not widely accepted. Many trail veterans, especially in California, had personally experienced attacks that they believed were orchestrated by Mormons. To them, the September 1857 massacre sounded simply like more of the same.

"More Outrages on the Plains!!
Two Men Wounded!! 320 Head of Cattle Run Off, &c, &c!,"
Los Angeles Star, 24 October 1857, 2/1–2.

The surprise and excitement, following the receipt of the intelligence of the late horrible massacre on the Plains, had not abated when we find ourselves called on to record another attack on peaceable citizens traveling along the common highway.

It was known that another train was following that which has been so ruthlessly assassinated, and but a few days march behind it, and great fear was entertained for its safety. This alarm has been but too well founded as the following detail of their sufferings will exhibit. No one who reads the statement given below by Mr. Honea, can for a moment doubt the complicity of the Mormon leaders in these scenes of crime and outrage. The immense sums paid to the interpreters, and their refusal to fulfill the terms of their contracts—not to say, what is very plainly charged against them by our informant—that they conspired with the Indians to commit the depredations and outrages complained of—would alone convict them of a participation in these murderous assaults. What course the Government will take in the matter we cannot say, but we think another year will not roll round without a sufficient force being stationed along the road to protect the people in their journey. This we think the Government owes to its citizens, whether or not it will inflict punishment on these wrongdoers.

From the statements made regarding the preaching of the Mormon Prophet, and the sentiments of the people, there can be no doubt but a deep rooted animosity exists amongst them against the people and Government of the United States. It will be seen that the Mormon troops had actually moved out to engage and drive back the men under the command of Col. Johns[t]on, who had succeeded Gen. Harney in command of the Utah expedition. What the result of this movement has been, a short time will tell; but the first shot fired against that band of "Uncle Sam's boys," will be the signal for lighting the torch of a long and sanguinary war, which will not be quenched till Mormonism is exterminated from the soil of the United States.

We commend the following statement to the careful perusal of our readers. We have full confidence in the candor and veracity of the gentleman who furnishes the information. He is well known to a large number of our most respectable citizens, who were formerly residents of Franklin county, in the State of Arkansas, from which he has just emigrated:—

S. B. HONEA, of Franklin county, State of Arkansas, left home on the 9th of May, 1857, for California, in company with the Crook & Collins company, and afterwards fell in with the Williamson company, from Pope county. With the exception of an attack by the Rappaho Indians, on the Arkansas river, on the 20th of June, on the company of Captain Henry of Texas, who lost 151 head of cattle, nothing of interest occurred on the journey, nor did they perceive any symptoms of opposition, or of armed bands, till they came to Fort Bridger, in Utah Territory. Here they saw a large quantity of provisions stored, a considerable number of Indians encamped all round the fort, and heard the people generally speaking of making preparations to go out and meet General Harney. At Fort Bridger, was told by a merchant that at Fort Supply over 400 Indians were encamped, awaiting orders to attack the U.S. troops. About thirty miles from Fort Bridger, met three companies of men, generally mounted, and all well armed, having abundance of baggage, their wagons being numbered in messes.

THE ARMY OF OBSERVATION.

Here had a conversation with one of the Mormon soldiers, an Englishman, who camped with our company, and over the camp fire became communicative. He referred in bitter terms to the treatment the Mormons had received in Illinois and Missouri, reflected on the unjustness and tyranny of the people of the United States, and said that the time was come to get even. He said they were on their way to meet Gen. Harney, to see what he was coming for; "if he was coming peaceably, we will let him come, but if not, we will drive him back," were the words used. Another Mormon, named Killion, an old man, who lives about seven miles [out] of Salt Lake city, spoke bitterly against the United States, denounced Judge Drummond, and all the Federal officers, and rejoiced that the time had come when the saints would be avenged on their enemies—that men were found who could face the enemy, and that Harney, with his 2,500 men, never would enter Salt Lake city. He also stated that Governor Brigham Young had ordered the people to prepare for war; that they should not sell emigrants anything; that they must lay up provisions; that the men and women must not dress up in store clothes any more, but that all must be saved to forward the cause of the church against the common enemy—that the men must be content with buckskin instead of broadcloth, and have plenty of guns and ammunition.

Declaration of Independence.

On the 17th of August, passed through the city of Salt Lake. Remained only three or four hours. Had a conversation with a merchant, a Gentile, who stated that on the previous Sunday, Brigham Young had declared, in the Temple, that henceforth Utah was a separate and independent Territory, and owed no obedience or allegiance to any form or laws, but those of their own enactment, and called upon the people to stand together, and support him in maintaining the cause of God and the church.[15] Was told that the house of Gilbert & Garrison, had orders from Brigham to pack up and leave before the 1st of November.[16]

Rumors of the Missing Train.

Nothing occurred worthy of not, till we arrived at Corn Creek. Here had a conversation with a man who represented himself as the Indian agent.[17] He told us that a train had passed a short time before us, who had poisoned an ox, and that they had been attacked by the Indians. He spoke in abusive terms of the men of that train, for having acted in an improper manner.

One of our company, named Joseph Lane, lost three oxen, which had been run off from him. He offered a reward to the Indians to bring them back, which they said they could not do, as they knew nothing of them, but three white men came into camp and offered to bring them back for $15, to which he agreed. They brought two of them and claimed the money, which was paid them. They then said the Indians had shot an arrow into the other, but that they would go and find him for $10, which was agreed to, and they then brought the missing animal into camp, which had no appearance of having been wounded. Here [we] traded off a horse with an Indian, the agent acting as interpreter. From this we proceeded to Beaver, passing Capt. Turner's train, of Missouri, about seven miles north of Beaver. Here we were informed that Capt. Baker's train, of Carroll county Arkansas, had been murdered, and that it would not be safe for us to proceed any further.

---

[15]This is one of many reports that Brigham Young on 16 August declared independence.

[16]Non-Mormon merchants Henry S. Gilbert and William Gerrish had been freighting goods to Salt Lake since 1850. Gilbert retreated to South Pass and opened a stage station there in 1858.

[17]Probably agent George W. Armstrong.

ATTACK BY INDIANS.

We camped that evening within half a mile of Beaver, and were informed that the Indians intended to attack Captain Turner that night. The Mormons proposed that five of their men would go back with five of our men, in order to assist Turner's train, but in reality to prevent us from firing on the Indians in their attack. Before we got there, firing had commenced, the Indians having begun to rifle the camp; one Indian was wounded. Turner's train was harnessed up to join our train, the Indians keeping up a fire on them, wounding some of the cattle, but doing no other injury. The interpreters prevented the men of the train from firing on the Indians, saying that if they injured an Indian we would all be killed. From this we became more apprehensive of the interpreters than of the Indians, feeling that we were completely in the power of an unscrupulous enemy.

INDIANS LEVYING CONTRIBUTION.

Next morning, the Indians sent down an order by the Bishop of Beaver [Philo Farnsworth], demanding cattle from us. Whilst in consultation on this demand, intelligence was received that five of the Corn Creek Indians had come down, and the Bishop went off with the Indians, without waiting for our answer. Here it was considered necessary to remain some time, as the grass was good, and our men went up to the Bishop to obtain permission to stop, and also to have smithwork done in town.

ANOTHER ATTACK BY INDIANS—TWO MEN WOUNDED.

At this place, we were joined by Turner's train. Whilst Turner, and Duke, our captain, were standing in the street, they were fired on by the Indians, and Captain Turner was shot through the hip, and Capt. Dukes was grazed by two or three bullets. Mr. Collins was standing in front of the blacksmith shop, and went in and begged protection, when he was pushed out of the house and the Indians shot him, breaking his arm, shattering the bone very loudly. A Mormon then came galloping to our camp, and told us to remain by the wagons. Supposing that something was wrong, four of our men started to the town to see what had happened, when we saw Turner, Dukes, and Collins coming to us in a circuitous route, who called to us to return, as they had been attacked by the Indians and were badly wounded. We then made preparations for a fight, made a corral of the wagons, and prepared our arms, but no fight took place.

This evening, an Indian chief, named Ammon came to our camp, in company with the Bishop, and said he had just come from Salt Lake city—that all was peace, and demanded cattle. We gave him six head of cattle. Here Mr. Honea had to give up the horse for which he he [sic] had traded with an Indian, because, it was said, the Indians knew the horse and were angry at seeing him in possession of an American.

Here heard a Mormon named Hooper say, that he was glad the train had been killed, for they carried poison with them, and had only got their just reward.

Next morning left Beaver. We now came to the conclusion that it would be better to hire interpreters, and we accordingly hired three Mormons, named David Carter, Nephi Johnson, and —— Shirts, who agreed to come with us to the divide between the Santa Clara and the Rio Virgin. Before we got to the divide, two of them turned back—Johnson came on, one of them, Shirts, stealing a horse. President Dame had been paid in advance for their services.

The Dead Unburied.

Dame advised us not to pass where the other train had been massacred, but to take a left-hand trail, which we finally did, having first proposed to go and bring [bury] our deceased countrymen, but the interpreters objected, saying that the Indians would serve us the same way. Here we met the two horse thieves, the brothers Young, who stated that the Indians were very troublesome on the Muddy, and advised us to hire additional interpreters, especially Hatch. We hired Hatch and four others, paying them $500 in advance. Their contract was, to come with us to the Cottonwood Springs.

The Interpreters Levy Blackmail.

While they were with us, they made us give beeves to the Indians on the Santa Clara, and advised us not to swear before the Indians, as they would know us to be Americans and probably kill us.

On passing down the Rio Virgen, we had to give more beeves to the Indians, who stole a horse from one of the company. We lost several head of cattle; [Oscar] Hamblin, the interpreter, sent Indians to search for them, who drove them back to Hamblin's house; other cattle strayed off, and were immediately killed by the Indians. On the Virgin, Mr. Samuel Weeks lost $302.50 from his wagon. A thorough search was made in the train, but it could not be found. The opinion was, that the interpreters had stolen it, as most of the company knew of the money being there. A man named Lovett,[18] joined us here, who had no ostensible reason for coming to us. He lived with Hamblin; and it was the opinion of the company afterwards that the plan was concocted here, between Hamblin and Hatch, for our robbery.

On leaving the Virgin, we were advised by the interpreters to make up a present of tents, blankets, &c, and send [it] to the Indians at the Muddy. This was done, to the amount of six or seven tents and several bundles of blankets, and a considerable amount of clothing. The interpreters took charge of the goods and left the same night in advance, for the Muddy.

Next night, we encamped about mid-way between the Virgin and the Muddy, where two of the interpreters came back to us, saying that the Indians were

---

[18]Dudley Leavitt.

peaceable, being well pleased with the presents sent them. Hamblin observed; that there was one captain, with 100 men, not there, and that there was nothing to fear, except from him, as he did not know where he was.

Next day we reached the Muddy. The interpreters told us the Indians wanted ten beeves. We gave them six, and thought they were well satisfied. Here we made particular observation to see whether any of the Indians had any of the tents or clothing sent them, but could not see any; we concluded that the interpreters kept them for themselves. We stayed here three or four hours, and then started for the Desert, leaving two of the interpreters, and Lovett with their own wagons, on the Muddy.

ATTACK BY INDIANS—LOSS OF STOCK.

Proceeded about eight or ten miles along the cañon. The cattle were in advance of our wagons about half a mile. The cattle were stopped to enable the wagons to come up. While waiting, [we] observed Hamblin on the top of the hill, apparently looking for Indians. He came down from the hill, and by this time the wagons had joined the advance party, and the train moved on. Before this, however, Hamblin had a conversation with a young Indian who accompanied us from the Muddy, and who pointed out to him where the Indians were located. When we started on, the Indian asked for water; there was none in any of the vessels, and he then ran in advance of the cattle and gave a whoop. The yelling then became general along the hills, where previously we could not perceive a single Indian. At this time, three of the four interpreters who remained with us were in the rear of the train. The other advised the captains to fall back and leave the cattle, and guard the wagons with the women and children. This was done—when a large body of Indians, over two hundred, made a descent on the cattle and run them off—to the number of 326 head, and five horses. Some of the party prepared to fire on the Indians, but the interpreter prevented them, saying we would all be killed. He then rode in among the Indians and soon returned, saying that they had sent word, if we wanted to fight to come on. He was requested to go again to the Indians, when he asked to exchange an old gun for a valuable navy revolver. It was given him; then he started off, in company with some of the train, on the condition that if danger threatened, he would fire the pistol, which would be the signal for them to return to the wagons. He fired the pistol, all the interpreters left the train, and were not again seen.[19]

---

[19]Honea's companions "noticed that some of the painted Indians had blue, gray, and different colored eyes; they had straight, curly, and fine hair, differing materially from the other Indians in this respect. Mr. Davis remarks, also, that a number of those painted Indians had streaks, and spots of white in the creases round their eyes, being in close proximity to the eyeballs; also around and behind the ears it was discovered that the skin of the white man was quite apparent. The painted *whites* were shy; they did not act with the same freedom and boldness as the aborigines did; but undoubtedly they were the leaders of the band of robbers that drove off the three hundred and twenty-six head of cattle that night." See "Letter from San Bernardino," *San Francisco Evening Bulletin*, 12 November 1857, 2/3.

We stayed here but a short time, and proceeded on our way to the Vegas, which we reached without molestation. The Indians were peaceable, and the interpreters not being with us, we had to give them only one animal.

From this we came to Cottonwood Springs, about 275 miles from San Bernardino. Here the Indians were also perfectly peaceable. The remaining cattle being almost wornout, it was resolved to remain here to recruit. Nine of the company started off on foot, and after enduring almost incredible sufferings from the want of food and water, reached San Bernardino almost exhausted.

It should be added that Hamblin, the interpreter, stated on being hired, that if there was to be any fighting the interpreters should take no part in it; that they were friendly with the Indians who were Mormons.

The train, at the time of the attack, consisted of 125 persons, forty-four of whom were men, bearing arms. They had 440 cattle, 130 work oxen, and forty-five mules and horses, and twenty-three wagons.

The party left at Cottonwood Springs, intend to remain until their animals are recruited, as the grass was good; and there being no Mormons, the Indians peaceable and friendly. They will probable arrive at San Bernardino within a week or ten days. The distance is 275 miles.

THE MURDERED TRAIN.

The train which has been so cruelly massacred, was under the charge of Captain Baker, familiarly known as "Uncle Jack," from Carroll county Arkansas—Silas Edwards and William Baker, son of the captain, are also known to have been in the train. At Cedar City, Mr. Honea saw President Haight riding a large bay horse which he recognized as having belonged to Mr. Silas Edwards. Was informed by Hatch, that young Baker had an opportunity of escaping, went a short distance but returned; was afterwards wounded in the arm; again escaped from the massacre, and had proceeded about ten miles this side the Muddy, when he met the Youngs who had escaped from San Bernardino.[20] He was advised to return to the Muddy, which he did, when he was met by Hatch and the Indians, and by them cruelly murdered.

AMMUNITION FOR SALT LAKE.

Mr. Honea says that in coming into San Bernardino, about fifteen miles the other side of the sink of the Mohave river, he met the mail wagon, for Salt Lake city, having a large quantity of pistols and ammunition. The driver wished to purchase arms from the party, but they refused to sell.

PAYING INTERPRETERS.

To give an idea of the fraud and extortion practiced by the Mormons on emigrants, Mr. Honea states, that their company paid to interpreters, six in all, the enormous sum of $1815. The duty to be performed by these guides

---

[20]Brothers Henry T. and Cau Young were allegedly non-Mormon horse thieves fleeing from justice in San Bernardino.

and interpreters, was, to conduct the company from Cedar City to Cottonwood Springs, a distance not over 300 miles. Yet this contract was not fulfilled, although payment was made in advance.

"LATER FROM THE SOUTH: THE MASSACRE AT MOUNTAIN CANON CONFIRMED.— MORE INDIAN OUTRAGES, & C.," ALTA CALIFORNIA, 27 OCTOBER 1857, 1/2–5.

OUR LOS ANGELES CORRESPONDENCE.

The massacre of more than a hundred American citizens by Mormon traitors and Indians, has created a great excitement among all classes in our community, and we hope that the tocsin is now sounded that shall rouse the nation
and compel the government to protect our countrymen from the additional danger which foreign traitors throw around them, in passing over the national territories. For long years outrage upon outrage has been committed and representations made imploring aid in that inhospitable region where nature herself
is so repulsive as almost to forbid travel, but their calls have been unheeded.

Our whole community has been deeply moved. Many of them are waiting
and wishing for a call, to go and abate the evils which arrest the weary traveler and consign him to an unknown and nameless grave, midway to his destination. Two large public meetings were held in this city last week, under the
circus pavilion, at which speeches were made by several who had been at Salt
Lake, and resolutions were passed, which, I believe, express the sentiments of
everybody here but Mormons. There is a sentiment of extermination, living
and intense, growing in the minds of all true Americans, against the traitors
who have planted themselves in our territory, and who have instigated the savages of the desert to slaughter and rapine. Will the government make any effort
to redeem its character for pusillanimity, in so long delaying to correct those
monstrous evils? does there need hecatombs more of victims, before anything
is done? What further outrage and insult is needed to prove to our rulers that
there is a band of armed traitors in our midst who are making indiscriminate
war upon men, women and children, simply because they are Americans, who
are more dangerous because they are blinded by fanaticism, and who are instigating the savages to slay all who are not saints? A terrible example seems necessary to prove to them the power of those they are thus taught to slaughter—
an example so fearful that it shall be remembered in all their villages, and shall
make them tremble with awe when they hear the American name.

The following statements (which I have already given to our public both
in English and Spanish) I took down from the lips of the gentlemen named.
The manner of these gentlemen was in their statements, which have been duly
authenticated and forwarded by mail to Washington. They arrived in town
on the 10th instant. It will be seen that they were not permitted to see anything of the massacre—that they were detained one day near Parowan, that

they might not arrive at the time of the massacre, and that they drove all night that the scene of the massacre might not be examined. Notwithstanding these precautions, it can scarcely fail to convince the unprejudiced reader that all these men saw and heard, goes to establish the complicity of the Mormons with the Indians in the wholesale butcheries reported—that if these Saints were not actually engaged in the slaughter, they must have stood pitilessly by, and encouraged the Indians, whose vindictive character they have so mould-ed as to make it unsafe for any American to travel in that region unless he be under their protection. [Here the *Alta* reprinted the Powers and Warn state-ments from the *Los Angeles Star.*]

The following statement is made to me by Mr. Henry Mogridge, with the request that I would give it publicity. He is a young man, and was once in high favor with the powers at Salt Lake. He says if called upon, he will make oath to the truth of his charges. He says:—

"In November, 1853, I resided at Salt Lake, and was sent for to attend a council. At the council I was solicited to take a mission to the Green River Indians. I did not consent, because I had just returned from Parowan, and the southern settlements, which I had been appointed to locate. Although not a member of the council, I was permitted to remain, and heard the charge given to the missionaries to those Indians by Willard Richards, now dead. First they were to establish missions, then they would form treaties and alliances with the Indians; the elders, both married and single, must marry squaws, partic-ularly the daughters of chiefs. Such ties as these could not be broken, and the Indians would be under their control forever.

"At that time, war against the United States was anticipated, and they pro-fessed according to the Book of Mormon, to use the Indians 'as the Lord's battle-ax.' A time would come when they would be of great service to the Saints, from their knowledge of the mountains. They were to teach the doctrines of Mormon, and baptize them into the church—they were also to monopolize all trade with them, and influence them to keep out the Gentiles.

"These missionaries did not at that time, go so far as Green River, but remained in the vicinity of Fort Bridger, to watch the movements of the moun-taineers, who were gathering there, indignant that Bridger had been driven off. In the following spring several other missionaries were sent to different parts of the territory. P. P. Pratt was sent to the Santa Clara for similar purposes.

"I had been an eye-witness to the baptism of scores of Indians at Parowan, and other southern settlements. The doctrines taught, are invariably, that the Americans are enemies to the Mormons and Indians, and they must kill them whenever they can find them.

"The Mormons have a school wherein the young men of the church are taught the different Indian dialects. These dialects are reduced to a system, and are printed in books. Many of the Mormon elders and missionaries have Indian wives, and are raising families of half-breeds.

"I have frequently heard Brigham Young declare that he could clean out the United States with the Shoshonees (Snake) and Utahs, and that he intended to do it."

At Painter Creek, which is but six or seven miles, on the other side of the scene of slaughter, there is a settlement of some fifteen or twenty families of Mormons. The people there knew of the beginning and end of the slaughter, but not one of them went to the assistance of the train.

Mr. Warn states that, two days before arriving at San Bernardino, a man named Bill Hyde, whom he learned was a noted Danite, and who is badly reported of in this town, joined the train, having come through with the mail. This Hyde reported that he went and saw the bodies lying scattered about upon the ground, most of them stripped naked—only a few of them being partially clothed. Dame and Haight, he said, staid there to bury the dead, but the bodies were so much decayed they could not endure the stench, and after throwing a few into a hole and covering them lightly with sage, the two Presidents departed. Decomposition must have been very rapid, to have produced so offensive results, the morning after the massacre!

Hyde also related to his Mormon brethren, that on arriving at the Santa Clara, where formerly there was a Mormon settlement, and is now occupied by the Chief Jackson, he saw in the hands of that chief, a little book, or journal, the name, "Wm. B. Jones, Caldwell County, Missouri." Again, Missouri! He offered to purchase it, but the chief refused to part with it. This is the first intimation we have that will in any manner serve to identify the train. Not a word, nor a sign, except this, has been given, which will rescue from oblivion the name or residence of those hundred and eighteen travelers, and the only monument left of them is their bones whitening upon the desert.

How were these deaths compassed? and who did it? It is charged upon the Indians, by Mormons. But what Indians? These two gentlemen have related all they saw along the whole route. Except the band of twenty, they met returning from the massacre, in company with nearly as many more white men, they say distinctly that they saw no Indians, going or coming; and at the various villages, from Corn Creek to the Muddy, they saw no suspicious movements among them—no preparations for attack—no rejoicing—no trophies of victory, except those already named, in possession of Haight and Dame's party. Those who were dressed as Indians in that party all talk English, and were on terms of equality with the Presidents. Is there any significance in this?

The significance of English-speaking Indians was no mystery to the *Star's* readers in California: the political situation in Utah was "the all-engrossing topic" of conversation and information poured into the newspaper. Early in November the paper printed several documents it considered "well worthy a careful perusal." The first was an affidavit filed on 2 November by overlander John Aiken.

"The Late Outrages on the Plains—Further Particulars,"
Los Angeles Star, 7 November 1857, 2/1–3.

I started from Port Gibson, State of Mississippi, in the summer of '56, to
New York, to engage a passage by steamer to California, but I was taken sick,
and returned to Texas, and thence to Kansas, where I took charge of a drove
of cattle, of 973, for Thomas Box, a Mormon, to deliver them at Salt Lake
city. We started from Leavenworth city on the 22d of June last. We proceeded quietly and uninterruptedly on our journey as far as Sweet Water. Here we
saw about one hundred and fifty armed men, (all Mormon); they had established an observatory to watch the approach and movements of Gen. Harney's army. We was informed by them, that the surrounding mountains were
alive with men, to watch the movements of the army. We understood that
there would be no danger if we turned our stock out unguarded; which we
found to be the case, because the proprietor was a Mormon. The owner gave
them some beeves; and was on very intimate terms. We proceeded on our way
as far as Fort Bridger; saw nothing of importance, except that several expresses passed us, to and from the various stations of their army. I learned nothing from any of the expresses, as they only conversed with the owner of the
stock. We camped near Fort Bridger, I suppose about one mile and a half; saw
nothing of their preparations, as I did not go nearer than a mile within their
battlements. We proceeded to Echo Cañon, forty miles from Salt Lake city.
We saw a number of Mormon soldiers in the cañon, guarding that pass, secreted in the brush; they made no fires at night and said that the U.S. army should
not pass them. They had great confidence in their allies, the Indians; they did
not intend to meet the army in open field, but to ambush them, and the Indians were to run off the horses, stock, &c. We next met a company of armed
men, with a train of wagons loaded with an outfit of provisions, munitions
of war, &c., about twelve miles from Salt Lake city, on the 20th day of September, early in the morning. We learned from Dr. Dunion, surgeon to Brigham
Young's army,[21] that they had taken a vote at Salt Lake city, that if the United States army forced its way into Utah, that they themselves would burn
their city, towns, forts, &c., and lay every habitation in ashes; they had already
picked out secret places in the mountains, to "cache" their provisions, and
make their future abode with the Indians. The Doctor stated that arrangements were already entered into, that provided the army should enter the settlements, *that every city, town and village in the States of California, Missouri and Iowa
should be burned immediately—that they had men to do this who were not known to be Mormons!*[22] And that they would cut off all the emigrant trains, army stores, stock,

---

[21]This was John L. Dunyon, listed as "Surgeon General" on a group of portraits of Nauvoo Legion
officers at the Utah State Historical Society.

[22]Brigham Young made a similar threat to Capt. Stewart Van Vliet. "If the Government Calls for volunteers in Calafornia & the people turn out to come to destroy us they will find their own buildings in
flames before they get far from home & so throughout the United States," Young told him. Kenney, ed.,
Wilford Woodruff's Journal, 13 September 1857, 96–97.

&c.; that no man, woman or child should hereafter cross the plains, without being scalped. That they depended and expected the Indians to perform this infernal and cowardly part of the their designs.

We arrived at the city in the afternoon of the same day. Here I found all that I had heard stated by the soldiers on their way out to their various stations assigned them, confirmed by the repetition of the same by the people of the city. I found here amongst the people of the city the most hostile feeling and bitter sentiments that the heart of man could possibly conceive. I was cautioned to be very cautious in my remarks, and say nothing against the Mormons, by a friend from Yankee land, who has to exercise the utmost discretion in all he said or done. Here I learned that it was necessary for me to get a passport from the War Department of Young's army, to secure my safety through the settlements, which I did, and found it very advantageous to me on my way through the settlements.

Adjutant General's office, Utah Territory
Great Salt Lake City, Sept. 21, 1857.

To all whom it may concern. This to certify that the bearer, Mr. John Aiken, who is peaceably traveling through the Territory, is permitted to pass on his way to California.

DANIEL H. WELLS,
Lt. General Commanding.

By order of the Lt. General Commanding,
JAMES FERGUSON, Adjutant General.
Endorsed by Col. Dame, of Parowan,
Sept. 28, 1857.   Wm. H. Dame,
Colonel Iron Military District.

This may seem strange to Americans, that they are not permitted to travel on their own soil, in Utah, without first obtaining passports; this may be accounted for, on the ground that Utah Territory is placed under martial law, and none but those who are considered friendly to their cause, can obtain passports out of the Territory. I obtained my passport through the recommendation of Captain Duncan, a Mormon, who traveled to Salt Lake in the company with which I was engaged. I started from the Mormon city on the 23d of September, and traveled three hundred and twenty-five miles on the southern route to California by myself. I passed through the principal towns on this route—being stopped by the Mormon officers and Indian chiefs, declaring that no American could leave the Territory without showing his authority and paying the Indians for the privilege; this I acceded to, by paying to the Indians about forty dollars, besides blankets and clothing, &c. All this occurred within the limits of the Mormon settlements. After I left the Mormons, I got along peaceably with the Indians, who are not directly under Mormon influence. I stayed at Painter Creek several days, within six miles of the scene of the late horrible massacre, where I joined the company of the U.S. mail to San Bernardino. John Hunt, the mail carrier, refused any protection whatever; said that I to fight my own battles, as they were friendly with the Indians, and did not wish to incur their displeasure. While at Painter Creek, I saw the Mormon drawing some of the wagons belonging to persons who fell in the late massacre towards Cedar City; they did not explain to me anything of their business, or of their possession of the wagons; seemed very distant and indifferent in their communications. I asked no questions; I wished to avoid suspicion.

After leaving Painter Creek, and arriving at the field of blood, I discovered several bodies that were slain, in a state of nudity and a state of putrefaction. I saw about twenty wolves feasting upon the carcases [sic] of the murdered. Mr. Hunt shot at a wolf, they ran a few rods and halted. I noticed that the women and children were more generally eaten by the wild beasts than the men. Although Cap. Baker and a number of others of the slain party were my acquaintans, yet I dared not express my sentiments in the company of Hunt and his companions, knowing that I was traveling with enemies to my country and countrymen. Mr. Hunt and his companions often laughed, and made remarks derogatory to decency, and contrary to humanity, upon the persons of those who were there rotting, or had become food to wild beasts. Although this terrible massacre occurred within six miles of Painter Creek settlement, and thirty from Cedar City, yet it appears that the Mormons are determined to suffer their carcasses to remain uncovered, for their bones to bleach upon the plains.

On the 17th day of October, I saw the tracks of a large herd of cattle going up the Santa Clara, toward the Mormon settlements, we supposed them to be the stolen cattle that were run off from the trains of Captains Dukes and Turner, as it was not customary for large herds of cattle to travel in that direction. I saw the tracks of several shod horses and mules following behind, supposed to be the animals used by the robbers. Where we first met the trail of these cattle, is where the road leaves the Santa Clara; ten miles from Hamblin's Fort, the residence of the Hamblins and Hatch, who were interpreters for the company. We continued on the trail of the cattle a distance of 100 miles, to the Muddy, near the place to where they were taken. I judge from the appearance of the trail that they were at least the number of 300 head. I know nothing more of importance. I arrived at San Bernardino on the 30th of October, and found the Mormons very distant and curious, very inquisitive about the affairs of Utah, but so far as I discovered, the Independent citizens are free and frank in their conversations and transactions.

I forgot to mention, in the proper place, that I met Nephi Johnson, one of the interpreters, at Painter Creek, of whom I inquired of the prosperity of the train to which he had been one of the interpreters and guides, to which he replied, that the train had passed safe; not even intimating that the emigrants had lost any of their cattle. Next day I met Mr. Hatch, at the same place, he told me that the train had lost over 200 head of cattle by the Indians.

A conversation between Mr. Hatch and Hamblin, occurred at this place, which seemed to betray something connected with the stolen cattle. Hamblin, the President of this fort, told Hatch to go and brand his own cattle, before he turned them out with his. This occurred on the 15th day of October, a few days after the robbery occurred. This conversation excited my curiosity to listen. Mr. Hamblin sold a steer to one of the Mormons; the steer was very poor; this was accounted for, because the steer had been driven to the Muddy and back.

Sworn and subscribed to, on this second day of November, 1857.

JOHN AIKEN.

The same article published a statement signed by members of William Dukes's wagon train, perhaps the men transmogrified years later into the Missouri Wildcats. It testified to the accuracy of S. B. Honea's earlier statement and pointed out the misinformation carefully distributed by Mormons at San Bernardino.

SAN BERNARDINO, Nov. 3d, 1857

Editor of Los Angeles Star,

Sir—After reading the statement of S. B. Honea, as published in the Star of the 24th ult., it appears to receive the approval of all the members of Captain Dukes' company. And desirous that the facts connected with our misfortunes whilst traveling through the Mormon settlements in Utah Territory, should be known, we hereby testify that Mr. S. B. Honea has simply stated the truth, and facts connected with the circumstances as described in his narrative, and not in any instance exaggerated. Signed,

Wm. C. Dukes, Captain;	from Missouri;	
James G. Bigham	"	"
Wm. Wilson,	"	"
Wm. Cooper,	"	"
James Cooper,	"	"
Wm. J. Dole,[?]	"	"
Wm. Combs,	"	"
Robert R. Hays,	"	"
James Wilson,	"	"
W. H. Horton	"	Arkansas;
W. Harton,	"	"
Orlon Horton,	"	"

Wm. Horton, sen.,	"	"	
Isaiah Baise,	"	"	
Wm. H. Harrington,	"	"	
John Daurity,	"	"	
Joseph F. M. Daurity,	"	"	
George W. Davis,	"	"	
W. B. Crook,	"	"	
Wm. L. Bevert,	"	"	
Abner Mount,	"	"	
John Hillhouse,	"	Salt Lake city, Utah;	
Wm. J. Hillhouse,[23]	"	" " "	
John Ashcroft,[24]	"	Battle Creek, Utah	
George Cook,	"	London, England;	
F. M. Nelson	"	Texas.	

Mr. G. W. Davis adds that when he was at Fillmore city, the Bishop [Lewis Brunson] said that he could scarcely withhold the brethren from following after the train (which was afterwards massacred) and cutting it into pieces; because parties of that train cursed the Mormons for not selling them provisions. The Bishop said that they had instructions from Brigham Young not to sell any provisions to emigrants unless they could get guns, revolvers, or ammunition for pay—this very much enraged a Dutchman, who threatened, or said, that if he had a good riding horse, he would go back to Salt Lake and kill Brigham. The Bishop said that the only way that he could control his men was that he promised them to set the Indians on the doomed train. Mr. Davis then proceeded as far as Beaver, where he found the Bishop very friendly with him; and as Davis had not attached himself to any train he deemed it necessary to do so, and accordingly he waited here two or three days for the arrival of Captain Dukes' company. During his stay here, the Bishop frequented Mr. Davis's wagon, and preached the Mormon doctrines, to which Davis listened without opposing it. Finally the Bishop solicited the hand of Miss Eliza in marriage, ("spiritual," of course,) at which Eliza, father, mother, and all the family, felt very indignant. The reverend gentleman almost insisted on the fam-

[23]William Hillhouse, age 46, John Hillhouse, age 22, and eight members of their family came to Utah in 1856 with the second handcart company. When John's family attempted to flee the next spring, "a posse of seven mounted Danites started rapidly in pursuit" and "drew down upon them with drawn revolvers and commanded them to retrace their footsteps under penalty of instant death." The posse arrested John, probably for failure to pay a debt to the church's emigration fund. Jeannette Hillhouse refused to return, saying her family "had starved while there for want of work." She pressed on with two children, Jesse, a toddler, and three-year-old William A., and set up a successful "dressmaking establishment" in Plattsmouth, Nebraska, where her husband found her more than two years later. See "Story of the Hillhouse Family," in Hollibaugh, *Biographical History of Cloud County, Kansas*, 539–45.

[24]John Ashcroft traveled to Utah in 1856 with Philemon C. Merrill's wagon train and was probably a defecting Mormon. The presence of Utah escapees such as the Hillhouses in the Dukes train supports the conclusion that fleeing Mormons were among the nameless dead at Mountain Meadows.

ily wintering at that place, but Mr. Davis thought that he would go as far as San Bernardino any way. The Bishop told Davis not to join the Missouri train that was then coming up, because the Mormons were all down on the Missourians; and he anticipated trouble would ensue between them and the Indians before they left the Territory; but if he could not better [betray] himself, he would give him information how to escape trouble: If he would drop the two hind-most bows of his wagon, he would vouch for his safety; that the Indians would not hurt the first hair of his head! However, Mr. Davis joined Captain Dukes company, without paying much heed to the advice which he had received; and shared in the perils and dangers which followed; which you have already published in the statement of Mr. Honea.

The first division of this company arrived in San Bernardino on the 31st of October, consisting of seventy-one souls altogether: twenty-two men, seventeen women, and thirty-two children; all enjoying good health. The second division of this train, under the supervision of Captain Nicholas Turner, is expected to arrive in the course of five or six days.

Having seen an article in the last issue of the Star, over the signature of Ellis Eames, to J. Ward Christian, giving a list of the names of the gentlemen who so liberally subscribed provisions, groceries, &c., for the relief of the suffering emigrants on the plains, I will say, for the benefit of those gentlemen who sent provisions to the emigrants, by Mr. Phineas Daley, that on his arrival at the first camp of the emigrants, he distributed a small portion of his load to the sufferers on the same terms as Messrs Van Luvan, J. H. Brooks, and P. Brown did theirs, namely "gratis." But Daley and his companions proceeded to the second encampment, where the provisions were most needed and passed themselves off as Anti-Mormons; and said that Van Luvan had sold all his load to the first camp (which was a lie.) Daley sold flour at eight cents per pound; coffee, twenty cents; sugar, twenty cents, tobacco, thirty-seven and a half cents per plug; and Spanish beef, which they killed on the Mohave, at eight cents; and some of the articles were not distributed on any terms. Respectfully yours, HENRY MOGRIDGE.

The *Star*'s eyewitness reports from southern Utah travelers ended with William Webb's sworn statement of 2 November 1857.

I arrived in San Bernardino, Oct. 17th, 1857. I was a member of Captains Dukes and Turner's train and in company with eight others left said train about 275 miles from San Bernardino, and traveled on foot to that city. We came in this way, because the train was not able to furnish us with animals to ride, and were nearly out of provisions, having been robbed of all their cattle, except those which were too lame to be run off, or too feeble to be driven by the robbers.

On leaving the train, we were told by the Captains and the company that on arriving in San Bernardino, we must say nothing against the Mormons, as that city was composed of Mormons, and that we must not excite them, as they might cut them all off before they could get in, and also fail to get them to forward supplies to keep the company alive. Immediately on arriving in the city, we were surrounded by the Mormons and taken to a corral, and they there commenced questioning us. Ellis Eames asked the questions, and J. Ward Christian done the writing. We had not been offered anything to eat, although we had had but one scanty meal for four days. They subjected us to an examination for several hours. The emigrants were not all together during the examination of this day. After they had got through questioning us, they asked myself and Mr. Baise to sign what they had written. J. Ward Christian read the document, and we affixed our names thereto. I have read the statement published in the Los Angeles Star of October 31st, 1857, over my signature, Messrs Baise, Bledsoe, Tannehill, and say, that I never signed that statement; that the statement read to me by Christian and which I signed without reading it myself, was altogether different from the published statement which is unqualifiedly false.

I have read the statement made by Mr. Honea, who came in with us, which was published in the Los Angeles Star of October 27, 1857, and that statement is true and not exaggerated.

I have no hesitation in saying, that from my knowledge and belief, the late horrible massacre and robberies, perpetrated upon emigrant trains in Utah Territory, were committed by the Mormons and Indians under Mormon influence.

WILLIAM WEBB

Despite efforts to control the flow of information that extended to forgery, the reports of southern Utah travelers published less than two months after the murders at Mountain Meadows left little doubt in the minds of most Americans about what had happened and who was responsible. Nonetheless, the treachery involved in the actual atrocity remained a guarded secret.[25]

JOHN D. LEE: BLOOD WAS IN THEIR PATH

According to John D. Lee, Brigham Young ordered him to tell no one else about the massacre and, as Indian farmer to the Southern Paiutes, to send a

[25]The newspaper reports in this chapter are not a comprehensive review of California press coverage. For other accounts, see: "The Emigrant Massacre," San Francisco Herald, 15 October 1857, 2/2; "Horrorosa Carnicerial" and Editorial, Los Angeles El Clamor Publico, 17 October 1857, 1/1, 2/1; "The Late Outrages on the Plains—Another Account," Los Angeles Star, 31 October 1857, 2/1–2; "The Late Massacre on the Plains—Additional Particulars," Nevada Democrat, 4 November 1857, 2/2; "Arrival of the Salt Lake Mail" and "More Outrages," Los Angeles Star, 7 November 1857, 4/1; "Letter from San Bernardino," San Francisco Evening Bulletin, 12 November 1857, 2/3; "Affairs in Utah," Los Angeles Star, 14 November 1857, 2/1; "Public Meeting," Los Angeles Star, 12 December 1857.

LOOKING NORTH FROM THE 1990 MONUMENT
The massacre probably took place in the fields and brush divided by Highway 18
in the upper-right section of this 1996 Will Bagley photograph.

letter to him, blaming the Indians. Lee waited nearly two months before writing the fable designed to conceal Mormon involvement. His letter did not mention that he had reported the atrocity to Young on 29 September and seemed to suggest that he was reporting it for the first time. His and Apostle Woodruff's strikingly similar account became the accepted versions.

My Report under date May 11th 1857 relative to the Indians over whom I have charge as Farmer showed a friendly relation between them & the whites, which doubtless would would [*sic*] have continued to increase, had not the white man been the first aggressor? As was the case with Capt. Fanchers co. of Emigrants passing through to California, about the middle of Sept. last, on corn creek 15 ms. South of Filmore city. Milliard county. The co. there Poisoned the Meat of an ox which they gave the Pah vant Indians to Eat, causing 4 of them to Die immediately. Besides Poisoning a number more the co. also Poisoned the water where they Encamped, killing many of the cattle of the settlers; This unguided Policy planed in wickedness by this co. raised the Ire of ~~all the~~ the Indians, which soon spread through the southren Tribes fireing them up with revenge till Blood was in their Path & as the breach according to their tradition was a national one, consiquently any Portion of that Nation was liable to attone for that offense; about the 22nd of Sept Capt Fancher & co. fell victim to their wrath near Mountain Meadows, their cat[t]le & Horses Shot do[w]n in every direction their waggons & Property Mostly committed to the flames & had they been the only ones that Suffered we would have less cause of complaint. But the following co. of near the same size; had some of their men shot down near Beave[r] city & had it not been for the interposition of the citizens, at that Place, the whole co would have been Masacreed by the enraged Pahvants, from this Place they were protected by mil[i]tary fource by order of Col. W. H. Dame through the Territory besides providing the co with Interpreters to help them through to the loss vagus on the Mudy. Some 3 to 500 Indians attacked the co while traveling & drove off Several hundred head of cat[t]le, telling the co that if they fired a single gun that they would kill every soul; the Interpreters tried to regain the stock or a Portion of them by Presants but in vain—The Indians told them to mind their own buisiness or their lives would not be safe.[26]

Apparently feeling safe by the date of his letter, Lee added phony claims against the federal treasury for goods and services to the very Indians who took part in the atrocity, which appear to total $2,920. He submitted charges to Superintendent Young for W. H. Dame totaling $415, P. K. Smith for $300, Jacob Hamblin for $300, and Henry Barney for $200, for services allegedly provided to Chief Owanup at Parowan, the "Wms" and Moquecheses bands at Cedar City, the Tatsegobbitts band on the Santa Clara, and the Youngquickes band at Harmony. Lee added on $600 for "my services the last six months & for provisions clothing &c." He ended the report, "I am your humble servant" and signed it "Farmer to Pahute Indians."[27]

PEYTON Y. WELCH: THE BLOOD OF THE AMERICANS

In contrast to the accounts of evil emigrants rampaging through Utah Territory that were offered to explain away the Mountain Meadows massacre, contemporary reports of men such as Peyton Y. Welch who were actually on the scene deal in cold, hard facts. Brigham Young himself later claimed Apostle Charles C. Rich warned emigrants to avoid the southern road to California,

[26]Lee to Young, 20 November 1857. Brooks, *The Mountain Meadows Massacre*, 151n11, published a transcription of this letter taken from a copy at the Huntington Library that had been prepared for the Lee trials. It closely matches our transcription of the original but gave the total charges as $2,220.

[27]Even more audacious was the compilation of these accounts in January 1858, when Superintendent Young billed the government for $3,527.43 in expenses paid to "Dr." Levi Stewart for purportedly distributing goods at Mountain Meadows on 30 September 1857. Lee and Dimick Huntington certified "on honor" they were present when the goods were delivered to Tat-se-gobbits, Non-cap-in, Mo-quee-tus, Chickeroo, Quo-na-rah, Young-quick, Jackson, and Agra-ootes and their bands. See "Accounts of Brigham Young," 1862, 100–102.

but Welch reveals why such advice would have been laughable in 1857, since Mormon-inspired Indian attacks on American travelers were already under way on the northern road to California. In a letter written only six weeks after the Mountain Meadows massacre, while still struggling across the Mojave Desert, Welch grimly reported he and his companions were "bound to travel or perish" and knew how narrowly they had escaped the fate that befell the Fancher train. "All this time," he observed, "the Mormons were working our ruin."

"MORE TRAINS DESTROYED BY THE MORMONS AND INDIANS," HORNELLSVILLE, NEW YORK, *TRIBUNE*, 21 JANUARY 1858.

Correspondence of the Missouri Expositor, Jan. 5.

Mohalia, California, Oct. 26, 1857.

We left Fort Bridger for Salt Lake City, as the news there was that Gen. Harney was on his way with a considerable force, in order to enforce the laws among the Mormons. We met Mormon soldiers every day, who showed us no favors, as they considered us Americans, and did not pretend to make any secret of the fact that their object was to intercept the United States troops.

Intelligence reached us that it would be dangerous to travel the Northern route, as the Indians had stopped it up, and had already killed several trains; and two trains had already turned off and taken the Southern route, and were but a few days ahead of us. As our train consisted of families moving, we concluded to incur as little danger as possible, and accordingly followed after. We had not traveled more than one hundred and fifty miles, when we were informed that the Indians were hostile on this route also. Our train had divided on account of scarcity of grass. We now came to Corn Creek, where we found the Indians very ill disposed toward us, and were informed that the Indians and Mormons together had stopped the trains ahead of us and killed a number of persons belonging to them.

We then left Corn Creek for Indian Creek, at which place the other part of our train joined us, but set out immediately for another camp, a Mormon settlement, about seven miles distant. We concluded to stay another day here, as grass was plenty.—Late in the evening we heard Indians, and later at night saw the lights from their fires. Still we thought of no danger, although they had told us that they intended to have the blood of the Americans.

We are now satisfied that the Mormons had hired the Indians to help them fight the Americans. We numbered seven wagons and twelve men, and about eight or nine o'clock the Indians made their attack on both sides. We drove them off in a few moments by wounding one of their men. About this time we saw eight men on horseback, who proved to be Capt. Luke's [Dukes's] company.

About dark the Mormons had gone to the other company and told them that the Indians were going to break up our company. That night four Mormons and four Americans came up to let us know what was going on. They told us that we must leave our camp that night, or we would all be destroyed before morning. It was now 10 o'clock, and we had to go to the other camp that night. But all this time the Mormons were working our ruin. We had not gone more than half way when the Indians commenced firing on us, but the Mormons refused to let us return the fire, although our boys were keen to fight them, and we thought *they* knew best what to do. There was no one hurt, though we lost some cattle and had holes shot in our wagons.

We now prepared to defend ourselves as best we could. In the morning, three Indians and the Bishop of that place came to our camp and called for a treaty. After breakfast Capt. Turner (formerly of Johnson County, Mo.,) Mr. Collins of Arkansas, and Capt. Luke of Missouri, went into the Mormon village, and, while in conversation with the Bishop, were attacked by some eight or ten Indians. Capt. Turner was shot through just above the hip; Collins was shot through the muscle of the arm, and Capt. Luke's belt was cut about two inches without any injury to his person. Capt. Turner called to the Bishop for protection, but the Bishop told him that he could not protect them. They then, after an ineffectual effort to get into one Mormon house, succeeded in getting into another, and put the inmates out of doors.—The Indians dared not attack them in the house, as they still had their pistols. They then offered a reward of $100 to any one who would let us at the camp know of their situation, but no one would do it.

The Bishop started a man for soldiers, and our men desired them to come by the camp and tell ten men to come to their relief, but, instead of doing as he was desired, he came to camp and reported that the Captain said not one of us should leave camp. In the course of three or four hours our wounded men came in.

We now numbered twenty-three wagons, and in a few days, after having hired some men to go with us and tell the Indians that we desired to go through the country peaceably, started out again. We traveled on without any loss, except what we gave away, until we got to Muddy, where we found about three hundred warriors. We gave them six beeves. Here was where they had killed the last of the train that was ahead of us.[28] One man said he had helped to bury sixty persons—men, women and children—all in on[e] grave.

We left the Muddy about 4 o'clock, in the evening, and traveled over the desert till 9 o'clock at night. We had about 440 head of loose stock in front of our train.—Our interpreter had told us that the Indians were not all at

---

[28]Welch confirmed reports that the last of the three Fancher party messengers sent to California died at the Muddy River, about fifty miles east of Las Vegas.

Muddy, and the moon had just begun to shine over the tops of the mountain when the yell of the savages was heard. The men all left the cattle and made for the wagons. There were about 400 Indians in this charge.

As the moon shone brightly on the desert they were easily seen. I mounted one of the mules which were at hand, and called for men for pursuit. Hays, Cooper and myself, of Lafayette County, Missouri, and five other men, were all I could get.—We made a charge on them, and drove them from the first lot. We were about to make a second charge, when our interpreters told us that we could get them back, if we would not fight them. We did not know at that time that four of our Mormons had already joined the Indians, and in a few minutes the last one of them had deserted us, although they had contracted to go one hundred miles further with us.

We lost at this place three hundred and thirty head of our best cattle, two mules and three horses. My loss about $3,000. We were now on a fifty-mile desert, and bound to travel or perish. Our teams were weak, and we had no fresh ones to put in, and consequently were compelled to leave wagons every few days.

Peyton Y. Welch.

Chapter 6

"Only Goin' over Home"
Not One Left to Tell the Story

The massacre at Mountain Meadows was an especially horrific act because it was so intimate. White men disguised as Indians, and perhaps a few Paiutes, struck down unarmed and helpless men, women, and children at close quarters. It is hard work to kill even an unarmed victim. At least fifty of those killed without mercy were children, more than twenty of them girls between the ages of 7 and 17.

Efforts to conceal a crime of such enormity began the day after the atrocity. The morning after the massacre, some seventy men met in a prayer circle at Mountain Meadows and gave solemn thanks to God that He had delivered their enemies into their hands. Then with their right arms raised to the square, they swore to keep their crime secret, to help kill anyone who broke this oath, and always to claim that the Indians alone did it. That this deceit held up as long as it did speaks for the silence of the perpetrators, the lack of an effective investigation, and the manipulation of the justice system in Utah Territory.

That the initial account was a fabrication is now apparent from its appearance in the same form at widely separated locations so soon after the atrocity. It took longer to reach Los Angeles because it had farther to travel, but it arrived as a detailed repeat of the same story that went to Salt Lake. This version put the full blame on the Indians while taking pains to justify their motives. The emigrants had provoked the attack by poisoning the Pahvant Indians at Corn Creek, more than a hundred miles north of the murder scene. As white involvement became known, tales of emigrant mistreatment of settlers along the trail were added. The accounts, then and now, portray the Indians and white settlers as the real victims. The Arkansans had not come to Utah simply to pass through on their way to California: they came to persecute the people and poison the Indians, and they got what they deserved. But the dead could not defend themselves.

George A. Smith: The Water Was Also Poisoned

If anyone knew the whole truth about what happened at Mountain Meadows, George A. Smith did. On the day the doomed train arrived in Salt Lake Valley, the portly apostle jumped off on his hasty tour of settlements in the south, where he gave verbal "instructions" to the local leaders who carried out the killing. He and Jacob Hamblin delivered the Southern Paiute chiefs to meetings with Brigham Young. Less than a year later, he discussed the massacre with Hamblin, who lived at Mountain Meadows and was not bound by a secrecy oath. While knowing the truth, Smith became a key figure in a disinformation campaign to hide Mormon involvement and blame the victims, Indians, and federal officials from President Buchanan to U.S. Indian agent Garland Hurt, a known Indian friend. His stories grew so outrageous that they speak for themselves, but he continued to spread them until he died in 1875.

George A. Smith to John Lyman, 6 January 1858, lds Archives.
As you are aware the Emigrants have made a business of shooting down the Indians of the Desert for many years. The same game was carried on this season by a Company from Arkansas; [on] the Santa Clara. Indians gathered and surrounded the Company and fought them for several days. It is rumored that one hundred of the Company were killed, the loss of the Indians is unknown, but must have been considerable, as the company fortified themselves with their Wagons, and made a Spirited defence. Wm. M. Wall who has just returned from Australia, passed over the ground where the engagement occurred, says if he had had command of the emigrant party he believes he could have whipt one thousand Indians. It was a terrible vengeance, and the first time they have ever taken such a step. It has rendered the greatest caution necessary even for our people to pass through their country, notwithstanding we have always treated them with the greatest kindness. The Indians spared the lives of the children, which have since been ransomed, and cared for by some of the Southern settlers, who speak the Indian language . . .

Smith to T. B. H. Stenhouse, 15 April 1859, lds Archives, 764–65.
. . . Many of the Indians gradualy became provided with rifles and other fire arms in addition to their bows and arrows (which with their poisoned

points are dangerous weapons). The party of Emigrants who were destroyed had about twenty wagons and a considerable amount of stock, they manifested a very singular hostility to the natives.

When encamped at the sinks of corn [sic] Creek they gave an ox which had died to a party of Indians they eat of it and ten of them died immediately. Some of the survivors said they saw the Captain of the company go to the carcass with a bottle after the main body of the camp had left the ground, the water was also poisoned so that several animals died from drinking of it.

The Indians poisoned were members of different bands of the "Pah Utahs" and "Pah Edes" who were up from the south on a visit to their friends the "Pahvantes".

The news of this tragedy spread through the different bands of Indians for hundreds of miles, and caused the concentration of reckless warriors who consumated the Massacre.

News of the attack of the Indians upon the emigrants, reaching the settlements; some interpreters repaired to the spot to effect a compromise. Some of the Indians had been wounded and others killed, and the whole emigrant party were closely invested, and all communication with them cut off the interpreters were prohibited from having any intercourse with them.

The Indians manifested considerable hostility towards them because they (the interpreters) were unwilling to assist them.

Finding that they were unable to render the emigrants any assistance, they returned to Cedar City, about fifty miles.

A party of about sixty volunteers were raised and repaired as speedily as possible to the spot, but Alas, too late to afford any other assistance than to rescue a few Children that had been preserved by the Indians, in accordance with their usual custom for the purchases of trade or slavery.

Whenever a fair and impartial investigation of this bloody Massacre is had, the establishment of the above facts will doubtless [be] the result.

G. A. Smith

THOMAS L. KANE: THEN THEY GOT SO MAD

Thomas L. Kane of Philadelphia was an influential and tireless Mormon friend who came to Utah via Los Angeles in February 1858 with a verbal offer from President Buchanan to settle the armed confrontation between the Great Basin theocracy and the United States without bloodshed. The self-appointed peacemaker finished his work in March and headed back to Pennsylvania. At Corn Creek, he apparently questioned Kanosh, the Mormon chief

of the Pahvant band, who owed his position to Brigham Young and faithfully repeated the official version of the events that led to the massacre.

Kane's account of the interview appears to be a memorandum composed
later that year, not an actual diary entry. If the document is fragmentary and
extremely difficult to read, it is important because it appears to explain what
Kane knew about the massacre and why he believed the Mormons' story.

Diary of Colonel Thomas L. Kane.

Kenosh Chief of Parvans near the sink of Corn Cr. This Company camped
at a kind of spring there. The Indians came in as usual [two words illegible]
to by and [sell?] [5 lines illegible]

they understood [two words illegible] The Indians went away they did not
want any fuss with them! they was careful about the [?] mules above, sold their

After the Camp had moved off they [the Pahvants?] went into the Camp
ground to move off. After the Indians had come into the Camp they noticed
a white like flour upon the grass and the Mormon cattle & the Indian cattle
was running around and they noticed one critter went off a little and died
right off. The Indians went to work & skinned this critter. One load[ed?] it
on his shoulder & took it up to Camp and it nearly killed him. One or two
of the Indians got thirsty and stooped down to drink at this Spr[in]g where
the Emigrants got their water and drank and one died and a number more
came very near dying. And ~~others~~ The friends of the man who died set up a
howl and followed them that night. Kenosh tried not to have them follow
them but he [cou]ld not prevent them.[1] They followed them that night shot
at their camp wounded one man & stole four head of cattle.[2] One of the
Emigrants on guard Supposing he shot an Indian killed his own mate. The
Parvans Indians passed this word on to the Pah éats in whose country is where
the Mountain Meadows are. It is about a hundred miles to the Mountain
Meadows from Corn Creek and there the Paheats boxed them again.

By law they [?] Indians wanted pay for their travelling through the country burning their wood wasting their grass &c. They killed a beef for them
but must have poisoned it. For four men and a number of women & children
(the number I don't remember[?] of them) died of eating that beef. That is
all I got from Kenosh. Then they got so mad! They passed the word around
[?] & gathered all together and used them up

The bands of the Paheats was there was

    Quanãras band

    Younggwitche's

    Tâts â gûbbét's

---

[1] Kanosh left for Salt Lake with George A. Smith and Jacob Hamblin after camping with the Fancher
party on 25 August 1857. It is unlikely that he was at Corn Creek as claimed.

[2] A possible reference to the Dukes train at Beaver.

(These were of the Paheats.)

Besides there were Indians from the Mõah pãh (Spirit Water) where the spirits of the dead go to to [two words illegible] and stay. (Indian for Sta Clara[3]) and the Rio Virgin whom Col K [?] has news of.

THE MORMONS CHEATED THEIR SAVAGE ALLIES

As noted, on 27 September 1857, Indian Agent Garland Hurt, the last non-Mormon federal officer in Utah, successfully evaded Brigham Young's orders to arrest him, vowing to escape or "die in the attempt." His Ute allies helped him do just that. By mid-November, he had found the U.S. army, and within days other government authorities had received the first accurate reports about who was responsible for the massacre at Mountain Meadows.[4]

A host of ink-stained wretches occupied a fair number of the shanties that made up the ramshackle civilian settlement dubbed Eckelsville near the Army of Utah's winter quarters at Camp Scott, but none of them were as widely published as James W. Simonton, a founder of the *New-York Times*. Writing as "S.," Simonton sent identical dispatches to both the *Times* and the *Evening Bulletin* of San Francisco throughout the spring and summer of 1858. Later that year he served as editor and half-owner of the *Bulletin*. Simonton returned briefly to the *Times* before going to work as the Associated Press general manager in New York, a job he held until 1881.[5] If Mormon leaders in Great Salt Lake City remained uninformed about what had happened at Mountain Meadows, they would have been well advised to read the stories Simonton filed based on the intelligence that Indian Agent Garland Hurt had collected the previous fall.

SIMONTON, CAMP SCOTT, 12 JUNE 1858,
"INTERESTING FROM UTAH," *NEW YORK TIMES*, 8 JULY 1858.

From all the information collected here by Dr. Hurt, the excellent and intelligent Indian agent, it does not seem probable that any large body of the Indians of Utah will, in any event, join the Mormons in offensive demonstrations against the United States Army, although there are a few bands which are and long have been under Brigham Young's control, doing his bloody work for him upon offending gentiles or apostate Saints, whenever it was desirable to transfer the responsibility of demoniac deeds to the savages, of whom little better

---

[3]Tonaquint was the Paiute name for the Santa Clara. Kane probably referred to the Moapits band that lived on the Muddy River in today's Nevada.

[4]Hurt to Forney, 4 December 1857, *The Utah Expedition*, House Doc. 71, Serial 956, 199–205.

[5]MacKinnon, "Epilogue to the Utah War," 224–25.

things could be expected . . . [Simonton next claimed the Utes provided "ample" evidence that Mormons helped instigate the Gunnison massacre, where Pahvant warriors killed the U.S. Army captain in October 1853.] It is also clearly established that it was this band which, under Mormon instigation, attacked several of the smaller parties of the Arkansas emigration last Fall, not long prior to the Mountain Meadow Massacre. This massacre was perpetrated by the Piades, or Santa Clara's, under Mormon Leaders. Your readers will remember the case—one in which one hundred and fourteen men, women, and children, were butchered almost before they had time to see their assailants.

A trusty Indian spy, who was sent down among the Piedes to ascertain the facts, reported that they expressed deep regret for this act, and said they never would have perpetrated the outrage, except for the counsel and exhortations of John D. Lee, President of the Mormon Stake at Cedar City, Iron County. Lee came to them, they said, told them that the Americans "always killed Indians whenever they saw them, and advised them, Therefore, to go and kill them." He stated, also, that the Americans killed Mormons, (this was not long after Parley P. Pratt was killed,) and therefore that they didn't like them either. The Indians expressed the fear that they were not strong enough to attack the large emigrant party with safety. Lee replied, that if they would undertake it, the Mormons would help them—a promise which they fulfilled by furnishing a party of Danites to lead the fray and make it horribly successful. Lee also told the Indians that they should have all the plunder, including the blankets and cattle, except the wagons, which the Mormons wanted for themselves. After the massacre, the Mormons cheated their savage allies, and appropriated the cattle also, which came near creating a row between them at the time, and left the Indians in no amiable mood toward their saintly employers, who left them with all the responsibility and scarcely any of the spoil. It was this bit of bad faith, probably, which made the Indians so ready to expose their prompters in the evil deed.

John A. Ray: The Emigrants Poisoned the Water

One of the more creative tales of emigrant wrongdoing was composed by John A. Ray of Fillmore and later quoted by Brigham H. Roberts in his *Comprehensive History of The Church*. Ray did not witness the events he described because he was not on hand when they supposedly took place.[6] After working for U.S. Indian agent Garland Hurt as an Indian farmer at Corn Creek, near Fillmore, he was called on a mission to Europe in 1855 and did not return until after January 1858. Taking the Spanish Trail from Los Angeles, Ray passed

---

[6]According to George A. Smith, Ray was in Europe when the Fanchers passed Fillmore. See Smith to Young, 17 August 1858, in Brooks, *The Mountain Meadows Massacre*, 254–55; and Roberts, *A Comprehensive History of The Church*, 4:143.

over Mountain Meadows on his way home, more than four months after the massacre. In 1859 he became bishop at Fillmore, succeeding Lewis Brunson, who was ordained in 1853.

Ray hastily wrote his account of the Arkansas company and their fate at the request of Albert Carrington, editor of the church-owned *Deseret News*, for James Ferguson and Seth M. Blair, who had founded *The Mountaineer* along with Hosea Stout as an "independent" newspaper to defend the Mormon cause against the new opposition sheet, *The Valley Tan.*

RAY TO *THE MOUNTAINEER*, 4 DECEMBER 1859,
UNPROCESSED ITEM, LDS ARCHIVES.

Fillmore City Dec 4th [18]59
Millard Cty U.T.

Gentlemen permit me through the columns of your paper to make a few statements concerning relative to the company that was Masacreed [*sic*] at "Mountain Meadows"

I find from perusing the States papers that blame is attached to the Latter-day Saints as a people because a company of Emigrants were Massacreed in the fall of fifty seven by the Indians who were probably aided by a few white-men. With much greater propriety the people of Nicuragua [*sic*] might charge the people of the United States with the murder of those slain by Walker in his military excursions in that Land for there were individuals in all parts of the Union that aided Walker & his band by their influence & contributions.[7] But not so with the Latterday Saints. They not only did not aid in the Massacre but were ignorant of the fact that such a thing was contemplated either by Indians or whitemen.

The blood stained soil of almost every state & Territory in the Union bears testamony that hundreds of incidents of a similar character have occured within their borders and that the citizens of such the states and Territories in which such scenes have been inacted [*sic*] might with equal propriety be charged with crime.

The company that were slain at "Mountain Meadows" brought destruction upon themselves by their own reckless conduct. While passing through the Territory upon their arrival at Fillmore they stoped near the State House block, & upon so some of our citizens passed by [and] they hailed them & inquired how far it was to any houses. And After a few such taunts had passed angry feelings arose between the parties upon which the emigrants then in a crowing & insulting maner inquired whether there were any men in the place and if their were let them come out & they were ready to fight them & able

---

[7]Walker was William Walker, "the gray-eyed man of destiny," a filibuster who seized Nicaragua in 1855 and ruled briefly before being executed in 1860 in Honduras.

to kill them. At the same time damming the "Mormons" in such a most wicked maner connecting the name of Deity with all their oaths. They also stated that [the] Government had sent Troops to kill every G— damed Mormon in Utah— they hoped they would do so & that they should like to help them do the job. From Fillmore they passed on to Meadow Creek Settlement where at the time some four or five families resided. There they acted more insolintly than at Fillmore. Upon being told by the citizens that they had no wheat to sell at their own prices when told they had none to spare upon which they armed themselves & advanced in a body upon the few citizens being at that settlement both parties in a threatening menacing maner cursing the Mormons & threatening them with the troops as at Fillmore. The few citizens that were there armed themselves & prevented the contemplated robery. From Meadow Creek they passed on to corn creek & incamped near the Indian Farm where they most likely did that which led to their destruction.

Contrary to law they induced the Indians to sell to them their grain & cattle purchased by the Government and purchased at half its value leaving the Indians to Starve or beg of the citizens as they did before the wise provision of Government supplied their wants. During their stay at Corn Creek one of their Oxen died, and as usual the Indians gathered around & skinned it. Immediately after it was skinned one of the Emigrant Company was observed by an Indian to go to the skinned animal & Sprinkle something white on it. The Indians not suspecting evil carried the meat to their encampments some carrying [it] on their backs & others on horse back. When the meat came in contact with the skin of the Indian or the horse it immediately broke out swelled & soon broke out in bad sores. All the Indians who ate of the meat were made very sick & one Squaw died supposed to have died from the poison thus taken. Immediately after the departure of the company from Corn Creek our cattle commenced dying in an unusual manner. some were observed to go to water drink & in a few moments fall dead. About twenty head of cattle died in the vicinity of their camp in less time than a week. I had two valuable Oxen to dye some three or four days after the company made their exit from Corn Creek. We succeeded in getting one of them home to Fillmore before he died. He was fat & [was processed?] for the Tallow. While rendering up the Tallow my wife cut her finger hand which immediately inflame[d] & swelled to the body. The finger flesh around where it was cut turned black & we had to employ costic [caustic] to separate the decayed from the sound flesh. She was very sick for a week from its effects. Joseph Robison a citizen of Fillmore also had an Ox to die about the time that mine did. One of his sons a youth of 15 years of age while skinning it scratched a small sore that was on his nose. It immediately commenced swelling & inlarged [sic] his head to an enormous size his whole head. He dyed [sic] on the fourth day from the effects of the poison thus taken into his system. Which was given to our cattle at Corn Creek near where the company had incamped. At Corn Creek there were a number of small pools of standing water. In the vicinity of these pools of water most of our cattle dyed & there is no doubt upon my mind but that the Emigrants poisoned the water & caused this death. About that time if the citizens had arrisen inmass [sic] & went to the company ferretted [sic] out demanded and executed the guilty sparing the innocent they would have done right. But this they could not do. As a company they were numerous strong and well armed & repeatedly made their boast that they were ready for a fight. Besides the masses At that time many of the community were paralyzed & hardly dare say that their Homes were their own. A large company of well armed Emigrants were passing a few small isolated settlement, threatening them with death & destruction while Bucanans [sic] Hell Houns [sic] were marching into our Territory from the East threatening to visit us with destruction upon their arrival.

The past History of the dealing of Mobs with us as a people whether voluntary or sent against us clothed with Government authority proved it was sufficient evidence that we had cause to be excited alarmed.

Some were excited and if while under the influence of the excitement of the times they should did unite with Indians & massacre a company that were continually Taunting them & rejoicing at the prospect of soon seeing us destroyed & our homes made a desolation, I should say that they thought they committed a great wrong for which they should be punished yet they are not guilty of murder as contemplated & defined in our statutes no more than our Troop[s] are guilty of murder when they attack an Indian settlement & make an indiscrimanate slaughter of men women & children. It is always to be regretted that the innocent should suffer with the guilty. But it has doubtless happened in this case as in a thousand others. And now the deed is done we should calmly consider all the circumstances & administer Justice and mercy to those whether red or white who are so unfortunate as to have participated in the Mountain Meadows Massacre.

The statement made in this communication relative to the conduct of the company can be substantiated.

J. A. Ray

NOTHING COVERED THAT SHALL NOT BE REVEALED

When Congress in 1850 rejected Mormon appeals for statehood and created instead a territory, Brigham Young reportedly said, "If they send a governor here, he will be glad to black my boots for me."[8] President Millard Fill-

[8]Bigler, *A Winter with the Mormons*, 50.

more spared other appointees such humiliation by naming Young himself to a four-year term as Utah's first governor, a title he held until 1857 for lack of a replacement.

The Mormon theocracy's submission to federal authority in March 1858 brought fulfillment of Young's earlier prediction. President Buchanan's choice for governor, Alfred Cumming, found himself no more able to govern the Mormon people than had the governors of Missouri and Illinois years before. From the first, the former Atlanta mayor adopted a peace-at-any-price policy. To the frustration of family members of the murdered emigrants and federal lawmakers, and to the contempt of western newspapers, Young's successor blocked any investigation.

Since "dead men tell no tales," Cumming found it easy to accept the counterfeit stories offered in convincing detail. Nor was he interested in investigating reported murders of other emigrants or apostates committed in 1857. Like others before him, he may have believed the false testimony and denials because they came from members of a religious body. But others were not as generous.

"Extract from a letter [from] Carroll Co.,"
Arkansas State Gazette and Democrat, 18 February 1858, 2/2.

Carroll co., Jan. 5 1858.

We have had a beautiful Christmas and New Year, and I think will have a warm winter. We have rather melancholy news from the Plains. Some of our best citizens murdered—at least supposed to be. Mr. Jno. T. Baker, son and daughter, and son-in-law; C. R. Mitchell, Joel Mitchell, sons of Gen. Wm. C. Mitchell; with several others known to be with the train. We get this news from a California paper, which states that the company was headed by a man familiarly known as "Uncle Jack of Crooked Creek, Carroll co., Ark."[9] If this be true, we have lost some of our best citizens, as Mr. Baker was one of that class. He was a warm friend and a bitter enemy; was possessed of good property, land, Negroes, &c. He started with a drove of cattle, intending to return and move to California, if he liked the country; he leaves a wife and several children in this county. What will the Government do with these Mormons and Indians? Will it not send out enough men to hang all the scoundrels and thieves at once, and give them the same play they give our women and children?

---

[9]This sentence appeared in "More Outrages on the Plains!" *Los Angeles Star*, 24 October 1857, 2: "The train which has been so cruelly massacred, was under the charge of Captain Baker, familiarly known as 'Uncle Jack,' from Carroll county Arkansas."

"PUBLIC MEETING OF THE PEOPLE OF CARROLL COUNTY,"
ARKANSAS STATE GAZETTE AND DEMOCRAT, 27 FEBRUARY 1858, 3:1.

PUBLIC MEETING OF THE PEOPLE OF CARROLL COUNTY.—At a public meeting of the citizens of Carroll county, held in Carrollton, on the 1st day of February, 1858, in pursuance of public notice, the following proceeding were had:

On motion, John Crump, Esq. was called on and unanimously selected to act as president of the meeting, and John Haggin was appointed secretary.

On motion, it was determined that the president should appoint a committee of three to draft suitable resolutions for the occasion, and such as would be expressive of the feelings and sense of the meeting.

Thereupon, the following named gentlemen were appointed such committee, to wit: Bryce Byrne, W. W. Watkins and John Haggin. The committee after deliberating and considering of their duty, reported the following preamble and resolutions which were unanimously concurred in and adopted:

WHEREAS, The painful intelligence has reached us that, in July last, an emigrant train with 130 persons from Arkansas was attacked by the Mormons and Santa Clara tribe of Indians near the rim of the Great Basin, and about fifty miles from Cedar City, in Utah Territory, and that all of the emigrants, with the exception of 15 children, were then and there massacred and murdered—that the children thus saved from the dreadful fate of their parents and the rest of their company were delivered over to the custody of the Mormons of Cedar city; and that among those who were with the said train at the time of the massacre were John T. Baker and sons, George and Able, Charles and Joel Mitchell, sons of Col. Wm. C. Mitchell, of Marion county, Allen Derhazo, George Baker's wife and four children, Charles Mitchell's wife and child, Milam Jones and his brother, and his mother-in-law and family, Pleasant Tacket and family, Alexander Fancher and family, Wm. Cameron and family, widow Huff (whose husband, Peter Huff, died after they had started on the route) and some others—all of whom were our neighbors, friends and acquaintances, and their families, and the same persons who constituted the company that left Carroll county in April last, for California, and which was known as Baker's company. And whereas it appears from many other instances of atrocity and crime which could be recited, that the Mormons are instigating the Indians to hostilities against our citizens, and are and have been as a community, systematically engaged in the infamous work of robbing and murdering peaceful wayfarers and emigrants and resisting the authority and laws of the United States—and in short of rebellion and treason against the general government; therefore be it

Resolved: That we, the people of Carroll county, feeling deeply aggrieved in consequence of the many and continued outrages committed upon the persons and property of our citizens, by the Mormons and Indians, acting under their instigation, and especially on account of the loss of such a number of our most estimable citizens, countrymen and friends, and their wives and children in the late massacre of an emigrant train near Cedar city, in Utah Territory, do hereby petition, and call upon the government of the United States to have thoroughly investigated the affair of said dreadful tragedy, and deal out retributive justice to the parties guilty of the monstrous deed.

Resolved, That as it appears from reliable information, there were spared and saved from destruction as many as fifteen infant children, in said massacre, that we hereby call on the general government for assistance and aid in rescuing said children from their captors, and restoring them to their relations and friends in Arkansas.

Resolved, That we request our representatives and senators in congress to use their influence and best exertions to have passed an act making an appropriation for the purpose of defraying the expenses which it may be necessary to incur in order to reclaim and bring home to their relations the children which were as aforesaid saved from the massacre.

Resolved, That we offer our condolence and sympathy to the distressed parents and immediate relations of the unfortunate adventurers who met on plains, as aforesaid, such a lamentable fate.

Resolved, That in our opinion the government should immediately adopt decisive measures for subduing the spirit of insubordination and treason, that is now rife amongst the Mormons, and to that end should call on Arkansas for volunteers, and that we, the people of Carroll county, hold ourselves ready to respond to any such call for volunteers, by tendering the services of at least four companies.

Resolved, That the True Democrat and the Gazette and Democrat, are hereby requested to publish the proceedings of this meeting.

A month later, the citizens of Newton County met in Jasper and held an indignation meeting that endorsed the resolutions passed in Carroll County. They expressed a similar sense of loss and outrage:

The painful intelligence has reached us that in July last, an emigrant train, with 130 persons, from Arkansas, known as Baker's train, was attacked by the Mormons and Santa Clara Indians, near the rim of the Great Basin, and about fifty miles from Cedar City, in Utah Territory, and that all the emigrants, except 15 children, were then and there inhumanly massacred—that the children, thus saved from the dreadful fate of their parent and company, were delivered over to the custody of the Mormons of Cedar City; and that among those who were with said train at the time of the massacre, were many of our most worthy, and much esteemed citizens from Carroll, Marion, Newton, and Johnson counties.

Individual resolutions called "on the general government for assistance in reclaiming said children from their captors, and restoring them to their friends in Arkansas" and offered "our heartfelt sympathy to the parents and relatives of those unfortunate emigrants, who, as above stated, met such a lamentable fate."[10]

William M. Gwin: The Blood of My Constituents

If Mormon leaders played Utah's new governor, Alfred Cumming, for a fool, few on the West Coast appeared to be deceived. The newly elected California governor John B. Weller warned on 8 January 1858 of the threat of "Mormons and Indians" to his state's lines of communication. "Hundreds of emigrants during the past year, who had abandoned their homes, and whilst wending their way over American soil to our shores, were inhumanly butchered," Weller said in his inaugural address. "Our people are certainly entitled to protection whilst traveling through American territory, and to secure this, the whole power of the federal government should be invoked."[11]

On the U.S. Senate floor, William M. Gwin of California took up the alarm to voice his state's interest in ensuring its immigration and protecting the lives of its future citizens. His call for an inquiry was opposed at first by Senator Sam Houston from Texas, a long-standing Mormon friend, but it would eventually bring an investigation by the U.S. Army.

"Massacre of Emigrants to California,"
The Congressional Globe, 18 March 1858, 1176–77.

Mr. GWIN. I offer the following resolution, and if there be no objection I should like to have it considered at the present time:

Resolved, That the Secretary of War be requested to communicate to the Senate what steps have been taken, if any, to punish the parties implicated in the massacre of one hundred and eighteen emigrants to California, at the Mountain Meadows, in the Territory of Utah.

There being no objection, the Senate proceeded to consider the resolution.

Mr. GWIN. I have not called attention to the subject-matter embraced in this inquiry before this for the reason that I had supposed that a military expedition would have been organized in California for the purpose of cooperating in Utah Territory with Colonel Johnston. When it is considered that a

---

[10]"Meeting in Newton County," *Arkansas State Gazette and Democrat*, 17 April 1858, 2/4.
[11]Inaugural Address, California Governor John B. Weller, 8 January 1858.

force composed of as fine a material as the world affords could have left California, and long before this could have traversed half their journey to Salt Lake City, it cannot be denied, if the Federal Government need additional troops in Utah, that my supposition had some foundation. Contrary to my own ideas and vote, the executive authority has been denied by Congress the increased military means which were asked; and hence it is now apparent that no large force can be sent from California to Utah.

I am afraid that in this we have committed a grave error. I am afraid that if the Federal arms should be resisted by misguided and rebellious men, the power and dignity of our country will not be vindicated by so imposing a force as the serious necessities of the case may require.

But, sir, I am induced by reasons peculiar to my position as Senator from California, to invite your attention to the incidents referred to in my resolution.

In September last, an emigrant train, composed of fifty-six men and sixty-two women and children, according to the best information that I can procure, were passing through Utah Territory, on their way to my own State. They were on our own soil, engaged in no unlawful pursuit; and yet, Mr. President, they were all murdered except a few children. I am unable to give to you the details of this horrid massacre, as they still remain shrouded in mystery. All that I can tell you, sir, is that one hundred and eighteen American citizens, including in this number sixty-two women and children, have been massacred without cause, and that as yet their blood is unavenged.

It is true, sir, that this outrage was not committed within the limits of California, or we, ourselves, without awaiting the tardy action of the Federal Government, would have sought and obtained a bloody vengeance; but the murdered victims had an intention to become Californians. They had left their homes in what you call the Far West, and, gathering their household goods, had taken up their march for our golden land of promise. Nay, sir, when they had reached the fatal Mountain Meadows, their longing eyes could almost behold the snow-covered peaks of our mountain ranges.

In all that constitutes unity of feeling and interest, they had become citizens of California, and as such, sir, as a Senator of that State, I am here to ask an account of the blood of my constituents.

As I before remarked, the details of this awful massacre are not known. There is no doubt that the various Indian tribes in the vicinity of the Mountain Meadows were the immediate agents in this butchery; and, sir, it is lamentable to say that, in the opinion of many well-advised parties, the Mormons themselves were their instigators and approvers. Upon this point no such positive evidence has been received as would justify me in asserting positively that they were guilty; and charity will gladly avail herself of any doubt which would hold our common nature to be free from so horrible a crime.

It is true, sir, that an intelligent and respectable meeting of citizens of Los

Angeles, after an examination into the facts, expressed their deliberate conviction that the Mormons were equally guilty with the Indians, and asked the interposition of the President.

But, sir, there is no doubt that the Indians are culpable, and whether their guilt be shared by the Mormons or not, still their responsibility is the same, and the exactions of vengeance against them are undiminished.

Mr. President, since the Americans commenced to travel over the plains, since our hunters and adventurous trappers penetrated the remote valleys and gorges of the vast country lying between the Mississippi and the Sierra Nevada, since the Indian tribes between the Oregon and Sonora lines first heard the American name, no such reverse, no such loss, has been inflicted on us as the destruction of these one hundred and eighteen emigrants. We are accustomed to pity the poor Mexicans along our frontier line who suffer from the fierce inroads of the Camanches and Apaches; but, sir, the sad history of their border warfare will show but few, if any, more mournful and disgraceful massacres than the one of which I am speaking.

The intelligence of this massacre has spread throughout the numerous Indian tribes. The impunity with which it was effected, and the richness of the plunder that rewarded it, will be incentive to similar acts. Heretofore, when American citizens traveled together, particularly in large numbers, no Indian tribe would dare to attack them, for fear of the vengeance of a Government represented to them as strong and warlike; but, sir, if this matter be permitted to go unavenged; if this reverse be unrepaired, our prestige is destroyed, and new and more frequent massacres will take place.

We are now opening up the center of this continent, we are crossing it with wagons roads and mail lines, and unless we crush these vile and savage tribes with a strong hand, we expose to dreadful massacres our citizens, invited to travel in these inhospitable regions by our own action.

I have before remarked that these emigrants were murdered without cause. There was a report, derived from the Mormons, that the emigrants had poisoned the Indians back at Corn creek; but investigation has proved this statement to be utterly unreliable, and I have no hesitation in stating my belief that it is a calumny on the unburied dead. Yes, sir, on the unburied dead! No Christian has ever extended the rites of sepulture to the bodies of these victims; and an American who traveled near there, in a Mormon train, a few days after, was informed, by Mormons living in the vicinity, that it would be unsafe to attempt their burial.

Therefore, sir, I ask that the Secretary of War may be charged to investigate this matter. If this be proved true, I hope that an expedition will be sent from southern California to inflict upon the guilty parties a vengeance so summary as to be talked of with terror in every wigwam in the great Salt Lake basin.

MR. HOUSTON. I think the resolution would be more perfect if it were to

require an inquiry to ascertain who did this act—to find out first who perpetrated the act. Before we punish them, I think we had better ascertain who
they were.

MR. GWIN. We know that our fellow-citizens were murdered. There is not
one left to tell the story.

MR. HOUSTON. Some persons killed them. The Mormons are suspected
of it. Some Indians must have been in the vicinity. Now, Indians frequently
go several hundred miles to start an expedition for the purpose of killing the
Indians resident near that place; and Indians from another quarter may come
there, and be inculpated and brought into jeopardy, while those who committed the crime escape. I think the inquiry would be more proper to ascertain who perpetrated the act, and not make war without any foundation.

MR. GWIN. It is well known that the Indians in the neighborhood had a
part of the spoils. That has been ascertained. They were implicated; they ought
to be punished, and every one to whom it can be traced. I have no doubt that
an expedition, if sent there, could soon ascertain the tribe of guilty Indians,
and the white persons, if any, who instigated it, as has been charged.

MR. HOUSTON. That would be very unsatisfactory evidence, because Indians traffic, as well as white people, and exchange commodities. The murderers may have stripped them, and in passing back may have disposed of the
articles to the tribes contiguous to where the massacre was perpetrated. I am
opposed to this indiscriminate warfare upon Indians, or Mormons, or any
other people, until their guilt is ascertained. I want the facts as to who perpetrated the crime ascertained, and then inflict punishment according to the
offense. But to imagine that somebody has done it, and therefore that some
one must be killed or massacred in retaliation, is not the way to retaliate; it
is the way to produce war by inflicting chastisement, as they call it, on people who have perpetrated no offense on the Government. That is the way our
Indian wars are kept up. The Treasury would be drained by hundreds of millions annually, if every occasion of an outrage were immediately to be redressed
by falling upon the first Indians upon our extended frontier that are suspected, or upon any tribe, because they had in their possession articles taken on
the occasion of a massacre.

A resolution requiring the Secretary to ascertain and to report the facts, I
should be glad to pass; and if it can be ascertained who were the perpetrators of the deed, inflict upon them a punishment commensurate with their
offense; but do not fall indiscriminately on the Indians who are at peace on
our borders, and thus provoke hereafter the massacre of perhaps ten for every
one that has fallen. We know that the Indians, if they can, never go unavenged
of injuries done to them, and you may attack an innocent tribe that had no
participancy in this transaction, and inflict on them a great wrong. Redress
on their part is the consequence, and other innocent persons have to fall vic-

tims to this indiscriminate mode of warfare that we are conducting on our frontier.

MR. GWIN. I did not think that a member of the Senate of the United States could be found who would object to punishing what we know has been one of the most outrageous massacres that has ever been committed in the country. What does the Senator propose? That we shall make inquiries; that is to say, send persons there to be murdered as these emigrants were. I ask that a force shall be sent there that shall punish these persons, and they will only punish them when it is ascertained who they are. That is what I propose. I want a force sent there of sufficient power to inflict the most condign and summary punishment on these murderers, who have massacred men, women, and children—American citizens—passing peacefully through the country, and then, after they are murdered and left unburied, bring forth a false accusation that they had attempted to poison the Indians, as some excuse!

It is a charge which has never been sustained by any testimony. All that I ask is that the murderers shall be punished. I do not want innocent Indian tribes attacked, and I do not expect they will be attacked. They have made this attack on American citizens. On nearly the only emigrant route now open to California this massacre has taken place. We hear a great deal of sympathy for the massacres of citizens by the Apaches and other tribes of Indians, but there is nothing like this atrocious deed in the history of our country. Not one of the whole party of one hundred and eighteen was left. They only spared a few children under five years of age, in order to make slaves of them; all the adults were murdered so that they should not have an opportunity to divulge who committed this terrible crime. I want force to be sent there to make the inquiry, and then to inflict punishment. That is all I ask.

The next day, Senator Houston withdrew his objection to Gwin's motion, since the resolution simply authorized an inquiry. The Senate resolved: "That the Secretary of War be requested to communicate to the Senate what steps have been taken, if any, to punish the parties implicated in the massacre of one hundred and eighteen emigrants to California, at the Mountain Meadows, in the Territory of Utah."[12]

LET THEIR BODIES EVER REMAIN SUSPENDED

While the Mormon "half-way house" favorably impressed many emigrants, others reported mistreatment and arbitrary lawsuits as they journeyed through Utah settlements. In the mid-fifties, California newspapers ran a number of

---

[12]"Massacre of California Emigrants," *Congressional Globe*, 19 March 1858, 1,187.

articles about Indian attacks on wagon trains, charging that they were incited by Mormon agents among the tribes. Even before the massacre, many Americans were ready to believe the worst about the religion. If some saw their coverage as unnecessarily inflammatory, it later proved to be remarkably accurate.

"THE FEDERAL GOVERNMENT AND UTAH,"
LOS ANGELES *SOUTHERN VINEYARD*, 29 MAY 1858, 2.

Fully sensible that the Utah question is one which presents difficulties of no ordinary kind, we are not disposed to hastily arrive at a conclusion of what is the wisest policy to be pursued by the government, in the prosecution to a settlement of this disagreeable subject.

The news from the East by the fast mail shows that the War Department is taking energetic and efficient measures to solve at an early day this difficulty.

On the other hand there are rumors and reports recently received here from Utah, which perhaps are entitled to some consideration, that a misunderstanding has occurred between Gov. Cummings [*sic*] and Col. Johnson [*sic*], and that the troops are not to advance, but that they will soon return East.

Unable to perceive why any difficulty should have taken place between the civil and military authorities sent to govern and preserve order in that Territory, we are not disposed to give credit to the report, much less to infer that the President is pursuing a wavering and vacilating course. It is not presumable, that while the President is occupied in providing for the forwarding of men and supply trains from the East, that he is countenancing a movement which must again leave the government of Utah at the mercy of those same persons whose acts have compelled the Federal Government to send an army into the field, and whose obstinacy has obliged that army to suffer the inclemency of a winter in the summits of the Rocky mountains, and who destroyed the few buildings that might have served as a partial shelter to that army from the storms of winter. The people of the United States will demand even if the present congress does not, a rigid investigation into certain transactions that have occurred in Utah, and which have been thus far permitted to sleep in almost forgetfulness.

The massacre of Capt. Gunnison's party has been laid at the door of the Utah Mormons, and justice requires an investigation that shall either relieve them of the charge, or stamp the cursed deed upon the foreheads of the guilty in letters of blood.

The massacre of the party of emigrants on their way to California in the past year must be enquired into. No sane man, acquainted with the character of Indians, with the testimony at present before the world, will believe that that act, of more than savage barbarity, was perpetrated by Indians. It is beyond the power of credulity to believe that Indians could, or would have done and acted as was reported, by the Mormons, to have been done by the incarnate devils who destroyed that party. The extermination of so large a number of men, without the escape of a solitary individual, is unheard of in Indian warfare. The preservation of the children is unprecedented in the barbarous acts of Indians. The return of those Indians along the highway that they knew was thronged with emigrants; and their undisguised entrance into a populous settlement, with the orphan children as trophies of their bloody deed, is beyond the limits of credence. If it were allowable to admit an impossible case, for argument, we would assume that the plan was concocted and the act performed by the Indians without the aid or knowledge of the Mormons.—In which case the whole body of Utah officers, from the Revelator himself, down to the constable of the town most remote from the scene, are guilty of murder in its most revolting form. Not only the officers, but the inhabitants throughout the length and breath of that Territory, are a thousand times more guilty than the Indians who imbued their hands with the blood of our country-men, their wives and their daughters. Months multiplied by months have passed on, and, until the present day no effort has been made by these saints to pursue after, and bring to justice those savages that had so cruelly murdered scores of their fellow citizens, and left the mutilated bodies of women to fester in the mid-day sun. The inhabitants of Utah cannot plead in excuse that the Indians were unknown, or that they were too numerous or powerful to be brought to justice, because they were known, and there are no mighty bands of Indians in that Territory, while there are resident Mormons in almost every Indian village in Utah. Neither was it because the Mormons felt themselves too weak to make the attempt; for almost immediately after that event they openly challenged and defied the combined civil and military powers of the United States.—Instead then of exerting themselves to avenge the horrid deed, they held up their hands before High Heaven, and shouted Hallelujah, rejoicing over the diabolical act.

The only conclusion at which any mind controlled by sound reason, can arrive, under the circumstances and the testimony thus far divulged, is that this unparalleled crime of fratricide was committed by the Mormons. And, we ask, shall this stigma be permitted to settle down and rest upon the people of America? Will the Government and the people of the United States follow the example of Brigham Young and the people of Utah; and suffer a crime of such enormity to attach itself to the skirts of our fellow-citizens, without an effort to clear up this charge.

It was charged at the time of the massacre, that it was the work of Mormons. The Mormons themselves knew that the circumstances were such as would cause the crime to be imputed to them by the unprejudiced and impartial of their fellow citizens of the United States.

This party of emigrants were murdered between the 12th and 15th of September last, and Mormon, J. Ward Christian, then a resident of San Bernardino, in communicating the circumstances, to the Los Angeles Star, writes as follows:

"It is absolutely one of the most horrible massacres that I have ever had the painful necessity of relating . . . it will be attributed to the Mormon people let the circumstances of the case be what the may."[13]

From the foregoing extracts, although written by a Mormon, and for the purpose of publication, we affirm that there is sufficient proof to satisfy every unprejudiced mind conversant with Indian character, that the deed was never performed by Indians. Further, we state with full confidence, that the emigrants knew at the time, that the attacking force was Mormon. No body of Americans, surrounded and reduced to such extremities, by enraged and savage Indians, would ever have thought of sending a little girl with a flag of truce, and more especially when these men were from Arkansas, where every inhabitant is familiar with the character of the Indian. But knowing them to be Mormons, and partly American, and not believing that they had lost all feelings of humanity, they would, in a case of extremity, make use of such a messenger as would be most likely to awaken their sympathy.

If the murderers had been Indians, they never would have killed, on the field, all tha [sic] females.—This party consisted almost entirely of families, and there must have been as many or more young women as there were infants. Indians would not have killed these; but would have carried them off as captives. Neither would they have preserved the infant children. The American history is full of instances where the brains of the infant have been dashed out in the presence of the parent, while the mother has been led into captivity. On the contrary, if they were Mormons, there were strong reasons that would urge them to adopt the course pursued by those murderers. The children would soon be of service to them. They would in a few years be men and women, and Mormons; while they could not spare the life of a grown person or youth,—no, not even the young and lovely females, because the risk of subsequent exposure and detection of participation in the harrowing deed, was too imminent.

This article has already exceeded our usual limits, or we would transcribe from the Star the statement made by Messrs. Powers and Warn, published in that paper in October last. These men were the first, except Mormons, that passed along the road after the massacre, and relate many circumstances that fix, in the most positive manner, the complicity of the Mormons in that tragedy.

We saw and conversed with Mr. Powers and Mr. Warn, [after] their arrival in this city, and it was at that time our deliberate opinion—derived not from prejudice, but from the testimony—that there were no Indians engaged in the affair, but that those Indians seen on the road by the men named above, were Mormons in disguise.

---

[13]Here the article repeats Christian's text, provided above in "Horrible Massacre of Emigrants!!" *Los Angeles Star*, 10 October 1857.

Both the editorials and the statements made in the Star at the time, imputed the act to the direct agency of the Mormons. A public meeting was held in this place, at which resolutions were passed declaring the conviction that the "attrocious [sic] act was perpetrated by the Mormons and their allies," and this belief was published to the world.

The representatives of the people of the entire Union, as well as those of the inhabitants of California, saw and read the history of this astounding crime, and what have they done or proposed in the premises? We have not seen that the subject has been urged upon, or has been brought up in Congress, save and except by Mr. Gwin. And the matter was not such as that, in his unaided hands, Congress could be induced to take any effective action.

That there has been a positive coldness, excited only to a slight lukewarmness, manifested in Congress by the California delegation, we think cannot be denied.

That hundreds of our fellow-citizens, while journeying over the domain of the people, should be so wantonly murdered, whether by Indians or Mormons, more than eight months since, and no steps taken either by the authorities of the Territory where it was committed, or by the Federal Government to investigate the occurrence, is an outrage upon humanity, and a scandal to ourselves and the Government.

Had this outrage been committed by the Chinese, or the cannibals of the Southern ocean, the halls of Congress would have echoed back in indignation of the representative of an incensed people, and our own California delegation would have cried for vengeance, and not have ceased until the manes of their fellow-countrymen had been appeased by an offering of blood, which should have satiated the god of justice.

There is no conceivable method by which these subjects can be investigated in Utah, but by the presence of an army which shall over awe the guilty, and protect those who would aid and assist in discovering the perpetrators. If they were Indians, thre [sic] is greater reason for bringing home the act to them, as, until this is done, the onus must rest on the Mormons. Justice, as well as our own good name, requires that they should not rest under so foul an imputation. But if they are guilty, the blood of our unburied sister, has ascended up to Heaven, and is demanding retribution.

If the performers in this outrageous tragedy were whites who masked themselves as Indians, that their darkened countenances might approximate the blackness of the crime which they committed, let them be pursued by long-suffering justice, until the vital air we breathe shall not circulate through the nostrils of one of the wretches; let them be forever hung upon the highest peaks of the overhanging mountains; let their bodies ever remain suspended in the frigid atmosphere of the mountain tops, as an example from ocean to ocean of retributive justice, and a warning to future and unborn generations.

Discursive Remarks: Inhuman Wretches

Of all the fabrications designed to excuse the murders at Mountain Meadows, the most creative was an anonymous fable entitled "Discursive Remarks."
Written in about 1860, this tale was allegedly the work of a "strictly impartial" non-Mormon, who had an eye only to "truth, justice and equity." Historian Glen Leonard has suggested that the author might be one of the editors of the Mormon newspaper *The Mountaineer*: either Seth M. Blair, James
Ferguson, or Hosea Stout.[14] But the statement's quaint handwriting on the
Utah State Historical Society's Photostat does not match that of any of these
men. (The long-suppressed original is at LDS Archives.)

This odd document is one of the earliest insider accounts of the atrocity
at Mountain Meadows. Discursive Remarks is significant for several other reasons: it sets a pattern that many later Mormon versions of the story followed,
notably its stirring conclusion and vindication of Brigham Young. It also reveals
how critical incidents in the "official" version of the massacre, such as the
poisoning of the Indians, could be relocated as required. The story has some
true surprises: it begins with the evil machinations of "a few Apostates" who
start the company on its path to destruction, and the message from Brigham
Young arrives *before* the massacre takes place. It may be that this is Isaac Haight's
only surviving tale of the murders that he ordered, but the document resem-
bles the stories that John D. Lee retailed for years. Discursive Remarks might
echo the statement Lee gave in 1859 that "somewhat impressed" Indian agent
Jacob Forney.[15]

ANONYMOUS, DISCURSIVE REMARKS, "MOUNTAIN MEADOW MASSACRE,"
UTAH STATE HISTORICAL SOCIETY.

... A company of Emigrants, mostly, I believe from Arkansas, passed through
the Southern Settlements of this Territory en route for California in the Month
of September 1857. Nothing very especial transpired, except the unlicensed
shooting of Chickens, purloining of hay, and frequent uncomplimentary remarks
bestowed upon the Mormons generally, until they reached Springville. Here
they were joined by a few Apostates, who not only requested the privilidge [sic]
of joining the Company but also solicited their protection; saying, "that since
they had abrogated their alligeince [sic] to Mormonism," they had not only
become objects of threats, but really apprehended an attempt on the part of

---

[14]Leonard made this observation in a paper given at the Western History Association conference in
October 2003.

[15]Curtis E. Bolton statement, 4 May 1859, LDS Archives.

the Mormons, to murder them. The Emigrants giving full credence to their averments, readily Complied with the request. On the following day (Sunday) the leader of the Apostates, delivered an address to the Company, Couched in terms, and uttered with seeming truthfulness, too well calculated to inflame the minds of the Strangers and Confirm all their preconceived opinions and sentiments, against the Mormons. This injudicious procedure was made no secret, and naturally produced Somewhat acrimonious feelings in the minds of those who heard the insulting discourse. The matter was Suffered to pass, however, unnoticed by the Citizens. On the following day a circumstance happened which had a strong tendency to augment the bitter feeling of animosity Entertained by the Strangers toward the Mormon people. The team and wagon, belonging to one of the Apostates was "Attached" to enforce the payment of an unliquidated claim. The proceeding elicited from the entire Company, an unqualified disapprobation; though they certainly manifested a cardinal folly, in this meddling with matters, to which they were utter strangers, and the issue of which Could in no wise have Compromised, or affected their interest. The defendant loudly and strenuously denied the existence of any just claim against him, the Strangers placing full confidence in his statements. However the case was tried, the claim clearly proven, and judgment rendered in favor of the plaintiff. The matter gave rise to much acrimonious discussion, but the man, in order to proceed with the Company, was finally constrained to comply with the judgment of the Courts; which I doubt not, was Just and Equitable in the premises. Frequent occurrences of a similar character have taking [sic] place subsequent to the above mentioned affair, to my own certain Knowledge. And I was unable to discover any injustice in a legal procedure, constraining a person, about leaving the Community, to pay his honest debts.

However the matter under present Consideration had the effect to add fuel to the flame of popular, and deep rooted prejudice, and to increase the vituperative taunts, and lawless liberties, hitherto indulged in by the Company, who were doubtless but too willing to receive, and give credence to the evil representations, and aspersory accounts, thus freely imparted to them by those, who, at one time would probably have resented the slightest insult or taunt, directed to the people, they now repudiated and bitterly denounced.

From this time on the travelers indulged more freely in their unjustifiable liberties and unmerited insults, and each day they Conduct became more reckless and reprehensible; so much so, that their character and general proceedure preceeded them, and settlements far in advance were fully apprised of their approach and doings. Not only would they appropriate without leave or asking, fowls, and such other things as they might happen to fancy, but in many instances, went so far as to break down fences and turn their cattle into fields and private pastures, ridiculing expostulation, and defying law. At one small settlement their conduct became so unrestrained and threatning, that the inhabitants deemed it prudent to send to the nearest town for assistance, not Knowing what excesses these reckless men might be led to Commit. In an incredibly short time a small party arrived, well mounted and armed, who Combined with the inhabitants Compelled the intruders to leave the place; the mounted party following in their wake, for the purpose of presenting further mischief, until they reached Cedar City.

Here their evil genious [*sic*] continued to lead them into the fatal Error of indulging in meddling propensities, unwise and dangerous in their nature. Hitherto, the Mormons had carefully avoided all discussion and collision, and treated as mildly as possible the ill, and ungenerous behavior of the Strangers. An unfortunate circumstance occurred at this place which ~~formed~~ probably formed the first stepping stone to their own destruction. In passing a farm yard, one of the Company, who had left the train some distance behind, coolly leveled his rifle and Killed a very fine specimen of the Shanghai Rooster. And that too in the presence of the owner, who resented the insult, with some Considerable warmth, and demanded payment for the loss of his favorite fowl. Whereupon he was Complimented with a tirade of abusive epithets, the fellow cursing him for a d——d Mormon Son of a bitch. The man was evidently under the influence of liquor, and probably made a more liberal use of his unruly member, than he otherwise would have done. In the meantime a few neighbors, together with two or three Indians had Collected; as had also a portion of the train arrived at the scene of the altercation.

"Damn you and your rooster," said the fellow. "I'd like to see you make me pay for it. I'd see you—

"Oh pay for the chicken and let the d——d Mormon go," said one of the Company.

"No I won't by God" vociferated the man; "and for two pins, I would serve him the same."

One or two others, who seemed likewise under "exhillerating [*sic*] influences" now took part in the dispute, in a strain, equally discourteous and insulting.

"Gentlemen," said the Mormon, "I wish to have no difficulty; and I highly valued the fowl, yet to preserve peace and good feelings, will let the matter drop, and say no more about it.

"You'll let the matter drop, will you," retorted the fellow contemptuously; "I thought you would," he added with a sneer.

"See here stranger," he continued, "do you know what I think of you? Well I will tell you. I think you are a pack of d——d thieving Scoundrels; and if half of you had your due, you would be hanged on trees, for the Crows to pick. But hold hard; go slow; the Army will be in here one of these days, and wipe ever d——d one of you out; which ought to have been long ago, and I for one, would help do it. And I tell you to your teeth my fine gentlemen, that I'll be d——d if I *do* get to California, till I have old Brigham's scalp, at least, to take with me." During this insulting speech, no one uttered a word, the Mormons evidently wishing if possible to avoid a collision.

"Damn you for a pack of rascals," continued the fellow, "You have gone too long, and ought to be jerked up; as you soon will be, for your damned rascality. That old humbug, Jo Smith paid for his imposture and the whole d——d pack of you ought to follow him; with old Brigham at the head, who is the biggest damned Scoundrel and murd—

"Liar!" exclaimed the insulted Mormon, no longer able to restrain his outraged feelings; and with a single stroke felled the insulter, stunned and bleeding to the earth. Every man instantly sprang for their wagons, with the evident intention of obtaining their arms; when a tall powerful built man suddenly leaped in their midst; holding in each hand a revolver, and in a voice of thunder cried Hold! Let the first man but dare lay a hand upon a gun, and he instantly dies.

This bold, and unexpected move had the desired effect. Every man halted, and gazed in astonishment upon the formidable opponent. "What would you do," said he slowly. "Would you shed innocent blood? And for what? Because an insulting Scoundrel has received what he but too justly deserved? Shame on you for men, thus to seek to add injury to insult. Have you not been treated with kind forbearance, and your wants cheerfully supplied; not withstanding your ill-governed, and ungenerous Conduct? Who has insulted or injured *you*? Point him out—name the person, and you shall have ample redress. You are silent. Then I say, shame on you, thus to turn like a Serpent, and sting those who have conferred nought but kindness upon you.

Meanwhile the discomfited braggadocio had risen to his feet, and stood confronting his opponent, with a look of dark implacable hatred; doubtless restrained from any further onslaught by the forcible argument of the new actor in the drama.

"Gentlemen," continued the speaker, "remove your comrade, that further mischief may be avoided. He has been somewhat severely chastised for his insolence, but not more so than his conduct justly merited."

The men instantly obeyed the suggestion in silence; apparently awed and crestfallen, but a shrewd observer might have detected the lurking demon "Revenge," beneath the assumed panoply of seeming submission.

"Now gentlemen," said the mediator, "depart in peace, and respect the rights, and feelings [of] *others*; insult no more, nor seek to bring trouble upon those who have never injured you."

"Gentlemen," said the humiliated insulter, while a furious glance of vindictive hatred flashed from his eyes, "I will yet be revenged, d——n you."

To this threat no reply was designed, and the Company moved on, and encamped, a short distance from the town for the night.

I would here observe that the same emigrant received in Great Salt Lake City, from one Mr. Pettit, a like chastisement for similar conduct. Thus ended a difficulty, apparently of little importance in itself, yet which, unfortunately led to more grave and deplorable results.

The Indians who had witnessed the whole affair, looked puzzled, unable to comprehend what it all meant. The matter being explained to them, they expressed their disapprobation in simple laconic sentences such as "Bad men, bad men—no good, no good."

As I before stated the strangers encamped for the night at no great distance from the spot where the unfortunate affair occurred. I say unfortunate, because the results inspired, not only the principle actor in the difficulty, but also many of his friends with a fatal spirit of revenge, which prompted them to acts, in their nature, too well calculated to bring destruction upon themselves.

The place created for their encampment was well chosen for good range, and water; the latter, supplied by two small springs.

During the evening a few Indians Came to the Camp, and asked for meat and bread. The strangers at first peremptorily refused, but suddenly, for some course or other, changed their minds, and bade the visitors come in the morning and they should have what they wanted. The Indians apparently satisfied with the promise, departed in peace.

The gentleman, who, by his firmness and presence of mind, had quelled the disturbance, and in all probability prevented more serious mischief saw the company under motion; and then quietly withdrew from the crowd, beckoning an elderly man to follow. "My friend," said he, after gaining a point beyond the danger of being overheard, "these reckless men must be closely watched to night; for if I mistake not, mischief is brewing, and there is no telling what they might be tempted to do, led on by their blind insatiate hatred, though God knows their vindictive animosity is unjust, and groundless. I fear that scoundrells [sic] threat will not altogether prove an idle boast, judging from the look of dark malignity that accompanied the words. A few proper persons must be chosen to watch their movements; and matters so arranged as not to attract the attention of those desperate characters. This arrangement was accordingly carried into effect; though the precaution proved unnecessary, as the night passed away without any disturbance.

The following morning some half-dozen Piede Indians approached the emigrant camp, in order to receive the promised gift. A goodly portion of fresh beef, and a small quantity of flour was distributed among them who received the donation with that imperturbable stoicism so peculiar to the race, and departed well satisfied with their success.

At an early hour the company raised Camp and proceeded on their journey; little dreaming of the dreadful fate that awaited them. The following day, they reached the "Mountain Medows," a small narrow valley and encamped about six miles south of Painter Creek, a small Mormon settlement. Here they proposed to remain a few days, in order to recruit their animals ere venturing forth upon the sterile and inhospitable deserts.

The Citizens of Cedar had witnessed the departure of the discourteous strangers with feelings of pleasure, their minds now relieved from an offensive and undefined sensation of a vague presentment of evil. But the following morning found the tone and aspect of things entirely changed. The people appeared to be laboring under some deep and sudden excitement, some hurrying to and fro, others gathered in small groups, engaged in earnest mysterious consultation. The cause is soon explained. On approaching the deserted campground, the herdsmen to their astonishment discovered the ground covered with dead cattle, in the vicinity of the springs, their bodies greatly swollen and bloated. The truth was too apparent—*the springs were poisoned.* Thus had these ill-advised and willing slaves to a sentiment of insatiate animosity, attempted to consummate their evil designs, and schemes of groundless vengeance.

A meeting was immediately called for the purpose of adopting measures of proceedure. Much excitement prevailed among the justly incensed people, who certainly did not merit so base an act of ingratitude and treachery. Many plans were suggested and debated. Some were in favor of summary chastisement being inflicted upon the guilty parties; which cannot be a matter of very great wonderment, under the circumstances, the excited state of the people and the aggravated Cause.

When the spirit of indignation had reached its height, and the deep wrought feelings of resentment was assuming a dangerous tone; a deep voice suddenly arrested the proceedings of the meeting, and produced a temporary silence. The speaker was our friend who had taken a prominent part in the affair two days previous whose name was withheld from the writer; but was assured of its publicity in the event of a legal investigation. "Gentlemen," said he, "without a doubt a dastard offense has been committed and a heinous evil contemplated, yet because they have done wrong it does not become us as men, as professed Christians, to follow their example. That you are justly incensed I grant, yet be calm and do nothing rashly, that you may no hereafter have cause to regret;—let not your anger allure you into the performance of acts, equally wrong, and unjustifiable. Remember, if you are asked what you profess to be, you owe a certain allegiance and respect to the authorities of this Church; then do not suffer excitement, and the errors of others to assume dominion over your judgment, and prompt you to acts of violence that would bring disgrace upon them, the Community, and your *selves.* This case can be reached and punished by law; and I therefore propose that the perpetrators of the treacherous act, be demanded and subject to legal investigation. This, gentlemen, is the only proper and legitimate plan of action. What say you?"

These simple and pointed remarks had the effect to calm the excitement of the enraged assembly, and reinstate, Reason in her wanted dominion. The property and justness of the views set forth, became at once manifest and clear to their understanding. The result was that the guilty parties should be apprehended and held subject to the order of a legal Court of Law. The people then quietly dispersed, and returned to their *homes.*

The "Mediator" as we shall term our friend of the "Revolver" argument, really felt more uneasiness as to the final result of the affair, than he chose to

betray. He foresaw the probability of a desperate resi[s]tence to any attempt
to apprehend the guilty ones; for he doubted not the cognizance, if not the
participation of the entire company, in poisoning the springs. Some of the
Company he knew to be desperate men, who would not lamely suffer themselves or their friends to be taken; & who would most likely resist any such
attempt, if necessary, with force of arms. These thoughts gave him much uneasiness of mind for he wished if possible, to prevent the serious results, the phase
of matters seemed to suggest.

Oppressed with these unpleasant reflections, he approached a young man,
and in a tone of deep earnestness, said, "Can you stand it to ride an express
to the City?"

"Certainly," replied the young man, "why do you ask?"

"Because," said the other, "I have strong fears for the issue of this affair.
Those men may, and I doubt not, will refuse to deliver up the perpetrators
of the foul deed; or they may all have been privy to the affair, in which Case,
and its more than probable that it is so, any effort to apprehend them will be
met with desperate resistence; and it is difficult to say how it would all end.
I would fain persuade the people to let the matter drop; though the treacherous ingrate well merit the severest punishment. But I fear this would prove
a hopeless task, under present excitement and indignation. I want you therefore to take the best horse in the settlement, and ride day and night till you
reach the City, and acquaint President Young with the whole particulars."

"It is a somewhat severe task," said the young man, "but I think I can stand
it."

"Then haste, and depart instantly, and change horses at each settlement.
The urgency of the Case admits of not the slightest delay; therefore neither
spare whip nor spur."

In less than thirty minutes, the Courier was en route for G. S. L. City.

Toward the close of the day, two or three Indians from an encampment
some two miles distant, came rushing into the settlement, whooping and screaming like mad men, apparently in a state of deepest excitement. From the wild,
and rappid gesticulations, and fierce angry yells, nothing for sometime could
be comprehended. They at length made the people understand that some of
their people were taken suddenly ill; the Cause, in some way connected with
the presence of the strangers. They desired that some of the whites should
immediately visit their camp and see for themselves. Accordingly our Mediator and two or three others, set forth in Company with the Indians.

A heart rending scene met their view on their arrival. Some dozen or more
Indians and Squaws lay here and there about the Camp, uttering alternate
screams and groans, betokening the presence of extreme suffering. Their features were horribly distorted and their bodies considerably bloated. The entire
Camp were gathered round the sufferers, consternation depicted on their countenances uttering discordant howls and yells of lamentations. To all enquiries

as to the cause of the sudden ailment, the Indians made no reply, but pointed to some beef hung up before one of the Lodges, and continued their wild
manifestations of mingled rage and sorrow. Upon examination, the meat was
found to have assumed a greenish hue, and emitted a nauseous odor, extremely unpleasant and sickening. The truth quickly flashed upon their minds—
the meat was poisoned.

"It is but too true," said the Mediator, "those inhuman wretches have certainly poisoned the beef, & given it to these poor Indians. God help them
should any of these unfortunate creatures die. Blood alone can appease their
anger, or satiate their thirst for vengeance."

The Mediator and his associates rendered every service, and assistance in
their powers; and administered such remedies as could be obtained. All was
done that could be accomplished; but despite every effort, three Indians died
during the night, in terrible convulsions.

The Indians evidently understood the fatal trick played upon them, and
after consigning the dead to the earth, with sorrow for the departed and exe-
crations upon the murderers, the male portion gathered up their ponies, mounted and struck out in a southerly direction.

This last inhuman deed, filled the minds of the people with horror, and
added strength to the sentiment of indignation, already sufficiently intense
to be safe. However, the original plan was adhered to, and a party of some
fifteen men, headed fortunately by the mediator, proceeded in pursuit of the
strangers; whom they found quietly encamped near the Mountain Medow
Spring. Their errand being declared, the demand was received with well feigned
astonishment and indignation.

"Gentlemen," said the Mediator, whom part of the Company recognized,
"it is useless to affect ignorance of a deed, your very looks too palpably betrays.
It is equally futile to attempt to screen yourselves beneath the false panoply
of ill-feigned innocence, when guilt too surely lies at your door. But we came
not to argue the matter, but demand the guilty parties; and if you are wise,
you will at once accede to the demand."

A somewhat rough looking personage now stepped forth, apparently the
leader or captain of the Company, and answered, "We deny any knowledge
of what you have stated, but," he added bluntly, "if you know better than we,
why take the perpetrators, if you know them."

"This, of course, we cannot do, unless we detain the whole Company,
which—"

"We shall not permit you to do," said the man quickly. "At least so long
as we can by any means prevent it. And now, once and for all," continued the
speaker, "you shall not detain the whole or any part of the Company. We
deny having any hand in poisoning the springs, and therefore do not wish to
be troubled."

"Gentlemen," said the Mediator in a calm tone. "'Tis not my province, nor wish to quarrel with you, neither is it my desire to upbraid you with the Commission of an act, your own consciences should but too severely condemn, and the memory of which, should consign you to a life of relentless remorse; and the fearful assurance of a hopeless hereafter. For the poisoning of the spring is not the least and only crime for which you are called upon to answer, and *alone.* Three of your unsuspecting victims, whom you heartlessly poisoned have died, and be assured they will not fail to wreak fearful vengeance upon the murderers of their people."

Several faces winced and became deeply suffused at this announcement. But the leader immediately came to the rescue; and said, "Again I tell you that we know nothing of what you are talking about. And," he added, viewing the speaker with an angry frown, "we do not want to be insulted with charges of which we are not guilty. As for the Indians, we are prepared for *them.*"

"My friend," observed the Mediator, eyeing the man closely, "I have said nothing *about Indians.*" The fellow became confused, aware that he had unwittingly betrayed himself. Quickly recovering, however, he replied, "Well, your words implied as much."

"Gentlemen," said the mediator, in a tone more of sorrow than anger, "You will certainly seal your own doom and I fear, a dreadful one it will be, if you thus persist in screening the *murderers* of those Indians. Look around you— do you wish to see your wives and helpless children butchered in cold blood before your very eyes? I tell you, those Indians will assuredly avenge the death of those who have perished, beyond a doubt by the hands of some person or persons belonging to this Company. They are, at this very moment, in quest of others to join them; and I feel confident will ere you are aware of it, fall upon you in force, and I need not tell you that their mode of warfare is to *spare none.* Therefore be wise, and reject not the only means of safety. For if you will surrender those who committed the deed, the Indians may be appeased; at least I will promise you the protection of the whites.

The leader, either conscious of the implication of most part, if not the entire Company in the affair, or placing but little credence in the words he had heard, still loudly persisted in his pretended ignorance of the matter.

"We are sufficiently able," said he, "to protect ourselves against any onslaught of the Indians, and shall be prepared to give them a warm reception if they make any attempt of the kind.

"This, then, is the determination of the Company?"

"It is," assured the man, "we do not intend to be detained upon an absurd charge which cannot be substantiated by proof. And as for the rest, we can take of ourselves."

"Then God help you," said the Mediator in a tone of deep regret. "You will repent the fatal step you have taken, when too late to repair the evil. I would fain have saved the innocent from a fate, I have too much reason to believe, is inevitable, Gentlemen. I have apprised you of impending danger; and would say, treat the warning not lightly, or your blind heedlessness may be attended with the most fearful results." So saying, the speaker, accompanied by his party, left the Company, and returned to their homes. Indeed, the Mediator had very little hopes, in setting out, of succeeding in his mission. But he had two motives in making the attempt. First, to satisfy the desire and allay the excitement of the people, and secondly, to gain, if possible, sufficient time for news to arrive from the City, having confidence that orders from the proper source, would restrain the enraged citizens and hold them in check.

It may be inquired, why a sufficient posse was not marshaled, and with a process the whole Company, detained until the culprits were ascertained. This was what the Mediator most feared, and labored to prevent. For it must be borne in mind that most part of the Company was composed of resolute, and reckless men, who were fully determined not to be taken; for they were not blind to the Consequences of their acts; and a successful attempt to arrest them would, in all probability have been attended with the shedding of blood on both sides.

Another feeling prompted the Mediator to visit the strangers camp; he felt a strong desire to warn them of—as he believed—the imminent danger to be apprehended from the justly excited indignation of the Indians, for his heart revolted at the probability of innocent women and helpless children being sacrificed to Indian vengeance.

Two more days passed, the fourth from the messengers departure for the city and nothing transpired to excite the suspicion of the Strangers or lessen their assurance of safety, who doubtless viewed—if they had not entirely forgotten—the warning voice of the Mediator, as a cunningly devised scheme to excite their fears, in the hope thereby of prevailing upon them to accede to his demand.

And yet these men must indeed have been deaf to the whisperings of conscience, not to have felt some compunction; and indeed reckless and indifferent to danger, not to have experienced some dubiety, as to the probable result of their diabolical trick upon the unsuspecting Indians.

That night those ill fated beings retired as usual with the pleasing confidence of peaceful slumber, and the happy waking to greet the smiles of another morn. The aged sire, the stalwart man in the vigor and prime of life, the youth, the child of tender years, and the prattling babe; all were buried in the oblivion of silent repose. Nor did, perhaps, even a flitting dream, impress them with a sense of impending danger, and that an implacable and savage foe, kept vigil while they slept. The moon had risen, filling the valley with a flood of mellow light, so that objects could be distinguished at some considerable distance, though not with any certain distinctness. Scarcely a sound relieved the monotony of the deathlike silence that reigned; not even the measured tread of a single watchman; so complete was their fatal assurance of safety.

But the deep stillness of the midnight hour, was suddenly broken, and the hapless sleepers aroused from their slumber, by the shrill whistling of the messengers of death, and the savage yells of a stealthy foe. The consternation, confusion and terror, combined with the shrieks of women and children, and the groans of the wounded, and dying must have presented a scene of horror, which may be imagined, but not described. The men, thus suddenly startled to a sense of the imminent danger that so unexpectedly beset them, rushed half awake, and wholly bewildered for their arms, and fired a random volley regardless of aim or object.

The Indians it seems, must have approached very near the waggons, well knowing the confusion, and terror that would naturally ensue in the camp, consequent upon the unexpected crack of the rifle, and the peaceful echoes of the savage war whoop, in order to direct more surely the messengers of death, with the comparative safety to themselves. Three or four volleys were poured in with deadly effect, upon the terrified emigrants, ere anything like order or discussion of action could be accomplished. The Indians then hastily retreated to an eminence which afforded them a secure shelter from the fire of their victims, who were left for a time, to waste their ammunition upon shadows, which their excited imaginations created into as many living enemies.

A desultory fire was kept up during the night, just sufficient to prevent the possibility of rest or sleep, if indeed such a things was thought of under such fearful circumstances, the wretched people suffering all the horrors of fearful suspense and dreadful uncertainty; ignorant as yet, of the full extent of the danger that encompassed them.

Morning came, but brought them no means or succor, or hopes of escape; but rather confirmed their worst fears, for Indians were seen prowling about in every direction, painted and decked in the wild fantastic costumes of war. They had, during the night, formed their waggons into a compact circle, and sinking the wheels into the earth, succeeded in producing a comparative shelter against the bullets of the enemy.

The fire was still continued at intervals, and often with fatal effect, though the Indians did not leave their hiding place nor attempt to approach the camp, which fact surprised and puzzled the emigrants not a little. But their wily enemy had determined upon a safer plan for the Consummation of their vengeance.

Thus passed the day and another sleepless night in the doomed camp; their numbers slowly, but surely decreasing, by the death-dealing bullet; or the equally fatal arrow.

A new terror now began to assail them; the horror of all horrors—*thirst*. The spring was situated at some considerable distance from the waggons, and to attempt to approach it, was certain death. Thus were these ill-fated beings made to suffer slow and torturing pangs far more intense and terrible than death itself. The low moans of the wounded and dying, and the touching appeals of helpless famishing children for water, had compelled two or three, in the recklessness of despair, to make an effort to procure the precious liquid, but a single expiring groan, announced the fearful result of the attempt. Wild, thrilling shrieks of hopeless despair wrung from the hearts of utter anguish, and uttered by lips withered and parched, by burning quenchless thirst—strangely blended with the mocking yells of the merciless savage.

But whey attempt to portray scenes of agony, suffering, and butchery, consequent upon a three days siege by an implacable and barbarous foe, the contemplation of which fills the soul with a sickening sensation of mingled horror and indignation. Three long days of untold anguish, human torture, and black despair. Then, thinned by death and weakened by continued exertion, ceaseless waiting and the soul-rending agony of consuming unquenched thirst, the wretched sufferers became an easy prey to the insatiate vengeance of a cruel foe; who neither asks for mercy, nor spares their victims.

The people of Cedar had been informed of the attack upon the emigrants and of course easily divined the cause. No disposition, however, was manifested to interfere in the matter. Indeed they would not dared have done so, even had they possessed the disposition; for to have taken part against the Indians, would have inevitably drawn future vengeance upon themselves; and rendered dangerous if not fatal, their longer stay in the country.

Late in the evening of the sixth day from departure of the Mediator's courier and the second of the attack, a messenger arrived from the city, bringing a letter from President Young. The laconic epistle, directed to the people, was in substance, the following: *Suffer the strangers to proceed, and on your lives commit no acts of violence.*

That night the Mediator succeeded in obtaining a few volunteers, and early the following morning set out for the "Mountain Medows," with the hope and determination of saving if possible, those [suffering] people, notwithstanding their evil deeds, and the cold indifference with which they had treated his words of timely warning. Away they sped, urged on by the importance of their mission, neither sparing whip nor suffering their jaded steeds to slacken pace, until they reached to within three or four hundred yards of the ill-fated camp. Here the wild despairing shrieks of the surviving victims, fell fearfully distinct upon their startled ears. The Mediator accompanied by a single attendant (he dared not take more, lest the Indians should turn their weapons upon them) instantly dashed forward and regardless of all consequences, plunged in the midst of the yelling savages, who had now taken full possession of the camp, dealing death at every blow. In a voice of thunder he shouted to them in their own language to desist; and holding forth the letter from Brigham, told them that the "Big White Chief," had sent to forbid them, harming the white people.

Whatever effect this might have had a few hours earlier, it is difficult to

say, but now it was too late. They had arrived only in time to witness the closing scene of the bloody tragedy. A few children only were spared of the entire
company.

The camp now presented a spectacle of revolting horror, far beyond the
possibility of an adequate description. Men, women, children and suckling
babes, indiscriminately covered the gory earth, weltering in warm pools of
blood, dreadfully disfigured and mutilated by the merciless tomahawks or scalp-
ing knife. The Mediator and his party, with painful reflections, and heavy
hearts returned to their homes.

Three nights hence, Brigham Young was a lone occupant of his cabinet,
apparently a prey to the pangs of bitter grief. With agitated steps, he paced
the floor the live long night, while at intervals tears of anguish trickled and
fell at his feet.

"My God! Tis horrible, horrible!" were sentences that fell from his lips,
indicating the nature of the painful reflections that oppressed and weighed
heavy upon his heart:—*He had learned the fate of the emigrants.*

So ends my narrative of the "Mountain Medow Massacre," one of the
most diabolical and cruel instances of human butchery on record. The statements embodied in the narrative are as many other reports, in relation to the
affair *have been said to be*, predicated upon "*information;*" and is in my opinion in
point of correctness, at least tantamount in worthiness of reception and credence as those that have heretofore been given to the public. For not withstanding the apparent unquestionable sources, from which other versions of
the matter has eminated, I am still inclined to believe the evil genious of
mankind, "Prejudice," to have had much to do in their construction.

In portraying the other side of the picture, I have been guided alone by what
I could gather from every source, which could throw the least particle of light
upon the subject, and have woven the different threads of information together, unbiased by interest and governed by no other motive than an honest desire
to strike a feeble blow in defense of those I firmly believe to be innocent.

If White men were participants in the murder of those unfortunate emigrants, I have been unable to glean any evidence of the fact; which might long
since have been determined by judicial investigation, had an unperverted and
impartial judiciary taken the matter in hand, and by a wise and proper procedure, sought to arrive at a truthful solution of this mystery.

But of one thing I am certainly convinced, that the "*Leaders*" of the Mormon people were neither directly nor indirectly in any way whatever concerned
in the affair; nor had they the slightest cognition of the matter til after the
consummation of the deed. This conviction is based upon evidence too strong
and palpable to admit of a doubt. With these few brief comments I have done.

Chapter 7

"THE SANTA CLARA EXPEDITION"
The Army Cracks the Case

It seemed as if everyone west of the Missouri River—except territorial officials in Utah and a national administration immobilized by larger events as the country moved toward civil war—knew what happened at Mountain Meadows. While angry voices in Arkansas and California cried for an investigation, the only man in the nation, or the rest of the world, who could have conducted one, chose to obstruct it instead. A shrewd judge of character, Brigham Young applied bribery and intimidation to frustrate justice and impose his will on federal appointees, who lacked not only support from President Buchanan but also the power to control events in a land where they were ignored or scorned. If not for a fearless judge and the integrity of the U.S. Army, it is possible that what is now known about the massacre would never have come to light.

In June 1858 Jacob Hamblin, Southern Indian Mission president, gave Brigham Young and George A. Smith a complete description of the Mountain Meadows massacre. Asked at John D. Lee's second trial in 1876, "Did you give them the whole facts?" Hamblin replied, "I gave them more than I have here, because I recollected more of it." His recital of the butchery had appalled those who heard it in the courtroom. Yet in 1858, only two months after Hamblin had given him an even more detailed description, Apostle Smith's own "investigation" placed all of the blame on the Indians. For twelve more years not one church official, including Lee, was called to account.

ALEXANDER WILSON: UNABLE TO OBTAIN ANY CLEW

Months passed before any government agency began to look into the massacre. As reports of Mormon involvement spread to the West Coast, Alexander Wilson, U.S. attorney for Utah Territory, finally asked Secretary of the Interior Jacob Thompson what to do. As this letter shows, Wilson was well aware of the horrific nature of the crime and knew it was his duty to prosecute, but he claimed it was the work of Indians, despite the common knowledge that white settlers had taken part. By now, Wilson had adopted the peace-at-any-price policy of Governor Cumming and Indian Affairs superintendent Jacob Forney. As part of his attempt to quell the rebellion in Utah, on 6 April 1857 President Buchanan had issued "to the inhabitants of Utah, who shall submit to the laws, a free pardon for the seditions and treasons heretofore by them committed."[1] Wilson's justification for doing nothing rested on the excuse that the president's pardon also forgave criminal acts, including the murder of 120 civilians.

A variety of motives drove Wilson's behavior. "I am sorry to say that District Attorney Wilson makes much use of liquor altogether too freely for his own good," Brigham Young told Thomas L. Kane, adding local gossip that claimed Wilson could not meet his bills after spending four thousand dollars on his wedding.[2] Jacob Forney and Alfred Cumming were also hard drinkers, and precisely the kind of outsider vulnerable to bribery and blackmail in Utah Territory. Less than a week after Wilson arrived in Great Salt Lake City, Brigham Young instructed Hosea Stout to hire him "to attend to all law suits that may come up against him or the Church before the Dist[rict] Courts; so far as it could be done without infringing upon the business of his office as U.S. Attorney."[3] For the next two decades, such semi-legal subornation supplemented simple cash bribery in a systematic campaign to induce congressmen and territorial officials to do Brigham Young's bidding—and obstruct justice for the murdered dead of Mountain Meadows.

WILSON TO JACOB THOMPSON, SECRETARY OF THE INTERIOR, 4 MARCH 1859, RG 60, NATIONAL ARCHIVES.

I have the honor of transmitting to you a statement concerning the massacre of certain emigrants who were passing through the Territory in the month of September 1857, for California. They were mostly, if not all, from the state of Arkansas, and were well provided with stock, wagons &c. to make permanent settlement in their proposed new home.

[1]The pardon appeared in 1858 in House Doc. 2, Serial 997, 69–72, and was reprinted in Roberts, *A Comprehensive History*, 425–28.
[2]Young to Kane, 17 September 1859, LDS Archives.
[3]Church Historian's Office Journal, 10 November 1858, cited in MacKinnon, "Epilogue to the Utah War: Impact and Legacy," 245n134.

The massacre, it appears, is laid to the charge of the Indians to whom, it is said, they became obnoxious while passing through their settlements in the southern part of this Territory. The first attack was made on them on the 8th of September, at which time a number were killed and wounded. Shortly after, either on that or the next day, the emigrants made a corrall with their wagons which afforded protection and enabled them to keep at bay their enemies. But owing to the absence of water in the corrall they were soon reduced to great distress and suffering.

After remaining in this condition for several days, being continually surrounded by their enemies, and several having been killed in the attempt to get water, it appears that an offer was made to spare their lives and let them go on their journey, if they would give up their arms and property. This proposition, it appears, was accepted, because, for the want of water, they were reduced to the last extremity. But after they had parted with their arms, and were marching out of the corrall, they were treacherously murdered—every living soul,—and cut off, save only seventeen children ranging from 3 to 7 years of age, but who are unable to tell their names or kindred. There were 119 killed. A more cold blooded butchering I have never heard of.

The massacre occurred on what is called the Mountain Meadows, about 300 miles south of Great Salt Lake City, and near the Santa Clara road to California, within the limits of this Territory.

Through the humane exertions of Dr. Forney, the Superintendent of Indian Affairs, the children that were saved, have been recovered from the Indians, and he has them in his charge, kindly cared for.

His Excellency Governor Cumming, and Dr. Forney, have been since their arrival in this Territory, diligently inquiring into the circumstances of this horrible massacre, with a view, if possible, to ascertain the truth concerning it, and the cause which prompted, as well as the parties engaged in it. But, as yet, they have been unable to obtain any clew, either satisfactory, or of a kind to warrant proceedings of a public nature.

A mystery seems to surround this wholesale butchery, but I entertain the hope that an avenging God will speedily bring to light the perpetrators.

My object in writing this to you, as I have no doubt you have been officially informed of the massacre from other sources previous to my arrival in this Territory, is to ask for instructions, as to how I shall proceed, and what I shall do in the matter. It is such a terrible affair, and its ramifications may involve such serious consequences, that I desire, if it is the wish of the Government that I should, in my official capacity, investigate it, to proceed according to instructions from your Department, from the proper sources at Washington, should it be determined not to come under your official cognizance.

May I respectfully ask for an early reply.

Secretary of the Interior Thompson informed Wilson that measures had been taken to return the children to their homes, and forthrightly told the U.S. attorney to do his job: "It is hoped that you will exert yourself within the line of your official duties, to bring the murderers to justice." Indian Affairs superintendent Jacob Forney could secure "all the information that can be obtained, and upon this, it will be your duty to act," he said.[4] But the tune from Washington soon changed.

Jacob Bigler: It Was Done by White Men

The veil of silence and secrecy was about to be torn by the new district judge whom James Buchanan sent to Utah in 1858 from Circleville, Ohio. John Cradlebaugh had just one eye (but that a very good one, a Mormon observer noted) and he brought an open mind about the Mormons. Before long, the judge saw things that Cumming and Wilson intentionally overlooked. Early in 1859 he opened an investigation into the massacre and other crimes that rocked the territory and sent settlement leaders running for the hills.

Cradlebaugh asked Gen. Albert Sidney Johnston at Camp Floyd, near present Fairfield, to send troops to serve as a *posse comitatus* to arrest and hold accused criminals when he began an investigation at Provo. The Army of Utah commander complied under his original orders to provide troops for this purpose and sent a company to Utah Valley's largest settlement, some forty miles south of Great Salt Lake.

Cradlebaugh seemed "the only authority with resolution and firmness to take up properly the matter of these murders and outrages," Capt. Albert Tracy concluded. By the time the judge opened his court in Provo in March 1859, Tracy's journal indicates that he had acquired detailed information about "the case of the massacre of Mountain Meadows, in '57, of more than a hundred people—men, women, and children, pertaining to an emigrant train originally from Arkansas." Tracy believed the murder of Parley Pratt was the primary cause of the atrocity: "it is told that Young vowed vengeance." Young's followers "were instigated to worry and harass them into quarrels and difficulties, until at last on their reaching the point called Mountain Meadows."

The hostilities of their persecutors reached a point of open warfare by Mormons in the guise of Indians who, with a few exceptions for show, were painted and costumed for the purpose. Finding, however, the Arkansas emigrants

---

[4]Thompson to Wilson, 25 April 1859, National Archives, 103–104.

too plucky and persistent for them, one, Lee, sent a deputation—divested, of course, of their Indian gear—to treat with the emigrants at the "corral" they had formed with their wagons. The Mormons said they were sorry difficulties had occurred, and as between the emigrants and the Indians, they would pro-cure peace, upon the contingency of certain supplies of powder, blankets, etc., to the latter. These terms being acceded to, the go-between retired professedly to consult with the Aboriginals over the hill—soon returning however, with the statement that all was agreed to, only that the Indians would not come into the corral to receive the gifts, fearing the rifles of the people therein. The people therein were therefore to lay aside all arms, and receive the Indians and turn over the powder and goods, after which they should suffer no further inconvenience or molestation. Procuring thus an entrance into the corral, among the emigrants disarmed, they fell to work, and slew to the right and left. Save and except one single man who hid himself, wounded, and ultimately escaped together with some four or five infants "who could not talk"—not one of all of that melan-choly band was left alive—men, women and children—they perished alike. This "Mountain Meadow Massacre," in short, for unmitigated treachery and bloody atrocity surpasses all of the description ever enacted upon our soil. Heading it was this rascal Lee, associated with others drawn in regular form of detail from villages throughout the valley, to the number of sixty or eighty. And Lee, it is, with several of his confreres in this awful crime, whom Judge Cradlebaugh has gotten fast, and whom he proposes to bring to account before the law.[5]

Tracy's limited knowledge may reflect an attempt to admit much but to obscure the most disturbing elements of the crime. A similar report appeared in the San Francisco press a month later: A purported eyewitness claimed "the unfortunate victims fell under the weapons of the Canosh band of Par-avant Indians," acting as "tools in the hands of the Mormons themselves." The purported witness claimed that "the massacre was designed and carried into execution for mere purposes of plunder." This version concealed the treachery of the massacre by claiming the Mormon militia "made a precip-itant rush at the poor defenceless victims" in their two wagon corrals, killed all the men, and then Lee "sent to the Indian chief, and his men in ambush," to kill the women and children.[6]

The Mormon bishop at Nephi, forty miles south of Provo, sat in on Judge Cradlebaugh's grand jury inquiry and described the hearings to the Church Historian's Office at Great Salt Lake City, which served as an intelligence communications center. Jacob G. Bigler's report made clear that the Ohio judge's crusade spelled real trouble for those involved in the massacre.

[5]Alter and Dwyer, "Journal of Captain Albert Tracy," 19 March 1859, 58–59.
[6]"The Mountain Meadows Massacre—A Tale of Horror," Daily Evening Bulletin, 23 April 1859, 2/2.

March 10 1859. Jacob Bigler called at the Historians office [and] brought a report of Judge Cradlebough Court at Provo which was opend on Tuesday 8th March at about 10 oclck. He empanelled the Grand Jury. He then gave them their Charge. He told them it was their duty to take notice of evry offen[s]e to the law which they had knowledge of or that should be brought before them by the Testimony of others. He commented on the massacre at the Mountain Meadows. He said he had the Testimony to prove it was done by white men [and] said it was the most outrageous massacre ever known. The evidence showed that it was not done by Indian[s] because they kept the Children. He took up an aumt [argument] to prove it was white man. He said in Court there was a company of men a wagon load & a Company on horseback went out of Ceder City a few miles & organized then went to the slaughter. A young man in Camp saw them start & return with the spoil and divided it among themselves. In Private He said that Isaac Haight was one of the Principle men and conveyd the Idea this was done under the sanction of the former Executive. He th[en] refered to the murder of Potter & Parrishes, & said that was done by the sanction of authority and young Parrish said he knew the man who commited the murder & they surrounded the House to kill him. He then refered to a Gentile who was killed in springvill, said Lysundengog had his horses and when the man was killed they let his wife & children suffer. The Judge then poored out all the Anathemis.[7]

FITZ JOHN PORTER: ENQUIRE INTO THE DEPREDATIONS

Spontaneous riots were hardly everyday occurrences in the Mormon theocracy, but Judge Cradlebaugh's Provo investigation appeared to cause an unprompted one. Alarmed by the civil unrest, Governor Cumming visited the town and assured General Johnston that he was satisfied that "the presence of the military force in this vicinity is unnecessary." The general replied that his orders required him to furnish troops on request by civil authority to execute the law and told the nervous governor that he was under "no obligation whatever to conform to your suggestions with regard to the military disposition of troops."[8]

Stung by Johnston's stiffly polite brush off, Cumming, with the backing of U.S. Attorney Wilson, sounded an alarm to his superiors in the nation's capital and warned that Cradlebaugh's conduct would lead to bloodshed.[9]

[7]Wilford Woodruff, Historian's Private Journal, LDS Archives.
[8]For this exchange, see Sen. Doc. 2, vol. 2, 36th Cong. 1st sess., Serial 1024, 150–52.
[9]Cumming to Cass, 25 March 1859, Alfred Cumming Papers.

He urged that the general's orders be changed to restrict authority to requisition troops as a *posse comitatus* only to himself. While he based his request on the unrest at Provo, it is possible, but not clear, that Cumming and Wilson also intended to kill any future investigation of the Mountain Meadows massacre. If so, they succeeded.

Being prior to the Pony Express, it would take nearly two months to receive a reply to this request. In the meantime, the U.S. Army ignored Cumming's fears and opened its own investigation. And without realizing how little time he had left, the relentless Judge Cradlebaugh made the most of every minute. He joined the army expedition to discover the truth about the atrocity on the headwaters of the Santa Clara River. Thanks to him and the U.S. Army, plus the pace of nineteenth-century mail delivery, the truth began to come out.

PORTER TO REUBEN CAMPBELL, 17 APRIL 1859,
FORT CRITTENDEN LETTERBOOK, NATIONAL ARCHIVES.

Head Quarters Department of Utah
Camp Floyd UT April 17th 1859

Campbell Captain R. P. 2nd Dragoons
Cmdg. Santa Clara Expedition

Sir,

The Commanding General designates you to command an expedition to a southern portion of this department, and has assigned to you in Special Orders, No. 26, one company of Dragoons and two companies of infantry.

The Commanding General orders that you proceed to Santa Clara and remain in that portion of the country as long as the interests of the Government and the objects of the expedition require.

The objects of the expedition are, the protection of travellers on the road to California; to enquire into the depredations that are reported in the accompanying letter as having been committed by indians in the vicinity of Santa Clara; and to furnish a company to escort to this camp Paymaster Prince in charge of public funds.

The Commanding General directs you to report the result of your examination into past depredations by indians, that, if necessary, additional force may be sent to you; and without his orders not to use your force to chastise indians except for depredations and murders committed while you are in the vicinity and which need prompt punishment . . .

I am very respectfully
Your obedient servant
F. J. Porter
Asst. Adjt. Genl.

Judge John Cradlebaugh, Porter informed Campbell two days later, "designs availing himself of the protection of your command to visit the southern portion of his District." Based on the fact that there was "no way to hold or secure offenders against the law, except through the aid of the army," General Johnston directed Campbell "to receive and detain, under the orders of the Marshal, such prisoners as he may turn over to you."[10] With these orders, Campbell and his troops set out for Mountain Meadows.

DR. CHARLES BREWER: PIERCED WITH BULLET HOLES

As Capt. Reuben Campbell's expedition and Cradlebaugh traveled south from Camp Floyd, the First Dragoons' Maj. James H. Carleton and a second column marched to the massacre ground from Fort Tejon in California. With Campbell's column was U.S. Army assistant surgeon Charles W. Brewer, who inspected the bones of the slain emigrants and described their location in relation to the slain emigrant camp. Dr. Brewer reported what he had found.

BREWER'S REPORT, IN "MASSACRE AT MOUNTAIN MEADOWS,"
SEN. EXEC. DOC. 42, 1860, 16–17.

CAMP AT MOUNTAIN MEADOWS,
Utah Territory, May 6, 1859

Captain: I have the honor to report, that this morning, accompanied by the detachment of men furnished by your orders, I proceeded to inter the remains of the men, women, and children of the Arkansas emigrant train, massacred by the Mormons at the Mountain Meadows, Utah Territory, in the month of September, 1857.

At the scene of the first attack, in the immediate vicinity of our present camp, marked by a small defensive trench made by the emigrants, a number of human skulls and bones and hair were found scattered about, bearing the appearance of never having been buried; also remnants of bedding and wearing apparel.

On examining the trenches or excavations, which appear to have been within the corral, and within which it was supposed some written account of the massacre might have been concealed, some few human bones, human hair, and what seemed to be the feathers of bedding, only were discerned.

Proceeding twenty-five hundred yards in a direction N. 15° W., I reached a ravine fifty yards distant from the road, bordered by a few bushes of scrub oak, in which I found portions of the skeletons of many bodies—skulls, bones,

---

[10]Porter to Reuben Campbell, 19 April 1859, Fort Crittenden Letterbook, National Archives.

and matted hair—most of which, on examination, I concluded to be those of men. Three hundred and fifty yards further on, and in the same direction, another assembly of human remains were found, which, by all appearance, had been left to decay upon the surface. Skulls and bones, most of which I believed to be those of women, some also of children, probably ranging from six to twelve years of age. Here, too, were found masses of women's hair, children's bonnets, such as are generally used upon the plains, and pieces of lace, muslin, calicoes, and other material, part of women's and children's apparel. I have buried thirteen skulls, and many more scattered fragments.

Some of the remains above referred to were found upon the surface of the ground, with a little earth partially covering them, and at the place where the men were massacred; some lightly buried, but the majority were scattered about upon the plain. Many of the skulls bore marks of violence, being pierced with bullet holes, or shattered by heavy blows, or cleft with some sharp-edged instrument. The bones were bleached and worn by long exposure to the elements, and bore the impress of the teeth of wolves or other wild animals.

The skulls found upon the ground near the spring, or position of first attack, and adjoining our camp, were eight in number. These, with the other remains there found, were buried, under my supervision, at the base of the hill, upon the hill-side of the valley.

At the rate 2,500 yards distant from the spring, the relative positions and general appearance of the remains seemed to indicate that the men were there taken by surprise and massacred. Some of the skulls showed that fire-arms had been discharged close to the head. I have buried eighteen skulls and parts of many more skeletons, found scattered over the space of a mile towards the lines, in which direction they were no doubt dragged by the wolves.

No names were found upon any article of apparel, or any peculiarity in the remains, with the exception of one bone, the upper jaw, in which the teeth were very closely crowded, and which contained one front tooth more than is generally found.

Under my direction, the above-mentioned remains were all properly buried, the respective locality being marked with mounds of stone.

I have the honor to be, captain, very respectfully, your obedient servant.

CHARLES BREWER,
Assistant Surgeon United States Army.

"THE MASSACRE AT MOUNTAIN MEADOWS, UTAH TERRITORY,"
HARPER'S WEEKLY, 13 AUGUST 1859, 513–14.

[FROM A CORRESPONDENT]

THE story of so horrible a butchery as that which occurred at Mountain Meadows, Utah Territory, in the autumn of 1857, has by this time, no doubt, reached the States; but as no account which I have seen yet can in the slightest degree approximate to a description of the hideous truth, being myself now on the ground, and having the opportunity of communicating with some who were no doubt present on the occasion, I deem it proper to send you a plain and unvarnished statement of the affair as it actually happened.

A train of Arkansas emigrants, with some few Missourians, said to number forty men, with their families, were on their way to California, through the Territory of Utah, and had reached a series of grassy valleys, by the Mormons called the Mountain Meadows, where they remained for several days recruiting their animals. On the night of September 9, not suspecting any danger, as usual they quietly retired to rest, little dreaming of the dreadful fate awaiting and soon to overtake them. On the morning of the 10th, as, with their wives and families, they stood around their camp-fires, passing the congratulations of the morning, they were suddenly fired upon from an ambush, and at the first discharge fifteen of the best men are said to have fallen dead or mortally wounded. To seek the shelter of their *corral* was but the work of a moment, but there they found they had limited protection.

To enable you to appreciate fully the danger of their position I must give a brief description of the ground. The encampment, which consisted of a number of tents and a *corral* of forty wagons and ambulances, lay on the west bank of, and eight or ten yards distant from, a large spring in a deep ravine running southward; another ravine, also, branching from this, and facing the camp on the southwest; overlooking them on the northwest, and within rifle shot, rises a large mound commanding the corral, upon which parapets of stone, with loopholes, have been built. Yet another ravine, larger and deeper, faces them on the east, which could be entered without exposure from the south and far end. Having crept into these shelters during the darkness of the night, the cowardly assailants fired upon their unsuspecting victims, thus making a beginning to the most brutal butchery ever perpetrated on this continent.

Surrounded by superior numbers, and by an unseen foe, we are told the little party stood a siege within the *corral* of five or seven days, sinking their wagon-wheels in the ground, and during the darkness of night digging trenches, within which to shelter their wives and children. A large spring of cool water bubbled up from the sand a few yards from them, but deep down in the ravine, and so well protected that certain death marked the trail of all who had dared approach it. The wounded were dying of thirst; the burning brow and parched lip marked the delirium of fever; they tossed from side to side with anguish; the sweet sound of the water, as it murmured along its pebbly bed, served but to heighten their keenest suffering. But what all this is to the pang of leaving to a cruel fate their helpless children? Some of the little ones, who though too young to remember in after years, tell us that they stood by their parents, and pulled arrows from their bleeding wounds.

Long had the brave band held together; but the cries of the wounded sufferers must prevail. For the first time, they are (by four Mormons) offered their lives if they will lay down their arms, and gladly they avail themselves of the proffered mercy. Within a few hundred yards of the *corral* the faith is broken. Disarmed and helpless, they are fallen upon and massacred in cold blood. The savages, who had been driven to the hills, are again called down to what was denominated the "job," which more than savage brutality had begun.

Women and children are now all that remain. Upon these, some of whom had been violated by the Mormon leaders, the savage expends his hoarded vengeance. By a Mormon who has now escaped the threats of the Church we are told that the helpless children clung around the knees of the savages, offering themselves as slaves; but with fiendish laughter at their cruel tortures, knives were thrust into their bodies, the scalp torn from their heads, and their throats cut from ear to ear.

I am writing no tale of fiction; I wish not to gratify the fancy, but to tell a tale of truth to the reason and to the heart. I speak truths which hereafter legal evidence will fully collaborate. I met this train on the Platte River on my way to Fort Laramie in the spring of 1857, the best and richest one I had ever seen upon the plains. Fortune then beamed upon them with her sweetest smile. With a fine outfit and every comfort around them, they spoke to me exultingly of their prospects in the land of their golden dreams. Today, as then, I ride by them, but no word of friendly greeting falls upon my ear, no face meets me with a smile of recognition; the empty sockets from their ghastly skulls tell me a tale of horror and of blood. On every side around me for the space of a mile lie the remains of carcasses dismembered by the wild beasts; bones, left for nearly two years unburied, bleached in the elements of the mountain wilds, gnawed by the hungry wolf, broken and hardly to be recognized. Garments of babes and little ones, faded and torn, fluttering from each ragged bush, from which the warble of the songster of the desert sounds as mockery. Human hair, once falling in glossy ringlets around childhood's brow or virtue's form, now strewing the plain in masses, matted, and mingling with the musty mould. To-day, in one grave, I have buried the bones and skulls of twelve women and children, pierced with the fatal ball or shattered with the axe. In another the shattered relics of eighteen men, and yet many more await their gloomy resting-place.

Afar from the homes of their childhood, buried in the heart of almost trackless desserts, shut up within never-ending mountain barriers, cut off from all communications with fellow-men, surrounded by overwhelming numbers, harmless citizens of land of justice and freedom, with their wives and families, as dear to them as our own to us, were coolly, deliberately, and designedly butchered by those professing to be their own countrymen.

I pause to ask one calm, quiet question. Are these facts known in the land where I was born and bred?

I have conversed with the Indians engaged in this massacre. They say that they but obeyed the command of Brigham Young, sent by letter, as soldiers

obey the command of their chief; that the Mormons were not only the instigators but the most active participants in the crime; that Mormons led the
attack, took possession of the spoil; that much of that spoil remains with
them; and still more, was sold at the tithing office of the Church.

Such facts can and will be proved by legal testimony. Sixteen children, vary-
ing from two to nine years of age have been recovered from the Mormons.
These could not be induced to utter a word until assured that they were out
of the hands of the Mormons and safe in the hands of the Americans. Then
their tale is so consonant with itself that it can not be doubted. Innocence
has in truth spoken. The time fast approaches when "justice shall be laid to
the line, and righteousness to the plummet."

James H. Carleton: A Great and Fearful Crime

Even more damning than the press reports was the report of the professional
soldier who inspected the field. Maj. James H. Carleton of the U.S. Army's
First Dragoons was deeply outraged by the evidence of a deliberate mass execution of men, women, and children. "There has been a great and fearful
crime perpetrated," he wrote, branding those who did it "relentless, incarnate fiends." Outraged at what he saw on the Mountain Meadows killing
ground, both he and Capt. Reuben Campbell denounced the Mormon settlers who had committed the atrocity.[11] Contrary to the abuse that Apostle
Smith dumped on Cradlebaugh, the officer praised the fearless judge for his
work and his determination to bring those responsible to justice. The reports
of their visit to the site are the earliest and best accounts of what happened
at the massacre from the initial attack, made largely by Mormons painted as
Indians, to the final act of betrayal.

J. H. Carleton, Special Report of the
Mountain Meadows Massacre, House Doc. 605,
57th Cong., 1st sess., 1902, 9–16.

Camp at Mountain Meadows,
Utah Territory, May 25, 1859

[Paiute leader] Jackson says there were 60 Mormons led by Bishop John
D. Lee, of Harmony, and a prominent man in the church named Haight, who
lives at Cedar City. That they were all painted and disguised as Indians.

---

[11]As a major general, Carleton commanded Union forces in the Southwest during the Civil War. A
colonel in 1862, Reuben Campbell was killed leading the 7th North Carolina Infantry at the Battle of Gaines
Mill on the Virginia Peninsula.

That this painting and disguising was done at a spring in a canyon about a mile northeast of the spring where the emigrants were encamped, and that Lee and Haight led and directed the combined force of Mormons and Indians in the first attack, throughout the siege, and at the last massacre. The Santa Clara Indians say that the emigrants could not get to the water, as the besiegers lay around the spring ready to shoot anyone who approached it. This could easily have been done . . . The following account of the affair is, I think, susceptible to legal proof by those whose names are known, and who, I am assured, are willing to make oath to many of the facts which serve as links in the chain of evidence leading toward the truth of this grave question: By whom were these 120 men, women and children murdered? . . .

John D. Lee, Isaac C. Haight, John M. Higby (the first resides in Harmony, the last two at Cedar City), were the leaders who organized a party of fifty or sixty Mormons to attack this train.

They had also all the Indians which they could collect at Cedar City, Harmony, and Washington City to help them, a good many in number. This party then came down, and at first the Indians were ordered to stampede the cattle and drive them away from the train. They then commenced firing on the emigrants; this firing was returned by the emigrants; one Indian was killed, a brother of the chief of the Santa Clara Indians, another shot through the leg, who is now a cripple at Cedar City. There were without doubt a great many more killed and wounded. It was said the Mormons were painted and disguised as Indians. The Mormons say the emigrants fought "like lions" and that they saw they could not whip them by any fair fighting . . .

On my arrival at Mountain Meadows, the 16th instant, I encamped near the spring where the emigrants had encamped, and where they had intrenched themselves after they were first fired upon. The ditch they there dug is not yet filled up . . . On the 20th instant I took a wagon and a party of men and made a thorough search for others amongst the sage bushes for at least a mile back from the road that leads to Hamblin's house. Hamblin himself showed Sergeant Fritz of my party a spot on the right-hand side of the road where he had partially covered up a great many of the bones. These were collected, and a large number of others on the left-hand side of the road up the slope of the hill, and in the ravines and among the bushes. I gathered many of the disjointed bones of 34 persons. The number could easily be told by the number of pairs of shoulder blades and by lower jaws, skulls, and parts of skulls, etc.

These, with the remains of 2 others gotten in a ravine to the east of the spring, where they had been interred at but little depth—34 in all—I buried in a grave on the northern side of the ditch. Around and above this grave I caused to be built of loose granite stones hauled from the neighboring hills, a rude monument, conical in form and 50 feet in circumference at the base and 12 feet in height. This is surmounted by a cross hewn from red cedar wood. From the ground to top of cross is 24 feet. On the transverse part of the

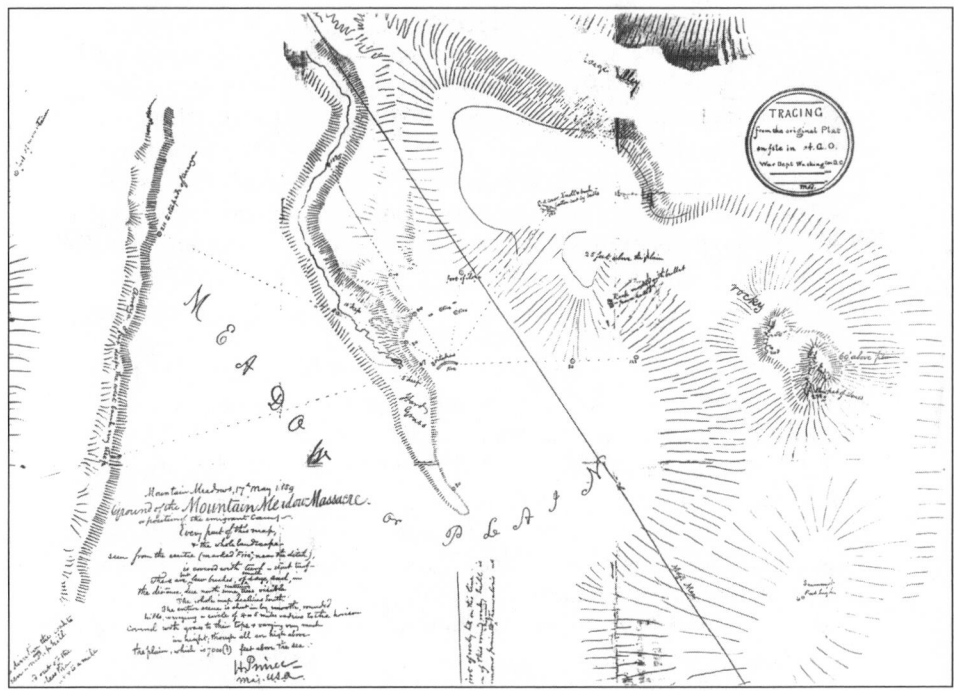

Army paymaster Maj. Henry Prince drew this map of the "Ground of the Mountain Meadow Massacre or position of the emigrant campground" at the site in May 1859. *Courtesy of Robert A. Clark.*

cross, facing toward the north, is an inscription carved deeply in the wood: "Vengeance is mine: I will repay, saith the Lord." And on a rude slab of granite set in the earth and leaning against the northern base of the monument there are cut the following words:

> Here 120 men, women, and children were massacred in cold blood early in September, 1857. They were from Arkansas.

I observed that nearly every skull I saw had been shot through with rifle or revolver bullets. I did not see one that had been "broken in with stones." Dr. Brewer showed me one, that probably of a boy of 18, which had been fractured and slit, doubtless by two blows of a bowie knife or other instrument of that character.

The scene of the massacre, even at this late day, was horrible to look upon. Women's hair, in detached locks and in masses, hung to the sage bushes and was strewn over the ground in many places. Parts of little children's dresses and of female costume dangled from the shrubbery or lay scattered about; and among these, here and there, on every hand, for at least a mile in the direction of the road, by 2 miles east and west, there gleamed, bleached white by the weather, the skulls and other bones of those who had suffered. A glance into the wagon when all these had been collected revealed a sight which can never be forgotten.

The idea of the melancholy procession of that great number of women and children, followed at a distance by their husbands and brothers, after all their suffering, their watching, their anxiety and grief, for so many gloomy days and dismal nights at the corral, thus moving slowly and sadly up to the point where the Mormons and Indians lay in wait to murder them; these doomed and unhappy people literally going to their own funeral; the chill shadows of night closing darkly around them, sad precursors of the approaching shadows of a deeper night, brings to the mind a picture of human suffering and wretchedness on the one hand, and of human treachery and ferocity upon the other, that can not possibly be excelled by any other scene that ever before occurred in real life . . .

Maj. Henry Prince, United States Army, drew a map of the ground about the spring where the entrenchment was dug, and embracing the neighboring hills behind which the Mormons had cover. On the crest of these hills are still traces of some rude little parapets made of loose stones and loopholed for rifles. Marks of bullets shot from the corral are seen upon these stones . . .

In pursuing the bloody thread which runs throughout this picture of sad realities, the question how this crime, that for hellish atrocity has no parallel in our history, can be adequately punished often comes up and seeks in vain for an answer. Judge Cradlebaugh says that with Mormon juries the attempt to administer justice in this Territory is simply a ridiculous farce . . .

James Henry Carleton,
Brevet Major, U.S.A., Captain in the First Dragoons.

William H. Rogers: Skulls Laying Grinning at You

William Rogers, affectionately known as "Colonel" and "Uncle Billy" in both California and Carson Valley, was already a western legend when he moved to Great Salt Lake City in 1858. There he quickly won "a legion of friends" and opened the California House, a hotel "fitted up in superior style."[12] Rogers accompanied Indian Affairs superintendent Jacob Forney to the Meadows and later returned as a deputy U.S. marshal with Judge Cradlebaugh. He described the massacre site to the newspaper in Ohio.

12"California House," The Valley Tan, 10 December 1858. For Rogers's career in Hope Valley, California, see Allen, The Tennessee Letters, 175.

Rogers, "Details of the Mountain Meadows Massacre in Utah—
Rescue of the Children—Escape of the Murderers,"
Painesville Telegraph, 21 July 1859, 2.

A letter from Salt Lake City June 6th, gives the harrowing details of the massacre of a train of emigrants from Arkansas to California, at Mountain Meadows, on the 19th of September '57, and the recovery of seventeen of the children carried off by the Indians. There were about one hundred and forty persons in the train, and the surviving children were about 350 miles south of Salt Lake City. The writer accompanied the Superintendent of Indian Affairs, and says:

The train passed through the upper part of the Territory unmolested. They were directed to go the southern route, as it was getting late in the season. After passing through all the settlements south for 360 [260] miles to the Mountain Meadows, they stopped to recruit their stock before they struck the Deserts, as they would have Deserts for 400 miles after leaving Mountain Meadows.

The Meadows is a beautiful spot, about four miles in length, and one fourth of a mile wide, and at the lower end is a fine spring.

They corralled their wagons and were there three days in quietness, 25 miles from any settlement, when, early on the morning of the 4th day, they were attacked, as they supposed, by a large party of Indians. The Indians fired on the emigrants and killed and wounded several. After this the emigrants set their wagon wheels in the ground, and threw the earth up against the bodies, making a snug defense. The Indians fought them for five days, having previously run all their stock off. The emigrants were within ten yards of as fine a spring as you ever saw, but could get no water, for whenever one came out to get it, he was shot down. The spring has a high bank, a deep ravine makes off from it, and in this the Indians were concealed. After fighting for five or six days, a party of Mormons approached the corral with a white flag in hand, to show the emigrants that they were friends.

The emigrants directly dressed a little girl in white and placed her at the mouth of the corral. The Mormon party then came in, sat down, and talked to the head man of the train for more than an hour, telling him that they had come as friends of the party to escort them back to Cedar City, about 35 miles behind, provided they would give up their arms, and leave all they had behind. They promised to protect them from the Indians. They marched the party in front of them baak [*sic*] on the road about 2,500 yards, where they had to pass through some sedge bushes—the Mormon escorts gave a signal, and all at once the Indians raised in the bushes—the Mormon escort fired first and killed all the men—then they went to work on women and children.

The spot can still speak for itself. When I first passed through the place I could walk for near a mile on bones, and skulls laying grinning at you, and women and children's hair in bunches as big as a bushel.

Judge Cradlebaugh and myself have the names of sixty white men who participated in this affair. It was done by council from Bishops in the Mormon Church. The Bishops were the head killers. They did not leave one to tell the tale. The oldest of the children is between seven and eight years of age. We have seventeen here. They are getting ready to send them to their friends in Arkansas, as there was $10,000 appropriated by Congress for that purpose—so you can see by what means the Mormons have lived and supported their Church. This was the richest train that ever passed through this country, and after killing all the party except 17 little children, they took cattle, wagons and horses back to Cedar City and sold them at public sale. The children were divided out to different ones—some who had no children took two.

All the above has been sworn to before Judge Bradlebaugh [*sic*]. He has issued warrants for all parties, but they fly to the mountains.

W. H. Rogers.

Marshal Rogers published the first detailed report in Utah on the massacre in *The Valley Tan*. To this day it remains one of the most accurate descriptions of the atrocity—and when it appeared on 29 February 1860, it ignited a firestorm. The issue would be the paper's last, wrote editor Stephen DeWolfe, due to a paper shortage and the harassment of his Mormon shop foreman by LDS authorities—but it seems he deliberately decided to save Rogers's damning indictment to mark the demise of the first non-Mormon paper in Utah.

"STATEMENT OF WM. H. ROGERS,"
THE VALLEY TAN, 29 FEBRUARY 1860, 2/4–3/3.

When we arrived here in April 1859, more than a year and a half after the massacre occurred, the ground, for a distance of more than a hundred yards around the central point, was covered with the skeletons and bones of human beings, interspersed in places with rolls or bunches of tangled and matted hair, which from its length, evidently belonged to females. In places the bones of small children were lying side by side with those of grown persons, as if parent and child had met death at the same instant and with the same stroke. Small bonnets and dresses, and scraps of female apparel were also to be seen in places on the ground there, like the bones of those who wore them, bleached from long exposure, but their shape was in many instances entire. In a gulch or hole in the ravine by the side of the road, a large number of leg and arm bones, and also skulls, could be seen sticking above the surface, as if they had been buried there, but the action the water and digging of the wolves had again exposed them to sight. The entire scene was one too horrible and sickening for language adequately to describe.

From this spot we proceeded south about one mile to a large spring, where the emigrants were encamped when the attack was first made upon them previous to the massacre. Here, within a few yards of the spring, we could distinctly define the form and size of the corral which they made, from a number of small holes, forming together a circle in the shape of a corral. These holes were dug for the purpose of lowering the wheels of their wagons in them, so as to form a better protection, after the attacks began. In the center of the corral a pit some twenty feet long, and four or five wide and deep, was dug for the purpose, no doubt, of placing the women and children in order to protect them from the fire of the assailants. To the left of this corral, and about one hundred and fifty or sixty yards distant, on a small mound or knoll, a number of stones were still piled up in a way to form a partial breastwork or protection against the fire which the emigrants no doubt returned for several days against their assailants. Numbers of the stones in this breastwork had bullet marks upon them on the side towards the corral, fully supporting the above construction as to its use. In places around the corral, human bones and imperfect skeletons were lying on the ground, indicating with the corral and the breastwork on the knoll, that it was here, and not at the place spoken of where the great body of the bones were found, that the work of slaughter began . . .

Owing to some disadvantages in the location of Cedar City, a large portion of the inhabitants that once dwelt there had moved away, and there was, in consequence, a good many vacant houses in the place. Judge Cradlebaugh obtained the use of one of these to stay in while he remained, and for the purpose of a courtroom. As soon as it became known that Judge C. intended holding a court, and investigating the circumstances of the massacre, and that he would have troops to ensure protection, and enforce his writs if necessary, several persons visited him at his room, at late hours of the night, and informed him of different facts connected with the massacre. All those that called thus, stated that it would be at the risk of their lives if it became known that they had communicated anything to him; and they requested Judge Cradlebaugh, if he met them in public in the day time, not to recognize them as persons that he had before seen.

One of the men who called thus on Judge Cradlebaugh, confessed that he participated in the massacre, and gave the following account of it: Previous to the massacre, there was a council held at Cedar City, which President Haight, and Bishops Higby and Lee attended. At this council they designated or appointed a large number of men residing in Cedar City, and in other settlements around, to perform the work of dispatching these emigrants. The men appointed for this purpose, were instructed to report, well armed at a given time, to a spring or small stream, lying a short distance to the left of the road leading into the meadows, and not very far from Hamblin's ranch, but concealed from it by intervening hills. This was the place of rendezvous; and here the men, when they arrived, painted and otherwise disguised themselves so as to resemble Indians. From thence they proceeded early on Monday morning, by a path or trail which leads from this spring directly into the meadows, and enters the road some distance beyond Hamblin's ranch. By taking this route they could not be seen by any one at the ranch. On arriving at the corral of the emigrants, a number of the men were standing on the outside by the camp-fires, which, from appearances, they had just been building. These were first fired upon, and at the first discharge several of them fell dead or wounded; the remainder immediately ran to the inside of the corral, and began fortifying themselves, and preparing for defence as well as they could, by shoving their wagons closer together and digging holes into which to lower them, so as to keep the shots from going under and striking them. The attack continued in a desultory and irregular manner for four or five days. The corral was closely watched, and if any of the emigrants showed themselves, they were instantly fired at from without. If they attempted to go to the spring, which was only a few yards distant, they were sure to fall by the rifles of their assailants. In consequence of the almost certain death that resulted from any attempt to pro-cure water, the emigrants, before the siege discontinued, suffered intensely from thirst. The assailants, believing at length that the emigrants could not be sub-dued by the means adopted, resorted to treachery and stratagem to accom-plish what they had been unable to do by force. They returned to the spring where they had painted and disguised themselves previous to commencing the attack, and there removed those disguises, and again assumed their ordinary dress. After this, Bishop Lee, with a party of men, returned to the camp of the emigrants, bearing a white flag as a signal of truce. From the position of the corral, the emigrants were able to see them some time before they reached it. As soon as they discerned it, they dressed a little girl in white, and placed her at the entrance of the corral, to indicate their friendly feelings to the per-sons bearing the flag. Lee and his party, on arriving, were invited into the cor-ral, where they stayed about an hour, talking with them about the attack that had been made upon them. Lee told the emigrants that the Indians had gone off over the hills and that if they would lay down their arms and give up their property, he and his party would conduct them back to Cedar City; but if they went out with their arms, the Indians would look upon it as an unfriendly act, and would again attack them. The emigrants, trusting to Lee's honor and to the sincerity of his statement, consented to the terms which he proposed, and left their property and all their arms at the corral; and, under the escort of Lee and his party, started towards the north in the direction of Cedar City. After they had proceeded about a mile on their way, on a signal given by Bishop Higby, who was one of the party that went to the corral with Lee, the slaughter began.

The men were mostly killed or shot down at the first fire, and the women and children, who immediately fled to different directions, were quickly pur-sued and dispatched.

Such was the substance, if not the exact words, of a statement made by a man to Judge Cradlebaugh, in my presence, who at the same time confessed that he participated in the horrible events which he related. He also gave Judge Cradlebaugh the names of 25 or 30 other men living in the region, who assisted in the massacre. He offered also to make the same statement in court and under oath, if protection was guaranteed to him. He gave as a reason for divulging these facts that they had tormented his mind and conscience since they occurred, and he expressed a willingness to stand trial for his crime.[13]

THE ARREST OF BRIGHAM YOUNG

The prying judge had been a worry even before Jacob Forney came back from the south with seventeen ragged orphans in tow. But when the agent reported in early May 1859 in *The Valley Tan* that "the Indians had material aid or assistance from whites," it appeared he was fishing for some very big fish.[14]

Two days after Forney's letter appeared, Brigham Young met with Daniel H. Wells, George A. Smith, E. T. Benson, Hosea Stout, and Territorial Attorney Seth Blair in the Beehive House to discuss "a question of accessory."[15] It shortly became apparent that the "question" involved the looming certainty that the former governor would be indicted for his role in the massacre and subsequent failure to arrest the perpetrators, rescue the survivors, and recover their property. It was decided that Young would surrender to a county probate court for a "fair and impartial trial." There could be but one reason that Young would submit to arrest on a warrant issued by the Mormon probate judge Elias Smith and served by Sheriff Robert T. Burton, one of his most trusted underlings: He wanted to make sure that any trial for his role in the massacre would be held before a court in which he would decide the outcome.

Young enjoyed this privilege because Mormon lawmakers had vested the probate courts, ruled by Mormon judges, with original criminal and civil jurisdiction, powers not intended by Congress when it created the territory

---

[13]Rogers's entire statement is found in *The Valley Tan*, 29 February 1860, 2/4–3/3; and in Brooks, *Mountain Meadows Massacre*, 263–78.

[14]*The Valley Tan*, 10 May 1859. Forney waited three months to report his findings to the office of Indian Affairs. Then he said evidence that justified "the declaration that this massacre was concocted by white men and consummated by whites and Indians." He also dismissed the poison story. "*In my opinion, bad men, for a bad purpose, have magnified a natural circumstance for the perpetration of a crime that has no parallel in American history for atrocity.*" See "Forney's Report," in Brooks, *The Mountain Meadows Massacre*, 253–60.

[15]Journal History, 12 May 1859; and Smith and Burton, Executed Warrant, LDS Archives. This file contains a draft of Young's affidavit and the executed warrant.

This little-known portrait of Brigham Young
appears to be part of a set that Charles W.
Carter shot in the mid-1860s. *Courtesy of the
Ken Sanders Collection.*

in 1850. Thus circumvented, the three district courts under judges appointed by the president were rendered virtually toothless. The tactic gave Young
control over the courts and stripped district benches under men like John
Cradlebaugh of any jurisdiction. Judge Smith issued a written warrant for
Young's arrest, stamped with the court's seal—"Be Just."

JUDGE ELIAS SMITH,
WARRANT FOR THE ARREST OF BRIGHAM YOUNG,
MAY 1859, LDS ARCHIVES.

To Robert T. Burton, Sheriff of said County and his Deputy
Greeting:—
      Whereas on this 12th day of May A.D. one thousand eight hundred and
fifty nine, Brigham Young Sen. of Great Salt Lake City in the County of Great
Salt Lake and Territory of Utah, filed in the Clerk's Office of the Probate
Court within and for the County and Territory aforesaid, the following information to wit:—"Territory of Utah, Great Salt Lake County, S.S. Personally appeared before me, Elias Smith Judge of the Probate Court within and
for the County of Great Salt Lake, Territory of Utah, Brigham Young Sen.,
who being duly sworn according to law, says that on or about the time between
the ninth and thirtieth day of September A.D. one thousand eight hundred
and fifty Seven, a company of Emigrants to the number of one hundred per-

sons, more or less, comprising men, women and children, names to the deponent unknown, while passing through the Territory aforesaid, on their way, as he supposes, to California, were, as he was informed, attacked by a party of armed men, and by them murdered in the region of Country known as the "Mountain Meadows," in the County of Washington, and Territory of Utah aforesaid. Deponent further says that in consequence of the disturbed state of affairs in this Territory during the fall and winter subsequent to the aforesaid murder, no court, to the knowledge of deponent, was held in the County or Judicial District in which said murder was said to have been committed, and that deponent was early in the subsequent spring succeeded as Governor by his Excellency Alfred Cumming, and as Superintendent of Indian Affairs by Dr. Jacob Forney.

Deponent further says that on the eighth day of March A.D. one thousand eight hundred and fifty nine, in a charge delivered in Provo City, County of Utah, by the honorable John Cradlebaugh associate Justice of the Supreme Court of the United States, for Utah Territory, to the Grand Jury for the Second Judicial district of said Territory, and in a speech delivered by said Judge at the discharge of the aforementioned Grand Jury on the (21) twenty-first of March A.D. one thousand eight hundred and fifty nine, he, deponent, was directly charged with interfering with the courts of justice, and preventing the punishment of offenders, thereby charging him as being accessory after the fact, to the murder of the aforesaid and other crimes, and that deponent was further charged indirectly, in the charge and speech aforesaid with instigating the committal of the murder aforesaid, thereby charging deponent as being accessory before the fact to the murder aforesaid. Deponent further says that he was during the whole of the year one thousand eight hundred and fifty Seven, and subsequently until succeeded in office as aforesaid by his Excellency Alfred Cumming and Dr. Jacob Forney, a resident of Great Salt Lake County in the Territory of Utah, and there kept his office, and discharged his duties as Governor and Superintendent of Indian Affairs, and that subsequent to the first of June in said year he did not leave the County of Great Salt Lake, nor until he was succeeded in office as aforesaid, so far as deponent at present remembers.

Now, therefore, owing to the aforesaid charges having been made and published to the world, by men in high authority, doubtless thereby acquiring more or less credence, and feeling unwilling to rest under the Stigma of such infamous charges and accusations, deponent claims the privilege of a fair and impartial investigation and trial and the rendition of a just verdict on the Judgment of his peers.

Sworn and subscribed to   "Brigham Young, Sen."
before me on this Twelfth day of May A.D. 1859
/s/ E. Smith

These are therefore to command you to arrest the said Brigham Young, Sen. and him safely keep subject to the order of this court, until an investigation of the matters set forth in the foregoing affidavit may be had in the premises, and the said Brigham Young, Sen. dealt with according to laws. Hereof fail not and of this writ make due returns, with your doings Herein endorsed.

Given under my hand and the seal of said court this 12th day of May A.D. 1859

/s/ E. Smith
Judge

As noted on the writ, the next day Salt Lake County sheriff Robert T. Burton returned the "Warrant for the arrest of Brigham Young" to the Probate Court, "having duly served the same by arresting Brigham Young Sen and having him now in my Custody Subject to the Court." If Young was "dealt with according to laws" in Judge Smith's courtroom, no trace of such justice survives.[16]

ATTORNEY GENERAL JEREMIAH BLACK: THE GOVERNOR OF THE TERRITORY ALONE

Even as Judge Cradlebaugh issued arrest warrants for more than three dozen men, including John D. Lee, orders from Camp Floyd ended his crusade. Acting on Cumming's recommendation, President Buchanan restricted the authority to requisition troops only to the governor. Since Cumming refused to authorize soldiers and since no one else was foolish or brave enough to become deputies of U.S. Marshal Peter Dotson, further investigation of the massacre and other crimes or the arrest of those responsible was cut short. Buchanan through his attorney general frowned on both Cradlebaugh and Associate Justice Charles E. Sinclair for exceeding their authority and causing all the trouble at Provo.

Encouraged by such support, Cumming pursued his appeasement policy so far as to urge Washington to recognize the territorial law giving probate courts original civil and criminal jurisdiction.[17] With his approval, the Utah legislature also redrew the judicial districts to pack Cradlebaugh off five hundred miles to a new post in Carson Valley in present western Nevada.

---

[16]Probate Court Criminal and Civil Case Docket, Great Salt Lake County, Utah State Archives.

[17]"Official report of Governor Cumming to General Cass," 2 February 1860, and Cumming to Cass, 22 March, 1860, Buchanan, *Territory of Utah*, House Doc. 78, Serial 1056, 44, 48.

J. BLACK TO J. CRADLEBAUGH, CHAS. E. SINCLAIR, 17 MAY 1859,
IN *CONDITION OF AFFAIRS IN THE TERRITORY OF UTAH*, 36TH CONG.,
1ST SESS., HOUSE EXEC. DOC. 78, SERIAL 1056, 1860, 2–5.

Gentlemen:

. . . assuming the legal right of the judge to put the marshal's business into the hands of the army without the marshal's concurrence, and granting, also, that this might be done by means of a requisition, was there, in this case, any occasion for the exercise of such power? When we consider how essentially peaceable is the whole spirit of our judicial system, and how exclusively it aims to operate by moral force, or, at most, by the arm of civil power, it can hardly be denied that the employment of military troops about the courts should be avoided as long as possible. *Inter arma silent leges*, says the maxim;[18] and the converse of it ought to be equally true, that *inter leges silent arma*. The President has not found, either on the face of the requisition, or in any other paper received by him, a statement of specific facts strong enough to make the presence of the troops seem necessary. Such necessity ought to have been perfectly plain before the measure was resorted to.

It is very probable that the Mormon inhabitants of Utah have been guilty of crimes, for which they deserve the severest punishment. It is not intended by the government to let any one escape against whom the proper proofs can be produced. With that view, the district attorney has been instructed to use all possible diligence in bringing criminals of every class and of all degrees to justice. We have the fullest confidence in the vigilance, fidelity, and ability of that officer. If you shall be of opinion that his duty is not performed with sufficient energy, your statement to that effect will receive the prompt attention of the President.

It is also very likely that public opinion in the Territory is frequently opposed to the conviction of parties who deserve punishment. It may be that extensive conspiracies are formed there to defeat justice. These are subjects upon which we, at this distance, can affirm or deny nothing. But, supposing your opinion upon them to be correct, every inhabitant of Utah must still be proceeded against in the regular legal and constitutional way. At all events, the usual and established modes of dealing with public offenders must be exhausted before we adopt any others.

On the whole, the President is very decidedly of opinion:

1. That the governor of the Territory alone has power to issue a requisition upon the commanding general for the whole or a part of the army.

2. That there was no apparent occasion for the presence of the troops at Provo.

3. That if a rescue of the prisoners in custody had been attempted, it was

---

[18]A Latin motto that means, "In time of war, the laws fall silent."

the duty of the marshal, and not of the judges, to summon the force which might be necessary to prevent it.

4. That the troops ought not to have been sent to Provo without the concurrence of the governor, nor kept there against the remonstrance.

5. That the disregard of these principles and rules of action has been, in many ways, extremely unfortunate.

J. S. Black

On the day he pronounced Cradlebaugh's actions "unfortunate," Attorney General Black praised the efforts of U.S. Attorney Wilson to keep the peace while contradictorily urging him on the other hand to pursue wrongdoers with vigor and impartiality. Black called Wilson's attention to the massacre of Arkansas emigrants at Mountain Meadows and asked him about it, but quickly added that his questions were only intended to reflect the government's interest, not tell him what to do. Wilson did nothing.[19]

JUDGE CRADLEBAUGH:
CRIMES WERE COMMITTED BY ORDERS OF COUNCIL

John Cradlebaugh was not a man to suffer silently unjust criticism for doing what he knew was just, necessary, and legal. Buchanan and Attorney General Black had accused him of exceeding his authority by requisitioning troops to carry out duties that properly belonged to the U.S. marshal "and all his deputies." Shortly after the judge came back from Mountain Meadows, U.S. Marshal Peter Dotson returned the warrants for the arrest of men charged with the massacre and other crimes to the judge with a letter explaining why "all his deputies" could not serve them. Cradlebaugh seized the opportunity to forward Dotson's letter direct to the president to show why he had requisitioned the troops and to illustrate the difficulties the federal judges faced in Utah. In another letter to Buchanan, the frustrated Dotson two months later blasted the president's appeasement policy and angrily resigned.

MARSHAL PETER K. DOTSON TO JOHN CRADLEBAUGH,
3 JUNE 1859, NATIONAL ARCHIVES.

Sir:

I have received from you certain warrants of arrest against many persons in your Judicial District charged with murder, including one against John D.

---

[19]See Black to Wilson, 17 May 1859, in Buchanan, *Territory of Utah*, House Doc. 78, Serial 1056, 9–10.

Lee, John M. Higbee (a Bishop—Haigh[t] (his and thirty six others for the murder of one hundred and nineteen men, women, and children at the "Mountain Meadows"—and against Porter Rockwell, John A. Wolf (President of the Seventies) Jacob Bigler (a Bishop) Samuel Pitchforth (President of the Seventies),—[Timothy B.] Foot[e] (Mayor of Nephi) and five others for the murder of the Aikins Brothers and ten others,—one against Lewis Bunty and three others for stealing six mules the property of the United States. I also have in my possession warrants against Aaron V. Johnson (a Bishop—[and James C.] Snow of Provo City, a President in the church) and certain others for the murder of the Parishes—also a warrant against Bishop Hancock and others for the murder of [Henry] Jones and mother. I regret to inform you that it is not in my power to execute any of these processes. I have made repeated efforts by the aid as well of the military as of the civil posse to execute the warrants last alluded to, but without success.

So large is the number of persons engaged in the commission of these crimes and such the feelings of the Mormon Church and the community in their favor that I cannot rely upon a civil posse to aid in arresting them. About the first of January last, holding a warrant issued by you for the arrest of Bishop Hancock and others, and being fully satisfied that I could not execute the command of the writ by any civil posse of that section of the Territory I called on Governor Cumming to make a requisition on the Commanding General of this Department for a small number of troops to assist as a posse. At the same time I made my affidavit to the fact of my utter inability to execute the warrants without such military aid, which affidavit I left with the Governor. His Excellency after considering the matter finally refused to make the requisition. I therefore do not feel warranted in again troubling his Excellency with another application. On account of the exclusive right claimed by Governor Cumming to call for troops to serve as a posse, I do not deem it proper to take the responsibility of making such a requisition until further advised by the Government.

In addition I beg leave to say that I have expended a considerable amount of my private means in efforts to execute writs for offences committee against Territorial laws which neither the Territory nor the federal Government provided for the payment of.

P. K. Dotson
U. S. Marshal

JOHN CRADLEBAUGH TO JAMES BUCHANAN,
3 JUNE 1859, NATIONAL ARCHIVES.

Sir:

I herewith enclose to you a letter addressed to me by P. K. Dotson Esq. U.S. Martial [*sic*] of this Territory. This letter taken in connection with the papers already sent on to Washington will serve to throw much light upon the conditions of affairs in this Territory.

In addition allow me to say I have lately visited the Southern Settlements of the Territory—Particularly the place where the 119 emigrants were massacred at the Mountain meadows on the 10th Sept 1857. Eighty or more white men were engaged in that affair. Warrants are now in the hands of the Marshal for forty of them. The entire white Population within 150 miles of the Mountain Meadows does not exceed 1100—with not more than 200 of an adult male population. About all of those engaged in committing that crime live within the limits I have stated and are connected with the remainder by church ties, endowment oaths & as relatives. So much of a church matter was this Mountain Meadow affair that much of the property was taken to the Tithing office and there sold out. I have made this statement to show you the impossibility of ~~execute~~ the marshal serving writs with the aid of a civil posse and also as reflecting upon the possibility of ~~executing~~ administering the law by jury trial.

It may be said in regard to all the murders for which writs have been issued that the perpetrators are now holding high civil & church offices and the evidence shows that the crimes were committed by orders of Council.

It is much to be regretted (sir) that there is not more coincidence of view and harmony of action ~~in~~ between the judges and executive of Utah. Without such concert the laws can neither be affectively nor worthily administered: with such concert the many atrocius crimes that have been committed could be [redressed] and although the perpetrators might not be punished through action of the juries—yet something in the way of establishing the Supremacy of the Laws for the future might thereby be achi[eved].

The immunity from punishment which criminals have enjoyed and still enjoy here tends to stimulate and multiply offences.

John Cradlebaugh

Smarting from Black's rebuke, in July 1859 Cradlebaugh and Judge Charles Sinclair sent the president a detailed defense of their actions and a report on conditions in Utah. U.S. Attorney Alexander Wilson had initiated "no criminal prosecutions whatever, although abundant evidence is attainable of mayhems, murder, and robberies." Wilson's prosecution of existing cases, Cradlebaugh and Sinclair charged, showed "neither vigilance nor ability," and his conduct exhibited "culpable timidity and neglect." In cases rising out of violations of individual rights and "crimes committed by the Mormons during their time of rebellion, he appears as their counsel to vindicate their conduct."[20]

---

[20]For Cradlebaugh and Sinclair's response to Black, see ibid., 11–21. Most of this document consists of Alexander Wilson's defense of his conduct.

Alfred Cumming blamed the federal judges and marshal for failing to accept his proposal to restart the stalled investigation into the massacre. The legislature had created territorial officers, such as prosecutor and marshal, whose duties were intended to preempt those of their federal counterparts. Cumming now advised "that John Kay, the *territorial marshal*, should be deputized" and given the writs that Dotson refused to serve without military protection. The judges rejected Kay as "a notorious Mormon" and said this strategy would simply "end in a Mormon whitewashing." Cumming stoutly insisted that Kay "was both able and willing to arrest the persons alluded to; and that I could perceive no material difference between the arrest and delivery of criminals by one person rather than another, whether Mormon or gentile."[21]

Buchanan, however, continued to press Wilson and Cumming to resolve the "mysteries" surrounding the massacre. In fall 1859, the territory's new surveyor general, Samuel C. Stambaugh, arrived with orders from the president. Buchanan reportedly "rapped Cumming over the knuckles" for his failure to execute the law, and Cumming assigned William Rogers to act as U.S. marshal for the inquiry.[22] Alexander Wilson had already asked Rogers "to collect evidence and summon witnesses in the case of the Mountain Meadow massacre" in early August. "No reasonable expectation of success can be entertained" for such an undertaking, Rogers replied, "unless a strong force, well equipped and furnished" accompanied the officer, and Wilson did not have a nickel to fund such an enterprise. "I would cheerfully undertake the business under auspices promising success," Rogers concluded.[23]

The posse that Governor Cumming recommended to Rogers speaks volumes about why Marshal Dotson had declined to accept John Kay's offer, as a Salt Lake newspaper correspondent explained:

> The advent of Col. Stambaugh has not been signalized by any remarkable act till to-night, when the fact is developed that he brought instructions to Governor Cumming to investigate the massacre at Mountain Meadows. This is part of the white-washing, perhaps, part of the combination—to shield crime, &c., mentioned by me in previous letters. The Governor designated a young man from Virginia (Mr. Rogers) to act as Marshal to inquire into this foul

---

[21]Buchanan, *Territory of Utah*, House Doc. 78, Serial 1056, 45–46.

[22]"The Mountain Meadows Massacre—Affected Inquiry Into It," *San Francisco Bulletin*, 28 October 1859, 3/4, from a transcription in the California State Library's Mormon file.

[23]Rodgers [*sic*] to General Wilson, 8 August 1859, in Buchanan, *Correspondence between the Judges of Utah and the Attorney General or President*, Sen. Exec. Doc. 32, Serial 1031, 41.

deed. He (Mr. R.) inquired who were to be his companions in the "civil posse" and affect the arrest of the murderers and aid him in the investigations. In answer, he was given the names of Bill Hickman, Porter Rockwell, and other notorious "Destroying Angels," and he indignantly spurned the proposition; and till today no one suspected what was the matter.[24]

Alexander Wilson successfully defended his failure to carry out the attorney general's orders. Superintendent Forney sent him eight names, including Lee, Haight, and Higbee, identifying Jacob Hamblin as a witness and promising to furnish others. This failed to satisfy Wilson, who was sick and had assigned the cases to his non-Mormon assistant, Stephen DeWolfe. Wilson wrote Forney on 19 August 1859 asking the agent to send DeWolfe "all the *evidence* you may have in your possession or under your command, or within your knowledge, in relation to the Mountain Meadow massacre." Wilson apparently believed there still was not enough evidence to indict anyone for the murders.

"Nothing has yet been done before the grand jury in regard to the Mountain Meadow massacre," DeWolfe reported. "I presume none of the witnesses regarding it are here, and I have called for no subpenas [*sic*] against them, regarding it, as you, no doubt, do, as altogether foolish and useless attempt to investigate into the matter, unless it can be gone into fully and thoroughly, and this I believe it is impossible to do at the present term of this court." Wilson discharged his grand jury on 29 August 1859 and left the territory three weeks later, appointing Hosea Stout, a veteran of the original Missouri Danite band, "to my office of public prosecutor."[25]

The territorial legislature redefined Utah's federal judicial districts and sent the troublesome Judge Cradlebaugh west to a new bench in Carson Valley. Here John Cradlebaugh become a leader in the movement to throw off Mormon rule and create in 1861 the Territory of Nevada. As its first congressional delegate, the territory chose the crusading judge himself.

Brigham Young: Crucifying to My Feelings

Having killed the investigation and returned power to Brigham Young, President Buchanan now had enough new problems to deal with as the nation

---

[24]"The Mountain Meadows Massacre," *San Francisco Bulletin*, 28 October 1859, 3/4.
[25]Buchanan, *Territory of Utah*, House Doc. 78, Serial 1056, 19, 32–33, 56.

headed into a civil war without worrying about trouble in a distant territory. Cradlebaugh's departure and Cumming's appeasement policy allowed Brigham Young to shelve the pretended arrest by the probate court and resume his duties as head of the Mormon domain without fear of prosecution. Still troubling, however, was the question of court jurisdiction. As was often his practice, Young assigned the real reason for his letter to its conclusion: he asked Thomas Kane to use his influence with the Buchanan administration to arrange for a ruling by the U.S. attorney general in favor of the probate courts that Young controlled.

BRIGHAM YOUNG TO THOMAS L. KANE,
15 DECEMBER 1859, LDS ARCHIVES.

My Dear Colonel Kane:—

. . . I occasionally perceive, from papers East and West, that the massacre at the Mountain Meadows still elicits more or less notice and comment, a great share of which is not very creditable either to candor or veracity. And some of the efforts made to arrive at the facts in that case have not been characterized by that good policy, impartiality, and observance of the people's rights which should accompany legal proceedings in a Republican Government, else I presume the affair, long ere this date, would have been thoroughly understood and correctly adjudicated.

Neither yourself, nor any one acquainted with me, will require my assurance that, had I been appraised of the intended onslaught at the Meadows, I should have used such efforts for its prevention as the time, distance, and my influence and facilities would have permitted. The horrifying event transpired without my knowledge, except from after report, and the recurring thought of it ever caused a shudder in my feelings.[26]

It is a subject exclusively within the province of judicial proceedings, and I have known and still prefer to know nothing touching the affair, until I in common with the people, learn the facts as they may be developed before those whose right it is to investigate and adjudicate thereupon. Colonel, you may think this a singular statement, but the facts of the massacre of men, women, and children are so shocking and crucifying to my feelings, that I have not suffered myself to hear any more about them than the circumstances of conversation compelled. But since some are prejudicially obtruding that affair upon public notice, and it appears uncertain when it will be better understood, unless we are privileged with a sound, intelligent adjudicators who, when claiming exclusive authority, will strictly adhere to the law and evidence, I have taken the liberty to transcribe, and herewith enclose, a letter addressed to me

[26]Why Young failed to quote or even mention his purported 10 September 1857 letter to Isaac Haight, responding to Haight's question as to what to do about the emigrants, is a mystery.

by Col. George A. Smith upon the subject.[27] Col. Smith is, and was at the time, a legislature Councillor [sic] from our southern counties, and had the opportunity of hearing many of the rumors afloat in that region. So far as I am able to judge, amid the few conflicting rumors I have suffered to be obtruded upon my feelings, I presume that Col. Smith's accompanying condensation, from the varied reports he deemed most worthy of notice, is the most reliable that can be obtained, until such time as the matter can receive an impartial judicial investigation.

Such investigation could long since have transpired, and the matter been thoroughly understood and justly disposed of, did we enjoy the court privileges which we deem the Organic Act[28] so plainly granted. But no, our Probate Courts, instead of jurisdiction as "limited by law" (acts of the Territorial Assembly relative to powers and jurisdiction), are debarred by the rulings and proceedings of the District Courts, upon every opportunity, from all actions in criminal cases, and from all of any moment in civil cases, there being a studied and persistent effort on their part to confine the Probate Courts to probate of wills, appointment of guardians, and like acts of minor import. Under these circumstances the Probate Courts decline acting as entertainers of business only to have it wrestled from them by courts whom they honestly deem have no superior legal authority in Territorial cases, save in the matter of appeals and a larger area for jurisdiction, the jurisdiction of a Probate Court being confined to one organized county, while that of a District Court embraces several counties. Bayonet courts have not made and, so far as yet appears, are not likely to make much progress towards bringing persons, whether guilty or not guilty, before them, and no true hearted citizen will marvel that such is the case, nor ever wish to have it otherwise, for such a course cannot lead to an impartial trial by one's peers.[29]

The Legislative Assembly and a very great majority of the people are sanguine of the justice, propriety, benefit, and legality of our legislation in regard to the powers and jurisdiction of our Probate Courts, and it is possible that the District Courts are candid in their interpretation of the Organic Act, and honest in their consequent efforts to so restrict our Probate Courts as to render them almost a nullity. But this difference of view and action causes great

---

[27]As part of George A. Smith's "investigation" of the massacre, he wrote two reports to Brigham Young that blamed the massacre on the Indians. See Brooks, *The Mountain Meadows Massacre*, 244–48, for the 17 August 1858 report that Young sent to Kane.

[28]Young referred to the act of Congress that established Utah Territory in 1850.

[29]"Bayonet courts" referred to the grand jury investigation that Judge John Cradlebaugh conducted in Provo in March and April 1859 under the protection of the army. Young's critique of Utah's federal courts did not find favor in the press, which complained that the secretary of the interior had sufficient evidence to convict John D. Lee "of having violated and murdered a young girl" at Mountain Meadows. Mormon authorities, reports claimed, "refuse to surrender this scoundrel for trial, unless he be tried before a Mormon jury; and as no Mormon jury has ever yet convicted any Mormon of any outrage on a Gentile, the offer is simply made to enable him to go scot free." See "Law in Utah," *New York Times*, 30 December 1859, 4.

hindrance in the conduct of judicial business, and affords opportunity for many plausible allegations as to tardy and inefficient administration of justice. Under these circumstances, if it will not be asking too much, nor trespassing to far upon the courtesy of the learned Attorney General of the U.S., I shall be highly gratified with a written statement of Judge Black's opinion upon this question.

Dear Colonel, please accept the gratifying assurance that your untiring and efficient services in behalf of the rights of mankind are highly appreciated by your numerous warm friends in Utah, who ever desire your welfare and that of your family, relatives, and friends, and who will not shrink from efforts to promote it.

And please accept for yourself and present to your mother, your true and noble hearted wife and beloved little ones the kinds regards of,

Truly Your Friend,
Brigham Young

As the nation slid toward all-out war during the next turbulent year, Attorney General Jeremiah S. Black's June 1859 instructions to Utah's federal attorney to "prosecute the rich and the poor, the influential and the humble with equal vigor" and his pointed questions about the murders at Mountain Meadows were entirely forgotten. The new judges for Utah Territory, Black assured the Mormon prophet in July 1860, "have been selected with a careful view to their moral as well as intellectual qualities. Their impartiality I am sure is above all dispute." They would "do their duty faithfully and uprightly and truly according to the best of their judgment and ability. This is what you need in order to give peace and security and safety to your rights of person, property and reputation." He regretted that the Senate had refused to confirm the pliant Alexander Wilson as U.S. attorney. (Mormon stalwart Hosea Stout served as U.S. attorney until 1867, but he never showed the slightest interest in prosecuting anyone for the massacre.) Black happily announced the appointment of territorial chief justice John Kinney, "against whom I believe no well-grounded accusation was ever made, though he served at a time when charges both true and false against the judiciary of the Territory were flying very abundantly."[30]

A confidential letter that Black had in his files from Kinney in March 1857 advising that an army regiment accompany a new set of federal officers to Utah may have made the attorney general feel he had made a clever choice. "Innocent and helpless men have been most cruelly murdered for no other

---

[30]Black to Young, 12 July 1860, LDS Archives.

reason than that they were gentiles or dissatisfied Mormons," Judge Kinney complained, and he denounced the Indian missionaries whom Young sent out annually "to poison their minds against the government and Americans and also to make them their allies in case of any difficulty with the U.S."[31] If Attorney General Black was confident that he had picked the right man to corner Brigham Young, he would not be the last lawyer to find himself outfoxed, for Kinney had learned a few hard lessons during his first term in Utah. As chief justice, legal historian Clifford L. Ashton reported, Kinney "had a change of heart, became pro-Mormon and ruled in favor of probate court jurisdiction." The judge told Wilford Woodruff that he had "not taken any step without Counciling" with Brigham Young, and he did nothing to seek justice for those murdered at Mountain Meadows or even for the four female and four male Mormon dissenters whom the Nauvoo Legion gunned down in June 1862 near Ogden while enforcing one of the judge's warrants. Ashton tells the happy ending of the tale: "The Mormon people and their leaders appreciated Judge Kinney's turnaround and returned his favors by unanimously electing him as their delegate to Congress" in August 1862.[32]

Black's conciliatory attitude probably reflected the Buchanan administration's desire to keep Young's vast domain among the states and territories loyal to the Union. If so, Utah's location athwart major east-west lines of travel and communication made securing the territory more important than pressing for an investigation that would provoke the Mormons. Abraham Lincoln, too, would see the need for federal control over the defiant territory, but typically he came up with a different solution. In 1862 he ordered the 3rd Regiment, California Volunteer Infantry, to Utah.

JOHN CRADLEBAUGH:
MORMONS PAINTED AND DISGUISED

As the Civil War raged, Brigham Young continued to cover up the murder of 120 American citizens, but the judge from Circleville, Ohio, refused to turn his blind eye on one of the cruelest crimes in U.S. history. The guns that fired

---

[31]Kinney to Black, 20 March 1857, Attorney General Files, National Archives, in MacKinnon, *At Sword's Point*, 109–11.

[32]Kenney, ed., *Wilford Woodruff's Journal*, 6:58; and Ashton, *The Federal Judiciary in Utah*, 21. The story of the "Morrisite Massacre" of June 1863, during which Maj. Robert Burton shot and murdered a woman who denounced the attack as "another Mountain Meadow Massacre," is summarized in Dwyer, *The Gentile Comes to Utah*, 107–10.

on Fort Sumter in April 1861 ended further investigations for a time, but they did not silence John Cradlebaugh either in Washington or on the field of battle. As Nevada Territory's first delegate to Congress, he took the floor in the U.S. House of Representatives to stop Utah's latest statehood bid.[33]

In his long address, the former judge reported how after the territorial marshal made a few arrests, "A general stampede immediately took place among the Mormons, and what I wish to call your attention to as particularly noticeable, is the fact that this OCCURRED MORE ESPECIALLY AMONG THE CHURCH OFFICIALS AND CIVIL OFFICERS." At his court, he heard complaint after complaint of murder and robbery, including the Parish and Potter murders, the killing of the Aiken party, "and worst, and darkest in this appaling [sic] catalogue of blood, the cowardly, cold-blooded butchery and robbery at the Mountain Meadows. At that time there still lay all ghastly under the sun of Utah the unburied skeletons of one hundred and nineteen men, women, and children, the hapless, hopeless victims of the Mormon creed."

CRADLEBAUGH, *UTAH AND THE MORMONS: SPEECH OF HON. JOHN CRADLEBAUGH*, 7 FEBRUARY 1863, 17–22.

The scene of this horrible massacre at the Mountain Meadows is situate[d] about three hundred and twenty miles west of south from Great Salt Lake city, on the road leading to Los Angelos, in California. I was the first Federal judge in that part of the Territory after the occurrence. My district extending from a short distance below Salt Lake city to the south end of the Territory, I determined to visit that part of my district, and, if possible, expose the persons engaged in the massacre, which I did in the early part of the year 1859. I accordingly embraced an opportunity of accompanying a small detachment of soldiers who were being sent to that section by General Johns[t]on, having requested the marshal of the Territory to accompany, or to send a deputy. He accordingly sent Deputy Wm. H. Rodgers, who went with me.

The command went as far south as the St. Clara, twenty miles beyond the Mountain Meadows, where we camped and remained about a week. During our stay there I was visited by the Indian chiefs of that section, who gave me their version of the massacre. They admitted that a portion of their men were engaged in the massacre, but were not there when the attack commenced. One of them told me, in the presence of the others, that after the attack had been

---

[33]The judge resigned his seat in Congress to recruit and command the 114th Ohio Volunteer Infantry Regiment. A minie ball struck Colonel Cradlebaugh in the mouth, knocked out many of his teeth, and shot away part of his lip, palate, and tongue as he lead his regiment in the first charge at Vicksburg. The disabling wound led to his death from pneumonia in 1872 in Nevada. His remains were later moved for final burial to Circleville, Ohio.

made, a white man came to their camp with a piece of paper, which, he said, Brigham Young had sent, that directed them to go and help to whip the emigrants. A portion of the band went, but did not assist in the fight. He gave as a reason that the emigrants had long guns, and were good shots. He said that his brother (this chief's name was Jackson) was shot while running across the Meadow at a distance of two hundred yards from the corral where the Emigrants were. He said the Mormons were all painted. He said the Indians got a part of the clothing; and gave the names of John D. Lee, President Haight, and Bishop Higbee as the big captains. It might be proper here to remark that the Indians in the southern part of the Territory of Utah are not numerous, and are a very low, cowardly, beastly set, very few of them being armed with guns. They were not formidable. I believe all in the southern part of the Territory would, under no circumstances, carry on a fight against ten white men.

From our camp on the St. Clara we again went back to the Mountain Meadows, camping near where the massacre had occurred. The Meadow is about five miles in length and one in width, running to quite a narrow point at the southwest end, being higher at the middle than either end. It is the divide between the waters that flow into the Great Basin and those emptying into the Colorado river. A very large spring rises in the south end of the narrow part. It was on the north side of this spring the emigrants were camped. The bank rises from the spring eight or ten feet, then extends off to the north about two hundred yards on a level. A range of hills is there reached, rising perhaps fifty or sixty feet. Back of this range is quite a valley, which extends down until it has an outlet, three or four hundred yards below the spring, into the main Meadow.

The first attack was made by going down this ravine, then following up the bed of the spring to near it, then at daylight firing upon the men who were about the camp-fires; in which attack ten or twelve of the emigrants were killed or wounded, the stock of the emigrants having been previously driven behind the hill and up the ravine. The emigrants soon got in condition to repel the attack, shoved their wagons together, sank the wheels in the earth, and threw up quite an entrenchment. The fighting after [this] continued as a siege, the assailants occupying the hill, and firing at any of the emigrants that exposed themselves, having a barricade of stones along the crest of the hill as a protection. The siege was continued for five days, the besiegers appearing in the garb of Indians. The Mormons seeing that they could not capture the train without making some sacrifice of life on their part, and getting weary of the fight, resolved to accomplish by strategy what they were not able to do by force. The fight had been going on for five days, and no aid is received from any quarter, although the family of Jacob Ham[b]lin, the Indian agent, were living in the upper end of the Meadow, and within hearing of the reports of the guns.

Who can imagine the feelings of these men, women, and children, surrounded, as they supposed themselves to be, by savages. Fathers and mothers
only can judge what they must have been. Far off in the Rocky mountains,
without transportation—for their cattle, horses, and mules had been run off—
not knowing what their fate was to be, we can but poorly realize the gloom
that pervaded the camp.

A wagon is descried far up the meadows. Upon its nearer approach it is
observed to contain armed men. See! now they raise a white flag. All is joy in
the corral. A general shout is raised, and in an instant a little girl dressed in
white is placed at an opening between two of the wagons as a response to the
signal. The wagon approaches—the occupants are welcomed into the corral.
The emigrants little suspecting that they were entertaining the fiends that had
been besieging them.

This wagon contained President Haight, and Bishop John D. Lee, among
others of the Mormon church. They professed to be on good terms with the
Indians, and represented the Indians as being very mad. They also proposed
to intercede and settle the matter with the Indians. After several hours of parley, they having apparently visited the Indians, gave the ultimatum of the Indians, which was that the emigrants should march out of their camp, leaving
everything behind them, even their guns. It was promised by the Mormon
bishops that they would bring a force and guard the emigrants back to the
settlements.

The terms were agreed to; the emigrants being desirous of saving the lives
of their families. The Mormons retired and subsequently appeared at the corral with thirty or forty armed men. The emigrants were marched out, the women
and children in front and the men behind, the Mormon guard being in the
rear. When they had marched in this way about a mile, at a given signal the
slaughter commenced. The men were most all shot down at the first fire from
the guard. Two only escaped, who fled to the desert, and were followed 150
miles before they were overtaken and slaughtered.

The women and children ran on two or three hundred yards further, when
they were overtaken, and with the aid of the Indians they were slaughtered.
Seventeen only of the small children were saved, the eldest being about seven
years. Thus, on the 10th day of September, 1857, was consummated one of
the most cruel, cowardly and bloody murders known in our history. Upon
the way from the meadows, a young Indian pointed out to me the place where
the Mormons painted and disguised themselves.

I went from the Meadows to Cedar city; the distance is 35 or 40 miles. I
contemplated holding an examining court there, should General Johns[t]on
furnish me protection, and also protect witnesses and furnish the marshal a
posse to aid in making arrests. While there I issued warrants on affidavits
filed before me for the arrest of the following named persons.

Jacob [Isaac] Haight, President of the Cedar City stake, Bishop John M. Higbee, and Bishop John D. Lee, Columbus Freemen, William Slade, John Willis, William Riggs, —— Ingram, Daniel McFarlan, William Stewart, Ira Allen and son, Thomas Cartwright, E. Welean, William Halley, Jabes Nomlen, John Mangum, James Price, John W. Adair, —— Tyler, Joseph Smith, Samuel Pollock, John McFarlan, Nephi Johnson, —— Thornton, Joel White, —— Harrison, Chas. Hopkins, Joseph Elang, Samuel Lewis, Sims Matheny, James Mangum, Harrison Pierce, Samuel Adair, F. C. McDulange, Wm. Bateman, Ezra Curtis, and Alexander Loveridge.

In a few days after arriving at Cedar City, Capt. Campbell arrived with his command from the Meadows; on its return he advised me that he had received orders for his command entire to return to Camp Floyd. The General having received orders from Washington that the military should not be used in protecting the Courts, or in acting as a posse to aid the Marshal in making arrests.

While at Cedar City I was visited by a number of apostate Mormons who gave me every assurance that they would furnish an abundance of evidence in regard to the matter, so soon as they were assured of military protection. In fact, some of the persons engaged in the act came to see me in the night, and gave a full account of the matter, intending, when protection was at hand, to become witnesses. They claimed that they had been forced into the matter by the Bishops. Their statements confirmed what the Indians had previously said to me. Mr. Rodgers, the Deputy Marshal, was also engaged in hunting up the children, survivors of the massacre. They were all found in the custody of the Mormons. *Three or four of the eldest recollect and relate all the incidents of the massacre, corroborating the statement of the Indians, and the statements made by the citizens of Cedar City to me.*

These children are now in the south part of Missouri, or north part of Arkansas; their testimony could soon be taken if desired. No one can depict the glee of these infants when they realized that they were in the custody of what they called "the Americans," for such is the designation of those not Mormons. They say they never were in the custody of the Indians. I recollect of one of them, "John Calvin Sorrow,"[34] after he found he was safe, and before he was brought away from Salt Lake City, although not yet nine years of age; sitting in a contemplative mood, no doubt thinking of the extermination of his family, say, "Oh, I wish I was a man, I know what I would do; I would shoot John D. Lee; I saw him shoot my mother." I shall never forget how he looked.

Time will not permit me to elaborate this matter. I shall barely sum up and refer every member of this house who may have the least doubt about

[34]William C. Mitchell correctly identified the boy as John Calvin Miller. William C. Mitchell to Commissioner of Indian Affairs Alfred B. Greenwood, 27 April 1860.

the guilt of the Mormons in this massacre, and the other crimes to which I have alluded, to the evidence published in the appendix hereto.

The Indians would not have saved the infant children from the slaughter. Neither could they have induced the "emigrants" to have left their protected position. It should also be borne in mind that Brigham Young at the time claimed to be, and was acting as Superintendant of Indian affairs in the Territory. There is now pending in this house a claim for thirty or forty thousand dollars, which includes about four thousand dollars for goods distributed by John D. Lee to the Indians about the Mountain Meadows, within twenty days after the massacre; and also includes pay to Lee while he was engaged in the commission of the massacre. Whether Brigham will get it or not, I do not know.[35] This, however, I do know, that some two years ago Congress passed an act to pay to the Territory of Utah some fifty-two thousand dollars, for [the] amount paid by the Territory in suppressing Indian hostilities in the Territory in the years 1852 and 1853. I have before me every law passed in the Territory, every appropriation made by the legislature, and the statement of the Territorial Auditor of Accounts. I defy the delegate from Utah to show that there was ever appropriated or paid from the Treasury of the Territory an amount to exceed three thousand four hundred dollars. It never was done. But you know Brigham says *"that he has the most adroit scoundrels in the world in Zion, and that he can beat their sharpest shavers."* So there is no telling but in his persevering he may succeed in procuring his demands for murdering, and expenses of endeavoring to purchase the Indians to aid him in his rebellion. The present claim was all made while Utah was in rebellion.

Why was it that Brigham did not report this massacre at the Mountain Meadows? Why, if he was acting as Superintendant of Indian Affairs did he not make report of the property taken at the massacre. And let me ask (my conjugal friend,) the delegate from Utah, why it was that the Deseret News, the Church organ and only paper published in the Territory, for months after failed to notice the massacre, even after it was well known in the States, and when it did so, only did it to say, the Mormons were not engaged in it. Will the delegate please answer me this question?

The motives which the Mormons had in the massacre was revenge for the killing of Parley Pratt, a leading Mormon, who, while in the act of running another man's wife and children through Arkansas to Utah, was overtaken by the outraged husband, and slain—the Arkansas courts refusing to punish the perpetrator. They, in addition, no doubt, were also actuated by a desire to possess themselves of the great amount of stock and property of the emigrants, supposed to be worth sixty or seventy thousand dollars.

This was emphatically "getting the Lord's property," as HEBER KIMBALL expresses it, "without getting in debt to the Lord's enemies for it."

---

[35]Congress paid Young's paid accounts, totaling $34,145, in 1866. Arrington, *Brigham Young*, 269.

The surviving children, after they were recovered and on the way back, frequently pointed out carriages and stock that belonged to the train, stating to whom it belonged.

A great portion of the property was taken to Cedar City, deposited in the tithing office, and then sold out; the bed clothes upon which the wounded had been laying, and those taken from the dead, were piled in the back room of the tithing office and allowed to remain for so great a length of time that when I was there, eighteen months after, the room was still offensive.

What a commentary upon the condition of affairs in our country! Mormonism revelling upon the spoils obtained by murder, while seventeen orphan children are turned penniless upon the world. Yet that world has "no ear to hear, no eye to see, no heart to feel, no arm to bring deliverance." That we should allow such a condition of affairs to exist is shameful, disgraceful to us all. The disgrace does not alone attach to the weak, imbecile administration of James Buchanan and his legal adviser, who lent himself to prevent the judiciary of Utah from investigating the horrible crimes that had been committed in that Territory, and aided in shielding the criminals, but we are all guilty, and should be so held until we, by force, if necessary, compel restitution to the fatherless children, so far as it can be made.

That you may not conclude that I do the Mormons injustice in charging upon them this horrible massacre, I shall publish in the Appendix to my remarks reports of different Government officials who have visited that section of our country.

Major, now General, Carl[e]ton, visited that region—he also corroborates all that is contained in the abstracts I make from official reports. At the time he was there, he erected a monument to the memory of the dead. It was constructed by raising a large pile of rock, in the centre of which was erected a beam some twelve or fifteen feet in height. Upon one of the stones he caused to be engraved "Here lie the bones of 120 men, women, and children, from Arkansas, murdered on the 10th day of September, 1857." Upon a cross-tree on the beam he caused to be painted—"Vengeance is mine, saith the Lord, and I will repay it." This monument is said to have been destroyed the first time Brigham visited that part of the Territory.[36]

---

[36]Cradlebaugh was correct.

Chapter 8

"Survivors of Sebastopol"
The Children

For almost a year after the massacre, no Mormon made an effort to identify the surviving children of the massacre and return them to their relatives. At the prompting of William C. Mitchell of Arkansas, who lost more than twenty family members in the massacre, the acting commissioner of Indian Affairs instructed Brigham Young in March 1858 "to use every effort to get possession" of the orphans. Nothing happened until Young's replacement as territorial superintendent of Indian Affairs, Jacob Forney, got around to this task in August 1858.[1] Ironically, on 3 August Brigham Young directed William H. Dame and Isaac C. Haight "to have Bro Jacob Hamblin make attempt to gather up those children that were saved from the Indian Masacre at Mountain meadows last fall with a view of delivering them over to Dr Forney." The next day, Forney assured Hamblin that he entirely approved his course among the Indians and said he would try to visit southern Utah in January. "Endeavor with all the diligence in your power, to discover the remainder of the unfortunate children still supposed to be among the Indians," Forney directed, repeating Mormon claims that the Paiutes had possession of the children. "All the children must be secured at any cost or sacrifice," he continued, indicating some skepticism, "whether among whites or Indians."[2]

---

[1]Charles E. Mix to Young, 4 March 1858, LDS Archives. Frederick W. Lander, superintendent of the Pacific Wagon Road Survey, thought Forney was "apparently a kind and quiet gentleman" but "a little too slow for this country." Forney impressed Mormon authorities even less. "Dr Forney was here a week ago today," Bishop Warren Snow said, "and if government cant raise better men than he is, they had better take some rotten wood and carve one out and let it stand and freeze over night and it would do better than him." Lander to Young, 23 September 1858; and Snow and Peacock to Young, 10 April 1859, both LDS Archives.

[2]Young to Dame and Haight, 3 August 1858; and Forney to Hamblin, 4 August 1858, both in Brigham Young Collection, LDS Archives.

Survivor Tryphena Fancher Wilson, pictured as a young mother, has grandchildren living in Arkansas today. *Courtesy of the Mountain Meadows Monument Foundation, Will Bagley Collection.*

Finally, prodded by the secretary of the interior, Forney took direct action in March 1859. He hired Mormon Indian missionary Ira Hatch, who surely knew where the youngsters could be found since he had played a leading role in killing their parents. An assistant, William Rogers, met the agent at Nephi and went on to Corn Creek, where the Mormon chief Kanosh joined his party.

JAMES LYNCH: WASHING THE PAINT FROM HIS FACE

Frontiersman James Lynch and a company of thirty-nine men from the U.S. Army post at Camp Floyd happened along and discovered the fearful Forney at Beaver, guarding his mules and wagons. Giving up his planned journey to Arizona, Lynch placed his party under Forney's command and later told a San Francisco newspaper what happened afterward. His haunting experience at Mountain Meadows became a turning point in his life.

JAMES LYNCH, "THE MOUNTAIN MEADOWS MASSACRE:
SURVIVING CHILDREN OF THE MURDERED FIX THE CRIME UPON
THE MORMONS," *SAN FRANCISCO EVENING BULLETIN*, 31 MAY 1859, 3/3.

We have received, from our Salt lake correspondent, a copy of the following thrilling statement, made by John [*sic*] Lynch, who accompanied Dr. Forney, the Utah Superintendent of Indian Affairs, to Mountain Meadows, on his recent trip in search of the surviving children of the Mountain Meadows massacre. It is the clearest and most interesting narrative of the facts, in connection with that terrible tragedy, which has yet been given.

About three months since, I started to go to Arizona. When I arrived at Nephi, I was overtaken by Dr. Forney, the Indian Superintendent, who was going to the Mountain Meadows for the thirteen surviving children of the Mountain Meadows massacre. He told me he was doubtful about the Mormons he had with him, and asked me if I would assist him if they deserted him. My party consisted of twenty-five men. I told him I would do so, and would return with him to Camp Floyd myself, if he could get no other assistance. When the doctor arrived at Beaver City, as was anticipated, the Mormons deserted him without apprizing him of their intentions—supposing he would be unable to go further in his unassisted condition. I found him about 11 o'clock at night guarding his mules—told him to go to bed, and I would relieve him. I persuaded two of my party to assist me; and with their aid, drove his teams down to Mountain Meadows, and gave up my intention of going further south.[3] We pursued our course to Parowan. In this place, which is inhabited almost entirely by English and Danes—as are most of the southern settlements—the greatest hostility was evinced toward us. The people would hold no communication with our party, and spoke in the most insulting terms of the Americans, as they designated all who are not Mormons.

We continued our journey to the Meadows, passing through Painter [Pinto] Creek and Cedar City. The scene of the massacre is a broad, level meadow, encompassed by a chain of hills. Upon careful inquiry, we learn[ed] that the emigrants had been harrassed by bands of men, whom they assumed to be Indians, during their journey from Cedar City to the Meadows, and, at the latter place, made a corral of their wagons for defense. The corral was near a spring, which is the source of a small stream running through the plain. Words cannot describe the horrible picture which was here presented to us. Human skeletons, disjointed bones, ghastly skulls and the hair of women were scattered in frightful profusion over a distance of two miles. Three mounds, partially exposing the remains of some of the murdered, indicated the careless attempt that had been made to bury the unfortunate victims. We remained two or three hours at the Meadows, and occupied ourselves in burying the uncovered remains of the massacred.

This done, we proceeded to the residence of the man Hamblin, a Mormon, in whose possession the children were. We found them in a most wretched condition, half starved, half naked, filthy, infested with vermin, and their eyes

---

[3]Lynch named the two men, Thomas Dunn and John Lofink, in his 27 July 1859 affidavit. He said Forney promised to employ them in Salt Lake, but "I am sorry to say, that he violated his plighted faith and his solemn contract, on reaching the city, but immediately discharging them, without cause, and hiring Mormons to take their place, as, I am informed, has been his custom since he came into the valley." Buchanan, *Massacre at Mountain Meadows*, Sen. Doc. 42, Serial 1033, 84.

diseased from the cruel neglect to which they had been exposed. After three
days at Santa Clara, where clothing was made for the children, we returned
with Hamblin and ten of the children, there obtained two more, and another at Painter Creek. When we passed through Beaver City, some of the Mormons hooted at the children, and called them survivors of Sebastopol and
Waterloo.[4] Among the children are some who retain a very vivid impression
of much connected with the massacre. A very intelligent little girl, named
Becky Dunlap [Rebecca Dunlap], pointed out the men at Santa Clara an Englishman named Tellus [David Tullis], whom she says she saw murder her father.
She also states that Hamblin's Indian boy killed her two sisters. Both she and
a boy named Miram [Emberson Milam Tackett] recognized dresses and a part
of the jewelry belonging to their mothers, worn by the wives of John D. Lee,
the Mormon Bishop of Harmony. The boy, Miram, also identified his father's
oxen, which are now owned by Lee. The two oldest boys told me that after
they had been fighting for eight days, during four of which they were in the
corral, from whence the water had been cut off, Bishop Hight [Haight], of
Cedar City, came into the corral, and told the emigrants that the Indians did
not want anything but their cattle, and if they would lay down their arms
their lives would be spared. They did so, and started to go to Santa Clara,
when they were attacked by a mixed group of whites and Indians, and all killed
except the children. The boy Miram stated, that after the massacre was over,
he saw the Bishop of Coal Creek [Philip Klingensmith] washing the paint
from his face, which he had used to disguise himself as an Indian.

The man Hamblin seemed perfectly conversant with the circumstances of
the massacre, and told me that at one time he had a good many of the cattle
in his possession. A Mormon named Ira Hatch also told me that he found
the only man that escaped about one hundred miles from the Meadows, persuaded him to return with him, but when they had gone about 40 miles, Indians murdered him in his presence.[5]

There were 18 wagons, 820 head of cattle, and 143 persons in this train. It
is supposed there was also a great deal of money, as the Mormons say it was
the richest train that ever crossed the plains. I believe Dr. Forney to be acquainted with all the circumstances I have narrated.

At Nephi, Forney's Mormon guides warned the agent "that if he went down
south the people down there would make an eunuch of him"—no idle threat
in Utah Territory. Lynch, Dunn, and Lofkin placed themselves at similar risk
when they escorted the terrified Forney to Mountain Meadows. Later, when

---

[4]The yearlong siege of Sebastopol by British and French forces during the Crimean War ended when
the Russians abandoned the city on 11 September 1855. The siege was reported in the *Deseret News*, and
"Sebastopol" became a code word for the Mountain Meadows massacre.

[5]Ira Hatch was a renowned Mormon Indian missionary and scout. Hatch was one of the Mormon
guards who abandoned Forney in Beaver.

confronted by Mormon Indian missionary, schoolteacher, and informer Marion J. Shelton, Forney returned Lynch's kindness by refuting his statement in the *San Francisco Evening Bulletin*. Shelton called on Forney and read Lynch's letter and asked the agent if he endorsed Lynch's report. The easily intimidated Forney said he did not, "as many of the statements made by Mr. Lynch were false."[6]

With this insult, James Lynch appeared before Chief Justice Delana R. Eckels of the Utah Supreme Court and repeated his story in the form of an official affidavit.[7] He further swore that Jacob Forney had told southern Utah Mormons that all who took part in the massacre had been forgiven by President Buchanan's pardon and that he would have Cradlebaugh removed from office. Lynch also gave a touching picture of the condition of the children that contradicted Forney's equivocations about how he found them. "The children when we first saw them were in a most wretched and deplorable condition; with little or no clothing, covered with filth and dirt, they presented a sight heart-rending and miserable in the extreme," Lynch said. "The scene of the fearful murder still bears evidence of the atrocious crime, charged by the Mormons and their friends to have been perpetrated by Indians, but really by Mormons disguised as Indians, who, in their headlong zeal, bigotry, and fanaticism, deemed this a favorable opportunity of at once wreaking their vengeance on the hated people of Arkansas." Lynch described the horrific scene that the agent and his men came upon at Mountain Meadows: he had witnessed many harrowing sights on battlefields, "but never did my heart thrill with such horrible emotions, as when standing on that silent plain contemplating the remains of the innocent victims of Mormon avarice, fanaticism, and cruelty."

John D. Lee, Lynch charged, was "in possession of a large quantity" of the ill-fated emigrants' property "Why not make him disgorge this ill-gotten plunder, and disclose the amount escheated to and sold out by the Mormon Church as its share of the blood of helpless victims?" Lynch said Lee "should not be allowed to make feasts and entertain government officials at his table as he did Dr. Jacob Forney," while Lynch's men refused "to share the hospitality of this notorious murderer—this scourge of the desert." More galling still, Lee admitted that "he was present at the massacre, but pretends that he was there to prevent bloodshed; but positive evidence implicates him as the leader of

---

[6]Church Historian's Office Journal, 25 June 1859, 18–19. This entry also mentioned Forney's application "to Elias Smith Judge of Probate for Utah Co. for letters of Guardianship of the children that were saved at the Mountain Meadow massacre; Judge Smith required bonds, which the Dr. refused to give."

[7]The three district judges appointed by the president comprised the supreme court of Utah Territory. Lynch's more detailed affidavit is Appendix 12 in Brooks, *Mountain Meadows Massacre*, 279–84.

the murderers too deeply for denial. The children point him out as one of them that did the bloody work." The children never were in the hands of the Indians, and both Hamblin and Forney knew it. The wealth of the Arkansas train "now makes rich the harem of this John D. Lee," Lynch said.

The Mormons had systematically tracked down and killed the messengers sent from the besieged train "to leave no witness competent to give testimony in a court of justice but God," whose inscrutable ways had left the orphaned children "to bring to light this most horrible tragedy and make known its barbarous and inhuman perpetrators." Lynch praised Judge Cradlebaugh's actions, which had led to "the flight of presidents, bishops, and elders to the mountains, to escape the just penalty of the law for their crimes." Cradlebaugh and Forney knew the names of "one hundred actors and accomplices," including the leaders, Lee, Haight, and Klingensmith. Jacob Hamblin, one of Forney's agents, "knows all the facts, but refuses to disclose them" and falsely told Forney "that the children we brought away were recovered by him from persons who had bought them from Indians," a lie intended "to cheat the government out of money [and] to again reward the guilty wretches for their inhuman butcheries."

Lynch accompanied Forney on his return north. During the trip he repeatedly heard the agent tell Mormons "'that they need not fear Judge Cradlebaugh,' (whose disclosures and energy had created some alarm;) 'that he (Forney) would have him removed from office; that the Mormons (murderers and all) were all included in the President's proclamation and pardon, and would not be tried or punished for any offense whatever committed prior to the issuing of the pardon; that Judge Cradlebaugh was not a fit man for office.'" No language was "too low or filthy" for Forney to use in abusing and slandering Cradlebaugh. "I could arrive at no other conclusion, from his conduct, than that the Doctor desired to influence the mind of the Mormons against the judiciary, and that he cared more to create a prejudice against Judge Cradlebaugh's course in attempting to bring these murders to light." It was to be regretted that Cradlebaugh had to be criticized "by such a man as Jacob Forney, a more veritable old granny than whom, in my opinion, never held official position in this country."

Men such as Lynch, Judge Cradlebaugh, Deputy Marshal Rogers, and Major Carleton, who had visited the scene of the massacre and had finally buried the victims' remains, expressed a bitterness against Mormonism that is still palpable. Ironically, their outrage against a theocratic system that would effectively shelter the murderers for another dozen years provided a handy excuse for Brigham Young and the federal officials he systematically bribed and intimidated to do nothing.

JACOB FORNEY: THESE ARE ALL THAT REMAIN

The Indian Affairs superintendent of Utah Territory arrived in Great Salt Lake City with all but one of the seventeen children who survived the Mountain Meadows Massacre and reported as much information about their identity as he could learn. Since the murder of their parents left the children "without natural guardians or protection in this territory," Jacob Forney petitioned the Mormon probate judge for Great Salt Lake County for approval to become their guardian.

FORNEY TO C. E. MIX, COMMISSIONER OF INDIAN AFFAIRS,
4 MAY 1858, *MASSACRE AT MOUNTAIN MEADOWS*,
SEN. EXEC. DOC. 42, 1860, 57–58.

Superintendent's office, Utah
Great Salt Lake City, May 4, 1859

Sir: I have just returned from a very laborious and difficult trip through the southern portions of this Territory.

I have succeeded in recovering sixteen children, and have them now in my possession. It is said these are all that remain of probably one hundred and forty men, women, and children, of the Mountain Meadows massacre in September, 1857.

In December last there was a small boy among the Navajos, near the Colorado, in Mexico Territory, who, it is supposed, also belonged to this emigrant train. I will allude to this boy in another communication.

I was positively assured by the settlers in the neighborhood where I got the children, that I have all that were saved. I have good reason for believing that none of these children have lived among the Indians at all.

These children average from about 3 to 9½ years old; are intellectual and good looking; not one mean-looking child among them.

I have collected the following particulars in relation to these children:

1st. Calvin, now 7 or 8 years old; does not remember his name; says they (his family) lived at Horse-Head, Johnston county, Arkansas. This boy had father, mother, and five brothers, older than himself, killed; brothers' names, Henry, James, William, and Larkin, and four sisters, Nancy, Mary, and Martha; his father, Joseph, and his mother, Matilda.

2d. and 3d. Ambrose Miram Taggit, about 7 years old, and William Taggit, now about 4½ years old. The elder boy says they had father, mother, and two older brothers killed; he says they lived in Johnston county, and when they left the States had a grandfather and grandmother living.

4th. Prudence Angeline, 6 years old; and,

5th. Annie; had father, mother, and two brothers, named James and John; all killed.

6th. A girl, about 4½ years old; says her name is Frances Hawn, or Kern.

7th. A boy, now three years old. I have no account of this boy; those with whom he lived called him William.

8th. Elisha W. Huff, 4 years old; and,

9th. Sophrania, or Mary Huff, about 6 years old.

10th. Charles Fancher, 7 or 8 years old; and,

11th. Annie, about 3½ years old; had sisters.

12th. Betsey, about 6 years old; and,

13th. Jane, about 4 years old; have no account of these.

14th, 15th, and 16th. Rebecca, Louisa, and Sarah Dunlap.

In conversation with these children, I learn that they resided in the same neighborhood; my impression is, principally in Johnston [sic] county, Arkansas.

I remain, very respectfully, your obedient servant,

J. Forney,
Superintendent of Indian Affairs.

FORNEY TO ELIAS SMITH IN THE MATTER OF THE ESTATE AND
GUARDIANSHIP OF MOUNTAIN MEADOWS CHILDREN,
JUNE 1859, UTAH STATE ARCHIVES.

To the Hon. Elias Smith Judge of the Probate Court of Salt Lake County Utah Territory.

Your Petitioner Jacob Forney Superintendent of Indian Affairs for Utah Territory respectfully represents that on the 8th or 9th day of September 1857 a party of Emigrants numbering as is believed between one hundred and thirty and one hundred and forty persons on their way from this Territory to California were massacred by a party of Whites and Indians at a place known as the "Mountain Meadows" in this Territory, that out of said party of Emigrants seventeen children between the ages of two months and eight years were spared alive and your Petitioner has by direction of the Department of the Interior collected said children for the purpose of sending them to Fort Smith Arkansas near which place the parents of most of them it is believed resided before starting on the trip which ended in their destruction. Your Petitioner further states that he has cause to believe that the Party of Emigrants refered to at the time they were murdered possessed a large amount of property and that a portion of this property can with proper diligence be recovered. Your Petitioner therefore asks as he has been already directed to take charge of the children by the "Department of the Interior" and as they are left by the massacre of their Parents without natural guardians or protection in this Territory that he be appointed guardian over said children with full power to collect and receive all property belonging to the murdered Emigrants rendering a deed account to the Probate Court of all property so received, and of the application made of the same.

The names of the children as far as your Petitioner has been able to learn them are as follows,

Rebecca Dunlap	Lewis Sorough
Louisa Dunlap	Mary Sorough
Sarah Dunlap	Francis Hawn
Ambrose Moran	Charles Francher
William Taggit	Anna Francher
John Sorough	Eligah Wm Hough
Sophnia Mary Hough	
Betsie Baker	
June Baker	
Prudence Angeline	Parents name unknown
Jane ———	" " "

Evidence indicates that Judge Smith turned down Forney's petition to be appointed guardian unless he provided an acceptable bond, which Forney at first refused to do. On the bond of federal Indian agent A. Humphreys and Mormon Curtis E. Bolton, however, Judge Smith issued the appointment just before the children left for Fort Leavenworth.

GEN. ALBERT S. JOHNSTON: I HAVE ORDERED SPRING WAGONS

At the end of June 1859, Gen. A. S. Johnston reported that the children who had survived the massacre left Camp Floyd to begin their long journey to Arkansas to be united with relatives. He did not state that the authorities had kept the two oldest boys at the post as possible witnesses. The party under Capt. Bradford H. Anderson also included three children who were not involved in the Mountain Meadows murder. Apparently thinking that the children who left Camp Floyd included all of the survivors, Mormon authorities at Salt Lake recorded the departure with a sense of relief.

JOHNSTON TO ADJUTANT GENERAL, 27 JUNE 1859,
FORT CRITTENDEN LETTERBOOK, NATIONAL ARCHIVES.

Colonel

I have the honor to report the departure from this place yesterday of companies A and C 2nd Dragoons under the command of Captain Anderson 2nd Dragoons . . .

I have sent forward with the Dragoons, the three children of the late Daniel Foster for whom application to the War Department was made for their restoration, by their mother Mrs. Verguson of Norwich Connecticut . . . At the request of Dr. Forney superintendent of Indian affairs, who informed me that the transportation provided by the Department of the Interior was unsuitable for the purpose, I have ordered spring wagons to be furnished for the conveyance to Fort Leavenworth of the 17 children whose lives were spared at the Mountain Meadow Massacre. I have directed that they shall also be provided with subsistence.

Major Whiting, who will be allowed to avail himself of his certificate of disability on his arrival at Fort Leavenworth, has been instructed to see that good care is taken of these children, and that they be provided with everything needful on the route. These children also accompany the Dragoons, and their commander is charged with their safety, as far as Fort Kearny, whence they will be furnished with a sufficient escort to Fort Leavenworth.

> With great respect
> Your obedient servant
> A. S. Johnston
> Colonel 2nd Cavalry
> Bvt. Brig Genl USA
> Comdg

On learning that two of the children had not departed from Camp Floyd with the others, Mormon authorities at Great Salt Lake became fearful that they had remembered enough of the massacre to blame white men for the killing. One LDS official, probably George A. Smith, found it necessary to discredit the children and malign their character. In contrast, messages from bereaved family members in California arrived too late to affect the departure of the children.

Captain Anderson, the redoubtable hero of the wheatfields in this city, with a detachment of troops, started east on the 28th inst., having under his "protection" 15 of the children who survived the Mountain Meadow Massacre, two others remaining here for ulterior purposes. When getting ready to start, several of the children bitterly opposed the efforts to get them into the carriages, declaring that they did not want to go with "those men", for the alledged reason that they "got drunk and swore so much." Two negros siezed [sic] one of the girls who lay down on the pavement and screamed, but, by the influence and persuasion of a citizen who was acquainted with her, she was finally put into the carriage. One of the children supposed to be old enough to testify to the massacre, was sent off, it is said because that she was such a liar, but probably because she would not swear and stick to just the things desired.[8]

FITZ-JOHN PORTER TO JOHN FANCHER, 6 JULY 1859,
FORT CRITTENDEN LETTERBOOK, NATIONAL ARCHIVES, 261.

Fancher John Esq
Visalia, Tulare County
    California.
Sir.

General Johnston desires me to acknowledge the receipt to day of your letter of the 12th Instant, and while awaiting the results of further inquiries which will be forwarded to you by next mail, to inform you that with the exception of two, all of the children spared from Massacre at the Mountain Meadows, were supplied by General Johnston with comfortable Army Transportation, and sent under safe escort to Leavenworth City. Whether either of those retained in Salt Lake City, are your relations or not I cannot say, but will inform you by next mail and also the mode of communicating with those in charge of them whoever they may be.

I am very respectfully
Your obedient servant
F. J. Porter
Asst. Adjt. Genl.

FITZ-JOHN PORTER TO JACOB FORNEY, 21 JULY 1859,
FORT CRITTENDEN LETTERBOOK, NATIONAL ARCHIVES, 261.

Sir:

In continuation of my letter of 6th Instant in reply to yours of the 12th Ultimo, I have to inform you that Charles and Annie Fancher, were on the 28th ultimo, sent, with the other children spared from Massacre at the Mountain Meadows, to Fort Leavenworth, whence, under the charge of the Superintendent of Indian Affairs Mr. Rector—they will be taken to Fort Smith, Arkansas, and delivered to their relations, if any there be. Communications in regard to them should be addressed to Superintendent Rector at Fort Smith.

The children are represented as very interesting and intelligent, the first named about 7, and the last about 3½ years old.

---

[8]Church Historian's Letterbook, 30 June 1859, LDS Archives. The cryptic reference to Capt. Bradford H. Anderson, Second U.S. Dragoons, and the wheat fields concerns a possible challenge to Mormon land ownership. Anderson encamped his company with 174 horses, mules, tents, and wagons on John Van Cott's five-acre plot in Great Salt Lake City's communal "Big Field." When Van Cott protested, the captain arrested him. The dispute ended peacefully when Anderson let him go.

Brigham Young:
An Expensive and Round About Method

As *ex-officio* superintendent of Indian Affairs, Brigham Young in 1857 submitted a voucher to the Office of Indian Affairs in the amount of $3,527.43 for articles given at Mountain Meadows nineteen days after the massacre to the Indians who allegedly committed the atrocity, as certified by "Indian farmer" John D. Lee. For the months before, during, and after the massacre, Young billed Washington more than $5,500, as certified by his adopted son Lee, for such items as 53 pounds of No. 1 tobacco, 2 dozen zinc mirrors, 100 stone pipes, 3 dozen fancy pipes, 7 pounds of Chinese vermilion, and other necessities for the same Indians. The Mormon leader's accounts for 1856–57 reveal no concern to control costs on behalf of the U.S. government.[9] Young's legendary sense of frugality surfaced only when it came to transportation for the surviving children to their families in Arkansas.

> Dr. Forney, Superintendent of Ind. Affrs, has lately returned from a trip to some of the southern Indian tribes, and has brought the children rescued from the Mountain Meadow massacre, to have them in readiness for the two commissioners appointed to come here and conduct them to their relatives. What an expensive and round about method for transacting what any company for the States could easily attend to at any time, and with trifling expense. While in the southern portion of our Territory, I am informed that Dr. Forney had more or less conversation with persons somewhat conversant with said massacre, and from the little I can or ever have learned of that affair, I feel sanguine that when the truth is fairly arrived at it will be found that had it not been for a few whites being near by at the time, not a child nor an animal would have been saved alive, as the Indians were exceedingly exasperated with the conduct of that and other emigrating companies.[10]

When Arkansas state senator William C. Mitchell first heard of the massacre in 1857 he demanded justice for the murder of two of his sons, Joel and Charles, a daughter, and possibly his infant grandson, John. He told U.S. senator W. K. Sebastian from Arkansas that the four new regiments that President Buchanan had asked Congress to approve were "too small a force to whip the Mormons and Indians" and said he was eager to volunteer. "I feel that I must have satisfaction for the inhuman manner in which they have slain

---

[9]Brigham Young's accounts as Indian Affairs superintendent in 1856–57 have never received the attention they deserve. For a revealing look, see "Accounts of Brigham Young," House Doc. 29, 1862.
[10]Young to George Q. Cannon, 5 May 1859, LDS Archives.

my children," he said. Later, he welcomed the task of meeting the surviving children at Fort Leavenworth and escorting them home. Sadly, his grandson was not among them.[11]

U.S. SENATOR JAMES H. BERRY:
THE BEST CITIZENS OF THAT COUNTY

U.S. senator James H. Berry of Arkansas was seventeen years old when William C. Mitchell brought the surviving children back to Arkansas. Not even the awful scenes that Berry later witnessed in the Civil War made a deeper impression than the sight. Testifying before the U.S. Senate in 1907, Berry refuted the accusations that had been leveled against murder victims by church authorities and historians for more than fifty years.

BERRY, SPEECH OF SENATOR FROM ARKANSAS,
CONGRESSIONAL RECORD, 11 FEBRUARY 1907.

In 1857 I lived in the County of Carroll, State of Arkansas. In the spring of that year there left that county, and two adjoining counties, between a hundred and forty and a hundred and fifty—including men, women and children—emigrants for California. They consisted of the best citizens of that county. It was a large train. It excited much interest throughout the section of country from which they went. They had about 600 head of cattle, several mule teams, a number of wagons, and each head of a family had more or less money; how much I do not know. Late in the fall or the early winter the news came back that the train had been assaulted by the Indians far out west, and that every soul had perished. Later on there came the news that some, the children—how many we did not at that time know—were saved and that they were in the hands of the Mormons in Utah. Our senators and representatives here called upon the Interior Department. An agent, a Mr. Forney, was sent there by the Commissioner of Indian Affairs. He gathered those children together, sixteen of them, who had been preserved from the massacre on that fatal 13th [11th] day of September. He brought those children back to Leavenworth, and there Colonel Mitchell of our county went and met them and took them in charge. I was a boy seventeen years old on that day when they were brought to the village court house. I saw them as they were lined up on the benches, and Col. Mitchell told the people whose children they were, at least, whose he thought they were. There were sixteen of them. One little girl, I distinctly remember had an arm broken by a gunshot wound. It

[11]Mitchell to Sebastian, 31 December 1857, Buchanan, *Massacre at Mountain Meadows*, Sen. Doc. 42, Serial 1033, 42–43, 90.

had not united and the arm hung dangling by her side. I have seen much of
life since that day; I have seen war along the lines of the Border States in all
of its horrors; but no scene in my life was ever so impressed upon my mind
as that which I saw there that day presented by those little children, their fathers,
mothers, brothers and sisters dead on the far-off plains of Utah, and they
absolutely without means, with no human being to look to. When he (Mr.
Forney) first got the children, he reported to the Secretary of the Interior,
and you will find it in the report of the Commissioner of Indian Affairs, that
they had been so frightened and scared by the Mormons that he could get
nothing from them; that they would not talk; and that it was long before he
could gain their confidence. The eldest of them was five or six years of age,
and perhaps there was one seven years of age. But when they got back to Leavenworth, and from there to Arkansas they had lost the fears that had been
instilled in them by the Mormon families in which they had lived. They could
not tell much, but they could tell that white men and not all Indians assisted in the massacre. They could tell it was a white man who came into their
corral and induced the emigrants to give up their guns; that it was white men
that drove the wagons in which they rode; that it was white men who shot the
wounded men who had been placed in one of the wagons.

The relatives and spectators who gathered on 15 September 1859 at the county courthouse in Carrollton, Arkansas, never forgot the homecoming of the
children. Mary Baker, Capt. John T. Baker's widow, spotted her son's daughters
by their sunbonnets. One of them, Sarah Baker, later remembered, "I called
all of the women I saw 'mother.' I guess I was still hoping to find my own mother, and every time I called a woman 'mother,' she would break out crying."[12]

"'CHILDREN OF THE MASSACRE' MAY MEET IN REUNION,"
ARKANSAS SUNDAY POST-DISPATCH, SEPTEMBER 1895.

... the reception of the surviving orphans at Carrollton is described as one
of the most affecting spectacles ever known and the old men and women who
still tell the story seldom get through with the incidents without shedding tears.

Some of the children were recognized by their relatives and claimed at once.
Others could not be clearly identified, as they were so young. The survivors
found homes among kindred or the friends of their parents, and each one of
them became an object of especial interest for all the people of the surrounding country. The elder children were talked to constantly for days about the
massacre, and no doubt the little ones learned to believe some of the stories
which fancy created where memory failed in trying to recall the details of the
tragedy and its consequences.

[12]See Sarah Baker Memoir, Chapter 15.

John C. Miller and Milum Tackett, the two witnesses, were taken to Washington City by Dr. Forney in January 1860. After being examined by the government authorities the boys were taken to Carrollton, Ark., by John Henry of Van Buren. These children, though the oldest of the survivors were too young to be legal witnesses and they did not testify in the trial of John D. Lee, which occurred after Tackett and Miller had grown to manhood.

WILLIAM A. ADEN: A NATURAL GENIUS

Young William Aden may have been a natural genius, as his father claimed, but he made a grievous error when he joined the Baker-Fancher company south of Provo to get away from Utah. His mistake later came to light only because his father wrote to inquire about him.

"INFORMATION WANTED," *THE VALLEY TAN*, 8 JUNE 1859, 4/2.

William A. Aden, who left St. Louis, Spring '57, and was last heard from in July of that year, in the South Pass, saying that he expected to spend the winter in Provo, and proceed to California in the spring of '58. Any information of his whereabouts, or probable fate will be thankfully received, and expense of same will be paid by his brother, Felen F. Aden, at Tennent & Co's 101 Main street, St. Louis.

A Daguerreotype can be seen at the office of the "Valley Tan," in Salt Lake City.

"$1,000 REWARD—WILLIAM A. ADEN," *THE VALLEY TAN*, 3 AUGUST 1859, 4/2.

I have learned through the Post Master, Lucius N. Scovil, of Provo City, Utah Territory, that my son, WILLIAM A. ADEN, left there about the 1st of October, 1857, for California, by the south route, aiming to overtake a party of emigrants, who were then some fifty miles ahead of them . . .

WILLIAM A. ADEN

If alive, is now about twenty-one years of age—pretty well grown—blue eyes—fair skin—hair curly, and rather dark—a pretty good talent for music (both vocal and instrumental)—writes poetry tolerable well—a natural genius—particularly at PAINTING . . .

Paris, Tennessee, May 27th, 1859.

[Dr.] S.B. ADEN

The Dr. is in deep distress.

BRIGHAM YOUNG TO S. B. ADEN, 27 APRIL 1859, LDS ARCHIVES.
Mr. S. B. Aden,
        Paris, Tennessee,
Dear Sir:—Your note of enquiry, concerning your son William A. arrived
per last Eastern mail, and I regret having to inform you that I have at no time
known either your son or his whereabout[s], nor have I as yet found any one
who has seen him or knows where he is. The Deseret News, printed in this
city, circulates throughout this Territory, and I caused an enquiry for your son
to be inserted in the columns of its this weeks issue, as the speediest and surest
method for learning his location, if in Utah, with the request that the information be promptly furnished to me or to yourself, as to your son or his whereabouts, will be cheerfully forwarded to you, at the earliest opportunity, by,

Respectfully,
Brigham Young

BRIGHAM YOUNG TO S. B. ADEN, 12 JULY 1859, LDS ARCHIVES.
Dear Sir:—Since my reply, of April 27th, to your letter of enquiry concerning your son William A, also advertising in the current number of the Deseret
News to learn his whereabouts, from all I can hear I am induced to believe
that he joined the Emigrant company that was massacred at the Mountain
Meadows. As all the reports that I have heard, or seen published, agree in the
statement that none of that company were saved, except some sixteen very
young children, it becomes my painful duty to inform you that, in case your
son was in that company, I know of no reliably stated fact or even report
upon which to ground the least hope that he is now alive.
    With the kindest sympathies in your affliction, and holding myself ready
to furnish you any additional information concerning your son William A.
that may come to my knowlege, I have the honor to remain, very respectfully,

Your Obt. Servt.
Brigham Young

William Leany had recognized William A. Aden at Parowan as the son of
a man who "had been a great friend" and defended Leany from a mob while
he was on a mission in Tennessee. William Dame, Leany recalled, sent Barney Carter, his son-in-law and "one of the Angels of Death," to reprimand
Leany for giving young Aden onions. Carter "tore a picket out of the fence
and hit Laney side of the head," inflicting serious damage.[13] Despite Brigham
Young's promises and Aden's good works, Samuel B. Aden never heard from
the Mormon prophet again.

---

[13]Baskin, *Reminiscences of Early Utah*, 112, citing the 1903 testimony of James McGuffie. Gibbs, *The Mountain Meadows Massacre*, 17–18, told the story with slightly different details.

Chapter 9

"A Dose of Rope"
Fire from Within and More Obstruction

With the coming of the Civil War and departure of U.S. troops from Utah, Brigham Young felt secure enough in 1861 to visit the Mountain Meadows killing ground. Two years later, Judge Cradlebaugh reported that Carleton's cairn was destroyed during Young's visit. The unpunished massacre would not go away so easily. Nor would the Civil War cause the United States to "be like water that is spilt upon the ground that Cannot be gathered," as Young predicted.[1] Instead, the attempt to cover up the truth about the massacre became an increasingly complicated operation, demanding that Young publicly denounce the massacre and the murderers while privately protecting them—and intimidate anyone who noticed the contradiction.

Yet what Brigham Young actually knew and believed about the atrocity is not the great mystery that some would like to pretend: He explained his reasons and his fears quite well to John D. Lee, the man most responsible for carrying out the orders "that the emigrants should be *decoyed* from their stronghold, and all exterminated, so that no one would be left to tell the tale, and then the authorities could say it was done by Indians."[2] A few days after directing the destruction of the rude monument that Major Carleton's troops had raised over the bones of the Arkansans, the Mormon prophet feasted with Judge Lee at his fort in Harmony and then unburdened himself to his adopted son.

Pres. Young Said that the company that was used up at the Mountain Meadowes were the Fathers, Mothe[rs], Bros., Sisters & connections of those that Muerders the Prophets; they Merittd their fate, & the only thing that ever trou-

---

[1]Kenney, ed., *Wilford Woodruff's Journal*, 6:92, 93.
[2]Bishop, ed., *Mormonism Unveiled*, 233–34.

bled him was the lives of the Women & children, but that under the circumstances [this] could not be avoided. Although there had been [some?] that wantd to betreyed the Brethren into the hands of their Enimies, for that thing [they] will be Damned & go down to Hell. I would be Glad to see one of those traitors, though I [don't] Suppose that there is any here now. They have run away. & when he came to the Monument that contained their Bones, he made this remark, Vengence is Mine Saith the Lord, & I have taken a litle of it.[3]

Defaced by Impious Hands

Three years after Brigham Young's visit to Mountain Meadows, the troopers of Company M, Second California Volunteer Cavalry, rebuilt the monument.

"General Items," *Union Vedette*, 8 June 1864, 2/2.

Salt Lake and Fort Mojave W R Expedition,
Camp No. 10. Mountain Meadow, U T,
May 25th, 1864

Captain:—It may be interesting to the General Commanding the District of Utah, to know that on yesterday and to-day I caused a monument to be erected beside the grave containing the bones of the victims of the Mountain Meadows massacre of September, 1857. Upon my arrival here on yesterday, I found the monument which was erected several years ago by an army officer, torn down—the cross taken away, and the stones forming the monument, scattered around the springs. Near the remains of this monument is the grave, giving evidence of much decay—both grave and monument have been defaced by impious hands. I immediately determined to repair the grave and rebuild the monument. Yesterday afternoon I had erected a substantial monument of stone of the following size and dimensions, viz: Twelve feet square at the base, and four feet high, compactly filled in with loose stone and earth. From the centre of this square, rises a pyramidal column seven feet high, of stone, compactly laid. We planted in the center a substantial cedar pole, on which was fastened a small cross, manufactured from one of our packing boxes. This cross reaches three feet above the apex of the pyramid—making the height of the monument fourteen feet. On the side of the cross facing to the East, so that the rising sunlight of God may each day cast its rays of beauty upon it, are these words:

"Vengeance is mine, I will repay saith the Lord."
Below these words on the arm of the cross, are these words:
"Mountain Meadow massacre, September 1857."

[3]John D. Lee, 30 May 1861, in Cleland and Brooks, eds., *A Mormon Chronicle*, 314.

The ruins of the 1864 U.S. Army monument
as they appeared in *Frank Leslie's Illustrated Newspaper* at the
time of John D. Lee's execution. *Courtesy of the Will Bagley Collection.*

"Erected by officers and men of Company M,
2d California Cavalry, May 24th and 25th 1864"

The monument, rudely but substantially erected, appears well from the
road, and will stand for years, if no impious hand destroy it. The grave has
also been neatly repaired, filling it with earth and rounding it on the surface—
covering the whole with a layer of stones. Myself, Lieut. Conrad, and every
soldier of my command, consider that the fatigues and hardships of a twelve
hundred mile march to the Mojave and back to Camp Douglas, are cancelled
in the privilege of erecting at this place beside the remains of the murdered
innocent, who were betrayed and massacred in cold blood by white fiends and
their Indians allies—a monument at once expressive of our horror at the act—
our respect for the memory of the murdered dead, and our sympathy for their
fate. I cannot refrain at this time, from entering my protest as a soldier and
as an American, at the delay of a powerful Government in at least attempting to bring the leaders of this infamous crime to justice, and holding them
up for the execration of the entire Christian world. The Mountain Meadows
are 302½ miles from Camp Douglas.

Very resp't, your obd't servant.
Geo. F. Price, Capt 2d Cal. Cav,
Commanding expedition.

Mormon diarist Lorenzo Brown visited the restored monument on 1 July 1864 and said it was "built of cobble stone at the bottom and about 3 feet high then rounded up with earth & surmounted by a rough wooden cross the whole 6 or 7 feet high & perhaps 10 feet square." The cross carried the same inscription as the one Carleton had raised, Brown noted, but below it someone had penciled an inscription: "Remember Hauns mill and Carthage Jail."[4]

George F. Hendrix: Every Thing Is Not Told Yet

One of the pesky issues related to the massacre that refused to disappear involved the cattle stolen from the trains that followed the Fancher party. Jacob Hamblin apparently believed that no one would cross the Mojave Desert to collect the animals, so he replied to a query from Joseph Lane and offered to return them.[5] Lane sent an agent to retrieve his livestock. Instead of surrendering the stolen cattle, Hamblin and his friends spent three weeks leading the man on a wild goose chase before giving up a few animals.

Despite his detailed report to Brigham Young, the identity of George F. Hendrix is a mystery, but his letter describing conditions in southern Utah provides a detailed perspective on how rural LDS leaders like Jacob Hamblin exercised their considerable powers. It also puts to rest the notion that anyone in Utah Territory could hide anything from the alleged prophet's all-seeing eyes.

GEORGE F. HENDRIX TO BRO BRIGHAM, 23 JUNE 1860, LDS ARCHIVES.

For information respecting the disposition of large [?] drove of Cattle in Washington County, in the year 1857.

Enquire of Ira Hatch the Indian interpreter, santaclara Fort. For I think that he was the principal actor, in taking and driving away. He has yielded explicit obedience to the council of his superiors. Enquire also of David Tullas [Tullis] respecting the intended appropriation by Brigham according to the declaration of Jacob Hamblin of this drove of cattle to the payment of the indians that assisted at the mountain meadows. Enquire of Robert Richey Pinta Creek, respecting the driving away and concealing in the mountain, of a large number of those cattle when Lane's agent came to the fort, for the cattle, after he had been promised, that he should have his cattle, if he would come or send.

---

[4]Brooks, "The Mountain Meadows," 183n16. During the conflict in Missouri in October 1838, the state militia slaughtered sixteen Mormon men and ten-year-old Sardius Smith. The event is still remembered bitterly, but no book addressed the subject until Beth Shumway Moore's *Bones in the Well: The Haun's Mill Massacre* appeared in 2007.

[5]Lane was the Joseph Lane who lost cattle in the raid on the Dukes train. See "More Outrages on the Plains!!" in Chapter 5.

These three Brethren will be able to tell you the present disposition and where abouts of the most of the cattle, at this time. Samuel Night [Knight] must know the history of this cattle affair from beginning to end, but whether he would disclose anything or not, I do not know, he is one of Jacob Hamblin's councillors, and his own interest seems to induce him to acquiesce in every thing that was done by the president and bishop, or to seem to do it.

David Tullas told me that Bishop Crosby had in his charge when I left santa Clara nine (9) of those cows belonging to Lane. Mother Crow told me he was conformed [?] in driving the cows away and hiding them, that the Bishop should have said it would break Brother Hamblin up if all these cattle should be taken away.

I am sure that the Bishop is in the secret; but whether he would expose Jacob Hamblin or not is doubtful in my mind. His son is married [to] Hamblin's daughter, the Bishop has lent Jacob considerable money, and Pres. Hamblin has appointed the Bishop to act as his [a]gent when the president is absent and I have heard the Bishop say that he was ready to do anything that Brother Hamblin wanted done and I know that there is a great intimacy between them.

Lane's drove of Cattle was called the public herd at santa Clara, and almost every body that lived there from '57 up to the time I went from there was acquainted with the affair. Jacob Hamblin told me that he had sent Lane word, that if he would come on [and] sent after his cattle he should have them for he did not want them nor did he know of any one else that did, so taking and having the cattle was no secret and almost any one out of the Hamblin connection would or could give a history of this matter. From all I have been able to learn Ausker [Oscar] Hamblin, Dudley Leavette, Samuel Night, and Jacob Hamblin's indian boy Albert, participated in the mountain meadow affair.

Brothers Richey and Riddle at one time had a grant from the court of Pine valley, for the purpose of building a saw mill. Jacob Hamblin requested them to let him bring his family and stock into the valley. They granted it to him, upon condition that he would have the stock herded in the upper end of [the] valley, as they had grain growing in the lower end. Jacob brought his stock and but in a few days they were let run at large. Brother Richey at length was compelled to save his crop, to take his bed at night and lay in his grain field. Jacob Hamblin reported around the county says Richey that Ritchey had taken the name of God in vain, that Ritchey should have sworn by God that he would kill enough of Hamblins cattle to make a fence a round his wheat field, and faced Richey down that he had said so. At the time of the reformation Brother Richey went to Jacob Hamblin and asked him if there was any way, that they could compromise and settle their difficulties. Jacob said yes, as far as I am concern[ed], for I knew that report about you killing the cattle to make a fence of, was a lie when I told it, and if you are willing to compromis[e], those difficulties and live in friendship, I am.

But unhappily hostility was again renewed between them last summer, some

time in June last while Jacob Hamblin was up to Salt Lake City. Bishop Judd
of Santa Clara, Hamblin['s] brother in law, authorized a clandestine marriage
between Lusias [?] Fuller and Ann Lay, a girl (16) years old, in the absence of
her father and unknown to her mother. This circumstance when discovered by
the people produced a great excitement amongst the people. John Young the
man that married them [took them] to a dark room, after night shut the door
with one witness who could hear the ceremony but could not see the parties,
as appeared on evidence afterwards, and performed the ceremony. Finally there
was a charge prefered against the Bishop, and tried before Brother Hamblin. Sister Lay employed Brother Richey to act for her as council in the trial. Brother
Richey felt very indignant at the conduct of the Bishop, considering that he
had treated his councillors, Father Crow and Brother Ritchey, with disrespect
in perpetrating of the act. Brother Ritchey and Bishop Crosby denounced the
conduct of Bishop Judd, in the strongest language, which brought down the
rath of Bishop Judd, Jacob Hamblin and all their family connection upon the
head of the old man Ritchey. Shortly after this Amasa Lyman and George A.
Smith came down to settle matters. while they were there they councied President Hamblin to have the town laid off in regular order and started the streets,
for the place was built up with no regularity or order, for there was a house
and a hog pen, a hogpen and a house, the stench of which with the litter of
horses, mules, and cattle added to the dead Coyotes or wolves, dead lambs,
skunks, calves and various other things that laid in the streets all last winter,
proved the saying of one of the brother Crows to Bishop Judd that we have
no law nor order here in fort Clara nor we have no Bishop.

The president and Bishop seemed to seize upon the Laying out of the town
as a suitable opportunity to oust the old man or otherwise to indirectly drive
him out of town. [When] the town was laid off, the lot that covered Brother Ritchey's house the president told his brother Francis M. Hamblin to build
a house on it. Arriminda Crow his wife refused to go on to the lot saying that
it of right belonged to Brother Ritchey. Jacob Hamblin told him the second
time to build his house there and being somewhat displeased said the old man
Ritchey had no lot. About this time brother Ritchey has two large American
mares larrietted in his field and some one went and stabbed one of them with
a large knife, in the thigh. The old man took this as a hint for him to leave
and so did I, but I kept quiet and said nothing. The old man went to Pinta
Creek to look out for a place to move to. While he was gone his crop of late
corn was destroyed. After he came back he told Bishop Judd that there was
men that herded their cattle on my corn, says he to keep them off their own
and you would go every morning before daylight and drive them out so that
it would not be known who done it or whose they were and says the old man
Bishop I can prove it. To conclude I must say there is no law nor order at Fort
Clara. The Bishop is of no force he is only a cats paw for the President [Jacob
Hamblin] and the people have no confidence in him and there can be an abun-

dance of evidence of the fact. Many of the people have expressed to me their
desire that I would report the state of things there, and feel that I have only
done my duty and every thing is not told yet.

George F. Hendrix

George Spencer: I Was in
That Horrid "Mountain Meadows Affair"

American soldiers returned to Utah during the Civil War, and as the nation
emerged from conflict with states rights weakened and federal authority
enhanced, voices across the country once more called for an investigation of
the massacre and punishment of the guilty. Mormon leaders responded to
this threat with more elaborate and detailed versions of the initial falsehood,
a deception made easier by the deaths or relocation of many who could con-
tradict them. Not so easily satisfied, however, were the cries for absolution,
like the plea of George Spencer, the former adjutant in Harrison Pearce's
Company I of the Iron County Brigade, Nauvoo Legion, and the demands
for an explanation that came from within the LDS church. For Mormon leaders, such voices were impossible to silence or reassure.

George Spencer to Erastus Snow, 26 March 1867, LDS Archives.

Dear Brother

I take pen to *write* to you because my heart is too full for utterance. I feel
that I shall break down if I should not undertake to *talk*. I feel like I was slowly waking from a hideous lethargic dream. It is now nearly fifteen years since
I first heard the gospel sound: but Oh! how little good have I accomplished?
what blunders have I committed? Instead of having faith in God "who feeds
the ravens when they cry!" I have been ever anxious lest my family should come
to want (and my fears have been realized). Instead of saying continually what
can I do to advance God's Kingdom? I have often so far forgot myself as to
be altogether absorbed with the question what can I do to make a living? Oh!
what a life I have led. I was in that horrid "Mountain Meadow affair" (which
was the grand cause of my moving back north).[6] And then Oh! that dear son
that I loved so much to think that his sweet life should be crushed out (last
summer) through my lack of watchfulness! through my not being humble and
full of the Holy Spirit!!

---

[6]Once George A. Smith granted permission to do so, hundreds of settlers abandoned southern Utah
in the wake of the Utah War. Spencer became one of the first pioneers of Peoa, now in Utah's Summit
County, while Samuel Knight and Ira Allen led a few Mountain Meadows veterans to Cache County.

What can I *now* do? What *can* I do to obtain eternal lives? Many are willing to *die* for salvation: but how few will live for it. Oh that God may direct me through his servants how to be of *some* use in His Kingdom! If it is necessary that my blood must be shed, and that *will* secure to me *life eternal,* let it run freely every drop of it. Without the hope of immortality and eternal lives: existence itself would be a burthen. I feel like a little child lost in the woods that needs a father to show me the path that leads to open ground. May God give you his spirit to direct me.

G. Spencer

In 1879 journalist J. H. Beadle reported "the confession of Spencer, a school teacher in St. George, who died of grief and remorse for his share in the act." Beadle claimed, "Young Spencer wasted to a skeleton, and wrote imploring letters to his bishop and to Brigham Young, begging for some word to relieve his remorse." The family preserves a tradition that Spencer killed himself.[7]

George Hicks: Pardon My Presumption

In a sermon in December 1866, Brigham Young referred to the murder of Dr. John Robinson, a non-Mormon physician who had tried to acquire land to build a hospital in Great Salt Lake City, which brought him into conflict with Mayor Daniel H. Wells. Eyewitness Fanny Brooks, wife of a prominent Jewish merchant, "was sure of one of the criminals but dared not tell" and took the secret to her grave, possibly because the killers were members of the city police force. "Fears of violence seized the whole non-Mormon community," her daughter recalled.[8] Gen. Patrick Edward Connor, former commander of U.S. forces in Utah, refused to be intimidated.

Patrick Edward Connor to Judge William Carter,
23 October 1866.

Dear Judge,
     I am in receipt of your 20th Inst. Am well, I feared we would have to postpone operations till spring, and perhaps it is all for the best.
     Dr. Robinson was foully assassinated, on Main St last night by Brighams destroying angels. Cause suit—with City—for possession of Warm Springs, north of the City. Great God how long is this state of things to last: A loyal american Citizen shot down like a dog, for appealing to the Courts, for his rights. The Gentiles are Panic Stricken and dare not express opinions of the foul deed.

---

[7]Beadle, *Western Wilds,* 497; and descendant Ken Sleight, personal communication to the editors.
[8]Ogden, ed., *Frontier Reminiscences of Eveline Brooks Auerbach,* 51.

If you have any friends in Washington beg of them to appeal to the President in our behalf. I may be the next, but as long as I have breath I shall denounce and cry aloud for vengeance on the foul assassins.

> Kind regards to you Family
> And believe me
> Your Friend
> Connor

National newspapers printed a series of damning remarks attributed to Brigham Young about the murder, and he was finally compelled to respond to charges that he had ordered the crime, among others.

REMARKS BY BRIGHAM YOUNG, 23 DECEMBER 1866,
DESERET NEWS, 9 JANUARY 1867, 10/3.

I see a notice in the *Daily Telegraph* that they are going to send a detective here to trace the murderers of Dr. Robinson. It is published to the world that the murdered man had no enemies only in the City Council. He had no enemies there. Were it not that there are many outsiders here to-day I would like the Saints to know how I feel about all such dastardly transactions. I will tell the Latter-day Saints that there are some things which transpire that I cannot think about. There are transactions that are too horrible for me to contemplate.

The massacre at Haun's mill, and that of Joseph and Hyrum Smith, and the Mountain Meadows massacre and the murder of Dr. Robinson are of this character. I cannot think that there are beings upon the earth who have any claim to the sentiments and feelings which dwell in the breasts of civilized men who could be guilty of such atrocities; and it is hard to suppose that even savages would be capable of performing such inhuman acts. To call a physician out of his bed in the night under the pretext of needing his services, and then brutally kill him in the dark, is horrible. "Have you any idea who did that horrible deed?" I have not the least idea in the world who could perpetrate such a crime. I say to all concerned, cease not your efforts until you find the murderers; and place the guilt where it belongs. I have not said this much before on that matter, and should not have spoken of it now, if the excitement which it created had not passed away. I do not care about the outsiders hearing this, as their opinion is neither here nor there to me; the Saints, however, are welcome to my views upon this matter. If the outsiders thank that I am guilty of the crime, let them trace it to me and prove it on me.

Old-time Latter-day Saints such as George A. Hicks might have chuckled at Young's challenge, which was similar to the gauntlet he had tossed down for anyone to prove he had more than one wife not long before the LDS church publicly admitted the practice of polygamy in 1852. The independent-minded

Hicks was unimpressed by his local priesthood authorities and persisted in going straight to the top rather than seeking answers from his file leader.[9] The Canadian, who lived in the same settlement as John D. Lee, kept demanding satisfaction on issues that troubled him.

GEORGE ARMSTRONG HICKS TO BRIGHAM YOUNG,
11 OCTOBER 1867, LDS ARCHIVES.

New Harmony Oct 11th 1867
Washington Co. U.T.

Pres Brigham Young dear bro

I hope you will Pardon my Presumption in adressing these Lines to you but I Know of no other way of Geting the information which I desire. On the 23rd of last Dec you Preached a Sermon in which you Spoke of the Mountain meadows Masacre. You classed it with the Hauns mill Masacre [and] the murder of Joseph and Hyrum Smith and the Murder of Dr. Robinson. Since your Discourse appeared in the Deseret News there has been considerabell talk about the afare. John D. Lee has said publick and Privatly that you did not mean what you said but Mearly said it to blind the eyes of the Jentiles and to Satisfy a few individuals. Now if you will please write and give me the real intentions which promted you I shall be mutch oblige[d] to you. If you are in favor of the Mountain meadows massacre I would like to know it if you are.

Now I would like to know it. Not that I pin my faith to your Sleave but I have allways believed that you are opposed to to [sic] the sheding of human-blood. John D. Lee is in full felow ship and is frequently Called upon to preach much to [the] anoyance of Good men. Last Sunday he asked the Bishop for and obtained a recommend to Get another wife and will.

[I] Start in a few days for the City. In the thirteenth section D&C and 21 verse Paragraph of the Doc and Covenants it claims [?] that such men are Condemed also in Psl [Psalms] 3 chapter and 15 ver[s]e.[10] Thes[e] things causes me some trouble of mind and a few words from you will dispose of all my dark fears.

I remain your brethren
George A. Hicks

[9]In classic Mormonism, one's "file leader" was a priesthood official. According to the current president of the Quorum of the Twelve Apostles, there is "an order of things as to where we go for counsel or blessings" that progresses from parents, home teachers, to one's bishop. "He may choose to send you to his file leader—the stake president. But we do not go to the General Authorities." See Boyd K. Packer, Devotional Address, BYU, 15 October 1996.

[10]"Lord, how are they increased that trouble me! many are they that rise up against me" was one of the lines from Psalms 3 Hicks cited. Another was, "I will not be afraid of ten thousands of people, that have set themselves against me round about."

HICKS TO YOUNG, 4 DECEMBER 1868 TO 21 JANUARY 1869,
ROMNEY TYPESCRIPT, LDS ARCHIVES.

Dear brother

I hope you will pardon my presumption in writeing this letter to you but you and you alone can give me enny peas of mind on the matter which rests with such might upon my mind tha[t] it is destroying my peace. On the 23d day of Dec 1866 you preached a sermon which was afterwards published in the "Deseret News" for Jan 8th 1867 in cou[r]se of your remarks you spoke of the Mountain Meadows Massacre. You classed it along with the Martyr-dom of Joseph Smith and Hyrum Smith. Now I was highly delighted to see it in print for I always had condemned that horable afair as being eaquiled in history only by such deeds as you compare it with: I felt in hopes that the perpitrators of that bloody deed would soon be punished for their Crimes or [if] they were not punished, their names would be stricken from the Church books. I carried the paper containing your sermon in my pocket and I read it to a great many people. Afterwards learned a song, descriptive of that mur-der which a gre[a]t many people came to my house to hear. In the Course of time my conduct made some excitement. I was persuaded to desist or rather advised but I continued to read and quote your remarks and to sing the song and at length I was gently warned that my course of conduct would be pun-ished if I continued. I took the revelations and the scripture generaly, in fact, for my guides at last but I find my self deserted. Reasone[ing] done no good, scripture done no good. I have been insulted in the public streets by some of John D. Lee's family only for encourageing the people to believe that the sixth commandment should be obeyed and that those who break it should be pun-ished according to the law of the Lord (see Doc & Cov sec XIII 21 paragraph also Ibid sec 110 and the 8th paragraph.) John D. Lee has said in public *and I have heard him* that you did not mean what you said about the Mountain Mead-ows Massacre but that you said it to *blind* the eyes of the gentiles and to sat-isfy a few individuals like myself. He is not generaly believed, however I heard one man say he believe[d] it. As for myself I scorned the idea at first but now I hardly know what to think, doubts and fears beginning to rise in my mind in relation to the matter, in short, my peace of mind is almost gone.

I wrote you once before on the subject but John Willis the P[ost] Master of Kannarah detained my letter and gave it to John D. and [?] Lee after keep-ing it for a long time on public exhibition at the post office.[11] I went to get it and *got nothing but insults for my trouble.* I have been a member of the church for over twenty five years—in fact the first thing that I remember was my father starting for Far west and from that time up to the present I have lived with the Latterday Saints.

---

[11] A common complaint by outsiders and many Mormons was that their letters were opened and read at territorial post offices.

I often ask my self the question "Can it be possible that the Church whose destiny I have so long followed through sufering privation and sorrow, to gain an exaltation not only fellowships a Company of men *whose hands have been stained with the blood of innocent women and children* but the gospel of Him who said "Thou shalt do no murder" (See Mathew XIX Chap 18 verse)

Some who pretend to be my friends advise me to pray to the Lord in relation to the matter. I have done so many a time but the bloody scene passes before my mind day and night. The fact stands upon our History "that the perpetrators are *still unpunished*" and have priveliges that I have not. If I was to venture to ask an action on your part it would be that John D. Lee if he is not punished for murder that he be deprived of a standing in the Church and then he can say what he pleases at his own option and not at the expense of the Church. No one knows the Contents of this letter but my self I have writen it with the best of feelings towards you and all good men hopeing [*sic*] you will give me such words of Consideration as will be for my best good.

> I remain your brother in
> the gospel of peace
> George A. Hicks

P.S. If you should condesend to answer direct to Harmony Washin[gton] Co UT.

BRIGHAM YOUNG TO GEORGE A. HICKS,
16 FEBRUARY 1869, LDS ARCHIVES.

President's Office, Feb. 16th 1869

Geo. A. Hicks,
Harmony, Washington Co.

Dear Brother: I received your letter reciting a tale of grievances at which I am not a little surprised.

What would be the judgment of any reasonable being after reading your letter, since you say, "The bloody scene passes before you day and night," and "it rests with such weight upon your mind" &c, why, that you yourself must have been a participator in the horrible deed. If this is correct, one can readily imagine why "it rests with such weight upon your mind," and "why you cannot sleep at nights"; the surprise would be that you could. In such a case, if you want a remedy—rope round the neck taken with a jerk would be very salutary.

There are courts of law and officers in the Territory, appeal to them, they would be happy to attend to your case.

If you are innocent you give yourself a great deal of foolish trouble. I would ask, why do not all the Latter-day Saints feel as you do? Simply because it does not concern them. As to your faith being shaken. If the Gospel was true before the "Mountain Meadow Massacre," neither that nor any other event that may transpire can make it false.

When Gov. Cumming was here, I pledged myself to lend him every assistance in my power, in men and means to thoroughly investigate that matter, but he declined to take any action. This offer I have made time and again, but it has never been accepted. Yet I have neither doubt nor fear on my mind but the perpetrators of that tragedy will meet their reward. God will judge this matter and on that assurance I rest perfectly satisfied.

If you are innocent, you may safely do the same; if you are guilty, better try the remedy.

> Yours in the Gospel
> /s/ Brigham Young

Even in the face of such intimidation, Hicks refused to back down. Instead, he turned to the *Salt Lake Tribune*, the newspaper that had done more to shed light on the Mountain Meadows massacre than any other institution in the United States, to tell his story.[12]

Hicks, "Some Startling Facts," ### Salt Lake Tribune, 21 August 1874, 2/2–3.

Hamilton's Fort, Aug. 12, 1874.

EDS. TRIBUNE: I ask the indulgence of a little space in your columns for the purpose of relating a few facts which pertain to myself, and may not be uninteresting to a majority of your readers. In the Semi-Weekly Deseret News, for Saturday, May 23d, 1874, appeared the following:

> "Excommunications:—At a public meeting held in Cedar City, Sunday evening April 26, 1874, Geo. A. Hicks, of Fort Hamilton, was cut off from the Church of Jesus Christ of Latter-day Saints, for apostacy."

The above is a very brief and unpretentious paragraph, which a business man might never notice—a paragraph which my friends who are still of the Mormon faith, would feel sad as they read it, and my enemies would rejoice at my downfall, and then it would be utterly forgotten. Not so with myself. In the notice of my excommunication, the readers only hear one side of the case, "apostacy." I shall endeavor to give

THE OTHER SIDE.

Of the forty years of my life, thirty have been spent in the Mormon Church. I, with my father's family, was expelled from Nauvoo. I thought it was very

---

[12]In its typical fashion, the *Tribune* ran a series of provocative subheadlines: "A Saint of Thirty Year's Standing Unburdens His Bosom. And Tells What He Knows of the Mountain Meadows Massacre. Brigham Young and John D. Lee, the Twin Assassins. Massacre of the Innocent Emigrants by the Profit."

cruel at the time and still think so in fact. I have shared the joys and sorrows, the victories and defeats of the Church for thirty years.

I came to Utah in 1852, strong in the faith of Mormonism. I have seen the church when it was full of Christian charity and brotherly love. In 1850 [1856] came what is called

THE REFORMATION,

which swept over the country like a tornado. It was then for the first time I heard the doctrine of Blood Atonement. Leading men in the church would say if you should find your father or your sister or your brother dead by the wayside, say nothing about it, but pass on about your own business. The wildest fanaticism prevailed everywhere. Secret deaths began to be

QUITE COMMON.

If we heard of a secret murder in San Pete or Cache valley, we knew the work of the Lord was progressing. I was then a citizen of Spanish Fork city and be it said to the honor of that place, no one has ever been killed by any priestly assassin inside of its borders.

WHOLESALE MURDER

In the year 1857, while Johnson's army was on the plains, a company of emigrants came into Utah. I saw them pass through Spanish Fork; they were quiet and orderly. They traveled on south and stopped on the bottom between Spanish Fork and Payson to rest their teams, and in a week or two continued their journey. The next news I heard of them was they had all been killed by the Indians. It was afterwards whispered that white men and Indians together, led by one John D. Lee, had done the deed, but nothing definite was known to the public. In autumn of 1863, I, with my family, was called on a mission to Washington county to raise cotton. In Washington I was told that many of the men there had been to Sebastapol. "Sebastapol," said I, "what do you mean?" "Oh, the Mountain Meadows—but don't say that I told you," said my cautious informer. I noticed that all those men were in full fellowship in the church and some of them were the loudest preachers and could bear strong testimony of

THIS WORK.

I thought I would soon be able to break down their influence in society, as soon as I got a little acquainted. I staid at Washington one year and a half and then removed to Harmony. That settlement was the residence at that time, of John D. Lee, and he was the presiding elder of that branch of the church. Surely, thought I, Brigham Young does not know that Lee is the man who led the Indians and whitemen who

MURDERED A TRAIN OF CHRISTIAN WHITE PEOPLE?

Lee is a Kentuckian.[13] He is an eloquent preacher of Mormonism, and has been very successful in making converts.

---

[13]Lee was actually born and raised in Illinois.

When I had been at Harmony one year, Brigham Young came to Harmony, passed through it, and drove up to the residence of John D. Lee! From that time my confidence in Brigham began to wane. Could it be possible that the Prophet of God could find no better men

TO ASSOCIATE WITH THAN JOHN D. LEE?

Then I began to argue the circumstance from my mind, by saying it was not my business where the servants of God should stop, or whom they should stop with.

Time passed on until the murder of Dr. J. K. Robinson. Soon after that event, Brigham Young preached a sermon in Salt Lake City, in which he used the following language: "These are some things which I cannot bear to contemplate, the hounds will [Haun's Mill] massacre; the Mountain Meadows massacre, and the murder of Dr. Robinson are atrocities of this sort. There," said he, "I cannot bear to think about; but

LET THE UNITED BRETHREN KEEP THEIR OATHS AND COVENANTS.

That last remark is significant. The sermon containing that extract, was published in the Deseret News. I read it, and re-read it; in my mind, which had wavered between two opinions—one in favor of Brigham Young's innocence, and the other against it. Brother Brigham is all right, I said, and is not in favor of Lee and his crime.

The people of Harmony had got tired of Lee, and had put another man in his place to preside over them, but Lee was still allowed to preach, two or three times a month. In one meeting I raised an objection, and used Brigham Young's sermon against Lee, and thought to silence him in public. Lee, who understood his "relations" to the Prophet better than I did, promptly informed me that I did not know Brother Brigham as well as he did; he (Brother Brigham)

DID NOT MEAN WHAT HE HAD SAID

in his sermon. He had talked that way to blind the eyes of the Gentiles, and to satisfy the disaffected individuals such as I was. I felt indignant to the highest degree that the character of a servant of God should be traduced by a man whose hand I believed to be

STAINED WITH INNOCENT BLOOD.

I immediately informed Brigham Young by letter, of Lee's slanderous statements, recommending that Lee be cut off from the Church. I waited for an answer; it came promptly to hand. The Prophet did not thank me for the information I had given him, but on the contrary he pretended to think that I had taken a part in the Mountain Meadows affair, and on that conclusion, advised me to take a

DOSE OF ROPE AROUND MY NECK

"with a jerk." That little bit of prophetic advice I did not obey. From that time forth, I have believed that Lee is better acquainted with the prophet than I am.

To the honest believing Mormon, these statements of mine will seem incredible, but they are nonetheless true. I do not wish to do Brigham Young any physical harm, but I will say to all men who read this article, that if I had only been

A PIOUS MURDERER,

I might have rode "cheek by jowl" with the Prophet as Lee has done, and been in good standing in the Church.

On the seventh day of April 1874, I saw John D. Lee ride into Kanarrah on horse back by the side of Brigham Young's carriage, and reported the same to THE TRIBUNE.[14] I was suspected of doing so. Bishop Henry Lunt of Cedar City, questioned me on the subject. I did not deny the fact, and was immediately cut off without even a hearing of any kind.

A few more words, and I will close. I was a member of the Mormon Church for nearly thirty years, and never had a charge of any kind brought against me. I have always lived a moral life. I have no faith in any of the religions of the day, but like [French novelist] Madam De Stael, I have loved God, my country, and liberty. The reader must judge whether I have or have not just grounds for apostacy.

Respectfully,
GEO. A. HICKS.

Hicks's stout refusal to be intimidated symbolized the revulsion many devout Latter-day Saints felt toward the 1857 massacre and the perpetrators who were shielded for so long. Hicks's resistance had its limits, however: eleven days after the Lion of the Lord roared his last, George A. Hicks made peace with his neighbors—for a while.

—TO ALL LATTER-DAY SAINTS: Inasmuch as I was cut off the Church of Jesus Christ of Latter-day Saints on the 28th of April, 1873, at Cedar City, for apostacy [sic], and published in the DESERET NEWS as such, and I have said and written many hard things about the people, and authorities of the church, I hereby confess my errors and acknowledge my follies, and ask forgiveness of all Saints who have been offended by my writings and sayings, for I desire to be restored to the fellowship of Saints, and to be forgiven of my heavenly Father. Geo. A. Hicks.[15]

[14]Lee, who had been hiding out on the Colorado River since 1872, visited Brigham Young's home in St. George on 5 April 1874, where Lee reported that Young "received me with the kindness of a Father" and then had "his wives and Family come & shake hands with me." On passing Lee's home in Washington the next day, Young "halted & bowed to My wife Emma." When the two men parted for the last time on 8 April 1874, Young chided Lee for playing cards and consorting with Gentiles, where once "he could trust Me to do anny thing on Earth that was wanted to be done." Young advised Lee to "be careful & stand to your integrity. Blessed me & drove on." See Cleland and Brooks, eds., A Mormon Chronicle, 5 to 8 April 1874, 2:336–38.

[15]"Public Confession," Mount Carmel, 9 September 1877, in "Local and Other Matters," Deseret News, 26 September 1877, 12/4. Hicks was again excommunicated after writing a play called "Celestial Marriage." His church membership was once more restored in the 1920s.

GEORGE A. SMITH:
THE DEATH OF THEIR FRIENDS BY POISON

Despite overwhelming evidence to the contrary, Mormon leaders as late as 1869 publicly professed that the massacre was purely an Indian affair and repeated the poison story. But that year saw the last official attempt to deny Mormon involvement, possibly because of the appearance of a series of open letters to Brigham Young by a former insider who knew a great deal about the massacre. (Those letters, signed "Argus," follow.) Apostle George A. Smith, whose own role in the massacre gave him a personal interest in deception, created the most elaborate of the last attempts to deny any and all Mormon involvement.

GEORGE A. SMITH TO MR. ST. CLAIR,
25 NOVEMBER 1869, LDS ARCHIVES.

Dear Sir:

I attended the interesting lecture of Madame St. Clair at the Theatre on the evening of the 23d inst. and in consequence of the reference made to the Mountain Meadow Massacre I have thought proper to furnish you some items in relation to that subject which came partly under my observation.

Very Respectfully,
/s/ G. A. Smith

A/C of Mountain Meadow Massacre sent to Mr. St. Clair.

In August 1857, I was returning from a visit to the Southern Settlements which were then few and far between. I left Beaver on the 25th at nine A.M., with two wagons, accompanied by Philo T. Farnsworth, S. S. Smith, Elisha Hoops and Jacob Hamblin. We traveled as the road then run, 52 miles en route for Salt Lake City. We arrived at Corn Creek Springs some hours after dark and found encamped a company of emigrants, with about thirty wagons and a considerable herd of stock. We drove across the creek and camped within forty yards of them. One of my companions remarked to me, that the emigrant company were excited, that they had eight men on guard on our arrival and had increased them to ten. We were soon visited by three gentlemen, one of whom was introduced to me as Captain of the company. He enquired where we were from; we told him our places of residence and that we had traveled from Beaver that morning, a distance of 52 miles. They enquired if there were any danger from the Indians who were encamped near us. I replied that if their party had not committed any outrage upon the Indians there would be no danger. They assured me that there had been no interruption whatever.

Next morning, soon after light while we were hitching up to continue our journey, I was again waited upon by the Captain of the emigrant company, who pointed out to me an ox which had died during the night, enquiring if the Indians would eat the animal. I answered, Yes; and informed him that they

were in the habit of eating the cattle that died, and that if he would give it
to them, they would be thankful. As we were starting, Elisha Hoops asked
me what the Captain was doing over at the dead ox with a bottle in his hand.
I informed Hoops that I had advised the Captain to give the Indians the ox
and that he was probably taking a drink. My company proceeded homewards.

On a subsequent visit I learned from Hon. John A. Roy [sic] and also from
herdsmen at Meadow creek that ten of the Indians who ate the dead animal
died and others were very sick and that thirty head of animals had died, apparently of poison from drinking the waters of Corn Creek, which the emigrants
were accused of poisoning.

A portion of these Indians were Pahvantes and the others were Pah-Utes
who lived in the vicinity of the Mountain Meadows and were on a visit to
the Pahvantes. I also learned that the remnants of these Indians returned home
with the news of the death of their friends by poison which, we [have no]
doubt, was the cause of the general rallying of the different tribes, which cul-
minated in the massacre of the arkansas company while camped at the Mountain Meadows early in September.

The massacre was charged upon the Mormons, as an excuse for keeping
an army in the territory, and those who were particularly interested in deplet-
ing the U.S. Treasury of its gold were most zealous in urging this charge.

I believe Gov. Alfred Cumming and U.S. District attorney Wilson were
desirous of complying with the earnest request of ex-Governor Brigham Young
and this community that a rigid investigation of this affair should take place;
but this was no part of the policy of the judges nor the attaches of the camp
who were interested in prolonging the difficulty.

Prest. Young proffered to go with the Federal officers to the vicinity of
the outrage and use every effort in his power to sift the matter to the uttermost and bring the guilty parties to justice.

In the Spring of 1859, a grand Jury on U.S. business undertook the investigation of the Mountain Meadow Massacre, at Provo. They requested the
U.S. district attorney, Mr. Wilson, a gentleman from Penn., to be present with
them & examine the witnesses. Two Indians, Mose and Looking glass, had
been committed for rape perpetrated upon a white woman and her daughter,
a girl of ten years. In the midst of the investigation of the Mountain Meadow case the Judge, John Cradlebaugh, called the Grand Jury into the court
room and administered to them an abusive lecture and summarily discharged
them: and at the same time, the Judge turned the savages Moses and Look-
ingglass "loose upon the community." The Grand Jury protested against this
unwarrantable proceeding by the court. Attorney Wilson reported that he was
present at the deliberations of the grand jury and at their request had examined the witnesses and that the jury were proceeding in the mater efficiently.

When Col. Fremont passed through the Southern part in 1844, his party
killed several Pah-Ute Indians near the Rio Virgin without any provocation. When
New Mexico was organized Gov. Calhoun, Supt. of Indian affair, recommend-

ed to the Department at Washington the extermination of the Pah-Utes, and it had been the practice of emigrants to shoot them upon nearing their camps without stopping to learn whether their intentions were friendly or otherwise.

When the party led by me made the settlement at Parowan, Iron Co., in Jan. 1851, then two hundred miles from our nearest neighbors on the north, and upwards of five hundred on the south, a delegation of Pah-Ute Indians from New Mexico, now Arizona, visited us and besought that the indiscriminate shooting of their people by emigrants should cease, as they were disposed to be friendly and wanted to trade with the emigrants. I told them I could not speak for the emigration, any farther than that portion thereof which was composed of our people.

There is no doubt but that the whole accumulated wrath of the Pah-Utes against american travellers from the wanton massacre by Fremont's men to the poisoning of the ox and the spring at Corn Creek by the Arkansas party was avenged at the Mountain Meadows, and all the Indians of that district were concerned in it except a small band of Piedes who resided at Parowan.

After hostilities had commenced the first intimation of it received at Parowan, was by Indian runners to Ouwanup, a chief of the Pi-Edes in Little Salt Lake Valley, who was summoned by the hostile Indians to assist them. Our people found out through the Pi-edes something pertaining to the matter and succeeded in keeping these Indians from participating in the outrage. Rumors still arriving that a battle was going on, a party of our people from Cedar started for the purpose of relieving the emigrants, but arrived too late, however they succeeded in rescuing a few children, who had been preserved by the Indians for the purpose of trading them.

It has been the custom of the stronger Nations of Indians for a long time to rob the weaker tribes of their children for the purpose of selling them to the Mexicans and these children were preserved for this purpose.

I am fully satisfied that it had been the determined policy of our enemies that this Subject should never be investigated, and from the fact that it never has been, it is plain that the charge is false; for during the years 1858 & 9, an army of Several thousand men were stationed in the territory in a state of complete idleness, and if there could have been the least pretense for the employment of these men against the Mormons any probability of criminating them, it would have been sought with avidity, but the news-paper rumor of this charge answered a better purpose in affording an excuse for keeping up the expense of Sustaining troops when they were not needed.

There has never been a time when President Brigham Young and his brethren were not ready to give every aid in their power to discover and bring to Justice the participators in this Massacre.[16]

Geo. A. Smith

---

[16]Editor George Q. Cannon reworked Smith's fabrications into a newspaper article, "Mountain Meadow Massacre," *Deseret News*, 1 December 1869, in Ekins, ed., *Defending Zion*, 387–90. Cannon had learned of white involvement in the massacre on his return to Utah with Charles Wandell in 1857.

THE ARGUS LETTERS: NOT ENOUGH OF BLOOD

"I notice in your paper of October 5 a partial account of the Mountain Meadow massacre, that took place ten years since," began an anonymous letter from
Nevada to a national religious newspaper in 1867. "A more hellish act or a
more terrible tragedy has not stained our record as a nation. The deed is here
not spoken of with any calmness."[17]

Frederic Lockley, the *Salt Lake Tribune* editor during the 1870s, noted that for
a Mormon who "vacates or is expelled from the fold" the purposes of life
become "jangled, out of tune and harsh."[18] The description fits Charles Wesley Wandell, who served the church faithfully from the day of his baptism in
1837 and probably wrote the angry letter from Nevada. He had labored as a
missionary, worked as a clerk to the church historian at Nauvoo, opened the
Australian mission in 1851, and later settled at San Bernardino. With the recall
of California Mormons at the start of the Utah War, he moved to Beaver,
Utah, a settlement some fifty miles north of Cedar City. There he taught school
and found himself excommunicated in 1864 for prospecting in the mineral-
rich region. He appealed to Brigham Young, who refused even to reply.

Wandell's anger grew, but he held his peace until the coming of the railroad to Utah in 1869 and the establishment of an independent newspaper
on the transcontinental line at Corinne, the new "Gentile Capital" of Utah.
Then at age 58 his indignation poured forth in more than twenty open letters to Brigham Young under the pen name "Argus," published in the *Utah
Reporter* at Corinne and later in the *Salt Lake Tribune.* Wandell's ornate prose did
little to soften his brutal story or raw accusations, and while he repeated much
of the mythology that had grown up about the atrocity, he also provided a
window on what curious southern Utahns believed about the event during
the 1860s. At the end of his first epistle, Wandell took up the subject that
became his main theme.

> At the time of that awful massacre at the Mountain Meadows, the Indians
> were called out in common with the Mormons to do that bloody deed, but
> to the honor of the savages be it known, that they refused to participate in
> that wholesale murder after the surrender; even Mormons shrunk back and
> refused to obey J. D. Lee's orders, until he made them a speech declaring that
> he was acting under your "counsel" in that affair, and even then, although the

---

[17]Americus, "Letter from Nevada," *Christian Advocate,* 19 December 1867, 402.
[18]Lockley, Recollections of Territorial Utah, Part 4, Chapters 1, 5.

Mormons felt compelled to obey your commands, "even to the shedding of blood," and did so, even to the "wiping out" of that ill-fated company, the Indians stood back amazed, without firing a gun or shooting an arrow. To first disarm men by lying promises of life and protection, and then deliberately slaughter an entire company of unoffending men, women and children, was more than even savages could do. At that time you had assumed, and had unquestioned control of the issues of life and death over the whole of old Utah, reaching from Bridger's Pass to the Sierra Nevadas, and from Bear River to the Rio Virgen; and you exercised that control without hesitation or stint; indeed, you appeared to have no more scruples of conscience in causing the murder of any one considered by you as an enemy, or that might become such, than you would to cut off a chicken's head. Your rule in all things in Utah, at that time, was despotic beyond example or precedent. No man knew this better than that same John D. Lee, and with such knowledge, for him to have acted as demon-in-chief in that most sanguinary, merciless and inhuman of all your crimsoned felonies, citing you there and then as his authority for so doing, was impossible.[19]

Wandell pointed his finger at the Mormon leader as fearlessly as the Prophet Nathan had rebuked King David. His letters kept the massacre before the public and led to the trials of John D. Lee. Five of them are presented below.

Argus, 17 February 1871, "Mountain Meadows,"
Daily Utah Reporter, 22 February 1871, 2/3–5.

Sir: The massacre at the Mountain Meadows was simply an effect resulting from a certain cause, which I now propose to notice. And right here I wish to state a proposition, which you will very much dislike to see, but one which is fully sustained by notorious facts; and that is, that the aforesaid massacre was but a realization, on a small scale, of a doctrine before enunciated by you, which had for years been publicly preached not only from your own stand in the old Tabernacle, but throughout the settlements in Utah; not only preached, but a prominence given to it second to nothing taught to your congregations, except polygamy . . . I mean your doctrine of "blood atonement." Almost immediately upon the introduction of your polygamous practices in Nauvoo did you announce, not publically, but privately, to your "secret police," that it was right to shed blood in defence of the Church and its (supposed) institutions. Upon your arrival at Salt Lake in 1847, the same idea begun to be preached to the congregations, and continued to be so taught for years, and until there became too many Gentile ears around to hear; and in secret it is so taught to-day throughout the Mormon settlements of Utah.

---

[19]"An Open Letter to Brigham Young," *Daily Utah Reporter*, 12 September 1870, 2/2.

Total Extirpation Taught.

You rejected the doctrine of atonement as given 1st John, II:2, and taught that the sin of apostacy could only be purged by the shedding of the blood of the apostate. You further taught that the killing of Joseph and Hiram Smith had to be atoned for by the shedding of blood, and, in that connection, I once heard you say that there was not enough of blood in the whole United States to make full satisfaction for their death. The results of such teaching were, as a matter of course, such scenes of blood as were common in Utah before the advent of the United States troops. The New Testament teaches us not to kill; but you taught murder as a precept of religion. You justified, applauded, sanctified, first, the killing of apostates; second, the killing of Gentiles. At that time there were no territories of Idaho, Montana, Wyoming, Colorado and Arizona; there was no State of Nevada, but this entire Rocky Mountain region was for the most part an unknown country to all except Mormons, and the peculiar isomorphism of Mormonism was such that you expected to maintain your position here on American soil until you got strong enough to turn your arms against the United States, and revenge the death of Joseph and Hiram. You taught us that in due time the Mormons and Indians were to make war on the entire American people. They were to "go through, tear down, break in pieces, and there should be none to deliver." They were to lay waste "counties, States, and the United States." They were to extirpate the populations in satisfaction for the blood of the Lord's Anointed, Joseph Smith and his brother. It is probable that you cared precious little about avenging the blood of those two men, but you were ruling over Mormons who loved the memory of their illustrious martyrs; you were using them as materials upon which to found your empire and dynasty, and the manner of the deaths of the founders of their faith afforded you a convenient hook upon which to hang your favorite way of disposing of your enemies.

The Crimson Track.

Now, Sir, this doctrine of the shedding of blood had been preached and enforced among the people of Utah for a period of twelve years up to the time of the Mountain Meadow massacre. During that time blood had been shed on the old overland road, on the Territorial road, at Salt Lake City, in the settlements, in the canyons, by the rivers' banks, among the sage brush, everywhere; and all to satisfy the Utah god, incarnated in your person, and portrayed in your treasonable ambition. And in no case has there been a man killed by your orders who was not less a criminal than yourself; no man but had less of lecherous practices, who was not less debauched and less dishonest and corrupt, less a falsifier of his word, and a better citizen than you. Even John D. Lee was, in my opinion, less a murderer than yourself . . .

Now as your death sentences have been invariably pronounced by yourself as President of the Church, and under conditions as above stated, you are in the eyes of the law a murderer, and are responsible for every death produced in pursuance of such sentence. They are fearful things to contemplate, those secret church trials, wherein men have been tried for their lives and condemned to death, knowing nothing of the matter until the assassin's bullet had executed the terrible sentence! And yet how often has that thing been done in Utah!

RESULTS OF TEACHING.

At the time of the Mountain Meadow massacre, the Mormon people had been long and persistently trained to the idea of the necessity, sinlessness, and even piety of church murders. Jedediah M. Grant, then your "Second Counsellor," was your chief apostle of blood and it was in your presence, and with your approval, in the old Bowery at Salt Lake City, he would get up and preach murder by the hour. Incredible as that may appear to the outside world, it was notorious enough at the time in Utah. Those blood sermons, preached by yourself, Grant, and Heber C. Kimball, were caught up by the bishops and missionaries, and preached to the settlements all over the Territory, and the man who would dare demur to them had need to lose no time in setting his house in order, for he would surely die. The scope of those sermons did not only include dissenting Mormons, but Gentiles also. In fact the whole American people were declared to be accessories, after the fact, to the murder of Joseph and Hiram and I am confident there was not at that time a sincere, full-faithed Mormon in Utah, but what considered it no crime against Heaven to kill a Gentile, and his bounden duty to kill a dissenting Mormon, when ordered to do so by you. In such a condition of public sentiment, with the moral sense of the people blunted by your preaching, with a thirst or blood as a matter of conscience and of duty, it only required your order to make the massacre at Mountain Meadows a matter of course.

LEGAL INQUIRY.

The question here arrises [sic] as to what [was] the relative degrees of responsibility that rests between you and your soldiers who did that deed. Your military order to them was a positive act, while the execution of that order by them was a negative act, and must have been so regarded by a court-martial had one been ordered in that case. And here I respectfully ask our present Governor and Commander-in-Chief, whether such court-martial must not yet be called? Now suppose it should be, and your subordinate, Colonel Dame should plead in his defense "obedience to orders," and should make it appear to the satisfaction of the court, that the massacre was the direct result of such order. You were at the time Governor and Commander-in-Chief, therefore said orders to him were legitimate, though commanding him to commit an act of hostility to a party of peaceable travelers. To what extent can the court hold him criminally responsible? And what is true in his case, must be equally true of every officer and soldier in the regiment. Did it ever occur to you that while the militia that served under Major Lee at the Mountain Meadows, have since scattered to different parts of the Territory and Arizona, the commanding officers have remained precisely where they are? That is so, and the reason is evident.

Fixing the Responsibility.

For while the ignorant masses only knew they had been engaged in a horrible massacre, Major Lee and Colonel Dame both knew that they were shielded by your order, and did not greatly fear trial, if one must be had. Do not suppose me to be the apologist of those murderers. The gusto with which many of them entered into that bloody work, and their persistent efforts since to justify the act, fixes their status as fiends, and excludes them from the sympathies of all proper-minded persons. My object is, simply, to bring you, the chief villain in that affair, to the light—to drag you from your hiding place—tear off your disguise, and exhibit you to my Mormon brethren and to the government as the champion monster of the continent . . .—Argus

The Weekly Reporter, Corinne, Utah, 15 July 1871, 2/2–3.

Sir: The company of emigrants slaughtered on the 15th of September, 1857, at the Mountain Meadows, and within your jurisdiction, was one of the wealthiest, most respectable and peaceable that ever crossed the continent by the way of Salt Lake City. They were American citizens—were within the territory of the United States, and when they encamped by the Jordan River, upon the free, unenclosed and unappropriated public domain, and by the laws of Utah their stock were "free commoners" on that domain. The most of those emigrants had unquestionably been farmers, all of them rural in their habits of life; and from the fact that you did not charge them with being thieves, or robbers, or of trespassing upon the rights of others, or disturbing the public peace, or with behaving themselves unseemly, it is fair to infer they were as upright and virtuous in their habits of thought, and as honest and honorable in their intercourse with others as people from country parts generally are. They came from Arkansas. When they encamped by the Jordan they were weary and foot-sore, their supply of food was well nigh exhausted, and their work cattle nearly "used up" by the labors of the long and toilsome journey. The necessity rested upon them of tarrying in Utah sufficiently long to rest and recruit their teams and replenish their store of provisions. The harvest in Utah that year, then gathering, was abundant, and mountain and valley were covered with rich and nutritious grasses. What was there to hinder this company from staying as long as they pleased, recruiting their stock, and pursuing their journey when they got ready? And, besides, what had they done that the protection of the law, represented in your person, should be worse than withdrawn from them? that they should be ordered to break up camp and move on? and, worse than all, that a courier should be sent ahead of them bearing your written instructions to the Mormons on said company's line of travel to have no dealing or intercourse with them; thus compelling them to almost certain death by starvation on the deserts? You was at that time the

GOVERNOR OF UTAH,

Commander-in-Chief of the militia, and Superintendent of Indian Affairs, a sworn officer of the United States and of the territory, upon whom devolved, and with whom were intrusted grave and important responsibilities affecting the liberties of the people, the rights of persons and property, and the welfare and happiness of all within the pale of your authority without regard to sect, creed, name, or nativity, or differences between individual opinions. In addition to your magistrature, you were the chief high priest of almost the entire body of the people, assuming to yourself extraordinary heavenly powers and an unusual amount of spiritual excellence. Without any modification of the term, you were professedly the earthly Vicar of the heavenly Savior . . . Not being allowed to remain, this weary, unrested company "broke camp" and took up their line of travel for Los Angeles. Their progress was necessarily slow. Arriving at American Fork settlement they essayed to trade off some of their worn-out stock for the fresh and reliable cattle of the Mormons, offering fine bargains; and also sought to buy provisions. What must have been their surprise when they found they could do neither? Notwithstanding that flour, bacon, vegetables in variety, poultry, butter, cheese, eggs, etc., were in unusual abundance, and plenty of surplus stock, not the first thing could be bought or sold! They passed on through Battle Creek, Provo, Springville, Spanish Fork, Payson, Salt Creek and Fillmore, attempting at each settlement to purchase food and to trade for stock, but without success. It is true that occasionally some Mormon more daring than his fellows would sack up a few pounds of provisions and under cover of night smuggle the same into the emigrant camp, taking his chances of a severed windpipe in satisfaction for such unreasonable contempt of orders; but otherwise there was no food bought by this company thus far. And here it is worthy to remark that up to this time no complaint had been made against these travelers. They had been accused of no crime known to the laws, and, undeniably, it had been a point with them to quietly and peaceably pass through Utah, in the hope of reaching some Gentile settlement where their gold and cattle could buy them something to eat.

THE QUERY ARISES HERE,

What caused so strange and unprecedented a proceeding towards this particular company? The custom of the overland emigration at that time was well known; which was to provision their trains for Salt Lake City, and met at that place for California. If other trains could rest and recruit, could buy, sell and refit in Utah, why not this? I answered these questions in a former letter; and shall here recall only one item of that answer, namely, That those people were from Arkansas, a State in which Parley P. Pratt, one of your fellow apostles,

had been killed for corrupting a man's wife and stealing his children. Parley was
an expert in the seducing business. He had already broken up a respectable family named Marden, in Boston, and one named Rogers, in New York, besides
some adventures in England; but then he was the Lord's anointed! He was the
Apostle of the pure Savior, and "to the pure, all things are pure," therefore his
inveigling McLain's wife and children from their once charming home, was a
pious and holy act! For that act he was killed by the outraged husband and
father, a Mississippian, who tracked them from New Orleans into Arkansas,
and there did to him precisely what you have many a time said should be done
to Gentiles in Utah under similar circumstances; and to avenge the blood of
this anointed lecher, was one of the alleged reasons for your holy (!) wrath against
these Arkansas emigrants. Mrs. McLain was living at Salt Lake City at the time
the company passed through, and it was reported that she had recognized one
or more of the party as having been present at the death of Pratt . . .

But to return. This ill-fated company were now at Fillmore. They had left
their camp at the Jordan with almost empty wagons, they had been unable to
purchase provisions, as before stated, they had but three or four settlements
yet to pass through; and then their way would pass over the most to be dread-
ed of all the America deserts, where there would be no possibility of obtaining a pound of food. What their prospects, feelings and forebodings were at
that time, I leave for your consideration; but, sir, I beg to call your attention
to the fact that, at the capture of their train at the Mountain Meadows, their
stores were found to be inadequate for the journey in contemplation. They
were, indeed, well nigh exhausted . . . There can not be a reasonable doubt that
they were already on short allowance when they reached that settlement . . .

Here we have in free America a peaceable company of emigrants who were
forced untimely into a journey, then half starved, and finally slaughtered in
cold blood! And this was the result of the apparent action of an entire people. Do you expect the world to believe that action to have been spontaneous
with them? That the whole people from the Jordan to Fillmore, should of their
own free will, uninfluenced, uninstructed, uncoerced, should all as one unite
in denying these strangers the right even of buying food? Impossible! For Mormons, after all, are men, and the mass of them can not be totally lost to the
promptings and sympathies of our better nature . . . Conscious guilt of multiplied criminalities perverted your judgment, causing you to see hostility in
the friendly action of the general Government toward Utah, and red-handed
enemies in this company of Arkansas farmers, traveling with their wives and
little ones. And they had now traveled through and by fifteen different settlements, large and small, peopled by Mormons under your absolute control in
all things, and had not been able to buy food. Oh! what a falling off was there
from the words of Him, who said, "If thine enemy hunger, feed him!"

I close, assuring you that you are faithfully remembered by —ARGUS.

"Argus," *The Weekly Reporter*,
Corinne, Utah, 22 July 1871, 2/1–2.

Sir: In my last, we left the emigrants of Mountain Meadow memory at Fill-more. Their store of provisions were too scanty to allow of delay; and so soon as they found they could do no trading there they moved on, and in due course reached Corn Creek. Here they saw the first kindly look and heard the first friendly word since they left the Jordan. And, strange to say, those friends were Indians! They sold the emigrants 30 bushels of corn—all they had to spare—and sent them away in peace. And, sir, these were the very Indians whom you afterward represented in the papers of California and elsewhere as having pursued this company and massacred them at the Mountain Mead-ows, alleging that the emigrants had poisoned an ox and certain springs which had caused the death of certain of their band.

Brigham as a Liar.

This lie, like other fabrications of yours, has done you some service; but the old settlers know it to be a falsehood. There was a company of *men* who started from Salt Lake City for Los Angeles about three weeks after the Arkansans had left the Jordan. This company had trouble with the Corn Creek Indians. And I am well persuaded that said trouble was another little trick of yours, to put them out of the way. They were driven from Salt Lake City. Some had been merchants there. You were preparing your campaign against the Government troops under Johnson. These Gentiles had to leave. But no sooner had they gone than you received the news of the massacre at the Moun-tain Meadows. It would not do for them to see the horrible sight presented there, and state the truth to the press of California. These are, as I believe, the reasons why they had trouble with the Corn Creek band, and why the sav-ages followed them as far as Parowan, expecting help from the Mormons to "wipe them out." But Colonel Dame had got an overdose of your Mormonism. He had sickened on the massacre, so most of this company were saved, but were not allowed to go by the way of the Meadows. They were compelled to make a rough and tedious detour via Washington settlement, avoiding the Meadows, so that when they arrived at Los Angeles they could give no cer-tain intelligence concerning the massacre. There is not a particle of evidence to show that any Corn Creek Indian was in Lee's fight with the emigrants.

The Trials of the Emigrants.

The Arkansas company passed on from Corn Creek, and, reaching Beaver, they found the same order of non-intercourse, the same prohibition as to trad-ing as before; and, passing on, they came to Parowan, *but were not permitted to enter the town.* Now be it known, and the books will show, that the General Government had paid twenty-five thousand dollars in gold coin for the sur-veying and opening of this road which passed directly through the town of

Parowan, and upon which this company was traveling and had traveled all the way from Salt lake City, passing through American Fork, and all the principal settlements on the route. They had passed through those settlements without let or hindrance; but here they were forced to leave the public highway and pass around the west side of the fort wall. When they reached the stream abreast of the town they encamped, and tried, as before, to trade for food and fresh cattle, but failed. There was a little Englishman who was determined to sell them some provisions; but Bishop Lewis' son and Counsellor advanced before him, and pressing the edge of a Bowie knife against his throat, compelled him to retreat without realizing his humane intentions. There was a grist-mill at Parowan, the first the company had "struck" since they left Corn Creek. They made application to have the corn ground which they had bought of the Indians, but were flatly refused.

A Pertinent Question.

Now, sir, why were these emigrants refused permission to enter and pass through Parowan? . . . You are quite competent to give the answer, so is your Aid[e]-de-camp and Brigadier-General, George A. [Smith]. So is Wm. H. Dame, the Colonel of the regiment forming a part of the militia under your supreme command—that same regiment that afterward fell upon that same unoffending company at Mountain Meadows and destroyed them. But you will not answer until compelled. Then let me suggest that Parowan was the legitimate head quarters of that particular regiment; that it was the place of residence of Col. Dame; that there was a certain military appearance inside the walls that it would not be prudent for the emigrants to see or suspicion, for their destruction had been decreed, and they must be taken at a disadvantage . . .

Opinion of an Old Pioneer.

Now, sir, I have consulted with one of the old pioneers of the road from Cedar City to the Mojave River, one whose judgment and experience are worthy of respect; one who saw that company in Utah as they were passing along on the Territorial road, and knew the condition of their teams. I asked him how long it would have taken them to go from Cedar to the Mojave? He reflected, then answered, "Sixty days." From there to San Bernardino would have taken six to ten days. Here was a company made up of men, women and children, with at least one child to be born on the road, whose mother would require a little rest and at least some comfort, forced to undertake this journey under circumstances beyond their control, but altogether under *yours*, who were obliged to put themselves on short allowance on the start. Think of that, sir, and say, whose fault it was! But methinks I hear you say, "We did not mean to starve them. We had intended to provide so bountifully at the crossing of the Clara, that they would hunger and thirst no more forever" . . .

During their journey to Cedar, and upon their arrival there, no person had been killed or suffered harm; they had stolen nothing, they had not meddled with your concerns, had created no riots, and, indeed, their whole conduct had been inoffensive and irreproachable, except the, to you, unpardonable offense of giving shelter and passage to at least one apostate Mormon. Do not be impatient, sooner than you wish, you shall [h]ear again from.—Argus.

"Argus," 27 July 1871, *The Corinne Reporter,* Corinne, Utah, 29 July 1871.

Sir: The Arkansas company remained at Cedar City but one day and then started on that fatal trip which was but too soon to come to a tragic and sanguinary end. And here I will state a fact well known at Cedar City and Pinto Creek, to prove that I have not overdrawn the picture when speaking of the jaded and worn-out condition of their teams.

The Militia start on their Bloody Errand.

It took them three days to go to Iron Creek, a distance of only twenty miles. The distance from Iron Creek to the Meadows, about fifteen miles, was made in two days. The morning they left Iron Creek, the fourth after leaving Cedar, your militia took up their line of March in pursuit of them, intending to make the assault at the "Clara Crossing"[20]—*your* militia! you, Brigham Young, was at that very time Governor of Utah, and Commander-in-Chief of the military forces of the Territory, and was drawing your salary as such from the treasury of the United States.

The Militia called out by Order.

These soldiers did not come together by chance. Indeed, sir, it is on oath and witnessed by the seal of the court, that the calling out of those troops *"was a regular military call from the superior officers to the subordinate officers and privates of the regiment."* And said sworn testimony further states that *"said regiment was duly ordered to muster armed and equipped as the law directs, and prepared for field operation."*[21] I am fully aware, sir, of the fearful import of these quotations, and how clearly and inevitably they point to you; yet, nevertheless, they are those which you cannot impeach, neither dare you gainsay or deny before a competent tribunal. How the order to make war on these emigrants passed from your office to the hands of Colonel Dame I have already suggested . . .

John D. Lee commands the Troops.

The regiment camped at Cedar City—was commanded by its Major, John D. Lee (who was also your Indian Agent for Southern Utah) and marched from that place in pursuit of the emigrants. It was accompanied by baggage wagons, and, with the exception of artillery, the other necessary "make up"

---

[20]The "Clara Crossing" was near the confluence of Magotsu Creek, which flows through Mountain Meadows, and the Santa Clara River. Evidence indicates the Mormons intended to attack the Fancher party as it made the sharp descent from the plateau that extends from the meadows to the canyon.

[21]Wandell is quoting Philip Klingensmith's 10 April 1871 affidavit.

of a military force in the field. Lee had extended an invitation to the Piede Indians to accompany him; and with these auxiliaries he had a force which the poor, hungry emigrants could not hope to resist.

Attack on the Emigrants.

The migrants were overtaken at the Mountain Meadows. Being entirely ignorant of the danger so near them, they "rolled out" from camp in a careless matter-of-course way, on the morning of the 12th of September, and as soon as the rear wagon had got a safe distance from the spring, the Indians, unexpectedly to Lee, commenced firing. The emigrants were taken completely by surprise. It is conclusive beyond a doubt from the loose and unguarded manner of their traveling, that they had no idea of the military expedition sent against them until they saw and felt it. Yet, unguarded as they were at the moment of the attack, they had traveled too far over roads infested with Indians to become confused. They immediately corraled their wagons and prepared for defense, fortifying as best they could; but, alas! they were too far from water.

A Desperate Resistance.

They fought your troops all that day, and all the next. Major Lee, beginning to think that he had waked up the wrong passengers, sent to Cedar City and Washington for re-enforcements, which were at once raised and forwarded, forming a junction with the main body on the morning of the fourth day's fight. This call for re-enforcements took every able-bodied man from Washington, and all but two from Cedar City.

Two Little Girls Shot.

During the third day's battle it became a necessity with the emigrants to get water. They were choking with thirst, and without water they could hold out but little longer. There it was, in abundance, in plain sight, but covered by the rifles of your troops. They made several desperate but fatal and unsuccessful efforts, and, finally, hoping there might be some little of humanity remaining with the Mormons, they dressed two little girls in white, and started them with a bucket toward the spring. *Your soldiers shot them down!*

Orders from Headquarters.

On the next morning, the re-enforcements having arrived, Major Lee massed his troops at a point about half a mile from the emigrants' fort, and there made a speech, during which he informed them that (I quote from a sworn statement,) His orders from headquarters were, *"To kill the entire company, except the children!"* Now, sir, as to whether those "headquarters" were located in your office at Salt Lake City, or at Parowan, is a matter to be settled between you and Colonel Dame; and, if I am not mistaken, you will yet have to settle it. If Colonel Dame shall ever confess before a proper tribunal that he issued that extraordinary order on his own responsibility, and, independently of you, I shall be very much mistaken. But of the fact that such an order was actually made, there can be no doubt. There had been two military councils held in Parowan—one before or about the time the emigrants passed that place, and one on the day they left Cedar. Haight and Lee were at both these councils, and from the last returned together to Cedar—the latter to take command of the troops, and the former to stand prepared to render him any service which might be needed.

Brigham Young Directly Responsible for the Massacre.

It is on oath, sir, that it was at Cedar City two days after the emigrants had left, that President Haight said to certain parties (who shall be nameless here), "that he had orders from headquarters to kill all of said company of emigrants except the little children!" This fixes the fact, beyond dispute that Lee and Haight were professedly acting under orders from headquarters; and to suppose that such profession was false—that two subordinates should take upon themselves the responsibility of such a bloody affair, professedly in your name, and yet without your authority, is out of the question. It is equally absurd to suppose that said order originated with Colonel Dame. All the reasons are against such a supposition. Besides no Colonel of a regiment would have the right or the authority to do anything in such premises except to promulgate and enforce the order of his superior officer. To do otherwise would be to subject himself to the eventualities of a military court; and it is certain that neither Colonel Dame nor Major Lee were ever court-martialed for their action in the military operations at the Mountain Meadows.

Negotiating Terms of Surrender.

After Major Lee had announced that fatal order to his troops, and instructed them as to how he intended to carry it out, "he sent a flag of truce into the emigrants' fort, offering to them that if they would lay down their arms he would protect them." This was on the 15th day of September, and the fourth since the battle, or, rather, siege had begun. You will not forget that the little band of Arkansans were not "whipped." Though well nigh exhausted with fatigue and loss of sleep, and burning up with thirst, they were not conquered. They were fighting for their wives and little ones more than for themselves, else, at any time, under cover of the darkness, they could have formed in solid column, broke through your lines and escaped. But to their honor be it said, they refused life when associated with the condition of deserting their families.

The White Flag.

But the flag of truce came into their little fort: That white flag held by all civilized nations and peoples from time immemorial as an emblem at once of peace, of truth, of honor. By the message accompanying this flag, they were promised protection. Alas! that it should prove to be "such protection as vultures give to lambs." But the message was not from Indians, it was from Major Lee, a regularly constituted officer of the military forces of the Territory of Utah, one of the Territories of the United States. What should they do but believe its promise. They marched out of their little fort, laid down their arms, marched up to the spring where Lee stood and placed themselves under his protection; and his promises of protection were yours.

A Scene of Blood Baffling Description.

But now was to be enacted one of those scenes which the pen is inadequate to describe, and the horrors of which it is impossible for one not then present to realize. Here were unarmed, unresisting men, innocent and inoffensive women, and helpless children, none of which had ever harmed you, or offended the majesty of the laws of Utah. They had every possible claim not only to Lee's protection, but to life, liberty and their property; Their right to be treated truthfully, honorably and humanely was perfect. But, sir, your order was practically as irrevocable as it was terrible. And it would not do for the troops to think long about it, lest conscience should assert rights which even the thought of you could not overcome. There must be no time for parleying between obedience to you, and duty to humanity. So, without allowing these famishing prisoners time even to refresh themselves, the women and children were separated from their husbands and fathers, and started on ahead toward Cedar City, the men following immediately in their rear, and all guarded by the entire command, with Lee at the head of the column. There is no reason to suppose that up to the moment of the massacre, the emigrants thought they were going to be shot down. After they had been marched about a half mile, Lee gave the word to "halt;" then immediately the command to "shoot them down" was passed down the column, and before the poor emigrants could realize their situation the first volley was delivered! Then from the survivors went up such a piercing, heart-rending scream!—such a shriek of blank dispair!—then the flight of all except one young woman, who sprang to Lee, and clinging to him for protection—then the chase—then another volley—and then another—and still another, and then—all was still! save the last death strugglings of the unhappy victims, the cries of the remnant of little ones who had been left behind in the flight, and the heavy breathings of soldiers, pale, trembling and aghast at the horrid scene before and around them! BRIGHAM YOUNG, THAT WAS YOUR DOING!

Reflection over the Innocent Dead.

And now, O, ye slaughtered ones! . . . What sins had you committed, that you should make so fearful an expiation?—that you should lie there baptized in your own blood? Methinks I hear you answer with your last grasp [*sic*], "This was Brigham Young's doings!" Sir, no explanations can relieve you from the charge of responsibility in this bloody matter. No man who knows you, and has a fair idea of your doctrines and "policy" can doubt. You stand condemned before the bar of an enlightened public opinion . . .—Argus.

"ARGUS," 17 AUGUST 1871, *THE CORINNE REPORTER*,
CORINNE, UTAH, 19 AUGUST 1871, 2/2–3.

SIR: That an entire company of peaceable families, as at the Mountain Meadows, could be butchered in cold blood, anywhere in the United States, upon
the public highway, and within the easy reach of the army of the civil power
created expressly for the protection of life and property; is a mystery which
the purely American mind finds very hard to understand. And the marvel is
only increased by the fact that no inquest was held over the remains of those
slaughtered ones—that no arrests were made of the murderers, although they
were well and notoriously known, and that no official notice was taken of the
matter (except as I have heretofore stated) during the remainder of your term
as Governor, and no apparent authoritative notice since, except to gather up,
by soldiers of the United States, what bones the wolves had left, and giving
them respectable sepulture. Based upon American ideas, and, indeed, upon the
more general notions of civilization, the whole story becomes incomprehensible. In order to understand this matter, it will be necessary for the reader,
first, to mentally segregate Utah geographically from the United States—to
consider it as absolutely a foreign State and nation, with a civilization such
as existed thirty-five hundred years ago, and a religion as antagonistic to Chris-
tianity as Moslemism itself, including within its creed a tenet more cruel and
bloody than the Thugism of India. Second, to consider this Deseret nation
as incensed to the last degree against the Government and people of the United States, for a series of wrongs committed against them, including exile and
the loss of life and property. Third, to take into the account, that the American Government, at that time had actually proposed to extend its jurisdiction over said Deseret (otherwise called Utah), and an army was then on its
way to occupy said Utah for the purpose of maintaining the sovereignty of
said Government there, and that a state of war was apparently existing between
said two nations. Fourth, that you were, at the very time of the massacre at
the Mountain Meadows, mustering and putting into the field an army of one
thousand two hundred men, which was known in Utah, as "The Standing
Army," and that said army was designed for active operations against the forces
of the United States, under Colonel Johns[t]on, then en route for Salt Lake.
Fifth, that *you* were the "Sovereign" Lord of Deseret—that your rule was an
absolute and unmitigated despotism—that your word was the only recognized
law . . . If the reader can grasp the ideas contained in the above items, and
arrange them into one compound proposition, he will be able to form some
idea of the causes which made the aforesaid massacre possible.

But the misfortune is that said proposition being based upon falsehood and
not upon the truth, affords you no justification whatever; for, first, Utah was
a part of the United States, and not a foreign state; second, your intense hatred
of Americans and their Government was without adequate cause; third, the

occupation of Utah as a Military Department was altogether a friendly act, and in strict accordance with the known military policy of the Government; fourth, that all your acts in relation to the State of Deseret were and are treasonable in their intent, and therefore, illegal and of no binding force. For these reasons, the American people will refuse to look upon that massacre from your stand point. They will and do hold you to your responsibility as a citizen of the Republic. And as you were at that time the Chief Magistrate of Utah, they have the right to demand why you took no official steps to inquire into that sanguinary affair which is *the shame and damning disgrace of your administration.* They have the right to demand why you took no official action in the case of Dame, Haight and Lee; and how it is that you have so far persistently and successfully screened those murderers from the officers and the action of the law. It is a foul blot upon the workings of the system of American jurisprudence that the Mountain Meadow massacre should have been committed nearly sixteen years ago, and to this present writing you, and Lee, and Dame, and Haight are at large, and come and go unquestioned by the proper authority . . .

It appears to have all along been the opinion that the investigation of the Mountain Meadow massacre must originate in the criminal courts. With that view, and the Grand Jury subject to your dictation, and under your complete control, what could be done? Nothing, absolutely nothing, but to wait. Murder is shielded by no statute of limitations. But I will here suggest, that such investigation should be made by a military court, for the reason that the operations of Lee were purely and undeniably of a military character . . . But no Mormon should be allowed to constitute a part of that court, nor any Gentile who could be allured from duty by your sirens or be purchased by your ill-gotten gold.

And now, in conclusion, as a Mormon, I demand of the proper authorities that this long-neglected affair be investigated, in order that the innocent may no longer suffer that reproach which belongs to Brigham Young and others only. In this connection it is proper to state that there is a strong and growing feeling in Southern Utah against Lee and his co-laborers on that bloody mission, and against their confederates, apologists and protectors. Even in Cedar City those characters are now known as "Mountain Meadow Dogs." As a citizen of the United States, I demand that the veil of mystery so long covering that butchery be rent asunder, and the foul deed exposed in all its repulsive hideousness, bringing to the light those latent agencies which superinduced its commission, in order that justice may be meted out to the guilty parties, thus wiping out a foul blot upon the American name. In the name of justice I demand it, that it may no longer be said that in Utah the direst of felonies may be committed with impunity. In the name of Truth, I demand that the facts concerning the Mountain Meadow massacre be ascertained and stated in official form by competent authority, in order that the people of the United States may know that said massacre, even to its most sickening details, was only too true. And I think, sir, that I but reflect the common sentiment of the country when I say that you and Lee, and the whole holy company of apostles, prophets and elders of Mountain Meadow notoriety should be punished to the full extent of the law; or, failing in that, be outlawed and driven beyond the pale of human society, to wander, as Cain, vagabonds and accursed upon the face of the earth.

For the present, adieu.—ARGUS.

Charles Wandell argued that the evidence he presented in his Argus letters showed that "the plan for the destruction of that company was laid in Salt Lake City, before they had left their encampment at the Jordan." The hostility that the emigrants encountered all along the southern route supported this view, he claimed. Not only was the plan concocted at Salt Lake, Wandell argued, but it was laid with great skill. "Had the original order to assault the emigrants in Santa Clara Cañyon been carried out, not one of them would have been living in fifteen minutes after the head teams had been shot down."[22]

JAMES GEMMELL:
MOWING THEM DOWN AS IF SO MANY BLACK BIRDS

Scottish immigrant James Gemmell's life reads like an adventure novel. He was imprisoned for his role in the 1837 revolt against British rule in Canada, escaped from exile in Tasmania, enjoyed a brief celebrity in New York in 1843, and went west over the Oregon Trail in about 1845. He accompanied Jim Bridger's 1846 brigade and left one of the first descriptions of today's Yellowstone Park. Gemmell (or Gammell, as he was generally known in Mormon records) had settled in Salt Lake Valley by 1849. Despite personal misgivings, he went on a mission to Texas in 1856—and somehow his name appeared as a suspect on the warrant used to arrest Parley P. Pratt in May 1857. That fall he campaigned against the U.S. Army during the Utah War. After the conflict, he served as a scout for Capt. James Simpson and accompanied Judge Cradlebaugh to Mountain Meadows as a translator and, perhaps, double-agent for Brigham Young. In the sixties the adventurous Scot abandoned Mormonism and moved north to the gold diggings in present Montana. There he told his story to Joseph C. Walker, who went on to become a prominent Montana businessman, rancher, and legislator.

Walker arrived in Montana in early June 1863. That fall he and his brother

---

[22]"Argus," 10 August 1871, *Daily Corinne Reporter*, 12 August 1871, 2/3.

built a sawmill in Madison County with Gemmell, who Walker said "had two wives and had raised two families, both of which were yet in Utah." Gemmell did not believe in polygamy, Walker recalled, "although he practiced it." The men spent the winter of 1863–64 on Mill Creek with a crew of about a dozen men that included five Mormons, "all being acquaintances of Mr. Gemmell in Utah. During the long evenings we had nothing to read, and therefore they were used in talking." Gemmell claimed that Brigham Young had appointed him territorial road supervisor and employed him to develop today's City Creek Canyon, statements supported in Mormon records.[23] But the stories Walker heard about Mountain Meadows were both colorful and chilling.

> Mr. Gemmell said that he was in Brigham Youngs office when a courier came to the office with the horrible news of the Mountain Meadow massacre. He said, he went with a party from Salt Lake City to Mountain Meadows and buried the dead. He said it was the most gruesome, pitiful, heart rending and sickening sight he had ever beheld. There, strung along the road lay the one hundred and seventeen bodies of men, women and children where they had fallen fatal victoms from the murderous treachery of the Mormons firing upon them from ambush and mowing them down as if so many black birds.

Gemmell's story, though filtered through Walker's memory, was based on his experiences with Cradlebaugh's 1859 investigation. His story provides another window into how much the federal authorities already knew about the nature of the massacre.

> Mr. Gemmell said they were well to do people, and had a good train, and that it was supposed they had one hundred thousand dollars of gold in the train. He said the Mormons dressed in Indian garb, hovered around them occupying menacing positions for some days. The people at the train dug trenches and formed embankments as best they could. Finally a few Mormons walked down the road leading to the train and carrying a white flag. The train people also hoisted a white flag. These Mormons continued on to the train, and when arriving there, they assured the people of the train that the Indians would not let one of them escape alive, but if they would leave their arms at the train and walk out with them, they would protect them. It seems there is a sweetness in life that often mars our best judgment and it was certainly so with these people. And then the horror even to men, but especially to all women at falling into the hands of Indians leads them to trust any people in prefference to the Indians. But see how unreasonable the proposition. Leave their arms at the train.

[23]Gemmell was in fact appointed territorial road superintendent on 5 October 1849. Three weeks earlier, Daniel H. Wells moved that the supervisor of roads "employ Mr. Gammel with his improved ditching machine and scraper, to work under his direction upon the public works." Morgan, *The State of Deseret*, 103–104.

Adventurer James Gemmell escaped from a British prison in Tasmania and later served as a Mormon missionary to Texas. His name appeared on the warrant used to arrest Parley P. Pratt. Gemmell claimed he was in Brigham Young's office when the governor told Jacob Hamblin "that if he (Brigham) was in command of the Legion he would wipe them out." Gemmell accompanied Judge John Cradlebaugh to Mountain Meadows as an interpreter. In the 1860s he departed for Montana, where as "Uncle Jimmy" he became a respected pioneer. *Courtesy of Reed A. Russell, Will Bagley Collection.*

Why if these train people were menaced by any foe, it was all the more necessary that they take their arms with them. But the treachery that day [that] was part of this proposition was not known to these people, but a few seconds before death came to all of them. Mr. Gemmell said these men, women, and children formed in line and marched up the road after these Mormons, till of a sudden, volley after volley was fired into them. He said a few small children were not killed at once, but on consultation it was agreed they could tell too much after they grew up. They were then slain. He said there were a few very young children whose lives were spared, Mormon families taking them to raise. He said there was one han[d]some young woman who went through the gauntlet unscathed. No doubt on account of her having been too close to these Mormons who were piloting them to their distruction and that she begged John D. Lee to spare her life, saying that she was betrothed to a young man in California and was to be married on her arrival. But John D. Lee drew his pistol and shot her. He also mentioned indignities that were perpetrated upon three persons after which they were shot. But they are too shocking to put on paper.

Walker felt there was "no darker page has ever been furnished in the American history than this Mountain Meadow Massacre." He resented that of "all that murderous company, but one was made to pay the penalty."[24]

---

[24]Walker, History of the Mormons in the Early Days of Utah, BYU Library.

After Gemmell's death in Montana in 1881, the Virginia City *Madisonian* published the old pioneer's obituary, which reported that Gemmell:

> was in Brigham's office when Bishop Hamlin came in and reported the Arkansas train near Cedar City, and heard Brigham tell Hamlin that if he (Brigham) was in command of the Legion he would wipe them out. About three weeks afterward the Mountain Meadows massacre occurred, which wiped out the Arkansas train, for which John D. Lee suffered the death penalty by being shot a few years ago. There were one hundred and twenty-five bodies found afterward and buried by United States troops sent out for that purpose. General Albert S. Johns[t]on was in command, and Judge Cradlebaugh was sent along to ascertain whether any white men were engaged in the massacre. The Indians said the Mormons incited them into it and gave them the plunder. Bishop Craig Smith [Klingensmith] afterwards acknowledged that he was there. Bishop Jake Hamlin lived within three miles of the battleground, and it was he that took the order from Brigham to John D. Lee. The foregoing history came under Mr. Gemmell's immediate observation and was written down at his request, and will no doubt be interesting to many.[25]

John Standifird "met Jim Gammel who took me to his home" in Salt Lake on 10 September 1857. This lends support to Gemmell's claim that he was in Brigham Young's office ten days earlier at his critical conference with southern Utah's Indian leaders.[26] Merely knowing about the meeting suggests Gemmell was there, since Young's encounter with them was a closely held secret well into the twentieth century.[27] Adding to this is the letter that Gemmell wrote to Salt Lake mayor Feramorz Little, Young's nephew and business agent, describing a federal investigation that was asking all the right questions.[28]

JAMES GEMMELL TO FERAMORZ LITTLE,
SHERIDAN, MONTANA, 14 OCTOBER 1872, LDS ARCHIVES.

Dear Sir

I have been very much annoyed lately by the officials of Montana, as they say through the request of their Friends in Utah, to accertain of me what took place, and what was said in President Youngs office, on my arrival from Texas, between Jacob Hamblin President Young and others, in regard to the Arkansas Train then passing through the southern settlements of the trouble

---

[25]Wheeler, "The Late James Gemmell," 334.

[26]Standifird, Recollection, in Papers, 1857–1909.

[27]To our knowledge, the first historian to describe the critical 1 September 1857 meeting was Juanita Brooks in 1950 in *The Mountain Meadows Massacre*, 41.

[28]The cover to Gemmell's letter at LDS Archives bears a clerical notation: "a witness in Mountain Meadow Massacre."

they had with the Inhabitants, and of their boasting, of Parley been [*sic*] killed in their neighborhood before they left. And of them threatening to Poison the springs and what Conversation took place between the President Hamlin and others at that time in the Presidents Office. And if I knew what was the purpose of the Instructions sent South, and if I thought the massacre was in retaliation for the killing of Parley, and of what I remembered of the evidence gleaned from the Indians and others from Judge Cradlebaugh when I was his Interpreter, when he was holden [*sic*] Court in Cedar City. Now where they got the Knowledge to interrogate me in this matter, is a mystery. I think they must have got it from Bill Hickman, in some of our whiskey sprees when we was togeather in Echo Canyon, but thank God those sprees are at a end for I have not drank any whiskey for over two years. Now, Ferry I expect to be put in restraint and compelled to go to Utah daily, and give evidence in that affair. I would much rather go to the end of the Earth, or Texas, than be compelled to go down there for that purpose, [but] go I must as that would be the only way I have of avoiding them, but I am dead broke as usual [and] have not the means of leaving a large family, please write as soon as you receive this. And give me Council for the best.

From your old Friend
James Gemmell

No record survives that tells how Brigham Young reacted to Gemmell's menacing letter, but Mormon authorities now knew that while the wheels of federal justice might grind slowly, they were grinding exceedingly fine.

Chapter 10

"THE BAR OF JUSTICE"
The Trials of John D. Lee

C harles Wandell's exposé of Brigham Young and the renewed attention his letters cast on Young's adopted son, John D. Lee, led to Lee's excommunication. This dampened much internal criticism, for many in Utah thought the ecclesiastical censure was the worst punishment anyone could suffer. But the loss of celestial glory was only the start of Lee's troubles. Two other developments would bring him to the worst of mortal penalties.

The first came when Philip Klingensmith, the former bishop at Cedar City, appeared on 10 April 1871 before the district court in Lincoln County, Nevada, and gave a sworn confession of his part in the crime. Soon after this news reached Salt Lake City, Lee received clandestine orders to relocate far from prying eyes. Although no longer a member, he dutifully obeyed an unnamed church leader's instructions to move to a hidden spot on the Colorado River known today as Lee's Ferry, a short distance downriver from Glen Canyon Dam.

Shorn of his church armor, Lee soon after lost the shield that he enjoyed under the Mormon-controlled judicial system. In 1874 Congress stripped Utah's probate courts of the powers so liberally bestowed by territorial lawmakers, and made clear that original jurisdiction in criminal cases belonged exclusively to the federal district courts. The law gave U.S. marshals and attorneys the sole authority to serve all writs and act as prosecuting officers in the district courts, which abolished the duplication of territorial offices and powers that had shackled justice in Utah to the territory's probate courts.

At the same time, the author of the measure, Rep. Luke Poland of Vermont, as an apparent gesture of good will, came up with a system for jury selection that invited further manipulation. To stop jury packing by either side, district court clerks and probate judges alternately selected the names of two hundred prospective jurors for trials. From this mixed pool, the U.S.

marshal was to draw by lot the names of jurors, thereby giving both sides balanced representation. Like others, Congress gave the Mormon theocracy the benefit of the doubt, but in so doing it invited jury tampering.

Nevertheless, the new law did introduce a period of sensational courtroom battles as U.S. prosecutors in Utah became more aggressive in seeking justice for crimes that had long gone unpunished, including the 1857 massacre. In little more than four months after its passage, Deputy U.S. Marshal William Stokes arrested John D. Lee as he visited to one of his families at Panguitch, Utah. His trials at Beaver electrified the nation and exposed the shortcomings of the Poland Act.

A feature of virtually every confession by a Mountain Meadows participant was how hard these men struggled to save the emigrants—at least by their own accounts. There were also stories about how orders to stop the murders were somehow waylaid, lost, or undelivered. None of these stories is convincing. "Whatever the details, the fact remains that the entire company was betrayed and murdered," wrote Juanita Brooks, "an ugly fact that will not be downed."[1] It is against this ugly fact that all self-serving confessions and historical apologias must be judged.

Philip Klingensmith:
I Did Not Stop to Count the Dead

The only eyewitness who broke the secrecy oath and described the massacre before the trials of John D. Lee was former bishop Philip Klingensmith, a native of Pennsylvania. Injured a year after the murders and apparently deeply troubled by the experience, he was released as bishop. When Judge John Cradlebaugh opened his investigation of the massacre in 1859, Klingensmith went into hiding and wandered around western mining camps until 1871. At the encouragement of Charles Wandell, he came before the clerk of the district court in Pioche, Nevada, and gave the stunning affidavit that led to the Lee trials.

Although it is easily accessible in Juanita Brooks's *Mountain Meadows Massacre*, the affidavit of the man who signed himself "Philip Klingon Smith" is too important not to summarize. He stated that "the militia was called out for the purpose of committing acts of hostility against" the Arkansas emigrants about four days after they left Cedar City. He characterized it as "a

---

[1]Brooks, *The Mountain Meadows Massacre*, 108.

regular military call from the superior officers to the subordinate officers and privates of the regiment." Lee sent word to Cedar City "after the fight had been going on for three or four days" reporting "that the fight had not been altogether successful, upon which Lieutenant-Colonel Haight ordered out a reinforcement." Capt. John M. Higbee ordered him to muster, "a matter of life or death to me to muster or not." Haight told him "that it was the orders from headquarters that all but the little children of said company were to be killed." Klingensmith did not know if headquarters were in Parowan or Salt Lake. After marching to Mountain Meadows, "Major Lee massed all the troops at a spring, and made a speech to them, saying that his orders from headquarters were to kill the entire company except the small children."

Lee arranged the emigrants' surrender:

the women and children were then, by the order of said Lee, separated from the men, and were marched ahead of the men; after said emigrants had marched about a half mile toward Cedar City, the order was given to shoot them down; at that time said Lee was at the head of the column; I was in the rear. I did not hear Lee give the order to fire, but heard it from the under officers as it was passed down the column; the emigrants were then and there shot down except seventeen little children, which I immediately took into my charge; I do not know that total number of said company as I did not stop to count the dead.

In their later confessions, a surprising number of the men who executed the massacre claimed their main duty was taking care of the surviving children. Bishop Klingensmith's statement that he, John Willis, and Samuel McMurdy "procured them homes among the people" is more credible than most. He provided the first account of a dispute between Dame and Haight, "in the course of which said Haight told Colonel Dame, that if he was going to report of the killing of said emigrants, he should not have ordered it done," an event that would pop up again in John D. Lee's memoir. Klingensmith said that Lee told him he reported the massacre to Brigham Young. He swore, "I gave no orders except those connected with the saving of the children." But he admitted "at the time of the firing of the first volley I discharged my piece; I did not fire afterward, though several subsequent volleys were fired." Klingensmith ended by saying that he made his statement in a Nevada court "for the reason that I believe that I would be assassinated should I attempt to make the same before any court in the Territory of Utah."[2]

Klingensmith's affidavit makes clear that Charles Wandell played an enor-

_____

[2]Ibid., 238–42.

mous role in bringing John D. Lee to justice. At Lee's trial, Klingensmith testified that he had confided in the author of the "Argus" letters, and on Wandell's death, newspapers throughout the West reported, "It was through his
labors that Bishop Klingan Smith was induced to make the confession of his
part in the Mountain Meadows massacre."[3] Wandell did not sign his name
to this 1872 letter, but he was no doubt the one who reported this pivotal
break in the case and pointed up its importance.

PIOCHE DAILY RECORD, PIOCHE, NEVADA, 20 SEPTEMBER 1872.

Editor Record: I was present at the time when Philip Klingen Smith made
his affidavit concerning the massacre at the Mountain Meadows. That affidavit is sealed with the seal of our District Court. Smith's statements were
straight-forward, and from his manner it was evident that he intended them
to be the truth, and nothing but the truth. The affidavit, though in narrative
form, was mainly taken by question and answer.

The Salt Lake Herald, in a late issue, in evident alarm, calls for the arrest
and punishment of Smith. That call is not sincere. They dare not face Philip
K. Smith in Court. He is ready to go at any time that he is wanted. From that
affidavit we learn, among other things, that Brigham Young was Governor of
Utah and Superintendent of Indian Affairs at the time and a long time after
the massacre, and that John D. Lee was his Indian agent for Southern Utah;
that the force sent against the emigrants was a regular military expedition—
a part of a regiment of the militia of Utah Territory, regularly called out, and
armed and equipped, officered by the proper regimental officers, and marching with regimental baggage wagons and a regular military outfit, except
artillery; that it was understood by the rank and file that the expedition had
been ordered by Gov. Young; that Major John D. Lee, who was in immediate
command, had invited the Indians within his superintendency to join the expedition, which they did; and finally, that Gov. Young never court-martialed Major
Lee for his action in that bloody affair, nor called him to account as Indian
Agent, nor as a fellow member of the Mormon church. These, Mr. Editor,
are some of the ugly facts contained in that affidavit; and neither the Salt
Lake Herald folks nor Brigham Young dare face them and Philip Klingen Smith
in open court.—Citizen.

COLLINS ROWE HAKES: THE TIME HAS COME

A letter that Arizona pioneer Collins Hakes wrote in 1916 recalled that he
was present when Brigham Young decided the time had come to make John

---

[3]"Death of a Noted Mormon," *Pioche Daily Record*, ca. 4 June 1875, citing S.F. *Chronicle*.

D. Lee a scapegoat. "He writes with the intention of showing that Brigham Young," the library catalog entry for the item says, "had nothing to do with the massacre." Ironically, the one-time stake president failed to appreciate that his story assumed that federal authorities never could have arrested Lee without the Mormon prophet's cooperation. Hakes described what happened when he alerted Young that Lee was about to be arrested.

COLLINS ROWE HAKES, TO WHOM IT MAY CONCERN,
MESA, ARIZONA, 24 APRIL 1916, BYU LIBRARY.

I am writing this to be used as a part or as an incident that came to me in relation to that horrid deed the Mountain Meadow Massacre. Which occur[r]ed on the 11th day of Sept. 1857 in the Southern part of the Territory of Utah.

At that time I was living in San Bernardino, Calif . . . When the news of the massacre reached San Bernardino, excitement ran high, for at that time all the world seemed determined to destroy the Mormons and their religion. A move was soon started to raise an army of men sufficient to wipe out the settlement of San Bernardino and it seemed that we either had to denounce our connection with the Mormon Church or break up and return to Utah, and I with most of the people chose the latter.

I reached Parowan, Iron County, Feb 28, 1858, where I lived 10 years, and where I became acquainted with most, if not all the men that were prominent in the planning and execution of that horrid deed. My whole soul longed to know whether the leaders of our Church had any responsibility in regard to it, and I determined to do all in my power to find out. As I became acquainted with those that were credited with the planning and executing of it, I tried in every way I could to get some of them to place the blame where it belonged, but in my ten years of residence and association with them I never heard one of them say one word that would in any way connect the Church or its leaders with the commission of the deed.

About two years after the deed was done, Pres. Young and a large party of the leading men of the church, made a visit to the southern part of Utah, and held a meeting at Parowan, at which he said word had come to him that some of those who were in hiding from officers to avoid arrest for the deed, had expressed themselves that they thought Brigham Young or the Church ought to help them in keeping away from the officers; and said, I want to say to those who planned and executed the horrid deed, that they did it on their own responsibility and without my counsel; and that I did not know anything about it until too late to prevent it. And I say to them, and wish the whole world could hear it: "You did it of your own volition and the responsibility rests on your own shoulders, for neither Brigham Young nor the Mormon Church will assist you to avoid the consequences of that terrible crime." This was one thing that helped to convince me that the leaders of the Church did not have anything to do with it and were not responsible for it.

In 1868 I moved to Kanab, Millard Co. I received another convincing testimony that our leaders were not responsible for it. On the evening before Lee was arrested, I was in Parowan visiting relatives. Pres. Young, with a large Company, were on their way to Salt Lake City, from Dixie.

In the evening, my brother-in-law came to me and said, Coll, I don't see things just like I used to, or as you do now. But Marshall Stokes is in town getting a party to go and arrest J. D. Lee at Panquitch; and if you want to go and tell Pres. Young, and he thinks it would be against the interest of the people of Utah to have him arrested, I will have two good horses saddled and ready, and we can beat the Marshall to Lee and prevent the arrest.

I went and told him and he called his men, and when they came he told me to tell them what I had learned, which I did. Then Pres. Young said, "Now what shall we do? If any one has any suggestion, make it freely but quick."

He dropped his chin into his hand and all was still. Then he raised his head and said, "If you will not talk, I will." Turning to me he said, "Bro. Hakes, we thank you and your brother-in-law for this information, but it is all right. The time has come when they will try John D. Lee and not the Mormon Church, and that is all we have ever wanted. Go to bed and sleep, for it is all right."

We went to bed. Lee was arrested, convicted and executed.

THE FIRST TRIAL OF JOHN D. LEE: A FULL EXPOSURE OF THE MURDEROUS CONSPIRACY

For two weeks in July 1875, the whole nation watched in stunned disbelief as the horrors of the 1857 massacre were rehearsed before Judge Jacob S. Boreman and a jury of eight good Mormons, one backslider, and three "Gentiles" in the town of Beaver, two hundred miles south of Salt Lake City. Interest in the trial of John D. Lee was intense and the little community was hard-pressed to provide rooms for all the lawyers, lawmen, soldiers, and curious outsiders who flooded the village. Leading the prosecution was U.S. Attorney William C. Carey, assisted by Robert N. Baskin. Former congressman Jabez Sutherland and George C. Bates headed a defense team bankrolled by the LDS church.

Lee's first trial was a costly charade. Not only did the refusal of a single Mormon in good standing to testify for the prosecution foretell the outcome. The make-up of the jury, as decided under the Poland Act's well-intentioned procedure, revealed beforehand how panel members would vote. In the meantime, Frederic Lockley, *Salt Lake Tribune* editor and correspondent for national news outlets, described the atmosphere and proceedings to his wife.

Beaver, Utah

~~Salt Lake~~ July 17th.

My Dear Wife,

Your very interesting letter was received on Thursday evening, much to my relief of mind. Dolly has arrived, it seems, safe and sound, and is even now enjoying herself on an excursion. I wish I had been home that you and I might have been on the party.[4] We must make up a little party on my return.

You see by my letters to the Tribune what is doing here. These trials are likely to lead to important results. The Church having given up the prisoner Lee as a sacrifice to popular indignation has seriously disaffected that old gentleman's affections toward his brother conspirators, and he is now writing out a full statement. Important witnesses have been brought in, who, if properly examined on the stand will be apt to tell the whole story of the massacre and bring proofs against the men who are responsible for the crime. But it is firm that Carey is not the right man for the work. Sutherland carries too many guns, for him, and will be apt to head him at every point. ~~The~~ Maxwell tells me that the miners in Star district will to-day petition Carey to associate one or two able lawyers with him in the prosecution, they offering to pay the expenses.[5] Unless this is done there is danger of Dame escaping on technicality and legal chicane. Lee will be admitted to States evidence, and his statement is depended upon for a full exposure of the murderous conspiracy . . .

My Dear Wife—

Your welcome letter just received. My last letter must have been detained at the Tribune Off. For I am certain a week did not pass between that and the former. The attorneys think the Lee trial will not last more than two weeks now the jury is impaneled—it was feared this would consume a week but it was done in one day. We shall commence upon the testimony to morrow, and look out for startling developments. It is distressingly dull here—I am as anxious to return home as you are to have me. Mr. Baskin's appearance upon the scene is our salvation. He tells me Carey wrote to him to come—but he did not like to neglect his business—his wife, however, insisted upon his coming, and for this public spirited action she is entitled to the thanks of the

---

[4]"Dolly" was probably one of the daughters Lockley had with his first wife, Agnes Jeannette Hill: either Josephine, born in 1853; or Gertrude, born in 1857. Agnes died in 1860 and Lockley married "Lizzie"—Elizabeth Metcalf—in 1861, who stayed in Salt Lake City during the Lee trial. They eventually had five children, including noted western journalist Fred Lockley. Rankin, "Type and Stereotype: Frederic E. Lockley," 78n17.

[5]George R. Maxwell was U.S. marshal. The crippled Civil War veteran was known as "the thunderbolt of Sheridan" when he commanded the First Michigan Volunteer Cavalry at age 22.

country. Without this able and fearless attorney, the prosecution would have made a complete failure of the trial. You need not mention this fact outside.

I have been sleeping in Judge Whedon's office, in a bed occupied by a Mr. Lee, secretary of some mining company. He returned to town on Tuesday, and I had to vacate my quarters. Mr. Baskin also wanted a room, so I hunted around and found an unfurnished bed apartment in a house kept by an old lady—widow of a Mountain Meadows assassin. But they tell me she is anxious to have the leaders of that inhuman butchery hung. She whitewashed the walls and ceiling, hung up some clean muslin curtains, at the windows, put in an old fashioned bedstead, and some plain furniture, and when the week was done I called to see if the apartment would suit. She and a married daughter showed me up to the room with an air of triumph. Seeing the old lady had done her best, I thought to encourage her by saying, "Why, I declare you have done wonders—it will answer admirably." The daughter explained, "I told you the gentleman would be hard to suit, if *this* didn't please him!" The simple creature evidently thought the room was something superb. We pay her enough for it—five dollars a week, but the town is choke full of strangers . . .

FREDERIC LOCKLEY TO ELIZABETH LOCKLEY, BEAVER, U.T., 26 JULY 1875.

My dear Lizzie—Your letter with Dollie's enclosed reached me yesterday and were read with interest & satisfaction. Would you believe I am really getting homesick? I keep constantly employed too. Get up at 5:30 to write my daily letter to the Tribune—have break fast at 8—attend court at nine—Read, gas and loaf two hours at recess—Court again till 5. Write out my telegram—then supper at 7—then the mail from Salt Lake and a discussion of the value of the evidence and the chances of the jury finding a verdict. Sunday I write long letters to the Chronicle and Inter-Ocean. So you see I am working like a beaver, while you are having a splendid time. It is probable the Lee trial will terminate next week. The prosecution has such an overwhelming case against the old assassin—that the scores of witnesses they had summoned to testify to minor details will not be needed. The court room being crowded, counsel and reporters have to sit where they can. I crowd in at the table set apart for the defense and jog elbows with John D. Lee. He offers his hand to me every morning—I don't like to hurt his feelings by refusing—and is as polite and attentive as he knows how. He's a bad egg, and if justice is awarded him he will soon dance on nothing . . .

We have been having a genuine norther this afternoon. It blew so savagely you could hardly keep your feet, and the whirling sand almost penetrated one's cuticle. I crawled to my lodging about 7-30—read ½ hour and then began a letter to you. Baskin came in shortly after—bringing a letter from Stenhouse and Sunday's Tribune. I sent a column dispatch on Saturday evening and there's not a word of it in the paper. The wonder is what became of it . . . Baskin persists in talking to me. I shall have to leave off writing. He is so choke [*sic*] full of the Lee trial, that we talk it over till 12 every night. He says he has waited ten ~~hours~~ years to see this day, and now like Samson of old, he is ready to say, "Lord, now lettest thou thy servant depart in peace."

Another commission. Will Josey ask Mr. Hamilton to search my table drawer for the letter written by anonymous giving the names of Dr. Robinson's murderers—There are two letters in one envelope. Please send them to me . . .

FREDERIC LOCKLEY TO ELIZABETH LOCKLEY,
BEAVER, U.T., 31 JULY 1875.

My dear Wife

I am so constantly employed attending court and writing correspondence, that I am unable to devote proper attentions to my family. Thank God! This Lee trial is approaching an end. The testimony is all in, and on Monday the arguments ~~will~~ of counsel will begin. [line illegible] the case will be given to the jury, and then lawyers and press correspondents will pack their carpet-sacks and return to the bosom of their families. This is a wretched little place to stay in, no where to go to, except the Marshal's office where a parcel of disconsolates congregate to talk over the Lee trial and speculate upon its probable close.

Baskin has done nobly, as he always does when he is working for the people. In his argument he intends to make a scathing arraignment of Brigham Young, the substance of which you will have the pleasure of reading in the Tribune the next morning. Carey has also done well, and it will afford me pleasure to bestow on him a mead of judicious praise. Maxwell and his deputies have acquitted themselves like heroes, but for their untiring exertions, the array of testimony which has set the Mountain Meadows butchery before the world in all its heart-sickening details, could never have been presented to the world. It is not likely we shall get a verdict. There are two or three men on the jury whose obligations to the Church will prevent them finding a verdict according to the evidence, and the most we can hope for is a divided jury. Strange to say we are all hoping this will be the result, as the attention of the whole country is directed to this trial, and if the jury fails to convict, it will render the insufficiency of the Poland bill so manifest, that Congress cannot fail to give us additional legislation at the next session.

John D. Lee is feeling terribly down-cast. I suppose he steeped his soul in the blood of mothers and children slain from a mistaken sense of religious duty, and the terrible rehearsals of his treachery made from the witness [box] must certainly appal him. Sitting at his elbow day after day, and seeing his deep afflictions, I cannot help but be a little moved at it; but when I think of his life of crime, I recognize the justice of his punishment, and am only desirous that law should take its way . . .

ROBERT N. BASKIN:
CRAVEN COWARDS AND OBEDIENT SERFS

Once described as "frowsy, cool and red-bearded," Harvard Law graduate Robert N. Baskin was age 28 when he came to Utah on his way west in 1865 and decided to stay. He was utterly fearless and became one of the most important if unsung figures in Utah history. Although territorial law prohibited any obligation to pay lawyers, he found a need for his services and became one of the Mormon theocracy's most relentless adversaries. Implored by the U.S. attorney to assist in prosecuting Lee, he left a heavy workload to take on the task. Frederic Lockley recorded his summation, which shows why Baskin was such a dangerous opponent of theocratic rule in Utah. From the Lee trial, he went on to become the second non-Mormon mayor of Salt Lake City and chief justice of the Utah State Supreme Court.

BASKIN'S SUMMATION,
FROM BASKIN, *REMINISCENCES OF EARLY UTAH*, 132–36.

Mr. Baskin made the closing argument for the prosecution. He commented upon the charge of the opposing counsel, that the case was being tried by popular clamor . . . [and that] a stranger would be in doubt who was really on trial. It had been admitted that murder was committed, heinous in nature and revolting in its details. The fact is well known that at the time of the massacre not over one hundred Gentiles were living in the Territory. The speaker dwelt briefly upon the organization of the Nauvoo Legion, and said that "it was a militia body obnoxious to public sentiment, a brutal instrument of an ecclesiastical despotism, and part and parcel of the Mormon church. Its highest officers were leaders of that church." He severely criticized the length of time the crime had been allowed to slumber . . . He said "the blame for delay in instituting a judicial investigation into the violation of crime rests solely with the Mormon authorities, who, having the power entirely in their own hands, have thrown every impediment in the way of executing the law." To make this disgraceful fact more apparent, the speaker pointed to one of the prisoner's counsel who long held the office of prosecuting attorney for the judicial district,[6] and whose duty during his tenure of office it was to bring his client to justice, and said that "Congress at last having acted, unpun-

---

[6]George Caesar Bates came to Utah from Chicago as U.S. attorney in 1871, vowing to prosecute perpetrators of the massacre, but somehow never got around to it. After his appointment, Hiram B. Clawson, son-in-law of Brigham Young, informed Young that Bates had lost his law library in the Chicago fire. "On learning his destitute situation, we telegraphed him to draw on the 1st National Bank of Chicago for *Five Hundred Dollars*, and come at once," Clawson reported. See Clawson to Young, 11 December 1871, LDS Archives. After President Grant removed Bates from office, Brigham Young hired Bates to defend of John D. Lee.

ished crimes are being investigated and offenders who have long enjoyed security brought to the bar of justice."

The counsel for the defense says that we ask you to "convict Lee, because he is a Mormon." Such an assertion is an insult to your intelligence. The first witness described the scene at the Mountain Meadows a few days after the occurrence, and the second witness a few weeks later. Their testimony established the corpus delicti. Klingensmith, a former bishop of the Mormon church, because of his position, was made a conspicuous actor in the crime. Because he was an active participant, and testified to that fact, he has been made the subject of vituperation and invective, and persistent effort is made to break down his testimony. If it were all stricken out, the charge is still conclusively proved. The prisoner's counsel have asked to what possible use a man like Klingensmith can be put. He is fit to obey counsel, a cardinal duty enjoined upon every good Saint. He is fit to be a polygamist bishop, and help build up "the Kingdom." He is fit to carry out the orders of his ecclesiastical superiors, and murder and spoliate at the command of alleged God-chosen servants. So long as he confined himself to these functions he was fit for preferment in the hierarchial [sic] ranks and not a word against his character was spoken, but now that he has come out from the charnel house, and has shaken his soul clear of the delusions that held it in bondage, and shown a willingness to atone for his past offenses by ridding his conscience of this appalling crime, he instantly loses all of his past sanctity and becomes "a monster of such hideous mien, that to be hated needs but to be seen."

From the accumulation of testimony upon the point there can be no doubt that the emigrants surrendered their arms and committed to Lee the care of their young children, and then followed in the death procession. Defendant's counsel asked the jury to believe that this was done in good faith with the intention of rescuing the emigrants from the Indians who were menacing them. Is not such a request an insult to common intelligence? If deliverance was meant, why compel them to surrender their arms? Why take from the mother's breast the nursing baby? Why lead them into an ambuscade of Indians? The whole execution of the plot shows murderous design, and to believe otherwise is to do violence to common sense. When the victims were slain, the whites dispersed unmolested to their homes. If the Indians had committed the massacre, their passions being whetted with blood, they would have further gratified their savage rage by an assault upon the white men present. But the testimony shows that, instead, Indians tricked out in the clothing of the slain, went to Cedar City and washed bloody garments in the ditches, and that there was no excitement among them, and none of the citizens feared any attack; that Brigham Young was governor of the Territory and exofficio Indian superintendent. Had he been an honest and faithful official—had be been a Christian gentleman—he would have diligently collected the vast property of the emigrants and sold it—at the high prices that such property brought at that time in the Territory—for the benefit of the innocent little children, made fatherless and motherless by the Mormon fiends who ruthlessly murdered their fathers, mothers, and their older brothers and sisters. But instead of performing that official and humane duty, he suffered much of the property to be sold at public auction to the assassins of the emigrants, and many of the cattle to be branded with the church brand.

If there is a man on this jury who has been through that sink of iniquity, the endowment house, and wears endowment garments on his limbs, he will not find a verdict according to the law and testimony. He parted with his manhood when he swore blashphemous [sic] oaths which bind him a lifelong slave to the Mormon priesthood. He divested himself of his individuality, and is under obligation to think and act as he is directed.

Judge Sutherland asks the question, Why did not the witness Klingensmith and Joel White object to the massacre, instead of engaging in it? I answer, simply because they were members of an organization in which upon their oaths, they had bound themselves to obey the priesthood, and in which they had been made cowards—craven cowards and obedient serfs. All of the defendants attorneys who have addressed you, have denounced Bill Hickman and have severely criticized the prosecution for summoning him as a witness. They failed, however, to state what has made him odious and notorious. Gentlemen, it was his connection with Brigham Young, and the crimes which he, as one of the chief Danites of the Mormon church, committed. Both Hickman, and [also] the fifty Mormons who participated in the massacre, have made themselves infamous by obeying their church leaders. I have no doubt that both Lee and the church officials of Cedar City under whose orders that crime was committed, at the October Conference following the massacre, which they attended, as usual partoook [sic] of the sacrament commemorative of the suffering and death of Jesus Christ, whose mission on the earth was one of mercy, and who said "Blessed are the Merciful."

With what joy must the beleaguered emigrants have hailed the approach of that white flag, the emblem of peace and mercy, in the hands of a man whose white skin denoted that he was a Christian and coming to their rescue? My God! what a sad mistake they made when they trusted that man who, with a lying tongue, induced them to give up their arms which was their only means of defense; and Oh! what must have been their horror when the onslaught upon them in their defenseless condition was began by the white men whose protection had been promised, and by the secreted Indians upon their helpless women and children. The horror of the scene is indescribable. About one hundred and twenty-five of the survivors of the emigrants were foully betrayed under a flag of truce, and in the space of a few minutes after the assault upon them began they were ruthlessly murdered by fifty-two white men called "Latter-day Saints," aided by an ambuscade of Indians. The evidence shows that the Mormons in the vincinity [*sic*] of the massacre, under the influence of the infamous organization to which they had subjected themselves, had lost their manhood and had become so servile that they made no effort to prevent that awful crime, and when those who participated in it were ordered out by their church leaders, they went to the scene of the slaughter like dumb cattle; and when they were at the Meadows, as testified to by young Pierce, Pollock and other witnesses, the talk among them was that the emigrants were to be destroyed; and yet not one among that assemblage of at least fifty-two members of the so-called Church of Jesus Christ of Latter-day Saints possessed manhood enough to make the least objection to the commission of that atrocious crime.

What was done with the property of the emigrants? The evidence shows that it was sold at auction and bought by the inhabitants of Cedar City; that the bulk of it was appropriated by the men who murdered the parents of those little orphan children. I arraign Brigham Young as an accessory of the massacre, because considering the power he had over his people, no man, bishop, or any other subordinate officer, would have dared to take such an important step, or engage in such heinous scheme, if he hadn't the direct or implied sanction of the head of the church. The evidence shows that the leaders in that massacre were leaders in the Mormon church at Cedar City. I not only arraign Brigham Young as accessory before the fact of the massacre, but also as having violated his oath of office in failing to do what both his official duty and the common dictates of humanity required of him, which was to prevent the little children who were saved from being robbed; to have the property of the emigrants collected and sold and the proceeds appropriated to the nurture and education of those children. In place of doing that, this man with almost omnipotent power over his people, when the news was carried to him that the fathers, mothers and friends of those children had been butchered like dogs by Latter-day Saints and savage Indians combined, ordered the property to be delivered to John D. Lee, one of the chief perpetrators of the massacre.

Gentlemen of the jury, in concluding, I again say, as I said before, I do not know whether any members of the Mormon church are on this jury, or even one man who has been bound by the shackles and subjected to the influence which led Klingensmith, Joel White, William Young, and each and all of the others engaged in that massacre, to march out to the Mountain Meadows and ruthlessly bathe their hands in the blood of offenseless men, women and children. If any one of this jury is a member of the Mormon church, I don't expect any verdict. In short, if any member of this jury has upon him the endowment garments received in that iniquitous grease-vat, the endowment house, where he took an oath of obedience and laid down his individuality, no evidence can be introduced in a case like this one that would induce such a man, as long as he is under that pernicuous [*sic*] influence, to find a verdict of guilty, and I do not expect it.

GEORGE Q. CANNON:
GIVING A FEW THOUSAND DOLLARS

Nine Mormon jury members upheld Baskin's prediction when they voted to acquit John D. Lee, while the three Gentiles on Lee's first jury voted to convict. Although no faithful Mormon had testified, enough evidence had come out that a wave of indignation swept across the country, including Utah. For years Mormon leaders had underestimated the magnitude of the crime and the outrage it evoked from the American people. Now it became clear that someone had to pay the price if the church was to clear the atrocity from its garments.

For eighteen years, using a combination of stalling, subornation, and intimidation, LDS church officials successfully prevented the prosecution of anyone for the 1857 massacre. They apparently used those same tactics to control the outcome of the second Lee trial. The appointment of a new U.S. attorney to prosecute the case became a critical issue. Despite George Q. Cannon's statements to the contrary, it is unlikely that Sumner Howard could have been confirmed if Utah's influential territorial delegate had opposed him.

GEORGE Q. CANNON TO BRIGHAM YOUNG,
31 MARCH 1876, LDS ARCHIVES.

A new District Attorney [is appointed], as you will see by the dispatches. I fear that we shall have one whom we cannot admire. I have learned of his character from various quarters. All admit that he has ability, a fine speaker, one of the best criminal lawyers, a man of about 40 to 45, in comfortable circumstances, has been a temperance lecturer, is a recent convert to Methodism and a licensed preacher. One who knows him tells me that he thinks he will be a fair man, not one to enter upon a crusade, that if he is inclined to take a wrong course, [Judge Phillip] Emerson and [Jabez] Sutherland can influence him. This informant is disposed to take a favorable view of his character. Another says that he thinks his surroundings were bad in early life, but that latterly he thought he was disposed to get rid of them; he thought, however, "he was on the make." He had employed him for a certain class of cases, not where calm, good judgment was required, for he said he did not give him credit for the possession of that, but where he wanted a case put through. He thought he was an unsuitable man for the place. Another asked me if we had plenty of money there, and plainly intimated that we could "fix" him. In reply to which I said that was not our style, and that if an officer thought he could be blackmailed, he had better not go there. He described him as unpopular at home, many people not having confidence in his integrity. He thought, however, that he could be managed if taken in hand before he took the wrong *chute*. He says Sutherland knows him well. I had a conversation with the Attorney General about him. He told me that Howard was highly recommended by the two Senators from Mich. and others, and he hoped we would find him a good man. He talked as if he did not want anything done, such as the "Ring" had been doing.[7] I shall inquire more about the new man, and if I do not learn something more favorable, I shall work for the defeat of his nomination, unless he has been confirmed in executive session this afternoon, the results of which I have not yet learned.

A subsequent letter to Brigham Young's first counselor about the Voorhees Bill, one of several unsuccessful statutes that attempted to outlaw polygamy, reveals that Mormon officials were not above the use of bribery to defeat legislation or "fix" the new U.S. attorney, Sumner Howard.

GEORGE Q. CANNON TO DANIEL H. WELLS,
16 APRIL 1872, LDS ARCHIVES.

Dear Bro. Daniel:

I have written to the President so fully upon all matters, which letters I have no doubt you have read, that I need not recapitulate their contents to you. Since my letters of yesterday's date, giving an account of the decision of the Supreme Court, the Bill (Voorhees') which is in the hands of the Judiciary Committee has assumed a more threatening attitude. Baskin is here; he and [James] McKean are laboring with might and main to strengthen themselves by suitable legislation.[8] My impression is that Bingham has been worked up. He is Chairman of the Judiciary Committee, and he tried to obtain the consent of the House this morning for that Committee to have two days. He will probably renew the attempt to-morrow when the House is thin, and so on from day to day until he obtains it. We have good reasons to be satisfied that it is for the purpose of introducing and passing this Bill. It is important that nothing of this kind should be done. With this Supreme Court decision in our favor, and no inimical legislation we can have peace and safety. But if this Bill, or any like it, should pass, we are launched again upon a sea of troubles. We shall do all in our power to prevent this. By proper exertions we think it can be kept from passing. With the aid of Bro Joseph F. I think you can make out the following.

Pono loa paha no kakou ke haa-wi aku ⟨in⟩ na dala i kela kanaka i keia kanaka o ke Ahanui, no lakou e hoopau i ka hana ma keia *"bill"* ino . . . [It would

---

[7]The "Ring" referred to the men who organized Utah's Liberal Party to oppose Mormon theocracy.

[8]Former congressman James B. McKean had served as a colonel in the Civil War before Ulysses S. Grant appointed him chief justice of Utah Territory in 1870, where his aggressive enforcement of the law alienated the Mormons and lost him the support of the president.

perhaps be well for us to fee some of the members of Congress, for them to stay proceedings on this infamous Bill. If this Bill passes and becomes the law of the territory our difficulties will be greatly increased. It is the aim of the ring to possess themselves of our wealth and to annoy us in every possible way, and also to take the lives of some of us . . . [It would] be better to kill this Bill now before its birth. It is now in the hands of the Committee. We had far better hire them to leave this Bill where it is, that it may not be born, or that it may not come out of their hands, but defeat it in the hands of the committee. We think so. If reported by the committee and it comes before the house it will cause a great deal of discussion and great difficulty to kill said Bill in that position; because the members are afraid to vote against it. We think its defeat is important, and we think we can defeat said Bill by giving a few thousand dollars. What is your mind? Shall we try? If you (the brethren) wish us to do this, it would be well for you (bro Wells) to arrange through Lew Hills, with Kountze Bro's. at New York, depositing the money with them in my name. If we do anything, or it is needed, I can send there and obtain it. But we shall go slow and in no way uselessly expend the money.][9] Such an enterprise will be a saving of money if it should succeed . . .

Your Brother, as ever,
Geo. Q. Cannon

Should the proposition meet your mind, and you do anything about it, a despatch by telegraph, might be a guide to us as to what to do.

The Second Trial of John D. Lee:
I Did Speak of It

With the pliant Sumner Howard in place as the new U.S. attorney, it was time to make a deal. Circumstantial evidence leaves little doubt as to the main elements of the bargain. Howard agreed to impanel only Mormon jury members and to drop charges against William H. Dame. In return, Brigham Young would provide witnesses and testimony to convict Lee and exonerate himself and other Mormon leaders. When Baskin learned the jury would be made up only of Mormons, he knew John D. Lee was doomed.

The contrast between Lee's first and second trials is instructive: "Now," Juanita Brooks observed, "there was no lack of Mormon witnesses" whose memories were much sharpened.[10] A parade of Mountain Meadows mur-

---

[9]The translation in the hand of Joseph F. Smith is interlined on original. Cannon and Smith both learned the language as missionaries to Hawaii. We are indebted to Ardis E. Parshall for this transcription.

[10]Brooks, *The Mountain Meadows Massacre*, 195.

derers appeared to blame the event on the victims, the Indians, and John D. Lee and Philip Klingensmith, who was not recalled to testify. The witnesses all sang from the same hymnbook, saying just enough without violating their oath of secrecy to convict Lee of killing a woman and implicate Klingensmith, while covering up their own roles. A rough draft of the evolving Mormon story of the massacre unfolded as Sumner Howard described James Haslam's heroic ride and argued that John D. Lee, in defiance of council, massacred the emigrants.[11]

Jacob Hamblin, the veteran Mormon Indian emissary, drove the final nail into Lee's coffin. "His lips had been opened," Judge Jacob Boreman recalled, but he was not impressed. "He was a rough—uncouth back-woodsman & was believed to be ready to do anything that the church desired him to do," the judge wrote.[12] Possibly because he had not sworn a secrecy oath, Hamblin gave the most explicit testimony. The "buckskin apostle" repeated the story that his Indian boy, Albert, had told Major Carleton about the two girls who had tried to hide in the bushes but were dragged out and killed; however, instead of Indians killing both, Hamblin said that Lee killed one by cutting her throat. He also testified that he had told Brigham Young and George A. Smith all he knew about the massacre soon after it happened, unwittingly contradicting the affidavits that both men submitted at the first trial.

TESTIMONY OF JACOB HAMBLIN,
IN BISHOP, ED., *MORMONISM UNVEILED*, 369, 375–76.

Question by Howard—Who else did [Lee] mention?

Hamblin: He mentioned my brother [Oscar Hamblin] being there, bringing some Indians there. Sent him word of this affair taking place, and for him to go and get the Indians, and bring up the Clara Indians.

Howard: Your brother, then, brought the Indians to the Meadows, and then left there?

Hamblin: Yes, he told me so . . .

Question by Bishop: Have you ever given a report of [the massacre] to any of your superiors in the church, or officers over you?

Hamblin: Well, I did speak of it to President Young and George A. Smith.

Bishop: Did you give them the whole facts?

Hamblin: I gave them more than I have here, because I recollected more of it.

Bishop: When did you do that?

---

[11]Bishop, ed., *Mormonism Unveiled*, 317–78, contains transcripts of selected trial testimony.

[12]Arrington, "Crusade Against Theocracy," 44.

Hamblin: Pretty soon after it happened.

Bishop: You are certain that you gave it fuller than you have told it here on the stand?

Hamblin: I told everything I could . . .

Bishop: Have you told it all?

Hamblin: No, sir, I have not.

Bishop: Then tell it.

Hamblin.—I will not undertake that now. I would not like to undertake it.

Brigham Young: Only by a Floating Rumor

Brigham Young and Apostle George A. Smith avoided personally testifying in Lee's defense during the first trial, claiming that they were too feeble to travel two hundred miles to attend court. Instead they submitted affidavits sworn before William Clayton and dated 30 July 1875. U.S. prosecutors objected and Judge Boreman refused to allow them as testimony in the first trial. At the second, however, the prosecution submitted the affidavits as part of its apparent commitment to clear Young and Smith of any wrongdoing.

Both affidavits have been widely reprinted.[13] George A. Smith asserted that attending the court at Beaver "would in all probability end his life." He denied having any military command during 1857 and claimed that he knew nothing of the Arkansas party until he "met said emigrant train at Corn Creek on his way north to Salt Lake City, on or about the 25th day of August 1857." He never "attended a council where William H. Dame, Isaac C. Haight or others were present, to discuss any measures for attacking or in any manner injuring an emigrant train from Arkansas or any other place, which is alleged to have been destroyed at Mountain Meadows." On his way south, he preached several times and "advised the people to furnish all emigrant companies passing through the Territory with what they might actually need for bread stuff, for the support of themselves and families while passing through the Territory, and also advised the people not to feed their grain to their own stock, nor to sell it to the emigrants for that purpose." Smith said he "never, at any time, either before or after that massacre, was accessory thereto; that he never, directly or indirectly, aided, abetted or assisted in its perpetration, or had any knowledge thereof, except by hearsay; that he never knew anything of the distribution of the property taken there, except by hearsay as aforesaid."

[13]Whitney, *History of Utah*, 2:806–12; and Brooks, *The Mountain Meadows Massacre*, 284–89.

"Brigham Young had been duly sworn to testify to the truth," his deposition began. The seventy-four-year-old prophet stated he was in his seventy-fifth year and said it would be a great risk to his health and life to travel to Beaver to testify in court. He claimed that he had been "for some time, an invalid," although he had been well enough to travel from St. George to Salt Lake the previous February, and he returned twice in 1876. He asserted that in the summer of 1857 "an army of the United States was *en route* for Utah, with the ostensible design of destroying the Latter-day Saints, according to the reports that reached us from the East." He "heard it rumored that a company from Arkansas, *en route* to California had passed through the city." He denied ordering the party away from Salt Lake. He admitted that "counsel and advice was given to the citizens not to sell grain to the emigrants to feed their stock, but let them have sufficient for themselves if they were out." No one was "ever punished or called in question for furnishing supplies to the emigrants, within my knowledge," the former governor said. He did not learn "anything of the attack or destruction of the Arkansas company until sometime after it had occurred,—then only by a floating rumor." He denied ever speaking with Philip Klingensmith "concerning the massacre, or anything pertaining to the property." He denied giving any directions about the train's stolen property "nor did I know anything of that property or its disposal; and I do not to this day, except from public rumor." He then told of receiving a letter from Cedar City on 10 September 1857. Asked if he had the letter from Haight, the Mormon prophet responded, "I have not. I have made diligent search for it but cannot find it." He then said that the substance of his reply "was to let this company of emigrants, and all companies of emigrants, pass through the country unmolested, and to allay the angry feelings of the Indians as much as possible."[14]

DANIEL H. WELLS: DAME WAS DISCHARGED

John D. Lee left home to stand trial filled "with a fearful dreads. I had presentements that I was betrayed & [a] deeplaid plan was on foot, to sacrifice and make a scapegoat of me for the sins of others."[15] Despite his doubts, he was stunned by the appearance of Daniel H. Wells at his second trial because it meant that Brigham Young's trusted second counselor had come to instruct Mormon witnesses and jurors to convict him. The LDS church now support-

---

[14]Brooks, *The Mountain Meadows Massacre*, 284–87.

[15]J. D. Lee to Rachel Lee, 24 September 1876, Huntington Library.

ed Lee's prosecution—to begin with, Brigham Young's son-in-law revoked Lee's bail and the First Presidency quit paying for his defense. U.S. Attorney Howard boasted that he won the church's support, but he never specified what he gave up in return. Moreover, the fearlessly honest Robert N. Baskin, the trial judge, federal marshal, defense attorney, jury members, and Lee himself all argued persuasively that such a deal was made. The telegraphic reports that Wells sent to Young from Beaver provide some of the best surviving evidence of the special arrangement that denied the fair trial that Baskin believed even Lee deserved under the law.

DANIEL H. WELLS, TELEGRAM TO BRIGHAM YOUNG,
14 SEPTEMBER 1876, LDS ARCHIVES.

To Prest B. Young—
Lee's trial commenced today jury empannelled this forenoon—I understand that they are all Mormons—Dame was discharged—will begin to take testimony tomorrow morning—Howard made no effort to get Gentiles on the Jury—In fact the word Mormon was scarcely mentioned in Court at all today—There is no excitement but the people were completely taken by surprise at the change from what things were here-to-fore—all well—D. H. WELLS

DANIEL H. WELLS, TELEGRAM TO
W.B.D. [WILLIAM B. DOUGALL], 15 SEPTEMBER 1876.

Documents were admitted to go before jury but not read—I was first witness for prosecution testifying simply as to Lee's position among Indians in Southern Utah—No cross examination—Joel W. White, James H. Haslem, Samuel McMurdy, Samuel Knight, Nephi Johnson and Jacob Hamblin were examined and cross-examined—Knight, McMurdy and Johnson testified positively to see Lee kill some of emigrations—Lee's admission to Hamblin that he led the attack was testified to by Hamblin—General tenor of testimony agrees very well and very damaging to Lee—The cross-examination though severe especially on Johnson elicited nothing to help the defense except to furnish some buncombe—Testimony for prosecution not yet closed—Lee's counsel find their hands full at present appearances.—D.H.W.

DANIEL H. WELLS, TELEGRAM TO W.B.D., 20 SEPTEMBER 1876.

Jury in Lee case just brought in a Verdict of murder in first degree—Counsel for defense asked time to file motion for new trial—Court adjourned until tomorrow at 10 AM jury were out nearly 4 hours—I expect now to start home in morning but am not yet certain—Bro Erastus [Snow] got here last night on way to Conference.—D. H. Wells

As John D. Lee watched the wheels of justice grind during his second trial, he abandoned hope and directed his attorney to mount no defense. In a letter written shortly after the verdict, he described what had happened:

> The names of each Jury man on the list was marked with an X & some with two XX = leading men of the church told my attorney W. W. Bishop to select the Jury from the Names that were marked = & to have no others = promising him that if he would do so, that—the Jury would acquit me = my attorney laid the matter before me; I told him that I was fearful, I thought that we had better retain some outsiders on the Jury? should we be sold [?] they will hang the Jury = my counsel thought that we had better trust a Mormon Jury that if they did not acquit me = the Jury would hang anyhow—we did so & the result was a verdict to hang me?—Daniel H. Wells was sent here to have the thing cut & dried which he did to perfection.[16]

JUDGE JACOB BOREMAN:
THE CHURCH WAS ON THE SIDE OF THE PROSECUTION

Although the American public was delighted with the conviction of John D. Lee, Sumner Howard's vindication of Brigham Young during the trial generated a storm of controversy in Utah. Three days after convicting Lee, Howard and U.S. Marshal William Nelson blamed the uproar on "certain functionaries here who have heretofore conducted the case . . . not for the purpose of convicting the prisoner, but to fix the odium of the Mountain Meadows butchery upon the Mormon Church"—an accurate assessment of Robert Baskin's strategy in the first Lee trial. They stoutly defended their conduct and praised the LDS church authorities for their "aid."

> It became apparent early in the investigation, that there is no evidence whatever to connect the chief authorities of the Mormon church with the Massacre, on the contrary those authorities produced documents and other evidence showing clearly that not only was that great crime solely an individual offense on the part of those who committed it, but that the orders, letters, proclamations etc. which issued from the central Mormon authority which was also at that time the Territorial authority were directly and positively contrary to all shedding of blood, not only of emigrants passing through Utah, but also forbade the Killing of the Soldiers of Johnsons [sic] Army which was marching on Utah. Being satisfied of this the prosecution laid the case before the Mormon leaders and asked their aid in unraveling the mystery of this foul

---

[16]Ibid.

crime. That aid was given and the horrid testimony is public from the mouths of eye witnesses, convicting the prisoner without the shadow of a doubt.[17]

Second District justice Jacob Boreman, who presided at both of John D. Lee's trials, had a different perspective on the U.S. attorney's conduct. Boreman was walking to the courthouse at Beaver on the first day of the September 1876 trial when he met Sumner Howard. Boreman did not realize it until later, but the plain-speaking judge was about to become a supporting player in a staged production. Howard described his conduct in securing the testimony and jurors whom he needed to convict John D. Lee in a very odd way. Boreman later told how Lee was sacrificed for the sins of many, including, the judge believed, high authorities of the church.

ARRINGTON, ED., "CRUSADE AGAINST THEOCRACY: THE REMINISCENCES OF JUDGE JACOB SMITH BOREMAN OF UTAH," 42–45.

Mr. Howard said to me about as follows & I replied about as I now give it. He said to me, "Judge, I have eaten dirt & have gone down out of sight in dirt & expect to eat more dirt, but I have done nothing wrong and all I ask of you is that you will not lose confidence in me but will give me a chance to show to the world that what I have done or may do is right, & I pledge you that I will leave no stone unturned to show who the instigators or promoters of the [sic] this Massacre were. Give me time only & I will show that my course has been proper &c." I replied substantially as follows, "Well, Mr. Howard, I do not know what you have done or what you propose to do, but I will try to have confidence in you as you do no wrong but if you do any wrong or have done any, you cannot expect [me] to retain confidence in you.

At the beginning of this (2d) trial, I noticed that Daniel H. Wells, first counselor of Brigham Young, had come all [the] way from Salt Lake City to Beaver, and located himself in a place facing the jury so that the jury could see him. I did not know whether he was there on behalf of the defendant or of the prosecution. As the forming of the jury proceeded, I observed that Howard made no objections to the exclusion of Gentile jurors from the jury on motion of the defendants' attorneys and seemed to be himself anxious to get Gentiles off of the panel. I felt that he did not know these people—that being a comparative stranger he was being misled & soon would be swamped in his efforts to convict Lee. The defense seemed in high spirits, believing, it seemed, that if they got some Mormons on the jury, Lee would not be convicted. The defense believed as any body did that the Mormons would be for the acquittal of Lee, regardless of the evidence.

When the jury was completed, it was composed wholly of Mormons and to my surprise the first witness of the Prosecution called to the witness stand

[17]Nelson and Howard to Taft, 23 September 1876, Letters Received, RG 60, National Archives, 2–3.

was Daniel H. Wells, one of the First Presidency of the Mormon Church, he being the 1st Counselor of Brigham Young. No question of any importance was asked Wells, and when asked, their irrelevancy being apparent & manifest, I ruled them out on objections by the attorneys for the defendant. No doubt, however, that the placing of Wells on the witness stand, as I afterwards concluded, served Howard's purpose, in his effort to let the jury see that the church was on the side of the prosecution. But when Howard got into the trial fully, he put forth witnesses that gave over whelming amount of testimony to the guilt of the defendant . . .

The evidence at this second trial was far more abundant to warrant conviction—the Church had evidently loosened the tongues of the witnesses—guarding, however, to protect the heads of the church in detailing the evidence. Every one could see that the mouths of the witnesses had, in some way, been loosened. It began slowly to dawn upon the minds of the people that Howard had made some kind of deal with the heads of the church, whereby witnesses who had been in hiding were brought forth and their tongues loosened . . .

Despite the pleas of his attorney, John D. Lee instructed William Bishop to make no defense. Lee understood how justice worked in Utah. The all-Mormon jury that Sumner Howard selected convicted Lee after a few hours' deliberation on 20 September 1876.

FREDERIC LOCKLEY: SOLD BODY AND BREECHES

The federal prosecutor's odd behavior during the trial raised a host of questions. "Sumner Howard is a Judas Iscariot," Pressly Denny, who assisted in the prosecution, reportedly said, "and I know it to be so!"[18] Sumner Howard's ambiguous performance did not impress the irreverent *Salt Lake Tribune* editor Fred Lockley, who had seen Mormon jury members nullify an obvious guilty verdict in the first Lee trial. To cover the second trial for the independent paper, he dispatched John C. Young, the Mormon chief's nephew. Later, in his recollection of territorial Utah, Lockley told what he thought of the actions of U.S. Attorney Sumner Howard in the second Lee trial.

FREDERIC LOCKLEY, RECOLLECTIONS OF TERRITORIAL UTAH,
SPECIAL COLLECTIONS, PRINCETON UNIVERSITY.

A year elapsed before further proceedings were instituted, and during this interval judge Carey was replaced by Sumner Howard as district attorney for Utah. Suspicion attaches to this man, of collusion with the church authori-

---

[18]Lockley, Recollections of Territorial Utah, Princeton University.

ties. His behavior was peculiar. When the question of a new trial was discussed, he would declare with offensive braggadocio that he was here to convict the wholesale assassin and bring him to punishment; an implication that others who had conducted judicial proceedings against the felon had lacked zeal or ability. When the second trial was in progress, this prosecuting officer, in his address to the jury made statements confirmatory of the belief that he was acting in bad faith. He gave emphasis to the declaration that his purpose was to try the prisoner at the bar, and not Brigham Young or the Mormon Church. He said he was ready to produce evidence going to show that Lee had acted against the wishes and authority of his leaders; that his own inherent depravity had prompted the betrayal of the emigrants to destruction; and, to load the prisoner with yet greater infamy, he was ready with witnesses to show that he had outraged two young girls who had appealed to him for rescue and brained a third; that he had cut the throat of a wounded man; and, finally, that he had gathered up the spoils of the massacre and disposed of them to his own emolument.

A prosecuting officer under engagement to Mormon leaders to rid this notorious criminal off their hands, would suffer from no lack of testimony. Men who had borne a prominent part in the massacre were dumb as oysters while they supposed it was the desire of Brigham Young to screen his guilty instrument; but now it was conveyed to their understanding that the prisoner was to be sacrificed, they were ready to come forward and swear to any sort of atrocity. Jake Hamblin, as an instance, who for many years had lived on a ranch in the vicinity, and had been mixed up with the whole murderous proceeding, on the first trial persisted that he had nothing to testify, and was not subpoenaed as a witness. But now he understood that Lee was to be made a victim, he readily went on the stand and filled the ears of the jury with the most atrocious lies in regard to the prisoner, which were accepted without question. Depositions of Brigham Young and George A. Smith were read. The first named, of course, avowed his entire ignorance of the tragedy until after its consummation, nor had he given directions as to the disposal of the spoil. Yet witnesses on the stand swore they had subsequently seen cattle on Church [Antelope] island, bearing the church brand and pastured with the sacred herd, which they recognized as the former property of the emigrants. Brigham Young's first counselor also solemnly disavowed any participation in the massacre. It may be said as pertinent to these denials that this party of emigrants had been banned during their painful travel thro' the territory, their animals deprived of pasture and they refused needed supplies; a rancorous hostility was shown, and in view of the fact that Brigham's ready way of disposing of "his enemies" was by the knife or the bullet in the hands of his guilty satellites, no great force of testimony was required to lay the guilt at the prophet's door. Judge Boreman in passing sentence on the betrayed criminal, made this remark: "The men who actually participated in the deed are not the only guilty parties. Altho' the evidence shows plainly that you were a willing participant in the massacre, yet both trials taken together show that others, and some high in authority, inaugurated and decided upon the wholesale slaughter of the emigrants."

This prostitution of justice—this flagrant subornation of perjury—was apparent to thousands who gave close heed to this second trial. The common talk on the street in Salt Lake (among the non-Mormon element) was that Sumner Howard had sold out, and the manner in which he was conducting the prosecution gave evidence of that fact. The flagitious Daniel H. Wells was in the court room, and was even placed on the witness stand to add to the weight of infamy being piled on the prisoner's shoulders; his nods and winks had a pernicious significance, and as he could not directly communicate with the jurors, some occult method was resorted to of making known his will. The result of the trial was a verdict of guilty, this being the fore-ordained ending of this grim judicial farce.

Our reporter, John C. Young, was present at the trial, and sent us daily detailed dispatches. He enclosed frequent private intimations that Sumner Howard was "playing us," that "he was sold body and breeches to Brigham Young;" the purpose of this alleged bargain and sale being to get rid of Lee, and thus satisfy the demand of the American people for a victim . . .

It may be proper to mention here that in 1885 I attended the sittings of the Montana constitutional convention, held in Helena, as reporter for the *Butte Inter Mountain*. Spending an evening, during my stay in the city with Col. W. F. Sanders and family, I found among my fellow guests a Mr. John S. Tooker, of Lansing, Michigan, appointed secretary of Montana territory, who had just come on to assume his duties. In conversation with this gentleman, I learned of his acquaintance with Sumner Howard, and he fully confirmed the reports that had already reached us, of this man's sudden rise in fortune, and the ostentatious display he made of his ill gotten wealth.

In fairness to U.S. Attorney Howard, he and Marshal Nelson sent repeated messages to the Justice Department asking for funds to track down Mountain Meadows suspects. Howard launched a grand jury investigation related to the murders of dissident Mormon leaders Joseph Morris and John Banks in 1862, charging that "this horrible crime was committed by the direct order of Brigham Young." He also gained firsthand experience with Mormon attempts to "bulldoze the Courts" when he arrested Robert Burton: Daniel H. Wells burst into the courtroom and used "threats and menaces" to intimidate the prosecutor.[19] One historian who evaluated his career observed, "Howard was neither corrupt nor unsuccessful as a prosecutor."[20]

---

[19]Nelson and Howard to Attorney General Alfonso Taft, 23 September 1876; and Howard to Attorney General Charles Devens, 28 July 1877, both in Letters Received, RG 60, National Archives, 3.

[20]Cresswell, "The U.S. Department of Justice in Utah Territory, 1870–90," 211.

In addition to winning the only conviction for the crimes at Mountain Meadows, Howard achieved another difficult feat: he alienated both the Mormon and non-Mormon citizens of Utah. The *Salt Lake Tribune* expressed its confidence in him in the wake of Lee's conviction: "Sumner Howard is a good man, a good lawyer, and knows his business." After the paper concluded that Howard had been corrupted, it proved judicious in its evaluation: "Great good has resulted from this perfidy, and according to the lax morals of many casuists, the end justifies the means. The dying prisoner left a confession which shows the active part taken by Brigham, and other Church leaders, in the betrayal and slaughter of the emigrants, thus convicting them of being accessory before the fact."[21] When Howard resigned in January 1878, the *Deseret News* insulted him as a "Methodist missionary, confession peddler, anti-Mormon crusader, fifth rate lawyer and nimble fee grabber."[22]

Howard went on to serve as a zealously anti-Mormon federal judge in Arizona Territory, where pioneer historian Joseph Fish complained that he "commenced lecturing of evenings against the Mormons" and "spoke in the most bitter and scandalous terms against the Saints, trying to excite the public mind against them." Howard's main topic, Fish wrote, was the Mountain Meadows massacre. "In these lectures he willfully misrepresented the Mormons and did not stop at the truth but went far beyond that point. Many of his statements were directly opposite to those made at the Lee trial."[23] Years later, the Salt Lake City bar reportedly petitioned the president not to appoint Howard as Utah's chief justice. Howard's reputation as U.S. attorney, his critics charged, "would break an elephant's back to carry. It is notorious that he drew a salary from Brigham Young all the time he was in the Territory." They said, "It would be a public disgrace to put him on the bench."[24] Sumner Howard's true character, like many elements of the Mountain Meadows saga, will remain a puzzle. But a report made on his resignation suggests that Brigham Young paid him well: Mr. Tilton, a former neighbor in Michigan, claimed Sumner Howard "made over $20,000 while in Utah and deposited the same in the Bank of Flint."[25]

[21]"A Good Word for Attorney Howard," *Salt Lake Tribune*, 22 September 1876, 1/3; and "Exit Sumner Howard," *Salt Lake Tribune*, 5 January 1878, 2/1.

[22]"Editorial Notes," *Deseret News*, 16 January 1878, 790/3.

[23]Fish, *The Life and Times of Joseph Fish, Mormon Pioneer*, 270.

[24]*Galveston News*, 8 December 1882, 4/2. Chester Arthur appointed Howard chief justice of Arizona Territory in 1884.

[25]Elder B. [R. N. Baskin?], "Washington: Howard and His Success," *Salt Lake Tribune*, 22 January 1878, 4/3.

Chapter 11

"THE OLD MAN NEVER FLINCHED"
Lee's Execution

The day after his conviction, John D. Lee wrote to his wife Emma that he was "perfectly whipped out" and had concluded that "some men will swear that black is white if the good Brethren only say so." He blamed Daniel Wells, "or the one Eyed Pirate as the *Tribune* calls him," for coming to Beaver "to advise & council & direct the Brethren how to swear."[1] Asked his preferred way to die—hanging, beheading, or firing squad—Lee chose the last, apparently in the belief that he had committed no sins that warranted blood atonement.[2] As his attorney, William W. Bishop of Pioche, Nevada, appealed his conviction, Lee wrote dozens of letters in which he pitied himself, raged at Young for betraying him, begged for money, and ordered his wives to find and send his journals so he could write his life story to cover legal expenses.

JOHN D. LEE: BARTERING MY LIFE AWAY

On 10 October 1876 Lee instructed Emma to help Rachel, another wife, "hunt up all my Journals & records = also all the money you can & let Rachel bring them to me. Whether I live or die I intend to have a History of my life published to the world."[3] Later he told her that he had been moved to the territorial prison in Salt Lake and seemed surprised by this. He continued to rail against Brigham Young and other church leaders and proclaim his innocence.

---

[1]J. D. Lee to Emma B. Lee, 21 September 1876, Huntington Library.
[2]Utah law at that time provided condemned men with the option of beheading.
[3]J. D. Lee to Emma B. Lee, 10 October 1876, Huntington Library.

EXECUTION OF JOHN D. LEE
Photographer James Fennimore took this photoraph of the condemned
and the federal officials gathered at Mountain Meadows to watch Lee
die on Friday, 23 March 1877. *Courtesy of the Will Bagley Collection.*

WILLIAM NELSON, COPY NO. 1 OF JOHN D. LEE TO EMMA B. LEE,
U.T. PEN, SALT LAKE CITY, 9 DECEMBER 1876, HUNTINGTON LIBRARY.
    Ever dear kind and affectionate Companion with pleasure I hasten to answer
acknowledge the receipt of your Truly Kind & interesting letter . . . I am fully
satisfied with the stand that you have taken & sincerely hope that you may
have nerve enough to carry it out, for I am satisfied, as you said that all Hell
will Boil over & evry effort will be made & used to turn you from your integrity. You know the policy of Brigham is to get into possession & control everything where there is a dollar to be made, & you are a good sister & I was a
good Bro. As long as he could make merchandize of me & when the time
came that he could do better & make more capital by bartering my life away;
he was just as ready to betray & sacrifice me in the most cowardly & dastardly manner, for sinister motive, if he considered me accessory to the deed why
would he bring men whose hands have been died in human Blood to swear
away my life & make an offering of me to save his guilty Petts.

Brigham Young himself declared, [in] public in 1848 at Winter Quarters that no man in this Church had done as much for the benefit of Widows and the poor as I have done acording to means & ability. That he did not accept himself & prophecied in the name of Iseral [sic] god that I would walk my Enemies underfoot in time and in Eternity & they could not help it . . . Brigham Young said Son of man prophecy and it shall all be fulfilled & these were his words. Br Heber C. Kimball prophecy upon the head of Bro John D Lee of whom many speak evil & say in the name of the God of Jacob of Joseph & the god of the Latter day Saints, that Bro John D Lee shall yet triumph over those that seek to oppress & brake him up in his house hold & will trample them under foot & walk over their graves in time & Eternity & his family that have left him thinking to better their condition shall yet come bending unto him. I say it in the name of the Son Jesus Christ Amen. Brigham also said Amen; it will be fulfilled every word of it. Couple those sayings & predictions of Brigham & Heber with his dastardly conduct towards me at Beaver & what Conclusion can any Consistant person come to, but one & that is this, that his words then give the lie to his conduct at Beaver, if he spoke by the Spirit of inspiration. Then he has certainly fallen from grace since; if I am to conquer and walk my Enemies under foot unless he thinks it a friendly act, to sacrafice me, to make me attone for the sins of his Pets as well as my own by shedding my blood. You know that is one of his peculiar ways of showing his kindness to some men by killing them to save them but that kind of Friendship is getting too thin, it is too much like the love that a hungry wolf has for an innocent lamb, but we have had enough of that kind of sympathy love & affection, to last us through the next thousand years & all I ask of him is to give us a rest. About 1 P.M. Rachel Arnold [came]. She was a little afflicted with breaking out in the face, like the small pox. Otherwise she felt first rate, and spoke very highly of you & of the family generally; said that you met her in tears with a warm open heart.—that her own sister could not have expressed more tender affection towards her than you did & said that your whole soul, mind & spirit was absorbed in my interest. In a word she said that you was nearer to her to day than you ever was before, she further said that your children was almost like her own = that when little Billy [William James Lee] & Isaac [Lee] they met at the riverside that they put their arms around her neck & wept for joy also little Dell [Frances Dell "Dellie" Lee] and Vic [Victoria Elizabeth Lee][4] ran to meet her with open arms—that theres an affinity & love between your children & her own, that is seldom seldom [sic] seen between half brothers & sisters . . .

I am glad that you found as many letters & Dockuments & sent as you did; I expect to send back to the Mow-E-yabba for my Journal & record, Caroline said that you & her found [one] from Brigham Young to me about the Indians preparing for war & that you put it away in one of your chests say-

---

[4] These were four of John D. and Emma Lee's eight children.

ing that it might be useful some day—I would like to have you look it up—Also the Journal that I carried in my pocket when Chas. Hopkins came to Harmony before day = when Judge Cradlebach was after him and &c when you & Mab [?] brought him to me in the big field to my retreat in the oak brush near the big wash. You doubtless remember, that he said to me Bro. Lee if I was in your place I would expose the whole thing, I know that you opposed it, & argued against it in tears, & I will swear to it. I replied that it was too late now the deed was done, he ought to have stood up like a man and backed me then; before the crime was committed, now if we hang let us hang together; that I could never could [sic] betray a friend in trouble. The Journal that I carried in my pocket there [?] it will doubtless refer to that circumstance & perhaps of many near, that Journal I want, it was yellow back sheep skin cover, made in pocket book style tolerably large should a letter come from me for those books and paper. My family record also please secure all that you can. I know that there are several at the Mow-E-Yabba = I think it be as well to send a letter over to Nancy to gether up all my Journals & Papers my family records also tell her to wrap them up carefully & stick the cloth that contains them that none may loose, if you have no chance to write & you could spair one of the little boys send them right away that the records may be at the river, should they be called for; I am writing up a History of my life & I much need them for references, as well as they may contain some valuable facts that may be of much value to me. I have not seen Col Nelson since I received your letter. He is gone to Provo to attend Court, while writing Col Nelson drives up & is glad that Rachel has come, but regrets that all the Journals & records were not brought to the Dell at once, but keep that matter to Yourself—It is more than likely that a messenger will be sent for them right away = if they are at the River, it will save the distance of travel from the Dell to the Mow-E-Yabba & back, besides the loss of time, I have received two letters from my attorney W. W. Bishop, at Pioche, in his last letter he said that Joseph had not put in his appearance yet with the stock or money & that he must have money to pay expenses District Clerks fees Traveling fees besides office at Salt Lake City & Beaver at least $5 a day—My case has been dragging over two years = & the expenses have footed to quite a Pile, & we have not paid over $1400 as yet & this appealing suits from one Court to another is attended with heavy expenses. He writes to me that he will stand by me to the last; if he can only have money to bear his expenses, but that he has no other money; of himself—& unless it can be raised, he will not be able to come to Salt Lake to attend to my case at the sitting of the Supreme Court in January at S. L. City, & if he does not, as a matter of course I must stand by the sentence that has been passed upon me by Judge Boreman, at Beaver, that is to be executed by shooting. Sometime matters look quite gloomy to me = Still I trust that Joseph will raise sufficient money, to enable Bishop to continue with my case. Rachel says that the stock got away from Joseph the first night after he left with them

& came back = that he went on to Pioche with his butter & cheese, to sell & let Bishop have what it brought & confer with Bishop, about bringing the Beef Cattle as soon as he should have & gether them up &c that Sam had gone to Leeds with a load of grain, to sell for money, for me and so &c don't know but Rachel will leave in a few days on business. The time is fast drawing to a close; & what is to be done must be done quickly.

Dearest Emma I am satisified that you will do for the best, but allow me to suggest a few ideas to you—you know that Uncle Tomy Smith owes $300 for work in that boat. I have done as much myself as Uncle Tommy had done. Bro Blythe & David Dennit [?] did the balance—hence you see that the boat is not church property but individual property hence they have no claim on it, whatever Rachel says that Tommy Smith wants his pay or he will cut the boat loose that he [will] never give it Brigham; But to admit that it was church property, we have set over church property & Missionaries = enough to double pay for the building of that Boat. If you feel to honor my request I want that matter stopt. Let no one cross hereafter without pay not even Brigham himself; unless it might be some poor destitute person who cant pay = You know that I never turned the hungry from my door. The telegram that Brigham sent me says that he never intended anyone to cross without paying & that when he and his Company crossed he would reward us liberally—for our services take him at his word = except no orders from any of them for crossing. If waren [Warren Johnson] will not do as you ask him send for Ralph to help Reiley [?] tend the ferry & let Johnson out.

I want you and the children to see better days with a house and comforts around you & the children educated = This can not be while we work for nothing. You should charge $3.00 for large wagons & $2. for light ones we have nothing to gain by working for blessings but loose everything. The more to do for some People the more ungrateful they are it is more charitable to pay our honest debts & help Pah out of trouble than it is to missionaries or church property for nothing—the men that have stood by us in trouble & in prision [sic] are our neighbors = & such we should treat as we do ourselves not those who pass by with groans & go by & leave us in trouble as many of our good Bretheren have done with us—the one eyed pirate for one. I think that you and your children should be as near & dear to me as Brigham Young & his children is. I don't think it is right, for you & my children to continue to be serfs & slaves to him & his children, I do not believe that the seller should eat the bread of the laborer nor wear the garments that the laborer has earned = neither am I willing that he shall continue to fleece me and mine as he has done in times past to keep up his profligate family in the most extravagant style. Thousands of poor honest people have denied themselves of almost every comfort of life & have turned in the last farthing to Brigham as trustee in trust for the Church & who is the Church. Brigham & his royal family; are the poor made equal with them (not yet) = have their wants been supplied & their conditions ameliorated from the

tithing & offerings of the Lords storehouse (I think not). Brigham says Bro.
John I want you to open up a road through into Arizionia secure the watering
places by the way; for the benefit of the Church, establish a ferry, for us to cross
= When trouble drives us to seek another place of retreat, & you shall be blest,
John goes and does everything that is told him until he is worn out & perhaps
he has property that is valuable & John gets tired of giving all he has & is not
willing to continue to be a serf & a slave any longer, John all at once is considered to be an enemy to the Church, but he must be saved, so we will make an
offering of him, to sacrafice him to attone for all our sins his included; Thus
end my reward, he says, and others for instance, Warren I want you to go & help
tend the ferry at the Dell, you must cross the missionaries over free & The Church
property = no no [sic] matter if your two wives have babes at their breasts &
have to eregate in hot burning & rain, the crop while you ferry the Church over
the river, you must not spend one cent to buy a little tea or Coffee to nurrish
& brace up nature. Let your wives do without it, & the Lord will bless them for
the church wants & must have all the money that the Saints can possibly raise
to build up the Kingdom (Brigham) & this you must do or you are dammed
and must die or be killed as soon as the honey making time is over & there we
are led as dupes to cary out a miserable life in sefdom & bondage & as a general thing when old age overtakes them their fate is but little better than mine.
The twelve & others off are but little better, = men are not servants according
to our faithfulness nor fidelity, after bearing the heat and burden of the day.
The Twelve must stand aside & give place to the spend thrift sons of Brigham
the fat boy who spent $26000 in one days spree in England of the money of
the poor fund. This man is set apart by father to be the President of the Church
& this man is set apart by his prolifgate Bro John W. who turned away his wives
= took up with an actress from the stage—is set apart for the first Counsellor, when Brigham knows well, that Jos Smiths sons was justly are [sic] entitled
to the place & position that he has filled with his own profligate sons.[5] This is
Brigham Youngs Justice & reward for services rendered him &c. But I must stop.
Young Joseph Smith has been holding forth in the Public Institute in this City
to crowded Halls who are attentive listeners the most of which are Mormons
who are tired of being in serfdom;[6] Col Nelson & Warden Crowe to treat me
as human beings not as a dog. Your present to the Col was left at his office. I
have not seen [it] but told him that you sent it he has not sen[t] it yet, but know
he will consider it as a token of respect. I have written perhaps more than was
advisable but I hope you will keep a close mouth. I hope to see better days yet.
Good bye dearest till you hear from me again.

To Emma B. Lee   J. D. Lee

---

[5]Lee referred to Brigham Young, Jr., and John W. Young, who both defended their profligate use of LDS
church funds as necessary to maintain their status as sons of the prophet.

[6]Joseph Smith III, oldest son of the Mormon prophet, visited Salt Lake City between 22 November
and 11 December 1876 and gave four sermons at William Godbe's Liberal Institute.

WILLIAM C. STEWART:
A WORD FROM YOU WITHOUT SIGNATURE

As federal officials prepared for Lee's execution in March 1877, the notorious William C. Stewart, whose conduct at Mountain Meadows appalled even his fellow participants, prepared to take flight. C. F. McGlashan, the California newspaper editor who became famous for his *History of the Donner Party*, visited Cedar City in 1874 and wrote a series for the *Sacramento Daily Record* on Mountain Meadows. In it he told the "horrible tale" of how Stewart murdered young William Aden.

McGLASHAN AND McGLASHAN, EDS.,
FROM THE DESK OF C. F. McGLASHAN, 142–43.

Aden and a companion were returning to the settlements, probably in an attempt to obtain assistance or food.[7] At all events, they met Bill Stewart and a companion at Pinto Creek, seven miles this side of the Meadows. Stewart had a revolver and his companion, a boy, had a shotgun. The former said he would shoot one and told the boy he must kill the other. As good as his word, Stewart sent a bullet crashing through Aden's brains while the horse of his unsuspecting victim was quietly drinking at a little creek. The boy's courage failed, and the other emigrant escaped to the train.

A HARDENED VILLAIN

Years after the murder, Stewart and a Mormon friend were passing the spot, and the former related the circumstance. The friend asked what had been done with the body, and Stewart pointed to a clump of bushes as the place where it had been concealed. "Is it there now?" asked the traveler. "I don't know," coolly responded Stewart. "Let's go see." Accordingly they went, and the horrified friend tells me to this day he shudders to think how Stewart went to the spot and brutally kicked about the bleached bones and examined the fragments of clothing and the scattered locks of hair . . .

I would not dare to publish this horrible tale, but I have it direct and positive from the lips of a highly respected gentleman, whose oaths are ready to back his assertions.

One of the suspects indicted with John D. Lee in 1874, Stewart had been on the run for years, but as Lee's execution approached, he was living in Cedar City. Having decided to flee the country, he sought the aid of the most powerful man in Utah.

---

[7]Since Aden and his companion avoided the Mormon settlement at Pinto, they were probably seeking help from the Dukes and Turner parties who were behind them.

WILLIAM C. STEWART TO BRIGHAM YOUNG,
10 MARCH 1877, LDS ARCHIVES.

Dear Br.

Please excuse me taking the liberty of writing these few lines to you.

For the last three years I have been an outcast and have not had the privilege of meeting and associating with my brethren. I have been on many missions to the Orabies [Hopis] and Navajoes and helped explore and make the road to the Colorado on both routes. I am getting tired of being hunted by Government Officials and in consequence of being so much away thro one cause and another am not so well off in this worlds goods as many who could stay at home, but I own one third share of the Cedar Grist Mill. There is two sets of stones the small ones are running and the large one set. I thought if you could help me in getting some one to purchase my share, I would like with your consent and approbation to go to Scotland and gather a geneaology of my friends, and perhaps do a little good there and also be out of the way untill this trouble is over. I will take 600 dollars for the share in the mill, if this meets your sanction and you deem it wisdom, direct under cover to Bishop Lunt, a word from you without signature will be sufficient.

Praying that the Lord will bless you with encreased good health and every wish your heart can desire I remain your brother in the Gospel,

Wm. C. Stewart

LT. GEORGE J. J. PATTERSON:
THE COMMAND "FIRE" WAS GIVEN

In March 1877 U.S. Marshal William Nelson ordered John D. Lee moved from the territorial penitentiary at Salt Lake City to the U.S. Army's Fort Cameron, near Beaver, Utah, to await execution. On 20 March 1877 the post's commander, Col. Henry T. Douglas, issued orders to Lt. George Patterson to "proceed with your Detachment to Mountain Meadows, Utah," and prevent any interference with the execution of John D. Lee. The orders made clear that civil officers, not soldiers, would "carry said sentence into effect." Patterson was to observe "the utmost secrecy" and his detachment of twenty men should avoid publicity. "Your simple duty is to prevent rescue or interference with the civil officers in the execution of their duty," the colonel directed. The enlisted men need not "know anything of the nature of their service." Escorted by Nelson and U.S. Attorney Sumner Howard, Lee left the post the next day for the eighty-mile buggy journey to site of the massacre nearly twenty years before. The escort preceded them to guard against an attack by Lee's sons. Douglas enjoined Patterson to employ the "utmost secrecy," but somehow a copy of his orders ended up in the files of the LDS church.

LT. COL. HENRY T. DOUGLAS, INSTRUCTIONS ON JOHN D. LEE, CITIZEN, TO LT. PATTERSON IN JOURNEYING TO M.M., LDS ARCHIVES.

Having received the foregoing instructions, I prepared my command and marched from this Post at about 7:30 P.M. of the same day. In order to be able to reach by daylight a place where my command could be concealed from the public highway, I was obliged to pass through the out skirts of Beaver City, but the men were so concealed in the wagons that no one knew or suspicioned even what they contained.

We travelled till about 6 A.M. of the 21st Inst. and then reached what is known as Red Creek Cañon and there our wagons were hid so that no one knew anything of our presence.

At about 6 P.M. the same day, 21 Inst: we started from our concealment which was twenty nine (29) miles from Fort Cameron U.T.—passed thru Paragoona, a small Mormon settlement at about 6:30 P.M. and Parawan [sic] at 8 P.M. The latter settlement is more extensive and contains about one thousand people. It is 35 miles from Beaver City, Utah. At about 1:20 A.M. March 22, we reached Cedar City in Iron Co, U.T. it being a distance of eighteen (18) miles from Parawan. From Cedar City the southern road was abandoned, the road to Mountain Meadows taking to the right hand, we traveled this new road in a south westerly direction and made camp at what is known as Leaches spring, at a distance of about thirteen miles from Cedar City. This camp was reached a short time before daylight on 22 Inst. At this point we were overtaken by United States Marshal and party with prisoner John D. Lee. This was the first intimation that the men of my command had, in regard to the nature of their duty. My command and the Marshal's party went into camp a short distance from each other, moving off the road and concealing ourselves and wagons as much as possible among the cedars.

At three P.M. my command, except the mounted men, left camp, the mounted party was left as a guard to the U.S. Marshal. We crossed little Pinto creek at 5 P.M. having made ten (10) miles from camp. Five miles farther is Big Pinto which was passed about 6:15 P.M. Big Pinto is also a Mormon Settlement containing about thirty-five (35) dwelling homes, one store and ten shops.

From this place our road passed over a large hill, and very steep in places on the south side, without any incident of note, [and] we reached Mountain Meadows, 12 miles from Big Pinto at about 9:30 P.M. 22 Inst.

On the morning of the 23rd, the day fixed for the execution of the sentence on John D. Lee, we found ourselves about one mile from the spot fixed upon by U.S. Marshal, for the carrying out of said sentence.

From our camp of the previous night being 22nd Inst., I marched my detachment across some low hills, sending the wagons around by an old road, to the spot before mentioned as fixed upon by the Marshal. I stationed two picket posts which could be seen constantly from where we stopped. They were ordered to give notice of the approach of any parties. The Marshal also requested that I protect him in his duty, from the encroachment of several parties who had arrived only a short time before the time fixed for Lee's execution, the request was fulfilled and guards for that purpose were stationed around the camp, permitting only those to enter who had authority from U.S. Marshal. At 11 A.M. everything being in readiness, as prepared by the Marshal, the command "Fire" was given and John D. Lee died without a struggle . . .

John D. Lee: I Am a True Believer

In his last speech, Lee proclaimed his innocence and his belief in the gospel of Jesus Christ as taught by Mormonism's founding prophet Joseph Smith. But he bitterly denounced Brigham Young for sacrificing him and teaching false doctrine. An early telegraph operator, Scipio Kenner, who had served as an apprentice and journeyman printer at the *Deseret News*, reported Lee's last words to the church-owned paper.

Scipio Kenner, telegram to *Deseret News*, Lee's Speech, 23 March 1877.

After Marshal Nelson concluded reading order of Court at 10:35 he asked Lee if he had anything to say before execution was carried into effect—Lee says I wish to speak to that man pointing to Mr. Fennemore who was fixing his instruments near by to take his Photograph preceding shooting—Lee calling to the artist Fennemore replied in a second Mr. Lee & waiting until artist assented his readiness to listen. Lee said "I want to ask you a favor I want you to furnish my three wives each a copy of my Photograph meaning the one being taken, a copy of the same to Rachael A Sarah & Emma B—Mr. Howard responded for artist; he says he will do it, Mr. Lee. Lee repeated over again carefully saying please forward them—& was answered I will Lee. He then arose & said I have but little to say this morning of course I feel that I am upon the brink of Eternity & the solemnities of Eternity should rest upon my mind at the present. I have endeavored to do so—I have written a short & abridged history of my life. This is to be published—I have given my views and feelings with regard to all those things—I feel as calm as a summer morning Have done nothing advisedly wrong—My conscience clear before God & Man & I am ready to meet my redeemer. It is this that places me upon this field. I have not denied

God or his mercy [for] I am a strong believer in those things. [What] I most I regret is parting with my family—many of them are unprotected & be left fatherless. When I speak of these little ones they touch a tender chord within me (Here Lees voice failed preceptably [sic].) I have done nothing designedly wrong in this affair—I used my utmost endeavors to save this people. I would have given worlds were it at my command to have avoided that calamity—But I could not—I am sacrificed to satisfy feeling and am shot to gratify parties but am nearly ready to die. I have no fear—death has no terror—of mercy I have asked none neither have I asked Court or officials to spare my life. I do not fear death—I should never have to go to a worse place than the one I am in now. I have said it to my family and I will say today that the government of US sacrifices their best friend & that is saying a great deal, but it is true. I am a true believer in the Gospel of Jesus Christ—I do not believe every thing that is now practiced & taught by Brigham Young. I don't agree with him. I feel he is leading people astray but I believe in [the] Gospel as was taught in its purity by Joseph Smith in former days—I have my reasons for saying this. I used to make this mans will my pleasure & did so for thirty years. See how & what I have come to this day—I have been sacrificed in a cowardly dastardly manner—Thousands of people in Church honorable good hearted that I cherish in my heart—I regret I leave my family they are dear to me, these are things to rouse my sympathies. I declare I did not do wrong designedly in this unfortunate affair—I did every thing in my power to save the Emigrants, but I am the one that must suffer. Having said this I feel satisfied—I ask Lord my God to extend his mercy and receive my spirit—my labors are don[e]—

John D. Lee: Shoot the Balls through My Heart

Frank Leslie's Illustrated Newspaper doubtless gave its readers the truest rendition of Lee's last words. Newspapers across the nation echoed the sheet's cry of satisfaction that the murderer of Mountain Meadows had finally gotten the justice he deserved. They also expressed wonder at Lee's tranquility in receiving it. "The old man never flinched," marveled the *Salt Lake Tribune*. "It made death seem easy, the way he went off."

"Justice at Last! Execution of John D. Lee for Complicity in the Mountain Meadows Massacre," *Supplement—Frank Leslie's Illustrated Newspaper* (14 April 1877), 109–12.

The circumstances of the terrible Utah tragedy of twenty years ago, known as the Mountain Meadows Massacre, are familiar to our readers, as well as the fact of the Mormon elder, John D. Lee having atoned for his complicity

in the affair, on March 23d, by his life. The details of this summary, if somewhat tardy, vindication of justice, have been published, with their terribly dramatic accompaniments. The proceedings attending Lee's execution were conducted with appropriate gravity and decorum. It had been determined by the
authorities that the execution should take place on the spot where the massacre, and, accordingly, the prisoner was conveyed, on Wednesday, March 21st.,
from his prison in Beaver City, the subject of our illustration last week, to
the hill-surrounded plain, known as Mountain Meadows. He was in the custody of Marshall Nelson, with an armed guard. The party camped out on
Thursday night, and, after making several brief halts along the road, reached
Mountain Meadows about ten o'clock, on Friday, the 23d.

SCENE OF THE MASSACRE

No more dreary scene can be imagined than those Mountain Meadows.
From the point of the massacre to the emigrant-camp measures a distance of
about a mile and a half. The meadows are cut up into deep gullies and covered with sage brush and scrub oak. At the lower part, where the immigrants
were encamped, is seen Murderers' Spring, the point where the first acts of
the assassins were perpetrated. This spring was twenty years ago on a level
with the surrounding country; but it has since been washed until it formed a
terrible gulch some twenty feet in depth and eight or ten yards wide.

Coming down to the easterly bank of this ravine is the monument of loose
stones erected by Lieutenant Price about thirteen years ago. Some of these
stones have slid down the declivity. The ravine monument is oblong in out-
line and about twenty feet in length, being some three feet high. Under the
monument at the time of its erection were placed all the bones that could be
obtained on the field; but on removing some of the stones, down to the level
of the earth, no trace of bones was discovered. Counting the military escort,
the marshal and his deputies and a few officials, there were probably eighty
persons present. A singular feature was the presence of a photographer, who
accompanied the solemn band, provided with his camera and paraphernalia,
for the purpose of taking pictures of Lee in his last moments, and of the
scene of the execution. As soon as the party arrived at the scene of the massacre a halt was called and Lee was ordered to descend from the wagon in
which he rode. Before the arrangements for his execution were completed, Lee
coolly pointed out to Marshal Nelson some points in the vicinity, with a view
evidently of showing the movements of the ill-fated people previous to their
being so cruelly massacred. The civilians accompanying the officers were still
kept back for a time. Some of the soldiers were posted on the adjoining hills
to guard against any surprise from any quarter.

CONCEALING THE FIRING SQUAD.

The wagons were meanwhile placed in line near the monument and the
army blankets fastened over the wheels. Behind this improvised screen the squad

of men who had been appointed to shoot Lee were to be stationed. The purpose of this concealment of the firing party was to prevent the men composing it from being seen by anyone, there being a reasonable fear that some of the numerous relatives of Lee might wreak vengeance on the heads of his executioners.

The boards of which the coffin was to be formed were next unloaded from a wagon and the carpenters began to nail them together. It was a rough pine box. While it was being made Lee sat at some distance away with Marshall Nelson, intently watching the scene around him.

The civilians, and those specially invited as witnesses, were allowed to come within the military enclosure. All of the others were allowed to witness the proceedings from a considerable distance east of the ravine. At Murderers' Spring there were only some twenty-five or thirty persons gathered from the neighboring settlements, for the time and place of the shooting had been very sensibly kept private.

Marshal Nelson then read the order and sentence of the court, directing the Marshal of the Territory to conduct his prisoner from the place were he was confined to the place of execution, and then to see that he was shot to death. The marshal read the order in a clear tone, his words being audible to everyone present. As he concluded the reading he asked Lee if he had anything to say before the sentence of the law was carried out. Lee looked up quickly and noticing Mr. Fennimore, the photographer, in the act of fixing up his canvas preparatory to taking a photograph of the prisoner, pointed with his finger towards him and said: "I wish to speak to that man. Come over here," at the same time beckoning with his hand. Mr. [James] Fennimore nodded and said: "In a second Mr. Lee." He, however, occupied over a minute before he was ready to comply with Mr. Lee's simple request. Lee said: "I want to ask a favor of you sir. I want you to furnish each of my three wives a copy of the photograph—one to Rachel A., Emma B., and Sarah C." Mr. Howard, the district attorney, who was standing by the side of the instrument, responded for the artist, whose head at the moment was covered by the hood as he was adjusting the camera: "He says he will do it." He replied: "Please forward them to my wives, Sarah C., Emma B., and Rachel A." As the prisoner uttered the names of his wives he seemed to pose himself involuntarily, and the picture was taken. He then rose from his seat, and looking around at his guards and the spectators, spoke as follows:

THE PRISONER'S LAST ADDRESS.

"I have but little to say this morning. Of course, I feel that I am upon the brink of eternity, and the solemnity of eternity should arrest upon my mind at the present moment. I have made out, or endeavored to do so, a manuscript and an abridged history of my life. This will be published. Sir."—Turning to the district attorney, Howard,—"I have given my views and feelings with regard to all these things. I feel resigned to my fate. I feel as calm as a summer morning. I have done nothing advisedly wrong. My conscience is clear before God and man, and I am ready to meet my redeemer. This it is that places me upon this field. I am not an infidel. I have not denied God or His mercy. I am a strong believer in these things. The most I regret is parting with my family. Many of them are unprotected and will be left fatherless. When I speak of those little ones they touch a tender cord within me."

At this moment the prisoner's voice trembled, and he perceptibly faltered in his words. He continued, however, as follows: "I have done nothing designedly wrong in this affair. I used my utmost endeavors to save those people. I would have given worlds were they at my command to have avoided that calamity, but I could not. I am sacrificed to satisfy feelings, and am used to gratify parties; but I am ready to die. I have no fear of death. It has no terrors for me; and no particle of mercy have I asked for from Court or officials to spare my life. I do not fear death. I shall never go to a worse place than the one I am now in. I have said it to my family, and I will say it to-day, that the government of the United States sacrifices their best friend, and that is saying a great deal, but it is true. I am a true believer in the Gospel of Jesus Christ. I do not believe everything that is now practiced and taught by Brigham Young. I do not agree with him. I believe he is leading his people astray. But I believe in the Gospel that as taught in its purity by Joseph Smith in former days. I have my reasons for saying this. I used to make this man's will my pleasure (evidently alluding to Brigham Young) and did so for thirty years. See how and what I have come to this day! I have been sacrificed in a cowardly, dastardly manner. There are thousands of people in the Church—honorable, good-hearted—whom I cherish in my heart. I regret to leave my family. They are near and dear to me. These are things to rouse my sympathy. I declare I did nothing designedly wrong in this unfortunate affair. I did everything in my power to save the immigrants, but I am the one who must suffer. Having said this, I am resigned. I ask the Lord, my God, to extend His mercy to me and receive my spirit. My labors are here done."

Last Offices of the Church.

It was then eleven o'clock, and as Lee ceased speaking he was informed that his hour was come, and he must prepare for execution.

He quietly seated himself on the coffin provided for his body, and coolly looked at the small group of spectators. He was still very calm and resigned. Parson Stokes, a Methodist minister, who was attending the condemned man as his spiritual advisor, then knelt on the sward and delivered a short prayer. The minister was quite affected by the solemnity of the occasion, and he was earnest in his prayer, and the prisoner listened with an attentive ear.

The prayer ended, the reporters withdrew, Lee took off his overcoat without assistance and shook hands with Mr. Stokes, Marshal Nelson, District

Attorney Howard and a few others. The handkerchief was next tied over his eyes, and as it was being done, he asked the Marshal not to tie his hands. This favor being granted, the doomed man clasped his hands over his head, bracing himself up tightly at the same moment, exclaiming: "Let them shoot the balls through my heart. Don't let them mangle my body." The marshal reassured him that the aim would be true and then stepped back. As he did this he gave the requisite orders, "Ready, aim, fire!" The five men selected as the executioners obeyed promptly. They raised their rifles to their shoulders, taking deliberate aim at the blindfolded man sitting on his coffin about twenty feet in front of them. As the fatal word: "Fire!" rang out clear and strong on the morning air a sharp report was heard, and Lee fell back on the coffin dead and motionless. He must have died in a single instant for there was not a cry or moan or not even a tremor of the body.

A few minutes then were allowed to elapse, all present standing motionless and with uncovered heads. The marshal stepped alone, moved and walked over to the body to examine and ascertain if death had resulted. At that moment the photographer was busy taking a view of the scene.

Contrary to the general anticipation, none of Lee's family were present; as Rachel was often heard to declare that she would be present if, indeed, her husband was executed, the change of program and scene of execution was no doubt the reason for this failure on her part.

Satisfaction of the Law.

The utter silence prevailing was at length broken by Marshall Nelson exclaiming: "He is quite dead. The law is satisfied at last."

Then a general movement was made by the party, and all gathered near to view the corpse. The features were quite composed, but ghastly white. After the body was picked up by the Deputy Marshall and placed in the coffin it was carried over to the wagon and put in, and the entire party began dispersing. The execution was a very remarkable one and was entirely successful. Subsequently the body was delivered to relatives at Cedar City.

Before his execution Lee gave what money he had to the District Attorney to be given to Rachel, one of his wives. He gave his coat to Marshal Nelson and his scarf to Howard. Lee's confession, made in view of death, of the history of the Mountain Meadows Massacre, so plainly incriminates Brigham Young as to leave no doubt on the mind of the unprejudiced reader that the Mormon leader was cognizant of that horrible slaughter, and a party to it. But this is a moral conviction only, and unless the crime can be legally brought home to him it would be unwise in [sic] the Government to initiate proceedings, for the failure to punish would have a bad effect. It is, therefore, a point of very great public interest whether or no it is not yet possible to obtain evidence to prove legally that guilt of which there is morally no doubt. Many stories that have appeared in Western papers since the publication of Lee's

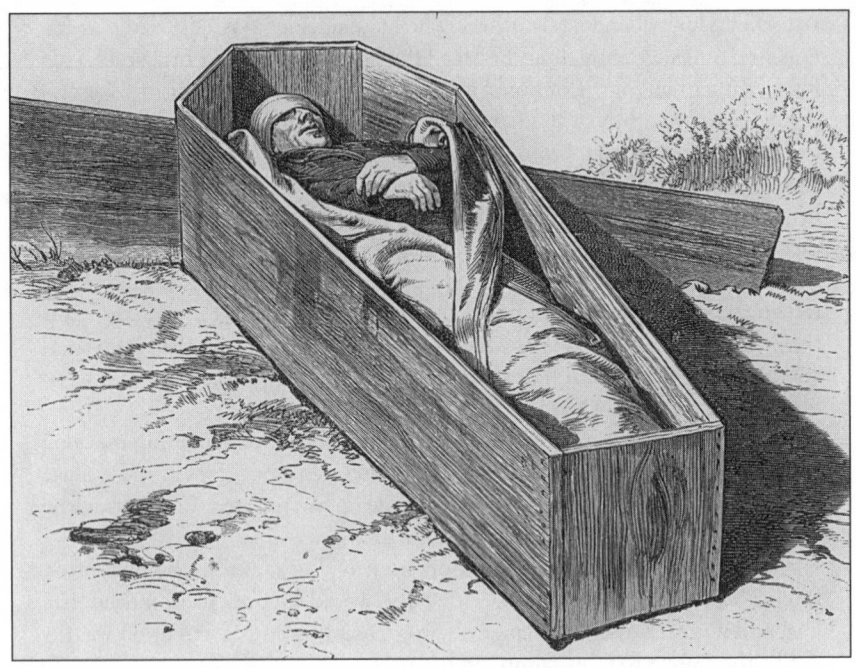

JUSTICE AT LAST!
John D. Lee in his coffin.
From *Frank Leslie's Illustrated Newspaper.*
Courtesy of the Will Bagley Collection.

confession, and many statements made by frontiersmen, seem to indicate that
there are persons having knowledge of the occurrence who are now willing
to tell all they know. Some of them may themselves have been accessories,
and are now frightened at the fate of Lee and the indication that the heads
of their capital church have given them up; but whoever they are, the occasion to make them of service in the enforcement of justice should not be lost.
It is just possible that the criminal law may yet resolve the most difficult parts
of the Mormon problem . . .

LEE's "LAST CONFESSION": THE HOWARD VERSION

The *Time* magazine review of *A Mormon Chronicle: The Diaries of John D. Lee* hailed
the work as "one of the most extraordinary documents ever written by an
American." As remarkable as the tale of "roughhewn courage and tenacity"

told in Lee's journals still stands, as a literary creation one must stand in awe of his autobiography, which he wrote while awaiting death. Here is a memoir whose protagonist describes in excruciating detail how he engineered the betrayal and murder of some 120 people, most of them women and children. Yet he manages to portray himself as another victim of his awful tale, and for all but the most skeptical reader, it is hard not to feel sorry for a man who suffered so much and tried so hard to save the Arkansans. But Lee is not to be trusted: much of his story is told with such compelling detail that it is impossible to tell when he is reporting the facts as he remembered them or when he is weaving an elaborate lie designed to vindicate himself and shift blame for a terrible crime to the victims, the Paiutes, his colleagues and superiors, and his own devotion to his cause and his adopted father.

All of Lee's many and varied "confessions" are calculated distortions of the truth, crafted to admit to much of what was already known about the atrocity but to conceal his role in launching the assault and ramrodding the operation to its brutal conclusion. When Brigham Young joked—or boasted—that Mormonism had "the greatest and smoothest liars in the world," he could have picked no better person to prove his point than John D. Lee.[8] In the twenty years between the crime and his death, Lee retailed convincing if contradictory "confessions" about his part in the massacre to almost anyone willing to listen, including Jacob Forney, journalist J. H. Beadle, his fellow Mormons, his attorneys, and even members of John Wesley Powell's second expedition. Lee's stories evolved as more became known about the details of the murders, but all were designed to shift the blame to any shoulders that did not belong to John D. Lee.

Lee dictated his final confession to William Bishop, his attorney, in March 1877, as part of an agreement to cover his legal expenses. Embittered against Young and those who had testified against him, he spared none of his enemies and made clear the Mormon leader's role as an accessory after the fact. This is the "last confession" that Bishop completed in May 1877 and published as *Mormonism Unveiled; or the Life and Confessions of the Late Mormon Bishop John D. Lee.* The work is a damning indictment not only of the men who shed so much blood but also of those who created the climate of fear and hatred that made the massacre possible.[9]

---

[8]Brigham Young, *Journal of Discourses*, 9 November 1856, 4:77.

[9]*Mormonism Unveiled* has been reprinted countless times and is now available on the Internet.

Lee gave an earlier statement to U.S. Attorney Sumner Howard that was published after his death in major newspapers, including the *San Francisco Daily Bulletin.* It included a number of interesting variations from the Bishop version.

"LEE'S LAST CONFESSION,"
SAN FRANCISCO DAILY BULLETIN SUPPLEMENT, 24 MARCH 1877, 1/2–5.

HIS VERSION OF THE MOUNTAIN MEADOWS MASSACRE.
HE CLAIMS TO HAVE SIMPLY OBEYED ORDERS AND PLACES
THE RESPONSIBILITY OF THE MASSACRE ON "OTHER DIGNITARIES"
OF THE MORMON CHURCH. HE PROFESSES TO HAVE PLEADED
WITH THE INDIANS TO SPARE THE LIVES OF THE EMIGRANTS.
HE TELLS THE FATE OF SOME OF THE SURVIVORS OF THE MASSACRE.

Appended is the last confession of John D. Lee. It was written by himself, without aid or advise, and with the certainty of death staring him in the face, having been penned by him subsequent to his second trial and sentence to die. The document was originally placed by Lee in the hands of United States District Attorney Howard, in the Penitentiary at Salt Lake City, last month, with the understanding that it should not be published until after his death. The same statement was repeated by Lee on the field at the scene of execution yesterday. As a gentleman, Mr. Howard kept the faith reposed in him, withholding its publication until the prisoner had suffered the extreme penalty of the law. Following is Lee's confession:

ARRIVAL OF THE EMIGRANT TRAIN IN UTAH.

In the month of September, 1857, the company of emigrants known as the "Arkansas Company" arrived in Parowan, Iron County, Utah, on their way to California. At Parowan young Aden, one of the company, saw and recognized one William Laney, a Mormon resident of Parowan. Aden and his father had rescued Laney from an anti-Mormon mob in Tennessee several years before, and saved his life. He (Laney), at the time he was attacked by the mob, was a Mormon missionary in Tennessee. Laney was glad to see his friend and benefactor, and invited him to his house and gave him some garden sauce to take back to the camp with him.

BISHOP DAME CROOKS HIS LITTLE FINGER—WHAT CAME OF IT.

The same evening it was reported to Bishop (Colonel) Dame that Laney had given potatoes and onions to the man Aden, one of the emigrants. When the report was made to Bishop Dame he raised his hand and crooked his little finger in a significant manner to one Barney Carter, his brother-in-law, and one of the "Angels of Death." Carter, without another word, walked out, went to Laney's house with a long picket in his hand, called Laney out and struck him a heavy blow on the head, fracturing his skull, and left him on the

THE MORMON MENACE
John Doyle Lee as he appeared in
the picture that accompanied his
confession in the *San Francisco Bulletin.*
Courtesy of the Will Bagley Collection.

ground for dead. Jacob Weeks [?] and Isaac Newman, President of the "High
Council," both told me that they saw Dame's manoeuvres. James McGuffee,
then a resident of Parowan—but through oppression has been forced to leave
there, and is now a merchant in Pahranagat Valley, near Pioche, Nevada—
knows these facts.

BRIGHAM'S RIGHT-HAND MAN
PAVING THE WAY FOR THE MASSACRE.

About the last of August, 1857, some ten days before the Mountain Meadows massacre, the company of emigrants passed through Cedar City. George
A. Smith—then First Counsellor in the Church and Brigham Young's right-
hand man—came down from Salt Lake City, preaching to the different settlements. I, at that time was in Washington County, near where St. George
now stands. He sent for me. I went to him, and he asked me to take him to
Cedar City by way of Fort Clara and Pinto settlements, as he was on business and must visit all the settlements. We started on our way up through the
cañon. We saw bands of Indians, and he (George A. Smith) remarked to me
that these Indians, with the advantage they had of the rocks, could use up a
large company of emigrants, or make it very hot for them. After pausing for
a short time he said to me, "Brother Lee, what do you think the brethren
would do if a company of emigrants should come down through here making threats? Don't you think they would pitch into them?" I replied that "they

certainly would." This seemed to please him, and he again said to me, "And you really think the brethren would pitch into them?" "I certainly do," was my reply, "and you had better instruct Colonel Dame and Haight to tend to it that the emigrants are permitted to pass if you want them to pass unmolested." He continued: "I asked Isaac (meaning Haight) the same question, and he answered me just as you do, and I expect the boys would pitch into them." I again said to him that he had better say to Governor Young that if he wants emigrant companies to pass without molestation that he must instruct Colonel Dame or Major Haight to that effect, for if they are not ordered otherwise, they will use them up by the help of the Indians.[10]

THE DECREE ISSUED NOT TO SELL ANY GRAIN TO THE EMIGRANTS.

He told the people at the Clara not to sell their grain to the emigrants nor to feed it to their animals, as they might expect a big fight the next Spring with the United States. President Young did not intend to let the troops into the Territory. He said, "We are going to stand up for our rights and will no longer be imposed upon by our enemies, and want every man to be on hand with his gun in good order and his powder dry," and instructed the people to part with nothing that would sustain life.

LEE'S INTERVIEW WITH PRESIDENT HAIGHT.

From the 1st to the 10th of September, 1857, a messenger came to me—his name was Sam Wood—and told me that President Isaac C. Haight wanted me to be at Cedar City that evening without fail. This was Saturday. He told me that a large company of emigrants had gone south. I then lived at Harmony, twenty miles south of Cedar City. I obeyed the summons. President Haight met me. It was near sundown. We spent the night in an open house on some blankets where we talked most all night. He told me that a company of emigrants had passed through some two days before, threatening the Mormons with destruction, and that one of them had said he had helped to kill old Joe Smith and his brother Hyram [sic]; that other members of the company of emigrants had helped drive the Mormons out of Missouri; that others had said they had come to help Johnston's army clean the Mormons out of Utah; that they had the halters ready to hang old Brigham and Heber, and would have them strung up before the snow flew; that one of the emigrants called one of his oxen (a pair a stags) "Brig." and the other "Heber," and that several of the emigrants had used all kinds of threats and profanity. John M. Higbee, the City Marshal, and [sic] informed them that it

---

[10]Compare with Bishop, ed., *Mormonism Unveiled*, 222–25. This much longer account of the conversation ends with Lee's conclusion that Brigham Young had sent Smith to southern Utah "to prepare the people for the work of exterminating Captain Fancher's train of emigrants." Some historians assert that Lee never accused Young of ordering the massacre, apparently in the belief that Bishop inserted this statement, but if Bishop were inventing spurious material, why not simply claim that Smith delivered Young's written order to Lee?

was a breach of the city ordinance to use profane language, whereupon one of them replied that he did not care a d—— for Mormon laws, or the Mormons either; that they had fought their way through the Indians and would do it through the d—— Mormons; and if their God, old Brigham, and his priests would not sell their provisions, by G—— they would take what they wanted any way they could get it; that thus raging, one of them let loose his long whip and killed two chickens, and threw them into his wagon; that the widow Evans said, "Gentlemen, those are my chickens; please don't kill them. I am a poor widow." That they ordered her to "shut up," or they would blow her —— brains out, etc.; that they had been raising trouble with all the settlements and Indians on their way; that we were threatened on the north by Johnston's army, and now our safety depended on prompt and immediate action; that a company of Indians had already gone south from Parowan and Cedar City to surprise the emigrants, who were then at the Mountain Meadows, and he wanted me to return home in the morning (Sunday) and send Carl Shurtz (Indian interpreter) from my home (Harmony) to raise the Indians south, at Harmony, Washington and Santa Clara, to join the Indians from the north and make the attack upon the emigrants at the Meadows. I said to him, "Would it not be well to hold a council of the brethren before making a move?" He replied that "every true Latter Day Saint that regarded their covenants knew well their duty, and that the company of emigrants had forfeited their lives by their acts," and that bishop P. K. Smith (Klingensmith) and Joel White had already gone by way of Pinto, to raise the Indians in that direction, and those that have gone from Parowan and here will make the attack, and may be repulsed. "We can't now delay for a council of the brethren. Return immediately and start Carl Shurtz; tell him that I ordered you to tell him to go, and I want you to try and get there before the attack is made, and make the plan for the Indians, and I will call a council to-day to talk the matter over and will send Nephi Johnson, the interpreter, to the Meadows as soon as he can be got, to help Carl Shurtz manage the Indians."

Lee Starts on His Mission.

I did just as I was ordered. The Indians from the north and about Harmony had already started for the Meadows before I reached home. Shurtz started immediately to do his part. I arrived at home in the night and remained till morning. I thought over the matter, and the more I thought the more my feelings revolted against such a horrid deed. Sleep had fled from me. I talked to my wife Rachel about it. She felt as I did about it, and advised me to let them do their own dirty work, and said if things did not go just to suit them, the blame would be laid on me. She never believed in blood atonement, and said it was from the devil, and that she would rather break such a covenant if she had to die for so doing than to live and be guilty of doing such an act. I

finally concluded that I would go; that I would start by daybreak in the morning and try to get there before an attack was made on the company, and use
my influence with the Indians to let them alone. I crossed the mountains by
a trail and reached the Meadows between nine and ten in the morning, the
distance from my place being about twenty-five miles.

THE EMIGRANTS ATTACKED.

But I was too late. The attack had been made just before daybreak in the
morning, and the Indians repulsed with one killed and two of the chiefs from
Cedar shot through the legs, breaking a leg for each of them.[11] The Indians
were in a terrible rage. I went to some of them that were in a ravine. They told
me to go to the main body or they would kill me for not coming before the
attack was made. While I was standing there I received a shot just above my
belt cutting through my clothes to the skin some six inches across. The Indians with whom I was talking lived with me at Harmony. I was Indian farmer.
They told me I was in danger and to get down into the ravine. I said that it
was impossible for me to do anything there, and I dare not venture to the camp
or to the emigrants without endangering myself. I mounted my horse and started south to meet Carl Shurtz. I traveled sixteen miles and stopped on the Megot-
sy to bait [feed] my animal, as there was good grass and water. I had rode it
over forty miles without eating or drinking. This is the place where Mr. Tobin
met his assassinators. About sunset I saw Shurtz and some ten or fifteen white
men, and about one hundred and fifty Indians. We camped. During the night
the Indians left for the Meadows. I reported to the men what had taken place.

They [the Paiutes] attacked the emigrants again about sunrise the next morning, which was Tuesday, and had one of their number killed and several wounded. I, with the white men, reached the Meadows about one o'clock P.M. On
the way we met a small band of Indians returning with some eighteen or twenty head of cattle. One of the Indians was wounded in the shoulder. They told
me that the Indians were encamped east of the emigrants at some springs.
On our arrival at the springs we found about two hundred Indians, among
whom were the two wounded chiefs, Moqueetus and Bill. The Indians were
in a high state of excitement; had killed many cattle and horses belonging to
the company. I counted sixty head near their encampment that they had killed
in revenge for the wounding of their men. By the assistance of Oscar Hamblin (brother of Jacob Hamblin) and Shurtz we succeeded in getting the Indians to desist from killing any more stock that night.

THE EMIGRANTS' CORRAL—LEE PLEADS WITH THE INDIANS.

The company of emigrants had corralled all their wagons but one for better defense. This corral was about one hundred yards above the springs. This

---

[11]This contradicts *Mormonism Unveiled*, in which Lee claimed the first attack was made on Tuesday morning. The attack took place on Monday.

they did to get away from the ravine south, the better to defend themselves. The attacks were made from the south ravine and from the rocks on the west. The attack was renewed that night by the Indians, in spite of all we could do to prevent it. When the attack commenced Oscar Hamblin, William Young and myself started to go to the Indians. When opposite the corral on the north, the bullets came around us like a shower of hail. We had two Indians with us to pilot us; they threw themselves flat on the ground to protect themselves from the bullets. I stood erect and asked my Father in Heaven to protect me from the missiles of death and enable me to reach the Indians. One ball passed through my hat and the hair of my head, and another through my shirt, grazing my arm near the shoulder. A most hideous yell of the Indians commenced. The cries and shrieks of the women and children so overcame me that I forgot my danger and rushed through the fire to the Indians, and pleaded with them in tears to desist. I told them that the Great Spirit would be angry with them for killing women and little children. They told me to leave or they would serve me the same way; that I was not their friend, but a friend to their enemies; that I was a squaw, and did not have the heart of a brave, and that I could not see bloodshed, without crying like a baby, and call me Cry-baby, and by that name I was known by all the Indians to this day. I owe my life on that occasion to Oscar Hamblin, who was a missionary with the Indians, and had much influence with the Santa Clara Indians. They were the ones that wanted to kill me. Hamblin shamed them and called them dogs and wolves for wanting to shed the blood of their father (myself), who had fed and clothed them.

A Temporary Truce.

We finally prevailed upon them to return to camp, where we would hold a council; that I would send for big captains to come and talk. We told them they had punished the emigrants enough, and may be they had killed nearly all of them. We told them that Bishop Dame and President Haight would come; and may be they would give them part of the cattle and let the company go with the teams. In this way we reconciled them to suspend hostilities for the present. The two that had been with Hamblin and myself the night before said they had seen two men on horseback come out of the emigrants' camp under full speed, and that they went toward Cedar City. Wednesday morning I asked a man—I think his name was Edwards—to go to Cedar City and say to President Haight, for God's sake, for my sake and for the sake of suffering humanity, to send out men to rescue that company. This day we all lay still, waiting [for] orders. Occasionally a few of the Indians withdrew, taking a few head of animals with them.

Lee Reconnoitres—The Wagon Fort.

About noon I crossed the valley north of the corral, thinking to examine their location from the west range. The company recognized me as a white man and sent two little boys about 4 years old to meet me. I hid from them, fearing the Indians, who discovered the children. I called the Indians, who wanted my gun or ammunition to kill them. I prevailed with them to let the children go back into camp, which they very soon did when they saw the Indians. I crept up behind some rock, on the west range, where I had a full view of the corral. In it they had dug a rifle-pit. The wheels of their wagons were chained together, and the only show for the Indians was to starve them out, or shoot them as they went for water. I lay there some two hours, and contemplated their situation, and wept like a child. When I returned to camp some six or eight men had come from Cedar City. Joel White, William C. Stewart and Elliot C. Weldon [Willden] were among the number, but they had no orders. They had come merely to see how things were. The Meadows are about fifty [thirty-six] miles from Cedar City. Thursday afternoon the messenger from Cedar City returned.[12] He said that President Haight had gone to Parowan to confer with Colonel Dame, and a company of men and orders would be sent to-morrow (Friday); that up to the time he left the council had come to no definite conclusion. During this time the Indians and men were engaged in broiling beef and making their hides up into lassoes. I had flattered myself that bloodshed was at an end. After the emigrants saw me cross the valley, they hoisted a white flag in the midst of their corral.

Arrival of Morman [sic] Reinforcements— The Decree of Extermination Goes Forth from the Mormon Council.

Friday afternoon four wagons drove up with armed men. When they saw the white flag in the corral they raised one also, but drove to the springs where we were and took refreshments, after which a council meeting was called of Presidents, Bishops, and other Church officers and members of the High Council, Societies, High Priests, etc. Major John M. Higbee presided as Chairman. Several of the dignitaries bowed in prayer—invoked the aid of the Holy Spirit to prepare their minds and guide them to do right and carry out the counsel of their leaders.

Higbee said that President J. [sic] C. Haight had been to Parowan to confer with Colonel Dame, and their counsel and orders were that "This emigrant camp must be used up." I replied, "Men, women and children?" "All," said he, "except such as are too young to tell tales, and if the Indians cannot do it without help, we must help them." I commenced pleading for the company, and I said though some of them have behaved badly, they have been pretty well chastised. My policy would be to draw off the Indians, let them have a portion of the loose cattle, and withdraw with them under promise

---

[12]Josiah Rogerson heard "from the lips of Bill Carter" that Dame "knew everything that went on at the Meadows every day before the finishing of that massacre." Carter told of carrying the messages back and forth. See Rogerson, "The Guilt of John D. Lee," LDS Archives.

that they would not molest the company any more; that the company would then have teams enough left to take them to California. I told them that this course could not bring them into trouble.

FATE OF THE EMIGRANT MESSENGERS.

Higbee said, "White men have interposed and the emigrants know it, and there lies the danger in letting them go." I said, "What white man interfered?" He replied that in the attack on Tuesday night two men broke out of the corral and started for Cedar City on horseback; that they were met at Richey's Spring by Stewart, Joel White and another man, whose name has passed from me. Stewart asked the two men their names when they met them at the spring, and being told in reply by one of the men that his name was Aden, and that the other man was a Dutchman from the emigrants' company, Stewart shoved a pistol to Aden's breast and killed him, saying, "Take that, d—n you." The other man, the Dutchman, wheeled to leave as Joel White fired and wounded him. I asked him how he knew the wounded Dutchman got back to the emigrants' camp. He said because he was tracked back, and they knew he was there. I again said that it was better to deliver the man to them and let them do anything they wished with him, and tell them that we did not approve of such things.

LEE REPROVED FOR TRYING TO DICTATE TO THE PRIESTHOOD.

Ira Allen, High Counselor, and Robert Wiley and others spoke, reproving me sharply for trying to dictate to the priesthood; that it would set at naught all authority; that he would not give the life of one of our brethren for a thousand such persons. "If we let them go," he continued, "they will raise h—l in California, and the result will be that our wives and children will have to be butchered and ourselves too, and they are no better to die than ours; and I am surprised to hear Brother Lee talk as he does, as he has always been considered one of the staunchest in the Church, now is the first to shirk from his duty." I said, "Brethren, the Lord must harden my heart before I can do such a thing." Allen said it is not wicked to obey counsel. At this juncture I withdrew—walked off some fifty paces and prostrated myself on the ground and wept in the bitterest anguish of my soul, and asked the Lord to avert the evil. While in that situation Counselor C. Hopkins, a near friend of mine, came to me and said; "Brother Lee, come get up and don't draw off from the priesthood. You ought not to do so. You are only endangering your own life by standing out. You can't help it; if this is wrong—the blame won't rest on you." I said, "Charley, this is the worst move this people ever made. I feel it." He said, "Come, go back, and let them have their way." I went back, weeping like a child, and took my place and tried to be silent, and was until Higbee said they (the emigrants) must be decoyed out through pretended friendship. I could no longer hold my peace, and said I, "Joseph Smith said that God hated a traitor, and so do I. Before I would be a traitor I would rather take ten men and go to that camp and tell them that they must die and how to defend themselves, and give them a show for their lives; that would be more honorable than to betray them like Judas." Here I got other reproof, and was ordered to hold my peace.

The Flag of Truce Decoy.

The plan agreed upon there was to meet them with a flag of truce, tell them that the Indians were determined on their destruction; that we dare not oppose the Indians, for we were at their mercy; that the best we could do for them (the emigrants) was to get them and what few traps we could take in the wagons, to lay their arms in the bottom of the wagon and cover them up with bed clothes and start for the settlement as soon as possible, and to trust themselves in our hands. The small children and wounded were to go with the two wagons, the women to follow the wagons and the men next, the troops to stand in readiness on the east side of the road ready to receive them. Shurtz and Nephi Johnson were to conceal the Indians in the brush and rocks till the company was strung out on the road to a certain point, and at the watchword, "Halt! do your duty," each man was to cover his victim and fire. Johnson and Shurtz were to rally the Indians and rush upon and dispatch the women and larger children.

Celestial Rewards for the Faithful.

It was further told the men that President Haight said, if we were united in carrying out the instructions, we would all receive a "celestial reward." I said I was willing to put up with a less reward, if I could be excused. "How can you do this without shedding innocent blood?" Here I got another lampooning for my stubbornness and disobedience to the priesthood. I was told that there was not a drop of innocent blood in the whole company of emigrants; also referred to the Gentile nation who refused the children of Israel passage through their country when Moses led them out of Egypt—that the Lord held that crime against them, and when Israel waxed strong the Lord commanded Joshua to slay the whole nation, men, women and children. "Have not these people done worse than that to us? Have they not threatened to murder our leaders and Prophet, and have they not boasted of murdering our Patriarchs and Prophets, Joseph and Hyrum? Now talk about shedding innocent blood." They said I was a good, liberal, free hearted man, but too much of this sympathy would be always in the way; that every man now had to show his colors; that it was not safe to have a Judas in camp. Then it was proposed that every man express himself; that if there was a man who would not keep a close[d] mouth they wanted to know it then. This gave me to understand what I might expect if I continued to oppose. Major Higbee said, "Brother Lee is right. Let him take an expression of the people." I knew I dare not refuse, so I had every man speak and express himself. All said they were willing to carry out the counsel of their leaders; that the leaders had the Spirit of God and knew better what was right then they did.

Lee Reluctantly Gives His Consent.

They then wanted to know my feelings. I replied, "I have already expressed them." Every eye was upon me, as I paused; but, said I, "You can do as you please, I will not oppose you any longer." "Will you keep a close mouth?" was the question. "I will try," was my answer. I will here say that the fear of offending Brigham Young and George A. Smith had saved my life. I was near being "blood-atoned" in Parowan, under J. C. L. Smith, in 1854, but of this I have spoken in my autobiography.

Saturday morning all was ready, and every man assigned to his post of duty. During the night, or rather just before daylight, Johnson and Shurtz ambushed [hid] their Indians, the better to deceive the emigrants. About 11 o'clock A.M. the troops, under Major Higbee, took their position on the road. The white flag was still kept up in the corral. Higbee called William Bateman out of the ranks to take a flag of truce to the corral. He was met about half way with another white flag from the emigrants' camp. They had a talk.

The Mormon Treachery.

The emigrant was told we had come to rescue them if they were willing to trust us. Both men with flags returned to their respective places and reported, and were to meet again and bring word. Higbee called me out to go and inform them [about] the conditions, and, if accepted, Dan McFarland, brother to John McFarland, lawyer, who acted as aide-de-camp, would bring back word, and then two wagons would be sent for the firearms, children, clothing, etc. I obeyed, and the terms proposed were accepted, but not without distrust. I had as little to say as possible—in fact, my tongue refused to perform its office. I sat down on the ground in the corral, near where some young men were engaged in paying the last respects to some person who had just died of a wound. A large, fleshy old lady came to me twice and talked while I sat there. She related their troubles—said that seven of their number were killed and forty-six wounded on the first attack; that several had died since. She asked me if I was an Indian Agent. I said, "In one sense I am, as [the] Government has appointed me Farmer to the Indians." I told her this to satisfy her. I heard afterward that the same question was asked and answered in the same manner by McFarland, who had been sent by Higbee to the corral, to "hurry me up for fear that the Indians would come back and be upon them."

The Emigrants Abandon Their Stronghold.

When all was ready, Samuel McMurdy, Counsellor to Bishop P. K. Smith (Klingensmith), drove out on the lead. His wagon had the seventeen children, clothing and arms. Samuel Knight drove the other team, with five wounded men and one boy about 15 years old. I walked behind the front wagon to direct the course, and to shun being in the heat of the slaughter—but this I kept to myself. When we got turned fairly to the east I motioned to McMurdy to steer north, across the valley. I at the same time told the women, who were next to the wagon, to follow the road up to the troops, which they did. Instead of my saying to McMurdy not to drive so fast—as he swore on my trial—I said to the contrary, to drive on, as my aim was to get out of sight before the firing commenced, which we did.

The Massacre—Revolting Scenes.

We were about half a mile ahead of the company when we heard the first firing. We had drove over a ridge of rolling ground, and down on a low flat. The firing was simultaneous along the whole line. The moment the firing commenced McMurdy halted and tied his lines across the rod of his wagon-box, stepped down coolly with a double-barrelled shotgun, walked back to Knight's wagon—who had the wounded men, and was about twenty feet in the rear. As he raised his piece he said, "Lord, my God, receive their spirits, for it is for the Kingdom of Heaven's sake that we do this," fired and killed two men. Samuel Knight had a muzzle-loaded rifle, and he shot and killed the three men, then struck the wounded boy on the head, who fell dead. In the meantime I drew a five shooter from my belt, which accidentally went off, cutting across McMurdy's buckskin pants in front, below the crotch. McMurdy said, "Brother Lee, you are excited; take things cool; you was near killing me. Look where the ball cut," pointing to the place on his pants.

Children Snatched from the Jaws of Death.

At this moment I heard the scream of a child. I looked up and saw an Indian have a little boy by the hair of his head, dragging him out of the hind end of the wagon, with a knife in his hand getting ready to cut his throat. I sprang for the Indian, with my revolver in hand and shouted to the top of my voice, "Arick, ooma, cot too sooet" (stop, you fool). The child was terror stricken. His chin was bleeding. I supposed it was the cut of a knife, but afterward learned that it was done on the wagon box as the Indian yanked the boy down by the hair of the head. I had no sooner rescued this child, than another Indian seized a little girl by the hair. I rescued her as soon as I could speak; I told the Indians that they must not hurt the children—that I would die before they should be hurt; that we would buy the children of them. Before this time the Indians had rushed up around the wagon in quest of blood, and dispatched the two runaway wounded men.

Lee's Demoralization—The Dead.

In justice to my statement, I would say that if my shooter had not prematurely exploded I would have had a hand in dispatching the five wounded. I had lost control of myself, and scarce knew what I was about. I saw an Indian pursue a little girl, who was fleeing. He caught her about one hundred feet from the wagon, and plunged his knife through her. I said to McMurdy that he had better drive the children to Hamblin's ranch and give them some nourishment, while I would go down and get my horse at the camp. Passing along the road I saw the dead strung along the distance of about half a mile. The women and children were killed by the Indians. I saw Shurtz with the Indians, and no other white man with them. When I came to the men they lay about a rod apart. Here I came up with Higbee, Bishop Smith and the rest of the company. As I came up, Higbee said to me, let us search these persons for valuables, and asked me to assist him. Gave me a hat to hold. Several men were already engaged in searching the bodies. I replied that I was unwell, and wanted to get upon my horse and go to the ranch and nurse myself. My request was granted.

Quarrel Between Dame and Haight.

Reaching Hamblin's ranch—being heart-sick and worn out—I lay down on my saddle blanket and slept, and knew but little of what passed through the night. About daybreak in the morning I heard the voices of Colonel Dame and Isaac C. Haight. I heard some very angry words pass between them, which drew my attention. Dame said that he would have to report the destruction of the emigrant camp and the company. Haight said, "How—as an Indian massacre?" Dame said he did not know so well about that. This reply seemed to irritate Haight, who spoke quite loudly saying, "How the h—l can you report it any other way without implicating yourself?" At this Dame lowered his voice almost to a whisper, I could not understand what he said, and the conversation stopped.

The Survivors of the Massacre.

I got up, saw the children, and among the others the boy who was pulled by the hair of his head out of the wagon by the Indian—and saved by me. That boy I took home and kept home until Dr. Forney, Government Agent, came to gather up the children and take them East. He took the boy with the others. That boy's name was Wm. Fancher. His father was Captain of the train. He was taken East and adopted by a man in Nebraska, named Richard Sloan. He remained East several years, and then returned to Utah, and is now a convict in the Utah penitentiary, having been convicted the past year for the crime of highway robbery. He is now known by the name of "Idaho Bill," but his true name is William Fancher.[13]

His little sister was also taken east, and is now the wife of a man working for the Union Pacific Railroad Company, near Green River. The boy (now man) has yet got the scar on his chin caused by the cut on the wagon-box, and those who are curious enough to examine will find a large scar on the ball of his left foot, caused by a deep cut made with an axe while he was with me.

[13]Richard Sloan had somehow conned Lee into believing that he was Lee's old ward, "Charley" Fancher. Christopher ("Kit") Carson Fancher actually died unmarried in 1873. See Fancher, *The Fancher Family*, 96.

BURYING THE SLAIN—CONDITION OF THE BODIES.

I got breakfast that morning, then all hands returned to the scene of the slaughter to bury the dead. The bodies were all in a nude state. The Indians through the night had stripped them of every vestige of clothing. Many of the parties were laughing and talking as they carried the bodies to the ravine for burial. They were just covered over a little, but did not long remain so, for the wolves dug them up, and, after eating the flesh from them, the bones laid upon the ground until buried some time after by a government military officer.

DAME TERROR-STRICKEN.

At the time of burying the bodies Dame and Haight got into another quarrel. Dame seemed terror-stricken, and again said he would have to publish it. They were about two paces from me. Dame spoke low, as if careful to avoid being heard. Haight spoke loud, and said: "You know that you counselled it, and ordered me to have them used up." Dame said: "I did not think that there were so many women and children. I thought they were nearly all killed by the Indians." Haight said: "It is too late in the day for you to back water. You know you ordered and counselled it, and now you want to back out." Dame said: "Have you the papers for that?" or, "Show the papers for that." This enraged Haight to the highest pitch, and Dame walked off. Haight said: "You throw the blame of this thing on me and I will be revenged on you, if I have to meet you in hell to get it." From this place we rode to the wagons. We found them stripped of their covers and every particle of clothing, even the feather beds had been ripped open and the contents turned out upon the ground, looking for plunder. I crossed the mountains by Indian trail—taking my little Indian boy [Clem] with me on my horse. The gathering up of the property and cattle was left in the charge of Bishop P. K. Smith. The testimony of Smith in regard to the property and the disposition that was made of it was very nearly correct. I must not forget to state that after the attack a messenger by the name of James Haslem [sic] was sent with a dispatch to President Brigham Young, asking his advice about interfering with the company, but he did not return in time. This I had no knowledge of until the massacre was committed.

LEE'S REPORT OF THE MASSACRE TO BRIGHAM YOUNG.

Some two weeks after the deed was done, Isaac C. Haight sent me to report to Governor Young in person. I asked him why he did not send a written report. He replied that I could tell him more satisfactorily than he could write, and if I would stand up and shoulder as much of the responsibility as I could conveniently, that it would be a feather in my cap some day, and that I would get a celestial salvation, but the man that shrunk from it now would go to hell. I went and did as I was commanded. Brigham asked me if Isaac C. Haight

Highwayman "Idaho Bill," Richard Sloan (*left*) met Lee in jail at Beaver, Utah, and convinced Lee that he was "the identical Chas. Fancher; the little boy that I saved from the Indians at Mountain Meadows." Sloan bore a passing resemblance to the real Christopher ("Kit") Carson Fancher (*right*). *Courtesy of the Will Bagley Collection.*

had written a letter to him. I replied not by me; but I said he wished me to report in person. "All right," said Brigham. "Were you an eye-witness?" "To the most of it," was my reply. Then I proceeded, and gave him a full history of all, except that of my opposition. That, I left out entirely. I told him of the killing of the women and children, and the betraying of the company; that, I told him, I was opposed to; but I did not say to him to what extent I was opposed to it, only that I was opposed to shedding innocent blood. "Why," said he, "you differ from Isaac (Haight), for he said there was not a drop of innocent blood in the whole company."

When I was through he said that it was awful; that he cared nothing about the men, but the women and children was what troubled him. I said, "President Young, you should either release men from their obligation, or sustain them when they do what they have entered into the most sacred obligation to do." He replied, "I will think over the matter and make it a subject of prayer, and you may come back in the morning and see me." I did so. He said, "John, I feel first rate. I asked the Lord if it was all right for the deed to be done, to take away the vision of the deed from my mind, and the Lord did so, and I feel first rate. It is all right. The only fear I have is of traitors." He told me never to lisp it to any mortal being, not even to Brother Heber. President Young has always treated me with the friendship of a father since, and has sealed several women to me since, and has made my home his home when in that part of the Territory—until danger has threatened him. This is a true statement according to my best recollection.

(Signed:) John D. Lee

Lee's Autobiography and Its Startling Revelations.

This statement I have made for publication after my death, and have agreed with a friend [William Bishop] to have the same, with very many facts pertaining to other matters connected with the crimes of the Mormon people under the leadership of the priesthood, from a period before the butchery of the Nauvoo to the present time, published for the benefit of my family, and that the world may know the black deeds that have marked the way of the Saints from the organization of the Church of Jesus Christ of Latter Day Saints, to the period when a weak and too pliable tool lays down his pen to face the executioners' guns for a deed which he is not more guilty than others who to-day are wearing the garments of the priesthood and living upon the "tithing" of a deluded and priest-ridden people. My autobiography, if published, will open the eyes of the world to the monstrous deeds of the leaders of the Mormon people, and will also place in the hands of the attorney for the Government the particulars of some of the most blood-curdling crimes that have been committed in Utah, which, if properly followed up, will bring many down from their high place in the Church to face offended justice upon the gallows. So mote it be.

As he noted, Lee gave a more detailed life history and massacre account to William Bishop, "a little man with a Big Heart," which Bishop subsequently edited and published.[14] The book became an immediate bestseller, and its story of the murders served as a basic source for all subsequent histories. Like Lee's other offerings, his confessions are a cunning stew of truth and fantasy, designed to protect some and blame others. Lee's argument that the Paiutes forced the Mormons to act, an especially clever piece of blame shifting, was happily repeated by generations of apologists. In the end, Lee kept the oath he had sworn on that bloody field and took the whole truth to the grave. Of all the ironies in the career of this highly capable and complex figure, perhaps the greatest is inscribed on his headstone: "Know the Truth, and the Truth shall make you free."

[14] J. D. Lee to Rachel Lee, 12 October 1876, Huntington Library.

A LUCRATIVE PRACTICE AMONG THE SAINTS

A year after Lee's execution, former U.S. attorney Sumner Howard touched off a new controversy by issuing a statement that John D. Lee had never confessed at all. If he had stopped there, the admission, contrary to all the headlines and book titles, was all too true. But he went beyond that and challenged the authenticity of the confession published by Lee's defense attorney, which included Lee's indictment of Brigham Young and other Mormon leaders as accessories after the fact to murder. In so doing, Howard accused Bishop of falsifying portions of Lee's actual "last confession" to point the finger at Young. The deal-making second trial prosecutor had come under fire himself for allegedly deleting any accusations against Young before he had Lee's earlier confession published right after the execution. If any altering was done either to blame Young or clear him, Howard was the likely culprit, for reasons set forth by Nevada's *Eureka Daily Republican.*

"MOUNTAIN MEADOWS MASSACRE:
THE ACKNOWLEDGEMENT OF ITS FORGERY BY MR. HOWARD—
WHY HE WANTS TO DISCREDIT IT—PROOF OF ITS AUTHENTICITY
IN THE POSSESSION OF MR. BISHOP, ETC., ETC.,"
EUREKA DAILY REPUBLICAN, EUREKA, NEVADA, 8 MARCH 1878, 3/3.

The telegram from New York, March 6th, having been published all over the country, making known to the world a statement, made by Sumner D. Howard, late United States Attorney for the District of Utah (not Marshal as stated), to the effect that John D. Lee, the Mountain Meadows murderer, never made a confession at all, and that he and Marshal Nelson tried in vain to get one, we yesterday waited on W. W. Bishop, of Lee's counsel, and the publisher of the "Life and Confession of John D. Lee," to ascertain what evidence he had of the authenticity of the manuscript from which the book was published. We found Mr. Bishop ready to converse upon the subject and to furnish all the evidence desired in order to brand the assertion of Mr. Howard as willfully false. Not only that, but the sketch of Mr. Howard's proceedings in Utah, given by Mr. Bishop, was such as to make the reason plain why that gentleman, now a resident of Salt Lake, desires to throw discredit on the published confession of Mr. Lee.

Mr. Howard went from Michigan to Utah to accept the office of United States District Attorney with the evident desire of making capital and not money out of the position, since it was one which no attorney of respectable practice and average ability would accept. In this desire he has been successful in one sense, for he has resigned his office and stepped into a lucrative practice among the Saints. In other words, from being a prosecutor of that people for their offenses, he has become their champion. No one will question his personal right to do so, but the fact that there were many cases which it rightfully devolved upon him to prosecute as District Attorney, and that he refrained from doing so and then went over to the enemy, shows that he must have had some powerful inducements. It becomes necessary for him in his altered position to do all he can to protect the members the One-eye-drily [*sic*] Association.[15] In order to do this he must throw discredit on Lee's confession.

But to the proof produced by Mr. Bishop of the genuineness of the manuscript from which the book was published. Mr. Bishop, in the first place, produces the hand-writing of Mr. Lee. This is not a difficult task, since he has not only numerous letters written to him as counsel, but a mass of manuscript, containing at least 1000 pages, which is unquestionably genuine. These are amply sufficient for the desired purpose, since they go back as far as 1846 and embrace a diary of his, the first entry being "Omaha Nation, November 21, 1846." This diary of Lee's contains detailed account of each day's transactions, journeyings, church meetings, teachings, etc., and is the only record remaining of all these things. This could not have been "composed" by Howard et al. Then Mr. Bishop has Lee's diary of the trial, etc., very voluminous.

The handwriting of Mr. Lee is peculiar, very difficult of imitation and easily recognizable. It corresponds throughout with the book manuscript. This manuscript consists of 335 pages of closely written legal cap, and on the margin of one of the rolls are traced the last words John D. Lee ever penned on earth. They comprise a short sentence, directed to the Marshal, and read as follows: "Please deliver to W. W. Bishop, Pioche, Nevada." The covers bear the direction and proof that the manuscript was sent by express as directed. The manuscript is unquestionably genuine, and just as it came from Lee's hands. Moreover, the orthography is as peculiar as the chirography.

It is a little singular, if, as is claimed by Howard, the confession was composed by himself, Marshal Nelson and a newspaper reporter, that it should bear the peculiar marks of identity which characterize the manuscripts of Lee, written 30 years before. If Howard's story is true, it shows these gentlemen to be as expert in forgery as in the manufacture of confessions.

The fact is, that the manuscript is genuine and that every word of it was penned by John D. Lee.

It is true, as telegraphed, that Mr. Howard did attempt to get a confession out of Lee and failed. The rough draft of what was to have been a confession, under which Lee was to have been pardoned, was made first by Mr. Bishop at a time when an agreement with Mr. Carey, the former District Attorney, to that effect was made. For six days Mr. Lee went to the office of Mr. Bishop and made his statements which were taken down by Mr. Bishop, and subse-

<hr/>

[15]This apparent reference to the LDS church's use of the "all-seeing eye" on many of its buildings may also be a backhanded salute to an obscene folksong, "One-Eyed Riley," which the U.S. Army's band played as it marched passed Brigham Young's Lion House in June 1858.

quently written out. This first draft was sent to Lee, Mr. Bishop keeping the copy written out, which he still has in his possession. This rough draft was the one which Howard undertook to publish to prevent the later publication by Mr. Bishop. It was all ready in type in the office of the Sacramento Record-Union and other papers on the coast when the day of execution came.

The fact is that Mr. Howard now seeks to discredit the real confession of Lee, so as to excuse himself for not prosecuting other offenders while he was in office in Utah. Lee, as is well known, was convicted under an agreement to that effect with the Mormon leaders. Mr. Howard's present Mormon practice probably presents another feature of that bargain, under which, also, all other participants with Lee must be allowed to go free.

Mr. Bishop has also many papers written by Mr. Lee after the confession and forwarded through the Marshal. These contain subsequent recollections, on the part of Mr. Lee, of occurrences which he had forgotten at the time of writing the large manuscript and which he wanted inserted. These all bear the same proofs of authenticity as the main manuscript itself. And even after the last of the manuscript was written Mr. Howard endeavored to keep Marshal Nelson from sending it to Mr. Bishop, as per agreement, but failed, Marshal Nelson insisting upon performing the trust reposed by Lee in him.

If Mr. Howard and others forged the confession, as he asserts, perhaps he would like to claim the authorship to the diaries referred to, the miracles claimed therein, the dogeral rhymes of still other manuscripts which were written by Lee, and have never been published, and which Mr. Bishop has in his possession.

We have other things in relation to this Mr. Howard and his actions in Utah which we shall make public soon.

BRIGHAM YOUNG: I NEVER KNEW THE REAL FACTS

Two days before the execution, James Gordon Bennett, editor of the *New York Herald*, telegraphed Brigham Young at St. George to warn that his paper was about to print Lee's confession and his claim that he was simply carrying out the orders of church authorities. Young wired back that the charge was "utterly false," but his denial did little to placate the national press. *Deseret News* editor David O. Calder telegraphed John W. Young on 31 March: "The only thing that will satisfy the country and the Press is a statement over the signature of your father giving the truth of his subsequent knowledge of the Mountain Meadow matter." Even Calder asked, "What is the story of this tragedy?"[16]

[16]Calder to J. W. Young, 31 March 1877, Telegrams 1877, LDS Archives.

That same day, Brigham Young telegraphed an odd appeal to President Hayes asking him to appoint a commission to investigate the massacre and punish the offenders. His wire was as much a challenge as it was a serious proposal, since federal officials in the territory were skeptical that anything would ever come of such an investigation. If nothing else, the Lee trials made it clear to the rest of the nation that the Poland Act, however well intended, had failed to break theocratic control of Utah's judicial system.

BRIGHAM YOUNG, TELEGRAM TO RUTHERFORD B. HAYES,
31 MARCH 1877, LDS ARCHIVES.

Petition—To His Excellency Rutherford B. Hayes President of the United States
I see by the New York Herald & press of the country generally that John D Lee who has recently been executed for his participation in the crime known as the Mountain Meadow Massacre has made a statement which if true directly implicates me as accessory after the fact by implication makes me liable as an accessory before the fact. I have before now publicaly [stated] that I was & had been at all times ready to render [any] aid I could to bring to justice the perpetrators of that great crime & especially did I on more than one occasion proffer my services & influence to the late Governor Cumming my successor in office to aid in obtaining the evidence necessary to furnish the guilty ones. These proffered services whatever they may have been worth have never been accepted. In view of the magnitude of the offense I now most respectfully ask you as the chief magistrate of the great nation in justice to the people who inhabited this Territory at that period if you have the power & if not to call the attention of Congress to the matter when it meets in June to appoint a commission fully authorized to investigate that inhuman slaughter & with jurisdiction to try & punish the offenders thereof.

With demand for answers unabated, Young at last relented and spent the last evening in April fielding questions from a *New York Herald* correspondent, probably E. N. Fuller. Also taking part were Young's second counselor, Daniel H. Wells, Apostle George Q. Cannon, and John W. Young. The three offered a rich assortment of evasions, misleading statements, and falsehoods. Among other things, Young said that blood atonement was equivalent to capital punishment, which was not how it was described in his sermons on the topic; claimed the emigrants first traveled north to Bear River and then laid over in Utah for six weeks before heading south, which was physically impossible; and took the opportunity to malign the victims. Wells said the emigrants were not even in the territory when George A. Smith headed south on 3 August.

And John W. Young stated he was in his father's office when Lee reported the massacre. Apostle Smith had died twenty months before, and Young would go to his reward only four months after. The church's official organ printed the interview without comment. The *Herald*'s correspondent began the article with a description of the national furor related to Lee's confession, particularly his statements about the role of George A. Smith in the crime.

"INTERVIEW WITH BRIGHAM YOUNG,"
DESERET EVENING NEWS, 12 MAY 1877,
REPRINTED FROM *NEW YORK HERALD*, 6 MAY 1877.

CEDAR CITY, APRIL 30, 1877

... *Brigham Young*—George A. Smith visited this whole southern region irregularly, and held meetings, as we are doing now. In fact, he was the founder of Parowan—the first settlement to the north—on his way home northward. This was the year of the massacre. They met the company of the Arkansas emigrants not far from Fillmore. It was at Meadow Creek, I believe. Some of the emigrant company came up to him and passed some remarks, inquiring about the route, &c. Brother George A. Smith gave them all the desired information. Some of the cattle belonging to the company died, which they poisoned, and from the effects of the poisoned meat some of the Indians who found and consumed the carcasses died. These carcasses also poisoned some springs. This raised the wrath of the Indians.

Here President Young turned to Daniel H. Wells, his second counselor, saying, "Brother Wells, do you remember if Brother George A. Smith was down here for anything special?"

Daniel H. Wells—No sir, he was not. He was preaching in the settlements between here and Salt Lake, as we usually do. He had part of his family living in Parowan, having built a residence there, and his being here was only one of several visits.

Brigham Young—Brother George A. Smith's testimony in regard to this has been published to the world, and I believe it to be true. It can be found among Howard's reports. George A. Smith knew nothing more about that company or their being interfered with than you did in New York. Had he possessed that knowledge I would certainly have heard of it, for he would have told me of it. He knew nothing about the company until he met them on his return north, near Fillmore. There was at that time no telegraph line running through here; no mails were carried to Utah. The United States government had stopped the mails, and we had no mails running from settlement to settlement as we have now.

Correspondent—The conviction is settled in the east, especially by the testimony in the Lee trial, that there was some powerful direction of the part taken by the whites in the massacre. This conviction is strengthened by the statements in Judge Cradelbaugh's [*sic*] speech.

Brigham Young—There is no doubt that the affair was directed by John D. Lee, and evidently he was a white man.

Correspondent—It appears incredible to outsiders that Lee would have undertaken a task like that on his own responsibility; the responsibility attaches, in their opinion, to the Mormon Church, even to its highest individual officers.

Brigham Young—My disposition is such that had I known anything about it I would have gone to that camp and fought the Indians and white men who took part in the perpetration of the massacre to the death, rather than such a deed should have been committed.

John W. Young—John D. Lee, in his testimony, says he informed President Young of the affair when he visited Salt Lake City. I happened to be present when he came in father's office, and I was present during the interview.[17] He commenced to relate the circumstances of the Indians killing the emigrants, but did not intimate a single word about the whites taking part in the killing. When he commenced to speak of the manner of the deed father stopped him, saying that the rumor which had already reached him was so horrifying that he could not bear to hear a recital of it.

Brigham Young—I never knew the real facts of the affair until within the last few years. I myself proposed to Governor Cumming, who came here soon after the massacre, to render him and Judge Cradlebaugh every assistance in hunting up the perpetrators and bringing them to justice, and if Mr. Cradlebaugh knows anything about this affair he must know that to be true.[18] That proposition was made in the spring of 1858.

Daniel H. Wells—There were plenty of witnesses to that, for I heard him make it in public.

Correspondent—What of your own experience as Governor and ex-officio Indian Agent at the time?

Brigham Young—Governor Cumming took it away from me. This point was too difficult to reach from Salt Lake, and besides, according to the rumors that reached us, the people thought themselves that they would do well if they escaped the vengeance of the United States troops. The burden of these rumors was that the Mormons were to be massacred.

---

[17]John W. Young would have been two days shy of his thirteenth birthday when Lee visited his father on 29 September 1857.

[18]As noted, Cradlebaugh was already dead. Shortly before Cumming left office, Charles Wandell wrote, Cumming told Brigham Young "to your face, and in your own office, that you had purposely lied to and deceived him" about arresting the Mountain Meadows murderers. See Argus, *Daily Corinne Reporter*, 7 October 1871, 2/3. An "old friend" claimed that Cumming complained Young broke his promise to "get out the whole truth" and never made an effort to track down the murderers. "God Almighty couldn't convict the butchers unless Brigham Young was willing," Cumming reportedly said. "Brigham Young deceived me." See "An Interview with Alfred Cumming," *Salt Lake Tribune*, 1 November 1876, 4/4.

Correspondent—To what do you ascribe the massacre?

Brigham Young—If you were to inquire of the people who live hereabouts, and lived in the country at the time, you would find, if it should be according to what I have heard, that some of the Arkansas company boasted that they had the promise from the United States that the Mormons were to be used up by the troops, and that they had boasted, too, of having helped to kill Hyrum and Joseph Smith and the Mormons in Missouri, and that they never meant to leave the Territory until similar scenes were enacted here. This, if true, may have embittered the feelings of those who took part in the massacre, and the probabilities are that Lee and his *confreres* took advantage of these facts and the disturbed state of the country to accomplish their desires for plunder, which under other circumstances would not have been gratified.

Correspondent—Have you an opinion of Klingensmith's testimony?

Brigham Young—I do not know anything about it.

Correspondent—How was it that Lee was at last, and not at first, convicted by a Mormon jury?

Brigham Young—The supposition is that there was not evidence enough against him at the first, that there was sufficient evidence against him at the last trial, and that the people of Utah could not obtain justice with any other jury.

Correspondent—Considering that your people believe they get their inspiration through you, do they not consider themselves responsible to you for their acts? What excuses them from crime?

Brigham Young—What causes men to steal or commit any sin? Do I prompt them? No; but the devil and his agents do. All evil doing is contrary to our covenants and obligations to God, and to one another as members of his Church.

Correspondent—Do you believe in blood atonement?

Brigham Young—I do, and I believe that Lee has not half atoned for his great crime. The Saviour [*sic*] died for all the sins of the world by shedding his blood, and then I believe that he who sheds the blood of man wilfully [*sic*], by man shall his blood be shed. In other words capital punishment for offenses deserving death, according to the laws of the land. And we believe that the execution should be done by the shedding of blood instead of by hanging. If the murderers of Joseph Smith were to come to me now, giving themselves up, I would not feel justified in taking their lives, but I would feel justified in having them taken to Illinois and there tried for murder.

Correspondent—Returning to the Mountain Meadow massacre, you are satisfied that John D. Lee could not have received previous intimation from the north as to what might be done in the case of the Arkansas company who were coming down from Salt Lake?

Brigham Young—None that I have any knowledge of, and certainly none from me.

Correspondent—You did not give any direction whatever as to the disposition of the emigrants' effects?

Brigham Young—I knew no more about it than you, nor do I to-day. I have heard that they have been made use of, which I suppose is correct. Klingensmith, who was a Mormon and an acting bishop, (I suppose) shared in the spoils, and because he held such a position, it is believed that the Church used it.

Correspondent—Was he the Church?

Brigham Young—No, he was only a poor miserable sinner.

Correspondent—In this southern country do the Bishops exercise the functions of the Justice of the Peace?

Brigham Young—I do not know that any of them do; and if any do it is not because they are bishops, but because they are elected justices according to the laws of the land.

Correspondent—The Mountain Meadows massacre was so unique that many curious questions are now asked in regard to it—for instance, why were the Indians angry against the Arkansas emigrants only? Other emigrant parties were passing through the country unmolested.

Brigham Young—As I understand it, for poisoning the water and poisoning dead cattle, which some of the Indians afterwards ate of and died. I would, however, refer you to the people of Crow [Corn] and Meadow creeks, who lived there at the time.[19]

Correspondent—Is it true that George A. Smith advised the people not to sell their grain?

Brigham Young—We had been scarce of breadstuffs, and the nature of his counsel was not to use their grain for feeding animals, neither to sell it to emigrants for that purpose, but no such word was ever uttered by him not to sell it for breadstuff. We have always made a practice of selling wheat and flour to the emigrants ever since we came here. And I will say that I am at the defiance of the world to prove that the heads of the church had anything to do with the Mountain Meadows massacre.

Correspondent—With regard to Haight and Higbee. Have you anything to say as to their reasons for getting out of the country?

Brigham Young—No sir. I presume, however, that they are trying to evade the law.

Correspondent—You do not consider yourself in the least degree responsible for them?

Brigham Young—No sir. Not any more than Mr. Beecher or any man of your city is.[20]

---

[19]Indian interpreter Nephi Johnson testified at Lee's second trial that no Pahvant Indians from Corn Creek took part in the massacre.

[20]As pastor of Plymouth Church in Brooklyn and editor of the *Christian Union*, Henry Ward Beecher (1813–87) was perhaps the most prominent Protestant preacher of his time.

Correspondent—It is understood in the East that the Mormon Church is a structure far more closely cemented than this would imply—an exclusive organization, standing in the midst of the continent, governed from the head downward by a system which renders leaders particularly responsible for the people over whom they preside?

Brigham Young—If the people over whom I preside do as I tell them to do there never would be such occurrences. But if a member of the Church lies, cheats, steals, or kills his neighbor, Brigham Young is not responsible for his evil acts any more than, if a Catholic were to kill, the Pope of Rome would be responsible for his crime. I am responsible only for the doctrines that I teach; but I cannot make people do right unless they choose to. I am responsible for no man's acts save my own.

Young Person (in shadow)—Then under no circumstances does the power of the President of the Church of the Latter-day Saints extend so far that men's lives are at its mercy. For example, were you to-day to say, "Let such a person be killed," would the wish be in any instance complied with?

Brigham Young—If I were to say, "Kill this man," I myself would be a murderer; or to say, "Take such a person's money," I would be a highwayman.

Correspondent—Yet, is it possible that such a thing could be?

Brigham Young—It never has been tried.

Correspondent—I want to find out what is the power of the Mormon Church.

Brigham Young—The Church has no power to do wrong with impunity any more than any single individual.

Correspondent—Yet we know, do we not Mr. President, that such power has been exercised in the world's history?

Brigham Young—You ask a question that does not apply to the Church of Jesus Christ of Latter-day Saints.

Daniel H. Wells—Judge Brocchus once said that if Brigham Young "had crooked his little finger, &c., he (the Judge) would have been torn to atoms;" but all there was to that was, President Young did not crook his finger.[21]

Correspondent (to Brigham Young)—What of the alleged order of Danites?

Brigham Young—That is all folly.

Correspondent—Then, as to the extent of the temporal power of the Church?

Brigham Young—It extends only as far as the membership is concerned. I may, however, advise a man how to build or improve his garden or field, and if he chooses to he may either receive it or reject it without involving his fellowship.

---

[21]Perry E. Brocchus of Alabama, one of Utah Territory's first district judges, almost caused a riot in 1851 when he appeared to impugn the patriotism of a large congregation at Great Salt Lake City. Later he told President Fillmore that Brigham Young said "that if he had crooked his finger, we would have been torn to pieces." See Fillmore, *Condition of affairs in the Territory of Utah*, House Doc. 25, Serial 640, 15.

Correspondent—Does not the temporal government of the Church, in extreme cases, assume the functions of courts?

Brigham Young—We have what we call bishops' courts, which amount to referees in ordinary cases of disagreement between members or immoral conduct. From these courts cases may be appealed to our High Counsel, which consists of a president, two councillors [*sic*] and twelve members. Their power extends no further than membership in the Church is concerned.

Correspondent—How far does the authority of the Church go in cases of apostasy?

Brigham Young—We have nothing to do with them; we let them seriously alone. They say the Church authorities injure them. They lie. We have no dealings at all with such men, for their acts prove their unworthiness of membership in our Church.

Correspondent—How do you protect your faith from outside influences?

Brigham Young—We are different from all other Christian sects. We are believers in the Bible, as well as all the revelations the Lord has given to the children of men, as contained in the Old and New Testament, Book of Mormon, and Book of Doctrine and Covenants, and also what he reveals through his authorized servant when speaking or preaching under the influence of the Holy Ghost. When a man speaks by the spirit it is revelation, and if his hearers are possessed of the same they are able to judge of the correctness of what he says. Job says, "There is a spirit in man, and the inspirations of the Almighty giveth him understanding." This is what I refer to. The object of my labors among the people is to get them the truth, and the whole truth, as it has been revealed. And they must live so that this good spirit can bear witness to them. Were it otherwise I might deceive them; but so long as they have this spirit no man can deceive them.

Correspondent—You, like the old prophets, receive direct revelation from God?

Brigham Young—Yes, and not only me, but my brethren also.

Correspondent—Does that extend to all the Church without reserve for rank?

Brigham Young—Yes; and it is just as necessary for the mother to possess this spirit in training and rearing her children as for any one else

Correspondent—Is it not absolutely necessary, then, that each person receive revelation through you?

Brigham Young—Oh no; through the spirit of Christ, the Holy Ghost, but to dictate [to] the Church is my part of it . . .

The Exposer of the Massacre Murdered

John D. Lee's death was not the only known execution of a massacre participant. The stolid Dutchman Philip Klingensmith had exposed the killers of

Mountain Meadows and predicted that sooner or later he would be killed for violating the oath he had taken to keep his mouth shut. Some four years after Lee's execution, the former Cedar City bishop met a somewhat similar fate.

> News has reached Pioche, says the Record, that bishop Philip Klingensmith, at one time a man of high standing and great influence in the Mormon Church, and the exposer of the Mountain Meadows massacre, and the names of the men who participated in the bloody deed, is dead. His body was found in a prospect hole, in the State of Sonora, Mexico, and a letter from there, which was received in the vicinity of Pioche, states that the mystery surrounding the body indicates that Klingensmith had been murdered. Klingensmith died just as he expected, for on his return from Beaver in 1876, after testifying in the trial of John D. Lee, we met Klingensmith in town, in a sort of secluded spot, and during the conversation Klingensmith remarked: "I know that the Church will kill me, sooner or later, and I am as confident of that fact as I am that I am sitting on this rock. It is only a question of time; but I am going to live as long as I can."[22]

The church-owned newspaper at Salt Lake City took sharp exception to charges that Mormon assassins had administered divine judgment on the errant former bishop who had revealed the truth about the massacre. In keeping with custom, it called Klingensmith an apostate, liar, and worse, and diagnosed accusing editors as insane.

"A FAR-FETCHED ASSUMPTION,"
DESERET EVENING NEWS, 16 AUGUST 1881.

We have refrained from noticing the report of the death of the confessed villain and murderer Klingensmith, and the absurd comments made by the press as to "Mormon" responsibility for his sudden taking off. But the reports concerning the affair are so wide spread that we take the opportunity of referring to them that it may not be stated truthfully that we dare not say anything about it.

Klingensmith, it will be remembered was an apostate who figured in the trial of John D. Lee, and by his own confession was as bad as the man whose life paid the forfeit for his terrible crime, after being convicted by a "Mormon" jury. Klingensmith's testimony was utterly unreliable, because he told so many different stories, made so many false pretenses and was evidently so bad a man that his oath was not worth anymore than his reckless, unsworn word.

---

[22]"Klingensmith. He is Supposed to Have Been Murdered by Mormons," Salt Lake *Daily Tribune*, 4 August 1881, 2/3.

It is now claimed that he is dead and that in some unexplained manner the "Mormons" killed him. As a specimen paragraph we take this from the Philadelphia News.

"There is no reasonable doubt that the Mormon authorities inspired the murder. Of course, this will not be proven, and even the murderers will with difficulty be caught and convicted. And yet all are morally sure as to the real responsibility. This evil of Mormonism, murdrous [sic] and corrupt as it is, must be dealt with. It is a fearful reproach to the country. It violates our laws. Its polygamy is a crime. Yet it artfully extends its political influence, and grows unchecked. Sooner or later rigid measures must be taken. It must be rooted out. Its crimes afford an ample reason for direct and repressive laws. The sooner they are enacted, the better. In the meantime such laws as we have are being rigidly enforced. They are sufficient, if vigorously pressed, to stop the growth, and seriously cripple the influence of the Mormon church."

Is not this a splendid sample of newspaper reasoning and consistency? Klingensmith, it is said, was found dead in Sonora, Mexico. It is not clearly established that the body found was that of Klingensmith. He was such an arrant liar that he may have started the story himself. But supposing he is dead and was killed, where is the connection between his decease in Mexico and the "Mormons" in Utah? There is none, except in the vivid imagination of some anti-"Mormon," who has started the absurd hypothesis, and it is seized at once by shallow writers ready to "pitch into the Mormons," on the shortest notice. There is about as much connection between Utah and Sonora as there is between Philadelphia and Peru. And then the "Mormons" are not a killing people. If they were given to deeds of blood, as falsely reported, there are infamous scoundrels right close to home who would be made to bite the dust. The fact that they are unhung is proof that the "Mormons" are entirely undeserving of the reputation for violence so lavishly manufactured for them . . .

Chapter 12

"Not an Accessory
before or after the Fact"
The Defense of Brigham Young

The defense of Brigham Young and the work of separating him from the massacre began on 29 September 1857, when John D. Lee reported to the Mormon leader. According to church records, Lee related that a notably harmless band of desert Indians had slaughtered the emigrants all by themselves. Recorded by assistant church historian Wilford Woodruff, this story has held up for a century and a half because it cannot be disproved. When Lee stuck to it as long as he did, he eventually sealed his own doom. It has been the heart of Young's defense, repeatedly used in published accounts ever since.

To Young's credit, dozens, if not hundreds, of his contemporaries made written statements of their conviction that "Brigham Young did not have anything to do with the Mountain Medow massacre nor did he know anything about it for a long time after it occur[r]ed," as Civil War veteran H. L. Halleck, a non-Mormon, wrote in 1900. "Brigham Young was one of the smartest men then in the United States and too smart to be mixed up in such a murder. No, it is against all reason and common sense. No, my friend, such a thing could not be. With all the abuse he got he never committed that crime."[1]

"I can say nothing from a personal knowledge of the Mt. Meadow Massacre," Jane Richards, wife of future church historian Franklin D. Richards, told Mrs. H. H. Bancroft in 1880, "but that Brigham Young was as innocent of any connivance in it or approval of it as I am myself."[2] According

---

[1]Halleck to Whiting, 6 November 1900, BYU Library. Halleck recalled visiting Mountain Meadows late in 1858 on his way to California.

[2]Richards, Reminis[c]ences, 1880, Utah and the Mormons Collection, LDS Archives.

to Eleanor Millick Woolley, a Mormon convert whose father had served in the Utah Expedition, even one of Philip Klingensmith's wives exonerated Young. "My husband was associated with John D. Lee, and he is now a fugitive from justice for this dreadful tragedy," Woolley heard Mrs. Klingensmith say in 1882. "Brigham Young was not responsible for the Mountain Meadow Massacre."[3]

Young's defense largely rested on several affidavits of Apostle Woodruff, who was present when Lee reported the crime to Brigham Young and a select audience. Each of Woodruff's subsequent statements about the meeting appears to address circumstances at the time it was written. The following differs from the original diary account in its emphasis on the original Mormon doctrine of innocent blood. Since the doctrine did not take into account women and older children in general, it was not likely that Young would have assumed that it did. Nor would there have been any reason to worry about the issue of innocent blood if Indians alone had committed the atrocity as Lee allegedly first reported. The apostle's mention of Lee's excommunication reveals that it was written after 1870.

> This is to Certify that I Wilford Woodruff being in Company with president Brigham Young at his Office on the 29 day of Sept 1857 and while present with him John D. Lee arrived and made a report to him of the Mountain Meadows Massacre. He did not at the time implicate himself or any white Men but said it was done by the Indians. President Young expressed much regret that such a thing should have been perform[ed] in this Territory especially that any innocent Blood should be shed in this Country. Lee remarked there was not a drop of innocent Blood in that Camp, president Young remarked what do you call the Blood of women & Children if not innocent Blood. Lee did not reply. This was the first information that president Young had of the Massacre.[4] As soon as president Young obtain[ed] testimony to satisfy him that Lee had a hand in the Matter he had him Cut off from the Church and was ever after ready to assist the United States Marshall to bring him to justice.[5]

---

[3] Woolley, Life of Andrew J. Millick, LDS Archives.

[4] The 28 September 1857 entry in the LDS Historian's Office Journal contradicts this statement. It states, "Reports reached town that the companies of Cala. Emigrants going south were all used up by the Indians—100 men & 1000 head of cattle,—at Mountain Meadows." Lee apparently made his first report to Brigham Young that evening and then told the story Woodruff recorded the next day. Young probably knew about the massacre and who did it more than a week before Lee's arrival.

[5] Woodruff, Undated Handwritten Affidavit, LDS Archives.

Brigham Young:
The Indians Will Do . . . as They Please

For years after Brigham Young's death in 1877, Mormon authorities maintained a firm silence on Mountain Meadows, but when H. H. Bancroft came to Utah in 1880 to research a volume for his history of the West, it became necessary finally to provide an explanation of the worst atrocity in the history of the overland trails. The task fell to Apostle Franklin D. Richards (who probably wrote much of the text printed in Bancroft's Utah volume) and *Deseret News* editor Charles Penrose, whose public address in October 1884 on *Who Were Guilty of the Crime?* became the story that the LDS church relied on thereafter.

Central to their task was the letter that Young sent to Isaac Haight on 10 September 1857 in reply to the Cedar Stake president's urgent request three days before to know what to do about the besieged emigrants. In his Lee trial affidavit, Young swore that a "diligent search" had failed to find Haight's letter carried by express rider from Cedar City. Asked for the substance of his reply, Young said it was to "let this company of emigrants" and other trains "pass through the country unmolested" and "allay the angry feelings of the Indians." This letter remained unpublished until seven years after Young's death, when it appeared in Penrose's 1884 defense. The letter, found in a collection of Young's retained copies, was only a few pages away from other materials the church had released during the Lee trial.

In a chatty missive hardly indicative of an urgent message intended to save dozens of lives, Young reported that the Utah Expedition could not reach the Salt Lake Valley "this season without we help them," clearly indicating "that the Lord has answered our prayers and again averted the blow designed for our heads." Typically, the Mormon leader then dropped the pleasantries and inserted what Juanita Brooks called "the real message in a single terse sentence or two in the very heart of his letter."

> In regard to the emigration trains passing through our settlements, we must not interfere with them until they are first notified to keep away. You must not meddle with them. The Indians we expect will do as they please but you should try and preserve good feelings with them. There are no other trains going south that I know of. If those that are there will leave, let them go in peace.

As Brooks observed, the letter deserves close scrutiny, and Young's key comment "sounds as though he might not condemn an Indian massacre."[6]

BRIGHAM YOUNG: DESTROYED BY THE INDIANS

Brigham Young saw the U.S. Constitution as a necessary step on the road to rule by the Kingdom of God and always presented himself as a stout defender of the document. "I stand for Constitutional law, and if any transgress, let them be tried by it, and, if guilty, suffer its penalty," he said in the following 1863 sermon, three days before his arrest for violating the Morrill Act "by taking another wife."[7]

As noted, the Utah territorial legislature had granted probate courts extraordinary powers: "Thus the probate courts, whose proper jurisdiction concerned only the estates of the dead, were made judges of the living, with powers almost equal to those of the supreme and district courts," H. H. Bancroft observed. Mormons argued that the federal district judges "were little with them and at such uncertain times that, save for the probate courts, they would have been practically without civil and criminal jurisdiction." Non-Mormons were skeptical: they felt the courts, whose judges were appointed in theory by the legislature but in reality by Brigham Young, were created "to nullify, so far as possible, the authority of the higher courts."[8]

Gov. Alfred Cumming was an enthusiastic supporter of the probate court's claim of "original jurisdiction, both civil and criminal, in chancery, as well as criminal law." In March 1860 Cumming recommended to the secretary of state that Congress "sanction the action of the probate court in the power claimed by it." If Congress should act, "I entertain little doubt that the community will, ere long, be relieved from the bands of desperadoes who have, by there presence, rendered the tenure of life and property so unsafe here for the last two months," Cumming wrote. The probate courts were "marked by calmness, justice, and decision, and I believe that, under the present circumstances, it is the only remedy for the existing evils."[9] Young agreed.

BRIGHAM YOUNG, 8 MARCH 1863, *JOURNAL OF DISCOURSES*, 10:109–10.

In 1857 it is estimated that eleven thousand troops were ordered here; some seven thousand started for this place, with several thousand hangers on. They

---

[6]Brooks, *The Mountain Meadows Massacre*, 63.

[7]"Arrest of Brigham Young For Polygamy," *Deseret News*, 11 March 1863, 292/4.

[8]Bancroft, *History of Utah*, 487–88.   [9]Buchanan, *Territory of Utah*, House Doc. 78, Serial 1056, 48.

came into this Territory when a company of emigrants were traveling on the south route to California. Nearly all of that company were destroyed by the Indians. That unfortunate affair has been laid to the charge of the whites. A certain judge that was then in this Territory wanted the whole army to accompany him to Iron county to try the whites for the murder of that company of emigrants. I told Governor Cumming that if he would take an unprejudiced judge into the district where that horrid affair occurred, I would pledge myself that every man in the regions round about should be forthcoming when called for, to be condemned or acquitted as an impartial, unprejudiced judge and jury should decide; and I pledged him that the court should be protected from any violence or hindrance in the prosecution of the laws; and if any were guilty of the blood of those who suffered in the Mountain Meadow massacre, let them suffer the penalty of the law; but to this day they have not touched the matter, for fear the Mormons would be acquitted from the charge of having any hand in it, and our enemies would thus be deprived of a favorite topic to talk about, when urging hostility against us. "The Mountain Meadow massacre! Only think of the Mountain Meadow massacre!!" is their cry from one end of the land to the other.

"Come, let us make war on the Mormons, for they burnt government property." And what was the government doing there with their property? They were coming to destroy the Mormons, in violation of every right principle of law and justice. A little of their property was destroyed, and they were left to gnaw, not a file, but dead cattle's bones. I was informed that one man brought five blood hounds to hunt the Mormons in the mountains, and that the poor devil had to kill them and eat them before spring to save himself from starving to death, and that he was fool enough to acknowledge it afterwards in this city. This is the kind of outside pressure we have to meet with. Who wanted the army of 1857 here? Who sent for them? Liars, thieves, murderers, gamblers, whoremasters, and speculators in the rights and blood of the Mormon people cried to government, and government opened its ears, long and broad, saying, "I hear you, my children, lie on, my faithful sons Brocchus, Drummond and Co.," and so they did lie on until the parent sent an army to use up the Mormons. Now I say, for the consolation of all my brethren and sisters, they cannot do it; and that is worse to them than all the rest; they cannot do it.

Young made it clear, again and again: All that was necessary to secure his full cooperation in 1859 to resolve the question of whether white men had been involved at Mountain Meadows would be to present the case to an unprejudiced judge in southern Utah. Both Young and Cumming considered the proper authority to be Judge James D. McCullough, chief magistrate of the Washington County probate court, who took office on 14 March 1859. Having no cases before the docket, his first act was to issue an order requiring

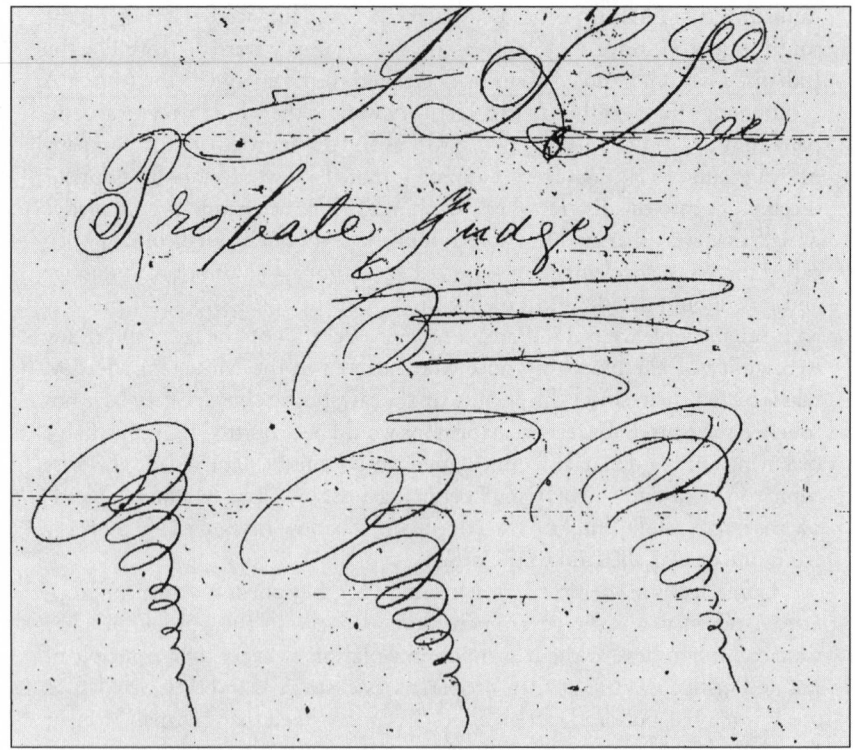

John D. Lee's flamboyant signature as the probate judge of Washington County
indicates both his pride and power. *Courtesy Utah State Historical Society.*

his predecessor, "The Honored J. D. Lee Ex Probate Judge Assessor & Collector & County Clerk," to turn over all "Books Records & Papers &c. that
you may have belonging to these offices," which Judge Lee did that very afternoon.[10] McCullough, no doubt, could have resolved any questions about
Mountain Meadows entirely to Brigham Young's satisfaction.

John D. Lee later mocked Young's claim that he had long sought justice for
Mountain Mountains as "another falsehood generally believed in Utah, especially among the Mormons." It was dishonest to pretend that "Brigham Young
was anxious to help Judge Cradlebaugh arrest all the guilty parties. There is
not one word of truth in the whole statement. Brigham Young knew the name

---

[10]Washington County Probate Court Minutes, Utah State Archives, 22. Judge Lee had no cases on his
docket when he held court on Monday, 14 September 1857.

of every man that was in any way implicated in the Mountain Meadows Massacre. He knew just as much about it as I did, except that he did not see it, as I had seen it," Lee wrote in his confession. "If Brigham Young had wanted one man, or fifty men, or five hundred men arrested, all he would have had to do would have been to say so, and they would have been arrested instantly. There was no escape for them if he ordered their arrest. Every man who knows anything of affairs in Utah at that time knows this is so." Lee charged "that Brigham made a great parade at the time, and talked a great deal about bringing the guilty parties to Justice, but he did not mean a word of it—not a word." This was simply another of "Brigham Young's cunning dodges to blind the government." His sermons in southern Utah, Lee wrote, "gave great comfort to all of us who were out in the woods keeping out of the way of the officers. It insured our safety and took away our fears."[11]

CHARLES W. PENROSE: HE WAS NOT A MAN OF BLOOD

On Sunday evening, 26 October 1884, British convert Charles W. Penrose, who eventually rose to the First Presidency of the LDS church, spoke for two and one-half hours to an overflow crowd at the Twelfth Ward Assembly Hall in Salt Lake City. For the first time a Mormon leader gave a detailed explanation of the subject that had bedeviled the religion for more than a quarter-century.

From the perspective of Salt Lake's Mormon press, Penrose's lecture was a great success. "There was literally a jam in the huge hall, and many were unable to gain admission," *The Herald* reported on 28 October. Penrose had, the paper claimed, correctly laid responsibility on "Lee and his assassins" and "the Indians, who did the greater part of the work." The non-Mormon press did not share this view, but that morning *The Daily Tribune* printed a remarkably straightforward summary of Penrose's remarks.

"MOUNTAIN MEADOW MASSACRE: DISCOURSE OF ELDER C. W. PENROSE
TRYING TO EXONERATE THE MORMON AUTHORITIES,"
THE DAILY TRIBUNE, 28 OCTOBER 1884, 4/2–3.

At the 12th Ward meeting house Sunday night there was a very large attendance to hear Mr. C. W. Penrose discourse on the Mountain Meadows Mas-

---

[11]Bishop, ed., *Mormonism Unveiled*, 258–59. Lee incorrectly recalled that Cradlebaugh visited southern Utah with Brigham Young, but his recollection of a sermon Young gave in Cedar City matches text recorded in his journal in 1861.

sacre. The reporter for The Tribune was courteously furnished by Bishop Clawson with a seat at a table on the stand, and after the choir had sung a hymn
and a prayer was uttered, Mr. Penrose addressed the congregation. He said
the subject upon which he was to speak had attracted a great deal of attention, had been mentioned in every part of the civilized world. Wherever the
elders have gone to preach the gospel they have been met with the statement
that the Mormon Church, with Brigham Young at the head, was a bloody
church, and believed in the shedding of human blood for apostacy; that there
is an organization in the midst of the people, called Danites, or destroying
angels, whose business it was to kill every one who attempted to escape from
Utah, or any obnoxious person, Mormon or Gentile, who may be in the midst
of the people. This has been denied frequently, and those who have made
these statements have been challenged to the proof, but it has not been furnished, because the statements were false. It has been claimed that the awful
tragedy known as the Mountain Meadow Massacre was perpetrated by the
Mormon Church, or that the church was responsible for it; that it was perpetrated at the command of Brigham Young, as the leader of the church, and
that it was in accordance with the doctrine of the church. This untruth has
been repeated so many times that the world has come to believe, in a great
measure, that it is true. He proposed to give a brief account of that occurrence and to trace the responsibility for it, who perpetrated it, and to show
whether the Mormon church is responsible for the deed, whether Brigham
Young was or was not an accessory before or after the fact, and hoped in so
doing that he would have the assistance of the faith of his brethren and sisters, that he might have the spirit of the Lord rest upon him, that he might
bring forward clearly the evidence which he had collected.

In the summer of 1857, a company of emigrants came into Salt Lake City
on their way to California. There were two ways to get there, one the Northern and the other the Southern. They went as far as Bear River, returned and
took the Southern route. On the way South they became very impertinent
and abusive. At that time news had been received here of the coming of
Buchanan's Army which was supposed to have been coming here to destroy
the Mormons. As the emigrants passed South they boasted to the people that
they were going to California, where they intended to get up a company to
return and attack the Mormons on the South. The company was composed
of from 120 to 150 persons; they were well armed, and when they came to the
small settlements they would rob hen roosts, and going through the streets
would flip off the heads of chickens with their whips. At one place, it is said,
they poisoned the springs, so that people who partook of the water died; they
poisoned beef and gave it to the Indians, and at another place they caught an
Indian, tied him up to a wagon wheel and whipped him severely. These are
the stories which were told concerning these emigrants; whether they are true
or false he was unable to say. On the way up they met Jacob Hamblin who

advised them to camp at Mountain Meadow. Their depredations had aroused the Indians to fury, who attacked them at Mountain Meadow, led by John D. Lee. At this time a council was held at Cedar City at which Philip Klingensmith, who was an acting bishop, Laban Morrill and some others, whose names I do not remember now, were present. These persons took into consideration the depredations which had been made by this party of emigrants. The people were very much excited; they had been persecuted and driven from their homes, and there seemed to be a prospect that they would be driven from here, and these emigrants had been making these threats, cursing Brigham Young, declaring that old Joe Smith ought to have been killed before he was and saying they had taken part in his killing. At this council some of those present advocated the interception and destruction of the emigrants, and Laban Morrill and others opposed it, and it was decided to send a messenger [to] Gov Young to find out what his mind was in regard to the matter.

James Haslam was sent to Brigham Young and was sent back with a letter and orders not to spare horseflesh, and arrived at Cedar City on Sunday, the 15th of September, two days after the massacre, and Haight "told him it was too late." The men had been called out by Klingensmith and Higbee, who claimed to be acting under the orders of Isaac C. Haight, but very few of them had an idea that they were going to perform a deed of blood, but thought they were going to bury the dead. On arriving a flag of truce was sent down into the camp, the emigrants were induced to give up their arms and they were all drawn out of the camp, and after they had passed a considerable distance away, the evidence is that some of the white men fired upon those emigrants, and they were all butchered except seventeen young children. It is related by the evidence that John D. Lee assisted in the slaughtering of the wounded emigrants who were in the wagons, those who were able to walk, without arms, were set upon by the Indians, and as stated, some white men fired upon them. It appears that John D. Lee and one of two others assisted in the killing.

It should not be laid at the door of the church because certain of them were Mormons. This church teaches that men shall not commit murder, and the church should not be held responsible, as a body, no matter what the position of the perpetrators. The speaker cited Stenhouse's book, The Tribune account of the Lee trial and other works, to show that the charges of guilt had been brought against the church as a body, and also read extracts from several books and papers, from the pens of non-Mormons, to the general effect that when the massacre became known a thrill of horror ran through the body of Mormons in Utah, thus showing that the sentiments and feelings of the people were against the commission of any such crime, and that it was condemned by them in toto.

The charges made against individuals, center in Brigham Young and George A. Smith; against Smith, that he preceded the emigrants south, told the people not to sell provisions to them, and arousing the hostility of the people, and as to him he would first analyze the evidence. Here the speaker read Geo. A. Smith's affidavit on the Lee trial; the testimony on the first Lee trial of Jesse N. Smith and his brother Silas S., as to what was preached by Geo. A. Smith on that southern trip, merely that the people were not to feed their grain to stock, nor sell it to the emigrants to feed. All who knew Geo. A. Smith know he was not a man of blood, and there is no reliable evidence that he did what has been imputed to him.

Next, it is charged Brigham Young was either an accessory before or after the fact, and, first, he would discuss the question as to his being an accessory before the fact; that he counseled or advised it, or that the people who were guilty were influenced by any message from him. He cited extracts from Brigham Young's instructions and statements in relation to retarding the advance of the army, showing that he uniformly ordered that no blood should be shed, and referred also to the circular in Bishop's book, dated Sept. 14th, 1857, in which he said he did not want a drop of blood shed.

The speaker also quoted from Sumner Howard's opening speech in the last Lee trial, imputing all the blame to Lee and exonerating the church and Brigham Young; and to Lee's confession reciting, among other things, the quarrel between Haight and Dame, and dwelt on the fears expressed by the former when Dame threatened to send a true report of the tragedy to the church authorities. If Brigham Young had counseled or advised it, why should Haight be afraid of its being reported to him? It was impossible that Young should have been an accessory before the fact.

Brigham Young kept a copy of his correspondence. The Salt Lake Tribune has repeatedly called for a copy of the dispatch from him to Haight, sent by James Haslam, and the speaker had made search for it and found it in a letter copying book in the President's office, which he read. It purports to be dated Sept. 10, 1857, gives information about the progress of the army, and closes by advising them to let the emigrants go in peace, that the people must protect their own lives but not interfere with the emigrants. (The letter, however, is not proven to be a genuine copy beyond that it is found in a letter-copying book in President Young's office—Rep.)

Now as to President Young being an accessory after the fact. It is claimed that Lee came to Salt Lake City about the latter part of September and made a full statement of the massacre to him, and the question is, is that true, or was he led to believe that it was done by Indians? Did he have a guilty knowledge of the matter? Lee in his alleged confessions says he started up here about a week after the occurrence, was about two days on the road, which would bring him here about the end of September, and that he then gave President Young a full statement of the facts.

A number of documents were then read by Mr. Penrose. First an Affidavit of Wilford Woodruff that he was present in President Young's office when Lee arrived, and that Lee stated the Indians had committed the outrage, that the white men were there only to restrain them and to bury the dead. That Young shed tears and said he was sorry that innocent blood had been shed in the Territory, Lee replied that there was not a drop of innocent blood in the company, and Brigham asked, "What do you call the blood of women and children?" Lee said that they were a wicked and corrupt lot; that he had two of the children at his house and could only make one of them kneel for prayer, and the other only laughed at her and that they both swore like pirates.

In support of this Mr. Penrose read his own affidavit, in which he had copied Wilford Woodruff's entry in his journal (under date of September 29, 1857) in which Woodruff had entered substantially the same facts set forth in his affidavit, and also read an affidavit of John W. Young that he was then thirteen years old, was in his father's office when Lee made his statement, and gives it the same as Woodruff; also the affidavit of Aaron F. Farr, that Lee came to his house the same day he reported to Brigham Young and made about the same statement, at the same time stating that he had told the matter to Young just as he had to affiant.

A portion of a letter dated May 21, 1862, from President Young to Secretary Belknap pledging himself to lend every assistance in men and money to thoroughly investigate the massacre, was read.

All the perpetrators were sworn to secrecy at Mountain Meadow, under penalty of death. That accounts for President Young's not knowing the real facts until a long time afterward.

All the investigations and prosecutions, except the last trial of John D. Lee, had been conducted with a view, not to convict the perpetrators, but the leaders of the Mormon church. This he attempted to show by quoting from Judge Cradlebaugh's speech published in The Tribune account of the Lee trial, and the speeches of Baskin and Carey on that trial.

He read the report made by Jacob Forney, Brigham Young's successor as superintendent of Indian affairs, dated Sept. 22, 1859, and claimed that before any steps were taken to investigate the massacre Brigham Young had been superseded both as governor and superintendent of Indian affairs, and was no longer responsible, officially, for the investigation. There were some feeble efforts made by the governors and judges who came along, but all directed to the implication of Brigham Young, until Sumner Howard prosecuted Lee on the second trial. An Affidavit of Erastus Snow was read, stating that President Young and the other authorities of the church in Salt Lake City were ignorant of John D. Lee's connection with the full facts relating to John D. Lee's connection therewith, by reason of the fact that Lee had falsely represented the matter to Young; that upon being sent to Washington county to preside he ferreted out the facts little by little; and in the year 1870 reported them to Young, who was astonished and said that Lee had added lying and deceit to his crime; that Lee was cut of[f] from the church never to be admitted again for his crime; and Haight for not restraining him, and for not taking prompt action against him.

The speaker said Lee was convicted finally on Mormon testimony, before a Mormon jury, a thing which the enemies of the church had said was impossible. Lee in his confession exonerates Hooper from the charge made against him of having received Mountain Meadow property.[12] There is an intimation in Lee's confession that he thought he might perhaps escape punishment. There was an agreement made between John D. Lee and Mr. Howard, the prosecuting attorney, and Nelson, who was the Marshal, and now is one of the editors of The Salt Lake Tribune, that John D. Lee should give them these confessions; that they might publish them to the world; and make considerable money out of it, but I will not enter into that tonight.

Lee was taken to Mountain Meadow and there shot on the 23rd day of March, 1878, [sic] for dramatic effect. Bishop's book is a dramatic one, and this was intended as a dramatic end to it.

The sermon was concluded by him saying that he thought he had established that the church was not responsible for the massacre; that George A. Smith was guiltless, and that Brigham Young was neither an accessory before nor after the fact; that his name stands clear from the crime imputed to him; he was not a man of blood nor even a warrior, but a statesman of a high order, who did not delight in physical conflict nor the shedding of blood.

Not Mormon Liars Enough in the World

While *The Daily Tribune* at Salt Lake City gave a straightforward account of Penrose's lecture, an editorial in the same issue portrayed the talk as a fabrication. The paper's fear that Penrose's vindication of Brigham Young and the church might be adopted as the customary explanation of the massacre proved to be prophetic. The "Penrose Defense" convinced H. H. Bancroft that the atrocity "was the crime of an individual, the crime of a fanatic of the worst stamp."[13] Bancroft's account became the generally accepted story of the murders for more than a century and remains the foundation of the LDS church's interpretation of its history.[14]

---

[12]A Marylander serving as Utah territorial secretary of state in 1857 and later Utah's delegate to Congress, William H. Hooper was Brigham Young's son-in-law. A prosperous businessman, he provided bail money for John D. Lee. James Martineau's report that Isaac Haight left Cedar City on 24 September 1857 "driving stock to W. H. Hooper" supports James Carleton's 1859 charge that the cattle Hooper sold to the U.S. Army in 1858 "were without doubt the cattle taken from the emigrants." See Martineau, My Life, Huntington Library.

[13]Bancroft, *History of Utah*, 543.

[14]Penrose's lecture was eventually published, and *The Mountain Meadows Massacre: Who Were Guilty of the Crime?* went through multiple editions.

"Penrose and the Massacre," *The Daily Tribune*,
Salt Lake City, 28 October 1884, 1/2.

Elsewhere we give a full synopsis of the lecture of Penrose, on Sunday night, on the Mountain Meadow Massacre. He opens by asking for the faith of the brothers and sisters present, that he might have the spirit of the Lord rest upon him, that he might bring forward clearly the evidence which he had collected. We do not wonder that he asked for help. He had started in to give such dignity as he could to a gigantic falsehood, to whitewash some wholesale murderers, and to traduce the innocent dead. It is hard to imagine what was in the mind of Penrose that induced him to make the extraordinary statements which he did make in that lecture, except that the Mormon Church leaders must in some way be whitewashed, and that he thought by persistent lying his lecture might some time be picked up and used as the real explanation of the affair. To begin with, one must remember the time and the circumstances. In 1857 Brigham Young was an absolute autocrat in Utah. To do anything like murdering a company of over 130 persons without his authority, or to have concealed the real facts from him had such a crime been committed; every Mormon knows would have been an absolute impossibility. Penrose knows that fact as well as he knows that he deliberately went to work to whitewash by falsehood the mightiest crime ever perpetrated west of the Rocky Mountains.

He declares that he has recently searched the Mormon records to get at the facts. If he has, he has seen that while yet these emigrants were in Wyoming or in Northern Utah, an order signed by Brigham Young was sent to the commander of the Nauvoo Legion to attack this particular company. That order in some way miscarried in the mountains, but the order, signed, "Your brother in Christ, Brigham Young," is in the records which Penrose says he has just been searching. It is known by all old Mormons that these poor people were persecuted all the way for 300 miles through this Territory; that not only grain was withheld from them but everything else, even to fresh eggs and vegetables, and that one man was cut off from the church for selling or giving some trifle to one of the company whom he had known. Penrose answers that by saying Geo. A. Smith, a most merciful man, was the one who went ahead and delivered the orders. That is another subterfuge. Mr. Dinwoodey, Bishop Clawson and John Taylor may be truthful men in their every day lives, but put them in court when there is a necessity to shield a criminal and see what they are. What was Geo. A. Smith when he was sent to deliver a message from Brigham Young? Of course his own individuality, almost his identity, was lost. He was simply a slave carrying an order from a master whom he did not dare to disobey, and under whose will he had no wish to disobey. Next Penrose tells of the stories which were circulated about the impudence [of the emigrant company, a] long string of falsehoods. A train of 130 or 140

emigrants in an enemy's country, followed, harassed, starved and finally driven
to their deaths, were impertinent and abusive? Shame! Even the "gall" of Penrose shrinks from vouching for the truth of the cowardly slander. Well, the
tragedy was consummated as we have often described it. The news was brought
to Brigham Young by Lee. The [Deseret] News says the record shows that
Lee reported it was done by savages, and that Brigham Young cried. If he cried
it was because some women were killed who might have done for Utah harems.
But the whole story is false. Lee told the exact truth. We have it on much better authority than that of Penrose. He may have made a second statement planned
by him and Young, at which he charged it upon Indians and Young might have
cried then. It would have been like him. Penrose finds a copy of an old letter
injected into Young's copy-book, purporting to instruct the murderers at Cedar
City to defend themselves only and to spare the lives of the women and children. But even the hardened soul of Penrose recoils against stating his belief
that the letter is genuine. There are other facts well known here. The next winter after the massacre Lee was a member of the Utah Legislature in this city.
He came up here, took a man's wife away from him a few miles from here.
Brigham Young gave the woman a divorce and married her to Lee, and that
winter she wore a silk dress which had belonged to one of the murdered women,
and every Mormon here knew the fact. Moreover, on one occasion he asked
the lady where he boarded, for paper, saying: "Brother Brigham wants the names
of all who participated in the Mountain Meadow business." "What!" said
the lady, "Brother Lee, you do not mean to say that our people were engaged
in that affair!" Lee simply laughed a brutal laugh, sat down and covered two
sheets with names. Afterward the lady counted the lines, and there were 55 on
the two pages. In point of fact 54 white Mormons were engaged in the killing.
More, soon after in a meeting of the Seventies in this city Brigham Young
justified the massacre. He went himself to the spot, read the inscription put
upon the tablet by the soldiers, who went there to bury the dead: "Vengeance
is mine, I will repay saith the Lord," turned around and said "vengeance is
mine, I have repaid, saith the Lord!" For years, whenever he went South, he
was the guest of John D. Lee. As late as 1868, he married Lee to a fifteenth
or sixteenth concubine.

Penrose says Lee was finally turned out of the Church. Yes, but how? He
was simply cut off and when he demanded a trial before the High Council,
something which the laws of the Church guarantee to him, he was refused
and covertly threatened with blood atonement if he persisted in demanding
it. The News charges that there was an agreement between Howard, Nelson
and Lee to publish Lee's confessions. Bishop, Lee's counsel, got the confession, and Nelson's only business in that connection was as Marshal, to receive
it, as it was prepared and turn it over to Bishop. This was by request of both
Lee and Bishop. Nelson never received or hoped to receive one cent from the

publication. When the firm which published the work wrote to Nelson about the proposed publication, he referred them to Mr. Bishop, as they say in their preface, he having no interest in the matter, and doing or hearing nothing more about it until he received a copy of the book, his sole reward.[15] Finally John M. Higby, who was in command of the white murderers on that day of blood, confessed the whole business to a gentleman in this city, whose word is worth a million affidavits made by Penrose. The above are the facts. They do not implicate the masses of the Mormons. They show that for revenge and plunder some 131 men, women and children were brutally murdered by Mormon chiefs, at the head of whom was Brigham Young, and there are not Mormon liars enough in the world to conceal the real facts.

Hamilton G. Park: Ride for Dear Life

The history of the American frontier is replete with heroic rides to save soldiers or settlers from hostile Indians, but James Haslam's story is in a class by itself. Only in Utah Territory did white settlers send a rider with only one horse on a five-hundred-mile round trip to tell a governor that Indians had attacked a wagon train and ask him what to do about it. And only in Utah would the messenger discover on returning that the settlers had helped the Indians murder the emigrants.

This singular episode began as the Arkansas emigrants neared their final resting place. A stake high council meeting of Mormon priesthood leaders at Cedar City on 6 September, a Sunday, apparently voted to "deal with the situation now, so our hands will be free to deal with the army when it arrives." Laban Morrill then suggested they should first send a messenger to Brigham Young and take no action until he returned with instructions on what to do.[16] The attack on the Fancher party was already well underway by the following afternoon, when Isaac Haight finally got around to sending express rider Haslam off to Salt Lake, where Hamilton G. Park served in 1857 as Young's business manager. By 1907 Park had seen many unusual events during his missions to Scotland, including missionaries raise the dead.[17] That year he reported what he had witnessed the day Haslam left Young's office with orders about what to do with the emigrants.

---

[15] William Nelson, *The Daily Tribune* editor and probable author of this editorial, took pains to deny Penrose's charge since he was the Marshal Nelson at Lee's second trial, referred to here.

[16] Brooks, *Mountain Meadows Massacre*, 53–54.

[17] Jenson, ed., *Latter-day Saint Biographical Encyclopedia*, 1:668.

TESTIMONY OF HAMILTON G. PARK, LDS ARCHIVES.

For many years I was President Brigham Young's steward and during that time it was my custom to call on him in his office to report and to receive instructions from him in relation to business affairs. On one of these calls, as I approached the President's Office, I observed a spirited horse, saddled and bridled, and hitched to a post near the outer gate. As I reached the office and took hold of the door, it opened from within and a man came out dressed in the riding costume of those days. He was equipped with leather leggings and large Spanish spurs and had a small rawhide riding whip in his hand. Close behind him was President Young. Seeing at a glance that the President was sorely troubled, I stepped aside, without speaking, to let them pass. President Young, as he came out of the office door, addressed this man with great feeling, saying: "Brother Haslam, I want you to ride for dear life; ride day and night; spare no horse flesh; that company must be protected and guarded out of the territory if it requires all the men in Iron County to do it." As the man thus addressed paused a moment to adjust the saddle girth on his horse, President Young repeated this emphatic command. The man then sprang into the saddle and shot off like an arrow down Theatre Hill and was soon out of sight. President Young went back into his office with a troubled face and bowed head, without noticing me. I did not understand what I had seen and heard until I entered the adjoining office and enquired of James Jack who the fast rider was and where he was going, when I obtained the information that he was James Haslam and that he was on his way to Iron County with instruction that a company of emigrants then in Southern Utah and bound for California were to be protected and assisted on their way.

JAMES HASLAM: HE CRIED LIKE A CHILD

Park's account of Haslam springing into the saddle and taking off like an arrow hardly goes with the lack of urgency shown in Young's letter of reply revealed in 1884 or the time it took to prepare it. Nor does it fit the express rider's own description of his trip from Cedar City to Salt Lake and back. His account shows that it took over sixty hours to cover the 250-mile northward leg of his journey. After Young reportedly told him to "ride for dear life," his return trip took a bit longer. He was too late: Colonel Dame and Major Haight did not wait for Young's answer.

Not long after Penrose's 1884 presentation, Haslam added his own testimony as a supplement to the lecture in defense of Brigham Young.

"TESTIMONY OF JAMES HOLT HASLAM," 4 DECEMBER 1884.
FROM PENROSE, *SUPPLEMENT TO THE LECTURE*
ON THE MOUNTAIN MEADOWS MASSACRE.

James Holt Haslam, being interrogated by S. A. Kenner, Esq., answered the interrogatories to him propounded as follows:

What is your full name?

James Holt Haslam . . .

In what part of Utah were you residing in the year 1857?

In the year 1857 I was residing at Cedar City, in Iron County.

What part of Iron County?

Cedar City.

Do you remember September of that year?

I remember it well . . .

Did you perform any office or any service in connection with those engaged in that transaction?

All that I performed was to carry an express from Cedar to Salt Lake City.

Who sent you on that errand?

Isaac C. Haight.

What position, if any, did he hold in that community where you lived?

President of Cedar City

By virtue of what authority was he president, if you know?

No more than he was called to that office.

I mean under what dispensation or government?

Under the church government of the Church of Jesus Christ of Latter-day Saints . . .

Do you remember the company of emigrants that were massacred at the Mountain Meadows?

I remember seeing them pass through Cedar City on their way south . . .

Was it before or after you received the dispatch?

Oh, before I received the dispatch.

About how many days before?

I should judge from one to two days, but I could not say positively.

State now, as nearly as you can, considering the state and circumstances leading to Mr. Haight giving that dispatch and with orders to convey it there.

Word came up to Mr. Haight from John D. Lee, stating that the Indians had got the emigrants corralled on the Mountain Meadows, and wanted to know what he should do . . .

What did Mr. Haight tell you in relation to the matter at that time?

He sent for me. He had a message written to send up to Brigham Young, and he wished to get a man to take it up. He had not found one when I went down there to his house, and he asked me if I would take it. I told him I would if it was possible to take it.

Did he then state the nature of that message that he wanted you to carry and deliver?

He gave me the message to read . . .

State the contents of it as near as you possibly can.

The same as I stated before: that the Indians had got the emigrants corralled at the Mountain Meadows, and Lee wanted to know what should be done. Lee at this time was major of what was called the Post, and he was the Indian agent . . .

Was that message placed in an envelope and sealed?

Yes, sir.

To whom was it addressed?

To Brigham Young, governor of Utah Territory . . .

Is it a fact that after the receipt of that message you were in the saddle ready to depart and did depart within fifteen minutes from the time of the reception?

Yes, sir . . .

Did you know about what time you arrived at Beaver?

To the best of my recollection now, Bishop P. T. Farnsworth was Bishop there, and to the best of my recollection when I arrived at Beaver he said it was nine o'clock, or a little past, in the evening . . .

Did you proceed immediately on your journey to Fillmore?

Right away . . .

How long did you ride after that?

From that to Fillmore.

Without stopping?

Without stopping, on the same horse, yes, on the on the same horse to Fillmore.

Can you remember the time you arrived at Fillmore—time of day or night?

I could not recollect exactly.

Can you remember how many hours?

No, sir; I got to Fillmore sometime before daylight, but I could not say exactly what time of the following day.

How long did you stay in Fillmore?

I had to stay till the Bishop came, and that was pretty near evening. He was off on a hunt, he and his horses too . . .

Were you resting during this time?

I had to: my horse could not go any further without urging him very much, as he had come from Beaver.

How long were you there waiting for the Bishop to arrive?

That day; and after he arrived I did not stop but a little while.

Did he get you a horse immediately?

Yes, sir; but it was a horse that I could only ride ten miles. I rode to Cedar Springs, or Holden.

Did you there obtain another horse?

They hadn't got one in Holden—had to send back to Fillmore and get another one.

How much time did that occupy?

That occupied, before they got back with another horse, till three o'clock in the morning next day.

Did you then immediately proceed?

Yes, sir . . .

What day of the week was it you arrived at Salt Lake City?

I can't remember that, but think it was Thursday morning.

Can you give me the time you occupied from Cedar City to Salt Lake City, altogether, including stoppages and everything?

I left Cedar at four o'clock in the afternoon, and it was the morning of the third day from then that I got to Salt Lake City.

After you left Cedar?

Yes, sir; I was at the Lion House just after daybreak, where Brigham Young had his office, or it was then.

That would be, then, about sixty hours, would it not, on your journey?

Yes, sir somewhere along there: two whole days and a little more than half of another.

Well, was it not about sixty hours?

Yes, about that time.

How many hours were taken up by these stoppages and delays altogether?

Well, about fifteen—yes, there was all of twenty hours taken up.

What was the first thing you did when you arrived at Salt Lake City?

To go to Brigham's office.

Did you see him there?

Yes, sir.

Immediately upon your arrival?

You might call it immediately. It was not over fifteen minutes.

Did you see him in his office?

Yes, sir.

What did you do when you first saw him?

I handed him my message . . .

What did he do?

He opened it and read it.

What, if anything, did he say after he read it?

He told me I had better go and lie down and take a little sleep.

What else, if anything?

He told me to be there again at such a time, and he would be ready to give me an answer.

Did he mention any time?

Yes, sir.

What time was it that he suggested?

One o'clock in the afternoon of the same day.

Were there any others present besides President Young on that occasion?

Yes, sir.

State, if you can recollect, who they were.

I can't recollect all, but Squire Wells, John Taylor and I should think about as many as half a dozen.

Do you remember George Q. Cannon and John Taylor?

I cannot say whether George Q. was there or not; I cannot say as to him positively, because I don't recollect.

Mention as many as you can remember.

That is about as many as I can remember—Daniel H. Wells and John Taylor.

How many were there altogether?

I should think there was all of half a dozen or more in a council.

Was this at the time you first went in—who was there when you first went to President Young?

I don't recollect only seeing one clerk in the office.

Was this at the time you first went into the office?

No, it was in the afternoon when I went for the answer . . .

As to the message—what did you do with reference to that?

He asked if I could stand the trip back; he said the Indians must be kept from the emigrants at all cost, if it took all of Iron County to protect them.

You remember he said that very distinctly?

I do, I know he said it . . .

Were you there at the time he mentioned for you to come?

I was.

What took place then?

He told me to start and not to spare horseflesh, but to go down there just as quick as possible.

Did he give you any written message?

Yes, sir.

Was it sealed or unsealed?

It was not sealed, but I never opened it.

Did you know the contents of it?

I did not—I could have done.

Did you see it subsequently or after?

When I handed it to Brother Haight he offered it to me to read.

About how long were you on the road taking the message down and going to Cedar City?

About the same as I was coming up, as near as I can think.

What did Mr. Haight say to you when you handed him the message or answer and he read it?

He said, "Too late, too late." The massacre was all over before I got home.

Did he say anything further on that subject?

No, sir; he cried like a child . . .

Do you know what became of that dispatch?

You mean the one I brought back?

Yes.

I do not.

Did you see what disposition Mr. Haight made of it?

He put it in his pocket after he read it.

Have you ever seen it since?

No, sir . . .

How long was it after that time that you next met President Young?

I can't say, for I don't recollect. I came up to Salt Lake City in 1859 and worked there till Fall; I can't remember any particular date.

But you have met him since?

Oh, yes, many times.

And heard him speak in places, in pulpits?

Yes, sir.

Have you ever heard him, in his house, in any place, or in any of the streets, or in any place of worship, or pulpit, or at any place whatever, make any reference to the subject that you have just testified to and under discussion?

I have.

Will you, according to your best recollection, give me, as near as possible, the nature of what he said at any of these places or times?

If I can recollect anything he said at all, he said it was one of the worst things that ever happened or could have happened in Utah, and those that had perpetrated that deed would go to hell for it. I have heard him use such an expression as that.

Then, to the best of your recollection, from what you have seen of him, what you have known of him, what you have heard him say, he was not only bitterly opposed to that whole proceeding, but discountenanced the men who engaged in it?

He did.

Do you know anything concerning any spoils or property that accrued from that massacre?

Only from hearsay.

Have you ever seen any of it?

Oh, yes.

In whose possession did you see it?

John D. Lee's.

Did you ever see any in anybody else's possession?

I can't say that I did, unless they bought it from Lee . . .

What was the state of the community at that time—at the time you took this dispatch to be carried to Salt Lake?

On the way through the Indians were very bad—they were excited, and they were up in arms on account of the treatment they had received from this company of emigrants.

Do you know anything of this treatment they complained of?

I know what the Indians told me when I was on the road carrying the dispatch.

State what it was.

They told me the emigrants had poisoned their water and had done everything that was mean for them, and that they were going to kill the emigrants for doing it . . .

Did the Indians point out to you, or tell you on your journey, where any of these poisoned springs were?

Yes, sir.

Where were they?

On the north of Salt Creek, where the Willow Creek is now.

Were there any other places?

Yes, sir; down below Fillmore, between Fillmore and Corn Creek, at some springs down there in the bottom

Do you know of any fatality resulting to the Indians by reason of this poisoning?

No.

Did the Indians claim of any?

No . . .

What, if anything, do you know concerning any orders issued to John D. Lee previous to the massacre by any one in authority?

There was an order issued to John D. Lee by Isaac C. Haight to keep the Indians in check till I came back from Salt Lake City, and that I was starting right then.

Did you see that order?

I saw that order and read it and those words were on it—I know this to be the fact . . .[18]

Do these answers that you have given here embrace the sum and substance of your testimony given at the second trial of John D. Lee, in Beaver City?

That is the sum and substance of it.

Does it embrace all you gave there?

Yes, sir; and more . . .

James Holt Haslam.
Subscribed and sworn to before me this 12th January, 1885.
Joseph Howell.

---

[18]Why Haight and Dame did not wait for instructions from Salt Lake is a puzzle.

James Martineau:
The Horde of Infuriated Savages

On his way to California in 1850, James Martineau converted to Mormonism and the next winter was assigned to be one of the first settlers of Iron County, where he became one of the most dedicated chroniclers of the community. As William Dame's adjutant in the local militia, on 4 September 1857 he left "on a scout, upon the upper Sevier, to watch for signs of troops approaching" southern Utah from the mountains to the east. He did not return from this wild-goose chase until a week later.[19] Hence, he was not present during many of the events he described half a century later to a friend who asked for information about the 1857 massacre.

For decades western historians and archivists have eagerly sought Martineau's diary, which was long sequestered in a descendant's safe in Los Angeles. Many hoped it would provide a unique document—a contemporary account of the events at Mountain Meadows. Unfortunately, when the Huntington Library recently acquired the manuscript, it proved to be a reconstructed rather than a contemporary record that repeated a wealth of misinformation and dated the massacre to 7 September 1857. The problems with Martineau's 1907 letter are similar and instructive: most significantly, several of its statements are obviously untrue. Some of these problems can be dismissed as typical of any recollection written fifty years after the events it describes, for human memory is notoriously unreliable. But some of Martineau's misrepresentations, such as his claim that the Fancher party spent a week at Cedar City and two weeks at the meadows, may have been an attempt to provide a more believable context for the traditional story. Perhaps he realized that the fact that the Arkansans did not reach southern Utah until early September did not leave enough time for the Indians to "have gathered in sufficient strength to have done them much harm," as the alibi required.

Other devout southern Utah pioneers denounced Colonel Dame as a poltroon and a coward, so Martineau's vindication of his old commander indicates an enduring loyalty to the enigmatic figure who served as president of the Parowan Stake of Zion from 1856 to 1880. But the loyal adjutant had been among those who spent four successive days in August 1858 with George A. Smith "carefully and patiently" investigating complaints made against

---

[19]Martineau, My Life, 4 September 1857, Huntington Library.

Dame, and he wrote the document that he and twenty-two other men signed that found the charges had no foundation in truth. Some may choose to pretend that the murderers somehow deceived Apostle Smith about what really happened at the meadows, but Juanita Brooks reported that Dame simply made a persuasive argument: "You can NOT lay this onto me! I will not take it!" the colonel allegedly declared. "If you dare try, I'll just put the saddle onto the right horse, and you all know who that is!"[20]

JAMES MARTINEAU TO F. E. ELDRIDGE, 23 JULY 1907, MARTINEAU PAPERS, BYU LIBRARY.

. . . The Company which perished at the Mountain Meadows was a part of a still larger company which entered Salt Lake City in the autumn, and there divided. Those who came to the meadows were such a disreputable lot that the more respectable part of the original party refused longer to travel with them, and remained at S. L. City while the others came South through Utah, making themselves very offensive to the Settlers as they journeyed.

At their camp at or near Corn Creek in Millard county an ox died, and the indians asked for the carcass for food. A man said, "No, leave it 'till morning and I'll fix it for them." He *did* fix it for them, inserting poison all through the carcass. Next morning it was given to the indians, a large number partaking of it. Six or Seven warriors died, with several squaws and children, and many were made very ill and the indians, knowing they had been poisoned without provocation became furious for reverse. To an indian, to revenge the death or to [?] neglects or refuses to redress the wrong; not necessarily upon the party actually guilty, but upon any one—man or woman—of the same race.

Accordingly the indians attacked the emigrants as they went onward, day after day, as opportunity offered, at the same time sending out runners to all surrounding bands, detailing the outrage and calling on them to come and help avenge it, only discontinuing when the travelers reached the Mormon colonies in Iron Co.

Arriving at Cedar City the company remained a week or more, their conduct becoming very offensive;—saying they would remain [illegible] until the U.S. troops arrived and then help kill every man and take the wives and daughters to do with as they pleased. Consequently altercations with the citizens were frequent and the presiding authorities had all they could do to prevent actual fights, until the situation became so unbearable a message was sent to Col. Dame showing the situation, and asking what could be done.

By Col. Dame's direction I wrote an order directing that all possible means should be used to keep the peace until the emigrants should leave and proceed

---

[20]Brooks, *John D. Lee,* 255.

upon their journey, and remember perfectly part of that order, which was in these words.—"Do not notice their threats, *Words* are but wind—they injure no one; but if they (the emigrants) commit acts of violence against citizens inform me by express, and such measures will be adopted as will insure tranquility."[21]

This order was directed to the authorities at Cedar City, from Col. Dame's headquarters in Parowan, 18 miles distant.

About this time the emigrant party proceeded onward to the Mountain Meadows, camping there a considerable time to recruit their teams for the desert country south. This delay was fatal. Had they not made these long halts, the indians would not have gathered in sufficient strength to have done them much harm, but during the two weeks of their stay indians gathered from a hundred miles around, until, emboldened by their number over 1000 they attacked the party. These things we did not understand or know of until afterwards, but learned that the emigrants parked their wagons in a circle, one behind another closely joined and dug a trench inside the wagon line throwing up the earth as a wall beneath the wagons, thus marking a strong fortification. Its fatal weakness was its distance from water, which could only be obtained by men going out in plain view of the enemy [illegible] yds. without the slightest shelter from their fire. But water they *must* have and day after day men were killed or wounded in getting it. This desultory warfare continued three or four days with loss on both [sides].

But indians cannot long continue a siege without a food supply; they cannot long continue an attack upon a fortification, and although hundreds in number did not dare attempt to assault their enemy. Enraged and determined not to allow their coveted prize to escape, they sent a demand to Maj. John D. Lee of Harmony to bring to their aid some of the settlers, with the threat that if help was not furnished, they would destroy the few Mormon Settlements in the south of Utah. It is probable they sent to him because he spoke their language and were well known to him ~~and frequently got them to work for him~~. I do not know if in going to help the indians, he knowingly disobeyed Col. Dame's order to preserve peace as he lived some distance south from Cedar City. I do know, however, he did not communicate with Col. Dame, but acted boldly upon his own volition. And the few whites he took with him to the Meadows have all testified they had no idea of what was expected of them, or they would not have gone with him ~~or taken any part in the tragedy~~. But on arrival, surrounded by the horde of infuriated savages [they] were compelled to choose between certain death at the hands of the Indians or to helping them in the fight.

---

[21]On 20 September 1857, Major Martineau filed a three-page "Topographical Report" to Col. Albert Carrington describing his survey of the Sevier River from 4 to 11 September. Utah Territorial Militia Records, 1849–1877, Series 2210, Utah State Archives, 1396. Martineau apparently had left Parowan before the Fancher party reached Cedar City and could not have drafted the order he describes.

Col. Dame was all this time in Parowan entirely ignorant of the situation at the Meadows, but when finally an express brought him intelligence, he instantly set out for the Meadows to put a stop to all hostilities. But he arrived too late. The tragedy was completed. The responsibility, so far as the settlers was concerned rests upon M̶r̶ Lee and a man of great influence commonly called Klinkensmith, who soon left the country and the church and died a miserable outcast in California.

Col. Dame arrived in time to save from the Indians about 40 little children, but i̶t̶ ̶w̶a̶s̶ with great difficulty. The Indians having tasted blood and lost numbers in the fight, were insatiable for more, like so many beasts of prey. The children thus saved were taken by various c̶h̶a̶r̶i̶t̶a̶b̶l̶e̶ ̶d̶i̶s̶p̶o̶s̶e̶d̶ families and tenderly cared for until friends and relatives came and claimed them.

Strenuous attempts were made by the Anti-Mormon officials of the Territory to implicate Brigham Young and Col. Dame as instigators of the tragedy, both of whom to my certain knowledge were absolutely ignorant of it until informed too late to prevent it.

As soon as Col. Dame received intelligence of the attack, he sent a messenger, a Mr. Haslam, well known to me, to inform Gov. Young. Haslam had orders to lose not a moment but ride for life no matter how many horses he might kill; and he did so, making a record rarely if ever equaled by any white man. He reached Salt lake City, a distance of 300 miles in 3 days accounting instantly to Gov. Young on his arrival. The Governor [gave] orders to all men in authority on his way back to furnish him with swift horses and all necessary aid to expedite his journey. Haslam made the return trip in three days, but three days too late. I believe no man ever before rode 600 miles in six consecutive days and lived. But Mr. Haslam did so. I saw him as he went through Parowan as he went and as he returned. He brought an order to Col. Dame to stop the attack upon the emigrants if it should require the entire military force of the Iron Military District to accomplish it . . .

William Dame, James Martineau claimed at the end of his defense, deserved credit for assigning the guides who turned "aside the threatened cyclone of destruction" and saved the train that followed the Fancher party from "the lust for plunder and murder" of the Indians. Without the Mormons' help, "another bloody page would have been added to frontier history," he asserted.

Chapter 13

"THE SHEEREST NONSENSE"
Damning the Dead and
Inventing the Missouri Wildcats

The failure of Utah authorities to identify the slain emigrants and inform relatives of what had happened to their loved ones deepened the grieving families' anger and distrust of the stories being told by Mormon officials. There was an obvious campaign to blacken the reputation and memory of this company, comprising some forty men, at least thirty women, and fifty or more children.

Not until one Sunday in 1955, when a petite teacher from the little town of Bunkerville, Nevada, came before a large crowd in Harrison, Arkansas, gathered to dedicate a monument to the memory of the massacre victims and survivors, did a Mormon spokesperson breech the wall of separation. Historian Juanita Brooks opened her talk with these words: "Nobody can forgive murder." She then gave the first honest, if incomplete, account of the massacre and how it came about. Later, Ronald E. Loving, a relative of Alexander Fancher, and Verne Lee, a descendant of John D. Lee, joined the state of Utah to build (with the full cooperation of the LDS church) a new monument at the massacre site. Largely thanks to the lifelong interest of Roger V. Logan, Jr., of Harrison, Arkansas, there is now engraved on a marker at Mountain Meadows the names and ages, listed by family, of the men, women, and children known to have died or been orphaned on that day of infamy.

WILFORD WOODRUFF:
THEY CURSED AND THREATENED THE PEOPLE

Knowledge gained from these developments and information that has come to light over the years exposes the falsehoods told about the victims for a century and a half. It makes clear that of all the untold thousands of emigrants who had passed through the territory before them, they would have been among the least likely to provoke a confrontation with local inhabitants. What is now known should put an end to the endless repetition of lies and slanders, usually based on second- or third-hand tales that had no other intent than to justify the unjustifiable. The drumbeat opened in 1857 when Apostle Wilford Woodruff put the initial cover-up story on record. His last version described many of the victims as being rotten from an abhorrent disease. It speaks for itself as to the truthfulness of all others before and since.

WILFORD WOODRUFF, HANDWRITTEN AFFIDAVIT, 1882, LDS ARCHIVES.

[Wilford Woodruff states] that on the twenty ninth day of September 1857, he was in Salt Lake City in conversation with President Brigham Young in the latter's office when John D. Lee arrived from Harmony in South Utah with an express.

Lee stated to President Young that a short time previously a company of emigrants to California consisting of about one hundred and fifty men, women and children passed south, many of whom belonged to the mob in Missouri and Illinois who had persecuted the Latter-day-Saints. They had many cattle and horses with them. As they travelled they did all the mischief they could, they cursed and threatened the people and their leaders, they poisoned beef and gave it to the Indians, some of whom died through eating it, they also poisoned springs of water near the settlements from drinking which some of the people died. The Indians became enraged at their conduct and they surrounded the Company on a prairie at the Mountain Meadows. The emigrants formed a bulwark of their wagons and dug an entrenchment up to the hubs of their wagons, and the Indians fought them five days until they Killed all their men about 60 in number, they then rushed into the corral and cut the throats of their women and children; except some 8 or 10 children which they bought and sold to the whites. They stripped the men and women naked and left them stinking in the broiling sun; when bro Lee went out and took some men and burried their bodies, it was a horrid job, the whole air was filled with an awful stench; many of the men and women were rotten with the pox before they were hurt by the Indians.[1] The Indians obtained all their horses, cattle, property, guns, &c.

President Young expressed deep regret and great sorrow that innocent blood had been shed in this Territory. To his expressions of regret Lee made no reply.

This is the first intimation that President Young had of the Massacre. As soon as he obtained testimony to satisfy himself that Lee had a hand in the matter he cut him off from the Church, and was ever ready afterwards to assist the United States Marshall to bring him to justice.

---

[1] Without defining words such as smallpox or chickenpox, "pox" usually referred to syphilis.

Cedar City Remembers:
Profaning and Threatening

Early sources provide vague indications that the Fancher party had some sort of conflict with the authorities at Cedar City in 1857, but starting thirty years later, local citizens recalled that the unruly Arkansans had made a number of threats and committed a variety of depredations against the community. English ironmonger Charles Willden came to Utah in 1852 when Brigham Young sent him to Cedar City to help the mission to produce iron from the ore in the region. He was fifty years old when the Arkansas train passed the settlement on its way to Mountain Meadows. In his confession, John D. Lee listed Willden's son, Elliott, as one of more than fifty men who took part in the massacre. Lee also named Alexander Willden, but may have gotten the first name of one of Willden's other sons wrong.

> I, Charles Willden, Sr., . . . depose and says that I resided in Cedar City, Iron County U. T. from the 29th of October 1852 till March 1861, that during the year 1857, was residing at the Lower Town about one mile from the present town site of Cedar City . . . and . . . on or about the 1st day of September of said year 1857, I saw a Company of Emigrants drive into said Lower Town consisting of Oxen and Horse teams, to the number of about twenty wagons. Said Company halted near the Grist Mill at the south east corner of said Lower Town where they went to get some grain ground. Returning from the mill, and between the latter and the distillery I heard some fifteen to twenty men of said company talking in a loud excited and boisterous manner profaning and threatening to do bodily harm and kill some of the citizens of said Lower town saying and affirming that they had helped to Kill Joseph Smith at Carthage, Hancock Co, Ills and other Mormons of Nauvoo and Missouri and that By G—— they would kill some more yet. That the United States troops were on the plains enroute to Utah, that they and said Company would go on to the Mountain Meadows, and wait there until the arrival of said troops into the Territory and would then return to Cedar and ~~Salt Lake~~ other towns through which they had passed in said Territory and carry out their threats . . .[2]

Anyone who knows Cedar City history might find it hard to imagine a whiskey distillery there in 1857, but since stake president Isaac Haight was its likely proprietor, its existence makes more sense. "Myself & Bro Western will not sell any more Liquir unless the people bring a recommend from the Bishop," Haight told his congregation in July 1857.[3] Telegrapher, court ste-

---

[2]Charles Willden Affidavit, 18 February 1882, LDS Archives.
[3]Cedar Stake Journal, 12 July 1857, 42–43.

nographer, and historian Josiah Rogerson remembered seeing the still, perhaps the same one referred to by Willden. As he recalled, there was an "illic-
it distillery" where the emigrants "obtained a too liberal quantity of whiskey,
which had a sad effect on several young male members of the company." After
that, the story goes, all hell broke loose.

> The young men became inebriated, going up and down the main street shot
> off their revolvers in the air and some shots becoming dangerous the consta-
> ble was ordered to arrest the reckless boys. Their friends resisted the demand,
> defying the officer, and the City authorities and some older ones joining with
> the defiant, and said that they had taken part in the massacre of the Patriarch
> at Carthage Jail and others in the mobbings at Far-west, and Nauvoo, and that
> when they got to California they would raise a sufficient force, and come back
> and wipe out the settlements in southern Utah. They went on by the way of
> Leach's Springs and Pinto Creek to the Mountain Meadows, where they made
> camp and intended to remain for at least ten days or two weeks . . .[4]

ELIAS MORRIS: BRANDISHED HIS PISTOL IN HER FACE

An English brick mason and furnace builder, Elias Morris constructed the
early iron-smelting furnaces still standing on State Highway 56 west of Cedar
City. He went on to become one of Utah's first industrialists. At the time
of the massacre Morris was captain of Company C in the Iron County Brigade
(which included such noted massacre participants as William Bateman and
Samuel McMurdy), and he served as counselor in the stake presidency. His
statement nearly thirty-five years later is problematic. Morris did not actually witness the emigrant provocations that he reports, claiming he was away
on a scouting mission, but he recalls attending a meeting two days after the
Arkansans passed through. He gives no information as to his own whereabouts when they were killed.[5]

ELIAS MORRIS STATEMENT TO ANDREW JENSON BY ELIAS MORRIS,
2 FEBRUARY 1892, LDS ARCHIVES.
Confidential so far as names are concerned
Elias Morris, Bishop of the Fifteenth Ward, Salt Lake City, was second
Counselor to Prest. Isaac C. Haight, in Cedar City, in 1857. Some time in August
of that year he volunteered to go east to watch for the arrival of a company

---

[4]Rogerson, "The Guilt of John D. Lee," 1913, LDS Archives.

[5]Further undermining his credibility, recently published statements in Milewski, ed., *Before the Manifesto*,
show that Elias Morris committed perjury during his trial for unlawful cohabitation.

of soldiers, which, according to rumor, might be expected to arrive in the Southern settlements from Texas. It was reported that a certain U.S. army captain had gone to Texas to beat-up volunteers to go against the "Mormons," and that they were to attack them from the South, while the regular army was approaching and attacking them from the East. This rumor, coupled with the idea which the people in the southern settlements had, that the Arkansas company of emigrants were, (as they themselves claimed) in some way connected with the incoming army, made the people feel very uneasy. Morris, with Joseph Pugmire as a companion, proceeded to Panguitch Lake, where they spent several days, and returned to Cedar in the beginning of September, after the Arkansas company had passed through. Men from Parowan are reported to have gone out by way of the Fremont road, looking for the same company of Texas soldiers, which, by the way, never arrived.[6]

About that time, or very soon afterwards he remembers seeing John D. Lee in Cedar City, counseling with Isaac C. Haight, about the emigrant company, who had acted very wickedly, and had threatened the people repeatedly with what they would do, while they also boasted of things they already had done. They had furthermore insulted several women, among whom [was] Barbara Morris, wife of John (Morris) and Mother of Elias Morris. This family (Morris) lived on the south street in the old town of Cedar, and Mrs. Morris happened to cross the street going toward the corrall when the company passed through. One man on horseback, a tall fellow, addressed her in a very insulting manner, and while he brandished his pistol in her face, he made use of the most insulting and abusive language, and with fearful oaths declared that he and his companions expected to return to use up the "Mormons." John M. Higbee, who, if Morris remembers right, was the marshall of Cedar City, tried to arrest this man, but he refused to be taken, and his companions stood by him, and dared the "Mormons" to arrest any of them. These matters were being discussed by Haight and Lee soon after Morris returned from Panguitch Lake, and Lee seemed very determined that the company should be made to suffer severely for their impudence and lawlessness, and said he had Indians enough around him to wipe the whole of them out of existence. Haight seemed to be more moderate in his feelings. On Sunday morning, Sept. 6th a prayer circle, composed of the members of the Cedar Stake Presidency, Bishop Klingensmith and Counselors, and the members of the High Council met as usual at the regular place of holding such meetings, and Prest. Isaac C. Haight here introduced the subject of the Arkansas company. Some of the more radical members present suggested harsh measures (none, however, favoring any wholesale killing), and others were in favor of letting the thing pass off and not

[6]Despite the vagueness of this description, Captain Morris probably ascended Coal Creek Canyon and crossed today's Cedar Breaks National Monument to Panguitch Lake. He may have continued eighteen miles to the northwest to the Sevier River, now the site of Panguitch. James Martineau was scouting John C. Frémont's 1854 route into Parowan at the same time.

bother the company. During the conversation, Elias Morris, although the youngest member present, suggested the idea of laying so important a matter before President Young, and not take any action until his judgment had been obtained in the matter. This suggestion prevailed, and the next day John Haslem [sic] started for Salt Lake City. Among those who attended that Council or prayer meeting and who opposed severe measures were John Morris, Laban Morrill,[7] [Charles] Hopkins, Pugmire, Elias Morris and others. The Bishopric of Cedar City at that time consisted of Philip Klingensmith, (Bishop) Samuel McCurdy and John Morris, (Counselors).

A few days later, perhaps on Wednesday evening, Sept, 9th, Isaac C. Haight called on Elias Morris and requested him to go with him to Parowan. His face and countenance indicated that something weighed heavily on his mind, and he desired to go and talk with Col. Dame, his superior in military command. They started late in the evening and traveled in a light wagon to Parowan, where they arrived about mid-night. Here they found Col. Dame at home, and he sent out for some of the leading men of the settlement to come to his house, where, after their arrival, a council was held, and the subject discussed was concerning the Arkansas company, who had been attacked by Indians at Mountain Meadows. The decision which was finally arrived at was to the effect that the company should be protected, if possible, from Indian violence. Brother Morris knows nothing of any other council being held in Parowan, at least this is the only council he ever attended in Parowan when the Arkansas company was under consideration. After the council was dismissed Haight and Morris returned to Cedar City, where they arrived early in the morning. The following day, if Bro. Morris remembers right, or at least not more than two days afterwards, he and C. J. Arthur went to the meadows, arriving there toward evening, and as they were traveling from Hamblin's Ranch in a southerly direction toward the place where the emigrants had encamped, they met the militia men returning from the massacre, going toward Hamblin's. Morris and Arthur were not called specially to carry any express to the Meadows, but hearing so many conflicting and terrible reports about what was going on at the Meadows, they agreed with each other that they would go out and see for themselves; but when they were about ready to start, Isaac C. Haight spoke to Morris and asked him to use his influence in the interest of peace, and do everything possible to avert the shedding of blood. Neither he nor Arthur carried anything in writing from Haight, Dame or any one else. Clewes' statement is correct, where he refers to his meeting Morris and Arthur, and a conversation like the one related by Clewes actually took place.

"Clewes" was actually Joseph Clews, a private in Company F of the Iron County Brigade. Like a number of southern Utahns, he decamped for Cali-

---

[7]Laban Morrill is usually credited with the messenger idea.

fornia shortly after the massacre, but Lee listed him among the participants at Mountain Meadows. Not long after his name appeared in the newspapers after Lee's execution, Clews apparently decided to confront his past but then reconsidered. His justification of his conduct appeared in the *Salt Lake Herald*.[8]

Joseph Clews was implicated in the Mountain Meadows massacre. Clews lives on Baseline St. [in San Bernardino, California]. He was informed of the accusation last Sunday, saddled a horse and started to overtake a man named Harris who was on his way to Utah across the desert (Mojave) with whom he intended to go to Beaver and give himself up to the authorities. While on his way he came to the conclusion that he had acted hastily and returned to Miller's Ranch on the Mojave River, where he was found by two gentlemen from San Bernardino to whom he gave a written statement of his connection with the massacre. He stated that he was not present at the massacre. He was employed as a messenger by the Mormon authorities and in that capacity was charged with a written message from J. [Isaac] C. Haight to John D. Lee. While on his way he became cognizant of the contents of the message, which was to the effect that Lee was to keep the Indians from molesting the emigrants further, etc. Clews gave the message to another to deliver to Lee, and whether it was delivered it was not known, but it was not acted on. When the troop was marched out on the morning of the massacre, Higbee told Clews he was not wanted there and to take a mule and go back. This he did, and therefore knows nothing of the slaughter.[9]

These and other accounts that try to blame the massacre on confused communications are dubious at best. Tales of misdirected orders may be comforting, but the facts show they are an illusion. Had Lee and Higbee, the senior officers, ignored or defied those orders, a court martial and the hangman's noose could have resolved all the legal questions about the massacre within months. Militia reinforcements arrived at Mountain Meadows on Thursday evening with explicit orders from headquarters to decoy and exterminate the emigrants, and those were the orders Higbee and Lee carried out.

Bishop Charles Adams of Parowan later told a compelling story about orders. Just a boy, Adams had tended the officers' horses as they conferred with William Dame before dawn on Thursday morning. As the men left Dame's house, Higbee told his commanding officer, "You know what the council decided," referring to the Stake High Council's decision to wait for word from Brigham Young. "I don't care what the council decided," said

---

[8]For the text of Clews's statement, see Walker, " 'Save the Emigrants,' " 139–52.
[9]Harshman, Notes of *Colton Semi-Tropic*, 31 March 1877, Feldheym Public Library.

Colonel Dame. "My orders are that the emigrants *must be* done away with."[10] For Dame, there was no need to wait a few days for clarification on how to proceed: he already had his orders.

An Exceedingly Fine Company of Emigrants: The Legend of the Missouri Wildcats Appears

How reliable are the "evil emigrant" stories that play such a key role in the traditional story of Mountain Meadows? A close examination reveals that they can be taken as folklore, but as historical evidence, they are worthless. Consider the legend of the "Missouri Wildcats," which does not appear in any of the contemporary reports of the massacre. Yet after springing onto the scene sixteen years later, it becomes an essential element in traditional accounts of the murders. No mention of these notorious land-pirates appeared anywhere until 1873, when purported eyewitnesses claimed to have traveled with them to Great Salt Lake City in 1857. T. B. H. Stenhouse mentioned none of these eyewitnesses by name, but his wife Fanny identified her main informant as Eli Kelsey, who abandoned the LDS church in the 1860s as a leading member of the "Godbeite" faction that opposed Brigham Young. Kelsey, however, was at Fort Bridger on 26 July 1857, when contemporary sources show the Fancher party was camped near Salt Lake.[11] Whomever Kelsey accompanied, it was not the Fancher family.

T. B. H. Stenhouse, *The Rocky Mountain Saints*, 424–28.

A few weeks in advance of the United States Expedition to Utah in 1857, there were two trains of emigrants crossing the plains with the purpose of going to southern California. One was from Missouri, the other from Arkansas. The former was composed chiefly of men who named themselves "Missouri Wild-cats;" the other train was a company of highly-respectable persons, sober and orderly, and in their associations seemed like a large gathering of kindred, or very near friends. The first were probably venturous spirits seeking fortune; the others, citizens seeking new homes . . . Those who passed the [Arkansas] company en route, or travelled with them a part of the way, were favourably impressed with their society, and spoke of them in the kindest terms as an exceedingly fine company of emigrants, such as was seldom seen on the plains.

---

[10]Brooks, *Mountain Meadows Massacre*, 80.

[11]Pulsipher, A Short Sketch of the History of John Pulsipher, 26 July 1857, Marriott Library.

OLD FOLKS' PARTY AT THE BUNKERVILLE OLD ROCK CHURCH, BEFORE 1908
The white-haired, bearded man at the front of the table may be Capt. Joel White,
who commanded a Nauvoo Legion company at Mountain Meadows, while massacre participants Nephi Johnson and Dudley Leavitt are seated at left side of the
table with their wives. *Juanita Brooks Collection, courtesy of Utah State Historical Society.*

Though utterly unlike themselves in character and disposition, the "Wildcats" contracted for them much respect, and came as near to them in travelling
as was convenient for the grazing of the cattle and the purposes of the camp
at night. Within sight of each other they would form their corrals, but, while
the one resounded with vulgar song, boisterous roaring, and "tall swearing," in
the other there was the peace of domestic bliss and conscious rectitude.

A gentleman, a friend of the Author, travelled with this Arkansas company from Fort Bridger to Salt Lake City, and speaks of them in the highest
terms: he never travelled with more pleasant companions. Hearing the night-
ly yells of the "Wild-cats," he advised the Arkansas company to separate from
them as much as possible while passing through the settlements, and in going
through the Indian country. At that time it was easy to provoke a difficulty;
the whole country was excited over the news of the "invading army;" and so
much was this gentleman impressed with the necessity of great prudence on
the part of the emigrants that, after he had left them on his arrival at Salt
Lake City, he afterwards returned and impressed upon the leading men the

urgency of refusing to travel further with the Missouri company so near to them. The kindly suggestions were appreciated, and they expressed their desire to act upon them.[12]

THOMAS W. CROPPER:
CALLED THEMSELVES THE MISSOURI WILD CATS

Few sources are more revealing of the difficulties in dealing with the myths about the Fancher party's ordeal than the tales told by Thomas Waters Cropper. Like much massacre folklore, Cropper's vivid account was created decades after the crime had occurred. It conflates dates and events, assigning every unhappy Mormon encounter with emigrants to the fall of 1857. His story is one of the favorite accounts of those who claim that the Fancher train included a band of hooligans known as Missouri Wildcats that had committed depredations against both Mormons and Indians.[13]

Born in Texas, Cropper was fourteen years old when his family migrated to Utah in 1856. In his early twenties, he recalled he met and married "one of the most beautiful girls in the country," the daughter of Colonel William Dame.[14] Cropper served in the Nauvoo Legion during the Black Hawk War and lived in Fillmore, Utah, for much of his life, but later moved to Deseret, where he wrote and dictated this life history at age 84, almost seventy years after the events he described. While many people retain remarkably accurate memories, Cropper's first line, which describes an 1858 event to begin his story of 1857, reveals that he was not one of them.

Cropper's memoir appears convincing, but a closer look reveals numerous problems. He recalled meeting the Fancher party *after* the establishment of Camp Floyd in 1858 and stated earlier that he was at Harmony in August and September 1857. He attributed an 1853 confrontation with Pahvants at Corn Creek to the 1857 Fancher party. He told of Proctor Hancock Robison's death in detail, but young Robison did not die until nearly a month after the Fanch-

---

[12]Stenhouse then presented "extracts" from the Argus letters in which Charles Wandell accused Brigham Young of ordering the Arkansans "to break up camp and move on." Interestingly, Stenhouse wrote that in the interest of brevity and fairness, Wandell's charges that Young ordered the massacre "have been nearly all left out." Stenhouse, *The Rocky Mountain Saints*, 430–31.

[13]Juanita Brooks quoted Cropper in *Mountain Meadows Massacre*, 47–48, and again in *John D. Lee*, 204–205, omitting material that reveals Cropper's poor memory.

[14]Ashby, ed., *Family History of Thomas Waters Cropper*, 38.

er train left Corn Creek. The quality of such sources claiming that the Arkansans or "Missouri Wildcats" poisoned Indians at Corn Creek validates the conclusion of historian Josiah Gibbs: "The charge that the emigrants poisoned the water is the sheerest nonsense."[15]

CROPPER, "MISSOURI WILD CATS—THEIR TROUBLE AT CORN CREEK," IN AUTOBIOGRAPHY, 29, 33–35.

The soilders [sic] having located at camp Floyd, I went with [A. F. Barron] to trade some butter and cheese for soldiers clothes.

The balance of that summer I was herding cows. In company with several other boys I was up on the benches when we saw the unusual sight of an immigrant train.[16] We ran down to where they were and accompanied them about two miles into Fillmore. They dared us to ride one of their wild steers and I got on it and it dashed into Cattelins Mill pond which caused them a lot of merriment. They moved on down to Meadow and camped just west of town. There appeared to be two companies of them joined together for safety from the Indians. One company which was mostly men called themselves the Missouri Wild Cats. One I heard one of them make the brag that he helped to mob and kill Joe Smith, and he further said, "I would like to go back and take a pop at Old Brig, before I leave the territory." They moved on over to what was know as the big Spring on the Corn Creek Sloughs. A lot of the Knosh Indians came to their camp to beg and trade. One man insisted on examining an indians bow and arrows but the indian refused and drew his [arrows and] jabbed an arrow into the man's breast the man whipped out a revolver and shot the Indian dead.[17]

SPRING POISONED: CATTLE DEAD: PROCTOR ROBINSON'S DEATH: MOUNTAIN MEADOWS

They poisoned the spring and a number of cattle died around the spring. The Indians ate some of the meat and several Indians died from the effects.

---

[15]Gibbs, *Lights and Shadows of Mormonism*, 238.

[16]Earlier, Cropper indicated he "went down into Utah's Dixie, camped at John D. Lee's (of Meadow Massacre fame)" during the summer of 1857. "While in Dixie I helped my half brother make mollasses or sorgham." John D. Lee's 1860 diary reveals that he typically did not begin harvesting sugar cane until late September, so if Cropper's memory is correct, he would have been at Harmony during the massacre. See Cleland and Brooks, eds., *A Mormon Chronicle*, 27 September to 16 October 1860, 1:274–77.

[17]Cropper recalled a real event, the Hildreth incident of 1853. On about 22 September "a party of emigrants, under command of Capt. Hildreth" killed a Pahvant chief. According to Solomon Carvalho, "some women and young men, went into Hildreth's camp merely to beg food. They were ordered out, and force was used to take away their bows and arrows; in the scuffle, one of the Americans got his hand cut with an arrow-head when they were fired upon with rifles, and several persons killed; among them this old chief." See Carvalho, *Incidents of Travel and Adventure in the Far West*, 197. The incident sparked the Gunnison massacre in October.

I went over and saw the cattle dead around the spring. Proctor Robinson [Robison] son of Joseph Robinson had been skining [*sic*] some of the cattle. He went back with me as far as Meadow and insisted on my going on to Fillmore with him. (I was staying at Barrons) He was on a poor rhone mare and I was afraid she would not carry us both—but we started for Fillmore about eight miles distant. When about two miles out it began to rain. He complained of his eye and kept rubbing it. It swelled shut and the rain came down in torrents. I slipped off from behind him and told him to whip the old mare through and get home for his face was getting very swollen.

I trugged on until I finally reached Fillmore. I was almost perishing with the cold and rain. I stopped in to warm and got something to eat at Theodore Rogers. Bro. Rogers went part way home with me and I succeeded in getting home alright.

Next morning early I went down to see Proctor. He was so swollen and bloated I would not have recognized him. He died that night. Next day I went on the range and saw a lot more dead cattle. This same company moved on South and met a sad fate at the Mountain Meadows.

SIMON WOOD: FIGHT OR PULL UP STAKES

When it comes to trespassing, reports of verbal clashes between the Fancher party and settlers at Provo and Nephi carry a ring of truth. Land in the Mormon kingdom belonged to God. It was either managed communally or parceled out to individual stewards to hold as long as they were faithful. To Mormon settlers, the emigrants' large herd destroyed grass being reserved as winter feed for the community's cattle. To the Arkansans, the communal fields near settlements belonged to the United States, pending sale under federal land laws. To them, the grazing lands in Utah were the common property of all American citizens.

Assistant LDS church historian William Lund collected an account of the Arkansas train's actions in the twentieth century, perhaps from John G. McQuarrie, a mission president and sometime resident of southern Utah. He also told Lund that "It was generally known that there was a secret police group in Utah just as there were vigelantees [*sic*] in other states, but few if any outside the group and officers who appointed them knew the extent of their operations." Lund's informant said he met Simon Wood while building a ranch near Hebron.

[Simon Wood] told me that while acting as a city Marshall [and as] an officer in the militia at Provo the company in question camped in the meadows just west of the town fields. He rode down to see that the hay meadows, which they saved for winter use, was not disturbed. By the height of the red top and timothy and the way the section was marked off no one could mistake the purpose for which the plot was saved. He found the intruders with near 400 head of livestock camped in the meadow. Wood rode up to the team captain, advised him in calm manners of the purpose and necessity of the winter feed for domestic animals, without which they could not winter through themselves. He informed him that there was a large valley of virgin grass and brouse [sic] a few miles to the west . . . and that he would assist in camp moving. The cocky captain answered with some feeling, "This is Uncle Sam's grass. We are his boys. We have a better claim on it than a bunch of rebel Mormons which had to be kicked out of one state to another and finally out of the United States. We are staying right here." Wood said "Your gauntlet is down" and gave the party "60 minutes to decide whether you want to fight or pull up stakes."

Lund's source said that the party left the contested ground. He had an equally interesting description of his meeting with the former president of the Southern Indian Mission, whom Brigham Young had replaced with Jacob Hamblin:

Rufus Allen . . . told me he was traveling north on his way to Beaver. About half way up the grade of the ridge he met the lead wagon of this California-bound company. He pulled his wagon out into the rocks and waited for the long caravan to pass. Soon the captain of the company rode along on a well-groomed, well-bred horse. I suppose [he was] trying to get to the head of the train. Allen saluted in a friendly way [and] said, "I see that you have not been killed yet by any of these Mormons." The captain instead of acknowleging [sic] the courtesy shown by Allen by giving them the right of way and sitting in the sun among the rocks for at least half an hour with an oath he answered, "No, the sons of bitches dare not tackle us or they would have done so before this."[18]

---

[18]Anonymous, MMM File, Folders 33 and 34, LDS Archives.

Chapter 14

"These Painted
Blood-Thirsty Indians"
Participant Accounts

A close look at Mormon culture, especially during the emotional firestorm
of 1856–57 known as the Reformation, provides part of the answer to
the question of what compelled seventy or so mostly respected, God-
fearing heads of families who cared for their wives and children to massacre
an emigrant party composed mostly of women and children.

Given the nature of early Utah's theocracy and the obligation to inform
on dissenters, it should be expected that some of the confessed perpetrators
of the atrocity claimed that they acted out of fear. Nor is it surprising that
among such deeply religious people a few found the courage to refuse to take
part in murdering unarmed men and helpless women and children. Pioneer-
ing Utah journalist Josiah Gibbs remembered that Nate Dodge once told
him how William Hawley was "chained to a wagon wheel during the massacre, as he threatened to fight for the emigrants. He went crazy, and remained
so until his death. Used to get up in ward meetings and curse Brigham, but
the brthren [sic] listened to him quietly. Then the Bishop would get up and
say: 'We will have to bear with brother Hawley, as we all know the things he
has gone through.' "[1]

Another striking aspect of the massacre is that so few of those who committed it, virtually none a criminal by nature, later came forward honestly to
confess their role in it. Only when ordered by Brigham Young through his
counselor Daniel Wells did selected participants speak out—and they only
said as much as it took to convict John D. Lee, not expose their own or any-

---

[1]Charles Kelly Papers, conversation notes with Josiah Gibbs, 19, 20 September 1931.

NEPHI JOHNSON, CIRCA 1880
While searching for remote, secure
locations with a Southern Paiute guide,
Nephi Johnson became the first Anglo to
visit Zion Canyon in 1858. As one of the
most sympathetic of the characters
associated with the massacre, his
experiences as a young lieutenant in
the Nauvoo Legion haunted him until
his dying day. *Courtesy Elsie Hewitt.*

one else's guilt. A handful in later life who felt a need to cleanse their consciences or restore their family reputation gave statements. But as the following examples show, they were careful not to incriminate themselves or anyone else then still alive.

As a result, there is not a single eyewitness account that is straightforwardly
honest and free of inconsistencies. Much like the confessions of John D. Lee,
each is an artful amalgam of fact and falsehood, created to absolve all but Lee
and Klingensmith of any personal responsibility whatever. Though haunted
by memories and destined to live on the outer fringes of society, Mormon or
otherwise, most refused to violate the oath they had sworn on that bloody
field and took to the grave the truth about what they did and why.[2]

NEPHI JOHNSON: DESTROY THE TRAIN

Nephi Johnson was born into Mormonism at Kirtland, Ohio. At the age of
17 he was sent as a member of the mission to establish an iron industry in

---

[2]Three of these unpublished participant accounts are from Collected Material Concerning the Mountain Meadows Massacre, LDS Archives, the "subject file" Andrew Jenson began assembling in 1892. In 1996,
it was still an "unprocessed item." In October 2002, archives officials denied graduate student Michael
Graffman and other scholars access to this trove of affidavits, alibis, and folktales. Archives managers say
the material, now reorganized, is again available.

southern Utah. Four years later he was called to become a missionary to the Southern Paiute Indians. Like other massacre participants, Johnson downplayed his own role in the sworn statement he gave at age 75 in 1908.

Johnson recalled that he had been harvesting crops "when two men came to my place and stated that Isaac C. Haight had sent them to request me to come to Cedar City immediately." Haight told him he wanted Johnson "to go to the Mountains and settle a difficulty between John D. Lee and the Indians, as the latter had threatened to kill Lee. Haight also said that Lee and the Indians had went to the Meadows to kill the emigrants, and had made three attacks upon them, but had found the emigrants better fighters than they had expected and as some of the Indians had been killed and quite a number had been wounded they were getting tired of it." Lee suggested withdrawing and letting the emigrants go, but Haight "sent word to Lee to clean up the dirty job he had started, and that he had sent out a company of men with shovels to bury the dead, but they would find something else to do when they got there."

Johnson claimed that he went to Mountain Meadows with John M. Higbee and others, arriving at Hamblin's ranch "about 10 o'clock at night where we found John D. Lee and the principal Indian chiefs were gathered. After discussing the trouble between Lee and the Indians, Lee stated that they would try and get the emigrants to leave their camp and give up their arms after which they would kill them. This satisfied the Indians." Johnson acted as interpreter while Lee made arrangements with the Indians.

No Indians were in sight the next morning when Lee sent "a man with a flag of truce" to the camp. On his return, "Lee stated they had agreed to come out under a promise to take them to Cedar City pending a settlement with the Indians."

> The arrangements were that the wounded emigrants and the little children should be put into wagons, the women followed on foot behind the wagons, and the men were drawn out single file behind the women, each man of the emigrants walked by the side of a white man, the white man walking on the right side of the emigrant along the road. After marching along for some time, the signal Halt was given, at which each white man was to kill the emigrant man at his side. The Indians were in ambush at the place where the signal was given, and at that signal quite a number of the posse failed to kill his man, for the reason that they did not approve of the killing.

The plan, Johnson claimed, "was for the Indians to kill the women and children and wounded and the white men of the posse to kill the men of the emigrants, but owing to some of the white men of the posse failing to kill their men, the Indians assisted in finishing the work. There were about 150 Indians present." Johnson did not think the killing required more than five minutes. "I was within 25 yards of the head of the column of men as they marched up the road and saw it all," he claimed. He thought fifteen or sixteen children were spared. After the killing, Johnson said he and a posse were sent to stop the Indians from looting the wagons. He let "them take what they had and stopped them from doing any more." Haight arrived from Cedar City about half an hour after the massacre. "Haight asked me what I would do with this property. I asked him if he wanted to know my real feelings about it and he said yes. Then I said you have made a sacrifice of the people, and I would burn the property, and let the cattle roam over the country for the Indians to kill, and go home like men." Instead, Lee auctioned off the cattle at Cedar City and gave most of the proceeds to the Indians.[3]

No one expressed the horror of the massacre and the wound it left on the souls of those who took part as vividly as Johnson while he lay dying. Despite the equivocations in his 1908 statement, as a Nauvoo Legion officer and interpreter he had played a central role in killing the women and children. Shortly before his death in 1919, he cried in delirium, "Blood! Blood! Blood!"[4]

Before then, he answered the request of LDS assistant church historian Anthon H. Lund in 1909 "to treat the subject as fully as you can within the range of your own personal experience."[5] Johnson replied in a painfully primitive hand, capitalizing all the words, almost a year after Lund had requested it. The affidavit differed substantially from the one he swore in 1908 and was probably among the documents that lay "a large brown envelope, so old that it was cracking" on the table between an LDS church official and Juanita Brooks when he denied her access to it.[6]

---

[3]Johnson Affidavit, in Brooks, *The Mountain Meadows Massacre*, 224–26.

[4]As described by Juanita Brooks, who stayed at his house for two days before he died at age 85, in *John Doyle Lee*, 15.

[5]Lund's letter on Office of the First Presidency letterhead commended Johnson for refusing to reply to any other requests and urged him not to deviate from that position. Johnson returned Lund's letter with his reply.

[6]Brooks, *The Mountain Meadows Massacre*, 217–18; and Peterson, *Juanita Brooks*, 159–61, 167–68, 176.

NEPHI JOHNSON TO ANTHON LUND, MESQUITE, NEVADA,
MARCH 1910, LDS ARCHIVES.

Dear Brother

Enclosed you will find my statement in relation to the Mountain Meadows Massacre. I will say by way of introduction to the Affidavit Enclosed that I came with my Father Joel H Johnson to Salt Lake Valley in the year 1848. We arrived where Salt Lake City now stands Oct 19 of that year and when the Wards were organized my father was appointed Bishop of Mill Creek Ward. He claimed a piece of land south of Mill Creek near Big Cottonwood where we lived until the Fall of 1850 when my father was called to go with President George A Smith to help make a settlement at Little Salt Lake (or Iron Co. Utah). My father not being able to settle up his business in time to go with the Company so he fitted up two teams & sent my oldest brother and myself with the company and we arrived where Parowan (Iron Co Utah) now stands by Jan 13 1851. My father came on in the spring bringing his family with him and in the fall of 1851 my father took all of the surplus stock of the 2 settlements Parowan & Cedar City to herd. We moved them to some springs six miles north of Cedar City now known as Enoch where I had to take care of them. I hired 2 young Indians to help me and keeping them near me most of the time I soon learned their language so I could converse with them on all common subjects. I was the first white man who learned the Piute language and for this reason I was cal[l]ed to go out with exploring parties and others who had business with the Indians. I was always kind to them and when I was present was successful in settling difficulties with them without killing them and I was known throughout Southern Utah as a friend to the Indians and in the fall of 1853 was called by Apostle Erastus Snow as a missionary to the Piute Indians of Southern Utah. And I often went with emigrant trains as far as the Muddy and Las Vagas to pilot them safely by the Indians who lived along the road. In 1854 or 5 Jacob Hamblin and other men were sent as missionaries to the Indians. They located at Harmony where John D Lee & others had a few Indians farming on Ash Creek. In 1856 the missionaries left Harmony & settled at Pinto Creek 25 miles west of Harmony. From there they visited the Indians on the Santa Clara[,] the Virgin and Muddy rivers.

In 1857 the US Army started for Utah which made considerable excitement among the people of Utah and sometime in September of that year a company of emigrants came south from Salt Lake City going the southern route to California which could be traveled during winter without danger of snow or cold. This company were defiant and aggressive and took delight in telling the people that the Army was coming to hang Brigham Young & the leading Mormons and they said many things to excite the people at Cedar City. (I was informed of this by people that lived at Cedar City.)

A few days after they had passed through President Isaac C Haight who presided over Cedar City and the settlements in Washington County sent a boy out to the ranch where I was living six miles north of Cedar City. He said Prest Haight wanted me to come to Cedar to talk with the Indians or the Squaws [who] were stealing wheat out of the Field—when I arrived at Cedar he saddled his horse and rode with me to the Indian camp about 4 miles distant and while riding to the camp he told me that John D Lee had been up from Harmony the day before and that Lee had proposed to him to gather up the Indians and distroy the train of Emigrants who had passed through Cedar two days before.

And said he had told him to go ahead & do so but Haight said he had sent a man to President Young to know what to do about it.[7] Then he asked me what I thought about it. I said to him it would be a fearful responsibility for a man to take upon himself to distroy that train of Emigrants and that I would wait until I rec[eived] word from President Young. He replied that Lee had already gone to raise the Indians. I said in reply that I would sent [sic] a man to tell him to wait if I was in his place. I also told him that there was a much better place on the Santa Clara to attack the train. I was in hopes he could put off the distruction [sic] of the train until he received word from President Young for I was satisfied what his answer would be. I then went home to the ranch and a day or two after an Indian runner came from the Mountain Meadows and stated that they had made an attackt [sic] on the emigrant train the night before & had been repulsed. He also said that the Indians wanted me to come out there for they were tired of Lee[']s Indian boy interpeter [sic] [as] he lied to them so much. I said to the Indian that I did not want anything to do with killing the emigrants for I was determined in my own mind that I would keep away from them but when the men came after me at the ranch they said to me that Haight said to them that I must come whether I wanted to or not [and] that he [Haight] would tell me what he wanted when I arrived at Cedar City (See Over). Bro Lund I have written the foregoing statement in a rather rough style but it is the best I can do for I am not educated but the statement is true as I saw it.

With Sincere Regards

I am as ever yours
Nephi Johnson

To Nephi Johnson's credit, he had been more forthright about what had happened when he spoke with Apostle Francis M. Lyman in 1895. Lyman had crossed Mountain Meadows with the Mathews-Tanner train the night after the massacre took place and had long been haunted by the event.

---

[7] An apparent reference to James Haslam.

DUDLEY LEAVITT, CIRCA 1890
Massacre participant Leavitt told his
granddaughter, Juanita Brooks, that he
witnessed Brigham Young order the
destruction of the 1859 U.S. Army cairn
marking a mass grave at Mountain Meadows.
Courtesy of the Utah State Historical Society.

FRANCIS M. LYMAN, DIARY EXCERPT, 19, 21 SEPTEMBER 1895,
FIRST PRESIDENCY VAULT, LDS CHURCH.

19 September 1895, St. Joseph, Nevada: After meeting bro George Adair told me all about the Mountain Meadow affair. There were but few White men who shed blood. John M. Higby and Joseph [Joel] White were the worst, having killed a dozen each. Haight did no killing. [William C.] Stewart was not there. Lee also did much killing. White fired on the camp.

21 September 1895, Bunkerville, Nevada: Bros Dudly Leavitt and Nephi Johnson were in the meeting. I talked with those two about the Mountain Meadows Massacre. The first gave me but little information. Bro. Johnson was the man who gave the word to the Indians to fire at the last general killing. He denies that Higby and White did the killing that Adair tells of. He says white men did most of the killing. He says Higby deserves mercy.[8]

Johnson's admission that "white men did most of the killing" completely undercuts the Mormon accounts claiming that "the Indians made us do it," making it the single most significant piece of new evidence about the massacre to appear since Juanita Brooks's groundbreaking work appeared in 1950.

---

[8]Since the original journal is unavailable to researchers at LDS Archives, this section relies on Edward Leo Lyman's transcription available in Lyman, "Diary Excerpt," *New Mormon Studies* CD-ROM. We have corrected "Kirby" to "Higby."

Maj. John M. Higbee's notoriety as the
Nauvoo Legion officer who gave the fatal order
at Mountain Meadows did not stop him from
serving as Cedar City's mayor from 1867 to 1871.
Courtesy Special Collections, Southern Utah University.

JOHN M. HIGBEE: LIKE A LOT OF INFURIATED WOLVES

From reading his 1896 statement, one would never imagine that Maj. John
M. Higbee was the commander of the Mormon troops on the field that day
who gave the order: "Halt!" that touched off a mass murder. As the slaughter wound down, Philip Klingensmith watched as Higbee murdered a man,
no doubt an apostate, in an apparent act of blood atonement:

> A: I didn't see but one man killed—and that man was wounded a little
> and was lying on the ground. And John M. Higbee went up to him and drew
> his knife and cut his throat. This man begged for his life, and he was lying
> on the ground when that was done.
> Q: How far from the ranks was he when that was done?
> A: Not more than a rod. He said, "Higbee, I wouldn't do this to you." He
> knew Higbee, it appears. And the reply was that, "You would have done the
> same to me, or just as bad."[9]

Higbee held the office of counselor to Isaac C. Haight in the Cedar Stake
of Zion. Years after the massacre and after serving as mayor of Cedar City,
he and others went into hiding and did not return to live in Utah perma-
nently until well after John D. Lee's execution.

---

[9]Backus, *Mountain Meadows Witness*, 137.

Posing as "Bull Valley Snort," Higbee had a written a detailed justification of his actions in 1894.[10] He made a second statement in June 1896, ten weeks after a Utah state court dismissed his 1874 indictment for murder in "the People of the United States in the Territory of Utah against John M. Higbee." Ironically, the motion to dismiss came from David H. Morris, the prosecuting attorney for Washington County, "and was made upon the grounds that there is no such sovereignty as that stated in the caption of the indictment, and for the further reason that evidence could not be secured that would warrant a conviction."

A turnout of surviving Mountain Meadows functionaries acted as Higbee's attorneys, including Jabez G. Sutherland, the legal defender who abandoned John D. Lee when his more powerful client, Brigham Young, withdrew his support, and J. Ward Christian, the man who on 4 October 1857 signed the first Mormon-vetted account of the murders that appeared in the *Los Angeles Star* six days later. Higbee's attorneys submitted "a petition for its dismissal signed by three hundred persons many of whom were leading citizens of the State," the *Salt Lake Tribune* reported. "This disposes of the last indictment pending found against those implicated in the Mountain Meadow massacre, except that against William C. Stewart, who is dead."[11]

Higbee signed the following statement on 15 June 1896 before notary public Mathew H. Dalley. It was witnessed by Henry Leigh and Andrew Corry, a member of the jury that convicted John D. Lee of murder. Its date indicates that the dismissal of charges did little to put the matter to rest. Higbee's account is now in the possession of the LDS church.

JOHN MOUNT HIGBEE, STATEMENT, 15 JUNE 1896, LDS ARCHIVES.
TO MY FAMILY, FRIENDS OF MY YOUTH AND EXILE, OR ANY WHOM IT MAY CONCERN:

I, John M. Higbee, after a forced absence of over 38 years, do now in all soberness and humility, herein express my gratitude to God, and all who have in any way befriended me, realizing in all my afflictions and wanderings, that if right and reason held sway, religious or political hatred could not have worked so great [a] hardship on me personally, as also the good people of Utah, by the overt act of one man.

The tragedy at "Mountain Meadows," Washington County, of which with others I was accused, was to us the most revolting. We used all the influence

[10]Brooks, *The Mountain Meadows Massacre*, 226–35.

[11]"Echo of Mountain Meadow: Indictment Against J. M. Higbee Dismissed. Impossible to Convict," *The Salt Lake Tribune*, 28 February 1896, 8/4.

we could to save the Company, and it is believed our efforts saved the children that were spared, yet I have been accused and represented as one of the worst.

The "Judge McKean raid" has been the cause of much unnecessary suffering; if the matter had been investigated when Johnston's Army came in, as requested by Brigham Young, Justice could have been vindicated and Mercy satisfied.

With Statehood, I think our friends need not be afraid of being implicated if they speak the truth on our behalf; though many of them are sleeping in the dust that knew our history best. Much has been written and more could be, of this event and the causes leading up to it.

It has not been popular to say anything in our favor for a generation past. I now wish to represent myself, hence, in an abriged [sic] form, [to] endeavor to give a few of the leading causes that led to that sad affair.

What is known as the "Buchannan" [sic] or "Mormon War" was one cause of the whole trouble. "Mormons" had been mobbed and driven time and again until they arrived in this Desert country, amongst the wild Indians and animals, poorly armed, clothed, and but poorly fed, without friends or sympathy.

September, 1857, news came of Buchannan's Army approaching (people called it a mob), which was heralded though the land; Leaders of the Church called on people to repent of all their sins; unite together, and prepare for the coming struggle at hand, and invoke the blessings of God on all their endeavors to protect themselves and families from Mob Violence, so there was with many a great reformation, with others a craze of fanaticism, stronger than we would be willing now to admit.

Former wrongs of mobbings and rapine were common topics of speakers to dwell upon. In the midst of this the "Nauvoo Legion" was fully organized and drilled, standing guard, building Forts and spying out passes in the mountains, discussing the best means for defending ourselves and families against the approaching army, looking out places of security for our families in case we had to burn our towns and flee to the mountains. Of course, with a people feeling thus, every means in right and reason was used to secure the Friendship of the surrounding Tribes of Indians, so they could be used as allies should the Necessity come to do so.

John D. Lee was, and had been Indian Farmer in Washington County for several years, having much influence with the "Natives." About this time word came from the far North, (there being no regular Mails), that some of the Army, and "Nauvoo Legion" had an engagement, so the word spread like "Wild Fire" that hostilities had begun. Major Lee, ambitious for Glory, as was thought at the time, without consulting his Commander, Colonel Dame, sent runners and gathered Indians from the surrounding country, and made a feast for them; then trained them on his own volition, disciplining them for service to be used as he affirmed against the approaching Army: About this time the Arkansas Company came along travelling South through the settlements. They had boasted of mobbing and made threats of what they would yet do, bringing on themselves some trouble with the Indians at Corn Creek, Millard County, by putting poison on the carcass of an ox that died, causing the death of several natives who had eaten the meat. Now whether Lee's Indians of their own accord got up the fight, or were otherwise prompted for revenge may never be known, but the fight was gotten up all the same, and this news spread over the Southern country. Isaac C. Haight hearing of it, sent word to Colonel Dame who at once sent an Express to Lee to do all he could to pacify the Indians, to let the Company go, and [make] the Indians go back to their own homes.

The next that I knew of, Lee sent an Express to Cedar stating that the Indians had killed all the Emigrants and asking for Volunteers to go out to help bury them. Some went to assist as requested but were deceived by Lee's report, for when they got there, thirty-five miles distant, the Indians were still fighting the remnant of the Company. The confusion and frenzy of these painted blood-thirsty Indians was terrible to behold; centered at that place were four to six hundred wild Indians engaged. An Express was immediately sent to Col. W. H. Dame, to Parowan, again reporting the facts; the Colonel took some interpreters and a squad of men and started as soon as possible for the scene of the trouble, distant about sixty miles from Parowan; when he arrived all was silent in Death, so all turned in and gave them a rude burial. Thus ended that part of the "Mountain Meadow" trouble.

The causes above named, the old settlers of that part of the country, will remember when they dare speak, as well as some that have had all the prejudice to bear, stirred up by irresponsible men.

To say that some of us have suffered and been obliged to leave our families and all that was near and dear or was worth living for, as wandering refugees to live an underground life, is putting it very lightly.

During the great interim another generation has grown up, who knows nothing of the calamity only by the overdrawn statements told about it, of the "Mormon War," and those exciting times, which has lost nothing by being repeated over and over for the last thirty-eight years. Any one can see at a glance by what I have written that Buchannan's Army coming against the "Mormons" through lies told, was the cause or foundation of the trouble, which led to the gathering of the Indians by Lee, and after they were gathered, all the men of Southern Utah could not control them, not even Lee himself, they were like a lot of infuriated wolves.

Major Lee was an aspiring Glory Seeking man, who ran before he was sent, [who] after getting into trouble himself, he with Klingen Smith sought to implicate all the leading men of Iron County, and the Leaders of the "Mormon Church" who did not know anything about the matter in time to save the Emigrant Company.

You may say: Can you prove what you have written? Most of it I can by many of the old settlers of that part of the country in 1857, wherever they may be, and I can and do solemnly affirm that this is literally true to the best of my memory, "So help me God."

John M. Higbee

I thought it right to say this much to all concerned and especially to my own family, who have suffered great indignities by being called the children of a man roaming over the earth without a name or a home.

Now I trust the most of the "Black Clouds of Prejudice" may disappear, Justice be vindicated, the bitter abuse of the Jury Law cease, and a candid Judge rule for Law and Right.

The foregoing statements of facts and sentiment of my mind were written for my family and friends, since which time, the Judge of the District Court at Beaver has recently decided the Grand Jury Indictment held against My Liberty, all these years, as faulty and obselete [sic], and my thanks and gratitude goes out to all my friends and honorable men, who united to petition the Court in my behalf, who have known my previous record and character, and laterly of my long and trying exile growing out of these peculiar conditions over which I had no control, in the proper discharge of my duty.

John M. Higbee

JOEL W. WHITE: I HAVE BEEN MISUNDERSTOOD

Joel W. White was a leading player in the massacre on several fronts. At age 28 he was captain of one of the Iron County militia companies that killed the unarmed emigrant men and was accused of murdering the older children. White's testimony in 1876 helped put John D. Lee in front of a firing squad. Later he denied rumors that he had also given damaging testimony against his commanding officer, John M. Higbee. In so doing, he upheld his oath of secrecy and indirectly confirmed that Lee's second trial was intended to convict Lee and exonerate all other participants in the massacre.

JOEL S. WHITE, TO WHOMSOEVER IT MAY CONCERN,
9 OCTOBER 1896, LDS ARCHIVES.

I, Joel W. White, having been told that I had given damaging testimony against John M. Higbee, in reply will say: I have been misunderstood if that is the case; for I could say nothing and tell the truth that would harm him (John M. Higbee) in the least; but whenever Higbee's name came up there was something I could never forget, viz: A base insult thrown at him by "Lee." "I will tell and swear to its truth whenever and whereever [sic] it can be used to counter [George W.] ADAIR's Lies." The disposition shown by the U.S. Federal Officers at Lee's trial at Beaver to "Hang the Mormon Church" or "Hang some of its Leaders," may have confused me; as anything said that did not accuse somebody was not wanted. If any words were construed to mean something different from what I intended I was not aware of it. I cannot remember saying anything to the detriment of John M. Higbee; but I shall always remember the insult thrown at Higbee by Lee! I think others can be found who heard what I refer to, without going over all that History, which for the sake of the living as well as the dead should be corrected and if possible forgotten. There were some merciful men that volunteered to go out there and bury the dead; for John D. Lee had sent an express from the "Mountain Meadows" to Cedar City stating that the Indians had killed all the Emigrant Company, and asked for volunteers to come and help bury the dead. I was one of the Company of Volunteers who went on that humane errand. When we reached the "Meadows" the Indians were still fighting the Emigrants. About this time Lee got an express from Colonel W. H. Dame telling him to treat with the Indians in some way to let the Emigrants go and [let] the Natives take part of the stock and go to their homes.

In addition to the above statement I hereby certify that I have carefully read the affidavits of Wm. Tate and Daniel S. Macfarlane (which are herewith attached) and I solemnly swear that to my best knowledge and belief they are true in every detail.[12]

Joel W. White

Subscribed and sworn to before me this 9th day of October A.D. 1896
James Jack
Notary Public

SAMUEL GOULD: THEY HELD TWO OF US AS HOSTAGES

Typical of the many fables about the massacre is the statement attributed to Samuel Gould. Gould was apparently the son of his long-lived Connecticut Yankee namesake, who was sixty-seven years old in 1846 when he enlisted in the U.S. Army's Mormon Battalion. As a captain of ten in Parley P. Pratt's 1849 expedition to southern Utah, the elder Gould was one of the first Mormons to visit the region. He helped found Parowan and died there at the age

---

[12]The Daniel S. Macfarlane affidavit of 29 June 1896, published as Appendix 3 in Brooks, *The Mountain Meadows Massacre*, 235–37, and the William Tait affidavit of the next day have only minor differences.

of 91. All that is known of the Samuel Gould who told the following tale to
Iron County chronicler Luella Dalton is that he had brother named Jacob.[13]

STATEMENT SIGNED BY SAM GOULD,
JUANITA BROOKS PAPERS, UTAH STATE HISTORICAL SOCIETY.

One evening I was spending with Jesse N. Smith in the early 70's, Smith
Rogers was also with us in the Smith home. Jesse N. was seated at his desk,
when a man came in whom I recognized as John M. Higbee was sitting near
him, and the following conversation took place. Higbee said, "Brother Smith,
what I am going to tell you must never be repeated until you are sure we have
all been dead at least two years. Now you must give me your word of honor
that it will never be repeated." Brother Smith gave this promise. Higbee than
made the following statement:

"I was walking down the street in Cedar City early one morning when I
met Bro. Philip Clingingsmith and he said to me John, I've got a scheme that
we can make some money easily and quickly. That of course interested me,
and I said, What is it, Bro Philip? He said the Indians are going to massacre
that train of emigrants, they are gathering by hundreds from all over the country for that purpose. I knew that to be a fact. Philip said, Let's go out there
and talk with the Indians and get them to let us have the property they don't
want, such as wagons, harnesses, tools, etc. That struck me as being just the
thing, so I suggested that we go see brother Isaac Haight and see what he
thinks about it. We walked over to talk with Haight, and when we told him
our plan, he fell right in with us. So we started right in to get ready to go. We
never told a soul, not even our wives.

After making preparations to leave we told our wives we were going up
north on some very important business, and if any one inquired for us, to
tell them we had gone North, and didn't know when we would return. Don't
make any inquiries for us nor look for us until you see us coming. After dark
we rode out of town to the North. We had a saddle horse and a pack horse
each. We traveled a short distance North, then separated, agreeing to meet at
a certain place—way out west of Cedar. This we did to cover up our tracks.
Then we traveled on together until we came to the Indian Camp. We stayed
there for four days among the Indians trying to make them understand that
we wanted the property that they did not want, after they had killed the emigrants. But we could not talk Indian very well and they couldn't talk English,
so we couldn't make them understand what we wanted. We decided then to
send for Brother John D. Lee to come and interpret for us.

We sent an Indian runner with a note to Brother John D. and in a very
short time the Indian and Bro John were back. We explained to him what we

---

[13]Dalton, ed., *History of Iron County Mission and Parowan, the Mother Town*, 2.

wanted, and instead of him interpreting for us he took the management of the whole thing. He talked to the Indians and we couldn't understand, then he talked with us and they couldn't understand. In a few days he helped the Indians plan an attack and two of the Indians were killed. Then the Indians told us we'd have to help them. They held two of us as hostages and sent the other two for help, telling them if they weren't back by a certain time, they would kill the other two and declare war on the Mormons. The two that went to town [and] sounded the call for minute men to gather at the meeting place, they quickly gathered and they said follow us.—and rode out of town. A very few men asked where are we going, and they said, follow us. There were a few who refused to go. The two men swore the others to secrecy.

When we reached Leeche's spring we met the other two and some Indians there, too. We told each man that we would be responsible for every act if they would obey orders. Then we went on and helped the Indians do the awful work.

Just after everything was over and quiet again, eight men from Parowan rode up, [and] Bro. Dame commenced wringing his hands and saying, Too bad, too bad. John spoke up in the presence of all the boys and said, It is too bad to see all these people lying dead around here, but wasn't it too bad for you to order it done. That was the way he had of throwing the responsibility on some one else, for they can't prove it on him. But Dame did not know anything about it, only [that] the militia had gone from Cedar—so Col Dame had took seven men, Edward Dalton, Jesse N. Smith and five others and rode out there and all the men believed he had ordered it—even Jesse N. Smith did not know but what he had.

(Statement written by Mrs. Luella Adams Dalton at the dictation of Sam Gould, and signed by him.)

SAMUEL R. KNIGHT:
THE BUTCHERY OF THE UNARMED AND HELPLESS

Samuel Knight's account, like many others, distances himself from the actual killing and volunteers no names but Lee, Klingensmith, and the dead. Knight told an LDS apostle his story almost four decades after the murders. Though often inaccurate—for example, martial law was not in force until 15 September—his description contains odd revelations.

ABRAHAM H. CANNON, JOURNAL, 11 JUNE 1895, MARRIOTT LIBRARY.
I had the pleasure of meeting Brother Samuel Knight with whom I conversed about the Mountain Meadows Massacre, he being able, of all living men to

give the best account of that miserable affair as he was an eye-witness to part of it. He informed me that there was only one man, and that Pres. D. H. Wells, to whom he had given the narration, but he seemed to have no hesitation in telling me of the event, though he expected me not to use it in any way: He had only recently been married when the news of the coming of this emigrant train reached his ears. He and his wife were living at the north end of the Mountain Meadows when the emigrants passed along, and they inquired of him where they could procure pasturage for their animals, and rest for themselves for a few days before starting out on the deserts to the west. He directed them to the south end of the valley where grass and water were abundant. Some of the emigrants were very boastful and seemed to be filled with a wicked spirit. The Territory was at that time under martial law, as the United States army was approaching from the east. These emigrants said they would go to California and raise a company of soldiers, returning to attack the Mormon people on the west, and thus destroy their homes. These boastings they had expressed through the settlements of the people on the north, and it had a tendency to aggravate the Saints who had already suffered so much at the hands of mobs. After the emigrants had been located at the south end of the valley a day or two, a messenger came from the authorities in Cedar City, but whether they were the military or ecclesiastical authorities who gave the command, Brother Knight does not now remember. This message, which he accepted as an order that could not be disobeyed without imperiling his own life, commanded him to go to the South, in the neighborhood of St. George and Santa Clara, and instruct the Indians to arm themselves and prepare to attack the emigrant train. This attack it was proposed to make at the junction of the Santa Clara and Magotsu [Creek], a point which we yesterday passed, as we came down a very steep incline, before we arrived in Gunlock. Brother Knight did not return with the Indians, but remained to do some necessary work on the ranch which he and another brother owned where Santa Clara now stands, but after laboring for two days he and his companion, feeling anxious to know what had occurred at the Meadows, mounted their horses and started for the place. While passing through the willows only a short distance to the south of the place, they were accosted by John D. Lee. He informed them that an attack had been made upon the emigrants, who had formed a corral of their wagons and were defending themselves. The Indians had surrounded them as far as they could, without exposing themselves to danger, and some of the emigrants had been killed. As Brother Knight passed on the way to his ranch at the north end of the valley, he saw the militia camped at the place where Joseph Burgess's house now stands, and on reaching his home he heard considerable shooting, which made his wife very nervous, she having but recently given birth to his first child. He did not go to the scene of the firing, however, but remained at his home until a message came requiring him to hitch his team to his wagon, there being only one other team in the valley, and proceed with it to the south end of the valley where the arms of the emigrants were to be loaded into his wagon, together with the children who were able to walk, he being thus informed that the besieged had surrendered. He refused to go at first but was told he himself would be punished if not slain, and his team and wagon would be taken any way. Against the protests of himself and wife he was thus forced to answer the call made upon him, though his feelings, as he says, were most terrible. Arriving at the place of the attack, his wagon was loaded with the arms of the emigrants, on top of which was piled some bedding and thereon some wounded and some of women and children were placed until his wagon was loaded to its utmost capacity. He then proceeded on his way, together with the other wagon, which was similarly loaded. Those who were able to walk were then formed in line and they proceeded towards the north end of the valley where his ranch was located. As they reached the summit of a slight elevation, shots were fired from the oak brush on the side of the road, and then occurred the butchery of the unarmed and helpless men, women and children, the Indians and the white men taking part alike in the slaughter. One man he particularly noticed as being blood-thirsty. His name was [William C.] Stewart, now dead. He seemed filled with an insane desire to slaughter as many as possible, and he hewed them down without mercy. The scene was most horrible, and the bodies of the victims were left upon the hill until the following day when a slight hole was dug in the ground and the slain were thrown into it, though the wolves subsequently uncovered the remains and picked the bones. Not until some years later were the skeletons buried decently. That same night Haight, Dame and others took supper at Brother Knight's house, and he learned that none of the general authorities of the Church had sanctioned or encouraged in any way the dastardly deed of which these fanatics were guilty. Indeed the authorities knew nothing about it until after the terrible event had occurred. The then bishop of Cedar City, Klingensmith, died alone and friendless on the desert, an outcast and haunted renegade. Some years after this occurrence Haight died in exile, despised and deserted, and all those who took part in this deed, so far as are known, lived miserable lives and died horrible deaths. It seems as if the hand of God was against them for their crimes, which no straining of their religion could excuse or justify.

GEORGE W. ADAIR: JOHN HIGBEE GAVE THE ORDER

Together with John D. Lee and William H. Dame, George Washington Adair was arrested in 1874 and held in custody for his part in the massacre, but he was freed in 1876 under the apparent agreement by the U.S. attorney to prosecute only Lee. If less openly frank than his namesake, Adair provided some useful information during a chance meeting a year before he died with future LDS church president David O. McKay.

GEORGE W. ADAIR, DAVID O. McKAY DIARY, 27 JULY 1907,
MARRIOTT LIBRARY, 28–29.

A pleasant morning. Made a fourth attempt to send a telegram home.

Met George W. Adair, an old pioneer, whose grandfather was at Valley Forge under Gen. Washington. He was in Washington Co. carrying mail from Parowan to Washington in the year when the Mountain Meadow Massacre took place. He saw the message that was sent by by [*sic*] John D. Lee & Higbee to Pres. Young. He saw the answer from Pres. Young. He said to me, "I am a living witness that the Church of Jesus Christ of Latter-day Saints had nothing to do with the massacre. Brigham Young, Geo. A. Smith knew no more about it than you did." Bro. Adair saw the white flag, saw the company disarmed, and saw the women's and children's throats cut. He said it was horrible. Not John D. Lee but John Higbee gave the order to kill the women and children. John D. Lee was with the wounded when the firing began behind him.

Next day after the massacre, Bro. Adair helped bury the massacred. They were stripped of their clothing and valuables. He picked up a long purse filled with gold, but held it away from him as a thing accursed, because John Higbee had said that if anybody took any property belonging to the company "it would burn them." As Bro. Adair was holding this purse, Mr. Higbee walked up, grabbed the purse, and pushed it in his pocket. "From that time," said Bro. Adair, "I had no use for him. It was then that he caught me by the hair, pulled my head back, and drawing a big knife across my throat, said if you ever divulge what you have seen, I will cut your throat from ear to ear."

WILLIAM EDWARDS:
REFUSED TO DISCHARGE HIS WEAPON

The wages for disobeying their file leaders frightened young William Edwards and others into participating in the atrocity. The demanding strictures of the Reformation compelled many decent men and their young sons to join in a massacre they later blamed on Indians. William Edwards, only fifteen years old when he marched to Mountain Meadows, later became a constable and postmaster at Beaver, Utah. For unknown reasons, he gave his sworn statement 180 miles from his home.

WILLIAM EDWARDS AFFIDAVIT, STATE OF UTAH, COUNTY OF CARBON,
14 MAY 1924, UTAH STATE HISTORICAL SOCIETY.

William Edwards, being first duly sworn, says: that he is 82 years of age, a resident of Greenville, Beaver County, Utah. That in September of 1857 your affiant resided at Cedar City, Iron County, in the Territory of Utah: that during said month your affiant accompanied about 30 men and older boys to Mountain Meadows where, we were told, an Indian massacre of a emigrant train had been consummated, and our services [were] needed to bury the dead.

We arrived at said Mountain Meadows early in the evening only to find John D. Lee and several other white men already present, and the said emigrants alive and well fortified against the Indian siege. After surveying the situation for some time we were called to a council of white men by said John D. Lee and by him ordered to assist the Indians in their purposes. Some of the council objected to the butchery but were silenced by said Lee and 2 or 3 others of our file leaders. The strategy, as laid out by said Lee, was that said Lee would trick the said emigrants into giving up their arms and fortifications by pledging them safe conduct to Cedar City. After the said emigrants were a safe distance from their defences [sic], a gunshot would signal us to keep our weapons conspicuous for the benefit of the Indians who would at that moment rush upon us, and that the best way to display them would be to join in the slaughter. The next day the said plan was carried out under the supervision of said Lee except that your affiant together with many of the other white men refused to discharge his weapon.

Your affiant further says: that he does not believe the reports that white men were knowingly sent to said Mountain Meadows by Isaac C. Haight for any other purpose than to bury the supposed dead: that your affiant was but 15 years of age at the time of the said Massacre, and that he and a few others who were nearly as young would not have been permitted to accompany the men if a battle were foreseen.

William Edwards died on 24 April 1925, the last known surviving participant in the massacre at Mountain Meadows.

Prudence Angeline Dunlap and Rebecca Dunlap Evins about 1897,
when Rebecca's statement appeared in the *Fort Smith Elevator.*
Courtesy of Judy Farris and Marian Crane.

Chapter 15

"You Don't Forget
the Horror"
The Survivors Remember

Among the saddest of Mountain Meadow's legacies are the few remembrances of the children whose lives were spared. Those who were under eight years of age met the church's criterion for innocent blood, and to spill such blood was considered a capital sin. John D. Lee sought to escape punishment for that crime by assuring Brigham Young that no one in the party met this exemption because even the surviving youngsters swore like pirates. He likely gave this tortured justification because he was fully aware that at least four, and probably more children under eight, had been butchered: none of the survivors had yet reached the age of 7.

From the viewpoint of the guilty, a benefit of the age limit of innocent blood was that the surviving children would supposedly be too young to remember what happened. The testimony of such young witnesses is problematic. When the massacre took place, Rebecca Dunlap Evins (often misspelled as "Evans") was six, Martha Elizabeth Baker Terry was five, her sister Sarah Frances (Sallie) Baker Gladden Mitchell was three, and Nancy Saphrona Huff Cates was four. At best, Sarah Baker was on the border of the age at which experts believe children can retain credible memories, but she never forgot her father gasping for breath or the spreading red splotch in the front of her mother's calico dress. Elizabeth Baker remembered her beautiful eight-year-old sister with the long black hair being led away, but never knew what happened to her.

Then Cut Their Throats with Knives

These documents speak for themselves. Unlike the "confessions" of the men who did the killing and the tales of the doomed train's depredations that grew more embellished over time, the survivors' statements share a remarkable consistency. Each makes an important point: the "Indians" at the massacre proved to be painted white Mormons and not Southern Paiutes. One can detect the influence of books about the atrocity such as Stenhouse's *Rocky Mountain Saints* and John D. Lee's confessions in the later recollections, but the earliest and best of them, Nancy Saphrona Huff's statement, was made eighteen years after the "terrible massacre" and shows little outside influence.

NANCY HUFF CATES, "THE MOUNTAIN MEADOW MASSACRE:
STATEMENT OF ONE OF THE FEW SURVIVORS,"
DAILY ARKANSAS GAZETTE, 1 SEPTEMBER 1875, 3/1.

The Dardanelle Independent published the statement of Mrs. Nancy S. Cates, of Yell county, one of the seventeen children who survived after the terrible massacre in 1857:

I am the daughter of Peter Huff; my mother's maiden name was Salidia Brown, daughter of Alexander Brown of Tennessee. I was born in Benton county, Arkansas, in 1853. My father started to move from that county in the spring of 1857, with the ill fated train bound for California. I was then a little past four years old. I can recollect my father and mother very well, as [well as] many little incidents that occurred about that time—our travels on the road, etc. I recollect passing through Salt Lake City, and passing through other places, and I recollect we were in a small prairie. One morning before day I was woke up by the firing of guns, and learned that our camp had been attacked, we suppose[d], by Indians. Some of the men folk were wounded. The men dug a ditch around our camp, and fortified [the camp] the best they could. The women and children got in the ditches, and were comparitively [*sic*] out of danger.

The fighting went on at intervals for six days, when failing to drive our men from their fortifications, the attacking party went off. Soon afterward a party that we thought to be friends came up with a white flag, and said that they could protect us. They said they were our friends, and if we would come out and leave what we had they would take us to Cedar City, where we would be safe, and that they would protect us, and see that none of us were hurt. Our people agreed to this, and all started out, men, women and children, and left everything we had behind. When we had got out a short distance from the wagons, where we had been fortified, we came to a place where tall sage brush was growing on both sides of the road, and as we were passing through this place we found we were trapped, as men had hid in it, and began to shoot among us, and then rushed upon our people from both sides, killing everybody they came to. Capt. Baker had me in his arms when he was shot down, and fell dead. I saw my mother shot in the forehead and fall dead. The women and children screamed and clung together. Some of the young women begged the assassins after they had run out on us not to kill them, but they had no mercy on them, clubbing [them with] their guns and beating out their brains.

Some of the murderers were white men and some I supposed were Indians from their dress. At the close of the massacre there was eighteen children still alive, one girl, some ten or twelve years old, they said was too big and could tell, so they killed her, leaving seventeen. A man, I afterwards learned to be named John Willis, took me in his charge (the children were divided) and carried me to his house next day in a wagon; he lived at Cedar City and was a Mormon; he kept me there that winter. Next spring he moved to a place called Topersville [Toquerville]. I stayed there about a year, until Dr. Forney had us children gathered up and carried us to Santa Clara, from there we went to Salt Lake City and remained two months, from there we came back to the states. I know that most of the party that did the killing were white men. The Mormons got all the plunder. I saw many things afterward.

John Willis had, in his family, bed clothes, clothing, and many other things that I recognized as having belonged to my mother. When I claimed the things, they told me I was a liar, and tried to make me believe it was the Indians that killed and plundered our people, but I knew better, because I recollected seeing them kill our folks, and knew many things that they carried off that I saw in their possession afterward. I saw Willis during the massacre; he carried me off from the spot; I could not be mistaken. Living with him made me know him beyond a doubt. I saw them shoot the girl after we were gathered up. I had a sister that was nearly grown, and four brothers that they killed. I was the youngest child of our family—the only one that was spared. They kept the children all separated whilst we remained with them. The scenes and incidents of the massacre were so terrible that they were indelibly stamped on my mind, notwithstanding I was so young at the time.

REBECCA DUNLAP EVINS, "MOUNTAIN MEADOW MASSACRE: THE BUTCHERY OF A TRAIN OF ARKANSANS BY MORMONS AND INDIANS WHILE ON THEIR WAY TO CALIFORNIA RELATED BY ONE OF THE SURVIVORS," *FORT SMITH ELEVATOR*, 20 AUGUST 1897, 2/1–3.

Monticellonian

Almost forty years have rolled away since this country was horrified from Maine to California by the report of what is known in history as the Mountain Meadow Massacre. The details of this bloody crime, that for hellish atrocity has no parallel in our history, are familiar to very few of the present generation, although they were impressed indelibly upon the minds of our elders. To the majority of people the story of this massacre has almost become a myth buried in the obscurity of a forgotten past.

What, then, was the surprise of some of our townspeople a week or two ago when an elderly gentleman who was in the city trading, incidentally remarked that his wife was a survivor of the Mountain Meadow massacre, and that he had rescued her from the Mormons while she was but an infant.

This old gentleman excited the curiosity of his auditors at once, being a very intelligent, interesting talker, but as his wife was waiting for him he did not have time to talk very much about the tragic drama in which his wife played such a thrilling part. In the course of his conversation, however, he said that his wife was the youngest of three sisters who survived the massacre, that he lived in Calhoun county and that he had brought his wife to this county on a visit to her eldest sister, Mrs. Rebecca Evans, who lived on a place belonging to Mrs. Lyle, about nine and one-half miles northeast of Monticello.

Learning that Mrs. Evans was about 7 years old at the time of the massacre, and thinking that she would be able to recall some particulars of that horrible butchery, in company with Dr. Tarrant of this city, we went out to call on her not long since. We found her living in an humble log house, with her husband and five children. They are merely tenants on Mrs. Lyle's place. Time has dwelt [sic] somewhat roughly with Mrs. Evans, and she does not look younger than her forty-six years imply. She is, however, a very pleasant lady and talked freely of the massacre through which she passed years ago, although she cannot speak even now without a great deal of emotion of this butchery of her loved ones; and an expression of horror appears at times upon her face, such as she must have felt when she saw on that fateful September day 120 of her people tomahawked and pierced with arrows, crushed with stones and mutilated with bullets and knives—victims of Mormon fanaticism and hatred.

Mrs. Evans says this train of emigrants left what was then Carroll county, Arkansas, in the summer of 1857. In the train she had a father and mother, five sisters, one brother, an uncle and an aunt and ten or twelve cousins. She says her father and uncle were well off and had $30,000 in money with them, besides a large number of fine stock. There were about forty heads of families in this train when it entered Utah, most of them hailing from Arkansas. It is said to have been one of the finest trains that ever crossed the plains. They were making their way to California. Mrs. Evans says they received hostile treatment from the time they entered Utah.

Early in September they came to the home of a prominent Mormon, Jacob Hamlin, on the northern slope of the Mountain Meadows. Here they were told that there was a large spring about four miles distant in the southern part of the Mountain Meadows. So the train, went on to the spring and encamped there for the night. After camping at this place for three days and nights, on the fourth day, in the morning just before light about sixty Mormons, disguised as Indians, and a number of Indians attacked the train. The Indians were ordered to stampede the cattle and drive them away from the train. They then commenced firing on the emigrants. The fire was returned by the emigrants, who had corraled their wagons. The Mormons and Indians had the train completely surrounded and they were cut off from the spring. For about eight days the siege lasted, the emigrants fighting like lions. The Mormons finding they could not whip them by fair fighting, decided to destroy them by treachery. Accordingly, John D. Lee, Haight and Higbee had their paint washed off, and dressing in their usual attire, took three wagons and drove down towards the emigrants' corral as if they were traveling on thesr [sic] ordinary business. Mrs. Evans says her 8-year-old sister, Mary Dunlap, who was dressed in white, went out towards them and waved a white handkerchief in token of peace. The Mormons in the wagons waved one in reply and advanced to the corral. The emigrants, no Indians being in sight at this time, came out, and walked [talked] with these leading Mormons for an hour or an hour and a half. The Mormons told the emigrants that the Indians were hostile, and that if they gave up their arms it would show the Indians that they did not want to fight. If the emigrants would do this the Mormons promised to pilot them back to the settlements.

Mrs. Evans, when asked if they did not suspect treachery, says that they did not, and if they did they were about famished from thirst, and were ready to accept almost any terms in order to get out of their distressing situation.

The emigrants having agreed to these terms, delivered up their arms to the three Mormons with whom they had counseled. The women and children started back towards Hamlin's house, followed by the men. The Mormons, with the arms, came along by the side of the men. Mrs. Evans says after they had proceeded about a mile on their way back to Hamlin's house they came to a cluster of scrub oaks and sage bushes on both sides of the road. About this time Higbee, who was with them, gave the signal to fire by shooting off his pistol, when a volley poured in from each side and the butchering commenced. Who can picture the horrors of the awful scene? From every bush, demons of destruction leaped forth to revel in crime and in blood. The Mormons and Indians shot down in cold blood the defenseless men, women and children, then pierced them with bows and arrows, then cut their throats with knives. With savage whoops and yells, these devils pursued their victims in every direction. Innocent girls fell upon their knees and prayed for mercy, but their cries were unheeded. The massacre commenced about 5 o'clock in the evening. In one-half hour's time, 120 men, women and children lay cold in death, horribly mutilated and disfigured.

Mrs. Evans says that she ran and hid behind a sage bush when the massacre began. Two of her older sisters were killed right near her, and were lying dead by her side. She heard her baby sister crying and ran to find her. She found her entwined in her mother's arms, but that mother was cold in death. This sister, whose name was Sarah, and who was about a year old at this time, had been shot through her right arm, below the elbow, by a large ball, breaking both bones and cutting her arm half off. Seizing her sister in her arms, Mrs. Evans rushed back to the sage bush where she had been hiding. She remained here until she saw a white man, who proved to be Jacob Hamlin.[1] She went up to him and begged him to save her and her little sisters. She says that Hamlin was the only white man that she saw who belonged to the massacreing [sic] party. She remembers distinctly that Hamlin was dressed in a suit of green jeans. After the massacre was over, she saw quite a number of white men washing the paint from their faces.

Mrs. Evans says that she and her sister Louisa begged not to be separated from their baby sister, Sarah. Jacob Hamlin finally agreed to take the three sisters to his home. Just seventeen children survived this horrible massacre, the oldest of whom was not over 8 years of age. All of them were placed in one wagon, several of them being wounded, while the clothing of nearly all of them was bloody with the gore of their kindred. A son-in-law of John D. Lee drove the wagon to Hamlin's house, where all the children were kept that night. What a pitiful sight these orphans, some of them moaning in pain, all of them bereft of parents and kindred, must have presented, as they were driven away from the scene of this horrible butchery!

On the day after the massacre, Lee and the other Mormons started off with the rest of the children, leaving Rebecca, Louisa and Sarah Dunlap with Jacob Hamlin. After the lapse of several weeks, Mrs. Evans says she went back to the scene of the massacre with some Mormon girls. None of the dead bodies had been buried, but wild animals and buzzards were eating the flesh from their bones. She was only able to recognize one corpse and that one was Jack Baker, a very prominent character among the emigrants. She recognized him by his long beard.

Mrs. Evans says the report they were kindly treated and well cared for while in hands of the Mormons, is false. To the contrary she says they were only half fed and half clothed and harshly treated.

Mrs. Evans and her sisters did not long remain at Mountain Meadows, but soon moved with Hamlin to the fort of Santa Clara. They remained in the hands of Hamlin for nearly two years, before they were rescued. The rescue of these children from the Mormons was an undertaking involving a great deal of difficulty and danger. United States Indian Agent Dr. Forney, Deputy Marshal [William] Rogers and Capt. James Lynch, with a body of United States troops, took part in the rescue. The children were kept for some time in Salt Lake City. Capt. Lynch then carried the children back to their homes in Arkansas and other states wherever they had relatives. He carried the three Dunlap girls back to Carroll (now Boone) county. Their uncle, James Dunlap, who was then living at Carrollton, took all three of them and treated them as his own children.

Here they lived uneventful lives, attending school, and doing pretty much what other girls do, until Rebecca was 23 years of age, when, as usually hap-

[1] Jacob Hamblin was in Great Salt Lake City during the massacre, but Mrs. Evans might have confused him with his brother, Oscar Hamblin, who was present.

pens, she, too, had her dreams of love fulfilled and was united in marriage to Mr. Evans, who carried her to Calhoun county to reside. There they lived until December 15, 1895, when they moved to Drew county, where they now reside. They have five children.

Louisa Dunlap was married to James Linton in Boone county in 1876. They have five children . . .

MARTHA ELIZABETH BAKER, "SURVIVOR OF A MASSACRE:
MRS. BETTY TERRY OF HARRISON VIVIDLY RECALLS
MASSACRE OF WESTBOUND ARKANSAS CARAVAN
IN UTAH MORE THAN 80 YEARS AGO,"
BY CLYDE R. GREENHAW, *ARKANSAS GAZETTE*,
SUNDAY MAGAZINE SECTION, 4 SEPTEMBER 1938, 6.

. . . Mrs. Terry celebrated her 86th birthday anniversary March 7. Even at her advanced age, she never ceases to work, and with eyes still strong enough to see to read, write and sew, she pieces quilts for her children and has completed many handsome articles. She finished a quilt last winter and spent many days this spring tearing carpet strings. She has lived most of her life here, and has been an active member of the Baptist church since early girl hood. She continues to attend services regularly. Mr. Terry died 11 years ago. The couple reared nine children, three boys and six girls, five of whom are still living. An entry in the family bible reads, "Married, January 25, 1874, J. W. Terry to Martha Elizabeth Baker, both of Boone county, by the Rev. Calvin Williams."[2]

When kinsmen press her for a story she sometimes tells that of the massacre, saying, "The wagon train to California made up of folks from our neighborhood and Missouri, was said to be the richest and best equipped that ever started across the plains, with goods, wagons, buggies, carriages and hacks. There were 30 extra good teams of mules and horses in addition to a large number of extra horses, and about 600 to 800 head of cattle, and one of the finest blooded stallions that had ever been seen in the Ozarks at that time.

[2]Ironically, George Calvin Williams, the itinerant Baptist minister who married Miss Baker, later joined the LDS church and became a polygamist. "I got along with the Mormon people alright until we were driven into Mexico for polygamy," he recalled. There he became acquainted with Apostle George Teasdale and "a man who went by the name of Horten and who was Sunday School Superintendent." Someone eventually told Williams the man was actually "Isaac C. Haight, the man that give the orders to kill all the women and children at Mountain Meadows Massacre." This information, Williams recalled, "made my blood boil for I had 13 blood relations murdered there by the orders of this man, now a High Priest in the same church with me." Williams held his tongue but went to Teasdale and "told him plainly that Mexico wasn't big enough to hold Horten and I both, and that one of us better get out of Mexico and do it quick." Williams never saw Haight again. He wrote to LDS president John Taylor "to know if the Church was held as a cloak to cover and conceal cold, black hearted murderers. He never answered my question but wrote me a very sympathetic letter, advising me not to let the misdeeds of others cause me to make a shipwreck of my faith." Williams was excommunicated for apostasy on 17 December 1895. See Williams, The Life and Religion, LDS Archives.

Survivor Martha Elizabeth "Betty" Baker Terry,
pictured with her husband James circa 1890.
Courtesy of the Will Bagley Collection.

Nearly a week was taken for the band to gather here. There were more than 200 in the train when it started out, but they split, part going a southern route and our division going on through the Utah way.

"My father, mother, grandfather and several uncles and aunts were among those killed in the massacre. Our family had a larger number in the company than any other family and we had an extra wagon and provisions besides the one that carried the family. My sister and younger brother, William Twittie [*sic*] Baker, who was only seven months old, were spared. My sister and I were both kept in the family of John D. Lee until the soldiers came and rescued us a year later. My brother was being cared for in another Mormon family. I played with Brigham Young's youngest children. My grandmother remained at Harrison, and when word came that the children had been rescued, she went out to bring us back."

"On the way out we stopped and made camp many times to rest the weary, footsore cattle, scouts going ahead to select camp sites."

It took nearly six months, she recalled, for the immigrants to reach Mountain Meadows, which is located about 160 miles south of Salt Lake City. Camp was made at the spring at the west end of Mountain Meadows, Friday night, September 2 or 3.

Mountain Meadows is named for the beautiful mountains on the northern and southern borders. There was good grazing for the cattle and it was a good place to camp and rest, so the leaders of the caravan of immigrants decided to remain there several days before pushing on into the plains country.

William Twitty Baker was one of the youngest
survivors of the Mountain Meadows massacre.
Courtesy of the Will Bagley Collection.

Early on Monday morning, September 6, about the time that the earlier
risers of the immigrants were moving about the camp near the spring, they
were fired upon from ambush, Mrs. Terry said. An alarm was sounded, the
entire party was aroused, and soon their more active men were organized with
firearms and they succeeded in temporarily frightening away the intruders.

During the quiet that followed the first brief battle, all wagons were put
into a circle, dirt was shoveled up under the wagon to serve as a breast works
for fort like protection.

Several of the men left the corral to investigate the cause of the earlier firing, and these again were engaged in another battle at close range, causing several fatalities to the stronger and braver group of immigrants, but little loss to
the enemy, who took advantage of the boulders and underbrush for shelter.

Preparations were made by the men in camp to conceal the women and
children and prepare for battle. The siege continued at intervals of four to
five days. Finally several white men, found to be Mormons and disguised in
Indian garb, under the leadership of three white men, posing as government
attaches, proposed to the wagon train group that if they would surrender their
arms and ammunition they would be escorted back east to the nearest village
of Cedar Valley. The immigrants surrendered all their arms and ammunition
and reluctantly agreed to retrace their steps under escort toward Cedar Valley. When the party had traveled about one mile from the spring and campsite the Utah group called a halt, placed all children under seven years old in
one wagon and sent them ahead. With the aid of a large number in hiding,

they immediately opened fire on the unarmed immigrants, killing the entire band.

The 17 children were sent ahead to the eastern end of the mountain valley to the home of one Hamblin, from which place they were distributed among the Mormons. The children were recovered by the government in the early summer of 1859, and were returned to Arkansas to their relatives. Names of the 17 children were as follows: John Calvin Sorel, Lewis and Mary Sorel, Ambrose, Miriam and William Tagget, Francis Horn, Angeline, Annie and Sophronia (or Mary) Ruff, Ephraim W. Huff, Charles and Triphenia Fancher, Betsey and Jane Baker, William Welch Baker, Rebecca, Louise and Sarah Dunlap.

Mrs. Terry sadly related that she never knew what became of her older sister, Vina. She was the prettiest of the three Baker girls, she said, and had beautiful long black hair. She was eight years old. The last time she remembers seeing her sister, she was being led away as a captive. "I do not know whether she was killed or what ever happened to her." Just before the last attack on the immigrants, Mrs. Terry said she heard her father tell her mother to get up and put the children in the wagon. That was the last time she saw her mother, she said. "I distinctly remember the group disguised as Indians. There was not a real Indian in the group, for they went to the creek and washed the paint from their faces."

"How was your grandmother able to identify and claim you?" Mrs. Terry was asked. "By clothing, and the sunbonnets which were quilted in a certain design still in our possession. My brother had a peculiar identification mark. The end of the index finger on each hand was smooth and glistening, without the sign of a finger nail, with but one joint to the finger, appearing much as a felon[3] leaves a finger." She explained that this disfigurement of the index fingers was a birthmark. "Our aunt lived with us and worked for our mother for months preceding my brother's birth. She suffered terribly from a felon and complained much. Her felon was on an index finger. So when the brother was born, the two index fingers were marked as if from felons. He carried them that way through life and never had a felon."

Before Caravan Springs are two huge flat rocks, where the family washing was done, she said: "They were long and broad and were on one side of the creek. Stately elm trees lined the creek banks, shading these rocks, where I spent many hours shedding tears."

"I do hope they get the marker at the right spring," she added. "Maybe I should go out there and point out the right place."

A number of descendants, great grandchildren of the wealthy Jack Baker who helped finance the emigrant train, now live in Harrison. Relatives of the Beller family who were members of the company, live there also.

---

[3]A felon is an abscess deep on the palm side of the fingertip.

This photograph, "taken shortly after the sisters had grown up," shows survivors Sarah Frances (Sallie) Baker Gladden Mitchell and Martha Elizabeth (Betty) Baker Terry. Both sisters left compelling accounts of the massacre. *Courtesy of the Will Bagley Collection.*

Sallie [Sarah Francis] Baker Gladden Mitchell,
"The Mountain Meadows Massacre—
An Episode on the Road to Zion,"
The American Weekly, 25 August 1940.

. . . I'm the only person still living who was in that massacre, where the Mormons and the Indians attacked a party of 137 settlers on the way to California, murdering everybody except 17 children, who were spared because they were all under eight years of age.

I was one of those children and when the killing started I was sitting on my daddy's lap in one of the wagons. The same bullet that snuffed out his life took a nick out of my left ear, leaving a scar you can see to this day.

Last November, I passed my 85th birthday and at the time of the massacre I wasn't quite three years old. But even when you're that young, you don't forget the horror of having your father gasp for breath and grow limp, while you

Sarah Frances (Sallie) Baker with her first husband, Joseph Allen Gladden, and her children (*left to right*) George William, Pearl, Claude, and Hugh Allen.
Courtesy of Judy Gladden, Will Bagley Collection.

have your arms around his neck, screaming with terror. You don't forget the
blood-curdling war-whoops and the banging of guns all around you. You don't
forget the screaming of the other children and the agonized shrieks of women
being hacked to death with tomahawks. And you wouldn't forget it, either, if
you saw your own mother topple over in the wagon beside you, with a big red
splotch getting bigger and bigger on the front of her calico dress.

When the massacre started, Mother had my baby brother, Billy, in her lap
and my two sisters, Betty and Mary Levina, were sitting in the back of the
wagon. Billy wasn't quite two, Betty was about five and Vina was eight.

We never knew what became of Vina. Betty saw some Mormons leading
her over the hill, while the killing was still going on. Maybe they treated her
the way the Dunlap girls were treated. Later on I'm going to tell about the
horrible thing that happened to them. And maybe they raised her up to be a
Mormon. We never could find out.

Betty, Billy and I were taken to a Mormon home and kept there till the
soldiers rescued us, along with the other children, about a year later, and carried us back to our folks in Arkansas. Captain James Lynch was in charge of
the soldiers who found us, and I've got an interesting little thing to tell about
him, too, when I get around to it . . .

There has been a lot of argument over how much part the Indians played
in the massacre and how much of it was due to the Mormons, some people
even saying that the Indians didn't have anything to do with it at all, and that
some of the Mormons disguised themselves as Indians just to lay the blame
on them. I can't say as to the truth of that but I do know that my sister Betty,
who died only a few months ago, always insisted that she had seen a lot of
the Mormons down at the creek after it was all over, washing paint off their
faces, and that some of them at least had disguised themselves as Indians.

At any rate, while the Indians, or a crowd of savage looking men that appeared
to be Indians, went around making sure that all the grown-ups were dead and
giving a final shot to any who looked as if they had a spark of life left in them
and also robbing the bodies of valuables—well, while that was going on the
Mormons rounded up all us children and took us off to their homes.

As I said, there were 17 of us—John Calvin Sorel, Lewis and Mary Sorel,
Ambrose, Miriam and William Tagget, Francis Horn, Angeline Annie and
Sophronia Mary Huff, Ephriam W. Huff, Charles and Triphenia Fancher,
Rebecca, Louise and Sarah Dunlap and us three Baker children, Betty, Sallie
and William Welch Baker.

I remember that we were treated right well in the Mormon homes where
we lived until we were rescued.

I recall, too, that we had good food, and plenty of it. We had lots of rice
and also honey right out of the comb. The only unpleasant thing that happened while we were there was when one of the older Mormon children in
the house got mad at me and pushed me down stairs. I hurt my right hand,

pretty badly and as a result of it I still have a long scar across the knuckles. That makes two scars I got from the Mormons.

The way Captain [James] Lynch and his soldiers found us was by going around among the Mormons in disguise. I got to know him right well later on, and, he used to slap his leg and laugh like anything, as he told how he said to those Mormons:

"You let those children go, or I'll blow you to purgatory."

I never will forget the day we finally got back to Arkansas. You would have thought we were heroes. They had a buggy parade for us through Harrison.

When we got around to our house, Grandma Baker, the one who refused to go to California, was standing on the porch. She was a stout woman and mighty dignified, too. When we came along the road leading up to the house she was pacing back and forth but when she caught sight of us she ran down the path and grabbed hold of us, one after the other and gave us a powerful hug.

Leah, our old Negro mammy, caught me up in her arms and wouldn't let me go. She carried me around all the rest of the day, even cooking supper with me in her arms. I remember she baked each of us children a special little apple turnover pie. We had creamed potatoes for supper that night, too, and they sure tasted good. I've been specially fond of creamed potatoes ever since.

I remember I called all of the women I saw "mother." I guess I was still hoping to find my own mother, and every time I called a woman "mother," she would break out crying . . .

Long after I had grown up and married and settled down, Captain Lynch, the man who rescued us, came to see me one day. He was in mighty high spirits and I could see right away he had something up his sleeve. He asked me if I remembered little Sarah Dunlap, one of the children he had rescued, and a sister of the two Dunlap girls who were killed. I said I sure did. Sarah was blind and had been educated at the school for the blind in Little Rock. I don't recall whether any injury she might have gotten in the massacre was what made her blind, but I do remember she grew up to be a really beautiful girl. Well, Captain Lynch said:

"Guess what? I'm on my way to see Sarah."

When he mentioned her name it looked like he was going to blow up with happiness. Then he told me why. He was on his way right then to marry Sarah—and he did. I guess he must have been forty years older than she was, but he sure was a spry man just the same. I never saw anybody could beat him when it came to dancing and singing.

Some time after the massacre, Federal Judge Cradlebaugh held an investigation and tried to bring to trial some of the Mormons. He was convinced [they] were responsible for the crime, but he never got anywhere with it, and he was finally transferred from the district at his own request. Then the Civil War came on and nothing more was done about it until 1875 . . . [4]

---

[4] Baker's account ends with derivative information on the capture and trial of John D. Lee.

Sarah Dunlap, the blind survivor
who married James Lynch. *Courtesy
of Judy Farris and Marian Crane.*

Rebecca Dunlap Evins: The Hero of Her Dreams

Traveling south from Camp Floyd in 1859, Mexican War veteran James Lynch
encountered Utah Indian Affairs superintendent Jacob Forney at Beaver, Utah,
abandoned by his Mormon guides and fearful. The romantic Irishman can-
celed his trip to Arizona and instead went with Forney to retrieve the surviving children of the atrocity at Mountain Meadows. Deeply moved by the
experience, he devoted much of his life to helping the massacre orphans.

Rebecca Dunlap Evins told the reporter who interviewed her forty years
after the massacre how Captain Lynch fell in love with her sister.

> Sarah Dunlap, the youngest, has never recovered the use of her arm, which
> was shot during the massacre. She has also been afflicted with weak eyes most
> of her life. She went to the blind school in Little Rock, and remained until
> she graduated. During all these years the memory of Capt. Lynch, who brought
> these girls away from the Mormons, had been cherished fondly by them. They
> were very much grieved to hear in January, 1893, that Capt. Lynch was seri-
> ously ill at his home in Washington City. In this letter it was stated that Capt.
> Lynch had signified his intention of leaving all his property to the survivors
> of the Mountain Meadows Massacre. Sarah, moved by a feeling of gratitude
> for all that Capt. Lynch had done for them, immediately wrote to him, offer-

ing to come to Washington and wait upon him as his nurse. He, in the meantime, had grown better, and responded to her letter. A lively correspondence was then carried on between the two for about a year by which time Cupid had done his work. The little infant, now 37 years old, gave her hand and heart to the hero of her dreams who had rescued her from the Mormons thirty-five years before, and who was now 75 years old. They are now living happily together at Woodbury, Calhoun county, Ark.[5]

Sarah Dunlap Lynch died on 13 November 1901, and Captain Lynch marked her grave in the Hampton Cemetery with an ornate headstone. Local tradition credits him with planting a bridal wreath bush that blossomed in the spring in "a mass of bridal whiteness." The old veteran died nine years later at about the age of 90.[6] He rested beside his bride in an unmarked grave until 21 March 1998, when the Arkansas State Society Children of the American Revolution dedicated a monument to his memory.

---

[5]Evins, "Mountain Meadow Massacre," *Fort Smith* (Arkansas) *Elevator*, 20 August 1897, 2/3.
[6]Willma Humphreys Newton, "Death at Mountain Meadows: The Story of Capt. James Lynch, Who Brought Back Arkansans Who Survived the Massacre," *Arkansas Gazette*, 6 September 1959, 2D.

Chapter 16

"THE SHADOW OF TREACHERY AND DEATH"
The Legacy of Mountain Meadows

W hen Sarah Frances Baker Gladden Mitchell died at the age of 93 in 1947, everyone who had been at Mountain Meadows on that fateful day in 1857 was dead, but wrangling over the event's contentious history has never ended. Frontier journalist Josiah F. Gibbs revived the controversy in 1909 with a chapter in his *Lights and Shadows of Mormonism*, which he followed the next year with a study focused on the massacre. LDS church officials felt so threatened by Gibbs's account that they commissioned Josiah Rogerson to write an approved history. They decided not to publish his study, "The Guilt of John D. Lee," perhaps because it unintentionally raised many questions about the Penrose defense, but more probably because they had long since learned that the less said about the massacre, the better.

JOSIAH F. GIBBS: LEST WE FORGET

Josiah Gibbs was born into Mormonism at Nauvoo, Illinois. Like many in his day and since, he loved the people of the faith and could never imagine life outside the unique culture they created. But like others, he could not accept the doctrines of unquestioning obedience and the profession of ultimate authority that went with belief in a prophet who literally spoke God's will in both spiritual and temporal realms. As a country newspaper editor he was an ardent opponent of church meddling in civic affairs, and as a self-taught historian he was indignant at the outright falsehoods told and repeated by respected Mormon historians.

CHARLES KELLY, JOSIAH F. GIBBS, AND FRANK BECKWITH, 20 SEPTEMBER 1931 Printer, artist, and author Charles Kelly became the first superintendent of Capitol Reef National Park in Utah. Newspaper editor, mining promoter, and reformed polygamist Josiah F. Gibbs fed Kelly and Beckwith fried chicken when they visited him at Marysvale, Utah. *Millard County Chronicle* editor Frank Beckwith played a leading role in the creation of the 1932 marker at Mountain Meadows. All three of these mavericks wrote histories of the 1857 massacre, but only Gibbs's account has been published. *Courtesy of Utah State Historical Society.*

Opinions like his could get one excommunicated, as they eventually did in Gibbs's case. Like the questioning newspaperman he was, Gibbs investigated several early Utah crimes, in particular the Gunnison and Mountain Meadows massacres. He exonerated Brigham Young of knowledge beforehand of either atrocity, but his dedication to the truth produced some of the earliest and most trustworthy accounts of both massacres. Most importantly, they ensured that the darkest stain on the state's history would never be forgotten.

JOSIAH GIBBS, "THE MOUNTAIN MEADOWS—PAST AND PRESENT," *SALT LAKE TRIBUNE*, 15 AUGUST 1909, 17/1–7.

Lest the Deseret News and some of the chief prophets of Mormondom have a "conniption" fit, or an attack of "blind staggers," when it, or they, read the above heading, they are assured that this communication is entirely peaceful, that it will be rather sentimental than warlike.

A few days since Frank Mayol of the Salt Lake Tribune, and the writer hereof, visited the Mountain Meadows for the purpose of obtaining pictures of the historic ground and to investigate present conditions that seemed imminent some four years since when the locality was visited by the writer.

At Modena, some 273 miles distant on the line of the San Pedro railroad, we secured a rig and a young Mormon driver to transfer us from the station to the Meadows, some thirty miles by wagon from Modena. The Meadows are about twenty-five miles in a direct line from Modena.

Our course was southeasterly over the southeastern portion of the Escalante desert, some twenty-four miles to Holt's ranch, situated at the base of the divide known as the "Rim" of the Great Salt Lake basin. From Holt's the road ascends the divide a distance of two miles, where, on turning a sharp bend in the road, we were face to face with a little hamlet of ranchers. The place is known as the Mountain Meadows, although it is several miles distant from the historic ground which was the point of destination. We left Modena a little after 12 and as it was late in the afternoon when we arrived at the ranches we were compelled to wait until morning to resume the trip.

The hamlet is situated in a picturesque little nook about 8000 feet above sea level. An agreeable surprise awaited us. Mr. Joseph Platt, a lifelong and intelligent Mormon, opened wide the door of his residence and bade us welcome. There was, however, no surprise in that for almost without exception every Mormon possesses in a large degree the time honored quality of hospitality. The surprise was to find our surroundings so entirely pleasant. Miss Platt, sister to the Platt brothers who own the ranch, is an ideal housekeeper and cook. Our appetites had been sharpened by a hurried meal at Modena, and the long wagon ride over the rough road. The "supper" call was quickly heeded . . . We were awakened early in the morning by the insistent conversation between the big and little bovines. Dear reader, gentle or otherwise, pardon the foregoing reminiscences which you may think have encumbered a lot of valuable space. We will now get down to business.

About one mile southwesterly from the Platt ranch the apex of the "Rim" is reached, and we look down on the historic ground of the Meadows proper. The road is the same as that traversed fifty-two years ago by the emigrant train of nearly 140 men, women and children whose destination was California, but over whose lives there was even then hovering the shadow of treachery and death.

Lest We Forget.

It is well to here state that there are many truly good and sentimental souls who object to any mention in public of the Mountain Meadows massacre. They object to having it mentioned because it is one of those "incidents of history which should be forgotten." Now, dear readers, whether Mormon or non-Mormon, let the fact be candidly stated that the Mormon people, as a people, past or present, cannot be held accountable for the tragedy enacted at the Mountain Meadows. There have been more falsehoods told by Mormon historians and speakers about that massacre than about any other incident of history. There was some justification for the falsehoods of those early years as they were then told in the interest of self-preservation. But the day has passed when falsehoods told of the tragedy will benefit the people of Utah or aid in the proselyting work of Mormon missionaries. Another justification for telling the truth about the massacre and for keeping it prominently before the public is found in the fact that every Mormon history of their church teems with stories of the "massacre of Haun's mill," the "persecutions" of Missouri and Illinois, and of the "martyrdom of Joseph and Hyrum Smith," and of the "expulsion" of the Saints from those states. And inasmuch as "persecution" is claimed by the Saints to be an evidence of the divine truth of Mormonism, those deplorable incidents in the history of their church are continuously kept before the public as an aid to proselyting. The Mountain Meadows massacre was the legitimate and logical outcome of the Mormon doctrines of unquestioning obedience and blood atonement, and the tragedy should be kept before the public as an aid in resisting the claims of divinity, and as an obstacle to conversion to a creed that recognizes no rights of men or women when those rights are in conflict with the revelations and dictates of the Mormon prophets.

It is about two miles southwesterly from the top of the divide down to where the small Mountain Meadows basin ends in a steep and narrow canyon through which the flood waters of the locality are carried to the Santa Clara river, some twelve miles to the south, and which, in turn, conveys the water to the Rio Virgin and thence to the Colorado river at Rioville on the Nevada-Arizona line. A half century ago a strip of meadow land about 200 yards wide occupied the lower portion of the basin and was a mile or so in length. Several tiny rivulets, formed by springs or the distant hillsides, reach the bottom land. On one of the northerly rivulets is now situated the Burgess ranch and which, in the practice of the present desolation, is a very oasis of shade and fruit. Well down toward the lower end of the basin is a spring which rises from the one time meadow. It was a few rods to the northwest of the spring where the emigrant train turned off the road to the left and made an irregular camp.

To the west, and distant from the spring just mentioned, is the north end of a basaltic dyke or ridge about 75 feet above the level of the valley. The sides of the ridge are covered with a dense growth of mountain sage, the apex of the ridge is strewn with boulders. Beyond the ridge toward the west, low basalt hills and ridges extend to the base of the Beaver Dam [Bull Valley] mountains, some two or three miles distant.

Some thirty rods east of the spring a hill covered with sage and clumps of scrub oak rises sharply from the bottom land. From that point the country rolls away to the east where a few miles distant, the higher land drops down to the Parowan valley; thence easterly a flat valley, marked here and there with volcanic cones, hills of almost pure iron, and isolated mountains of eruptive origin, extends to Cedar City. Beyond, the Tushar and Kolob mountains rise to the region of perpetual snow. And such is the topography that environs the last resting place of the Arkansas emigrants.

It is reported by some of the Mormon people that, while the emigrants were en route to the Meadows, some of the latter boasted of having aided in killing "old Joe Smith" at Carthage jail in Illinois, and with having conducted themselves in a boisterous and domineering manner toward the Mormon people. Others now living—men and women who mingled with the emigrants at their

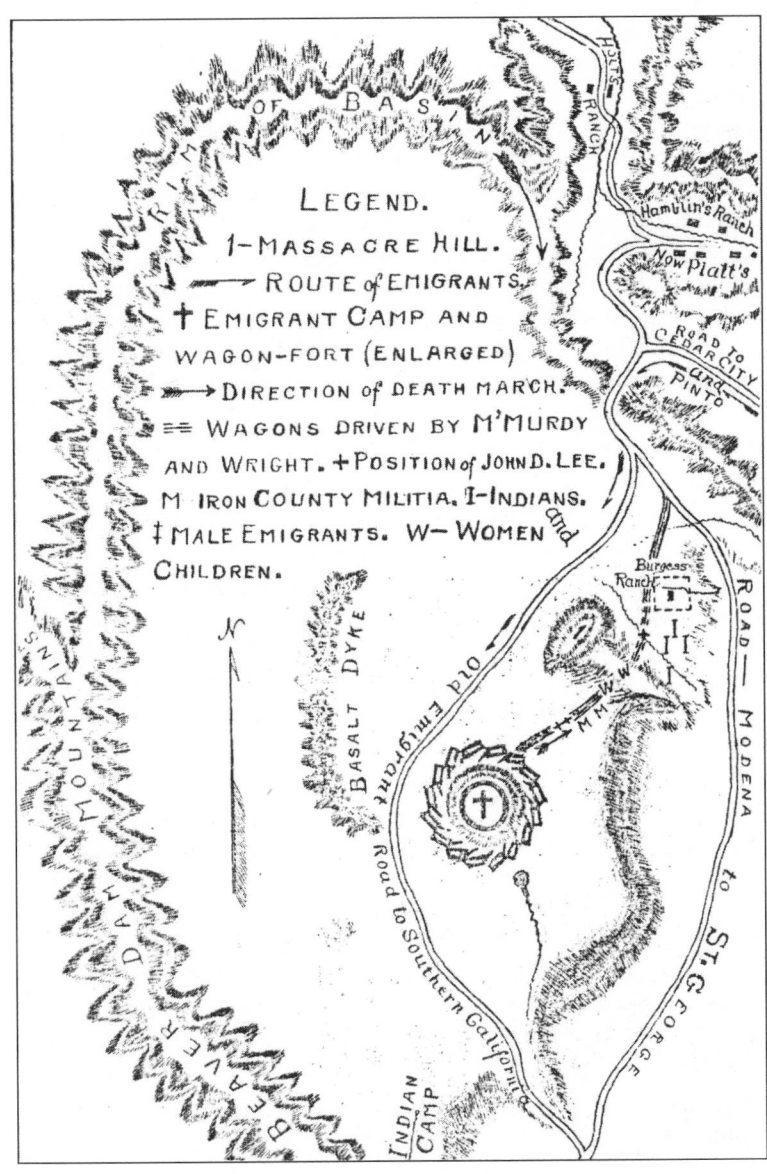

This 1910 map from Josiah F. Gibbs's *The Mountain Meadows Massacre* significantly misrepresented distances and locations and contributed to decades of confusion about the topography of Mountain Meadows. *From Josiah Gibbs,* The Mountain Meadows Massacre *(Salt Lake City: Salt Lake Tribune Publishing Co., 1910).*

several encampments—aver that the men and women conducted themselves as gentlemen and ladies, and were sociable and hospitable. And there is absolutely no evidence that more than one of the emigrants made the boast above referred to.

Along about the middle of September, 1857, and while the emigrants were lingering at the Meadows, the presiding priesthood of Iron county held a "council" meeting at Cedar City, about thirty miles easterly from the camp of emigrants, and consulted as to whether or not the emigrants should be permitted to go in peace or should be exterminated. Only one man's name has thus far been recorded who opposed the massacre of the emigrants. To appease that one stalwart, it was agreed to send a messenger to Gov. Brigham Young at Salt Lake City and learn his wishes in the matter. So cocksure were these priestly fanatics that President Young would approve of the extermination of the Arkansans that they detailed certain men to collect the Indians of Iron and Washington counties for the murderous work. And at least two days before the messenger arrived at Salt Lake the Indians were on the ground and ready for the slaughter.

Attack Upon the Emigrants.

The wagons of the emigrants were not arranged in the circular form which was usual when danger was imminent. It was not yet daylight, but a half dozen campfires were burning brightly. A score or so of men were grouped around the fires when, from the east hillside, a volley of bullets rained upon them. Several men were killed and wounded. Hastily securing their guns, and guided only by inferred direction, the men returned the fire and killed two redskins and wounded several. Disgusted with their luck, and terrified at the fierce resistance, the Indians withdrew. Hastily moving their wagons into a circle the emigrants barricaded their camp as best they could. A rifle pit was digged in the center of the "corral," and every effort made for stubborn resistance.

The second attack of the redskins was made from behind the basaltic ridge to the west. They were again repulsed with serious loss to themselves.

This letter is not intended as a history of the Mountain Meadows tragedy. The brief reference to it is made for the purpose of enlightening the young and others who may have but a dim idea of the tragedy and the locality in which it was enacted.

Butchered in Cold Blood.

Suffice it to say that two or three days after the first attack fifty-five white men were on the ground. A flag of truce was sent down to within about forty rods of the camp of the emigrants who, after a short parley, surrendered themselves to the protection of the white men. Within a half mile of their encampment the emigrants were shot, brained and otherwise butchered. On the pretext that their weapons might excite the animosity of the redskins the arms of the emigrants were taken from them, and which left them as helpless as so many babes in the clutches of a band of religious fanatics. Seventeen of the children, too young, as the fanatics believed, to tell the story of the massacre, were saved from the slaughter.

The following spring Jacob Hamblin, a Mormon Indian interpreter, who owned a ranch some two miles from the Meadows, gathered up more than one hundred twenty skulls and other parts of skeletons and buried them in the rifle pit digged by the emigrants. The common grave of the members of the Arkansas company is now marked with a mound of boulders which, at the west end, forms a monument about four feet high.

Present Condition on the Meadows.

Several of those who were present at the Meadows on March 23, 1867 [sic], when John D. Lee was executed for participation in the massacre, say that a small gully about six feet deep had formed in the lowest part of the basin, and which formed a trough into which the flood water and summer rains quickly found an escape from the bottom land. The result was that the meadow grass had disappeared and that mountain sage then covered the basin. Some four years ago the writer passed through the Meadows and camped on the ground during twenty-four hours. The gully had increased to a depth of twenty to thirty feet where an uneven bed of basalt near the grave had prevented the flood water from cutting a deeper channel. While the gully is not now deeper, it is rapidly widening and, unless measures are soon adopted to protect the last resting place of those stranger dead, the remains of those so ruthlessly murdered fifty-two years ago will be swept away. Several years ago a portion of the grave caved into the channel, and Joseph Platt assured us that a number of skulls were scattered in the bottom of the gully. At the present time the earth descends from the east end of the grave at angle of about 35 degrees to the bottom of the gully or wash. The small spring from which the emigrants obtained water during the siege is now about ten feet below the surface and forms a swampy patch some two or three rods in diameter on a small bench about half-way down from the brink of the wash. A hundred feet or so to the north of the cairn the force of the flood water is projected directly toward the grave, then turns directly east and passes it as before described. And unless the burial spot is protected not more than two or three years will pass before the remains of those victims of blind obedience and blood atonement will be swept into the Santa Clara river, or buried in the silt along the intervening wash. A few short pilings, backed by a wall of sagebrush will be sufficient to deflect the water from the grave until such time as the vertical banks will have caved down and the channel become fixed and the sides protected by sage and grass which will naturally take possession as soon as caving ceases.

Shaft Should Be Erected.

And there is yet another obligation that is due from the living to the dead at the Mountain Meadows. A granite monument of modest proportions and price should be placed over the grave. There should not be any offensive inscription thereon, just the names of those, so far as obtainable, the bare fact of their death, and the exact date if that can be fixed from the conflicting data.

We were assured by Mr. Joseph Platt that if the measures of protection, as enumerated herein, and a monument be erected that he will do all in his power to care for the grave and will plant trees around it and otherwise improve the surroundings. So far as we could learn there is a general desire on the part of the people of southwestern Utah to have the grave protected and cared for.

Modena is the distributing point for St. George, Washington and the towns on the Rio Virgin. The road from those places to Modena passes within 300 to 400 yards of the grave, the condition of which is cause for deep regret to the inhabitants of that isolated locality.

Almost Unbelievable.

And as unbelievable as it may appear to many, there is not one in 100 of the younger men and women of southwestern Utah who know anything of the actual details of the massacre, or of the influences that led up to it. Our driver, an intelligent Mormon of about 25 years, asked the writer what caused the Mountain Meadows massacre. He was frankly informed of the causes and was visibly worried over the recital.

With each passing year the doctrine of the brotherhood of men is being more and more recognized. Selfishness is being slowly driven from the hearts of men. The sons and daughters of northern veterans now strew flowers on the graves of once hated "rebels." On each recurring Memorial day Salt Lake men and women gently lay the emblems of purity on the graves of the stranger dead in the cemeteries near our city. Then why should we not remember those whose remains occupy a grave in the wilderness of southwestern Utah? If someone will take the initiative there will be no difficulty in securing the necessary funds. The subscription should be popular with every Utahn irrespective of creed or nationality.

In memoriam.
J. F. Gibbs.
Salt Lake City, August 11, 1909.

Anthony W. Ivins: The So-Called Missouri Wildcats

Apostle Anthony W. Ivins was only five years old when the massacre took place, so he had no memory of it when he answered the questions of a concerned church member. He was, however, a leading citizen of southern Utah and later directed the Mormon colonization of Mexico. Known for his exceptional energy and ability, he became an apostle and, as first counselor to President Heber J. Grant, a member of the First Presidency. For decades, he was the church's "point man" on Mountain Meadows.

ANTHONY W. IVINS TO MRS. G. T. WELCH,
ANSWERS TO QUESTIONS ABOUT MMM,
16 OCTOBER 1922, LDS ARCHIVES.

Dear Sister Welch:

Your letter of the 7th, addressed to President Grant, has been handed to me for answer. You enclose a newspaper clipping containing a report of the so-called Mountain Meadows Massacre, and ask the President to give you some information in regard to this unfortunate affair.

First, let me say that I went to Southern Utah with my parents in the winter of 1861, at which time I was eight years of age. We located at St. George, about thirty miles from the spot where the unfortunate affair to which you refer occurred. I was frequently on the ground, frequently met the Indians who were the perpetrators of this offense, and a number of the few white men who were connected with it. After I had grown to manhood, at the time that John D. Lee was executed, I was present at the execution. I heard the last words that John D. Lee uttered and saw the firing squad at whose hands he met his death. Because of these conditions, and my intimate association with that section of the country, I feel as well competent to speak in regard to the matter as any one with whom I am acquainted.

The story in brief is as follows: About the first of August, 1857, the exact date I do not know, a party of emigrants arrived in Salt Lake City on their way to California. The majority of the party were from Arkansas and were led by a man whose name was Fancher. Fancher appeared to be a very honorable man, and his party was made up of intelligent, well-behaved and well-to-do people. But there was with them a small party of men who had joined them on the way, who called themselves the Missouri wildcats. The party was advised by Charles C. Rich and others to proceed to California by the northern route via the Humboldt river and over the pass down to San Francisco. But some of them insisted on taking the southern route, notwithstanding the fact that they had been made aware that the Indians in that neighborhood were hostile and that the road was an exceedingly difficult one because of lack of water on the long desert stretches which intervened. They started on the northern route, but some of them desired to go to southern California, and after having reached Bear River they returned to Salt Lake and started for Southern California via the route known as the old Spanish trail. As they traveled through the settlements to the South of Salt Lake City it is said they had difficulty with the settlers, the so-called Missouri wildcats assuming to take property which did not belong to them, turning their animals into the people's fields, and otherwise making themselves obnoxious.

Finally, at Corn Creek, about half way between Salt Lake City and the Mountain Meadows, it is said these people poisoned an ox, which had died, and that the Indians eating the carcass were made sick, ten of their number dying from the effects of the poison. However much of truth there may be in these stories I do not know, but it is certain that upon arrival at the Mountain Meadows, just on the edge of the desert country through which they were obliged to pass in order to reach California, they stopped to recruit their cattle and rest at a little mountain valley called the Mountain Meadows. While in camp at a spring here they were unexpectedly attacked by a body of Indians. At the time that this attack was made there was but one white man present among the Indians. That man was John D. Lee. For three days the emigrants, who were brave men and well armed, defended themselves against this attack. About this time the Indians were joined by other white men who came to the place pretending that it was their purpose to rescue the travelers from the Indians and convey them to a point of safety. A number of Indians had already been killed and it appears that nothing but the blood of the emigrants would satisfy their thirst for revenge. The result was that the white men who latterly joined the Indians themselves through treachery induced the emigrants to lay down their arms and then mercilessly slaughtered them. That this act was committed by the Indians and the white men with them without any knowledge whatever so far as the authorities of the Church were concerned and who were at that time at Salt Lake City, three hundred miles distant, is amply proven.

When word reach the settlements in Southern Utah the emigrants had been attacked by the Indians, an expressman was immediately sent to notify Brigham Young who was at the time Governor of the Territory. James Haslam left Cedar City September 7th and arrived in Salt Lake City on the morning of the 10th, delivered his message to Governor Young, the Governor made the following reply, after asking Haslam if he felt able to make a hurried return, for he was very much fatigued upon reaching Salt Lake. Haslam answered yes. Governor Young then said to him: "Go with all speed, spare no horseflesh, The emigrants must not be meddled with, if it takes all of Iron County to prevent it; they must go free and unmolested." Haslam immediately mounted a fresh horse and started back to Cedar City, where he arrived on the 13th, and delivered the message of the Governor to Isaac Haight who was in command of the militia in that part of the State. Upon receiving the letter Haight burst into tears, exclaiming, "Too late, too late." The battle had already ended and the bloody deed been accomplished.

My brother-in-law was one of the jurymen which convicted John D. Lee at the time he was tried for the offense. When it became known that he would be taken to the Mountain Meadows for execution, I, then a young man with other companions, rode all night to reach that point and was present the following morning when the execution took place. I stood near John D. Lee at the time he was executed. I heard the last words he ever uttered, and saw the men who fired the rifle shots that ended his life. He did not, as has been so often stated, incriminate the leaders of the Mormon Church in anything he said. He said simply that he had been misled; that he had done what he thought was a justifiable thing, but which he now fully realized was an error, and met his death without fear and without asking favor.

This in brief is the story of that great tragedy which we all so sincerely deplore. That the men connected with it and responsible for it will be held accountable before the bar of justice in the life to come for the commission of this awful act there can be no doubt, but that the Church at large, or the presiding authorities of it were in any way connected or responsible for it is not true. It occurred at the time when there was great excitement in the then Territory, the time when an army was marching to Utah, and the people of the outlying districts, with the little opportunity that they had of receiving news or communicating with headquarters of the Church, some of these rough wild men of the frontiers did unite with the Indians in the battle which resulted in the death of these people. They alone are responsible for it, and they alone will answer for it. Much has been written in detail recounting the actual truth, and much has been written by enemies of the Church in which an endeavor has been made to involve the leaders in it, but these efforts have always been in vain. There is no evidence at all except that from statements of irresponsible men—men who were enemies of the Church and who desired to bring reproach upon its leaders—to justify any such accusation. I know this from my own experience, my own contact with some of the Indians and some of the white men who were associated with it.

I trust that this will be satisfactory, but should you need other information I can cite you to [sic] books in which full accounts may be found. I remain,

Your Brother,
A. W. Ivins

Frank J. Cannon:
Brigham Knew the Whole Ghastly Story

Frank Jenne Cannon was known as "a militant spirit," always ready to fight for what he believed to be right. Born in Salt Lake City in 1859, he possessed many of the qualities that made his father, Apostle George Q. Cannon, one of the leading figures of the faith for decades. He worked as a newspaperman in San Francisco, Ogden, and Salt Lake City and in 1891 helped found the Utah Republican Party. He was elected territorial delegate to Congress and, after statehood in 1896, as Utah's first senator. In Washington, D.C., Cannon fought hard for church interests until he discovered that Mormon leaders had broken their vows to Congress to end polygamy as a condition of statehood. He then battled with equal vigor to expose the practice. Excommunicated, he authored several books on Mormonism and died in Denver at age 74.

Haslam's ride convinced Cannon that Young did not order the 1857 massacre and cleared him "of direct complicity in the slaughter." But Cannon argued that the massacre "was the logical culmination" of the Reformation that Young had sanctioned and "the legitimate result of the doctrine of blood atonement. It was no more than the translation into deeds of sermons which Brigham and his aids had preached for years." Their leaders' violent rhetoric led "simple savages like Lee or covetous savages like Haight or Klingensmith" to conclude that "if the sermons of the 'reformation' meant anything, the Mountain Meadows massacre was justified. If they meant nothing, why were they uttered?" Cannon said it was "absolute certainty that whether from Lee or from another, Brigham knew the whole ghastly story within a few days. His mastership of the territory in those days has never been questioned. Yet to the day of his death, Brigham never lifted a finger to bring to justice the perpetrators of this massacre." But as horrible as was the crime was, Cannon claimed that "the excuses offered for it by Mormon historians add a touch of infamy not often achieved. The Arkansans, being safely dead, are maligned." He dismissed the massacre's connection with the murder of Parley Pratt, asking if it "was a crime properly punishable by the murder of one hundred and twenty persons who had no part in it, merely because they came from the same state?" He concluded:

> The charges against the emigrants themselves are quite as idle. Had they been guilty of any such disturbance, they would have been laid by the heels within forty-eight hours after they entered the Mormon kingdom. In one point, the absurdity of the charges becomes grotesque. Since no Arkansans were present at the murder of Joseph Smith, it became necessary to invent a party of "Missouri wildcats" who were traveling in company with the party from Arkansas. These Missourians are as mythical as the poisoned spring. It is passing strange that intelligent men, such as some of the Mormon historians are, cannot see that by repeating these absurd slanders, they are making themselves apologists for the most atrocious massacre that has stained American annals.[1]

---

[1]Cannon and Knapp, *Brigham Young and His Mormon Empire*, 279–83.

Blaming the Indians: It Is All One Lie

Over the years, the mythology about the Mountain Meadows made it appear that some forty men and about twice as many women and children came to Utah with the intent of tormenting more than thirty thousand white people and poisoning natives along the trail. At first, this cover story laid the blame for the massacre entirely on the Indians, but excused them for doing it. Under mounting pressure, Mormon leaders gave up John D. Lee as a scapegoat, but held that he acted alone or with only a few other renegades. Still today, the usual account is that the desert bands along the Santa Clara River were the primary actors in the awful tale, but fully justified in what they did. This story, by inference, portrays these natives as fearsome and warlike.

In 1859 Indian Agent Garland Hurt gave a harsh but accurate description of these bands. "The [Southern Paiutes] are perhaps the most timid and dejected of all the tribes west of the Rocky Mountains," the non-Mormon agent said, noting it was "utterly absurd and impossible" for them to mount an assault like the one at Mountain Meadows. To the contrary, he felt safe "in asserting that ten men well-armed could defend themselves against the largest force this band could muster."[2] After seeing the massacre site, Nauvoo Legion officer William Wall told George A. Smith that "if he had had command of the emigrant party he believes he could have whipt one thousand Indians."[3] Distinguished trails scholar John Unruh concluded the Paiutes at most served "merely as lackeys carrying out Mormon plans."[4] The Indians themselves agreed with his assessment.

"Interview with the Chief of the Beavers," clipping from *San Francisco Morning Call*, 4 August 1875, in Ichel Watters Papers.

BEAVER, Utah, August 3, 1875.

So much has been said about the Indians at the [Mountain Meadows] massacre, that your reporter has for several days been in search of the Chief of the Beavers. To-day he found him and held an interview by the aid of an interpreter. This chief's name is Beaverite. He became Chief by the recommendation of the Mormons and the ratification of the Indian agent, on account of his good character. He is aged about 46, and is afflicted with partial blind-

---

[2]Simpson, *Report of Explorations across the Great Basin of the Territory of Utah*, 462,
[3]Smith to Lyman, 6 January 1858, LDS Archives.
[4]Unruh, *The Plains Across*, 184.

ness. He said, "I was not at Corn Creek, but am brother to the mother of Kenosh [*sic*], Chief of the Corn Creek Indians, and I am a warm friend of the Pahvants. I often talked the matter over with them. The story of the poisoned ox is not true, nor of the poisoned springs. The water talked of is not a spring, it is running water. No persons ever poisoned it as the Mormons say. The Indians never told me of it, and I being with them must have heard it. No Corn Creeks, Pahvants, nor Beavers ever went to Mountain Meadows. It is all one lie, whoever says so. All the Indians there were not more than one hundred, for I knew Moquepus, who was there with his Cold Creek Indians. He is my friend: so were all his Indians. I have often talked with them during the last seventeen years. Moquepus and his warriors always said they were making a living round Cedar, when John D. Lee came and told them to come and help kill the emigrants. Moquepus replied that he had not guns nor powder enough. Lee said the Mormons would furnish guns and powder. Moquepus said, "What will the Indians get?" Lee said, "Clothing, all the guns and horses, and some of the cattle to eat." So they went out. Moquepus was wounded and died a year after of his wounds. All the Indians tell the same story. No Indians in Utah had any animosity against the whites. Then all was peace with the Indians. One Indian tried to steal a horse of Drake's [Dukes's] party, and a guard shot him, and for a day or two there was trouble and some shooting. That was the only trouble we ever had. I know all these Indians. I know all Indian traditions. I know what I tell is true. I tell it because they are cowards, and had tried to throw all the blame on the Indians. Lee is like an Indian who shot two miners long ago. He got caught, and when brought here he got scared and shook like a coward. So with Lee. He has got scared and says the Indians did it. Lee led the Indians at the massacre, and Moquepus always said Lee was the Chief over him in that fight. That was the bargain.

Clifford Jake: We're Going to Get Blamed for It

Evidence confirming Indian involvement in the massacre at Mountain Meadows appears at first to be compelling. Consider the October 1857 report in which George Powers described seeing Colonel Dame "coming from the scene of the slaughter" with a "band of some twenty Indian warriors." The best sources on the murders—the first federal investigators—provide Paiute accounts that admit they played a limited role, but the earliest investigations consistently note that Mormons solicited Indian participation, provided the leadership, seized all the booty, and were the primary perpetrators of the massacre. Yet the more closely one examines this evidence, the more suspect it becomes: for example, his conversations with eyewitnesses Powers and Warn convinced one Los Angeles editor that "there were no Indians engaged in the affair, but that those Indians seen on the road by the men named above, were Mormons in disguise."[5]

Among all the lies told about the massacre, the vast mythology related to Indian participation became the ugliest and most enduring falsehood. The attempts to shift responsibility to the Indians were untrue then, and to the extent that they continue, are even more shameful now. "The confusion and frenzy of these painted blood-thirsty Indians was terrible to behold; centered at that place were four to six hundred wild Indians engaged," John Higbee claimed in 1896. It now is difficult to give such blame-shifting any credibility: no modern expert on the Southern Paiutes accepts such fables. Even John D. Lee's contemporaries disputed his claim that hundreds of Indians were the driving force behind the slaughter. On the day Lee died, the *San Francisco Call* published an interview with one Captain John Morse, "a frontiersman, prospector, trapper and trader," who claimed to know both Lee and Utah's tribes well. "Morse disputes Lee's statement, that there were 500 Indians present, claiming there were not more than 300 in that whole section of country," the *Call* reported. "The butchery was planned by Mormons, and almost entirely done by them, the Indians not killing over half a dozen."[6]

"It is beyond the power of credulity to believe that Indians could, or would have done and acted as was reported, by the Mormons," a Los Angeles newspaper observed in 1858, and what it said then remains true today.[7] Anthropologist Martha C. Knack's prize-winning study on the Southern Paiutes spelled out five reasons it was unlikely that they acted on their own: the military strategy was totally uncharacteristic of the tribe; the number of warriors required for such an assault and siege "far exceeded the capacity of local Paiutes bands"; such a coordinated, inter-band operation "would have required an obedience to authority that did not exist in Paiute culture"; the attack came in September during the pinion pine nut harvest, "the busiest time in the Paiute year," which was essential to the people's survival; and finally, "logistical support for such a large party on the march, during the siege, and for their return would

[5]See "The Federal Government and Utah," *Southern Vineyard*, 29 May 1858.

[6]"Mountain Meadows Massacre, Brigham Young Charged as Accessory Before and After the Fact," *Morning Oregonian*, 26 March 1877, 1/4.

[7]"The Federal Government and Utah," *Southern Vineyard*, 29 May 1858, 2.

require an unlikely level of surplus production" and the participation of family members "over an extended period during which they were themselves unproductive. The Paiute economy in late summer could not have done this." Knack concluded, "it seems clear that Southern Paiute culture, political structure, and economy could not have produced an action like the Mountain Meadows Massacre without Mormon stimulus and support."[8]

So, what was the extent of Indian involvement in the massacre? To this day, Mormon historians avoid addressing the question directly, preferring to cite the incredible numbers reported by the murderers at the John D. Lee trial. Participant estimates were as high as Lee's "wild and excited band of several hundred Indians" to John Higbee's four to six hundred "savages."[9] When asked how many Indians were present at the slaughter, Philip Klingensmith said, "I could not tell you, but the hills were pretty full around there." He became even more evasive when Lee's defense council asked how many he actually saw: "I could not tell." The defense asked again, and the witness said, "I saw a good many around there." Finally, Bishop asked, "How many did you understand, from those in authority, were there?" Klingensmith had "heard it talked of that there was something more than a hundred Indians there." Bishop asked if, "of your own knowledge, that there was over three hundred there?" Klingensmith's answer is illuminating: "I do not."[10]

In contrast to the talk of hundreds of Indians, participant Joel White testified there "might have been 40 or 50, somewheres along there."[11] Beaverite said there were not more than one hundred Indians involved, which appears to be a reasonable upper limit for the total number of native participants over the entire week. However, given the conditions Professor Knack describes, even these numbers appear improbably high, a fact that other experts confirm. LaVan Martineau collected twenty-six accounts of war and conflict from Southern Paiute informants, but the largest war party he identified consisted of only twelve members.[12]

Assembling even a few dozen Indian "warriors" to attack a wagon train would require considerable effort, but their numbers were augmented by recruits from among the "several hundred Indians, held in servitude" in Utah

[8]Knack, *Boundaries Between*, 79–80.

[9]Brooks, *The Mountain Meadows Massacre*, 228; and Bishop, ed., *Mormonism Unveiled*, 227.

[10]Klingensmith testimony, digital copy at http://www.mtn-meadows-assoc.com/klingensmith.htm [9 January 2006].

[11]White testimony, Lee Trial Transcripts, 155.

[12]Martineau, *Southern Paiutes*, 47–68. Thanks to Logan Hebner for this observation.

Territory.[13] Surviving accounts place at least three "adopted sons" at the massacre: Hamblin's Albert, a Shoshone; Samuel Knight's John from the Las Vegas Band; and John D. Lee's Clem. As early as 1851 Brigham Young had directed southern Utah settlers "to buy up the Lamanite children as fast as they could, and educate them and teach them the gospel, so that many generations would not pass ere they should become a white and delightsome people." By the middle of September 1851 the pioneers of Parowan had purchased ten Indian children. The stalwarts of the Southern Indian mission, including Lee, Hamblin, Klingensmith, and George A. Smith, all participated in the Indian slave trade: when it came to kill the Arkansans, the Nauvoo Legion's native auxiliaries may have consisted almost exclusively of such "adopted" servants.[14]

In the fall of 1995 spiritual leader and tribal elder Clifford Jake told the story of the Mountain Meadows massacre that he had learned from Paiute elders, including George Hunkup. "They tell stories about what happened over there and the way" it happened, Jake said.

CLIFFORD JAKE, INTERVIEW WITH WILL BAGLEY,
29 NOVEMBER 1995, PAIUTE INDIAN TRIBE
OF UTAH HEADQUARTERS, CEDAR CITY, UTAH.

Bagley: [Gary Tom said] your parents might have told you something about Mountain Meadows?

Jake: I used to hang among the older Indians around here.

Bagley: Yes.

Jake: The old people, and old ladies, too, and some people come from my area, too, they used to talk Indian. They tell stories about what happened over there and the way. According to two guys from Shiv-Wits, there were two brothers that were hunting. On that day, on that morning they came up and they go hunting over to Pine Valley there and during the day, I guess early some time during the day they heard these guns popped out like a firecrackers or something like that. Well these two brothers went along towards that place, and they went up the hill, and looked down, now I don't know which mountain or hill they were looking down like that, maybe on this side, maybe on that side, and looking down, they say, sure enough they [the Mormons] were shooting down at a wagon train come from, going down towards the south. They had seen that they were dressed up in Indian, all Indian paint, paint up like Indian, ride the horses bareback. They seen that. After they got done and they looked all over, after they shot, they killed all them, and the people were gone from that wagon

[13]Browne, "The Utah Expedition: Its Causes and Consequences," 581.
[14]Brooks, "Indian Relations on the Mormon Frontier," 6; and Edson Whipple, Diary, 17 September 1851, BYU Library.

train, they looked all over the things to pick up some animals and horses and things. [They seen them down washing off the paint in the creek.] . . . so many distant, see what they doing.

Bagley: Ah hum.

Jake: They come to New Harmony. They take all the Indian stuff what they was wearing and burn it. I don't know what they done with the guns, the guns they had, whether they buried or put them away somewhere else in a cave. So these two Indians went back to warn his people. He wanted to warn his people, see, tell them that something going to, something going to be. They went down to the place towards Shiv-wits. They had seen something really bad happen. So they said I want you people to get prepared, for we're going to get blamed for it. These two Indians [went] to the Indian over there, the chief, whoever it was, the old people over there, they warn the people to get on the saddle horses, quick, the saddle horses and travel, go to warn those people. Over here, this area here, they didn't even know about what was going on over there. They don't know nothing. That's exactly the way I heard it among the old people tell the story about it. They said we pretty nearly got killed for the things that we didn't do.

Bagley: Yes. Did you hear this from the [Shiv-wits] brothers?

Jake: From the rest of the Indians, the older Indians, they used to gather round and tell us about it, about what the white people did at that time.

Bagley: Yes.

Jake: They used to tell about it, tell a story about it. It comes from that, the stories come from all the different Indians, old people come and tell the story about it.

Bagley: Sure, sure.

Jake: They discussed it, they discussed it.

Bagley: Um hum.

Jake: That was the wrong thing what the white people do, did. That people that wanted to live, they just want to live, just like we all. That's what the old Indians used to say. Some older ones. I don't mean just one or two of the Indians, I mean four or five of them sit together and tell the story while the others are listening.

Bagley: Yes.

Jake: They answer the questions, too, in their own language.

Bagley: Yes. I'm glad you listened.

Jake: I was a young guy, only a teenager. I used to chop wood for the older Indians. That's exactly what happened . . .

Jake: Some kind of a major, or some kind of [officer], come from Salt Lake to investigate that down here.

Bagley: Yes.

Jake: But they said the Indian don't do this thing . . . They don't do that thing.

Bagley: Major Carleton?

Jake: I think he was, he was some kind of soldier. But that's what the old Indians say.

Bagley: But he remembered the army officers coming down to find out about it?

Jake: Probably some of them seen him at long distance, when they hunting, coming down. The army was coming down, then tell it together. That's exactly, that's the way I heard it. They trace those people to New Harmony. Later on they found out the leader of the massacre over there.

Bagley: Yes.

Jake: It was John D. Lee or something like that.

Bagley: Yes, it was John D. Lee

Jake: He was the one that got us in trouble.

Bagley: Hmm, hmm. Interesting that when [the Paiutes] saw it happen they knew that the Indians would be blamed for it.

Jake: Yes.

Bagley: And they were right . . . Did the Mormons give the Indians anything from the [massacre]?

Jake: Never receive anything from them. They made a lot of promises, but the promises never worked out.

Bagley: Hmm.

Jake: It still was that way. It still is now that way. You have to go by the papers in order to get help.

Bagley: Some things never change.

Jake: There's a lot of Indians talk about those things, the government put them into reservations, they say they're going to take care of the Indians. They put them on reservations. They couldn't get out and hunt like they used to do in early days. They promised them they were going to give them some clothing, everything they need, food and everything, that never happened.

Bagley: Yes.

Jake: There's something still then that not come out right. I think about it some times. Brigham Young he send a big old wagon train came down through here. They had some people out killing Indians, killing Indians by the head, $20 a head, all the way down, small ones, little ones. And they had a big load of wagon of head hunters. They take it back and get paid for that.[15] And quite a lot of Indians had a good place . . . They been driven out of that place too.

Bagley: You heard these stories from Shivwits?

Jake: No, from Indian Peak people. This one here was George Hunkup.

Bagley: And he told you . . .

Jake: He used to tell the story about what happened. He told the story I told you about what happened at Mountain Meadows.

---

[15]This tradition may reflect an incident following the Battle of Provo River in 1850. After Daniel Wells ordered the execution of eleven Ute prisoners at Utah Lake, two local militiamen under the direction of U.S. Army contract surgeon James Blake decapitated their bodies for "scientific purposes." See Carter, *Founding Fort Utah*, 208, 223.

A Feather Lying Down

There is enough historical evidence to argue that a few Paiutes were more than mere spectators at Mountain Meadows. But in many ways, the Indian perspective is the reverse side of the coin of Mormon stories that put responsibility for the atrocity on the Indians: both cultures need to lay the blame at someone else's door. Like the survivor accounts and much of the Lee trial testimony, traditions about the massacre from Paiute bands share a remarkable consistency. "My Grandfather was involved in all this Mountain Meadows. He saw everything. Saw the White people dressed as Indians. There were two Indians that saw what was happening with the White people dressed as Indians," Eleanor Tom remembered. "They knew right then and there they'd be blamed. They blamed all that on the Indian People. Now, nobody'd listen to an Indian any way," she told a local writer, concluding with an inarguable truth: "The Whites, they won that story."[16]

At the dedication of the Mountain Meadows memorial on Dan's Hill, held in Cedar City in 1990, southern Utah politician Dixie Leavitt asked Clifford Jake to conduct a prayer ceremony. After the Mountain Meadows Choir sang "I Sing the Greatness of our God" and before Gordon B. Hinckley's dedicatory prayer, tribal chairwoman Geneal Anderson introduced Jake to the audience. He then led them in prayer.

"I told them people that come from far off, I want you people to stand up and rise. They all rise up, started praying. After that I felt some tears," Jake recalled. He prayed "to give us strength, give us heart, even if it's that way it had to be done, nobody can help it. That's the way the great spirit felt about it. The time, their time was up. That's what's taken place. Forgive. Forgive, it's hard, but you have to forgive. That's the way I prayed."

After the prayer, Stewart Udall told Jake he was moved by a "great feeling when you were talking." To his surprise, Jake's wife told her husband, "There was two of you standing down there." Clifford said, "No, I don't see nobody there but me." His wife disagreed: "He was standing on this side of you, all buckskin and buckskin trousers on, with a feather lying down."

Some spirits refuse to die, and some stories should never be forgotten.

---

[16]Hebner, "Stop Blaming the Paiutes," *The Spectrum* (St. George, Utah), 11 September 2007, A6.

AFTERWORD

I will beg leave to lay down, as a standing rule in such cases, that the suppressing of evidence ought always to be taken for the strongest evidence.
Andrew Hamilton, at the trial of John Peter Zenger, 1735.

The Southern guns that announced the start of the Civil War in Charleston harbor in April 1861 also signaled the effective end to the initial federal investigation into the massacre at Mountain Meadows. A month later, Brigham Young made his only visit to the site and saw the monument of granite stones and the cedar cross that Major Carleton and his men had erected and inscribed with the words, "Vengeance is mine: I will repay, saith the Lord." Young studied it a moment, then said: "It should be Vengeance is mine and I have taken a little."[1] That was all he said, Dudley Leavitt recalled. "He just lifted his right arm to the square and in five minutes there wasn't one stone left upon another." Even more revealing was the fact that Young gave no spoken order. "He didn't have to tell us what he wanted done," Leavitt said. "We understood."[2]

There was no need to say more. In those few words Brigham Young revealed why the massacre took place and the authority for it. As he silently directed his escort to tear down the monument, his act announced that the truth would never be told; any investigation would be relentlessly opposed. Five days later, Young told John D. Lee that the only thing that ever troubled him about the atrocity was the killing of women and children, "but that under the circumstances [it] could not be avoided." Anyone who wanted to betray the Brethren into the hands of their enemies would be damned and go to hell, but such

---

[1]Kenney, ed., *Wilford Woodruff's Journal*, 5:577.
[2]Brooks, *The Mountain Meadows Massacre*, 183. The sign Young made when he raised his right arm "to the square" was used in the Mormon temple rites.

traitors had all "run away."[3] Young's words reveal that the charge James Buchanan made in the pardon that the Mormon leader accepted was still true: "a strange system of terrorism" had brought the territory's inhabitants to a point where "no one among them could express an opinion favorable to this government, or even proposed to obey its laws, without exposing his life and property to peril."[4]

True to Young's example, the pattern of cover-up and denial continues even today. When asked who was to blame for the slaughter, former LDS church president Gordon B. Hinckley told the *Salt Lake Tribune* in February 2000, "Well, I would place blame on the local people." The religion's leaders and even its scholars insist that the massacre is an impenetrable mystery: "We can't understand it in this time, but none of us can place ourselves in the moccasins of those who lived there at the time," Hinckley said. More recently distinguished Mormon historian Thomas Alexander asserted, "I don't think we'll ever really understand why this massacre took place."[5] Yet the documents assembled in this volume provide a wealth of evidence about what happened at the massacre and why it happened. Of course, the surviving evidence is only that part of the historical record which has not disappeared or been altered, suppressed, or destroyed. Among a people as dedicated to record keeping as the Mormons, the fact that so many manuscript sources have had pages ripped from them should raise a host of questions.[6]

Contemporary reports reveal that the charges Brigham Young leveled not long after the massacre against the murdered dead, which argued that the victims provoked the Indians and local settlers and basically got what they deserved, are simply false. The Arkansas company was similar to hundreds of others that passed through Utah during and after the California gold rush. A few attributes made it distinctive: the train was larger than most, and women and children outnumbered the adult males by about three to two. Nearly half were children, including as many as twenty girls between the ages of 7 and 17. Its

---

[3]Cleland and Brooks, eds., *A Mormon Chronicle*, 1:314. Since Wilford Woodruff's diary contains the same quotation, Lee's next comment makes it difficult to challenge the authenticity of his journal entry: "when he came to the Monument that contained their Bones, he made this remark, Vengence is Mine Saith the Lord, & I have taken a litle of it."

[4]Roberts, *A Comprehensive History of the Church*, 4:426.

[5]Smith, "The Dilemma of Blame," *Salt Lake Tribune*, 14 March 2000, 1/1–3; and Morgan, "Professor Investigates Mountain Meadows Massacre," *BYU Universe*, 15 February 2007.

[6]Among such documents: the August–October 1857 pages from the southern Utah journals of Preston Thomas and Isaac Coombs, John D. Lee's 1859 journal, the autobiographies of Jacob Hamblin and Nephi Johnson, and Isaac Haight and William Dame letters to and from Brigham Young.

members also carried an unusually large amount of property, mostly in the form of a large herd of cattle, but their possessions included horses, wagons, equipment, excellent weapons, and a considerable amount of money.

The picture of this party, as known today, is of closely interconnected farm families moving to California to make new homes. They left Arkansas weeks before Parley P. Pratt was murdered and had nothing to do with his death or the failure to bring his assassin to justice. For the mature men who led the train, its many women and children added up to a compelling reason to avoid trouble. Evidence shows that they respected this obligation and backed away from confrontation. Save for seventeen little ones, all its members were murdered and everything they owned stolen, even their bloody clothes. The serving Indian superintendent did nothing to recover the property of the murdered parents for the young survivors. No attempt was ever made to identify the victims, notify relatives, or bury them properly. Their naked bodies were left as food for the coyotes.

The historical record is indebted to survivors such as Malinda Cameron Thurston, who later testified in separate affidavits that her company left home on 29 March 1857 and reached Great Salt Lake City on 3 August. She survived because her husband decided to take the northern route, while her father and the rest of her family, including brothers and sisters, took Mormon advice and went south. The "southern route" was indeed the best because it was an all-season route and the desert natives on the Virgin River and its tributaries and at Las Vegas Springs posed no threat to a large company.

Every American train that followed that trail after 1851, especially those driving cattle or sheep, experienced harassment, but the treatment of the Fancher party was unique from the day it reached Great Salt Lake City. Early that morning, 3 August, Apostle George A. Smith left on his flying trip to the Mormon villages along the trail south. After more than four months on the overland road, the Arkansans needed fresh vegetables and flour, especially for the children. But as their wagons and cattle slowly followed Smith, the emigrants met only hostility in the wake of his passage.

Moving fast, the apostle averaged over 40 miles a day on the 250-mile trip to Iron County. As he went, he delivered written orders from Brigham Young to sell no food to the emigrants and to tell the Indians "they have either got to help us or the United States will kill us both."[7] At each settlement Smith

---

[7] Young to Hamblin, 4 August 1857, Brooks, *The Mountain Meadows Massacre*, 34–35.

fanned the flames of the Reformation. Joseph Woods, Thomas Willis, and others recalled George A. Smith telling a congregation at Cedar City that the emigrants were coming, "and he told them that they must not sell that company *any grain or provisions* of any kind, for they were a mob of villains and outlaws, and the enemies of God and the Mormon people."[8]

An omen of what the future held was Young's appointment of frontier zealot Jacob Hamblin to replace the moderate Rufus Allen as president of the Southern Indian Mission. Hamblin could be trusted to do what he was told. "For the general news I refer you to Elder G. A. Smith who is well acquainted with the things transpiring in the lower world," Young told Isaac Haight in a letter informing him of Allen's replacement. "I wish you to pay strict attention to the instructions which I forwarded to you by him." If nothing else, Smith's visit eliminated the need to create a paper trail of written orders that might threaten "the interest of the 'Kingdom.' "[9]

The first large company to go south that year, the Fancher party traveled at a leisurely pace to allow their cattle, variously estimated from three hundred to a thousand head, to graze along the well traveled road. The refusal of settlers to sell them food no doubt provoked an angry reaction. Sparks also flew when their cattle grazed on fields reserved for Mormon livestock, producing a clash over national land laws and local ideas about land ownership. To settlers the lands of God's Kingdom were assigned to individual stewards or placed under communal control. To the Arkansans, the settlers were squatters on public range owned by the United States.

Reports of disputes at Provo and Nephi indicate that the emigrants prudently backed down rather than let such quarrels get out of hand. Later tales of emigrant misdeeds do not square with what is now known about the party, its makeup, and its leaders; in our opinion, these stories appear to be an orchestrated effort to slander the emigrants and justify killing them. Brigham Young's replacement as Utah Indian superintendent made "strict inquiry" into the Arkansans' behavior in 1859. Jacob Forney concluded "they conducted themselves with propriety."[10] At worst, these allegations accused the party of mean-spirited insults that may have offended the settlers. They provide no evidence whatsoever that its members harmed any person or property. Nor was there

    [8]Bishop, ed., *Mormonism Unveiled*, 225.

    [9]Young to Haight, 4 August 1857, LDS Archives.

    [10]Forney to Greenwood, August 1859, Buchanan, *Massacre at Mountain Meadows*, Sen. Doc. 42, Serial 1033, 75–80.

reason to think that the train was any different from hundreds of others that went through Utah, except that its members had better reasons to be well behaved than most.

As the Arkansas emigrants journeyed south, Apostle Smith scurried about, meeting with the men who would soon execute them. During his tour, he met with all of the primary participants in the massacre, including Indians. He talked with Col. William H. Dame, the Nauvoo Legion's Iron County Brigade commander and Parowan Stake president, and reviewed the Cedar City companies. He met with John D. Lee; Isaac Haight, president of the Cedar Stake of Zion; and Maj. John M. Higbee, who would give the order to kill the emigrants. And he told Hamblin, the new head of the Santa Clara Indian Mission, to accompany him back to Great Salt Lake City and escort the Southern Paiute chiefs to see Brigham Young. Smith recorded these meetings in his diary, but chose not to say what was discussed. He "expected every emigrant to be killed that undertook to pass through the Territory while we were at war with the Government," John D. Lee concluded. "I thought it was his mission to prepare the people for the bloody work."[11]

As if to confirm Lee's opinion, Young at Great Salt Lake gave dire warnings of Indian trouble to justify stopping travel on the overland trails while his agents at the same time urged the tribes to join the Mormons in their conflict with the United States. In a 16 August discourse filled with malice toward the federal government, the Mormon prophet said that he wished to tell all the Gentiles "they must stop crossing the continent to California for the Indians will use them up."[12] But of all of the tribes on the overland trails, the Southern Paiutes were the least warlike or dangerous.

Brigham Young knew the president had appointed his successor, but he continued to act as governor of Utah Territory. He warned the commissioner of Indian Affairs on 12 September to keep U.S. soldiers away or he would have "the utmost difficulty" controlling the Indians.[13] When news of the massacre spread, it made his warning appear prophetic. It also gave him an alibi, justified stopping overland travel, and made it possible to blame the Indians.

---

[11]Bishop, ed., *Mormonism Unveiled*, 225. Our interpretation owes much to Robert N. Baskin. It is not reasonable, he concluded, to believe authorities "at Cedar City would have taken steps to murder the emigrants had they not been instructed to do so by an order of their superior officers." Baskin acknowledged there was only circumstantial evidence of such an order, whose existence could have been verified "only by the church officer at Cedar City to whom it was (in my opinion) communicated by George A. Smith on his southern trip, made for that purpose." See Baskin, *Reminiscences of Early Utah*, 147.

[12]Woodruff, Synopsis of an address by Brigham Young on 16 August 1857.

[13]Young to Denver, 12 September 1857, *The Utah Expedition*, House Doc. 71, Serial 956, 183–85.

The poison story provides more circumstantial support to the view the massacre was planned in advance. First invented to justify the Indians in committing the atrocity, it belongs with the original claim that they did it without Mormon help. Since the tale of the poisoned spring reached the southern Utah settlements ahead of the Arkansans, it appears that George A. Smith concocted the story after meeting the Fancher train at Corn Creek and sent it south with his cousin, Silas S. Smith. As time passed and Mormon involvement became known, the falsehood became the centerpiece of the campaign to smear the emigrants, but it failed to convince those on the scene who heard it first. Traveling ten days behind the ill-fated train, emigrant George Davis camped at Corn Creek and "never heard anything of poisoning" before reaching Beaver. The members of the Dukes train thought the story was a Mormon fabrication "to clear themselves of suspicion, and to justify the Indians in murdering that company of emigrants."[14] All that has been learned since confirms the finding of Superintendent Jacob Forney, who looked into the charge. "Why an emigrant company, and especially farmers, would carry with them so much deadly poison is incomprehensible," he said. "I regard the poisoning affair as entitled to no consideration."[15]

The significance of the encounter at Corn Creek was not about poison. It was the reaction of the ill-fated train's leaders, who immediately doubled their guard when they saw Apostle Smith escorting native chiefs to Salt Lake. From Corn Creek to their last resting place, the Arkansans stepped up their pace and traveled about as fast as they could go with a large cattle herd. They were not looking for trouble. They were trying to get away.

The people they feared reached Great Salt Lake City, where Hamblin delivered the Paiute chiefs to a conference with Brigham Young and his interpreter, Dimick B. Huntington. No detailed record was made of the session, but the Mormon officials gave them "all the cattle that had gone to Cal[ifornia] by the south rout[e]."[16] The chiefs knew which cattle he referred to, because they had seen them at Corn Creek. Young's generosity with other people's property was a criminal act that betrayed his oath as a federal officer, but it also can be seen as an invitation to attack the Fancher train with an implied promise of support if needed.

Meanwhile, even the evasive and self-serving recollections of Nauvoo

[14]"Letter from San Bernardino," *San Francisco Daily Bulletin,* 12 November 1857, 1/3.
[15]Forney to Greenwood, August 1859, *Mountain Meadows Massacre,* 75–80.
[16]Dimick B. Huntington Journal, 1857 August–May 1859.

Legionnaires suggest that William Dame ordered southern Utah's best Indian interpreters—Carl Shurtz, Nephi Johnson, and Samuel Knight—to begin recruiting local Paiutes and any handy Indian freebooters shortly after Smith's departure. Colonel Dame apparently sent orders to outlying militia units along the Virgin and Santa Clara rivers to attack the first wagon train to reach Santa Clara Canyon: the Washington County men whom John D. Lee found approaching Mountain Meadows shortly after the ambush were more than a hundred miles of rugged road from the Iron Brigade's headquarters in Parowan. According to the diary of Jesse Smith, the best Mormon source to provide a date, the Fancher party did not reach Cedar City until Friday, 4 September. The size of the attack force that was in place at dawn three days later indicates that Colonel Dame had to begin issuing orders to attack the Fancher party by the first of September, days before the wagon train reached southern Utah. This begs a critical question: why would a military officer issue orders to attack an emigrating party he had never seen? The implied answer helps explain why Haight and Dame did not wait for clarification from Salt Lake when they issued the order to decoy and exterminate the Arkansans: they already had their orders.

The earliest and most reliable sources paint a clear picture of the initial assault on the emigrant camp.[17] Despite the Mormons' best efforts, they probably had collected only a few Indian auxiliaries. Most of these partisans were sent up the nearby hollows to run off the emigrants' cattle before daylight, and the rest were used as rifle fodder for the first attack. The earliest federal investigators reported that sixty to seventy white citizens, painted and disguised as Indians, formed the backbone of John D. Lee's ragtag bandit band. The devastating nature of the initial attack, in which Judge Cradlebaugh reported "ten or twelve of the emigrants were killed or wounded" and Lee claimed seven emigrants were killed and forty-six wounded, indicates that the sharpshooters were Mormons. The lack of known white casualties suggests that Lee, who said the Indians "had been told that they could kill the emigrants without danger to themselves," persuaded his allies to make a half-hearted frontal assault. When Lee's magic failed, most of the Indians decamped. "Now we knew the Indians could not do the work," John D. Lee wrote later in his carefully calculated confession, "and we were in a sad fix."[18]

---

[17]These sources were the reports of the 1859 federal investigators, notably Carleton, Cradlebaugh, and Rogers. They spoke with Indians and peripheral witnesses, and Cradlebaugh heard confessions from at least two massacre participants.

[18]Bishop, ed., *Mormonism Unveiled*, 227–28.

Out of ammunition and cut off from water, the victims were in desperate shape at the end of a siege that lasted for five days. They had dispatched as many as five messengers sent on a hopeless bid for help. Indians and Ira Hatch would track down the three men sent to California and kill them, and Mormon militiamen had already murdered William Aden and a possible companion, who had been sent east to try to contact the wagon trains still coming down the trail. Lee's claim that one of the messengers returned to the Fancher party and warned that white men were involved in the assault appears invented to justify the subsequent atrocity: would the Arkansans have surrendered had they known that Mormons were among those attacking them?

The bones of the unburied dead in that valley would have remained silent if the Mormon theocracy had successfully thrown off the federal yoke and gained its independence. As the Utah War turned out, however, in 1858 Brigham Young accepted President Buchanan's pardon, agreeing that he and his followers would "submit themselves to the authority of the federal government."[19] Whether he intended to abide by the condition is arguable, but his acceptance made it necessary to conduct an ongoing defense against accusations that he was an accessory to the massacre. This campaign goes on today.

Young's defenders seem unaware that a centerpiece of their defense is also its most bizarre element: the epic ride of James Haslam. Late on the day the attack began, Haslam left Cedar City with only a single horse to ride five hundred miles; even in Mormon Country, other couriers dispatched on critical missions set out with several of the best mounts available. In no other frontier territory would settlers need to ask the governor what they should do about a party of emigrants, many of them women and children, under Indian attack. Anywhere else, without a "by your leave" volunteers would surely have saved those in peril. Nowhere else would the governor have pondered for six hours before sending word, in effect, that Indians will do what Indians do, but do not get in the way. Where else in the annals of heroic western rides for help does one find a case where the courier returns to find that white settlers have joined the Indians in murdering the emigrants? Rather than buttress Young's innocence, his reply provided both an alibi and scapegoats: the Indians who would "do as they please." If the perpetrators had truly wanted confirmation of what they were supposed to do, they would have waited for Haslam's return. Instead they hurriedly finished the job before he got back.

---

[19]Buchanan, *A Proclamation*, House Doc. 2, 35th Cong., 2d sess., vol. 1, Serial 997, 69–72.

Four days later, just as long as it would take for another express rider to carry word of the massacre to Great Salt Lake, Young declared martial law, ordered Mormon troops to confront U.S. soldiers, and stopped all travel "into or through or from this Territory without a permit from the proper officer." For over five months, he pretended he was still governor but made no effort to investigate an unparalleled atrocity and punish those who committed it, whites or Indians. Later, he looked the other way and moved only under pressure. When it came, he imposed on his pacifist successor, Alfred Cumming, to allow him to handle the investigation, which he placed in the hands of none other than George A. Smith, who proceeded to display his remarkable gifts for mythmaking.

More than a half-century ago, without the insights found in her subsequent work or much of the evidence presented in this volume, Juanita Brooks concluded, "While he did not order the massacre, and would have prevented it if he could, Brigham Young was accessory after the fact, in that he knew what happened, and how and why it happened. Evidence of this is abundant and unmistakable, and from the most impeccable Mormon sources."[20] The evidence contradicts the notion that for years southern Utah leaders lied to and deceived men as well-informed as George A. Smith and Brigham Young. That Lee, Dame, Haight, Klingensmith, and the other massacre participants who visited their prophet less than a month after the murders would all lie to Brigham Young about such an important matter and not be severely punished is wishful thinking. Even if Young were the victim of such an unlikely conspiracy, the truth was impossible to hide.

Instead of ferreting out the truth, Young dispatched Apostle Smith to "investigate" the massacre and then sent Smith's report blaming the emigrants and the Indians to Thomas Kane to pass on to the attorney general of the United States. It is hard to find a more open-and-shut case of a conspiracy to obstruct justice. Local Mormon leaders headed for the hills in 1859 when Judge John Cradlebaugh investigated the massacre and other crimes and moved to arrest them.[21] Unable to join them, Brigham Young took cover in the local judicial system of probate courts that he had created and controlled. It was odd behavior for someone who bore no guilt.

The U.S. Army conducted the first investigation worthy of the name. Maj.

---

[20]Brooks, *The Mountain Meadows Massacre*, 219.

[21]Isaac Haight and other Mountain Meadows offenders joined central Utah settlement leaders at a location in Juab County identified only as "old Castle Ballagarth" or "Balleguarde," near Nephi.

James H. Carleton inspected the site in 1859 and saw that there had been "a great and fearful crime perpetrated."[22] Two years later Carleton made clear why no one had ever been punished. Said the officer: "Who compose the jury to find the indictment? The brethren. Who are generally the witnesses before the Jury? The brethren. Who are the officers and jailers who have custody of the prisoner before and after the trial? The brethren. Who are the members of the jury before whom the trial takes place? Still the brethren. Who are the witnesses for the prosecution, and, more particularly, who are those for the defense? The brethren."[23]

As Carleton reported, a pre-millennial theocracy used democratic institutions to create a separate judicial system to protect those who lived under a higher law. But as millennial expectations diminished, the wall eroded. The first crack opened in 1874 when Congress stripped the probate courts of the extraordinary powers bestowed by Mormon lawmakers. The Poland Act restored exclusive criminal jurisdiction to the district courts as Congress intended under Utah's 1850 organic act. It also returned to U.S. attorneys and marshals the sole authority to serve all writs and process, which made it possible to prosecute crimes committed many years before.

The new federal law introduced sensational courtroom battles, the most famous of which were the John D. Lee trials, but the passage of time was the least of the reasons it failed to bring convictions. Shorn of judicial control, Mormon leaders adopted tactics such as testifying falsely, jury tampering, and apparent bribery to gain acquittals. If effective, the illegal tactics imposed a heavy cost.[24] They hurt the faith's reputation and convinced leaders of a reform movement that stronger laws were needed to break theocratic rule.

Former Cedar City bishop Philip Klingensmith put his life in danger at the first trial when he told the truth about the atrocity and his own role in it. Two important witnesses escaped from the perils of cross-examination: Brigham Young and George A. Smith said they were too feeble to travel to the Beaver City court. When testimony appeared to implicate them, however, they were not too weak to send affidavits in the form of answers to questions they had drafted themselves, which the judge rejected. At the end of the first trial, the evidence against Lee was overwhelming, but in a society

---

[22]Carleton, "Special Report of the Mountain Meadows Massacre," 17.

[23]Carleton, "The Mormons as a People," 50:550–53.

[24]For an example of these tactics, see Sylvanus Collett's trial for the 1857 murder of John Aiken in Bigler, *Fort Limhi*, 189–92.

where higher justice prevailed, proof had even less to do with verdicts than it does in man-made judicial proceedings. A jury of eight active Mormons, one backslider, and three non-Mormons voted nine to three to acquit Lee. A wave of outrage rolled across the country that shook even Mormon leaders and produced another trial.

The second tribunal was so contrived that it denied spectators the suspense they expected from a sensational court case. Either from a payoff or pressure to convict at any cost, a new prosecutor agreed to drop charges against other massacre leaders and not pursue the LDS church—meaning Brigham Young. In return Young sacrificed Lee and sent his trusted counselor, Daniel H. Wells, to direct the choreographed performance. The compact would have saved George A. Smith, too, but the creator of the poison myth passed away between trials. His physician reportedly said he died of fright, but it was probably a lung infection.

At the second trial the judge accepted the affidavit that Brigham Young had tried to enter during the first trial. In it he swore he did not investigate the crime when acting as the governor in fall 1857 because his successor and new federal judges had not arrived, which was a lie by omission. He failed to say that they would have come, but were stuck in the snow at Fort Bridger because he had ordered Mormon troops to keep them out. By what is now known, Young's affidavit speaks more loudly of guilt than of innocence.

The proceeding was designed to clear Young and close the book on Mountain Meadows. With the seating of an all-Mormon jury, Lee's fate was sealed. A unanimous conviction by a Mormon jury was needed to mollify the public and take the heat off Young and his church. At the first trial, prosecution witnesses were hard to find. At the second, they turned up in whatever number was required to say whatever was called for to pin the blame on their former friend and brother, John D. Lee. As expected, the jury found Lee guilty. In sentencing Lee, Judge Jacob S. Boreman, who presided over both trials, said the evidence demonstrated that authorities at the highest level had "decided upon the wholesale slaughter of the emigrants." From the time the massacre occurred, he went on, there had been "persistent and determined opposition to an investigation." Both of his conclusions were clear then and even more so today—but not to everyone.[25]

The trials put the final touches on the morality that tale apologists have

---

[25]Whitney, *History of Utah*, 2:822–24.

faithfully followed ever since to tell the story of Mountain Meadows. Under it, the victims were mainly to blame. They came from Missouri to Utah to poison the Indians and maltreat innocent religionists who had already suffered years of persecution. President Buchanan was also culpable when he sent troops to Utah. The U.S. Army was guilty, too, because it was determined to carry out sealed orders to wipe out Mormonism, forcing believers to take up arms against a despotic government. The emigrants' evil deeds goaded the Indians into attacking them. A little-known Indian farmer and a few white renegades helped kill the emigrants, but only because they feared the savages would kill their own families if they did not help them destroy the train. Having no choice, they killed a few of the men but saved the youngest children.

Those who expected Lee to escape the firing squad by fingering Brigham Young once again underestimated his zealotry and the Mormon prophet's talent for evading justice. In 1839 Joseph Smith, the faith's founding prophet, had warned against betraying a brother, "lest innocent blood be found in your skirts, and you go down to hell." Smith then added a second mortal sin to the one that Jesus Christ gave. "*All other sins are not to be compared to sins against the Holy Ghost and proving a traitor to thy brethren,*" he said.[26] Lee made the perfect scapegoat, since his instructions came through a clever wink and a nod from Apostle George A. Smith, while his immediate superiors in the Nauvoo Legion issued his direct orders. Even if he had wanted to, John D. Lee could not have "put the saddle on the right horse," as Major Haight and Colonel Dame threatened to do. Their ability to do just that meant they would never be brought to the bar of justice. If Haight endured a symbolic temporary excommunication from the Kingdom, Brigham Young restored his priesthood rights and privileges in 1874, and after 1867 the twelve-hundred-mile Deseret Telegraph that Young controlled insured that federal marshals would never catch him.

So Lee accepted his assigned role as sacrificial lamb to save the faith. His reward would be a passport to celestial glory. LDS authorities in 1961 restored his church membership and former priesthood blessings. At last, the book on Mountain Meadows was closed.

Except for the bones. Over the years they would not keep silent. The bones cried from the ground in 1859 when Maj. James Carleton and Company K, First Dragoons, heard them and collected many from victims of all ages. Saved for a time by the Civil War, Brigham Young said that vengeance had been

---

[26]Smith, ed., *An Intimate Chronicle,* 513–14. Emphasis in the original.

taken and oversaw the destruction of the marker Carleton raised over one of their graves. But the bones would not keep quiet. In 1864 Capt. George F. Price and his California Volunteers heard them and rebuilt the monument. The bones again cried from the ground in 1999 when a backhoe operator began work on the foundation of a new monument constructed by the LDS church as a memorial to the victims. He scraped the earth and uncovered the human remains that Major Carleton's men had gathered from the sagebrush and buried: broken children's bones, the skull of a young woman with a bullet hole in the crown, bones of arms and legs torn by coyote teeth. When he saw the children's bones, a veteran county sheriff was deeply moved. "That was what really hit me hard," he said.[27] The bones now rest on the ground where the victims died, but they are still not silent.

The bones speak of original Mormonism. They tell of forgotten doctrines and beliefs that no longer energize true believers: the Kingdom of God as an earthly state—the imminent coming of the Son of Man—oaths to avenge the blood of the prophets—American Indians as instruments of divine justice—the shedding of human blood for the remission of sins not forgiven by Christ's sacrifice—divine land ownership—unthinking obedience to higher authority—revealed justice—the sealing up against all crimes save shedding innocent blood—the law of adoption—and others. All can be found at Mountain Meadows. All are consistent with the actions and refusal to act by their most fanatical proponent, Brigham Young, and the events that took place under his hand that day.

The bones also speak of Arkansas farm families seeking a better life in the West. These closely knit families did not come to torment the Mormons, but just to pass through their domains on their way to California. They rebuke the contrivances, elaborate falsehoods, slanders, and false testimony that their killers created to conceal their involvement or to justify those most responsible. They proclaim vengeance that fell on innocent heads. They tell of men, women, and children slain for no rational reason or purpose.

A harmonious sequence of events reveals the Fancher train was marked for destruction at least as early as the day it arrived in Salt Lake Valley. The only spontaneous or unplanned thing that happened afterward was the stiff resistance of the Arkansans and the need to deploy too many Iron County militiamen to keep the awful secret. Stripped of fabrication and slander, the

---

[27]*New York Times*, 15 August 1999, 22.

episode has all the marks of a planned operation that goes in a straight, consistent line to a preordained finish without internal contradictions.

The massacre at Mountain Meadows raises much harder issues than the question of whether Brigham Young ordered an atrocity. The most haunting problem is explaining how deeply religious nineteenth-century men, who grew up in a culture that required a man to lay down his life rather than see violence done to females or the young, could participate in the murder of some fourscore helpless women and children.

"I did not act alone," John D. Lee wrote as his prepared to meet his fate. Despite his uncounted lies, Lee's confession helps answer the massacre's most troubling question. The men who assisted him at Mountain Meadows "were acting under the impression that they were performing a religious duty," Lee concluded. "I know all were acting under the orders and by the command of their Church leaders; and I firmly believe that the most of those who took part in the proceedings, considered it a religious duty to unquestioningly obey the orders which they had received. That they acted from a sense of duty to the Mormon Church, I never doubted."[28]

It is impossible to know what is in someone else's head or heart or to know how many men at Mountain Meadows acted out of fear for their own lives if they defied their "file leaders." But it is hard to imagine that many who committed murder on that awful day did not share the belief Samuel McMurdy expressed before executing two unarmed men: "Lord, my God, receive their spirits, for it is for the Kingdom of Heaven's sake that we do this." The men who perpetrated a horrific crime at that remote oasis on the road to California did not act in defiance of Brigham Young's will. To the contrary, the fire-and-brimstone sermons of the Reformation had taught them to obey their superiors in the priesthood absolutely and without question. Lee said that the senior officers on the field asked that "every man speak and express himself" about the terrible act they were about to commit. "All said they were willing to carry out the counsel of their leaders; that the leaders had the Spirit of God and knew better what was right then they did." Jacob Hamblin claimed years later that a few brave men defied their orders, but those who betrayed their better selves and violated their own sense of right and wrong to ruthlessly shed so much innocent blood on that dark afternoon did so in the belief that they were doing God's work.

[28]Bishop, ed., *Mormonism Unveiled*, 213–14, 242.

Mountain Meadows Massacre Timeline

The intent of this appendix is to provide readers with a basic sequence of events leading to and following the massacre at Mountain Meadows. Specific dates are usually documented, but some are "best guesses" and are open to revision should new information appear.

Apr. 1857	Fancher, Baker, Mitchell, Dunlap, Cameron, Jones, and other families leave their homes in Arkansas for California.
13 May 1857	Parley P. Pratt murdered in Arkansas.
July 1857	A California-bound party met "the Arkansas companies" camped "six miles from Salt Lake" including Fanchers, Camerons, and Dunlaps, waiting for the Bakers.
20 July 1857	First overland emigrants, mostly from Illinois, arrive in Salt Lake.
23 July 1857	Eleanor Pratt arrives in Great Salt Lake City with Porter Rockwell.
24 July 1857	Tenth Pioneer Day celebration interrupted to announce approach of the U.S. Army. Young declares independence.
1 Aug. 1857	Wilford Woodruff interviews Eleanor McLean Pratt.
3 Aug. 1857	George A. Smith leaves Salt Lake for the south. Fancher party "arrived in G.S.L. City with a large herd of cattle."
4 Aug. 1857	Brigham Young appoints Jacob Hamblin president of the Southern Indian Mission and orders Fancher party to depart.
8 Aug. 1857	George A. Smith arrives in Parowan.
15 Aug. 1857	Samuel Pitchforth reports Fancher party camped near Nephi. George A. Smith goes to Cedar City.

16 Aug. 1857   George A. Smith preaches twice at Cedar City. Spends night with John D. Lee. Brigham Young says in sermon: "I will say no more to the Indians, let them alone, but do as you please. And what is that? It is to use them up; and they will do it."

17 Aug. 1857   Samuel Pitchforth reports Fancher party passes through Nephi.

18 Aug. 1857   George A. Smith "Arrived at Washington City . . . Preached in afternoon. Dame drilled the militia." Visited Tutsegabbit.

24 Aug. 1857   Woodruff hears Eleanor Pratt describe Parley's death. George A. and Silas S. Smith travel to Beaver.

25 Aug. 1857   George A. Smith, Hamblin, and Indians camp at Corn Creek "with a party of emigrants who seemed to be much excited and placed on a double guard." Woodruff again interviews Eleanor Pratt.

28 Aug. 1857   Fancher party camps on Indian Creek near today's Manderfield. Silas Smith has supper with the Fancher party.

1 Sept. 1857   Mormon interpreters begin recruiting Indians.

3 Sept. 1857   Jesse N. Smith reports Fancher party at Paragonah. Train arrives later at Parowan and is kept outside the town wall.

4 Sept. 1857   Fancher party stops briefly at Cedar City and camps west of town.

5 Sept. 1857   Rachel Lee says John D. Lee "went on an expedition south."

6 Sept. 1857   Fancher party arrives at Mountain Meadows. Cedar City High Council Meeting votes to "do in" the emigrants and then decides to send a message to Brigham Young asking for orders.

7 Sept. 1857   At dawn, Lee and his men attack the emigrants. Emigrants "drew their wagons near each other and chained the wheels one to the other." James Haslam departs Cedar City a "little past four o'clock in the afternoon."

10 Sept. 1857   Haight meets with Dame at 2:00 A.M. and returns to Cedar City with orders. Militia assemble in Cedar and depart. Indians attack Dukes train at Beaver. At dawn Haslam arrives at Young's office, leaves at 1 P.M. Garland Hurt hears emigrants "on the southern route had got themselves into a very serious difficulty with the Piedes." Nauvoo Legion leaves Cedar City and arrives at Mountain Meadows about 10:00 P.M. Militia leaders hold a council. Three emigrant messengers escape.

11 Sept. 1857	William Batemen and Lee enter emigrant camp. Emigrants surrender and march up Mountain Meadows in late afternoon and are slaughtered near the rim of the Great Basin. Militia leaders loot corpses and make speeches. Haight and Dame arrive at the Meadows.
12 Sept. 1857	Militia hurriedly buries the dead, gathers property, take "a most solemn oath" of secrecy. "All the leading men made speeches."
13 Sept. 1857	Lee and Indians arrive at Harmony, where Lee stages a feast. Haslam arrives in Cedar City from Salt Lake.
14 Sept. 1857	Brigham Young issues declaration of martial law. Ira Hatch and others kill the last of the Fancher party messengers.
17 Sept. 1857	Garland Hurt sends a Ute, Pete, to ask the Paiutes "what the nature of the difficulty was, and who were the instigators."
20 Sept. 1857	Dame issues orders to protect trains in southern Utah. Arapene tells Brigham Young of the massacre. Lee departs for Salt Lake.
23 Sept. 1857	Pete tells Garland Hurt that Paiutes "participated in the massacre of the emigrants, but said that the Mormons persuaded them into it." Lee meets Hamblin and tells him of the massacre.
27 Sept. 1857	Lee speaks at Provo. Garland Hurt escapes Nauvoo Legion.
28 Sept. 1857	Lee arrives in Salt Lake and meets with Young.
29 Sept. 1857	Lee tells "awful tale of blood" to Young and selected Mormon authorities, including Wilford Woodruff.
30 Sept. 1857	Indian Agent George Armstrong reports massacre to Young. News of the massacre reaches San Bernardino.
2 Oct. 1857?	Massacre participants Klingensmith, Haight, Dame, and Charles Hopkins meet with Brigham Young.
3 Oct. 1857	*L.A. Star* publishes first rumors of the massacre.
7 Oct. 1857	Mormons and "Indians" steal cattle from the Dukes train.
12 Oct. 1857	A mass meeting in Los Angeles denounces massacre.
17 Oct. 1857	First members of the Dukes train arrive at San Bernardino. *Star* and *Alta California* publish detailed reports on the massacre.
4 Dec. 1857	Garland Hurt submits first federal report of the massacre and says John D. Lee recruited Indians to attack emigrants.
15 Dec. 1857	*New York Times* first reports massacre.
6 Jan. 1858	Young tells Indian Affairs commissioner that as the "natural consequence" of poisoning at Corn Creek, the Fancher party fell "victims to the Indians' wrath."

June 1858	Hamblin tells Young and Smith "everything I could" about the massacre.
8 July 1858	*New-York Times* reports John D. Lee's involvement in "the Mountain Meadow Massacre."
Aug. 1858	George A. Smith investigates massacre and writes two letters blaming the emigrants and the Indians.
15 Dec. 1858	Young sends Thomas L. Kane one of Smith's Aug. 1858 letters.
May 1859	Indian Agent Forney retrieves seventeen orphans and U.S. Army and Judge Cradlebaugh investigate the massacre.
17 May 1859	U.S. Attorney General Black orders judges not to use army to support prosecutions, effectively ending the federal investigation.
23 Dec. 1866	Brigham Young sermon calls the massacre one of the "transactions that are too horrible for me to contemplate." Those who claim he ordered any crime "are liars in the face of heaven. If I am guilty of any such thing, let it be proved on me, and not go sneaking around insinuating that Brigham knows all about it . . . Let the fraternity of the brotherhood keep their oaths and covenants and vows."
12 Sept. 1870	"Argus" (Charles Wandell) publishes first "Open Letter to Brigham Young" in the *Daily Utah Reporter*.
8 Oct. 1870	Lee, Haight, and George Wood are excommunicated from the LDS church "for Committing a great Sin."
10 April 1871	Participant Philip Klingensmith provides an affidavit to a Nevada district court describing the massacre in detail.
Sept. 1874	The first grand jury called under the Poland Bill indicts Lee, Dame, Haight, Higbee, Klingensmith, Stewart, Samuel Jukes, George W. Adair, and Elliot Wilden (or Willden) for the murders at Mountain Meadows.
8 Nov. 1874	Deputy U.S. Marshal Stokes arrests John D. Lee at Panguitch.
July 1875	First Lee trial ends in hung jury.
Sept. 1876	All-Mormon jury convicts John D. Lee of murder.
23 Mar. 1877	Lee executed at Mountain Meadows.

Selected Bibliography

This is not a comprehensive bibliography: a complete list of all the sources related to the Mountain Meadows massacre would fill its own volume. Readers are referred to the more extensive surveys in our books Blood of the Prophets *and* Forgotten Kingdom. *This bibliography includes works located while working on* Innocent Blood *and the books, periodicals and essays, pamphlets, newspapers, manuscripts, and government documents cited in this volume.*

Books

Alexander, Thomas G. *Utah, The Right Place: The Official Centennial History.* S.L.C: Gibbs Smith, Publisher, 1995. 2nd revised edition, 2003.

Allen, Richard N. *The Tennessee Letters: From Carson Valley, 1857–1860.* Ed. by David Thompson for the Danberg Historical Series. Reno: The Grace Danberg Foundation, 1983.

Arrington, Leonard J. *Brigham Young: American Moses.* New York: Alfred A. Knopf, 1984.

Ashby, Robert L., ed. *Family History of Thomas Waters Cropper and Hannah Lucretia Rogers: Also, short sketches of their immediate ancestors and the lives of their daughters.* Downey, Calif: By the author, 1957.

Ashton, Clifford F. *The Federal Judiciary in Utah.* S.L.C: Utah Bar Foundation, 1988.

Backus, Anna Jean. *Mountain Meadows Witness: The Life of Bishop Philip Klingensmith.* Spokane, Wash: Arthur H. Clark Company, 1995.

Bagley, Will. *Blood of the Prophets: Brigham Young and the Massacre at Mountain Meadows.* Norman: University of Oklahoma, 2002.

Bancroft, Hubert Howe. *History of Utah, 1540–1886.* San Francisco: History Company, 1889.

Baskin, Robert N. *Reminiscences of Early Utah.* S.L.C: By the author, 1914. Reprinted S.L.C: Signature Books, 2006.

Beadle, John Hanson. *Western Wilds, and the Men Who Redeem Them.* Cincinnati: Jones Brothers & Co., 1879.

Berrett, William Edwin. *The Restored Church.* S.L.C: Deseret Book Co., 1961. Fourteenth edition, 1969.

Bigler, David L. *A Winter with the Mormons: The 1852 Letters of Jotham Goodell.* S.L.C: The Tanner Trust Fund, Marriott Library, University of Utah, 2001.

————. *Forgotten Kingdom: The Mormon Theocracy in the American West, 1847–1896*. Spokane, Wash: Arthur H. Clark Company, 1998.

————. *Fort Limhi: The Mormon Adventure in Oregon Territory, 1855–1858*. Spokane, Wash: Arthur H. Clark Company, 2003.

Bishop, William, ed. *Mormonism Unveiled; or the Life and Confessions of the Late Mormon Bishop, John D. Lee*. St. Louis: Bryan, Brand & Company, 1877.

Brooks, Juanita, ed. *On the Mormon Frontier: The Diary of Hosea Stout*, 2 vols. S.L.C: University of Utah Press, 1964.

————. *John Doyle Lee: Zealot, Pioneer Builder, Scapegoat*. Glendale, Calif: Arthur H. Clark Company, 1961. Reprinted S.L.C: Howe Brothers, 1982.

————. *The Mountain Meadows Massacre*. Stanford, Calif: Stanford University Press, 1950. Reprinted Norman: University of Oklahoma Press, 1962. Third revision, fourth printing, 1970. First paperback edition, with a foreword by Jan Shipps, 1991.

Cannon, Frank J. and George L. Knapp. *Brigham Young and His Mormon Empire*. New York: Fleming H. Revell Co., 1913.

Carter, D. Robert. *Founding Fort Utah: Provo's Native Inhabitants, Early Explorers, and First Year of Settlement*. Provo: Provo City Corporation, 2003.

Carvalho, Solomon Nunes. *Incidents of Travel and Adventure in the Far West with Colonel Frémont's Last Expedition*. New York: Derby & Jackson, 1856.

Cleland, Robert Glass and Juanita Brooks, eds. *A Mormon Chronicle: The Diaries of John D. Lee, 1848–1876*, 2 vols. San Marino, Calif: The Huntington Library, 1955. Reprinted S.L.C: University of Utah Press, 1983.

Clemens, Samuel. *Roughing It*, 2 vols. 1871: Author's National Edition. New York: Harper & Brothers Publishers, 1913.

Collier, Fred C. *Adoption—Law of the Kingdom—Forgotten Doctrine of Mormonism*. S.L.C: Collier's Publishing Co., 1991.

Cradlebaugh, John. *Utah and the Mormons: Speech of Hon. John Cradlebaugh, of Nevada, on the Admission of Utah as a State. Delivered in the House of Representatives, February 7, 1863*. Privately printed, 1863.

Dalton, Luella Adams, ed. *History of the Iron County Mission and Parowan, the Mother Town*. 2d ed. Provo: Simon K. Benson, n.d.

The Doctrine and Covenants of The Church of Jesus Christ of Latter-day Saints. S.L.C: The Church of Jesus Christ of Latter-day Saints, 1921.

Dwyer, Robert Joseph. *The Gentile Comes to Utah: A Study in Religious and Social Conflict (1862–1890)*. Washington, D.C: Catholic University of America Press, 1941.

Ekins, Roger Robin, ed. *Defending Zion: George Q. Cannon and the California Mormon Newspaper Wars of 1856–1857*. Spokane, Wash: Arthur H. Clark Company, 2002.

Fancher, Burr. *Captain Alexander Fancher: Adventurer, Drover, Wagon Master and Victim of the Mountain Meadows Massacre*. Portland, Ore: Inkwater Press, 2006.

Fancher, William Hoyt. *The Fancher Family*. Milford, N.H: The Cabinet Press, 1947.

Fish, Joseph. *The Life and Times of Joseph Fish, Mormon Pioneer*. Ed. by John H. Krenkel. Danville, Ill: Interstate Printers and Publisher, Inc., 1970.

Gibbs, Josiah. *Lights and Shadows of Mormonism*. S.L.C: Salt Lake Tribune Publishing Co., 1909.

————. *The Mountain Meadows Massacre*. S.L.C: Salt Lake Tribune Publishing Co., 1910.

Hollibaugh, Mrs. E. F. *Biographical History of Cloud County, Kansas: Biographies of Representative Citizens*. Kansas City?, 1903.

Howe, Irving. *Orwell's Nineteen Eighty-Four: Text, Sources, Criticism*. N.Y: Harcourt Brace Jovanovich, Inc., 1963.

Jarvis, Zora Smith, comp. *Ancestry, Biography, and Family of George A. Smith*. S.L.C: By the Family, 1962.

Jenson, Andrew. *Latter-day Saint Biographical Encyclopedia*, 4 vols. S.L.C: Andrew Jenson History Company, 1901.

Journal of Discourses, 26 vols. London: Latter-day Saints Book Depot, 1854–86.

Kenney, Scott G., ed. *Wilford Woodruff's Journal*, 10 vols. Midvale, Utah: Signature Books, 1983.

Knack, Martha C. *Boundaries Between: The Southern Paiutes, 1775–1995*. Lincoln: University of Nebraska Press, 2001.

Larson, Andrew Karl and Katharine Miles Larson, eds. *Diary of Charles Lowell Walker*, 2 vols. Logan: Utah State University Press, 1980.

Lee, John D. *Mormonism Unveiled*. See Bishop, William, ed. *Mormonism Unveiled*.

[Lockley, Frederic]. *The Lee Trial! An Exposé of the Mountain Meadows massacre: Being a condensed report of the prisoner's statement, testimony of witnesses, charge of the judge, arguments of counsel, and opinions of the press upon the trial by the Salt Lake Daily Tribune reporter*. S.L.C: Tribune Printing Company, Publishers, 1875.

Martineau, LaVan. *Southern Paiutes: Legends, Lore, Language and Lineage*. Las Vegas: KC Publications, 1992.

Milewski, Melissa Lambert, ed. *Before the Manifesto: The Life Writings of Mary Lois Walker Morris*. Logan: Utah State University Press, 2007.

Moore, Beth Shumway. *"Bones in the Well": The Haun's Mill Massacre*. Foreword by Will Bagley. Norman, Okla: Arthur H. Clark Company, 2007.

Morgan, Dale L. *The State of Deseret*. Logan: Utah State University Press, 1987.

Ogden, Annegret S., ed. *Frontier Reminiscences of Eveline Brooks Auerbach*. Berkeley, Calif: Friends of the Bancroft Library, 1994.

Parker, Basil G. *The Life and Adventures of Basil G. Parker: An Autobiography*. Plano, Calif: Fred W. Reed, American Printer, 1902.

————. *Recollections of the Mountain Meadows Massacre*. Plano, Calif: Fred W. Reed, American Printer, 1901.

Penrose, Charles W. "Testimony of James Holt Haslam." *Supplement to the Lecture on the Mountain Meadows Massacre: Important Additional Testimony Recently Received*. S.L.C: The Juvenile Instructor Press, 1885.

————. *The Mountain Meadows Massacre: Who Were Guilty of the Crime?* S.L.C: The Juvenile Instructor Press, 1884.

Peterson, Levi. *Juanita Brooks: Mormon Woman Historian*. S.L.C: University of Utah Press and Tanner Trust Fund, 1988.

Pratt, Ann Agatha Walker. "His Last Mission," in "The Pratt Story as Told by the Tenth Wife," in Carter, ed., *Our Pioneer Heritage*, 17:223–45.

[Pratt, Parley P.] *Proclamation of the Twelve Apostles of the Church of Jesus Christ of Latter-day Saints to All the Kings of the World, to the President of the United States of America; to the Governors of the Several States, and to the Rulers and People of All Nations.* N.Y: Pratt and Brannan, 1845.

Rea, Ralph R. *Boone County and Its People.* Van Buren, Ark: Hugh Park, Publisher, 1955.

Roberts, Brigham H. *A Comprehensive History of The Church of Jesus Christ of Latter-day Saints,* 6 vols. S.L.C: Deseret News Press, 1930.

Schindler, Harold. *Orrin Porter Rockwell: Man of God, Son of Thunder.* S.L.C: University of Utah Press, 1966. Second Edition, 1983.

Shirts, Morris A., and Kathryn H. Shirts. *A Trial Furnace: Southern Utah's Iron Mission.* Provo: Brigham Young University Press, 2001.

Shirts, Morris A., and Frances Anne Smeath. *Historical Topography : A New Look at Old Sites on Mountain Meadows.* Cedar City, Utah: Southern Utah University Press, 2002.

Skogen, Larry C. *Indian Depredation Claims, 1796–1920.* Norman: University of Oklahoma Press, 1996.

Smith, George D., ed. *An Intimate Chronicle: The Journals of William Clayton.* S.L.C: Signature Books, 1991.

Smith, Oliver R., ed. *Six Decades in the Early West: The Journal of Jesse Nathaniel Smith.* Provo, Utah: Jesse N. Smith Family Association, 1970.

Stenhouse, T. B. H. *The Rocky Mountain Saints: A Full and Complete History of the Mormons, from the First Vision of Joseph Smith to the Last Courtship of Brigham Young.* New York: D. Appleton and Co., 1873.

Unruh, John D., Jr. *The Plains Across: The Overland Emigrants and the Trans-Mississippi West, 1840–1860.* Urbana: University of Illinois Press, 1979.

Waite, Catherine Van Valkenburg. *The Mormon Prophet and His Harem: An Authentic History of Brigham Young, His Numerous Wives and Children.* Cambridge: The Riverside Press, 1866.

Whitney, Orson F. *History of Utah,* 4 vols. S.L.C: George Q. Cannon & Sons Co., Publishers, 1892.

PERIODICALS AND ESSAYS

Aird, Polly. " 'You Nasty Apostates, Clear Out': Reasons for Disaffection in the Late 1850s." *Journal of Mormon History* 30:2 (Fall 2004), 129–207.

Alter, J. Cecil and Robert J. Dwyer, eds. "Journal of Captain Albert Tracy." *Utah Historical Quarterly* 13 (1943).

Arrington, Leonard J. "Crusade Against Theocracy: The Reminiscences of Judge Jacob Smith Boreman of Utah, 1872–1877." *Huntington Library Quarterly* 24:1 (November 1960), 1–45.

Bagley, Will ("Brigham Did It"), and Ron Walker ("No He Didn't"). "Did Brigham Young Order a Massacre?" *True West: Celebrating the American West* (April 2003), 31–34.

———. " 'They Have Slain My Children': The Rescue of the Orphans of Mountain Meadows." *Wild West* 17:5 (February 2005), 28–36.

Bigler, David L. "The Crisis at Fort Limhi, 1858." *Utah Historical Quarterly* 35:2 (Spring 1967), 121–36.

————. "Garland Hurt, the American Friend of the Utahs." *Utah Historical Quarterly* 62 (Spring 1994), 149–70.

Briggs, Robert H. "The Mountain Meadows Massacre: An Analytical Narrative Based on Participant Confessions." *Utah Historical Quarterly* 74:4 (Fall 2006), 313–33.

Brooks, Juanita. "An Historical Epilogue [Speech Given at the Dedication of a Monument Honoring the Victims of the Massacre at the Mountain Meadows]," *Utah Historical Quarterly* 24 (January 1956), 71–80.

————. "Indian Relations on the Mormon Frontier." *Utah Historical Quarterly* 12 (January–April 1944), 1–48.

Cresswell, Stephen. "The U.S. Department of Justice in Utah Territory, 1870–90." *Utah Historical Quarterly* 53:3 (Summer 1985), 205–22.

Foreman, Grant. "Missionaries of the Latter Day Saints Church in Indian Territory." *Chronicles of Oklahoma* 13:2 (June 1935), 196–213.

Hebner, Logan. "Warriors and Chiefs: 'Angry and thirsting for blood' Indians have been blamed for the Mountain Meadows Massacre." *Wild West* 17:5 (February 2005), 10–12, 68–69.

Logan, Roger V., Jr., "New Light on the Mountain Meadows Caravan." *Utah Historical Quarterly* 60:3 (Summer 1992), 224–37.

Loving, Ronald E. "Captain John Baker." *Mountain Meadows Newsletter* 1:2 (June 1990), 2.

————. "The Fanchers of California." *Mountain Meadows Newsletter* 1:2 (June 1990).

MacKinnon, William P. "Epilogue to the Utah War: Impact and Legacy." *Journal of Mormon History* 29:2 (Fall 2003), 186–48.

Mitchell, Sarah Francis [Sallie] Baker. "The Mountain Meadows Massacre—An Episode on the Road to Zion," *The American Weekly*, 25 August 1940. Utah State Historical Society, PAM 16316.

Morgan, Dale L. "The Administration of Indian Affairs in Utah, 1851–1858." *Pacific Historical Review* 17 (November 1948), 383–409.

Novak, Shannon A., and Derinna Kopp. "To Feed a Tree in Zion: Osteological Analysis of the 1857 Mountain Meadows Massacre." *Journal of the Society for Historical Archaeology* 37:2 (Summer 2003), 85–108.

Novak, Shannon, and Lars Rodseth. "Remembering Mountain Meadows: Collective Violence and the Manipulation of Social Boundaries." *Journal of Anthropological Research* 62:1 (Spring 2006), 1–25.

Parshall, Ardis. "'Pursue, Retake & Punish': The 1857 Santa Clara Ambush." *Utah Historical Quarterly* 73:1 (Winter 2005), 64–86.

Rankin, Charles E. "Type and Stereotype: Frederic E. Lockley, Pioneer Journalist." In Robert C. Ritchie and Paul Andrew Hutton, eds., *Frontier and Region: Essays in Honor of Martin Ridge*. San Marino: The Huntington Library Press, 1997, 56–81.

Scott, Stuart D. "A Frontier Spirit: The Life of James Gemmell." *Australasian Canadian Studies* 25:2 (2007), 55–115.

Walker, Ronald W. "'Save the Emigrants': Joseph Clewes on the Mountain Meadows Massacre." *BYU Studies* 42:1 (2003), 139.

Wheeler, William F. "The Late James Gemmell." *Contributions to the Historical Society of Montana* 2 (1896), 331–36.

PAMPHLETS

History of the Mountain Meadows Massacre, Butchery in Cold Blood of 134 Men, Women and Children by Mormons and Indians, September, 1857, Also A Full and Complete Account of the Trial, Confession and Execution of John D. Lee, The Leader of the Murderers, Illustrated by a True Likeness of John D. Lee. For Distribution with Their Celebrated Picture of Mountain Meadows. San Francisco: Pacific Arts Press, 1877. Copy at BYU Library.

Mountain Meadows Association. "Memorial Service at the Re-internment of Remains of Victims of the Mountain Meadows Massacre [at] Mountain Meadows Emigrant Campsite." Harrison, Ark: Harrison Daily Times Print Shop, 1999. Contains a revised list of victims and survivors.

———. "Mountain Meadows Memorial Dedication Program." Cedar City: Mountain Meadow Memorial Steering Committee, 1990.

MANUSCRIPTS

Adair, George W. Statement in David O. McKay Diary, 27 July 1907. MS 668, University of Utah Library.

Anonymous. Discursive Remarks. MSS A 628, Utah State Historical Society.

Anonymous. MMM File, Folders 33 and 34, LDS Archives.

Bigler, Jacob G., to Pyper and Webb, 23 December 1856. Minute Book of the Mass Quorum of Seventies, Nephi, Utah. MSS SC 3244, Brigham Young University Library. Ardis Parshall transcription.

Black, Jeremiah S. Letter to Brigham Young, 12 July 1860. Brigham Young Collection, LDS Archives.

Bolton, Curtis. Statement. Church Historian's Office Journal, LDS Archives.

Boreman, Jacob S. Correspondence, 1875–1880. Manuscripts MSS A 61-2, Utah State Historical Society.

Borrowman, John. Extracts, Journal of John Borrowman. Joel E. Ricks Collection of Transcriptions, Item 4, Vol. 1, MIC 341, Utah State Historical Society.

Bradshaw, Hazel B. Letter. 12 December 1963. Manuscripts MSS A 5231, Utah State Historical Society.

Brewer, Charles W. Letter to Dear Captain, 6 August 1860. Wisconsin State Historical Society, Madison. Copy courtesy of Vickie Speek.

Brocchus, Perry E. "Extract of a letter from a judicial officer of the government, at Great Salt Lake City," 20 September 1851, in House Exec. Doc. 25, 32d Cong., 1st sess., 1852, Serial 640, 8–22.

Brooks, Juanita. Collection. B-103, Utah State Historical Society.

———. Papers. MS 486, University of Utah Library. Consists mostly of Dale Morgan's letters to Brooks.

Brown, Homer. Journal. LDS Archives, Keith Franklin Larson transcription.

Calder, David O., to J. W. Young, 31 March 1877. Telegrams 1877, Brigham Young Collection, LDS Archives.

Cannon, Abraham H. Journal. Vol. 19, MS 3, Marriott Library, University of Utah.

Cannon, George Q. Letter to Daniel H. Wells, 16 April 1872. Ardis Parshall transcription and translation, Brigham Young Collection, LDS Archives.

Cedar Stake Journal, December 1856–August 1859. MS 1, Box 89, Folder 12, William Rees Palmer and Kate Vilate Isom Palmer Western History Collection, Southern Utah University Library.

Church Historian's Letterbook, 30 June 1859. Edyth Romney Typescript, MS 2737, Box 26, Folder 4, 790, LDS Archives.

Church Historian's Office Journal, 24 August 1857, Edyth Romney Typescript, CR 100 1, Box 22, Folder 1, LDS Archives.

Church Historian's Office Journal, 28 June 1859, Edyth Romney Typescript, MS 2737, Box 22, Folder 3, 23, LDS Archives.

Clawson, Hiram B. Letter to Brigham Young, 11 December 1871. Brigham Young Collection, LDS Archives.

Clements, John Moon. Diary. LDS Archives.

Connor, Patrick Edward. Letter to William Carter, 23 October 1866. Ron Kezar Collection. Copy in possession of the editors from Carter Papers sale.

Cradlebaugh, John. Letter to James Buchanan, 3 June 1859. U.S. Attorney General, Records Relating to the appointment of federal judges, attorneys, and marshals for the Territory and State of Utah, 1853–1903, National Archives; microfilm copy, Utah State Historical Society.

Cropper, Thomas Waters. Autobiography. Mss 654, Brigham Young University Library.

Cumming, Alfred. Letter to Lewis Cass, 25 March, 1859. Alfred Cumming Papers, Duke University.

———. Papers. Duke University, Durham, North Carolina; microfilm copy at Utah State Historical Society.

Dame, William Horn. Papers. Vault MSS 55, Brigham Young University Library. Copies in MS 2041, LDS Archives; and Utah State Historical Society

Dotson, Peter K. Letter to John Cradlebaugh, 3 June 1859. U.S. Attorney General, Records Relating to the appointment of federal judges, attorneys, and marshals for the Territory and State of Utah, 1853–1903, National Archives; microfilm copy, Utah State Historical Society.

Douglas, H. Orders to Lt. George J. S. Patterson, 20 March 1877, Fort Cameron, Utah. MS 6568, LDS Archives. These are Lt. Patterson's orders to escort John D. Lee to his execution.

Duffin, James. Journal, 3 September 1903. James Orme's account of Parley P. Pratt's murder. Journal History, 13 May 1857, 7–8.

Edwards, William. Affidavit, 14 May 1924. MSS A 1112, Utah State Historical Society.

Forney, Jacob. Letter to A. B. Greenwood, August 1859. "Mountain Meadows Massacre," Sen. Exec. Doc. 42, 1860.

———. Letter to Elias Smith [June 1859] in the Matter of the Estate and Guardianship of Mountain Meadows Children. Utah State Archives.

Gemmell, James. Letter to Feramorz Little, 14 October 1872. Brigham Young Collection, LDS Archives.

Gould, Sam. Statement. Juanita Brooks Papers, B-103, Box 25, Folder 15, Utah State Historical Society.

Hakes, Collins Rowe. Affidavits, 3 and 16 June 1859. Collected Materials Relative to the Church Historian's Office, MS 5020 Box 4, LDS Archives.

————.To Whom it May Concern, 24 April 1916. Brigham Young University Library.

Halleck, H. L., to W. E. D. Whiting, 6 November 1900, MSS 65, Special Collections and Manuscripts, Brigham Young University Library

Hamblin, Jacob. Daybook, Journals and Letters. Amer M270.1 H17, Brigham Young University Library.

————. Journal, 1854–1859. Typescript, MS A 567-1, Utah State Historical Society.

————. Testimony, Second John D. Lee Trial. Bishop ed., *Mormonism Unveiled*, 375–76.

Hammond, Milton D. Journal. PAM 2068, Utah State Historical Society.

Harker, Joseph. Journal. BX 8670.1.M782, Brigham Young University Library.

Harshman, Virginia W. Notes of *Colton Semi-Tropics*, 31 March 1877, Feldheym Public Library, San Bernardino.

Haslam, James Holt. Testimony, 4 December 1884. From Penrose, "Supplement to the Lecture on the Mountain Meadows Massacre."

Hawley, John Pierce. Autobiography. P13.F317, Library & Archives, Community of Christ Archives, Independence, Missouri.

Hebner, Logan. Paiute Interviews. Copy in possession of the editors.

Hendrix, George F. Letter to Brigham Young, 23 June 1860. MS 1234, Brigham Young Collection, LDS Archives.

Hicks, George Armstrong. Family Record and History of George Armstrong Hicks, Containing the principle events of a life among the poor of Utah and the "Saints" generally. Written by himself. ca. 1874. Copy in possession of the editors.

————. Letters to Brigham Young, 11 October 1867 and 4 December 1868–21 January 1869, Brigham Young Collection, LDS Archives.

Higbee, John Mount. Statement, 15 June 1896. MMM File, LDS Archives. [Folder label: 1896 John M. Higbee trial]

Hinckley, Gordon B. Dedicatory Prayer, 15 September 1990. Mountain Meadows Memorial Dedication Ceremonies File, Mo-2-2, Southern Utah University Library.

————. Remarks, 15 September 1990. Mountain Meadows Memorial Dedication Ceremonies File, Mo-2-2, Southern Utah University Library.

Huntington, Dimick Baker. Journal. 1857 Aug–1859 May. MS 1419-2, LDS Archives.

Hurt, Garland. Letter to Alfred Cumming, 17 December 1857. U.S. State Department, Territorial Papers, Utah Series, National Archives, vol. 4–6, Utah State Historical Society.

Ivins, Anthony Woodard. Letter to Mrs. G. T. Welch, 16 October 1922. Ms d 4222, LDS Archives.

Johnson, Nephi. Testimony, Second John D. Lee Trial. Lee Trial Transcripts, W. L. Cooke Papers, Manuscript Division, Library of Congress.

————. Letter to Will Lund, March 1910, MMM File, LDS Archives.

Johnston, Albert S. Report to Adjutant General, 27 June 1859. RG 393, Part 1, Old Military Records, Series 5029, Vol. 2 of 3, Fort Crittenden Letterbook, National Archives, 250–52.

Journal History. Historical Department, LDS Church.

Kane, Thomas Leiper. Diary of Colonel Thomas L. Kane. Mormon File, The Huntington Library, FAC 515.

————. Papers. MS 8829, LDS Archives.

Kelly, Charles. Collection. MSS B-114, Utah State Historical Society.

————. Papers. Conversation notes with Josiah Gibbs. MS 100, Box 12, folder 5, University of Utah Library.

————.Utah's Black Friday: History of the Mountain Meadows Massacre of 1857. Charles Kelly Collection, MS 100, University of Utah Library.

Kenner, Scipio. Telegram to *Deseret News*, 23 March 1877. Brigham Young Collection, LDS Archives.

Kimball, Heber C. Journal. LDS Archives. Also see Smith, George D., ed. *An Intimate Chronicle: The Journals of William Clayton*, 223.

King, Hannah Tapfield. Journals. MS 628, LDS Archives.

Lander, Frederick W. Letter to Brigham Young, 23 September 1858. Brigham Young Collection, LDS Archives.

Leany, William, Sr. Letter to John Steele, 17 February 1883. John Steele Papers, Vault MSS 528, Box 1, Folder 30, Brigham Young University Library.

Lee, Ann Gordge. Autobiography. MSS SC 1706, Brigham Young University Library.

Lee, John D. Collection, B116-1, Utah State Historical Society.

————. John D. Lee Collection. The Huntington Library.

————. Letter to Brigham Young, 20 November 1857. Brigham Young Collection, LDS Archives.

————. Letter to Emma B. Lee, 9 December 1857. John D. Lee Collection, The Huntington Library.

————. Letter to Emma B. Lee, 21 September 1876. John D. Lee Collection, The Huntington Library.

————. Letter to Emma B. Lee, 10 October 1876. John D. Lee Collection, The Huntington Library.

————. Letter to Rachel Lee, 24 September 1876. John D. Lee Collection, The Huntington Library.

————. Letter to Rachel Lee, 12 October 1876. John D. Lee Collection, The Huntington Library.

————. Trial Papers. Clerk of the Court, District Court for Beaver County, Fifth District of Utah, Beaver City, Utah.

————.Trial Transcript, 1875. Utah State Historical Society, Mss B 915.

————. Trial Transcripts. W. L. Cook Papers, Manuscripts Division, Library of Congress.

Lee, Rachel. Diary. Mormon File, HM 26338, The Huntington Library.

————. Journal of Rachel Andora Woolsey Lee. Typescript, Brigham Young University Library.

Lee, Verne, and Ronald E. Loving. The Fancher Train of 1857. Utah State Historical Society.

Lockley, Frederic E. Collection, including Letters to Elizabeth Metcalf Campbell Lockley, 1869–1904. Box 6, The Huntington Library.

————. Recollections of Territorial Utah. Fred Lockley Papers, Typescript NjP mss CO199, Dept. of Rare Books and Special Collections, Princeton University.

Lyman, Francis M. Diary Excerpts of Francis M. Lyman, 1892–1896. The original diaries are in possession of the First Presidency of the LDS church and are not available to the public. Edward Leo Lyman transcription, *New Mormon Studies CD-ROM: A Comprehensive Resource Library.*

Martineau, James H. My Life. New Acquisition 2292, Huntington Library. Robert Briggs transcription.

———. Topographical Report from J. H. Martineau to Col. A. Carrington, Parowan Sept. 20/57. Utah Territorial Militia Records, 1849–1877, Series 2210, Utah State Archives, 1396.

———. Letter to F. E. Eldridge, 23 July 1907, James Martineau Papers, MSS 467, Brigham Young University Library.

Mathews, William. Letter to Brigham Young, 7 October 1857. Brigham Young Collection, LDS Archives.

McComb [McLean Pratt], Eleanor J. Account of the death of Parley P. Pratt, ca. 1857. MS 525, LDS Archives.

———. Letter to Erastus Snow, 14–15 May 1857. MS 2099, LDS Archives.

McKay, David O. Diary, 27 July 1907. MS 668, University of Utah Library.

Minutes of the Female Benevolent Society of Cedar City, 10 September 1857. Ms 1, Box 89, Folder 14, Southern Utah University Library.

Miscellaneous Minutes Collection, 1 May 1865, LDS Archives.

Mitchell, William C. Letter to Alfred B. Greenwood, 27 April 1860. Letters Received, Bureau of Indian Affairs, National Archives.

Morgan, Dale L. Collection. MSS B-40, Utah State Historical Society.

Morris, Elias. Papers. Bancroft Library; microfilm copy at, University of Utah Library.

———. Statement [Holograph], 1892. Communicated to Andrew Jenson by Elias Morris, 2 February 1892. MMM File, LDS Archives.

Mountain Meadows Massacre File, Collected Material Concerning the Mountain Meadows Massacre. MS 2674, LDS Archives. Unprocessed subject file formerly maintained at LDS Archives, cited as MMM File.

"The Mountain Meadow Massacre," undated clipping circa 1916 from Berryville, Arkansas paper, California State Library.

Park, Hamilton G. Testimony. MMM File, LDS Archives.

Pitchforth, Samuel. Diary, 1857–1868. Typescript, Mor M270.1 P68d, Brigham Young University Library.

Porter, Fitz-John. Letter to Jacob Forney, 21 July 1859. Fort Crittenden Letterbook, National Archives, 2:273–74.

———. Letter to John Fancher, 6 July 1859. Fort Crittenden Letterbook, National Archives, 2:261.

———. Orders to Reuben P. Campbell, 17 April 1859. RG 393, Part 1, Old Military Records, Series 5029, Vol. 2 of 3, Fort Crittenden Letterbook, Vol. 2 of 3, National Archives, 2:183–84.

———. Orders to Reuben P. Campbell, 19 April 1859. Fort Crittenden Letterbook, National Archives, 2:188.

———. Papers. Manuscripts Division, Library of Congress. Includes Extracts from the Diary of Maj. Fitz-John Porter. Container 53.

Pratt, Parley P. "Reminiscences and Testimony," 7 September 1856. *Journal of Discourses*, 5:197–98.

Probate Court, Great Salt Lake County. Criminal and Civil Case Docket. Series 3914, Reel 2, Utah State Archives.

Pulsipher, John. A Short Sketch of the History of John Pulsipher: the Son of Zera Pulsipher. MS 92, Marriott Library, University of Utah.

Ray, John A. Letter to *Mountaineer* re MMM, 4 December 1859. Unprocessed item, LDS Archives.

Richards, Jane Snyder. Reminis[c]ences of Mrs. F. D. Richards, San Francisco, 1880, Utah and the Mormons Collection, Bancroft Library, MS 8305, Reel 2, LDS Archives.

Robinson, Oliver Lee. Diary. Book 1, box 1, MS 24, University of Utah Library.

Rogerson, Josiah, to W. B. Dougall, 22 and 23 March 1877. MS 1234, Box 46 Folder 15: Telegrams 1877, Brigham Young Papers, 1801–1877, LDS Archives.

———. "The Guilt of John D. Lee." Collected Material Concerning the Mountain Meadows Massacre, MS 2674, LDS Archives.

Salmon River Mission Journal, LDS Archives; photocopy , folder 2, box 27, series 9, LJAHA-I, Utah State University Library.

Seventies. Record of the Nephi Mass Quorum of Seventies, 1857–1859. MSS SC 3244. Special Collections, BYU Library.

Shelton, Marion Jackson. Affidavit. Unprocessed Documents, Church Historian's Office Journal, May–June 1859, LDS Archives.

———. Church Historian's Office Journal, 25 June 1859. Romney Typescript, LDS Archives.

———. Diary, 1858 March–1859 June. MS 1412, fd. 1, LDS Archives.

Skinner, James. Reminiscences. MS 6587, LDS Archives.

Smith, Elias, and Robert T. Burton. Executed Warrant for the Arrest of Brigham Young, 12 May 1859. Church Historian's Office Unprocessed Documents, LDS Archives.

———. Draft Arrest Warrant for Brigham Young, May 1859. Collected Materials Relative to the Church Historian's Office, MS 5020, Box 4, LDS Archives.

———. Journal. See Thomas, Sarah C., ed., *Elias Smith's Journal.*

Smith, George A. Letter to John Lyman, 6 January 1858. Romney Typescript, Church Historian's Office, CR100/38, Vol. 1, LDS Archives, 508–509.

———. Letter to Mr. St. Clair, 25 November 1869. Typescript Collection CR 100/38, vol. 2, MS 2737, LDS Archives, 941–49.

———. Letter to T. B. H. Stenhouse, Provo, 7 [?] June 1858. Historian's Office Letterpress Copybooks, CR 100 38, Reel 2, LDS Archives, 521.

———. Letter to T. B. H. Stenhouse, 15 April 1859. Typescript, Church Historian's Office Letterbook, MS 2737, 26:4, LDS Archives, 764–65.

Snow, Warren S., and George Peacock. Letter to Brigham Young, 10 April 1859. Brigham Young Collection, LDS Archives.

Spencer, George. Letter to Erastus Snow, 26 March 1867. Brigham Young Collection, LDS Archives.

Standifird, John Henry, 1833–1923. Papers, 1857–1909. Vault MSS 44, Brigham Young University Library.

Thomas, Sarah C., ed. *Elias Smith's Journal*, 3 vols. S.L.C: By the family, 1984. Copy at Utah State Historical Society, 921 SM5th 1984.

Thompson, Jacob. Letter to Alexander Wilson, 25 April 1859. Letters Sent Concerning Judiciary Expenses, 1849–84, PI 194, Entry 78, Vol. 5, Record Group 60, 103–104, National Archives.

Utah Stake Minutes, General Meetings 1855–60. Romney Typescript, Ms 2737, Box 53, Folder 4, LDS Archives.

Walker, Joseph C. History of the Mormons in the Early Days of Utah. Joseph C. Walker Papers, Brigham Young University Library.

Watters, Ichel. "Interview with the Chief of the Beavers," clipping from San Francisco Morning Call, 4 August 1875. A 1588, Utah State Historical Society.

Weller, John B. Inaugural Address. Governors' Gallery, California State Library, Sacramento.

Wells, Daniel H. Orders to William H. Dame, 1 and 13 August 1857. Palmer Collection, Southern Utah University Library.

———. Telegram to Brigham Young, 14 September 1876. CR 1234/1, Box 43, Folder 20, Reel 56, Brigham Young Collection, LDS Archives.

———. Telegram to W.B.D. [William B. Dougall], 15 and 20 September 1876. Brigham Young Collection, LDS Archives.

Whipple, Edson. Diary, 1842–1851. MSS 691, Brigham Young Library.

White, Joel W. To Whomsoever It May Concern, 9 October 1896. MMM File, LDS Archives.

Willden, Charles. Affidavit, 18 February 1882. LDS Archives.

Williams, George Calvin. The Life and Religion of George Calvin Williams. Typescript, MS 13382, LDS Archives.

Wilson, Alexander. [Letter] to Jacob Thompson, 4 March 1859. RG 393, Letters Received Concerning Judiciary Accounts, PI 194, Entry 59, RG 60, National Archives.

Woodruff, Wilford. Historian's Private Journal, LDS Archives; copy in possession of Michael Marquardt.

———. Affidavit [handwritten, undated], describing Lee's 29 September 1857 report. MMM Files, LDS Archives.

———.Affidavit, 1882 [not notarized]. Folder labeled WW Aff re MMM, MMM File, LDS Archives.

———. Report of Brigham Young's remarks to Van Vliet on 12 September 1857, Woodruff Collection, LDS Archives, 178–90.

———. Synopsis of an address by Brigham Young on 16 August 1857. Romney Typescript, Ms 1737, Box 35, Folder 1, Woodruff Collection, LDS Archives.

Woolley, Eleanor Millick. Life of Andrew J. Millick, MS 3800, LDS Archives.

Young, Brigham. Collection. B-93, Utah State Historical Society. Includes "Three Weeks in Brigham Young's Office," a typescript of the Brigham Young office journal.

———. Discourse on 16 August 1857, reported by George D. Watt. Brigham Young Collection, LDS Archives.

———. Letter to Andrew Cunningham, 4 August 1857. Brigham Young Collection, LDS Archives.

———. Letter to George A. Hicks, 16 February 1869. Letterbook No. 11:362–63, Edyth Romney Typescript, Brigham Young Collection, LDS Archives.

———. Letter to George Q. Cannon, 5 May 1859. Brigham Young Collection, LDS Archives.

————. Letter to Isaac C. Haight, 4 August 1857. Letterbook No. 3, Brigham Young Collection, LDS Archives, 742

————. Letter to Jeter Clinton, 12 September 1857. Brigham Young Collection, LDS Archives.

————. Letter to J. W. Denver, 12 September 1857. *"The Utah Expedition,"* House Exec. Doc. 71, 183–85.

————. Letter to Lewis Brunson and I. C. Haight, 2 August 1857. Brigham Young Collection, Letterbook No. 3, LDS Archives, 732.

————. Letter to Philip Klingensmith, 7 January 1857. Letterbook 3, MS 1234, Brigham Young Collection, LDS Archives.

————. Letter to Rufus C. Allen, 4 August 1857. Letterbook 3, Brigham Young Collection, LDS Archives, 745–46.

————. Letters to S. B. Aden, 27 April and 12 July 1859. Brigham Young Collection, LDS Archives.

————. Letter to Thomas L. Kane, 17 September 1859. Brigham Young Collection, LDS Archives.

————. Letter to Thomas L. Kane, 15 December 1859. Letterbook No. 5, Brigham Young Collection, LDS Archives, 325–28; corrected with a photostat of Kane's copy.

————. Office Journal, Unprocessed item, LDS Archives. See also Brigham Young Office Journals—Excerpts, 1853–62, *New Mormon Studies CD-ROM: A Comprehensive Resource Library.* S.L.C: Smith Research Associates, 1998.

————. Telegram to Rutherford B. Hayes, 31 March 1877. CR1234/1, Box 46, Folder 15 (Reel 59), LDS Archives.

Government Documents

"Accounts of Brigham Young, Supt. of Indian Affairs in Utah Territory," 37th Cong., 2d sess., House Exec. Doc. 29, 1862, Serial 1128.

"An Act to Establish a Territorial Government for Utah," *Statutes at Large of the United States,* Vol. 9, 458.

Baker, Shane, Richard K. Talbot, and Lane D. Richens. "Archaeological Remote Sensing Studies and Emergency Data Recovery at 42WS2504, Washington County, Utah." Provo: Brigham Young University Museum of Peoples and Cultures, Technical Series No. 03-8, 2003.

Buchanan, James. *A Proclamation of the President, offering to the inhabitants of Utah, who shall submit to the laws, a free pardon for the seditions and treasons.* 35th Cong., 2d sess., House Exec. Doc. 2, vol. 1, 1859, Serial 997, 69–72.

————. *Message of the President communicating correspondence relative to the condition of affairs in the Territory of Utah,* 36th Cong., 1st sess., House Exec. Doc. 78, 1860, Serial 1056.

————. *Message of the President communicating information in relation to the massacre at Mountain Meadows, and other massacres in Utah Territory,* 36th Cong., 1st sess., Senate Exec. Doc. 42, 1860, Serial 1033.

————. *Message of the President communicating the correspondence between the judges of Utah and the Attorney General or President, with relation to the legal proceedings and conditions of affairs in that territory,* 36th Cong., 1st sess., Sen. Exec. Doc. 32, 1860, Serial 1031.

————. "The Utah Expedition." Message of the President of the United States, Transmitting Reports from the Secretaries of War, of the Interior, and of the Attorney General, relative to the military expedition ordered into the Territory of Utah, 35th Cong., 1st sess., House Exec. Doc. 71, 1858, Serial 956.

Carleton, James Henry. Report on the Subject of the Massacre at the Mountain Meadows, in Utah Territory. by Brevet Major James Henry Carleton, U. S. Army, and Report of the Hon. William C. Mitchell relative to the seventeen surviving children. Little Rock, Ark: True Democrat Steam Press Print. 1860.

————. Special Report of the Mountain Meadow Massacre, by J. H. Carleton, Brevet Major, United States Army, Captain, First Dragoons, 57th Cong., 1st sess., House Doc. 605, 1902, Serial 4377.

————. "The Mormons as a People" in Maj. George W. Davis, Leslie J. Perry, and Joseph W. Kirkley, eds. The War of the Rebellion: A Compilation of the Official Records of the Union and the Confederate Armies. Series 1, Vol. 50, Part 1, Serial 3583. Wash. D.C: Government Printing Office, 1897, 550–53.

Fillmore, Millard. Information in reference to the condition of affairs in the Territory of Utah, 32d Cong., 1st sess., House Exec. Doc. 25, 1852, Serial 640.

Forney, Jacob. "Annual Report," in Report of the Secretary of the Interior, Office of Indian Affairs, New Mexico, Utah, Oregon and Washington Superintendencies, 1859, 35th Cong., 1st sess., Senate Exec. Doc. 2, Serial 1023.

————. Annual Report in Message from the President of the United States, 36th Cong., 1st sess., House Exec. Doc. 10, Report of the Secretary of the Interior, Serial 956. Washington: George W. Bowman, Printer, 1860.

Nelson, William, and Sumner Howard to Attorney General Alphonso Taft, 23 September 1876, National Archives Microfilm Publication NNO-170A-3015, Mountain Meadows Massacre Reference Microfilm, Source—Chronological Files: Utah, Department of Justice, Record Group 60, National Archives.

Salt Lake County, Probate Court Criminal and Civil Case Docket, Series 3944, Reel 2, Utah State Archives.

Simpson, J. H. Report of Explorations Across the Great Basin of the Territory of Utah for a Direct Wagon-Route from Camp Floyd, to Genoa, in Carson Valley, in 1859. Washington: GPO, 1876. Reprinted Reno: University of Nevada Press, 1985.

Thurston, Malinda Cameron Scott. Depositions in support of H.R. 1459 and H.R. 3945, 15 October and 18 December 1877. Thurston vs. the United States and the Ute Indians, Record Group 123, Indian Depredation Claim 8479, National Archives.

————. Depositions, Malinda Thurston, Joel Scott, Frederick Arnold, and Andrew Wolf, 2 May 1911, Thurston vs. the United States, Indian Depredation Claim 8479, RG 123, National Archives.

Washington County Probate Court Minutes, Record Book A. "A Book Containing the Records of the Probate Court of Washington County." Utah State Archives.

Welch, Peyton Y., vs. the United States and the Ute Tribe. Record Group 205, Records of the Court of Claims Section (Justice), Indian Depredations Case No. 9239, National Archives.

INDEX

242–44; hosts Young at Harmony, 250, 251; says Young publicly disapproves atrocity to blind the gentiles, 264, 265, 266; involvement of whispered, 268, 269; escorts Young, 270; visits St. George home, 270n; allegedly knew Young's role, 275, 276; shielded by orders, 278; commands troops, 283, 284; never court-martialed, 285; at head of the column, 286; military operations of, 288, 293; ordered to secluded location on Colorado River, 295; arrested, 296; plan for emigrant surrender, 297–99; first trial of, 202, 300–10; second trial of, 310–20; massacre participants testify against, 310–12; gives up all hope, 315; Mormon jury convicts, 315–17; chooses firing squad, 321; letter of, to Emma B. Lee, 322–26; seeks journals, 324; rails against Young, 325, 326, 327; escorted to Mountain Meadows, 329, 330; execution of, 327–36; last words of, 330, 331, 333, 334, 335; confession of (Howard version), 336–52; admission of guilt disputed, 353–55; trials of and Poland Act, 356, 358, 359, 365; alleges no innocent blood, 366, 367; replaced as probate judge, 370, 371, 373; and Young's defense, 373–76, 378, 382; ordered to keep Indians in check, 386, 390–92; names participants, 393, 395, 397; confessions mix fact and falsehood, 406; sends white flag, 407, 409; also did much killing, 411, 412; legal defenders abandon, 413; sends runners to Indians, 414; as glory-seeking man, 415, 416; told to let emigrants go, 417, 418, 420, 421; with the wounded, 422; supervises plan, 423; and innocent blood, 425, 426; washes off paint, 429, 430; keeps Baker sisters, 432, 447, 450; incites Southern Paiutes, 454; blames Indians for massacre, 455; adopted Indian son of, 457, 459, 461, 465; Indian allies of not up to job, 467, 468–70; takes the blame, 471; reward of celestial glory, 472; did not act alone, 474
Lee, Joseph H: 324
Lee, Nancy: 324
Lee, Rachel A: 321–24, 333, 335, 341
Lee, Rachel Woolsey: 99n, 130; says Lee returned with Indians, 131
Lee, Samuel: 325
Lee, Sarah C: 333

Lee, Victoria Elizabeth: 323
Lee, William James: 323
Lee's Ferry: 295
Lehi, Utah: 98
Leigh, Henry: 313
Leonard, Glen: 186
Lewis, Samuel: 98, 235
Lewis, Tarleton: 100, 282
Lincoln, Abraham: 231
Lincoln County, Nev: 298
Linton, James: 431
Linton, Louisa Dunlap: 431
Little, Feramorz: 292
Little, Lewis Henry: 80
Little Rock, Ark: 32, 438, 439
Little Salt Lake Valley: 109, 273
Lockley, Frederic: on dissident Mormons, 274; letters on first Lee trial, 300–303; reports Baskin's summation, 304; on second Lee trial, 317–19
Logan, Roger V., Jr: 43, 391
Lonely Dell, Ariz: 324, 326
Looking Glass (Ute Indian): 272
Los Angeles, Calif: 32, 41, 129, 138, 150, 178, 232, 279, 291, 387
Los Angeles Star (newspaper): 32, 138–40, 142, 143, 151, 152, 155, 156, 158, 159, 167, 170, 184, 413
Loveridge, Alexander: 235
Loving, Ronald E: 42, 391
Lund, Anthon H: 408–10
Lund, William: 402, 403
Lunt, Ellen: 66
Lunt, Bishop Henry: excommunicates Hicks, 270; intermediary for the indicted W. C. Stewart, 328
Lyman, Amasa: 260
Lyman, Francis M: 410
Lyman, John: 166
Lynch, James: describes massacre site, 240–44, 430, 438, 439; as "old gentleman," 427–28

Macfarlane, Daniel S: 66, 70n, 235, 347, 417
Macfarlane, John M: 66, 235, 347
Macfarlane, Tillie: 66
Magotsu Creek: 420
Mangum, James: 235
Mangum, John: 235
Margetts, Philip: 91

THE EDITORS

David L. Bigler was born in Provo, Utah, and served in the U.S. Navy in World War II and the Korean War. He graduated from the University of Utah in 1950 with a degree in journalism. Southern Utah State College, now Southern Utah University, at Cedar City, awarded him an honorary Doctor of Letters degree in 1979. He is retired as Director of Public Affairs for U.S. Steel Corp. Since 1986 he has devoted full time to the study of Utah and western history. Mr. Bigler is a past president of the Oregon-California Trails Association and a founder and first president of the Utah Westerners. He has served on the Utah Board of State History and is a former officer of the Friends of University of Utah Libraries. Winner of the Utah State Historical Society's Dale L. Morgan Award, he is the author of several award-winning books, including three previous volumes in this series. Mr. Bigler and his wife, Evah, now live in Roseville, California.

Will Bagley lives and writes in Salt Lake City. He attended Brigham Young University and graduated from the University of California at Santa Cruz. He has edited more than a dozen historical studies, including *Frontiersman: Abner Blackburn's Narrative*. He helped Harold Schindler revise Dale L. Morgan's classic *West from Fort Bridger*. With his brother, cartoonist Pat Bagley, he published the children's book *This Is the Place: A Crossroads of Utah's Past*. Mr. Bagley serves as editor of the Arthur H. Clark Company series, KINGDOM IN THE WEST: *The Mormons and the American Frontier*. The series has won awards from the Mormon History Association, the Utah State Historical Society, and Westerners International. His study of the Mountain Meadows Massacre, *Blood of the Prophets* (University of Oklahoma Press, 2002), has won numerous awards, including the Denver Public Library's Caroline Bancroft History Prize and the Caughey Western History Association Prize for the Best Book of the Year in Western History.

KINGDOM IN THE WEST SERIES

The role of the Church of Jesus Christ of Latter-day Saints in the settlement of the American West has been a subject of controversy and fascination for 150 years. Using primary source documents, most of them never before published, KINGDOM IN THE WEST: *The Mormons and the American Frontier* explores the story of the Mormon people and their part in the wider history of the American West.

1. *The Pioneer Camp of the Saints: The 1846 and 1847 Mormon Trail Journals of Thomas Bullock,* edited by Will Bagley. 1997.

2. *Forgotten Kingdom: The Mormon Theocracy in the American West, 1847-1896,* by David L. Bigler. 1998.

3. *Scoundrel's Tale: The Samuel Brannan Papers,* edited by Bagley. 1999.

4. *Army of Israel: Mormon Battalion Narratives,* edited by Bigler and Bagley. 2000.

5. *Defending Zion: George Q. Cannon and the Mormon California Newspaper Wars of 1856-1857,* edited by Roger Ekins. 2002.

6. *Fort Limhi: The Mormon Adventure in Oregon Territory, 1855-1858,* edited by Bigler. 2003.

7. *Gold Rush Saints: California Mormons and the Great Rush for Riches,* edited by Kenneth N. Owens. 2004.

8. *On the Way to Somewhere Else: European Sojourners in the Mormon West, 1834-1930,* edited by Michael W. Homer. 2006.

9. *Doing the Works of Abraham: A Documentary History of Mormon Polygamy,* edited by B. Carmon Hardy. 2007.

10—11. *At Sword's Point: A Documentary History of the Utah War, 1857-1858,* edited by William MacKinnon. Two volumes, 2008 and 2010.

12. *Innocent Blood: Essential Narratives of the Mountain Meadows Massacre,* edited by Bigler and Bagley. 2009.

Subsequent volumes will include studies of Mormon-Indian relations, dissenters in the Mormon West, and the trail to southern California from Salt Lake.

Series subscriptions are welcomed. Manuscript proposals of a documentary nature may also be submitted. Address inquiries to the publisher:

THE ARTHUR H. CLARK COMPANY
2800 Venture Drive
Norman, Oklahoma 73069-8218
(405) 325-5609